THE BLACK JACOBINS
READER

| | | | |

THE BLACK JACOBINS

C. L. R. JAMES

TOUSSAINT LOUVERTURE
AND THE
SAN DOMINGO R...

Original dustjacket from the first edition of *The Black Jacobins*,
Secker and Warburg, 1938. Image of Toussaint Louverture
by (William) Spencer (Millett) Edge (1872–1943). Reproduced
with thanks to Marika Sherwood, and with kind permission
from The Random House Group Limited.

C. L. R. James, circa 1938.
Courtesy of National Library & Information
System Authority.

THE C. L. R. JAMES ARCHIVES
recovers and reproduces for a contemporary
audience the works of one of the great intellectual figures of the twentieth century, in all
their rich texture, and will present, over
and above historical works, new and current
scholarly explorations of James's oeuvre.

Robert A. Hill, Series Editor

THE BLACK JACOBINS
READER

| | | | |

CHARLES FORSDICK AND

CHRISTIAN HØGSBJERG, EDITORS

DUKE UNIVERSITY PRESS   DURHAM AND LONDON   2017

Printed in the United States of America on acid-free paper ∞
Typeset in Arno Pro by Westchester Publishing Services

Library of Congress Cataloging-in-Publication Data
Names: Forsdick, Charles, editor. | Høgsbjerg, Christian, editor.
Title: The Black Jacobins reader / Charles Forsdick and Christian
Høgsbjerg, editors.
Description: Durham : Duke University Press, 2016. | Series:
The C. L. R. James Archives | Includes bibliographical references
and index. | Description based on print version record and CIP data
provided by publisher; resource not viewed.
Identifiers: LCCN 2016031242 (print) | LCCN 2016030242 (ebook)
ISBN 9780822373940 (e-book)
ISBN 9780822361848 (hardcover : alk. paper)
ISBN 9780822362012 (pbk. : alk. paper)
Subjects: LCSH: James, C. L. R. (Cyril Lionel Robert), 1901–1989.
Black Jacobins. | Toussaint Louverture, 1743–1803. | Haiti—
History—Revolution, 1791–1804.
Classification: LCC F1923.T853 (print) | LCC F1923.T853B53 2016
(ebook) | DDC 972.94/03—dc23
LC record available at https://lccn.loc.gov/2016031242

Cover art: François Cauvin, *Toussaint L'Ouverture*, 2009. Cauvin
depicts Louverture wearing a guinea fowl as a cap. This is Cauvin's
reference to the history of the guinea fowl, or *pintade*, as a symbol
of Haitian resistance to slavery.

FOR STUART HALL

CONTENTS

Foreword | ROBERT A. HILL xiii

Haiti | DAVID M. RUDDER xxi

Acknowledgments xxiii

Introduction: Rethinking *The Black Jacobins*
CHARLES FORSDICK AND CHRISTIAN HØGSBJERG 1

Part I. Personal Reflections

1   *The Black Jacobins* in Detroit: 1963
DAN GEORGAKAS 55

2   The Impact of C. L. R. James's *The Black Jacobins*
MUMIA ABU-JAMAL 58

3   C. L. R. James, *The Black Jacobins*, and *The Making of Haiti*
CAROLYN E. FICK 60

4   *The Black Jacobins*, Education, and Redemption
RUSSELL MAROON SHOATZ 70

5   *The Black Jacobins*, Past and Present
SELMA JAMES 73

Part II. The Haitian Revolution: Histories and Philosophies

6   Reading *The Black Jacobins*: Historical Perspectives
LAURENT DUBOIS 87

7   Haiti and Historical Time
BILL SCHWARZ 93

8   The Theory of Haiti: *The Black Jacobins* and the Poetics
of Universal History
DAVID SCOTT 115

9   Fragments of a Universal History: Global Capital,
Mass Revolution, and the Idea of Equality in *The Black Jacobins*
NICK NESBITT 139

10   "We Are Slaves and Slaves Believe in Freedom": The Problematizing
of Revolutionary Emancipationism in *The Black Jacobins*
CLAUDIUS FERGUS 162

11   "To Place Ourselves in History": The Haitian Revolution in
British West Indian Thought before *The Black Jacobins*
MATTHEW J. SMITH 178

Part III. The Black Jacobins: *Texts and Contexts*

12   *The Black Jacobins* and the Long Haitian Revolution:
Archives, History, and the Writing of Revolution
ANTHONY BOGUES 197

13   Refiguring Resistance: Historiography, Fiction, and the
Afterlives of Toussaint Louverture
CHARLES FORSDICK 215

14   On "Both Sides" of the Haitian Revolution? Rethinking Direct
Democracy and National Liberation in *The Black Jacobins*
MATTHEW QUEST 235

15   *The Black Jacobins*: A Revolutionary Study of Revolution,
and of a Caribbean Revolution
DAVID AUSTIN 256

16   Making Drama out of the Haitian Revolution from Below:
C. L. R. James's *The Black Jacobins* Play
RACHEL DOUGLAS 278

17   "On the Wings of Atalanta"
ALDON LYNN NIELSEN 297

Part IV. Final Reflections

18   Afterword to *The Black Jacobins*'s Italian Edition
     MADISON SMARTT BELL   313

19   Introduction to the Cuban Edition of *The Black Jacobins*
     JOHN H. BRACEY   322

Appendix 1. C. L. R. James and Studs Terkel Discuss
The Black Jacobins on WFMT Radio (Chicago), 1970   329

Appendix 2. The Revolution in Theory
C. L. R. JAMES   353

Appendix 3. Translator's Foreword by Pierre Naville
to the 1949 / 1983 French Editions   367

Bibliography   383

Contributors   411

Index   415

FOREWORD

... It is of the West Indies West Indian.

—C. L. R. James

What an education it would be—whether as to the God of yesterday or today—
were we able to hear the true prayers on the lips of the humble!

—Marc Bloch

In the preface of the first 1938 edition of *The Black Jacobins*, C. L. R. James announces the first move in the argument to come in the book. "By a phenomenon often observed"—the phenomenon being the Haitian Revolution of
1791–1804—"the individual leadership responsible for this unique achievement was almost entirely the work of a single man—Toussaint L'Ouverture."
The history of the Haitian Revolution, James explains, "will therefore largely
be a record of his achievements and his political personality." He goes further
and confidently declares: "The writer believes, and is confident the narrative
will prove, that between 1789 and 1815, with the single exception of Bonaparte
himself, no single figure appeared on the historical stage more greatly gifted
than this Negro, a slave till he was 45." No sooner are these broad claims
made than James seems to attenuate his argument with an important pair of
qualifiers.

The first of the pair is: "Yet Toussaint did not make the revolution. It was
the revolution that made Toussaint." The second qualifier follows immediately: "*And even that is not the whole truth*."[1]

The first qualifier is what propelled James's interpretation of Toussaint and
the Haitian Revolution into becoming a historical classic and as such prove
foundational for all subsequent investigation of the revolution. It provides
evidence of James's penetrating historical insight: the profoundly dialectical

nature of the relationship between Toussaint and the revolutionary movement, such that, as James explains, it becomes almost impossible to determine where one began and the other ended. "The revolution had made him
[Toussaint]," he asserts once more,

> but it would be a vulgar error to suppose that the creation of a disciplined
> army, the defeat of the English and the Spaniards, the defeat of Rigaud, the
> establishment of a strong government all over the island, the growing har-
> mony between the races, the enlightened aims of the administration—it
> would be a crude error to believe that all these were inevitable.

He goes on to add:

> At a certain stage, the middle of 1794, the potentialities in the chaos began
> to be shaped and soldered by his powerful personality, and thenceforth it is
> impossible to say where the social forces end and the impress of personal-
> ity begins. It is sufficient that but for him this history would be something
> entirely different.[2]

The latter statement reflects the aphoristic clarity of James's literary style.
Another example of his deployment of stunning aphorism occurs in his account
of Toussaint's "extraordinarily difficult"[3] position when faced with France's
preparation to restore slavery in Saint-Domingue. "It was in method, and not in
principle, that Toussaint failed," James informs the reader. By way of underscoring the underlying factor in Toussaint's quandary, he adds: "The race question
is subsidiary to the class question in politics, and to think of imperialism in
terms of race is disastrous. But to neglect the racial factor as merely incidental
is an error only less grave than to make it fundamental."[4]

The same legibility, however, is not evident where the preface's second
qualifier—"And even that is not the whole truth"—is concerned. The reader
is left to ponder James's meaning. Why does he not say it? If "It was the revolution that made Toussaint," and that was not "the whole truth," where does
one find the missing part, the "truth" that is left unsaid? These questions induce a slightly unsettling experience once the reader begins to ponder them,
mainly because it starts to dawn on the reader that perhaps one of the key
analytic coordinates on which the analysis hinges and turns remains hidden
from view.

Since my first encounter with James's preface, I have wanted to test my
understanding, in the hope that I would be able to discern their real meaning
and the search would clarify what James left unsaid. I ask myself: Was it one

of those sudden leaps of understanding that occurs in the very act of writing, which the writer expects to revisit but never does? Perhaps. What if James was engaged in a kind of subterfuge or subversion of Enlightenment rationality? The hint of sarcasm accompanying the statement makes one suspicious. Or was James simply indulging his love of aphorism? Could it be that the force of the argument exceeded his capacity to represent it? It might have been proleptic, in the sense that the argument simply exceeded the framing of the question. In that case, the argument was not indeterminate; rather, it was overdetermined, but before there was a language or set of concepts to describe what James was striving to express.

I suspect the idea came to him all in a flash. We hear an echo in the text when James notes: "We have clearly stated the vast impersonal forces at work in the crisis of San Domingo. But men make history, and Toussaint made the history that he made because he was the man he was."[5] Moreover, Toussaint was not alone: "Toussaint was no phenomenon, no Negro freak. The same forces which moulded his genius had helped to create his black and Mulatto generals and officials."[6]

Intellectually, it is important to recognize that James was writing before the emergence of cultural studies in the 1950s, 1960s, and 1970s, which, inspired as it was by a vision of the countervailing power of popular culture, transformed the whole approach to the study of culture. He was writing before E. P. Thompson's *The Making of the English Working Class* (1963) ushered in the practice of writing history from below and cemented the field of social history. He did not have available Benedict Anderson's *Imagined Communities* (1983), which gave us, in its treatment of the effect of print capitalism on the day-to-day imagining of new kinds of solidarities, a new way to think about languages, literature, and cultural symbols and their role in generating a concept of nationhood and peoplehood. In this context, what I find remarkable is that by the time the second edition of *The Black Jacobins* was published in 1963, James had already arrived at the idea Anderson's name would become associated with twenty years later. Here is James writing about the Caribbean in 1963:

> The people of the West Indies were born in the seventeenth century, in a Westernized productive and social system. Members of different African tribes were carefully split up to lessen conspiracy, and they were therefore compelled to master the European languages, highly complex products of centuries of civilization. From the start there had been the gap, constantly

growing, between the rudimentary conditions of the life of the slave and the language he used. There was therefore in West Indian society an inherent antagonism between the consciousness of the black masses and the reality of their lives, inherent in that it was constantly produced and reproduced not by agitators but by the very conditions of the society itself. It is the modern media of mass communication which have made essence into existence. For an insignificant sum per month, the black masses can hear on the radio news of Dr. Nkrumah, Jomo Kenyatta, Dr. Julius [Nyerere], Prime Minister Nehru, events and personalities of the United Nations and all the capitals of the world. They can wrestle with what the West thinks of the East and what the East thinks of the West. The cinema presents actualities and not infrequently stirs the imagination with the cinematic masterpieces of the world. Every hour on the hour all variations of food, clothing, household necessities and luxuries are presented as absolutely essential to a civilized existence. All this to a population which over large areas still lives in conditions little removed from slavery.[7]

It is all the more remarkable, then, that James, working practically alone and before the radical transformation in the understanding of culture that did not emerge until after World War II, was able to anticipate so many of the key ideas that we take for granted today. What he inherited and had available to him, he used brilliantly. This was set out in the 1938 preface:

Great men make history, but only such history as it is possible for them to make. Their freedom of achievement is limited by the necessities of their environment. To portray the limits of those necessities and the realization, complete or partial, of all possibilities, that is the true business of the historian.[8]

The year 1963 also marked the publication of James's other major classic, *Beyond a Boundary*. A transformative study not only of cricket but also the aesthetic of organized sport and games, *Beyond a Boundary* was animated throughout by a similar conception of culture hinted at in the 1938 preface. Although the subject matter of *Beyond a Boundary* may have been quite different, the same radical ideal of cultural emancipation supplied the framework. This explains, in my view, the continuing appeal *Beyond a Boundary* exerts on each new generation of readers—exactly as is the case with each new set of readers of *The Black Jacobins*. James tells us that the idea for the book on cricket, as was also the case with *The Black Jacobins*, originated in the West Indies, but it was in Britain that the material was shaped and imbued with the cultural figuration that received explicit formulation in the 1963 preface to *Beyond a Boundary*. "If the ideas originated in the West Indies it was only in England and in English life and history that I was able to track them down and test them," he declares, then pointedly adds: "To establish his own identity, Caliban, after three centuries, must himself pioneer into regions Caesar never knew."[9]

Today we are better able to appreciate the idea that James was alluding to in the 1938 preface of *The Black Jacobins* with his set of qualifiers. I believe that what he was gesturing to there was the idea of *cultural revolution*. Seen against the backdrop of the broad turn toward cultural history that has transformed the discipline of history today, we can begin to appreciate the revolutionary use to which James put the concept of culture in his study of the Saint-Domingue revolution. In this context, we ought to note, in the words of David A. Bell, that today we have available a whole series of "cultural histories of revolution that center on close readings of the language, symbols, imagery, and festive practices of individual revolutions, in a manner that [have] tended to highlight the particularities of each."[10] Obviously, none of these were available when James was writing *The Black Jacobins*, which makes his achievement all the more remarkable as a pioneering statement of the cultural study of revolution. Thus, it is only now, in the light of history's cultural turn, that we are able to appreciate *The Black Jacobins* as a study of cultural revolution avant la lettre.

What James was trying to get across in the 1938 preface was his conviction that the revolutionary culture of Saint-Domingue provided the critical variable in the revolution. Few people at the time appreciated this. Conversely, we might say that the idea of the Haitian Revolution as a cultural revolution fuels the tremendous outpouring of scholarship on the revolution in recent times.

In seeing himself as "specially prepared to write *The Black Jacobins*," James claimed that "not the least of my qualifications [was] the fact that I had spent most of my life in a West Indian island not, in fact, too unlike the territory of Haiti." This feeling of cultural consanguinity made the cultural aspect of the revolution especially vivid for him:

> In addition, my West Indian experiences and my study of marxism had made me see what had eluded many previous writers, that it was the slaves who had made the revolution. Many of the slave leaders to the end were

unable to read or write and in the archives you can see reports (and admirable reports they are) in which the officer who made it traces his name in ink over a pencil draft prepared for him.[11]

The Black Jacobins contains numerous allusions to James's consciousness of the West Indian dimension of the revolution. He points out, for example, that "those who took the trouble to observe them [the slaves] away from their masters and in their intercourse with each other did not fail to see that remarkable liveliness of intellect and vivacity of spirit which so distinguish their descendants in the West Indies today."[12] In a similar vein, "it is as well to remind the reader that a trained observer travelling in the West Indies in 1935 says of the coloured men there, 'A few at the top, judges, barristers, doctors, whatever their shade of colour, could hold their own in any circle. A great many more are the intellectual equals or superiors of their own white contemporaries.'"[13]

Despite the fact, as James tells us, that "the book was written not with the Caribbean but with Africa in mind," it remains the case that it could only have been written by a West Indian. Analyzing the agonizing dilemma Toussaint faced when confronted with the reality of Napoleon's plan to restore slavery in Saint-Domingue, James feels obliged to warn his European readers that it would be "a mistake to see him [Toussaint] merely as a political figure in a remote West Indian island."[14]

The conjoined theme of cultural consanguinity and cultural revolution reaches its apotheosis in James's lengthy appendix to the 1963 edition of *The Black Jacobins*, when he speaks, in the concluding sentence, of "Toussaint, the first and greatest of West Indians."[15] Titled "From Toussaint L'Ouverture to Fidel Castro," the appendix was completed in January 1963, five months after James had returned to England from the West Indies, where he had spent the previous five years. The appendix attempts to bring up to date the historical significance of the Haitian Revolution within the context of the unfolding Cuban Revolution and sum up the insights gained from his experience in the West Indies. According to James, "What took place in French San Domingo in 1792–1804 reappeared in Cuba in 1958." The slave revolution in French Saint-Domingue marks the beginning of the Caribbean quest for "national identity." "Whatever its ultimate fate," he goes on, "the Cuban revolution marks the ultimate stage of a Caribbean quest for national identity. In a scattered series of disparate islands, the process consists of a series of uncoordinated periods of drift, punctuated by spurts, leaps and catastrophes. But the inherent movement is clear and strong."[16] What James refers to as "the development of the West Indian quest for a national identity"[17] is another name for the cultural revolution that started in Haiti and continued throughout the Caribbean.

And even that is not the whole truth . . .

We are back where we began. It should be clear that James's recognition of the truth of the Haitian Revolution as a cultural revolution was not the result of some abstract or objective historical exercise. It required "something other, something more, than a matter of strict historiography"—that is, it operated less on the plane of historiography than on the powerfully introspective terrain of "historical truth."[18] That, I realize now, is the meaning James was driving at in 1938, the truth which at the time was lacking the requisite language but which he ultimately found in 1963 with "It was of the West Indies West Indian. For it, Toussaint, the first and greatest of West Indians, paid with his life."[19]

My last and final conversation in person with C. L. R. James took place sometime around 1980–1981. It took place in Washington, DC, in a small room in a house where he was living. He had moved from his apartment shortly before then and was living temporarily with a former student. He was returning to England after a decade of living and teaching in the United States. I was helping him sort through and pack up his books and personal effects.

I told James of my wish one day to organize an edition of his books and collect and edit his papers. He seemed puzzled at the thought. As I had just purchased some of the titles in the new Penguin Books edition of the works of Freud, I mentioned this to him, hoping to provide an example of what might be done with his work. Much to my disappointment and amazement, he looked at me and responded: "Who is going to be interested in my work?"

I must have tried to mutter something, too incoherent to remember now. Although it has been a long time in the making, I believe the answer to James's querulous response that day in his room, as he was preparing to depart, is contained in the present collection of reflections on *The Black Jacobins*. I think he would be pleased to welcome it, just as I am, to applaud and welcome its auspicious entry into the world.

Robert A. Hill
Literary Executor
The C. L. R. James Estate

Notes

1. C. L. R. James, *The Black Jacobins: Toussaint L'Ouverture and the San Domingo Revolution* (New York: Vintage, 1963), ix–x; emphasis added.

2. James, *The Black Jacobins*, 248–49.

3. James, *The Black Jacobins*, 284.

4. James, *The Black Jacobins*, 283.

5. James, *The Black Jacobins*, 91.

6. James, *The Black Jacobins*, 256.

7. James, *The Black Jacobins*, 407.

8. James, *The Black Jacobins*, x.

9. C. L. R. James, *Beyond a Boundary* (Durham, NC: Duke University Press, 2013), xxvii.

10. David A. Bell, "Renewing the Comparative Study of Revolutions," AHA *Today* (a blog of the American Historical Association), December 7, 2015, http://blog .historians.org/2015/12/comparative-study-of-revolutions/.

11. C. L. R. James, *The Black Jacobins: Toussaint L'Ouverture and the San Domingo Revolution*, with an introduction and notes by James Walvin (London: Penguin Books, 2001), xvi.

12. James, *The Black Jacobins* (New York, 1963), 17.

13. James, *The Black Jacobins*, 43. The quotation was from W. M. Macmillan, *Warning from the West Indies: A Tract for Africa and the Empire* (London: Books for Libraries Press, 1936), 49.

14. James, *The Black Jacobins*, 291.

15. James, *The Black Jacobins*, 418.

16. James, *The Black Jacobins*, 391.

17. James, *The Black Jacobins*, 396.

18. Nathan Gorelick, "Extimate Revolt: Mesmerism, Haiti, and the Origin of Psychoanalysis," *New Centennial Review* 13, no. 3 (2013): 117.

19. James, *The Black Jacobins*, 418.

HAITI | DAVID M. RUDDER

In 1988, the Trinidadian calypsonian David M. Rudder composed "Haiti," which was inspired by C. L. R. James's The Black Jacobins *and performed at James's funeral in Tunapuna in 1989.*

VERSE 1

Toussaint was a mighty man
And to make matters worse he was black
Black and back in the days when black men knew
Their place was in the back
But this rebel still walked through Napoleon
Who thought it wasn't very nice
And so today my brothers in Haiti
They still pay the price.

CHORUS

Yeah, Yeah,
Haiti I'm sorry
We misunderstood you
One day we'll turn our heads
And look inside you
Haiti, I'm sorry
Haiti, I'm sorry
One day we'll turn our heads
Restore your glory.

Many hands reach out to St. Georges
And are still reaching out
To those frightened
Foolish men of Pretoria
We still scream and shout
We came together in song
To steady the Horn of Africa
But the papaloa come and the babyloa go
And still, we don't seem to care.

When there is anguish in Port au Prince
It's still Africa crying
We are outing fires in far away places
When our neighbours are just burning
They say the middle passage is gone
So how come
Overcrowded boats still haunt our lives
I refuse to believe that we good people
Would forever turn our hearts
And our eyes . . . away.

ACKNOWLEDGMENTS

This collection emerged originally out of some of the proceedings of a one-day conference, "Seventy Years of *The Black Jacobins*" at the Institute of Historical Research in London in February 2008, organized by the London Socialist Historians Group. Our first thanks go to all those who attended, particularly our speakers, who made that conference such a successful event, with particular thanks to Rachel Cohen, Keith Flett, and David Renton. Over the intervening years as this collection has come together, we have accumulated many debts of gratitude for various forms of assistance and help with finding rare material, and we thank Talat Ahmed, Henrice Altink, Gaverne Bennett, Weyman Bennett, David Berry, Ian Birchall, Paul Blackledge, Jennifer Brittan, Sebastian Budgen, Paul Buhle, Margaret Busby, Graham Campbell, Pierre Cours-Saliès, Alissandra Cummins, Allison Edwards, Merryn Everitt, Alan Forrest, Camille George, David Goodway, Juan Grigera, Catherine Hall, Donna Hall-Comissiong, Julie Herrada, Richard Hart, Paget Henry, Darcus Howe, David Howell, Leslie James, Phoebe Jones, Aaron Kamugisha, Nina Lopez, Michael Löwy, F. Bart Miller, Olukoya Ogen, Gregory Pierrot, Matthieu Renault, Giorgio Riva, Penelope Rosemont, Frank Rosengarten, Alyssa Goldstein Sepinwall, Marika Sherwood, Patrick Silberstein, Andrew Smith, Matthew J. Smith, Joseph Tennyson, Maurice Valère, Daniel Whittall and Yutaka Yoshida. Very special thanks also to Selma James. We thank the archivists and librarians of various institutions, including the Alma Jordan Library, University of the West Indies, Saint Augustine, Trinidad and Tobago; the British Library, London; the George Padmore Institute, London; the National Archives, London; the Quinton O'Connor Library, Oilfield Workers' Trade Union, San Fernando, Trinidad and Tobago; the University of Michigan Library, Ann Arbor; and Wayne State University Archives of Labor and Urban Affairs in Detroit, Michigan.

We were also privileged to be part of a conference organized by Rachel Douglas and Kate Hodgson to mark the seventy-fifth anniversary of the publication of *The Black Jacobins*, "*The Black Jacobins* Revisited: Rewriting History Workshop and Performance," held in October 2013 at the International Slavery Museum and Bluecoat Arts Centre, Liverpool.

For permissions, we thank the C. L. R. James Estate, Véronique Nahoum-Grappe (for the material by Pierre Naville), Gloria Valère and the National Library and Information System Authority (NALIS) in Trinidad and Tobago (for permission to reproduce the image of C. L. R. James from the Constantine Collection), David Michael Rudder, Tony Macaluso of the WFMT Radio Network, and Allison Schein of the Studs Terkel Radio Archive (for permission to publish the transcript of the interview between Studs Terkel and C. L. R. James). We also thank Grace Q. Radkins for her transcription of this interview. David Scott's essay in this collection, "The Theory of Haiti: *The Black Jacobins* and the Poetics of Universal History," was first published in *Small Axe* 45 (2014): 35–51.

This volume was completed while Charles Forsdick was Arts and Humanities Research Council Theme Leadership Fellow for 'Translating Cultures' (AH/K503381/1); he records his thanks to the AHRC for its support.

Finally, we thank the team at Duke University Press, particularly Gisela Fosado, Danielle Houtz, Amy Ruth Buchanan, Valerie Millholland, and Lydia Rose Rappoport-Hankins; Mark Mastromarino for his work on the index; the anonymous readers for their expertise and constructive comments on this work; Robert A. Hill for his assistance and editorial expertise; and last but far from least, all our contributors for agreeing to be part of this project—and for their support, assistance, and especially patience.

INTRODUCTION | Rethinking *The Black Jacobins*

CHARLES FORSDICK AND

CHRISTIAN HØGSBJERG

In September 1938, the small, independent British left-wing publisher Secker and Warburg published one of the first major English-language studies of the Haitian Revolution of 1791–1804, *The Black Jacobins: Toussaint Louverture and the San Domingo Revolution*. Its author was the black Trinidadian writer, historian, and revolutionary C. L. R. James, and the completion of the book constituted the culmination of his active and productive period in Britain since his arrival in London in 1932.[1] The dust jacket informed its readers that "the black revolution in San Domingo is the only successful slave revolt in history," the most "striking episode in modern history" and of "immense political significance." As Secker and Warburg stressed to their readers at the time:

> Far from being the chaotic bacchanalia of oppressed savages, the revolution followed with precision the rise and fall of the revolutionary wave in France; and the drama of Toussaint's career is played out on the surface of a social revolution, unfolding with a logical completeness to be found only in the Russian Revolution of 1917.[2]

The reference to the Russian Revolution was telling, for James's previous work with Secker and Warburg was *World Revolution, 1917–1936: The Rise and Fall of the Communist International* (1937), a pioneering political history of the rise of the revolutionary movement after 1917 and its failure and collapse amidst the degeneration of that revolution and the rise of a counterrevolutionary Stalinist bureaucracy.[3] Yet if the writing of *World Revolution* had clearly emerged out of James's turn to Marxism and decision to then join the Trotskyist movement in Britain in 1934, the roots of *The Black Jacobins* were more numerous and deep and were first nourished in the soil of his native Trinidad.

The Emergence of *The Black Jacobins*

In "The Old World and the New," a lecture delivered on his seventieth birthday in Ladbroke Grove, London, in 1971, James describes with characteristic evasiveness the genesis of his history of the Haitian Revolution: "I don't know why I was writing *The Black Jacobins* the way I did. I had long made up my mind to write a book about Toussaint L'Ouverture. Why I couldn't tell you."[4] The idea of writing a book on the Haitian Revolution clearly preceded his journey from colonial Trinidad to England in 1932. "Stuck away in the back of my head for years," he commented in *Beyond a Boundary*, "was the project of writing a biography of Toussaint Louverture."[5] The initial emergence of this book remains unclear, though as Matthew J. Smith shows in his contribution to this volume, the Haitian Revolution had been a subject of discussion by nationalists in the British West Indies since the nineteenth century. For James, it seems that his particular interest in Louverture was actively sparked by his exchanges with Sidney Harland in *The Beacon* the year before his departure from Trinidad. As Selwyn Cudjoe has suggested, it is also clear that James was influenced from an early stage in his thought by the work of J. J. Thomas, the schoolteacher whose 1889 rebuttal to J. A. Froude's *The English in the West Indies* (1887) was one of the first assertions that Caribbean people had a legitimate claim to govern themselves.[6] Froude had dismissively referred to the Haitian revolutionary: "There has been no saint in the West Indies since Las Casas, no hero unless philonegro enthusiasm can make one out of Toussaint. There are no people there, with a purpose and character of their own."[7] In his article "Racial Admixture," Harland had developed a pseudo-scientific account dependent on heavily racialized taxonomies of IQ, arguing along the same racist lines as Froude's and presenting Toussaint Louverture as belonging to what he called "class F" in intellectual terms.[8] Dismissing Harland's article as "antiquated," naïve, and characterized by "monstrous blunder[s]," James was particularly critical in his response to comments on Louverture, to whom he devotes a long paragraph. In a *reductio ad absurdum* of Harland's statistics, he claimed:

> among every 4,300 men the Doctor expects to find a Toussaint L'Ouverture. He will pick a Toussaint from every tree. According to this theory, Port-of-Spain has fifteen such men, San Fernando two, there is one between Tunapuna and Tacarigua. Or if Dr Harland prefers it that way there are about 80 in Trinidad today. I need carry this absurdity no further. But what respect

can anyone have for a man who in the midst of what he would have us believe is a scientific dissertation produces such arrant nonsense![9]

In embryonic forms, we see questions that interested James throughout his later life about the exceptionalism (or otherwise) of Louverture, as well as an implicit reflection on whether the revolutionary hero might emerge in other contexts in need of revolutionary change. In the exasperated final section of the article, reflecting on the racial and educational implications of Harland's piece, James concludes: "I think I have written enough. I would have far preferred to write on Toussaint Louverture, for instance."[10]

In suggesting that the Haitian revolutionary might one day be the subject of his own attentions, James includes in his text in *The Beacon* a telling observation about his own sources—"All my quotations," he writes, "are from white historians."[11] The only life of Louverture that is mentioned directly is Percy Waxman's *Black Napoleon*, published in 1931, a work that was dismissed in the bibliographical notes of *The Black Jacobins* as a "superficial book."[12] It is clear that in response James was already envisaging a study of the Haitian Revolution and its inspirational leader that would challenge this prevailing historiography and provide a perspective on this key Caribbean event that would restore an understanding of its world historical significance. Shortly after the exchange with Harland, the catalyst for writing on Louverture presented itself in James's journey to Europe—in particular in his contact with the working people of Nelson, Lancashire, and his observation of their organization industrially in the Nelson Weavers' Association and politically in respect to their historic support for the socialist Independent Labour Party. In *Beyond a Boundary*, James describes his voyage in these terms: "The British intellectual was going to Britain."[13] Edward Said categorizes this transatlantic crossing as a "voyage in," that is, as a destabilizing process whereby the integration of thinkers from colonized countries into metropolitan culture serves as a "sign of adversarial internationalization in an age of continued imperial structures." In Said's terms, "the separations and exclusions of 'divide and rule' are erased and surprising new configurations spring up," and the genesis of *The Black Jacobins* can clearly be seen as symptomatic of such processes and as a key contribution to the challenge to the sense of racial and cultural inferiority James felt had been a central aspect of his British Caribbean education.[14] Such is the importance of writing this history of the Haitian Revolution and the biography of its principal leader in the work produced during James's first stay in Britain that Stuart Hall commented in a 1998 interview with Bill

Schwarz that it was "almost as if it's one of the reasons for his coming to Europe in the first place."[15] In the draft of his autobiography, James endorsed this view, associating the interest in the Haitian Revolution with the turning point of his arrival in England:

> My concern with being a novelist or a writer was soon to be blown away into dust invisible. The only thing that I took with me and settle [sic] down to work with was the idea of showing that the blacks could do things and from my first day in England I began to look for books on the Haitian Revolution.[16]

The Black Jacobins would indeed be one of the most significant products of the 1932–38 period in Britain, a period in which—amidst the Great Depression and the rise of fascism in Europe—James intellectually radicalized toward revolutionary Marxism and militant Pan-Africanism and produced a work that itself continued to evolve during the remaining five decades of his life and beyond. Not only does the text in which the history appeared travel through a number of rewritings (in the course of which James increasingly rethought his initial premises and assumptions), it is also central to a constellation of other writings, lectures, and other interventions, ranging from the pre-text found in the 1936 dramatic version *Toussaint Louverture* (itself reworked in 1967) to constant references to Haiti, its revolution, and its revolutionary leaders in correspondence and talks until James's death. As such— and as this volume attempts to illustrate—*The Black Jacobins* is much more than a book: borrowing a term from Dan Selden, Susan Gillman identifies the text as part of a "text-network," made up of a series of "translations without an original";[17] it is the protean centerpiece of the set of reflections on revolution, history, culture, personality, and the urgent need for sociopolitical change that characterizes James's life; it is a key part of a prolific body of work that reveals the evolving thought of one of the twentieth century's most significant intellectuals; it is a site in which struggles over the relationship between theory and praxis play themselves out. It remains a major element of James's legacy and the vehicle whereby his life and work continue to influence action and debate today.

The Black Jacobins in Context

It is important to trace the emergence of *The Black Jacobins* in the context of James's intensive production of a number of other writings, not least another (more contemporary) biographical text, *The Life of Captain Cipriani:*

An Account of British Government in the West Indies (1932). The earlier work similarly engages with questions of Caribbean self-government and the place of the charismatic individual in political movements through a discussion of Captain Arthur Andrew Cipriani, leader of the Trinidadian Workingmen's Association. Whereas the work on Cipriani—an abridged version of which was published as "The Case for West Indian Self-Government" by Hogarth Press in 1933—drew on interviews and material James had gathered in colonial Trinidad, his writings on the Haitian Revolution depended on extensive research that formed part of an energetic engagement with radical historiography and more general Marxist writings. In *Beyond a Boundary*, James suggests that shortly after his arrival in Nelson he began to import from France the books required to consolidate his knowledge of Haitian history and write *The Black Jacobins*. His wider reading at the time—of radical and socialist historians of the French Revolution such as Jean Jaurès and Jules Michelet—provided further impetus to write the Haitian Revolution back in to the period historians came to call "the age of democratic revolution." Together with his studies of two massive works which—as Bill Schwarz explores in his contribution to this volume—would help make him a Marxist, Oswald Spengler's *The Decline of the West* and Leon Trotsky's *History of the Russian Revolution*, James was, in his own terms, "reading hard"; "Night after night," he adds, "I would be up till three or four."[18]

James's securing of work as a professional cricket reporter for the *Manchester Guardian*, together with generous financial support from Harry Spencer (a friend in Nelson), meant that the study of books ordered direct from France was soon complemented by regular research visits to archives in France throughout the 1930s. As soon as the 1933 cricket season was over, James was able to visit Paris and consult documents that had rarely received such serious attention since they had been read by the first generation of Haitian historians—figures such as Thomas Madiou and Beaubrun Ardouin—in the mid-nineteenth century.[19] He originally had the good fortune to be shown around various archives and bookshops in Paris in the winter of 1933 by Léon-Gontran Damas, a black poet from French Guiana who would be central to the development of the philosophy of négritude.[20] As the foreword that James wrote in January 1980 for the Allison and Busby edition of *The Black Jacobins* makes clear, in Paris James also met the Haitian historian and diplomat Colonel Auguste Nemours, who served as Haiti's permanent delegate to the League of Nations in the 1930s before being appointed to the post of minister plenipotentiary to France in 1937.

Nemours is perhaps best remembered for his intervention at the League of Nations in 1935, when he protested against the Italian invasion of Ethiopia with the call: "Craignons d'être, un jour, l'Éthiopie de quelqu'un" [Be afraid of becoming one day someone else's Ethiopia].[21] Yet Nemours was also the author of a book on Toussaint Louverture, *Histoire de la captivité et de la mort de Toussaint Louverture* (1929), which was described by James in the bibliography of *The Black Jacobins* as a "thorough and well-documented study." He would later publish several more, including *Histoire de la famille et de la descendance de Toussaint Louverture* (1941), *Quelques jugements sur Toussaint Louverture* (1938), and *Histoire des relations internationales de Toussaint Louverture* (1945). By the time they met in the 1930s, Nemours had also written a two-volume account of the Haitian war of independence, dedicated to Louverture, *Histoire militaire de la guerre d'indépendance de Saint-Domingue* (1925 and 1928), and James records having consulted him particularly on tactical aspects of the revolution, which the Haitian historian had demonstrated "using books and coffee cups upon a large table to show how the different campaigns had been fought."[22] In the draft of his autobiography, James also notes other contacts that Nemours facilitated: "He introduced me to the Haitian Ambassador in Paris who told me a great deal. Whether he knew it or not he gave me great insight into the Mulatto side of the Haitian people."[23] The nexus of race and class—and the critique of pigmentocracy—that underpins *The Black Jacobins* was clearly embedded in James's observations of contemporary Haiti as reflected by its representatives in Paris.

We get some additional glimpses of James's research trips to Paris during the 1930s from the memoir of Louise Cripps, a friend and comrade in the tiny British Trotskyist movement that James joined soon after his return from France in spring 1934. According to Cripps, James took her and a friend, Esther Heiger, to Paris, probably in spring 1935. The three stayed in Montparnasse in Paris, where the local cafés were "favourite meeting grounds for the Trotskyists at that time (as well as the rendezvous for artists and writers)."[24] James did not miss out on sampling the culture of "black Paris," and one evening, he took Cripps to one of the black nightclubs, Le Bal Nègre. "It was not a very fancy place, but it was filled with people. There were blacks of every height, weight, and shades of colour from all parts of the world where there are Africans or people of African descent . . . we danced and danced."[25] The little party also took in French Impressionist art in the Jeu de Paume in the Tuileries Gardens, and in general did a lot of sight-seeing, visiting Le

Louvre, the Bastille, Napoleon's tomb at Les Invalides, and the Palace of Versailles, with James "giving us several lectures as we wandered from place to place."[26] In the drafts of his autobiography, James alludes to visits to Paris with his compatriot and former student Eric Williams, during which the two historians would work together in the archives and at the Bibliothèque nationale:

> He covered a lot of work for me, he is a wonderful man at research, collecting information and putting it in some sort of order. [...] And there are certain pages in the *Black Jacobins* where most of the material and all the footnotes (I would put them in some time) are things that Williams gave to me, I never had occasion to look them up.[27]

The insight into James's working practices is illuminating, and the understanding of *The Black Jacobins* as a collaborative project is one that merits further investigation (not least in the light of James's claim that Williams's Oxford D.Phil. thesis, "The Economic Aspect of the Abolition of the West Indian Slave Trade and Slavery," also completed in 1938, was the result of similar collaboration).[28]

From 1932 to 1934, James had turned his research into the Haitian Revolution into a play, *Toussaint Louverture: The Story of the Only Successful Slave Revolt in History*, a drama in which one of his main concerns was challenging the ideological tenets behind European colonial domination in general and educating the British public about colonial slavery and abolition during the national commemoration of the centenary of the abolition of slavery in the British Empire.[29] Stuart Hall, in his 1998 discussion of how James came to write *The Black Jacobins*, stressed the importance of his campaigning anticolonial activism and his raising of "The Case for West Indian Self-Government" in particular, noting that "what is riveting . . . is the way in which the historical work and the foregrounded political events are part of a kind of seamless web. They reinforce one another."[30] Clearly there was the plight of occupied Haiti itself, under U.S. military domination from 1915 until 1934.[31] In 1935, the question of rallying solidarity with the people of Ethiopia in the face of Mussolini's barbaric war came to the fore, and James played a central role alongside Amy Ashwood Garvey and others in the Pan-Africanist movement in Britain to form the International African Friends of Abyssinia (IAFA). Hall also had in mind the way James was "fired" by the arc of heroic Caribbean labor rebellions that swept the British West Indies from 1935 onward as "those workers involved in the sugar industry, in oil, and on the docks—the most proletarianized sectors—became conscious of their power."[32]

This "seamless web" has really yet to be adequately mapped by scholars, and though some have drawn attention to the apparent silence with respect to the Caribbean labor revolts in the work itself, we get glimpses of it nonetheless.[33] For example, on August 9, 1937, several hundred people assembled in London's Trafalgar Square at a rally organized by the International African Service Bureau (IASB) to hear speeches urging solidarity with Trinidadian and other West Indian workers by James and also his compatriot and friend George Padmore and Chris Braithwaite (who used the pseudonym "Chris Jones") from Barbados, which itself had also just been rocked by riots.[34] Two Africans, Jomo Kenyatta, the nationalist leader from Kenya, and I. T. A. Wallace-Johnson, a towering figure of West African trade unionism from Sierra Leone, were among the other speakers. According to the Special Branch agents present,

> James gave a resume of the history of the West Indies, explaining that, after the native Caribs had been wiped out, negro slaves had been imported to labour in the islands. Slavery had only been abolished when the British bourgeoisie realised that it was less expensive to pay the negroes starvation wages than to feed them. He compared the West Indian general strike of 1919 with the recent one, saying that black workers had learned much during the last 18 years from events throughout the world. They now knew how to enforce their rights, and how to remain solid in the face of threats and persecution. They were no longer afraid of strike-breaking police, militia and marines.[35]

One of James's particular leadership roles within the Pan-Africanist movement in Britain during this period seems to have been to put his historical consciousness and knowledge to the service of building solidarity with the various liberation struggles across the African diaspora. As Mussolini's war drums beat louder in Ethiopia's direction in summer 1935, James had spoken at a meeting of the newly formed IAFA, an organization he chaired, on July 28 (see figure I.1). According to the *Manchester Guardian*, their cricket correspondent "gave a lucid history of the European treaties with Abyssinia," and declared that "Abyssinia is a symbol of all that Africa was and may be again, and we look on it with a jealous pride."[36] James's passionate speeches in defense of Ethiopia also give a sense of how his study of the Haitian Revolution—and the ruthless guerrilla warfare waged from the mountains

FIG. I.I C. L. R. James speaking on Ethiopia at a rally in Trafalgar Square, London, 1935. Courtesy of Getty Images.

of Haiti by Toussaint's army—clearly fired his imagination about how the coming war against Italian imperialism might be won. On August 16, 1935, at another IAFA rally, James suggested for example that should the Ethiopians find themselves unable to get to grips with the Italian forces in conventional combat, he would "look to them to destroy their country rather than hand it over to the invader. Let them burn down Addis Ababa, let them poison their wells and water holes, let them destroy every blade of vegetation."[37]

The heroic Ethiopian resistance to fascist Italy's barbaric invasion and occupation after the war began in October 1935 was not the only symbolic demonstration of what Africa "may be again," as 1935 also saw Copperbelt mineworkers strike in what is now Zambia. As Frederick Cooper has described,

> The Northern Rhodesian mineworkers strike of 1935 was organized without benefit of trade unions, and it spread from mine to mine, from mine town to mine town, by personal networks, dance societies, religious organizations, and eventually mass meetings. The movement embraced nonminers in the towns, women as well as men.[38]

For James, after reading about the official British Government Commission of Inquiry into these "disturbances," the parallel between the movement of Zambian Copperbelt miners and the seditious midnight gatherings of enslaved Africans of French Saint-Domingue could not have been clearer. "Let the blacks but hear from Europe the slogans of Revolution, and the *Internationale*, in the same concrete manner that the slaves of San Domingo heard Liberty and Equality and the *Marseillaise*, and from the mass uprising will emerge the Toussaints, the Christophes, and the Dessalines."[39] If, as James warned in his pioneering 1937 history of "the rise and fall of the Communist International," *World Revolution*, and elsewhere, as in his discussion of the Spanish Civil War, Stalinist counter-revolution endangered the possibility of the slogans of the Russian Revolution flowing out of metropolitan Europe to the colonial periphery in the same "concrete manner" as they had in 1789, he retained his optimism nonetheless, insisting the history of the Haitian Revolution pointed to the future for the African continent.[40]

If *World Revolution* focused on the dissipation of revolutionary impetus, *The Black Jacobins* instead told the story of a revolutionary movement that delivered not only emancipation from slavery but also independence from colonial domination. The Haitian example also allowed James, as Anthony

Bogues has suggested, to move away from the factionalism of contemporary politics "to hone his political ideas and elaborate a political theory of revolutionary struggle, national oppression and resistance of the colonial people in Africa and the West Indies."[41]

The Black Jacobins and Contemporary Historiography

Leon Trotsky once remarked that "what has been written with the sword cannot be wiped out by the pen ... at least so far as the sword of revolution is concerned."[42] As James noted, this had not prevented "Tory historians, regius professors and sentimentalists," "the professional white-washers" of the historical record, putting their pens to the task of trying to wipe out all trace of what had been written in blood and fire by the black rebel slave army under Toussaint Louverture for well over a century.[43] Eric Williams, whose classic work arising out of his doctoral thesis, *Capitalism and Slavery*, was published in 1944, was right to note that "no work of scholarly importance had been done in England" on the abolition of the slave trade, and that "the British historians wrote almost as if Britain had introduced Negro slavery solely for the satisfaction of abolishing it."[44] For Western scholars, the Haitian Revolution, when it was mentioned at all, was essentially portrayed as Froude had described it in *The English in the West Indies*—simply as a bloodthirsty and savage race war, without reason or rhyme.[45]

James systematically demolished this racist argument in *The Black Jacobins*, stressing how race and class were intrinsically intertwined in Saint-Domingue, and so understanding the tumultuous upheaval that was to be so critical to the abolition of the entire Atlantic slave trade through the prism of class struggle remained fundamental. "Had the monarchists been white, the bourgeoisie brown, and the masses of France black, the French Revolution would have gone down in history as a race war. But although they were all white in France they fought just the same."[46] For the first time James brought cold hard rationality to the history of the revolution, while also developing a pioneering Marxist analysis of Atlantic slavery and the slave trade. In a more sophisticated analysis of the relationship between capitalist accumulation and the barbarism of slavery than what was soon to be advanced by Williams, James noted that the plantations and the slave ships were fundamentally modern capitalist institutions in themselves, things that did not just enrich but had been themselves formed by "the French bourgeoisie" and "the British bourgeoisie." He described the plantations as "huge sugar-factories" and the slaves as a proto-proletariat, indeed, "closer to a modern proletariat than any group of workers in existence at the time," and when they rose as "revolutionary labourers" and set fire to the plantations, he compared them to "the Luddite wreckers."[47]

James later, with characteristic generosity, praised W. E. B. Du Bois's achievement in his monumental 1935 work *Black Reconstruction in America* as greater than that of his own in *The Black Jacobins*, where apparently "there is no understanding of when you go beyond the economic and the social and political and you get deep into the psychology of the people who made the revolution."[48] But this was surely too modest an admission on James's part, for despite the difficulties in getting source material on the importance of African "survivals" for the Haitian Revolution in the 1930s, he was arguably able to suggestively point to the blackness of the "black Jacobins," for example, demonstrating how the African cult of Vodou allowed those without "education or encouragement to cherish a dream of freedom."[49] Moreover, in his artistic portrait of the leaders of the Haitian Revolution, above all Toussaint Louverture, James showed a biographer's grasp of individual psychology as well as the mass collective psychology of the revolutionary slaves.

Yet James's critical stress on black agency—making the central plot of his "grand narrative" the dramatic transformation in consciousness and confidence of the Haitian masses—was combined with a masterful grasp of the totality of social relations in which they acted. His reading of the Marxist classics, above all Trotsky's masterful *History of the Russian Revolution* (1930), saw James make a pioneering and outstanding application to the colonial Caribbean of the historical "law of uneven but combined development" of capitalism. As Trotsky had noted, the peculiarities resulting from the "backwardness" of Russian historical development had explained the "enigma" that "a backward country was the *first* to place the proletariat in power":

> Moreover, in Russia the proletariat did not arise gradually through the ages, carrying with itself the burden of the past as in England, but in leaps involving sharp changes of environment, ties, relations, and a sharp break with the past. It is just this fact—combined with the concentrated oppressions of czarism—that made the Russian workers hospitable to the boldest conclusions of revolutionary thought—just as the backward industries were hospitable to the last word in capitalist organization.[50]

One of James's most striking achievements in *The Black Jacobins* was his demonstration that just as "the law of uneven but combined development" meant the enslaved laborers of Saint-Domingue, suffering under the "concentrated oppressions" of slavery, were soon to be "hospitable to the boldest conclusions of revolutionary thought" radiating from the Jacobins in revolutionary Paris, so the Marxist theory of permanent revolution illuminated not just anticolonial struggles in the age of socialist revolution but also the antislavery liberation struggle in the age of "bourgeois-democratic" revolution. The bold Haitian rebels were, James insisted, "revolutionaries through and through . . . own brothers of the Cordeliers in Paris and the Vyborg workers in Petrograd."[51]

Throughout his study of the Haitian Revolution, James ably demonstrated that it was not simply an inspiring struggle on a tiny island on the periphery of the world system, but was inextricably intertwined with the great French Revolution throughout, pushing the revolutionary process forward in the metropole and investing notions of human rights with new meanings and universal significance. In writing about the Haitian Revolution, he rewrote the history of the French Revolution as well.[52] In *The Black Jacobins* he fused classical and Marxist scholarship to resurrect a vivid panorama of the Haitian Revolution, stressing that it was not simply the greatest event in the history of the West Indies but took its place alongside the English Civil War, the American War of Independence, and the French Revolution as one of the great world-historical revolutions in its own right, a revolution that had forever transformed the world and laid the foundation for the continuing struggle for universal human rights. "The work of Toussaint, Dessalines, Christophe, and Pétion endures in Hayti, but what they did went far, far beyond the boundaries of the island."[53]

Edward Said once suggested that *The Black Jacobins* might be usefully compared with George Antonius's *The Arab Awakening: The Story of the Arab National Movement*, which also appeared in 1938.

> Despite the differences between the indigent and itinerant West Indian Black Marxist historian and the more conservative, highly educated, and brilliantly well-connected Arab, both addressed their work to a world they considered their own, even if that very European world of power and colonial domination excluded, to some degree subjugated, and deeply disappointed them. They addressed that world from within it, and on cultural grounds they disputed and challenged its authority by presenting alternative versions of it, dramatically, argumentatively, and intimately.[54]

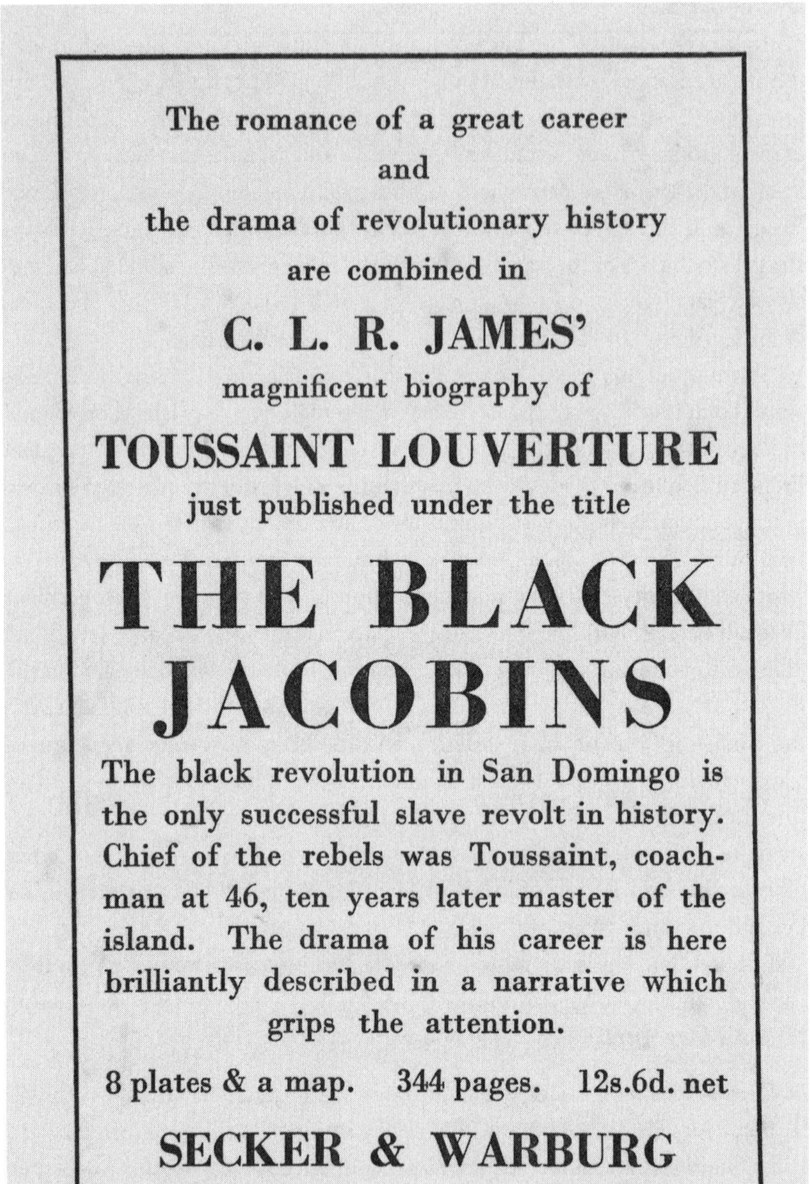

FIG. I.2 Image of Secker and Warburg's 1938 advertisement for *The Black Jacobins*. Courtesy of the C. L. R. James Estate.

The Black Jacobins has other contemporary "others." Alex Callinicos has usefully described how "the example offered" by both Leon Trotsky's political writings in the 1920s and 1930s and by his *History of the Russian Revolution*

> inspired some of the ablest of his followers to write contemporary histories of other twentieth-century revolutions that sought to trace the interplay of class interests and political forces that in each case led to defeat—Harold Isaacs on the Chinese Revolution of 1925–7, Pierre Broué on the German Revolution and on the Spanish Civil War, Adolfo Gilly on the Mexican Revolution.[55]

In many ways, James's work should also be located within this tradition, with respect to charting contemporary revolutionary defeats in *World Revolution* and an eighteenth-century revolutionary victory in *The Black Jacobins*. As he famously put it in his 1938 preface to *The Black Jacobins*, evoking John Keats's "Ode to a Nightingale," he felt "the fever and the fret" of the Spanish Revolution when writing up his magisterial history of the Haitian Revolution in Brighton in the winter of 1937. "It was in the stillness of a seaside suburb that could be heard most clearly and insistently the booming of Franco's heavy artillery, the rattle of Stalin's firing squads and the fierce shrill turmoil of the revolutionary movement striving for clarity and influence."[56]

Contemporary Responses to *The Black Jacobins*

It is tempting to follow David Patrick Geggus and retrospectively conclude that ever since its publication in 1938, *The Black Jacobins* "has dominated study of the Haitian Revolution in the English-speaking world."[57] In reality, the reception to the work was a little more complicated. For the activist audience who mattered most to James, above all George Padmore and Paul Robeson, his account of the Haitian Revolution was immediately celebrated. As James recalled, both Padmore and Robeson responded in essentially the same fashion: "James, I always knew the history was there, that we had it."[58] Padmore's review of *The Black Jacobins* emphasized how "the author has done justice to his subject."

> He has combined with great skill history and biography without sacrificing one to the other. Mr James is a real historian, with the sensitive mind of the scholar and an excellent literary style ... who writes with vigour and incisiveness ... *The Black Jacobins* is a fascinating story, brilliantly

told, and should be an inspiration to Africans and other colonial peoples still struggling for their freedom from the yoke of white imperialism.[59]

Members of the IASB in Britain, including such figures as Jomo Kenyatta and Amy Ashwood Garvey, would have read *The Black Jacobins* in 1938, and Amy Ashwood would later hail it as "the most revolutionary book on Toussaint L'Ouverture."[60] Copies were quickly sent out to contacts in the colonial world as James prepared to leave Britain for a tour of the United States. It is noteworthy in this regard that the British state intercepted a letter dated October 19, 1938, that Secker and Warburg sent to one of James's comrades in the Pan-African movement, I. T. A. Wallace-Johnson, who was back in Freetown, Sierra Leone.

> At the suggestion of George Padmore, I send you herewith a review copy of C.L.R. James's THE BLACK JACOBINS for review in the *West African Standard*. I feel sure you will do what you can to promote the book and Padmore thinks you will be able to sell in your district a dozen or so copies. I hope this may be the case.[61]

On January 6, 1939, Wallace-Johnson, in the midst of organizing a highly successful branch of the militant nationalist West African Youth League in Sierra Leone in the context of a growing political and economic crisis in the colony, launched a new paper. The first editorial of the *African Standard* was certainly in keeping with the spirit of *The Black Jacobins*, boldly declaring that "the crowning victory of our warfare is the end of the structure of capitalism, the complete collapse of imperialism and the triumph of the cause of self-determination for the oppressed sections of humanity the world over," and it seems they also carried Padmore's review of *The Black Jacobins*—also published in *The People* (a Trinidadian paper).[62] In Britain, despite several worthy reviews, including two by comrades of his (the British Marxist Arthur Ballard and Dorothy Pizer, Padmore's partner), the work was all but ignored outside the Pan-Africanist and Trotskyist movement.[63]

Flora Grierson in the *New Statesman* famously dismissed *The Black Jacobins* because of its "bias," noting James was "a Communist and wants us to see the worst."[64] Leaving aside the question of quite which "best" bits of the slave experience Grierson had hoped to see James highlight, the awful truth was that if he had actually been a Communist with a capital C, the work would have received greater attention on publication. *The Black Jacobins* certainly did not warrant anything like the attention given to Soviet novelist Anatolii

Vinogradov's 1935 *The Black Consul*, which James later recalled enjoyed an "enthusiastic welcome in almost the whole British press."[65] As Eugene Genovese noted, *The Black Jacobins* "deserves to rank as a classic of Marxian historiography but has been largely ignored, perhaps because of the author's Trotskyist politics."[66] There was no "perhaps" about it. In 1934, in a review of the powerful antifascist novel *Fontamara* by the anti-Stalinist writer Ignazio Silone, Trotsky asked, "has this book been published in the Soviet Union? Has it come to the notice of the publishing houses of the Third International? This book deserves a circulation of many million copies."[67] Six years later, after Trotsky's murder in 1940, James praised Trotsky's *History of the Russian Revolution* and made a similar point, noting "had the Third International been a revolutionary organization, this book, with its knowledge, its confidence, and its will, would have inspired, directly and indirectly, millions of political leaders all over the world."[68] The argument here stands with respect to James's *Black Jacobins*, too.

If general indifference among British intellectuals might have been inevitable by 1938 as the clouds of war gathered overhead, *The Black Jacobins* nonetheless found an audience among a select few. The work inspired many socialists in and around the Independent Labour Party and it had been a leading member of this organization, Fenner Brockway, who had first introduced James to the publisher Fredric Warburg, of Secker and Warburg, back in 1936.[69] The young future Labour leader Michael Foot also recalled reading it at the time and being "swept along, like most other readers, by the excitement and the passion, the sheer narrative drive."[70] The Communist Eric Hobsbawm recalled that "C.L.R. James' *Black Jacobins* was read, in spite of the author's known Trotskyism" by some of those who went on to form the Historians' Group of the Communist Party of Great Britain, so crucial to helping develop the tradition of "people's history" and then "history from below" after World War II.[71] These intellectuals aside, Peter Fryer accurately judged that James "might have been writing in German for all the notice that was taken by historians" in Britain.[72]

When Dial Press published a U.S. edition in November 1938, the reception was rather better, perhaps helped somewhat by James's presence in the United States as well as the contemporary interest in Haiti in the period immediately following the 1915–1934 occupation. William Seabrook, a U.S. writer who had visited occupied Haiti and was the author of an influential work on Haitian Vodou, *The Magic Island* (1929), wrote a very perceptive review in the *Journal of Negro History*:

Mr. James has rendered the public a service for which he merits the attention due a scholar who blazes the way in an all but neglected field ... with this comprehensive view of the history of the island and those who made it the author has given the public a work which surpasses any production in this field hitherto published ... *Black Jacobins* deserves a warm welcome and an extensive circulation.[73]

Harold Courlander, a U.S. anthropologist who had been influenced by Seabrook and soon published his first book about Haitian life, *Haiti Singing* (1939) (he later wrote a classic work on Haitian culture, *The Drum and the Hoe: Life and Lore of the Haitian People* in 1960), reviewed the work in the *Saturday Review of Literature*:

> *The Black Jacobins* is not a simple account of this epic revolt in the West Indies. Nor could it be simple. But for the first time the scene is viewed with complete perspective and the theme recorded with understanding. It is not only one of the most sharply defined stories of the period to be published in our time, it is told in terms which have contemporary significance. "To the African robbed of his land and segregated, what does it matter whether the robbers are fascists or democrats?" It may prove to be the text of tomorrow's events in Africa.[74]

Rayford W. Logan, a leading black U.S. historian at Howard University who had links to the Roosevelt administration, and who had also conducted research in occupied Haiti, was more reserved in his praise than were Seabrook and Courlander. Nonetheless Logan concluded his review for *Opportunity: Journal of Negro Life* by noting that

> *The Black Jacobins* is a notable contribution to the history of the Caribbean and of the class struggle ... this study definitely established Mr. James as an historian from whom other authoritative monographs may be expected. This is certainly one of the books that our libraries will want to display during Negro History Week.[75]

Other scholars such as Ludwell Lee Montague, based at the Virginia Military Institute and soon to publish *Haiti and the United States, 1714–1938* in 1940, were also appreciative, with Montague noting that James "finds his way with skill through kaleidoscopic sequences of events in both Haiti and France, achieving clarity where complexities of class, color, and section have reduced others to vague confusion."[76]

While African American journals such as *The Crisis* and Trotskyist journals like *New International* were naturally enthusiastic, even *Time* magazine hailed *The Black Jacobins* as

> an impassioned account of Toussaint L'Ouverture and the Santo Domingo revolution, written from the Marxist point of view by a young British Negro. It bristles with harrowing atrocities, fiery denunciations of imperialism, but manages to give a vivid account of a revolution which greatly influenced U.S. history before the Civil War.[77]

An equally glowing review followed in the *New York Times*, which noted that "Mr. James is not afraid to touch his pen with the flame of ardent personal feeling, a sense of justice, love of freedom, admiration of heroism, hatred for tyranny—and his detailed richly documented and dramatically written book holds a deep and lasting interest."[78]

Underground Histories: The Persistent Presence of *The Black Jacobins*

Despite such praise, as James went "underground" in the United States in 1939, living a pseudonymous existence to be able to stay and work with Raya Dunayevskaya and the other members of the Johnson-Forest tendency within U.S. Trotskyism, *The Black Jacobins* also became something of an underground text, rapidly going out of print. One rare intellectual in the United States who did manage to make use of it was the Austrian radical anthropologist Eric R. Wolf (1923–1999)—later author of the classic studies *Peasant Wars of the Twentieth Century* (1969) and *Europe and the People without History* (1982)—who had come across James's writings as a seventeen-year-old refugee from fascism while interned in England in 1940 with other "aliens" at an Alien Internment Camp at Huyton near Liverpool. "I learned about Marxism by reading C.L.R. James," Wolf recalled.[79] "C.L.R. James . . . got me to think of Marxian methods to understand colonialism and global inequalities. That gave me an entry into the so-called underdeveloped world. From there, I read some political science, social science, and finally, just before the war, anthropology."[80] Studying anthropology at Columbia University after World War II, Wolf formed a study circle with others, including Sidney Mintz. As Wolf recalled,

> during those years I read three landmark books which suggested that anthropology could gain much from the infusion of Marxian understandings . . .

Karl Wittfogel's *Wirtschaft und Gesellschaft Chinas* (1931), an extraordinary, ecologically orientated study of the Chinese economy... Paul Sweezy's *The Theory of Capitalist Development* (1942) ... the third was C.L.R. James's *The Black Jacobins* (1938), on the slave rebellions in Haiti in the wake of the French Revolution, one of the first attempts to write a history of a people supposedly "without history."[81]

Yet James remembers how the few African intellectuals who managed to get hold of a copy were certainly impressed by its thesis that "placed the revolutionary struggle squarely in the hands of the Africans."[82] Among these was the future leader of Ghana, Kwame Nkrumah, whom James met in the United States during World War II. As James recalled, "Nkrumah read the book and we talked about it."[83] Indeed, if "C.L.R. James" had somewhat faded from view, his reputation as the author of *The Black Jacobins* persisted. Though James—unlike Nkrumah—was not present himself at the historic Fifth Pan-African Congress held in Manchester in October 1945, the official report edited by George Padmore included *The Black Jacobins* in its list of suggested reading.[84] In the summer of 1947, Raya Dunayevskaya visited Britain and attended a left-wing demonstration in London's Trafalgar Square. As she wrote to James back in the United States, "I noticed one of the Negro RAF men had the identification 'Trinidad', so I proceeded to introduce myself and ask whether he had ever heard of fellow Trinidadian [C.L.R. James]. An author? Yes. 'Black Jacobins'? Yes."[85] In the Caribbean, the work clearly proved an inspiration. A young Trinidadian radical, John La Rose, recalled coming across "the world classic *The Black Jacobins*" long before he was able to meet James. "I remember I had been so moved by his description of Boukman and his fellow revolutionaries on the mountain making the blood sacrifice amid thunder and lightning in 1791 at the start of the Haitian revolution that I wrote my first poem there and then."[86]

During the war, a French Trotskyist, Pierre Naville—who had first met James in Paris in 1936—translated the work into French in 1943–1944, when France itself was under Nazi occupation.

> My opinion at that time was that if France succeeded in restoring its national sovereignty—with the help of the Anglo-American forces—her first duty would be to give back freedom to its colonial empire as it existed before 1939. I thought that the publication of this book by James, whom I had known before the war, dedicated to the freedom struggle of the 'Hai-

tians' in Saint-Domingue during the first French Revolution, would serve this purpose.[87]

Les Jacobins noirs, Naville's French translation, eventually appeared in 1949, but David Geggus has noted that "the book has never been very popular with Francophone readers," perhaps, he suggests, because of superficial factual errors that might have been noticed by an educated French audience.[88] In February 1950, in *Les Temps Modernes*, Louis Ménard declared *The Black Jacobins* "most topical and most useful, as Naville stresses in his preface. The analysis and the way he [James] disproves a thousand abusive or calumnious tall stories about the cruelty of the Black insurgents are particularly instructive." Nonetheless, Ménard wondered at whether the Haitian Revolution really represented "the revolutionary success" that James saw it as, noting

> there is a problem: to what extent was the framework of bourgeois principles which Toussaint used not a new form of exploitation of the Black proletariat, but more subtle, and still far from a true liberation? . . . The fight of San Domingo only appears to be a revolutionary fight when viewed with the perspective afforded by other times and other events.[89]

This review forced James to protest by letter to the editors of *Les Temps Modernes*, noting the Haitian Revolution was "a revolution for the abolition of basic slavery; to assure their liberty, the Blacks judged it necessary to establish an independent State. I feel uncomfortable to have to declare that I consider these goals to be valid in themselves." As he continued,

> The revolution of San Domingo received its impetus from the French Revolution, and could not have been achieved without it, but reciprocally, the Blacks' fight proved a powerful contribution to the victories against the counter-revolution in France. In this way the slaves' revolution does not only have an immediate justification, but also an historic justification.

As for Ménard's argument that Toussaint did not deliver "true liberation" for the enslaved of Saint Domingue, James was scathing:

> Of what does this "true" liberation consist? The only meaning I can give him is the socialist abolition of all exploitation of man by man. It is not reasonable to blame Toussaint for not having tried to achieve that. The only liberation in question was the liberation from basic slavery and it was a liberation that was fairly "true." Mr. Ménard passes over this point as if it were

without importance. I insist—if I insist on something—on the fact that it was of a great importance, in the sense that I have talked about above . . .

As to the particular type of thought that this review seems to me to reveal, I abstain from any comment. But my book is a study of revolutionary theory and practice, referring especially to colonial revolution, and it really was not possible for me to let the interpretation of it given by Mr. Ménard stand without correcting it.[90]

Causing a stir in *Les Temps Modernes* aside, the French translation enabled the work to reach at least some Francophone anticolonialists, including, it appears, Frantz Fanon.[91] It also ensured the work finally made an impact in Haiti itself, where James recalled it quickly became something akin to a Bible. "When *The Black Jacobins* was published in French, it was read and deeply admired in Haiti. I unreservedly took the side of the slaves. Yet it was years before they discovered that the book was written by a Negro and a West Indian. That testifies to the historical objectivity."[92]

The appearance of the 1949 edition helped facilitate a dialogue between James and the Haitian historian Étienne Charlier, a member of the Déjoie Party, who wrote one of the first Marxist critiques of Haitian history (*Aperçu sur la formation historique de la nation haïtienne*, 1954). Charlier was also one of the first to stress the role of the maroons in helping ignite the Haitian Revolution, provoking historiographic controversy in Haiti and further afield. As W. E. B. Du Bois noted in 1955,

> from the time of Columbus . . . in every island . . . there were hundreds of slave revolts which prove, as Haitian historians say, that the French Revolution did not spread from France to the West Indies but from the West Indies to France. Negro revolt under the Maroons culminated in Haiti where Britain, France and Spain were worsted and the United States was frightened into stopping the slave trade.[93]

Another of Charlier's arguments—which triggered a robust response from a number of Haitian intellectuals, including Jean Price-Mars—was that 150 years after the revolution, pigmentocracy continued to determine social class in Haiti. Emmanuel Paul attacked Charlier for perpetuating the "mulatto legend" of Haitian history through suggestions that maroon revolt was precursory to the revolution that began in 1791,[94] and James—in a 1955 letter to Charlier—contested the claim that Louverture was "a man of the ancient regime." Repeating the key thesis of *The Black Jacobins*, James again presents the leader of the Haitian Revolution as "a revolutionary who had gone a long way but could not continue to what the situation actually demanded, the independence of the island," but he concedes that this is "a question more of the biographical analysis of Toussaint than of the fundamental analysis of the classes and forces in conflict." "And there," he adds, "I have learnt much from you!" In anticipation of his future interest in this key aspect of the history of the revolution, the letter goes on to question Charlier on material available about Toussaint's nephew, Moïse, "the man of the minor figures who interests me most," before James concludes with a statement underscoring what principally draws him to the Haitian Revolution: "the revolutionary and creative power of untaught slaves is what interests me about the revolution in San Domingo more than anything else." What he appreciated in Charlier was his central thesis that warns against versions of history that privilege "a few great men" to the detriment of any recognition of "the only great midwives of history," the people themselves.[95]

From the perspective of French revolutionary historiography, James had already been influenced here by Daniel Guérin's controversial argument in his substantial study *La Lutte de classes sous la première République: bourgeois et "bras nus" (1793–1797)* (published by Gallimard in 1946), a book that outlined a then-unorthodox critique of Jacobinism that explored the progressive domestication of the anonymous popular vanguard that drove the revolution in its early years. From the late 1940s, James worked on an English translation of Guérin's study, a section of the introduction to which appeared in French in 1958 in *Perspectives socialistes*.[96]

Perhaps part of the reason James never completed his intended translation of Guérin's work was the thrilling political developments taking place as national independence movements rose across Africa and the Caribbean after World War II, vindicating the prophetic conclusion to *The Black Jacobins*. On March 6, 1957, James—alongside many other distinguished black activists and writers from across the African diaspora, including Martin Luther King Jr. and George Padmore—was present for the Independence Day celebrations in Ghana, having been invited by Kwame Nkrumah.[97] While in Ghana, James discovered that *The Black Jacobins* had served as an inspirational underground text of the antiapartheid movement in South Africa. In his foreword to the 1980 edition, he recalled that "during the celebrations of the independence of Ghana in 1957, I met some Pan-African young men from South Africa who told me that my book had been of great service to them." After being recommended to the work by a white university professor, the young black students found it "a revelation, particularly in the relation between the blacks and the mulattoes . . . they typed out copies, mimeographed them and circulated the passages from *The Black Jacobins* dealing with the relations between the blacks and the mixed in Haiti."[98] James's experience more generally on this visit was incredibly stimulating, and as he wrote to his comrades back in the United States on his return to London, he felt it critical to begin writing "a 70,000 word book on Ghana." This eventually emerged in 1977 as *Nkrumah and the Ghana Revolution*, and contained a significant chapter on "The Revolution in Theory," written around 1957, discussing how he came to write *The Black Jacobins* and outlining some thoughts on how the Marxist theory of permanent revolution needed to be updated in light of decolonization. As James put it in a letter written to his comrades on March 20, 1957,

> I propose to review past writings particularly *Black Jacobins*. I shall quote and show how clearly the future was foreseen there, when practically everybody thought they were crazy. (Read in particular pp. 314–316; p. 11; p. 222.) . . . I shall review Nkrumah's book [*The Autobiography of Kwame Nkrumah*] and break completely with, or rather develop qualitatively the theoretical premises of the *Black Jacobins* and the Leninist theory of the colonial revolution. The African revolution (as a process) is no longer to be seen as supplementary to or subordinate to the revolution in Western Europe. I shall examine it in relation to the French Revolution, the Russian; the Chinese and the Hungarian.[99]

The next day, James wrote again to his comrades, explaining that he had begun his rethinking of *The Black Jacobins* in the light of inspiring recent political developments. "You will note that at last the two strands which I have worked on for the last twenty years, beginning with *The Black Jacobins* and *World Revolution*, have at last merged quite naturally into one."

> Please remember that the last part of the book is going to pose very sharply the enormous difficulties which face Nkrumah and the CPP [Convention People's Party] . . . The central question is Nkrumah's rejection of armed revolution. He says, and he tells me that I can quote him on this, that looking over the experience taking over the government and between 1957 he is not certain that the method he adopted was correct. I am fairly certain that it is. But the real danger comes now, and originates with the lack of momentum with which he was compelled to approach the problems

of government. Revolutionary it was, profoundly so, as Luther King in Montgomery, Alabama was revolutionary.[100]

Three days later, on March 24, 1957, James again met with Martin Luther King Jr. and his wife, Coretta, as they passed through London. Together with Selma James, George Lamming, and David Pitt, they discussed the Montgomery bus boycott and the wider civil rights movement that had erupted in the United States.[101] On April 5, 1957, James, who had been forced to return to Britain from the United States in 1953 amidst the rise of McCarthyism, wrote the following letter to King:

Dear Dr. King,

I expect that you are safely home by now. I hope you and your wife had a pleasant journey and that when you reached home you found the baby well, and the organisation in good shape.

I have by now been able to send a copy of THE BLACK JACOBINS to Louis and Lucille Armstrong and have asked them, when they have finished with it, to send it on to you. You will have realised by now that my political frame of reference is not 'non-cooperation', but I examine every political activity, strategy, and tactic in terms of its success or failure.

I wish you the best of success and hope to hear from you periodically.

I am thinking in terms of re-writing THE BLACK JACOBINS. The facts of the case and my general interpretation will remain the same, but there are many references and certain tones and attitudes which I think spoil the book for the general public.

With best wishes for yourself and the family, and with warm greetings to all your fellow workers.

Yours sincerely,
C. L. R. James[102]

On April 30, 1957, King replied to James, noting that "I am looking forward with great anticipation for a copy of *The Black Jacobins*. [Lawrence Dunbar] Reddick has already told me what an excellent piece of work it is."[103]

Amidst the exciting contemporary political changes under way, epitomized by "the Ghana Revolution," James actively reengaged with Haiti's revolutionary history. Although it remains unclear whether he ever visited Haiti himself, he actively planned to do so in this period. In March 1958 he corresponded with the poet, politician, and diplomat Jean-Fernand Brierre about his discussions with Félix Morisseau-Leroy and others regarding a possible trip that year.

> You would be interested to know that my book on Haiti has formed an indispensable basis for my study of Ghana. The basic parallels, both in the course of political events and in the shaping on individual character, are astonishing. In tracing what was immanent in Haiti and has now reached full flower in the political development of Ghana, we walk along the very high road of modern history.[104]

James's role in interpreting the legacies of the Haitian Revolution in wider frames, not least those of contemporary postcolonial politics, was recognized in Haiti, and his papers contain a letter to Morisseau-Leroy from Lamartinière Honorat, undersecretary of state and representative of the recently elected president François Duvalier, in which he recognizes the existence of "une dette à acquitter envers le grand intellectuel noir antillais" [a debt to be paid to the great Black Antillean intellectual].[105] It seems that at the time there were plans to produce a Haitian edition of *The Black Jacobins*, and it is clear that by this stage James was keen to engage contemporary Haitian historians in discussion of his work.

Rewriting *The Black Jacobins*

In the British West Indies, triumphant nationalist politicians also realized their debt to James and *The Black Jacobins*. On May 30, 1960, Eric Williams, now leader of the People's National Movement in Trinidad, publicly praised in front of a large crowd "the trail blazed" since "C.L.R. James's monumental analysis of the Haitian segment of our history" in exposing the "great lie of West Indian history."[106] That year James returned the compliment, noting "for my part I had had plans for doing more work on the West Indies. I put that aside for other things when I saw the powers [Eric] Williams had developed and the direction of his mind. I felt the intellectual basis of West Indian nationalism was in safe hands."[107] Williams's warm sentiment about *The Black Jacobins* was eloquently expressed the same year by the Barbadian poet and novelist George Lamming, who had first met James in 1950s London. In an important reflective essay in *The Pleasures of Exile*, Lamming declared *The Black Jacobins* "a West Indian classic . . . the product of a West Indian working at the height of his powers." "It is not by accident that a document so rich in facts, so beautiful in narrative organisation, should have remained out of print for over twenty years." Yet

> it is wonderful that this epic of Toussaint's glory and dying should have been rendered by C.L.R. James, one of the most energetic minds of our time, a neighbour of Toussaint's island, a heart and desire entirely within the tradition of Toussaint himself, a spirit that came to life in the rich and humble soil of a British colony in the Caribbean.[108]

Encouraged by Lamming's endorsement of his book, James began to sense the political and intellectual urgency of making *The Black Jacobins* available in an accessible format once again. This comes through in a letter to Fredric Warburg in September 1960: "With the situation what it is in South Africa, the Rhodesian Federation, in Kenya, the Congo and the West Indies, there is an insistent demand that the book be republished, not least in America. The general idea is that the edition should be paper-covered."[109] The idea soon became a reality, for North American publishers were beginning to see the commercial potential of republishing *The Black Jacobins* amidst the civil rights movement. As Selma James recalled in 2013, "the reason *The Black Jacobins* was republished was because black people in the United States were requesting it and the publishers said 'Ah, this is a chance to make some money.' And so we got the call. We were absolutely astonished. It came out of the blue."[110]

Having produced the first edition in the interwar context of emerging anticolonial and Pan-African activism, James was committed to recasting it in the altered, postindependence context of the 1960s. In his rewriting of the book, he concentrated on a very different set of highly complex circumstances. In the Caribbean, newly won independence in the former British colonies (most notably in Trinidad) is to be contrasted by accentuating a colonial relationship through departmentalization in the French territories of Guadeloupe, Guiana, and Martinique. Led by activist-intellectuals such as Édouard Glissant, an autonomist movement was growing in the Francophone Caribbean, the direction of which was modulated in part in response to the inspiration of the Cuban Revolution and the anxiety generated by the rise of Duvalierism in Haiti. In a wider Atlantic frame, the sharpening of the politics of race, in particular the growing militancy that later became known to the world as Black Power, granted the Haitian Revolution a renewed resonance.

James's rewriting began in earnest in the context of his return to Trinidad from 1958 onward in advance of independence. He noted in a 1961 letter to Morris Philipson—his editor at Random House—the existence of "a lot of excitement in the West Indies" about the new edition, "especially in view of the approaching independence, the emergence of Castro, and the recent death of Trujillo."[111] In a letter earlier the same year to John G. Patisson at Secker and Warburg, James had similarly referred, in the context of the Cuban Revolution, to "excitement among the politically-minded all over the West Indies with frequent references to *The Black Jacobins*, and the historic revolution in San Domingo which is so near to them."[112] Indeed, the correspondence with Philipson allows tracking of this process of translation of the 1938 edition into its new context and reveals James's freedom to reshape the work as he saw best. In November 1960, Philipson stated that if the new edition were contracted, "it would be entirely agreeable with us to have you make any changes, omissions, or alterations that you should wish to make for such a new edition."[113] The implications of this rewriting have been studied in detail by David Scott in his important intervention in postcolonial studies, *Conscripts of Modernity*. Scott focuses on the addition of six new paragraphs to chapter 13, "The War of Independence," to describe the way the anticolonial romanticism of the 1938 edition is translated into a form of postcolonial tragedy. There is still a need for a more thorough genetic analysis of the complete set of transformations in the text, for although the alterations to chapter 13 are clearly very significant, there are rewritings evident throughout the text (not least in terms of a lightening of the Marxist-inflected language of 1938). In letters to Philipson, James referred to "a number of political references, in themselves very slight, but nevertheless obtrusive, which I want to take out," and Philipson also suggested a reduction of the accounts of the military campaigns while urging James to consider whether "to change some of the phrasing of your analysis of relations among the classes of people involved, since you yourself indicated that it is now rather questionable whether the particular sets of Marxian terms used for such analysis are the most appropriate."[114]

In a subsequent letter to the editor of the *New Statesman* after the new edition had been published, James outlined the extent of his revisions, highlighting the updating of sections relating to the historiography of the French Revolution and the refined assessment of the world historical role of Louverture (and its links to Haiti), concluding that the 1963 edition would find a readership that eluded its precocious 1938 predecessor: "It has been agreed that the book appeared before its time and that it is events in the colonial world after World War II that make what was envisaged in 1938 actual history of the 1960s and the times ahead."[115] The paratextual addition of a new appendix was, however, clearly the element of the new edition, situating the Haitian Revolution in the "spurts, leaps and catastrophes" of Caribbean history, to which James anticipated the most significant reaction. The genesis of the appendix can be tracked in James's correspondence with Philipson, who encourages the author to develop the modest textual addition to which he first refers: "I shall also write an introduction of a few pages in which I shall link up what took place in the Caribbean in the eighteenth century with what is taking place there today, what is known in general as the passing of colonialism."[116] Philipson, understanding the potential significance of such an essay, encouraged James to produce "an essay of whatever length you would wish to make it,"[117] and in a subsequent letter repeated the invitation "to write as extensive an introduction as you wish to, in order to make the point that we discussed concerning the reflections that may well be drawn for contemporary colonial problems from the Haitian experience."[118]

In a letter to George Lamming after the new edition had appeared, James highlighted the importance of his new appendix, "From Toussaint L'Ouverture to Fidel Castro," and commented: "I am still amazed at what you did for *Black Jacobins* in *The Pleasures of Exile*. I send you a revised copy and I eagerly await what you will have to say about the Appendix."[119] There has been much debate as to the respective emphases of the 1938 and 1963 editions, triggered not least by James's later claim that the first version of *The Black Jacobins* was written "with Africa in mind."[120] Although the new edition was produced in a rapidly changing Caribbean context—in the tension between disappointments regarding Trinidadian independence and continued hope associated with Cuba—its resonance remains multiple and its relevance for newly independent sub-Saharan African states evident. James wrote to Basil Davidson that the appendix "poses West African development in pretty stark opposition to African," but nevertheless saw his focus on "the fundamental conception that goes under the name of Negritude" as a persistent link.[121] He continued this argument in a letter to Colin Legum of *The Observer* in which he stated that the new edition constituted "the beginning of much clarification about the things that are disturbing people who are concerned with the future of African development."[122]

The 1963 edition of *The Black Jacobins* was complemented by a new version of the play describing the same events, rewritten for a performance produced by Dexter Lyndersay at the University of Ibadan, Nigeria, in 1967, and discussed by Rachel Douglas in her contribution to this volume. There is also further evidence of James's ambitions for rewriting the work across media, and in a 1967 letter to his fellow Trinidadian Marina Maxwell, he mentioned the possibility of a film version of the work: "I am on the verge of sending a copy of my book and a copy of the play to the Rank Organization where I understand there is an excellent possibility that they will take out an option, for them of course to us as and when they please."[123] Susan Gillman notes that the appendix to the 1963 edition was part of an expansive gesture, with the text's original opening in 1938, presenting the landing of Columbus in the New World, extended to the present day:

> Expressed mathematically: from Columbus to Toussaint + from Toussaint to Castro = from Columbus to Castro. The total evokes a strikingly open-ended comparative history that outdoes even Eric Williams's book of the same title, *From Columbus to Castro: The History of the Caribbean, 1492–1969*, that would not appear until 1970.[124]

When the revised edition of *The Black Jacobins* was published by Random House in 1963, David Geggus notes that its prestige was now "enhanced by the wave of decolonisation that it had predicted and by the onset of the new social history," epitomized by E. P. Thompson's monumental *The Making of the English Working Class* (1963).[125] Professional historians found the work more difficult to avoid now, and in a sign of things to come, in a footnote to the second volume of his *Age of Democratic Revolution* (1964), R. R. Palmer recommended James's work as one of "the best" of the "many books on the revolution in Haiti."[126] *The Black Jacobins* finally began to receive the kind of recognition and attention it deserved amidst the rise of the New Left and the Black Power movements in the Caribbean and internationally. In his contribution David Austin explores some of the intense and urgent discussions about the work's meaning and message among young black radical activists and scholars on the Caribbean New Left, including the Canadian-based C. L. R. James Study Circle, which came together in Montreal around figures such as Franklyn Harvey, Tim Hector, Anne Cools, Alfie Roberts, and Robert A. Hill.[127] James had added six new paragraphs discussing the tragedy of Toussaint Louverture in this new edition, noting that his hero "was attempting the impossible—the impossible was for him the only reality that mattered." The revolutionary energy of the 1960s, captured in the slogan "Be realistic—demand the impossible!" thus found its echo consciously or unconsciously in

James's *Black Jacobins*, helping make it "a book of the Sixties" for many young black revolutionary activists.[128]

The young Trinidadian who became a key figure in the Black Power movement of the United States, Stokely Carmichael, has described how he was "thrilled—moved and inspired" when he read "this great book," which "just overwhelmed" him.[129] Third Worldism was also at its height, and as Dan Georgakas, a young radical in Detroit, once recalled, there was a tendency among others of his generation to interpret *The Black Jacobins* "in a kind of Maoist fashion as an example of how an underdeveloped Third World nation could defeat the most powerful imperialists of its day through a protracted people's war."[130] Yet importantly those engaged with local race and class struggles also found the work an inspiration. Georgakas and Marvin Surkin, in their history of the League of Revolutionary Black Workers, a U.S. organization described by historian Manning Marable as "in many respects the most significant expression of black radical thought and activism in the 1960s," recalled that "James's ideas were well known to League activists and *Black Jacobins* was the work which struck the deepest chord."[131]

By the late 1960s, the rise of the civil rights and Black Power movements enabled James to return to the United States to lecture. As Selma James recalled, "CLR was not able to even pass through the States, or even Puerto Rico on his way to London from the West Indies until Black students demanded that he come and lecture. . . . The movements were great and were immediately beneficial to us."[132] From 1968 to 1969, thanks to the demands of black students at Northwestern University, James was invited to be a visiting scholar, which enabled his legal return to the United States. He later moved to Washington, DC, where he briefly taught black studies at Federal City College (now the University of the District of Columbia).[133] In a letter to Fredric Warburg in January 1969, written after the international revolutionary turmoil of 1968, James noted: "*Black Jacobins* in the new edition is a great success and I found the book well known on campus after campus in the United States and Canada."[134] The impact it made on the emerging field of black studies in the North American academy should not be underestimated, and distinguished scholars such as Manning Marable and David Levering Lewis have paid tribute to the powerful impact of the work.[135] In 1968, the work was translated into Italian, and despite a misleading rendering of the work's subtitle as "La prima rivolta contro l'uomo bianco" ("The first uprising against the white man"), Ferrucio Gambino recalled "the publication of *The Black Jacobins* led to some radical rethinking not only of world history and world accumulation but also of the very notion of imperialism, class, and social formation" among the Italian left.[136]

The work also made an impact in Britain, in particular among young West Indian intellectuals. As Stuart Hall, a young Jamaican scholar then in London, remembered, "although of course I knew of its existence, I'm pretty certain that I didn't read it until the paperback publication of 1963, and so far as I remember it wasn't prominent in public discussion. So for me, and for many others, it is in fact a text of the sixties." As Hall notes,

> the West Indian intellectuals who came to London in the fifties and sixties . . . knew C.L.R. through *The Case for West Indian Self-Government* and his connections with the West Indian labour movement, but not through his histories. So I don't think it really becomes an active text again until the sixties . . . it was a long while before people in Britain understood that, in addition to the other ways in which they knew James, he was also an important historian.[137]

One exception to this general rule was Walter Rodney, the outstanding Guyanese historian and political activist, who had come across *The Black Jacobins* in the library while studying as an undergraduate at the University of the West Indies in the early 1960s. He later declared the work together with Williams's *Capitalism and Slavery* as "two of the foremost texts that informed a nationalist consciousness" among his fellow students in this period. On moving to Britain to undertake his doctorate at the School of Oriental and African Studies, he joined a study circle on Marxism for West Indian students in London around James himself.[138] Rodney later presented *The Black Jacobins* as James's "major effort to project a past revolt into present consciousness," declaring it to be a "remarkable study of the momentous victory of the enslaved African population of San Domingo against white plantation society, against the Thermidorean reaction in France, and against the expansionism of British capital."[139] The next generation of black radicals in Britain would often come to know James after first hearing about and reading his historical work. As Jamaican dub poet Linton Kwesi Johnson once recalled,

> I came into contact with the work of C.L.R. James when I was a young Black Panther, a member of the Black Panthers Youth League and the Black Panther Movement in England, in the late 1960s, early 1970s. We studied the book *The Black Jacobins*, chapter by chapter. It was the begin-

ning of my political education and my having a sense of what black history meant.[140]

Among a new generation of African intellectuals, the work struck a chord. The Kenyan novelist Ngũgĩ wa Thiong'o first met James at Makerere, while James was visiting Uganda in 1969, and James later actively supported the struggle to free political prisoners such as Ngũgĩ in Kenya. Ngũgĩ met James again in London during the 1980s at the annual International Book Fair of Radical Black and Third World Books (1982–1995), established by Bogle-Louverture Publications, New Beacon Books and the Race Today Collective.[141] As Ngũgĩ wrote in 1993, in *Moving the Centre: The Struggle for Cultural Freedoms*, "if I could make every black person read one book on the history of black people in the West, that would have to be C.L.R. James's *The Black Jacobins*."[142] That was easier done in some places than others. In apartheid South Africa, Scott McLemee notes of the banned 1963 edition that "copies were scarce, and the potential audience was large so people had to improvise," continuing that one group

> tore James's thick book into clusters of a few pages, to be circulated a little at a time. Members would study each fragment closely and then pass it on to the next eager reader. They doubtless memorized large parts of the book this way, while waiting for the next instalment to reach them. Few writers ever find their work treated with such passionate intensity.[143]

Rethinking *The Black Jacobins*

It is difficult to talk of the impact of *The Black Jacobins* in terms of the afterlives of a text because the work continued to expand and evolve, not least as it was discovered by new readerships in newly politicized contexts. In James's lectures in the United States in the late 1960s, the Haitian Revolution continued to be a key subject in his repertoire, largely because be found that his history had attracted new audiences. What becomes increasingly apparent is that *The Black Jacobins* had begun to take on a life of its own—as is the case with many of the other so-called great books about which James himself wrote extensively—meaning that telling divergences may appear between the text and James's commentary on it, not least in terms of the work's historiographic underpinnings.

In "The Old World and the New" (with reference to which this introduction opened), James may have discussed with a certain vagueness his personal motivations for writing *The Black Jacobins*, but he remains very clear about two aspects of the text. The first is the way the history of the Haitian Revolution reacted to a certain zeitgeist: "Something was in the atmosphere," he writes, "and I responded to it." The second is the extent to which the text had by then achieved a wider resonance of unprecedented scope and scale:

> What is remarkable is that today, in 1971, that book is more popular, more widely read than at any other previous time. In other words, though it was written so long ago, it meets the needs of the young people in the United States today, and I am very pleased about it, in Britain, Africa, the Caribbean and other places. There has been a French translation, there has been an Italian translation. . . . But the book was written in 1938 and still has a validity today, 1971, because I came originally from the kind of territory which produced René Maran, Marcus Garvey, George Padmore, Aimé Césaire and Frantz Fanon, and we were prepared not only to say what should be done in the Caribbean, but we were trained and developed in such a way that we were able to make tremendous discoveries about Western civilisation itself.[144]

James gives a sense of the continued engagement with a text that had been published three decades earlier. He focuses on translation as a key element of the work's wider dissemination but does not make explicit the ways he had continued to revisit his account of the Haitian Revolution, in a process that could be seen as self-translation, in the light of changing circumstances in the Caribbean and in the wider global frame to which he alludes. In his foreword to the 1980 Allison and Busby edition of *The Black Jacobins*, an edition which helped ensure the work made an impact on a new generation of radicals and anti-racists, James acknowledged the limitations of his original history: "1938 is a long time ago, however, and I waited many years for other people to enter the lists and go further than I was able to go. I was never worried about what they find, confident that my foundation would remain imperishable."[145] He went on to reference two projects—Jean Fouchard's *Les Marrons de la liberté* (1972), which built on the work of Charlier and provided the first detailed study of the maroons and for the English translation of which (*The Haitian Maroons: Liberty or Death* [1981]) he wrote a preface, and Carolyn Fick's doctoral thesis that was published as *The Making of Haiti: The Saint Domingue Revolution from Below* (1990). Both of these works signal the emergence of an alternative historiography of the Haitian Revolution, one in which the formerly enslaved play a key role.[146]

James's characteristic conviction regarding the "imperishability" of *The Black Jacobins* is tempered by a firm sense in his 1980 foreword that "further study of the revolution in French San Domingo will reveal more and more of its affinity with revolutions in more developed communities"—a reflection that continues to echo the shuttling in the 1930s between the historical moment of the Haitian Revolution and the interwar niche in which James was interpreting it.[147] He had been aware for some years that the historiographic underpinnings of *The Black Jacobins*—in particular his reliance on narrating the revolution primarily through the figure of Toussaint Louverture—were increasingly under scrutiny. The emergence of alternative modes of narrating the past, in which the agency of the people was granted the greater recognition it merited, undermined the emphases on the revolutionary leaders by which the writing of Haitian history had long been characterized. *The Black Jacobins* had challenged such tendencies, not only by resisting hagiography and by drawing political meanings from the flaws evident in a character such as Louverture but also by alluding to the role of the formerly enslaved masses in inciting, driving, and shaping the revolution.

In essence, this recalibration of the relative emphases on the role of the leaders of the revolution and that of the formerly enslaved masses characterized James's continued reflection on Haiti in the final years of his life.[148] It is a theme particularly evident in the "Lectures on *The Black Jacobins*" delivered at the Institute of the Black World in Atlanta in 1971, given alongside a series of other lectures (including one on the Trinidadian Marxist sociologist Oliver Cromwell Cox). Aldon Nielsen studies James's 1971 lectures on *The Black Jacobins*—that appeared in print for the first time in *Small Axe* in 2000—in the current volume. Perhaps more than any other source, the transcripts capture James's constant reengagement with, reevaluation of, and rewriting (literal and otherwise) of the work that already had begun to multiply in the 1930s. The three lectures have a clear structure, moving from a detailed account of the genesis of the text, locating it in relation to his other writings in the 1930s in "How I Wrote *The Black Jacobins*" (June 14, 1971), establishing the credentials of the book in a differential comparison with Du Bois in "*The Black Jacobins* and *Black Reconstruction*: A Comparative Analysis" (June 15, 1971), and concluding with a self-reflexive account of what a new and fully revised 1970s edition of the work might look like in "How I Would Rewrite *The Black Jacobins*" (June 18, 1971). The final lecture underscores the extent to which new material—drawing on the work of contemporary French historians such as Lefebvre and Soboul—included in the footnotes of the 1963 edition would, in a rewritten version of the text, even more radically affect the historical analysis of the Haitian Revolution. James claimed a new version would foreground the formerly enslaved as the chorus of the narrative and focus on the "obscure leaders" or on the "two thousand leaders to be taken away" whom Leclerc describes in a letter to Napoleon in which he outlines the implications of removing Louverture from the Caribbean.[149] The work he imagines builds on the research of Haitian scholars such as Jean Fouchard and anticipates the writings of other key scholars of the Haitian Revolution, such as Laurent Dubois, Carolyn Fick, John Thornton, and Michel-Rolph Trouillot. The invitation implicit in the lectures is summarized by Anthony Bogues in his afterword to their publication in *Small Axe*: to "think *with* and then *beyond* James."[150] It is striking that the author himself, in his reflections on and revisions and rewritings of *The Black Jacobins* over a period of five decades, demonstrates the potential of such a project and encourages the reader to use the book in the light of such a challenge.

Now in its eighth decade, *The Black Jacobins* continues to attract new readers and new readings, as a result of the new editions in which it appears (most recently and notably the 2001 Penguin version, with an introduction by James Walvin) and of the translations in which it continues to circulate.[151] Translation has constituted a key mechanism in the text's circulation; to reflect this, the volume contains English versions of the prefatory material to the French and Cuban editions (by Pierre Naville and John Bracey, respectively) as well as the afterword to the 2006 Italian edition (by Madison Smartt Bell). Having been almost lost from view (except among a dedicated readership in the immediate postwar period), the second edition of 1963 propelled the work into the midst of debates on decolonization and its aftermath, transforming it into a handbook for revolution in the context of the emerging black power movement and other ongoing struggles. For some, James's political partisanship and lack of status as a professional historian sometimes made him somewhat vulnerable to the charge that *The Black Jacobins* was not somehow adequately scholarly. Although it is the case, as Geggus notes, that "relying heavily on secondary sources, *The Black Jacobins* has its share of factual errors, but probably, fewer than most of its competitors," historians of the Haitian Revolution (such as Thomas O. Ott) who have tried to insist that these mistakes somehow flowed naturally from flaws in James's Marxist ideology have never been convincing.[152]

In particular, Ott's accusation that James's "stumbling attempt to connect the Haitian and French revolutions through some sort of common mass movement is a good example of 'fact trimming' to fit a particular thesis or ideology" now looks more than a little short-sighted in light of the way it anticipated subsequent scholarship around transnationalism and Atlantic history.[153] As Catherine Hall and Keith McClelland have noted recently,

> the injunction to place metropole and colony within the same analytic frame, practised so brilliantly by C.L.R. James in the late 1930s in his classic text on the Haitian and French revolutions, *The Black Jacobins*, but neglected by historians for decades, has been widely adopted. As metropolitan societies once at the heart of great European empires struggled to adapt to and understand their own forms of postcolonial melancholia and to transform themselves into multicultural and creolised societies, historians thought anew about their paradigms.[154]

Although Franklin Knight could suggest in 1974, in a review of Ott's work, that "curiously, however, the historiography of the Haitian revolution fails to yield any competent scholarship of the quality readily available for the American, French, Mexican, Russian, Turkish, or Cuban revolutions," what seems most remarkable today is that *The Black Jacobins* has established itself as not simply the classic Marxist account of the revolution but the classic introduction to the Haitian Revolution in its own right.[155] As Paul Buhle once put it, "*The Black Jacobins* is the novelistic account of the first successful slave revolt in two thousand years; like W.E.B. Du Bois's *Black Reconstruction*, it will never be out of date."[156] As well as various and continuing new translations of the text, James's insights and analysis have been taken up and developed by numerous historians of race and slavery in the Americas, including Robin Blackburn, Carolyn Fick, Eugene Genovese, and George Rawick.[157] Testimony to the power of the work to inspire might also be seen by the fact that as well as David M. Rudder's 1988 calypso song "Haiti," *The Black Jacobins* has inspired at least one opera, at least one play, and one art exhibition.[158]

Conclusion: *The Black Jacobins* in a Contemporary Frame

In an overview of James's political legacy, Selma James criticizes the tendency of a number of contemporary critics and readers to defuse the incendiary implications of works such as *The Black Jacobins*. "It was often more convenient," she writes, "in the mushrooming CLR James industry for most of his political history to be dismissed as either a detour in an otherwise brilliant career or the foibles of a genius."[159] The frustration evident here is over what might be seen as a "cultural turn" in studies of James, resulting in the presentation of his work "in a political and organizational vacuum."[160] A postcolonial engagement with James began with the work of Edward Said, most notably in the chapter of *Culture and Imperialism* cited already, in which James's journey to England in the 1930s is seen as an archetypal "voyage in," between colonized and colonizing worlds, with the Caribbean thinker challenging and reorienting intellectual and political life in Europe and its colonies as a result.

In another essay, in which James does not play a role, Said describes "travelling theory," by which he understands the shift of ideas between contexts and the dissipation of their original insurrectionary, revolutionary impact in the process.[161] Said asks what happens when a theory, idea, or text is tamed and instrumentalized as it undergoes multiple displacements. Taking as his example the work of Georg Lukács, he tracks the analysis of reification in *History and Class Consciousness*, the transfer of which from 1919 Budapest to mid-twentieth-century Paris (in the work of Lucien Goldmann) and finally to later twentieth-century Cambridge (in the work of Raymond Williams) is seen in terms of dissipation, degradation, and domestication. Said emphasizes the importance of recognizing both current context and point of origin; transfer is seen in terms of the loss of incendiary power and revolutionary impact. For Said, when a book with an incendiary power first emerges, it possesses what he considers to be a worldliness or organic connection to lived experience or contemporary history that is lost as it is progressively distanced from its origins. In identifying the cultural turn in discussions of works by James, Selma James may be seen to describe the type of traveling to which Said alludes. It is clear that studies of *The Black Jacobins* in a number of fields, not least postcolonial studies, have heavily underplayed the book's political underpinnings and implications.

It is important to note, however, that the dissipation he originally describes is eschewed in Said's later corrective essay, "Travelling Theory Reconsidered," in which he considers alternative trajectories of Lukács's work; in Adorno's and Fanon's respective engagements with his writings, there emerges an alternative type of "travelling theory gone tougher, harder, more recalcitrant," as if reinterpretation has become not so much a repetition as a reignition of original impact in different contexts and different situations.[162] *The Black Jacobins* has been subject to both of these processes, and this introduction has endeavored to track the shifting influence of the work in a range of different situations—geographical, historical, and intellectual. What remains clear is its continued potential to illuminate and inspire—and contribute to the process of "setting the past in relation to the present in order to distil from it a politics for a possible future."[163]

| | | | |

While we were preparing this volume for submission, the sad news reached us of the passing of Stuart Hall. Given that Hall was one of the most profound and thoughtful readers of *The Black Jacobins*, which he suggested was "the first work to centre slavery in world history," and that we had hoped he might honor us by contributing an afterword to this volume, we felt it was only fitting to salute his rich life, work, and legacy by dedicating this volume to his memory.[164]

Notes

1. On James's political and intellectual evolution in Britain, see Christian Høgsbjerg, *C.L.R. James in Imperial Britain* (Durham, NC: Duke University Press, 2014).

2. Our thanks to Robert A. Hill for providing the text from the original dust jacket from the 1938 Secker and Warburg edition.

3. James's first work to be published with Secker and Warburg was his novel *Minty Alley* (1936).

4. C. L. R. James, "The Old World and the New," in *At the Rendezvous of Victory: Selected Writings*, vol. 3 (London: Allison and Busby, 1984), 211. It is interesting to note in passing that the French ornithologist Louis Jean Pierre Vieillot (1748–1831), who had experienced the Haitian Revolution firsthand, coined the term "Black Jacobin" in 1817 to name a type of hummingbird (*Florisuga fusca*) found in parts of Latin America. On Vieillot, see Paul H. Oehser, "Louis Jean Pierre Vieillot (1748–1831)," *Auk* 65, no. 4 (1948): 568–76.

5. C. L. R. James, *Beyond a Boundary* (London: Hutchinson, 1969), 122.

6. See Selwyn R. Cudjoe, "The Audacity of It All: C.L.R. James's Trinidadian Background," in *C.L.R. James's Caribbean*, edited by Paget Henry and Paul Buhle (Durham, NC: Duke University Press), 46–50.

7. James Anthony Froude, *The English in the West Indies; or, the Bow of Ulysses* (London: Longmans, Green, 1888), 347.

8. Sidney C. Harland, "Race Admixture," *Beacon* 1, no. 4 (July 1931), 27.

9. C. L. R. James, "The Intelligence of the Negro: A Few Words with Dr. Harland," *Beacon* 1, no. 5 (August 1931), 7–9. For a full discussion of this exchange, see Aldon Lynn Nielsen, *C.L.R. James: A Critical Introduction* (Jackson: University Press of Mississippi, 1997), 8–12.

10. James, "The Intelligence of the Negro," 10.

11. James, "The Intelligence of the Negro," 9.

12. C. L. R. James, *The Black Jacobins: Toussaint L'Ouverture and the San Domingo Revolution* (London: Penguin, 2001), 336.

13. James, *Beyond a Boundary*, 114.

14. Edward W. Said, *Culture and Imperialism* (London: Chatto and Windus, 1993), 295.

15. Stuart Hall, "Breaking Bread with History: C.L.R. James and *The Black Jacobins*: Stuart Hall Interviewed by Bill Schwarz," *History Workshop Journal* 46 (1998): 24.

16. C. L. R. James, "Autobiography, Section 4, 1932–38," University of the West Indies (UWI), Box 14, file 309.

17. Susan Gillman, "Black Jacobins and New World Mediterraneans," in *Surveying the American Tropics: A Literary Geography from New York to Rio*, edited by Maria Cristina Fumagalli, Peter Hulme, Owen Robinson, and Lesley Wylie (Liverpool: Liverpool University Press, 2013), 171, 172.

18. James, *Beyond a Boundary*, 124.

19. David Nicholls, *From Dessalines to Duvalier: Race, Color and National Independence in Haiti* (Cambridge: Cambridge University Press, 1979), 87–102.

20. See C. L. R. James, "My Knowledge of Damas Is Unique," in *Leon-Gontran Damas, 1912–1978: Father of Negritude: A Memorial Casebook*, edited by Daniel L. Racine (Washington, DC: University Press of America, 1979), 131–34. Thanks to F. Bart Miller for this reference.

21. In *The Black Jacobins*, James recalled how Lord Robert Cecil, representing the British government at the League of Nations in 1935, tried to counter Nemours by bringing up the historic massacre of many French whites in Haiti by the new Emperor Dessalines, at the time "supported by the King of England" in 1805. As James noted, Cecil "would have been more cautious if he had known the part his own highly civilized country played in this supposedly typical example of black savagery." See James, *The Black Jacobins*, 299.

22. James, *The Black Jacobins*, xvi, 336. For more on James and Nemours, see Charles Forsdick, "The Black Jacobin in Paris," *Journal of Romance Studies* 5, no. 3 (2005): 9–24.

23. James, "Autobiography, 1932–38."

24. Louise Cripps, *C.L.R. James: Memories and Commentaries* (London: Cornwall Books, 1997), 48–55.

25. Cripps, *C.L.R. James*, 50.

26. Cripps, *C.L.R. James*, 48–50. Though James could clearly read French well, Cripps recalled his spoken French in comparison was less strong, something that "really angered him" as "he could not fully express his views." On this 1935 trip, apparently "he became almost fluent in French in three weeks."

27. C. L. R. James, "Eric Williams," UWI, Box 16, folder 338.

28. For further discussion on the intellectual relationship between James and Williams with respect to their work overthrowing the conventional historical understanding of Atlantic slavery and abolition, see Aaron Kamugisha, "C.L.R. James's *The Black Jacobins* and the Making of the Modern Atlantic World," in *Ten Books that Shaped the*

British Empire: Creating an Imperial Commons, edited by Antoinette Burton and Isabel Hofmeyr (Durham, NC: Duke University Press, 2014), 190–215. For recent scholarship on the material legacies of colonial slavery in Britain that build upon the pioneering work of James and Williams, see Catherine Hall, Keith McClelland, Nick Draper, Kate Donington, and Rachel Lang, *Legacies of British Slave-Ownership: Colonial Slavery and the Formation of Victorian Britain* (Cambridge: Cambridge University Press, 2014).

29. The play was performed at the Westminster Theatre in London by the Stage Society in March 1936, with Paul Robeson in the title role. See C. L. R. James, *Toussaint Louverture: The Story of the Only Successful Slave Revolt in History: A Play in Three Acts* (Durham, NC: Duke University Press, 2013). For a recent discussion of twentieth-century theatrical engagements with the Haitian Revolution, see Jeremy Matthew Glick, *The Black Radical Tragic: Performance, Aesthetics, and the Unfinished Haitian Revolution* (New York: New York University Press, 2016).

30. Hall, "Breaking Bread with History," 21.

31. On the occupation, see Mary Renda, *Taking Haiti: Military Occupation and the Culture of U.S. Imperialism, 1915–1940* (Chapel Hill: University of North Carolina Press, 2001), and for some suggestive comments about James's thoughts on this, see Raphael Dalleo, "'The Independence so hardly won has been maintained': C.L.R. James and the U.S. Occupation of Haiti," *Cultural Critique* 87 (spring 2014): 38–59.

32. Hall, "Breaking Bread with History," 21.

33. For discussion of James's apparent "silence," see Bill Schwarz, "Not Even Past Yet," *History Workshop Journal* 57 (2004): 104–5. For a response, see Christian Høgsbjerg, "'A Thorn in the Side of Great Britain': C.L.R. James and the Caribbean Labour Rebellions of the 1930s," *Small Axe* 35 (2011): 24–42.

34. On Padmore, see Leslie James, *George Padmore and Decolonization from Below: Pan-Africanism, the Cold War, and the End of Empire* (Houndmills: Palgrave Macmillan, 2015); and on Braithwaite, Christian Høgsbjerg, *Mariner, Renegade and Castaway: Chris Braithwaite: Seamen's Organiser, Socialist and Militant Pan-Africanist* (London: Socialist History Society and Redwords, 2014).

35. National Archives, London, KV/2/1824/13a; Public Record Office, London, CO318/427/11; quoted in Bill Schwarz, "C.L.R. James and George Lamming: The Measure of Historical Time," *Small Axe* 14 (2003).

36. *Manchester Guardian*, July 29, 1935.

37. S. K. B. Asante, *Pan-African Protest: West Africa and the Italo-Ethiopian Crisis, 1934–1941* (London: Longman, 1977), 46.

38. Frederick Cooper, *Decolonization and African Society: The Labor Question in French and British Africa* (Cambridge: Cambridge University Press, 1996), 58.

39. C. L. R. James, *The Black Jacobins: Toussaint Louverture and the San Domingo Revolution* (London: Secker and Warburg, 1938), 314–15. See also *Report of the Commission Appointed to Enquire into the Disturbances in the Copperbelt, Northern Rhodesia*, Cmd. 5009 (London, 1935), 19.

40. See Christian Høgsbjerg, "'The Fever and the Fret': C.L.R. James, the Spanish Civil War and the Writing of *The Black Jacobins*," *Critique* 44, nos. 1–2 (2016): 161–77.

41. Anthony Bogues, *Caliban's Freedom: The Early Political Thought of C.L.R. James* (Chicago: Pluto, 1997), 41.

42. Leon Trotsky, *How the Revolution Armed: The Military Writings and Speeches of Leon Trotsky*, vol. 1 (London: New Park, 1979), xviii.

43. James, *The Black Jacobins*, 11, 15.

44. Eric Williams, *Inward Hunger: The Education of a Prime Minister* (London: Deutsch, 1969), 49; Eric Williams, *British Historians and the West Indies* (New York: A and B, 1994), 182.

45. This was essentially the thesis of the most "serious" official account of the Haitian Revolution before James, the U.S. academic T. Lothrop Stoddard's *The French Revolution in San Domingo* (New York: Houghton Mifflin, 1914). On Stoddard's "vendetta against the Negro race," see James, *The Black Jacobins*, 335.

46. James, *The Black Jacobins*, 104.

47. James, *The Black Jacobins*, 69, 71, 73.

48. C. L. R. James, "Lectures on *The Black Jacobins*: *The Black Jacobins* and *Black Reconstruction*: A Comparative Analysis," *Small Axe* 8 (2000): 94.

49. James, *The Black Jacobins*, 14. Although James's work does have important parallels with Du Bois's *Black Reconstruction*, and his discussion of the American Civil War in *A History of Negro Revolt* suggests an awareness of the work, there remains no evidence he had actually read Du Bois's classic itself while writing *The Black Jacobins*. For James's appreciation of Du Bois, see C. L. R. James, "W.E.B. Du Bois [1964]," in C. L. R. James, *The Future in the Present: Selected Writings*, vol. 1 (London: Allison and Busby, 1977).

50. Leon Trotsky, *The History of the Russian Revolution* (London: Pluto, 1977), 19–20, 33.

51. James, *The Black Jacobins*, 224.

52. This was suggestively pointed toward in a remarkable earlier work apparently unknown to James, a 1925 dissertation at the University of Paris on "L'Attitude de la France à l'egard de l'esclavage pendant la revolution" [The Attitude of France toward Slavery during the Revolution], submitted by the black U.S. scholar Anna Julia Cooper. This was published in 1988. See Anna J. Cooper, *Slavery and the French Revolutionists (1788–1805)* (New York: Edwin Mellen Press, 1988); Vivian M. May, "'It Is Never a Question of the Slaves': Anna Julia Cooper's Challenge to History's Silences in Her 1925 Sorbonne Thesis," *Callaloo* 31, no. 3 (2008): 903–18.

53. James, *The Black Jacobins* (1938), 311. James's use of the phrase "beyond the boundaries" in 1938 is quite striking.

54. Said, *Culture and Imperialism*, 299.

55. Alex Callinicos, "The Drama of Revolution and Reaction: Marxist History and the Twentieth Century," in *Marxist History-Writing for the Twenty-First Century*, edited by Chris Wickham (Oxford: Oxford University Press, 2008), 160–61. See Harold Isaacs,

The Tragedy of the Chinese Revolution (Stanford, CA: Stanford University Press, 1961); Pierre Broué, *The German Revolution* (Leiden: Brill, 2004); Pierre Broué and Emile Témime, *The Revolution and the Civil War in Spain* (London: Faber and Faber, 1972); Adolfo Gilly, *The Mexican Revolution* (London: Verso, 1983). James may have played a role in helping Isaacs, then a member of the American Socialist Workers' Party, publish his *Tragedy of the Chinese Revolution* with Secker and Warburg in 1938 (the first edition carried a long introduction from Leon Trotsky). See Paul Collin, "The Tragedy of the Chinese Revolution: An Essay in the Different Editions of that Work," *Revolutionary History* 2, no. 4 (1990). James wrote an admiring review of Gilly's study of the Mexican Revolution. See C. L. R. James, "A Revolution Ignored," *Third World Book Review* 1, no. 1 (1984): 36–37.

56. James, *The Black Jacobins*, xix–xx.

57. David Patrick Geggus, *Haitian Revolutionary Studies* (Bloomington: Indiana University Press, 2002), 33.

58. James, "Lectures on *The Black Jacobins*: *The Black Jacobins* and *Black Reconstruction*," 85, 91.

59. George Padmore, "Toussaint, The Black Liberator," *People* (Trinidad), November 12 and 19, 1938. This review was syndicated in the British journal *Socialist Vanguard: Monthly Journal of the Militant Socialist International* 4, no. 12 (December 1938).

60. This comment was made by Amy Ashwood Garvey in August 1940 in a speech on "The Contribution the West Indian Negro had made to the Social and Cultural Development of the U.S.A. Negro" at Edelweiss Park, Kingston, Jamaica. See "Important Work Done in U.S.A. by West Indians," *Daily Gleaner*, August 13, 1940. Thanks to Matthew J. Smith for this reference.

61. National Archives, London, KV2/1824/36a, Letter from Secker and Warburg to I. T. A. Wallace-Johnson of the West African Youth League, Trelawney Street, Freetown, Sierra Leone, October 19, 1938.

62. LaRay Denzer, "Wallace-Johnson and the Sierra Leone Labor Crisis of 1939," *African Studies Review* 25, nos. 2/3 (1982): 172. In Trinidad, the *Port of Spain Gazette* noted, "Mr. C.L.R. James, Trinidad-born writer and politician who has been residing in England for the past few years is once more in the lime-light as an Author. His latest book is *Black Jacobins* which deals with Haytian History." See *Port of Spain Gazette*, November 6, 1938.

63. See the review by "K.A." in *The Keys: The Journal of the League of Coloured Peoples* 6, no. 2 (October–December 1938); Arthur Ballard, "The Greatest Slave Revolt in History," *New Leader*, December 9, 1938; Dorothy Pizer, "A Lesson in Revolution," *Controversy* 28 (January 1939). For James's later reminiscences of Ballard, see Al Richardson, Clarence Chrysotum, and Anna Grimshaw, *C.L.R. James and British Trotskyism: An Interview* (London: Socialist Platform, 1987).

64. Flora Grierson, "Man's Inhumanity to Man," *New Statesman*, October 8, 1938.

65. James, *The Black Jacobins*, 336.

66. Eugene D. Genovese, *In Red and Black: Marxian Explorations in Southern and Afro-American History* (London: Allen Lane 1971), 155. On November 29, 1979, Genovese wrote to James in praise of *The Black Jacobins*, noting that his wife, Elizabeth Fox-Genovese, and he "independently came to the conclusion many years ago that it is about the best one-volume Marxist history of any revolution, and it has deeply influenced our thinking on many questions." See letter from Eugene Genovese to C. L. R. James, November 29, 1979, Box 1, File 11, C. L. R. James Collection, Quinton O'Connor Library, Oilfield Workers' Trade Union, San Fernando, Trinidad and Tobago.

67. Leon Trotsky, "Fontamara," *New International* 1, no. 5 (December 1934): 159.

68. C. L. R. James, "Trotsky's Place in History," in *C.L.R. James and Revolutionary Marxism: Selected Writings of C.L.R. James, 1939–1949*, edited by Scott McLemee and Paul Le Blanc (Atlantic Highlands, NJ: Humanities Press, 1994), 123.

69. Fenner Brockway would later become the founder and chairman of the Movement for Colonial Freedom (later Liberation) in Britain.

70. Michael Foot, "C.L.R. James," in *C.L.R. James: His Intellectual Legacies*, edited by Selwyn R. Cudjoe and William E. Cain (Amherst: University of Massachusetts Press, 1995), 102. The work also inspired Michael's nephew, the revolutionary socialist Paul Foot. See Paul Foot, "Black Jacobin," *New Statesman*, February 2, 1979.

71. See Eric J. Hobsbawm, "The Historians Group of the Communist Party," in *Rebels and Their Causes: Essays in Honour of A.L. Morton*, edited by Maurice Cornforth (London: Lawrence and Wishart, 1978), 23. In *The Age of Revolution* (1962), Hobsbawm recommended *The Black Jacobins*. Eric J. Hobsbawm, *The Age of Revolution: Europe, 1789–1848* (London: Abacus, 2002), 389. Brian Pearce, another member of the Communist Party Historians' Group (who became a Trotskyist and was expelled after leaving the party in 1957), praised *The Black Jacobins* in the British Trotskyist paper the *Newsletter*, on October 10, 1959, together with Eric Williams's *Capitalism and Slavery*. Pearce noted that both works threw "Marxist light" on the abolition of the slave trade in the British Empire, "one of the most mystified and sentimentalized in our history."

72. Peter Fryer, *Staying Power: The History of Black People in Britain* (London: Pluto, 1987), 207.

73. See William B. Seabrook, "*The Black Jacobins*," *Journal of Negro History* 24, no. 1 (January 1939).

74. Harold Courlander, "Revolt in Haiti," *Saturday Review of Literature*, January 7, 1939.

75. Rayford W. Logan, "Reviews—Caribbean History," *Opportunity: Journal of Negro Life* 17, no. 2 (1939).

76. Ludwell Lee Montague, "*The Black Jacobins*," *Hispanic American Historical Review* 20, no. 1 (February 1940): 129–30.

77. *Time*, December 5, 1938. See also James W. Ivy, "Break the Image of the White God . . . ," *Crisis* 46, no. 8 (August 1939); George E. Novack, "Revolution, Black and White," *New International* 5, no. 5 (May 1939).

78. "The Black Jacobins of San Domingo's Revolution," *New York Times*, December 11, 1938. See also "W.N.," "Black Majesty's War Has Pointers for Today," *Los Angeles Times*, January 8, 1939.

79. Eric R. Wolf, "Encounter with Norbert Elias," in *Human Figurations: Essays for Norbert Elias*, edited by Peter Gleichmann, Johan Goudsblom, and Hermann Korte (Amsterdam: Amsterdams Sociologisch Tijdschrift, 1977), 30.

80. Gerd Baumann, "Interview: Eric Wolf: How Ideological Involvement Actually Operates," *European Association of Social Anthropologists Newsletter* 25 (March 1999): 11.

81. Eric R. Wolf, *Pathways of Power: Building an Anthropology of the Modern World* (Berkeley: University of California Press, 2001), 4.

82. Alan J. Mackenzie, "Radical Pan-Africanism in the 1930s: A Discussion with C.L.R. James," *Radical History Review* 24 (1980): 70.

83. C.L.R. James, "Interview [1972]," in Ian Munro and Reinhard Sander (eds.), *Kas-Kas: Interviews with Three Caribbean Writers in Texas: George Lamming, C.L.R. James, Wilson Harris* (Austin: University of Texas Press, 1972), 35.

84. Hakim Adi and Marika Sherwood, *The 1945 Manchester Pan-African Congress Revisited* (London: New Beacon Books, 1995), 122.

85. Letter from Raya Dunayevskaya to C. L. R. James, July 29, 1947, Raya Dunayevskaya Collection at Wayne State University Archives of Labor and Urban Affairs, Detroit, MI.

86. John La Rose, "CLR James—The Revolutionary as Artist," in John La Rose, *Unending Journey: Selected Writings* (London: New Beacon Books/George Padmore Institute, 2014), 52–53.

87. Pierre Naville, "Avant-propos," in C. L. R. James, *Les Jacobins noirs: Toussaint L'Ouverture et la Révolution de Saint-Domingue* (Paris: Editions Caribéennes, 1983), xix–xxi, quoted in Frank Rosengarten, *Urbane Revolutionary: C.L.R. James and the Struggle for a New Society* (Jackson: University Press of Mississippi, 2008), 228–29. On Pierre Naville, see Michael Löwy, *Morning Star: Surrealism, Marxism, Anarchism, Situtationism, Utopia* (Austin: University of Texas Press, 2009), 43–62. For Naville's recollections of James, see Pierre Naville, letter to Franklin Rosemont, June 20, 1989, Franklin and Penelope Rosemont Papers, Joseph A. Labadie Collection, University of Michigan Library, Ann Arbor.

88. Geggus, *Haitian Revolutionary Studies*, 33. Geggus cites French colonial historian Gabriel Debien's discussion of *The Black Jacobins* in 1947. Gabriel Debien, "Les travaux d'histoire sur Saint-Domingue (1938–1946): essai de mise au point," *Revue d'Histoire des Colonies* 34 (1947): 31–86.

89. Louis Ménard, "*Les Jacobins noirs*," *Les Temps Modernes* 52 (February 1950).

90. C. L. R. James, "Correspondence [27 February 1950]," *Les Temps Modernes* 56 (June 1950). Our thanks to Merryn Everitt for her translation of these pieces from *Les Temps Modernes*.

91. There is a copy of *Les Jacobins noirs* in Fanon's personal library. See Ministère de la Culture, *Bibliothèque Fonds Frantz Fanon*, 60. We are indebted to Matthieu Renault for this reference. For James on Fanon, see C. L. R. James, "Fanon and the Caribbean," *International Tribute to Frantz Fanon: Record of the Special Meeting of the United Nations Special Committee Against Apartheid, 3 November 1978* (New York: United Nations Centre Against Apartheid, 1979), 43–46. Growing interest in James in France is signaled by the recent appearance of Matthieu Renault, *C. L. R. James: La vie révolutionnaire d'un "Platon noir"* (Paris: La Découverte, 2016).

92. C. L. R. James, "A Convention Appraisal: Dr. Eric Williams, First Premier of Trinidad and Tobago; A Biographical Sketch [1960]," in *Eric E. Williams Speaks*, edited by Selwin R. Cudjoe (Wellesley, MA: Calaloux, 1993), 338. The 1949 edition had referred to "P.I.R. James" as the author. Geggus, *Haitian Revolutionary Studies*, 226.

93. W. E. B. Du Bois, "Two Hundred Years of Segregated Schools," in *W.E.B. Du Bois Speaks: Speeches and Addresses 1920–1963*, edited by Philip S. Foner (New York: Pathfinder, 2000), 304.

94. See Emmanuel C. Paul, *Questions d'histoire* (Port-au-Prince: Imprimerie de l'Etat, 1955).

95. C. L. R. James, letter to Étienne Charlier, August 24, 1955, UWI, Box 7, folder 190.

96. C. L. R. James, "L'actualité de la Révolution française," *Perspectives socialistes: revue bimensuelle de l'Union de la Gauche Socialiste*, February 15, 1958, 20–21. On Guérin's *La Lutte de classes sous la première république. Bourgeois et "bras nus," 1793–1797*. (Paris: Gallimard, 1946), see Norah Carlin, "Daniel Guérin and the Working Class in the French Revolution," *International Socialism* 47 (1990): 197–223.

97. Independent Ghana became a kind of home for an entire generation of West Indian migrants; it was also visited by Ras Makonnen, George Lamming, Kamau Brathwaite, Jan Carew, the Nobel Prize–winner Arthur Lewis, Amy Ashwood Garvey, and Frantz Fanon. See Bill Schwarz "Crossing the Seas," in *West Indian Intellectuals in Britain*, edited by Bill Schwarz (Manchester: Manchester University Press, 2003), 27n41. For more on James in Ghana, see Kevin K. Gaines, *American Africans in Ghana: Black Expatriates and the Civil Rights Era* (Chapel Hill: University of North Carolina Press, 2006).

98. James, *The Black Jacobins*, xvii.

99. C. L. R. James, "Letters on Politics: III. 20 March 1957," in *The C.L.R. James Reader*, edited by Anna Grimshaw (Oxford: Blackwell, 1992), 269.

100. C. L. R. James, letter to friends, March 21, 1957, in possession of Robert A. Hill.

101. For James's letter on March 25, 1957, about this meeting, see C. L. R. James and Martin Glaberman, "Letters," in *C.L.R. James: His Life and Work*, edited by Paul Buhle (London: Allison and Busby, 1986), 154–58.

102. C. L. R. James to Martin Luther King, April 5, 1957, quoted in *The Martin Luther King Jr. Papers Project: Vol. IV: Symbol of the Movement*, edited by Clayborne Carson, Susan Carson, Adrienne Clay, Virginia Shadron, and Kieran Taylor (Berkeley: University of California Press, 2000), 149–50.

103. Martin Luther King to C. L. R. James, April 30, 1957, quoted in *The Martin Luther King Jr. Papers Project: Vol. IV*, 194. Reddick served as curator of the New York Public Library's Schomburg Collection from 1939 until 1948 and may have met James while he was in the United States.

104. C. L. R. James, letter to Jean Brierre, March 1, 1958, UWI, Box 7, folder 190.

105. Letter from Michel Lamartinière Honorat to Félix Morisseau-Leroy, April 16, 1958, UWI, Box 7, folder 190.

106. Quoted in Anthony P. Maingot, "Politics and Populist Historiography in the Caribbean: Juan Bosch and Eric Williams," in *Intellectuals in the Twentieth-Century Caribbean: Volume II, Unity in Variety: The Hispanic and Francophone Caribbean*, edited by Alistair Hennessy (London: Macmillan Caribbean, 1992), 153.

107. C. L. R. James, "A Convention Appraisal: Dr. Eric Williams," 334. See also Williams's 1964 comment on James, who "in his *Black Jacobins*, rescues the Haitian slave revolution and the rise of Toussaint L'Ouverture from historical oblivion, and his analysis is of profound and enduring significance, if only as one of the first challenges to the British interpretation of the abolition of the slave system." However, by then James and Williams had split politically, and Williams also suggested that James's "incursion into West Indian history was only a temporary deviation from the author's preoccupation with Marxism and the world revolution." Williams, *British Historians and the West Indies*, 164.

108. George Lamming, *The Pleasures of Exile* (1960; London: Pluto, 2005), 119, 150.

109. C. L. R. James, letter to Fredric Warburg, September 1, 1960, UWI, Box 7, folder 179.

110. Selma James's comments at "Every Cook Can Govern: C.L.R. James and the Canon," London, November 23, 2013.

111. C. L. R. James, letter to Morris Philipson, June 23, 1961, UW, Box 7, folder 181. In the same letter, James mentions plans for a Caribbean edition of the book, with a print run of two thousand copies. There were also discussions, ultimately abortive, in 1961 regarding a Spanish translation with the Imprenta Nacional de Cuba (see James's correspondence with John G. Pattisson at Secker and Warburg, February 9, 1961, UWI, Box 7, folder 179).

112. C. L. R. James, letter to John G. Pattisson.

113. Morris Philipson, letter to C. L. R. James, November 7, 1960, UWI, Box 7, folder 181.

114. See correspondence between C. L. R. James and Morris Philipson, December 10, 1960, and February 24, 1961, UWI, Box 7, folder 181.

115. *New Statesman*, April 3, 1964.

116. James to Philipson, December 10, 1960, UWI, Box 7, folder 181.

117. Philipson to James, December 21, 1961, UWI, Box 7, folder 181.

118. Philipson to James, February 24, 1961, UWI, Box 7, folder 181.

119. C. L. R. James, letter to George Lamming, March 15, 1964, UWI, Box 7, folder 190. James makes a similar point in a letter of the same date to V. S. Naipaul, to whom, following Naipaul's review of *Beyond a Boundary* in *Encounter*, he wrote: "I am looking forward to what you may have to say about *Black Jacobins* and in particular about the Appendix." UWI, Box 7, folder 190.

120. James, *The Black Jacobins*, xvi.

121. C. L. R. James, letter to Basil Davidson, March 15, 1964, UWI, Box 7, folder 190.

122. C. L. R. James, letter to Colin Legum, March 15, 1964, UWI, Box 7, folder 190.

123. C. L. R. James, letter to Marina Maxwell, 29, October 1967, UWI, Box 7, folder 190. Marina Maxwell, a singer, poet, playwright and performer, was the wife of the Jamaican journalist John Maxwell.

124. Gillman, "Black Jacobins and New World Mediterraneans," 174.

125. Geggus, *Haitian Revolutionary Studies*, 33.

126. R. R. Palmer, *The Age of the Democratic Revolution: A Political History of Europe and America, 1760–1800, Volume II: The Struggle* (Oxford: Oxford University Press, 1964), 514.

127. On this group, see David Austin, *Fear of a Black Nation: Race, Sex, and Security in Sixties Montreal* (Toronto: Between the Lines, 2013), 73–93. See also Paul Buhle, *Tim Hector: A Caribbean Radical's Story* (Kingston: Ian Randle, 2006) and Kate Quinn (ed.), *Black Power in the Caribbean* (Gainesville: University Press of Florida, 2014).

128. James, *The Black Jacobins*, 236.

129. Stokely Carmichael and Michael Ekwueme Thelwell, *Ready for Revolution: The Life and Struggles of Stokely Carmichael (Kwame Ture)* (New York: Scribner, 2005), 105.

130. Dan Georgakas, "Young Detroit Radicals, 1955–1965," in *C. L. R. James: His Life and Work*, edited by Paul Buhle (London: Allison and Busby, 1986), 187.

131. Dan Georgakas and Marvin Surkin, *Detroit: I Do Mind Dying: A Study in Urban Revolution* (London: Redwords, 1998), xi, 16, 261. For more on James's general influence among the League of Revolutionary Black Workers, see the essays by Modibo M. Kadalie and Matthew Quest in the updated edition of Kimathi Mohammed's 1974 text, *Organization and Spontaneity: The Theory of the Vanguard Party and Its Application to the Black Movement in the U.S. Today*. See Modibo M. Kadalie, "Introduction" to Kimathi Mohammed, *Organization and Spontaneity* (Atlanta, GA: On Our Own Authority!, 2012); Matthew Quest, "Afterword: C.L.R. James and Kimathi Mohammed's Circle of Black Power Activists in Michigan," in Kimathi Mohammed, *Organization and Spontaneity* (Atlanta: On Our Own Authority!, 2012).

132. Personal correspondence with Selma James, May 28, 2014.

133. Martha Biondi, *The Black Revolution on Campus* (Berkeley: University of California Press, 2012), 94–95.

134. C. L. R. James to Fredric Warburg, January 10, 1969, George Padmore Institute, 429/4.

135. As Marable put it in 2000, "there is no more powerful history in the English language, in my judgment, than James's classic study of the Haitian Revolution." Manning Marable, "Black Studies and the Racial Mountain," *Souls: Black Politics,*

Culture, and Society 2, no. 3 (2000): 20. See Onwubiko Agozino, "The Revolutionary Sociology of C.L.R. James: An Interview with Manning Marable," *Transition* 106 (2011): 127–38. See also David Levering Lewis's praise for the "superb analytical synthesis of race, class and color" and great narrative style of *The Black Jacobins*; James P. Comer, Paula J. Giddings, Richard A. Goldsby, William Chester Jordan, Randall Kennedy, David Levering Lewis, Albert J. Raboteau, and Ronald Waters, "Books That Changed the Lives of Black Scholars," *Journal of Blacks in Higher Education* 19 (1998): 102.

136. Ferrucio Gambino, "Only Connect," in *C.L.R. James: His Life and Work*, edited by Paul Buhle (London: Allison and Busby, 1986), 198. Thanks to Giorgio Riva for alerting us to the problematic Italian translation. In 1968, James made efforts to encourage translations of *The Black Jacobins* into German, Japanese, and Spanish, as well as trying to interest British Lion Films into making a film based on *The Black Jacobins* playscript. See the correspondence in UWI, Box 10, file 241.

137. Hall and Schwarz, "Breaking Bread with History," 22.

138. Kamugisha, "C.L.R. James's *The Black Jacobins*," 204–5. Another exception was Darcus Howe, a relative of James, who was presented with an original first edition copy of *The Black Jacobins* in 1962 when he met James in London after Howe had arrived from Trinidad the year before. Personal information from Darcus Howe, December 15, 2014. For Howe's brief reflections on *The Black Jacobins*, see "Red Reads: Fifty Books that Will Change Your Life," *New Statesman*, August 10, 2009, 21.

139. Walter Rodney, "The African Revolution," in *C.L.R. James: His Life and Work*, edited by Paul Buhle (London: Allison and Busby, 1986), 35.

140. Quoted in David Austin, *The Black Jacobin* (Canadian Broadcasting Corporation, 2006).

141. The inaugural Book Fair was opened on April 1, 1982, by C.L.R. James, while Ngũgĩ opened it in 1987. See Sarah White, Roxy Harris, and Sharmilla Beezmohun, eds., *A Meeting of the Continents: The International Book Fair of Radical Black and Third-World Books—Revisited* (London: New Beacon Books, 2005).

142. Quoted in Patrick Williams, *Ngũgĩ wa Thiong'o* (Manchester: Manchester University Press, 1999), 8. See also Abdilatif Abdalla's 2011 interview with Ngũgĩ wa Thiong'o about C. L. R. James, http://vimeo.com/37375273.

143. Scott McLemee, "C.L.R. James: A Biographical Introduction," *American Visions* (1996).

144. James, "The Old World and the New," 211.

145. James, *The Black Jacobins*, xvi.

146. For more evidence of James's continuing interest in the developing historiography of the Haitian Revolution, see his review of Wenda Parkinson's biography, *"This Gilded African": Toussaint L'Ouverture*; C. L. R. James, "Romanticising History," *New Society*, February 15, 1979.

147. James, *The Black Jacobins*, xvii.

148. The consequences of this shift in his thinking by the 1970s are well brought out by the late Jamaican Marxist historian and politician Richard Hart, author of classic works such as the two-part history *Slaves Who Abolished Slavery* (1980, 1985). As Hart later recalled, "It was C.L.R. James who, in his *Black Jacobins* impressed upon me how important the individual can be in expediting or delaying the development of historical events and in diverting the course of historical events as they unfold in one direction or another. In this book he illustrated this in the person of Toussaint Louverture. However, in a later period, C.L.R. set off in the opposite direction. In his 'New Beginning' period he was at pains to denigrate the importance of the individual in historical events, attributing the course of developments almost entirely to 'the masses'. I will never forget my meeting with a then young man in Trinidad, whose name I forget but who was introduced to me by James Millette, who complained that he had been misled by C.L.R. into failing to recognise the importance of the individual in history. C.L.R. James had profoundly influenced both of us, but at different times and in opposite directions!" Richard Hart, personal correspondence with Christian Høgsbjerg, September 3, 2005.

149. C. L. R. James, "Lectures on *The Black Jacobins*: How I Would Rewrite *The Black Jacobins*," *Small Axe* 8 (2000): 107. C. L. R. James's lecture on Oliver Cromwell Cox's *Caste, Class, and Race*, given at the Institute of the Black World, Atlanta, Georgia, on June 16, 1971, has also now been published. See C. L. R. James, "The Class Basis of the Race Question in the United States," *New Politics* 60 (Winter 2016).

150. Anthony Bogues, "Afterword," *Small Axe* 8 (2000): 117.

151. In 1991, Ohmura Shoten published a Japanese translation of the 1963 Vintage edition of *The Black Jacobins*, which was reprinted in 2002. The main translator was Yoshio Aoki. We are indebted to Yutaka Yoshida for this information. The first Spanish editions of *The Black Jacobins* appears to have been released in 2003—by Fondo de Cultura in Mexico and Turner Publicaciones in Spain—while there was a Portuguese Brazilian edition in 2006 published by Boitempo.

152. Geggus, *Haitian Revolutionary Studies*, 33. For discussion of inaccuracies in *The Black Jacobins*, also see David Patrick Geggus, *Slavery, War and Revolution: The British Occupation of Saint Domingue 1793–1798* (Oxford: Oxford University Press, 1982), 82, 85–86, 103. In his history of *The Haitian Revolution*, Ott claimed to set out to "bring the Haitian Revolution into clearer historical perspective" against those who in the past "often viewed much of the conflict ideologically, varying from T. Lothrop Stoddard's white racism to C.L.R. James's Marxism." Singularly sure of his own total freedom from any kind of ideological shortcomings, Ott promptly slandered James as a "Negro racist." Thomas O. Ott, *The Haitian Revolution 1789–1804* (Knoxville: University of Tennessee Press, 1973), 199, 204.

153. Ott, *The Haitian Revolution*, 185.

154. Catherine Hall and Keith McClelland, "Introduction," in *Race, Nation and Empire: Making Histories, 1750 to the Present*, edited by Catherine Hall and Keith McClelland (Manchester: Manchester University Press, 2010), 2. See also Ann Laura Stoler and

Frederick Cooper, "Between Metropole and Colony: Rethinking a Research Agenda," in *Tensions of Empire: Colonial Cultures in a Bourgeois World*, edited by Frederick Cooper and Ann Laura Stoler (Berkeley: University of California Press, 1997), 1–56. For a valuable recent discussion of the "particular, insurgent, imaginative geography of the Haitian revolution" and "the dynamic geographies of connection between the French and Haitian revolutions" as uncovered in *The Black Jacobins*, see David Featherstone, *Resistance, Space and Political Identities: The Making of Counter-Global Networks* (Chichester: Wiley-Blackwell, 2008), 23–28. James's approach has still not been accepted by all historians, and one of the most celebrated liberal histories of the French Revolution avoided even a passing mention of the Haitian Revolution. See Simon Schama, *Citizens: A Chronicle of the French Revolution* (London: Random House, 1989).

155. Franklin W. Knight, "Toussaint, the Revolution and Haiti," *Reviews in American History* 2, no. 2 (1974): 200.

156. Derek Seidman, "An Interview with Paul Buhle," *Counterpunch*, March 8, 2004. Buhle wrote the authorized biography of James. See Paul Buhle, *C.L.R. James: The Artist as Revolutionary* (London: Verso, 1989).

157. There was a German translation in 1984. Geggus, *Haitian Revolutionary Studies*, 33. Eugene D. Genovese, *From Rebellion to Revolution: Afro-American Slave Revolts in the Making of the Modern World* (Baton Rouge: Louisiana State University Press, 1979); Carolyn E. Fick, *The Making of Haiti: The Saint Domingue Revolution from Below* (Knoxville: University of Tennessee Press, 1997); Robin Blackburn, "Haiti, Slavery and the Age of the Democratic Revolution," *William and Mary Quarterly* 63, no. 4 (2006); Robin Blackburn, "*The Black Jacobins* and New World Slavery," in *C.L.R. James: His Intellectual Legacies*, edited by Selwyn R. Cudjoe and William E. Cain (Amherst: University of Massachusetts Press, 1995); Robin Blackburn, *The Overthrow of Colonial Slavery, 1776–1848* (London: Verso, 1988). On the work of George Rawick, author of the classic study *From Sundown to Sunup: The Making of the Black Community* (Westport, CT: Greenwood, 1972), see David Roediger and Martin Smith (eds.), *Listening to Revolt: The Selected Writings of George Rawick* (Chicago: Charles H. Kerr, 2010). *The Black Jacobins* continues to inspire new historiographic approaches. See, for example, Gerald Horne, *Confronting Black Jacobins: The United States, the Haitian Revolution, and the origins of the Dominican Republic* (New York: Monthly Review Press, 2015).

158. See David Blake and Anthony Ward, *Toussaint, or The Aristocracy of the Skin: Opera in Three Acts* (Sevenoaks: Novello, 1977), and Tariq Ali, "Nothing to Lose but Their Manacles," *Guardian*, June 6, 1989, about his 1989 play *Liberty's Scream*, which was screened on Channel Four's Bandung File shortly after James's passing on July 11, 1989. The art exhibition "Black Jacobins: Negritude in a Post Global 21st Century" was an initiative developed by Black Diaspora Visual Arts—a partnership based in Barbados with major sponsorship from the Andy Warhol Foundation for the Visual Arts—which held a five-day symposium in 2011 in Barbados and Martinique that examined the influence of James and Aimé Césaire on visual artists in the region. It was followed by an exhibition of commissioned works titled "Black Jacobins at the Caribbean Pavilion," held at the Barbados Community College. Many thanks to Alissandra Cummins for information about this art exhibition. *The Black Jacobins* was also among inspirations for several works by Lubaina Himid in the 1980s, including "Scenes from the Life of Toussaint Louverture" (1987).

159. Selma James, "Striving for Clarity and Influence: The Political Legacy of C.L.R. James (2001–2012)," in Selma James, *Sex, Race and Class: The Perspective of Winning: A Selection of Writings 1952–2011* (Oakland, CA: PM Press, 2012), 283.

160. S. James, "Striving for Clarity and Influence," 285.

161. See Edward W. Said, "Traveling Theory," in *The World, the Text and the Critic* (1983; London: Vintage, 1991), 226–47.

162. See Edward W. Said, "Travelling Theory Reconsidered," in *Critical Reconstructions: The Relationship of Fiction and Life*, edited by R. Polhemus and R. Henke (Stanford, CA: Stanford University Press, 1994), 255.

163. Scott, *Conscripts of Modernity*, 21.

164. Hall, "Breaking Bread with History," 22.

PART I.
PERSONAL REFLECTIONS

| | | | |

1 | *The Black Jacobins* in Detroit: 1963

DAN GEORGAKAS

The paperback edition of *The Black Jacobins* issued by Vintage Books in 1963 was a timely catalyst to the emerging radical movement in Detroit in that era. The book was read and admired by most of the individuals who were active in Detroit radical politics for years, including many who would be in the leadership of the League of Revolutionary Black Workers. The impact of *The Black Jacobins* in particular, and Jamesian ideas in general, were less a wow factor in the sense of awakening a body of enthusiastic supporters than a stimulus to the political and cultural momentum already in motion.

The most consistent and influential advocate of Jamesian thought in Detroit was Martin Glaberman. He was among the Jamesians who had moved to the city to take part in the radical labor environment that had taken shape there since the founding of the United Automobile Workers (UAW). There were numerous splits in the Jamesian camp. The first came in 1955 when Raya Dunayevskaya with the support of half the membership formed a new organization named News & Letters. A second schism in 1962 was led by James Boggs and Grace Lee. They took the name Correspondence. Martin Glaberman, Seymour Faber, Jessie Glaberman, and other James loyalists eventually adopted the name Facing Reality. All three groups had public meetings that attracted the emerging radical generation of the 1960s. Each had literature tables and a publication.[1]

Perhaps the most influential aspects of Jamesian thought was the attention it brought to the nature of radical newspapers and the view that African American workers would be at the forefront of revolutionary change in the United States. The Jamesian critique of vanguard parties was not universally accepted, but it led to wariness about rigid organizational forms. The League of Revolutionary Black Workers, for example, initially avoided a vanguard party ideology, but when the League began to dissolve, one sector gravitated to Maoism.

James's views on newspapers deeply influenced John Watson, one of the founders of the League. His ideas about publishing grew out of a study group of black radicals taught by Glaberman. A number of other future League leaders were part of that group. Among the texts that had considerable impact on them was Lenin's "Where to Begin."

In a prelude to the agitation that led to the Dodge Revolutionary Union Movement (DRUM) and then the League, in 1967 John Watson, Luke Tripp, General Baker, and Mike Hamlin began to publish the *Inner City Voice*, an agitational popular newspaper designed to air the grievances of black Detroiters. All four became part of the six-man leadership committee of the League. Watson was the editor and the driving force in the publication. Later he was elected editor of Wayne State's daily newspaper and transformed it into a de facto daily of the League. Mike Hamlin played a key role in that effort, and General Baker was the major organizer at DRUM, which was formed at Chrysler's Dodge Main plant in 1968. Baker continued to focus on in-plant organization while Hamlin headed the League's efforts to create a printing house able to produce the League's own newspaper, handouts, and books.[2] Attorney Ken Cockrel, another of the six-man leadership group, worked with Watson to add cinema to the League's outreach assets.

All of these efforts were based on addressing the immediate problems of African Americans with a view that blacks in general and the black working class in particular would lead a new U.S. revolution. The paperback edition of *The Black Jacobins* helped provide a theoretical and historical framework for what was being currently experienced and observed in contemporary life. That Toussaint Louverture, despite meager resources and an undereducated mass base, had led a black revolution that defeated powerful European armies was inspiring. This history gave an emotional boost to black radicals who were aware of the tremendous power the UAW, the auto industry, and the U.S. government could amass to defeat them.

The Black Jacobins also confirmed the need to politically educate the black masses, a concern many in the Black Power movement found paramount. The story of the rebellion led by Toussaint Louverture, like similar historical portraits of renowned black figures, had not been offered in many college courses, much less in high schools. That the author of *The Black Jacobins* was an Afro-Trinidadian and not a sympathetic white historian underscored the ability of black intellectuals to create powerful works that spoke to general readers and specialists of all ethnic heritages. Unlike so many accounts of revolutions, the immediate outcome in Haiti had not been a glorious defeat but a spectacular victory. *The Black Jacobins* provided an example of how seemingly impossible rebellions could be successful, and it was a warning that military victory was only a prelude to even more perilous challenges.

A group of Detroit radicals including Baker had gone to Cuba in 1964 to speak with Che Guevara and other revolutionaries. Some of them also supported Robert Williams, an advocate of armed self-defense for blacks. The Detroit radicals found strategies that included armed defense more appealing than the nonviolent strategy of Dr. Martin Luther King Jr., a leader they respected but did not wish to emulate. *The Black Jacobins* was a chronicle of fighters with whom they could readily identify.

Another aspect of the impact of *The Black Jacobins* on radicals in Detroit involved the historical development of Haiti. The impoverished and under-educated Haiti of the 1960s was clearly not a consequence of Louverture's victory but the result of long-term and short-term extremely hostile U.S. actions that went into effect well before the American Civil War and continued through the twentieth century. Radicals saw that rather than welcoming Haiti as North America's second democracy, the U.S. government, driven by racism and the possibility of a slave revolt in the South, had shunned Haiti and deliberately worked against its well-being.

What had happened in Haiti supported the view that similar U.S. policies were now operative wherever reformers and revolutionaries arose in the world, particularly in what was then called the Third World. The problems these nations faced were not solely due to the United States or other colonial powers, but the United States and its allies actively suppressed rebellions wherever they gained popular support. There was no reason to doubt the United States would react any differently to domestic rebels.

Notes

1. For a more extensive account of these groups and their impact on Detroit as I experienced them, see Dan Georgakas, "Young Detroit Radicals: 1955–65," in *C.L.R. James: His Life and Work*, edited by Paul Buhle (London: Allison and Busby, 1986).

2. Black Star, the publishing arm of the league, printed James Forman, *The Political Thought of James Forman* (Detroit: Black Star, 1970). It was a 192-page paperback.

MUMIA ABU-JAMAL

There is, as ever, an interregnum of ignorance between the time one knows of a book and when that book is read. Mine was extended for perhaps a decade. A radical book review (now defunct) featured *The Black Jacobins* on its front page (c. 1987) and glowed with praise for it. It was 1998–1999, when studying for a master's degree, before I used it to research the Haitian Revolution.

My mind was blown by its sheer brilliance, its prodigious research, its stellar writing, and the panoramic quality of this hidden, little-known, stunning account of the heroism of the Haitian people.

I knew, even before finishing *The Black Jacobins*, that here was James's masterpiece. I learned a great deal and have used his lessons in almost all of my written works of history, either covertly or overtly. Indeed, for any student of James, there must be many lessons, not least that of his lived experience, which proved one could be a committed activist, even a revolutionary, and yet be a scholar (albeit an independent one) of the highest order.

Among his lessons is one, which is quite recurrent and found not in the text proper of *The Black Jacobins* but in its preface. Here James writes:

> Great men make history, but only such history as it is possible for them to make. Their freedom of achievement is limited by the necessities of their environment. To portray the limits of these necessities and the realisation, complete or partial, of all possibilities, that is the true business of the historian.

Lo and behold, this very day, as if by sheer serendipity, I received a book, the introduction of which was titled "White Zombies, Black Jacobins."[1] The influence of James goes on!

Note

1. Patricia E. Chu, *Race, Nationalism and the State in British and American Modernism* (Cambridge: Cambridge University Press, 2006).

3 | C. L. R. James, *The Black Jacobins*, and *The Making of Haiti*

CAROLYN E. FICK

This essay is in many respects a journey into the past, for it is now over forty years since I first met C. L. R. James and soon thereafter, intellectually and politically, became one of his many protégés and he one of my most influential mentors. Yet that distant past is very much with us today, as we see the actuality of James's views on world politics and mass movements of a revolutionary nature being played out daily.

In 1971 the seeds were first planted for the project that eventually culminated in the publication of *The Making of Haiti*, a study of the Saint-Domingue, or Haitian slave revolution "from below."[1] The idea for the project came from James, but initially it had to do not with the Haitian Revolution but with the French Revolution. James's feeling at the time was that it would be worthwhile to do a study of the French Revolution that took account of the new and older social history scholarship in French revolutionary historiography. He was referring to works such as Gaetano Salvemini's *The French Revolution, 1788–1792*;[2] Richard Cobb's *The Police and the People: French Popular Protest, 1789–1820*;[3] George Rudé's *The Crowd in the French Revolution*;[4] and even R. R. Palmer's *The World of the French Revolution*;[5] not to mention Albert Soboul's *The Parisian Sans-Culottes and the French Revolution, 1793–4*.[6] With regard to Richard Cobb's treatment of the sans-culottes of 1789–1795, it constituted in James's view "an analysis such as I have never seen bettered," and he was convinced that the study of the French Revolution was still making great strides.[7]

This popular study of the French Revolution that he was proposing I write would have been directed at the youth of the 1970s, particularly U.S. youth, whom he believed had their own outlook on the world and revolutionary change. Based on his understanding of the questioning and groping for answers to the crisis of bourgeois society being expressed by university students to whom he spoke on campuses throughout the United States, James was convinced that a popular study of the French Revolution—one that focused on the role and influence of the popular movements and their "obscure leaders" at various stages of the revolutionary process, and in regard to the politics and policies of the official leadership—was needed not only for general knowledge but as some sort of guide in the uncertainty and searching that was going on in the United States at that time, both in political and historical matters, especially with regard to "the relation of past historical periods to the present day."[8]

That study was never written, in part because I was leaving the United States for Montreal to pursue my graduate studies, hoping initially to be able to find a way of working the French Revolution project into a doctoral dissertation, something that proved to be unrealistic. Upon arriving in Montreal, my first impulse was to address my concerns to the chair of the History Department at McGill University, hoping to be accepted for admission and allowed to pursue this rather unconventional project in a very conventional academic setting. Fortunately, I was redirected to one of Montreal's other Anglophone universities, then known as Sir George Williams University (later Concordia University), just a stone's throw away from McGill, where to my astonishment I learned that George Rudé, whose pioneering work had already made an impact on my studies in the United States, had just been hired and was now teaching in the History Department. Naïvely optimistic, I proposed my French Revolution project to Rudé, who with characteristic diplomacy and tact (and a slight bit of amusement), suggested perhaps I think of some other historical moment in which popular forces played a distinctive role and on which I could write a dissertation—perhaps the revolutions of 1848—intimating of course that this perspective on the French Revolution had already been masterfully taken on by its most distinguished historians. Indeed it had, and I believe the study James was proposing I undertake would have added very little if anything to the then recent, primarily Marxist scholarship on the French Revolution.

The outcome to this academic impasse came in 1973 in a three-way meeting in the faculty lounge at Sir George Williams between James, Rudé, and myself, with James proposing a possible alternative: a study of the "crowd in the Haitian Revolution," of the slave masses and their popular leaders, their self-defined aspirations, objectives, and forms of self-mobilization—in other words, a history of the Haitian Revolution from below, something that had not yet been done. Here were two distinguished Marxist historians, both residing in England at the time, who regretted they had not had the occasion to meet in the past and promising to do so again. Mutually acknowledging and praising each other's work, and with similar perspectives on the writing of history, they were discussing (if not deciding) my academic future from above. Thus the groundwork for *The Making of Haiti* was laid.

James was convinced that there was enough documentation—indeed, an immense amount of material—in the Archives Nationales in Paris alone to make such a study not only feasible but historically significant. Citing several passages from the 1963 Vintage edition of *The Black Jacobins* in his correspondence with a New York–based Haitian archivist, James made it explicitly clear what he meant. "On page 243 of my *Black Jacobins*," he wrote, "there is a paragraph which explains very fully what I am talking about":

> The change had first expressed itself in August 1791 . . . In the North [the slave masses] came out to sustain royalty, nobility and religion against the poor whites and the Patriots. But they were soon formed into regiments and hardened by fighting. They organised themselves into armed sections and into popular bodies, and even while fighting for royalty they adopted instinctively and rigidly observed all the forms of republican organisation. Slogans and rallying cries were established between the chiefs of the sections and divisions, and gave them points of contact from one extremity of the plains and towns of the North to the other. This guaranteed the leaders a means of calling out the laborers and sending them back at will. These forms were extended to the districts in the West Province, and were faithfully observed by the black laborers, whether fighting for Spain and royalty or for the Republic.[9]

Here he had summarized "for the historical thinking of those days" a mass of material he believed could be examined in detail in the material with which scholars were most familiar and in new investigations. For James, the time for merely summarizing the actions and movements of the masses was long past. He insisted that every sentence of that paragraph could be made actual and vivid by a careful selection and accumulation of archival material of what the masses actually did. He went on to point to another passage, one of his few additions in the 1963 volume to the first edition of 1938. It was a statement by Georges Lefebvre in one of his mimeographed lectures on the French Revolution, given at the Sorbonne in 1947:

It is wrong to attach too much importance to any opinion that the Girondins or Robespierre might have on what needed to be done. That is not the way to approach the question. We must pay more attention to the obscure leaders and the people who listened to them in stores and the little workshops and dark streets of Paris. It was on them that the business of the day depended and for the moment, evidently, they followed the Girondins. . . . It is therefore the popular mentality, in the profound and incurable distrust which was born in the soul of the people, in regard to the aristocracy, beginning in 1789, and in regard to the king, from the time of the flight to Varennes, it is there that we must seek the explanation of what took place. The people and their unknown leaders knew what they wanted. They followed the Girondins and afterwards Robespierre, only to the degree that their advice appeared acceptable.

Who, then, are these leaders to whom the people listened? We know some. Nevertheless, as in all the decisive days of the revolution, what we most would like to know is forever out of reach; we would like to have the diary of the most obscure of the popular leaders; we would then be able to grasp, in the act so to speak, how one of the great revolutionary acts began; we do not have it.[10]

It is a lengthy citation, but it summarizes what in James's view could, with an immense accumulation of material from the French archives, elucidate what the crowds and the mass of the Saint-Domingue population actually did and their effect on the development of the revolution and the speeches and policies of the acknowledged leaders. Finally, in reference to the revolt of the plantation workers in 1801 in the colony's North Province, led by Toussaint Louverture's nephew Moïse, just months before Napoleon Bonaparte's expeditionary army arrived to return them to slavery, James referred once again to Lefebvre's comments on the Parisian sans-culottes, who, in contrast to the Jacobins as authoritarian "enlightened despots," were basically extreme democrats who wanted direct government and wished to make their leaders do what they wanted. James's instinctive understanding of Lefebvre's characterization of the sans-culottes was that

the sansculottes, of Paris in particular, saw very clearly what was required at each stage of the revolution at least until it reached its highest peak. Their difficulty was that they had neither the education, experience nor the resources to organize a modern state if only temporarily. *This was pretty much the position of the revolutionaries of Plaisance, Limbé and Dondon in relation to*

Toussaint. Events were soon to show how right they were and that in not listening to them Toussaint made the greatest mistake of his career.[11]

Contained in these passages, which only summarized the activities and mentality of the masses, were what was important not only to the further clarification of the history of the Saint-Domingue revolution but "to what we call today history."[12] James often referred to these passages in his public lectures and speeches on the French Revolution and on revolutionary politics generally in the 1970s. They provided me the perspective and concrete guidelines I needed for a study of the popular movements and mentality of the slave masses, and later the emancipated plantation workers, in relation to the acknowledged leaders of the revolution, in particular in regard to the policies and politics of Toussaint Louverture himself. Thus an analysis of the problematic relationship between revolutionary leadership and the mass movements from below, the driving forces shaping the revolution, was as much at task as the identification of those obscure people, their chosen leaders, and what they did and thought. It was a daunting task, all the more so because these slaves and their leaders left no written records of their own. But James was convinced and absolutely right in his conviction that the abundance of material in the French archives would make this possible.

In many ways, James's evolving politics of the 1970s set the stage for my writing of *The Making of Haiti*, although I was totally unaware that by 1971 James was moving toward a refiguration or reconsideration of how he would revise *The Black Jacobins* were he to write it again. Nor was I aware of his correspondence, as early as 1955, with the Haitian socialist historian Étienne Charlier, in which James was already thinking beyond the biographical analysis of the revolutionary personality of Toussaint Louverture in *The Black Jacobins* toward an analysis of "the classes and forces in conflict" during the Saint-Domingue revolution, with a primary interest in "the revolutionary and creative power of untaught slaves."[13] His thinking along those lines evidently progressed and was expressed far more explicitly in his 1971 lecture at the Institute of the Black World in Atlanta, in which he stated that if he were to reconstruct *The Black Jacobins*, he would "write descriptions in which the black slaves themselves, or people very close to them describe what they are doing and how they felt about the work that they were forced to carry on."[14]

Had I known this in 1973, when James was encouraging and unequivocally pushing me to undertake such a project for my doctoral dissertation (and eventually a book) when he could have done so himself, and much more eloquently at that, I would have been terrified to the point where I may never have agreed to do it. Fortunately, I remained in the dark on James's public pronouncements about how he would revise *The Black Jacobins*, although he hinted in some of our preliminary conversations that this needed to be done. He acknowledged that his primary concern in writing the book in 1938, while active along with George Padmore in the International African Service Bureau in London, had been with issues revolving around revolutionary politics and political leadership in the liberation struggles waged around the world, as well as with the idea and ultimately the realization of African independence. As such, James's history of the Saint-Domingue revolution, the first successful antislavery and anticolonial liberation struggle of its kind in the history of the modern world, focused on the leadership of its most prominent figure, Toussaint Louverture, and was written in part as a forecast of the independence movements that emerged in Africa during the late 1950s and early 1960s. But in the context of the 1970s, with new approaches to the writing of history and the emergence of what came to be the field of social history, any new history of the Saint-Domingue revolution would have to be written from the bottom up. As James read over and commented on my preliminary drafts, he had to keep driving it into my head that the obscure, largely local, and unknown insurrectionary leaders of the masses all had names, and *they* had to come first:

> After all, we are dealing with the revolt of the masses. I don't see a number of the mass leaders; Jean-François, Boukman, etc., are well known but there are a number of leaders who were actually leaders of the mass, and they I should think should figure prominently in your list. I have got a few down in *The Black Jacobins*. If you look carefully you will see them. But there are many others and I think those are the names that should go in instead of Barnave, Brissot, etc. They could just be mentioned, it is true ... but it is the mass movement which must be our main concern. And with the mass movement their leaders I believe should be very important and stand out.[15]

He repeatedly marked up the margins of my drafts with his characteristically handwritten notations: NAMES, NAMES, NAMES.

Even more so, James felt that the revolt of the Saint-Domingue masses constituted a book that ought to begin with a fully detailed statement of who they were and where they were in 1789 at the beginning of the revolution, after which one could write on "how they reached there historically, what was the preceding movement, and what was the situation of the other classes." James suggested that the very first chapter should place the reader "right in the centre of the people whose history you are going to deal with substantially."[16] Were he to redo his own history of the Saint-Domingue revolution, I have no doubt this is how he would have undertaken it as "a new kind of historical work," in his words. Still, he was hesitant about insisting on such an idea too forcefully, because he knew it would break with historical orthodoxy and "fly in the face of the normal." Given my academic background and training, and my understanding that full-scale revolutions rarely begin with a revolt of the oppressed but with an irreversible crisis of the ruling class and a breach in the power structure supporting it, then opening the way for the emergence of the masses to take hold of the revolutionary process in transforming society, I chose, for better or worse—academia oblige—not to adopt his bold proposal for an opening chapter.

Where *The Making of Haiti* does, I think, go a long way in doing what James was spelling out is in the third section on the popular movements of the South Province, a region of the colony either neglected altogether or subsumed by most historians of the revolution who focused their attention, as James did, largely on the explosive mass insurrectionary movements of the North. Here the Haitian historian Jean Fouchard, with whom James put me in touch when I began my foray into the Archives Nationales in Paris and whose work on the Saint-Domingue maroons, *Les Marrons de la liberté*, had just appeared,[17] directed me to an amazingly rich and abundant source of planter, governmental, and military correspondence located in the Public Record Office (today the National Archives of the United Kingdom) covering the daily activities and firsthand accounts of resistance and insurrection among the slaves and their chosen leaders of the South. In the mountains surrounding Les Cayes, the capital city and administrative center of the province, with a concentration of over one hundred sugar plantations in the plains, the slaves of the South launched their own movements in what had become by 1792–1793 a multifaceted and regionalized mass liberation struggle to overthrow slavery. In *The Black Jacobins*, James had characterized the South, the last of the colony's three provinces to be settled, as both "backward" and underdeveloped in comparison with the North, but he failed to realize that the plains of Les Cayes contained as high a concentration of sugar plantations as that of many of the key parishes of the great northern plain. Thus his argument that the particular requirements of sugar production and the organization, concentration, and division of labor—combining field and skilled factory labor in the same process—had proletarianized the slaves of the North and provided them with the discipline and the organizational tools to overthrow their masters is equally true for this region of the South. Where the South differs significantly from the North Province is in its demographic composition and high concentration of free coloreds, or mixed-race people, many of whom owned plantations and slaves of their own, chiefly the coffee and indigo estates, and rivaled their white counterparts in education and wealth.

Even more fundamental to James's line of thinking on how to rewrite the history of the Saint-Domingue revolution "from below" and bring to the forefront the masses and their obscure unknown leaders, is the fact that they were overwhelmingly African-born, and by 1789 they constituted nearly two-thirds of the entire colonial slave population. They had brought with them memories of the Middle Passage and how their lives—their social and kinship relations; their cultural, religious, and linguistic practices; their political views; their landholding and agricultural practices, not to mention their acquired military skills—had all been shaped and structured in their native African communities. Far from being the dull and simple-minded field laborers who carried the weight of slavery and the plantation system on their backs and were thus conditioned to see no further than their immediate existence, as James had initially characterized them,[18] the African masses—those to whom he would have had to redirect his attention and was urging me to do—were the backbone of the revolution and the war for independence. As such, their own vision of freedom and of how to make the promises of the revolution work for them and allow them to recast their lives as free and independent individuals with access to land, ran head-on in collision with that of Toussaint Louverture and the "black Jacobin" leadership. In the end, if independence was won, it was in spite of and not because of the revolutionary leadership. It was out of a crisis of leadership in the early stages of the war against Napoleon, with the knowledge that slavery had been restored in Guadeloupe in the summer of 1802, that the masses of Saint-Domingue took the initiative to organize themselves throughout the colony to fight both the French expeditionary troops and, until their defection from the French army, their own leaders who had failed them.[19]

James's *The Black Jacobins* was written in 1938. On the eve of World War II, with the emergence of fascism in Europe and "the turmoil of the revolutionary movement striving for clarity and influence," his book was, "with something of the fever and the fret," a part of that age.[20] So, too, was the writing of *The Making of Haiti* during the 1970s and 1980s as popular insurrectionary movements swept through Central America, in Guatemala, El Salvador, and Nicaragua, and as other movements of resistance emerged throughout Latin America, striving for clarity and influence in the face of military and fascist repression of the regimes in place. In Haiti, it was the growing popular movements that emerged in full force in 1985–1986, and the creative energies and grassroots organizational capacities of the Haitian people, "with no single leader and without arms," that ultimately brought down twenty-nine years of the Duvalier dictatorship and terror.[21] Thus my work bears the stamp of that period, as it does the mark of James's overpowering influence. In less turbulent times and in the absence of these influences, *The Making of Haiti* (to paraphrase James's own reflections in his preface to the first edition of *The Black Jacobins*) would have been quite a different book, but certainly not a better one.

Notes

1. Carolyn Fick, *The Making of Haiti: The Saint Domingue Revolution from Below* (Knoxville: University of Tennessee Press, 1990).

2. Gaetano Salvemini, *The French Revolution: 1788–1792*, trans. I. M. Rawson (London: Jonathan Cape, 1969). First published in 1954; reprinted in 1963, 1965 and 1969.

3. Richard Cobb, *The Police and the People: French Popular Protest, 1789–1820* (New York: Oxford University Press, 1970).

4. George Rudé, *The Crowd in the French Revolution* (London: Oxford University Press, 1969).

5. R. R. Palmer, *The World of the French Revolution* (New York: Harper and Row, 1971). The book was first published in French under the title *1789: les révolutions de la liberté et de l'égalité* (Calmann-Lévy, 1967).

6. Albert Soboul, *The Parisian Sans-Culottes and the French Revolution, 1793–4* (London: Oxford University Press, 1964). This is a shorter English version of Soboul's master work, *Les Sans-culottes parisiens en l'An II: mouvement populaire et gouvernement révolutionnaire, 2 juin 1793—9 thermidor An II* (Paris: Librairie Clavreuil, 1962).

7. C. L. R. James to Fick, London, January 11, 1971, personal correspondence.

8. C. L. R. James to John Higham (Chair and Program Director in American Studies, University of Michigan), London, January 4, 1971.

9. C. L. R. James to Laurore St. Juste, Washington, DC, June 26, 1973.

10. James to St. Juste, June 26, 1973. Quoted in C. L. R. James, *The Black Jacobins: Toussaint L'Ouverture and the San Domingo Revolution* (New York: Vintage, 1963), 338.

11. In James, *The Black Jacobins*, 276n6; emphasis in original.

12. James to St. Juste, June 26, 1973.

13. Quoted in chapter 13 of this volume.

14. Quoted in chapter 13.

15. James to Fick, London, August 15, 1974, personal correspondence.

16. James to Fick, August 15, 1974, personal correspondence.

17. Jean Fouchard, *Les Marrons de la liberté* (Paris: École, 1972). The English translation by Faulkner Watts, to which James wrote the preface, appeared in 1981. See Jean Fouchard, *The Haitian Maroons: Liberty or Death*, trans. Faulkner Watts (New York: Blyden Press, 1981).

18. James, *The Black Jacobins*, 15–17.

19. Carolyn E. Fick, "The Saint Domingue Slave Revolution and the Unfolding of Independence, 1971–1804," in *The World of the Haitian Revolution*, edited by David P. Geggus and Norman Fiering (Bloomington: Indiana University Press, 2009), 188–92.

20. James, *The Black Jacobins*, xi. From the preface to the first edition (London: Secker and Warburg, 1938).

21. Fick, *The Making of Haiti*, xi. A revised and expanded French edition, *Haïti, Naissance d'une Nation: la Révolution de Saint-Domingue vue d'en bas* (Rennes: Éditions Les Perséides; Montreal: Éditions du CIDIHCA), appeared in 2013 and 2014, respectively.

4 | *The Black Jacobins*, Education, and Redemption

RUSSELL MAROON SHOATZ

The ruling elites of societies use prisons both to punish those they label as law breakers and to terrorize those "free" citizens they hold sway over. In these hellholes, boredom and "nothingness" grips one, as you watch your life drift away.

To reverse that, early on during my decades in prison (c. 1984–1989 at State Correctional Institution, Dallas, Pennsylvania), I helped establish seminars where, prior to preparing and subsequently bringing their work to the floor, prisoners would choose the subjects to be presented. We demanded excellence, even though many of the participants had very little formal education. That research and study served to defeat our captors' objectives.

As the moderator of many of these sessions, I was expected also to be fully prepared—and I always tried to live up to those expectations.

One seminar developed into a lively debate as to whom did we believe should be considered the most impressive historical individual of African descent (seeing how the seminars were almost always made up of African American prisoners). By that time many of the participants had read so deeply and so widely, I believe they could have received degrees in various fields.

Thus the prisoners vied for a chance to present their choices, while being allowed a brief biographical sketch, which was followed by a Q&A session. We heard of Queen Hatshepsut of ancient Egypt, Kwame Nkrumah of Ghana, and Julius Nyerere of Tanzania as well as Shaka of the Zulus, and so it went. We were in no rush, only having to periodically break for meals and other prison routines.

As moderator, and by then respected for my learning, I was looked to as the party who would guide the session to a satisfactory decision. Personally I was leaning toward the choice of Shaka. Pontificating like a judge delivering a decision in a court of law, I summarized all the arguments I had kept notes on. Then I went on to highlight why Shaka was "obviously" the best choice. While those hardened prisoners respectfully awaited what was by then clearly going to be my judgment of Shaka as the most qualified individual, a low voice eight cells away interrupted by saying he had listened to everything, but with all due respect, we were all on the wrong wavelength. It was Moukie, a smallish, thirty-something prisoner, who was also respected as a "thinker."

By that point I couldn't imagine that my judgment could be swayed, and to reinforce my coming decision I stopped Moukie to add a few finishing touches to my paean-like comments on Shaka.

When I finished, Moukie, in a quiet voice, one that forced the prisoners to strain to hear, said we all should recognize that Toussaint Louverture was clearly the most impressive individual of African descent. Dead silence followed . . .

I was stunned! We were "on the wrong wavelength!" By failing to consider individuals outside of the African continent, we had seriously erred. Moreover, I instantly knew Moukie's choice was right. By their continuing silence—no Q&A followed—it was clear that the other prisoners did also.

How could all of these otherwise opinionated prisoners be so quickly turned around? Because we had all read C. L. R. James's *The Black Jacobins*. . . . In fact, it was so popular there we could never keep copies on the cell block. Prisoners would go to lengths to engineer ways to have borrowed copies packed with their other personal possessions when they were being transferred to other cell blocks. They would swear to either return the book or have a new copy mailed to the owner. Everybody loved that book!

Even so, the book often caused prisoners to fly into rages. Simply because James's portrayal of pre- and revolutionary Haiti can only be described as searing. The prisoners could vividly imagine the suffering their African ancestors had endured; I've also known white prisoners who were also deeply moved by that book—my comrade Nuno Pontes for instance, who was a Portuguese national.

The other side of the coin was the ability of *The Black Jacobins* to almost instantly begin to effect a change in the most antisocial prisoners, causing them to become hungry to learn what else remained hidden from them. Thus *The Black Jacobins* was one of our best educational and organizing tools.

So there I was, stunned and wordless. Like a judge who has to reverse a decision, my mind was furiously working to formulate a face-saving response, and all the time Moukie did not offer a word to bolster his choice of Toussaint, although I have to imagine he felt satisfaction in having bested all of us in that protracted debate.

Bowing to the inevitable, I swallowed my pride and announced my judgment that Moukie had been right, then opened the floor to objections—to which there remained only silence.

Consequently, we moved on to another seminar subject.

Here I need to say that the late C. L. R. James was loved by those prisoners for writing that book. His other writings and work were also highly respected and valued.

To those not in prison, if you want to help orient and educate those prisoners who will be returning to your communities, I urge you to find a way to send copies of *The Black Jacobins* to them. That book is capable of speaking to all those of African descent or otherwise who find themselves on the bottom rungs of society.

SELMA JAMES

In 1804 the independent republic of Haiti was born. Seizing on the revolution in France, the slaves had taken their freedom and gotten revolutionary Paris to ratify it. But as the French Revolution's power waned, to prevent slavery's return the Haitians had to defeat the armies of Spain and Britain as well as Napoleon. Amazingly, they did.

| | | | |

The Black Jacobins, published in 1938, was part of the massive working-class movement of the 1930s in many countries, including in the British West Indies. Its impact has been overshadowed by World War II, which it tried but failed to prevent (including trying to defeat Hitler in Spain in 1936–1938) and then the movement of the 1960s, which built on the 1930s and the experience of world war. The book was a contribution to the movement for colonial freedom—for Africa first of all, when few considered this possible. (A quarter of a century later, Ian Smith of apartheid Rhodesia was still able to say he could not conceive of Black majority rule "for a thousand years.")

The book came from the pen of an anti-imperialist campaigner who was also a leader of the Trotskyist movement in Britain; not long after, he began to break with its premises. But both framed the book.

By 1963, an exploding anti-imperialist movement and the civil rights movement in the United States had created a new market for republication after years out of print.

Between 1938 and 1963, it had been read and studied first of all by colonials in the English-speaking and French-speaking Caribbean islands (in the translation by C. L. R.'s Trotskyist comrade Pierre Naville).[1] Frantz Fanon and Aimé Césaire probably read it. Trinidadians told us in the late 1950s that *The Black Jacobins* had sustained them trying to build not only the movement for independence but an anticapitalist youth movement. People from the Pan Africanist Congress in South Africa told us in the 1960s that they had typed and copied sections for comrades to read clandestinely. It must have been known to people in the colonies wherever English was a second language. In 2011 when former Haitian president Jean-Bertrand Aristide returned home from exile in South Africa, he told me that *The Black Jacobins* had put Haiti on the map; people didn't know where it was before. He also told me that former South African president Thabo Mbeki said he knew they would win against apartheid when he read *The Black Jacobins*.

The book was called on when the 2010 earthquake in Haiti, whose destructive power was increased manifold by dire poverty,[2] reignited interest in Haiti and its revolutionary past. Many who wanted to know who Haitians were seem to have turned to *The Black Jacobins*, the classic history of the revolution the slaves made.

Later research has added substantially to our information and therefore our understanding of the revolution, but this has not challenged its classic status. It's worth asking why.

First, C. L. R. stands uncompromisingly with the slaves. Now we read about "partisan historical scholarship"; the historian was expected to be "neutral," especially seventy-five years ago—that is, not on the side of the subversives. In academia, few ignored that then or ignore it now. They did not commit themselves entirely to the slaves. Even today most historians find it hard to call the revolution anything more profound than a revolt or rebellion—not to demean the significance or the courage and organization demanded by every rebellion (and there have been many), but a revolution is qualitatively broader and deeper—it overthrows the state.

C. L. R. has all the time in the world for antiracist whites who loved the revolution and its leaders, but his point of reference, particularly in the first ten chapters, is the struggle of those who were wresting themselves away from being the property of others. Above all the book recounts their determination to be free, whatever it took.

C. L. R. doesn't glamorize; rather, he demands that we see the slaves' actions from their point of view: "The slaves destroyed tirelessly. . . . And if they destroyed much it was because they had suffered much. They knew that as long as these plantations stood, their lot would be to labour on them until they dropped. The only thing was to destroy them."[3]

Nor does C. L. R. shield us from the terror and sadism of the "civilized" masters. But the catalog of tortures, rather than merely torturing the reader, deepens our appreciation of the former slaves' power to endure and overcome, and their self-transformation from victim to protagonist. We are thrilled and inspired, learning from the Haitians' determination to be free what being human—and free—are about.

Second, Toussaint Louverture possessed all the skills of leadership the revolution needed. An uneducated, middle-aged Caribbean creole when the revolution began, he was soon able to handle sophisticated European diplomats and potentates who foolishly thought they could manipulate him because he was Black and had been a slave.

C. L. R. liked to say much later that while the establishment's authorized version of U.S. history was that Abraham Lincoln had freed the slaves, it was in fact the slaves who had freed Lincoln—presumably from his personal limitations and the conservative constraints of high office. Here C. L. R. says that "Toussaint did not make the revolution. It was the revolution that made Toussaint." Then he adds: "And even that is not the whole truth."[4]

In other words, while the movement chooses and educates its leadership, an observer is unlikely to trace this ongoing process however accurately events are recorded. We can be sure, however, that the great leader is never a "self-made man," free of the influence of those of us more lowly, as he or she is sometimes presented in an almost religious way. Leaders are a product of their individual talents and skills (and weaknesses), shaped by the power of the movement they lead in the course of social upheavals. The Haitian Jacobins chose and educated Toussaint Louverture, and he led them to where they had the will and determination to go—up to a point, which I touch on later.

This was groundbreaking considering that in 1938 there were and still are those organizations that claim that their vanguard leadership was crucial for a revolution's success. C. L. R. had something to do with the movement breaking free of such dangerous delusions. On the other hand, trying to avoid betrayal, many believe leadership is unnecessary and inevitably holds the movement back. In Haiti the slaves made the revolution, and Toussaint, one of them, played a vital role in their winning their freedom.

Third, C. L. R. compares the revolutionary slaves with how class is traditionally defined. They were not proletarians, "But working and living together in gangs of hundreds on the huge sugar-factories which covered the North Plain, they were closer to a modern proletariat than any group of workers in existence at the time, and the rising was, therefore, a thoroughly prepared and organized mass movement."[5]

This is C. L. R. the Marxist rejecting rigid definitions of class. It was those who did collective forced labor who ensured collective planning of the insurrection. The result is to open further the question of how to define who is working class long before this was on the movement's political agenda. What about not only unwaged slaves but others who don't sell their labor power on the market—subsistence farmers (often women) and other unwaged women and men: Should they be excluded from definitions of who is a worker?

By the time he wrote the 1980 foreword, C. L. R. was more confident in his assertion. By then some of us in the women's movement had helped change the climate. And new research showed that the unwaged slaves were found to have made wage slave demands! "They wanted to have three days off from work or two and a half days or at least two days."[6] He refers to Haitian historian Jean Fouchard, who had found evidence also that as early as 1793 "black women dared to demand wages equal to those of the men."[7]

There is more to learn about these revolutionaries. In 1938 C. L. R. knew that the revolution was spearheaded by the Maroons, the runaway slaves, some of whom formed their own alternative fortified societies, which lasted for years and even decades. (The Brazilian Quilombo dos Palmares lasted almost a century.) C. L. R. tells us about François Mackandal, one of Haiti's great Maroon leaders and an enormously talented orator and organizer. Two things are of particular interest here. First, Mackandal was from Guinea, an African, not a creole born in the Caribbean. Second, "He was fearless and though one-handed from an accident, had a fortitude of spirit which he knew how to preserve in the midst of the most cruel tortures."[8] He had built an organization of slaves over six years to prepare for the murder of the entire white plantocracy.

Fouchard confirmed that it was the Maroons who had led the Haitian Revolution. C. L. R. made clear that overwhelmingly the slave population was, like Mackandal, African. "The enormous increase of slaves [due to a thriving economy and—not unconnected—to people being worked to death] was filling the colony with native Africans, more resentful, more intractable, more ready for rebellion than the creole Negro. Of the half-a-million slaves in the colony in 1789, more than two-thirds had been born in Africa."[9]

Fouchard's detailed research proves that the dominant force among the Maroons were the Africans who had made the Middle Passage. He is justifiably indignant that "Those who have previously studied the Maroons have not considered the runaway new Negroes [that is, new to Haiti and slavery] with the attention they deserved yet they are the most significant expression of absolute refusal of the slavery they condemn." The new Negroes were "newly disembarked, ignorant of the language and the geography of the country" and thus "their necessary dependence for escape on accomplices."[10] That is, the Maroons must have organized to help those escaping—already revolutionary organizing.

Marcus Rediker indicates an early source of the slaves' collective rebellion. The slave ship was not only a chamber of horrors, a prison, a death trap but a training ground. Rediker indicates some of the ways that "a multiethnic mass of several hundred Africans, thrown together . . . learned to act collectively."[11] To do this, he says, they had to learn to cross language and culture divides among the various tribes and nations represented by the captive passengers.[12] Those who were more likely to survive the Middle Passage were the strongest, possibly the more able, and may have learned about organizing across divides. Wouldn't they most likely become runaways and join or form a Maroon encampment?

When C. L. R. first read Fouchard's book with its new and precise information, he was delighted. He thought it outdated *The Black Jacobins*: "It lasted for thirty-five years. That's long enough for any history book!"

| | | | |

In chapter 11, *The Black Jacobins* takes a quite different turn. Slavery has been abolished but Haiti is still a French colony and will soon face the attempt of postrevolutionary France to reimpose it. While the story of the revolution expresses the movement of the 1930s, the story of postslavery, preindependent Haiti tells us what that movement had to confront.

C. L. R. must present Toussaint's clash with those he had led to victory. As with so much else, Haiti faced earlier than others all the problems of shaping its course following the overthrow of the state. Theirs is also the story of what happens to the leader who, having led the revolution, believes he knows better than his people what is best for their future.

We are told that to restore order from the chaos and blood-letting after years of war, Toussaint "instituted a military dictatorship."[13] This is a shock.

Worse follows. C. L. R. tells us that Toussaint believed the Haitian economy demanded the plantation system. "The ultimate guarantee of freedom was the prosperity of agriculture. This was Toussaint's slogan. The danger was that the blacks might slip into the practice of cultivating a small patch of land, producing just sufficient for their needs. He would not allow the old estates to be broken up."[14]

The 1930s had struggled to make sense of Stalin's forced collectivization in the Soviet Union. In that decade the world, and C. L. R. with it, had been shocked into slow recognition that forced labor could be imposed by the very organization that had led a revolution. How different was that from Toussaint reimposing the plantation system? We must bear in mind that Trotskyism, from which C. L. R. had not yet broken, characterized the Soviet Union of forced labor as a workers' state.[15]

> He confined the blacks to the plantation under rigid penalties. He was battling with the colossal task of transforming a slave population, after years of licence, into a community of free labourers and he was doing it in the only way he could see. On behalf of the labourers he saw to it that they were paid a quarter of the produce. This alone was sufficient to mark the change from the old to the new despotism.[16]

But it was despotism. After all, the revolution had begun by burning the plantations to the ground. Ultimately the laborers fought and won. How much do we know of the society that replaced the plantation? We are told:

> Left to themselves, the Haitian peasantry resuscitated to a remarkable degree the lives they had lived in Africa. Their method of cultivation, their family relations and social practices, their drums, songs and music, such art as they practiced and above all their religion which became famous, Vodun.[17]

If this is so, the Africans were likely to reproduce the communal societies they had brought with them; they knew only this and the hated slavery. The general view at the time (and even today) was that communal village life was "primitive" and had to be superseded for there to be progress. In the 1960s, President Julius Nyerere of Tanzania had a different perspective. He characterized the village he had grown up in as "tribal socialism." It had weaknesses, he said, but with independence it could become the way Tanzania could develop, ending poverty and women's subordination while bypassing capitalism.[18] Of course we cannot say for sure, but it may well be that this was the course the population chose once they had won the right to do as they wished on the land.

For Toussaint, the French, not the Africans, had "civilization." Once Toussaint and the Black population diverge, C. L. R. had to choose his point of reference. It was not always the ex-slaves who provided his direction.

When C. L. R. tells us that Toussaint "had no interests apart from theirs," that is, the laborers,[19] it is unclear whether this is what Toussaint thinks or whether C. L. R. agrees. His later statement is unambiguous: "Between Toussaint and his people there was no fundamental difference of outlook or of aim."[20]

C. L. R.'s restrained critique was, I think, not to risk undermining our appreciation for what Toussaint accomplished despite acts that were "worse than errors." The revolution itself had powerful enemies even at the distance of well over a century. He is more protective of Toussaint in 1938 than in the 1960s, when he decided to revise his 1936 play about him, giving his nephew Moïse more of a role and enhancing his case against his uncle.

The crisis over imposing the plantation leads Toussaint into killing the leader who fought him on behalf of the laborers' movement—Moïse. "Moïse . . . beloved by the blacks of the North for his ardent championship of them against the whites. He stood high in Toussaint's favour until he refused to carry out Toussaint's severe labour legislation in the North."[21]

It is clear from C. L. R.'s evidence that Moïse was the person Haiti needed after slavery. Moïse sought to have unity among the Blacks and mulattoes. It certainly seems that he was killed not only because he was the leader of a movement against Toussaint's plantation but because of the superiority of his leadership. C. L. R. comments to underscore the enormity of Toussaint's "crime" that "to shoot Moïse . . . was almost as if Lenin had had Trotsky shot for taking the side of the proletariat against the bourgeoisie."[22]

In the constitution Toussaint wrote and imposed, "he authorized the slave trade because the island needed people to cultivate it. When the Africans landed, however, they would be free men."[23] Commenting on the constitution, Moïse "called Toussaint an old fool. 'He thinks he is the king of San Domingo.' "[24]

It was ambition for power, a kind of madness that often afflicts those who have been put into positions of authority by the movement; this leads them to believe they have earned the right to impose their will.

Toussaint could not conceive of Haiti moving forward independent of what he calls French civilization; the African and creole population could not move up from slavery without what the French had to teach them— although what that is exactly is not spelled out. At first he considers that Haiti would be a French colony and that the population would become French. We must assume he was not thinking of Napoleon's imperialist France, which later attempted to reimpose slavery, but of the revolutionary population that agreed to abolish it.

Unlike Toussaint, who was ultimately kidnapped and murdered by the "civilized" French, C. L. R. had a chance in the 1963 appendix to spell out his contempt for the Haitian elite which venerated "French civilization." But C. L. R. is not cleared of the charge that he too had a belief in what Europe calls "civilization."

This term is at best unhelpful and usually dresses deep racism in respectability. Who is not civilized? When Mahatma Gandhi visited London in the 1930s, he was asked what he thought of British civilization. His reply was filmed and became famous: "I think it will be a good thing." We can all agree.

Ten years after *The Black Jacobins* was published, C. L. R., immersed in working-class organizing and having broken with Trotskyism, completed a study of Hegel and Marx. In *Notes on Dialectics*, he not only breaks with the vanguard party but identifies and analyzes the corruption in the new governing class, of which Toussaint was an example.[25] In this light, the delusions of grandeur Moïse describes is for C. L. R. no longer merely a personal failing of Toussaint but a class characteristic. This enables us to call Toussaint on the class nature of his ambition without demeaning the great Haitian Revolution or his enormous contribution to making it.[26]

| | | | |

Some of us feel strongly the need to acknowledge and support today's Black Jacobins. Actor-activist Danny Glover is a shining example. Speaking after the U.S.-led coup that overthrew President Aristide, he wrote:

> The first time I went to Haiti was 30 years ago . . . I'd read C.L.R. James's *Black Jacobins* in college, about a country and a revolution I had never heard about. I wanted to see who these people were. Haiti did the unthinkable . . . it undermined the whole premise of white supremacy by overthrowing slavery. It was the first victory over slavery of Africans. And for that it has continued to be dismissed, beaten and just torn apart . . . we have to find ways on every level to come to the aid of Haiti. My position is that President Aristide remains the duly elected president of Haiti, that position I will not waver from or be moved from.[27]

When I visited Haiti for the first time, I saw the names of places associated with individuals, battles, events that I knew from the book. I also saw the revolution.

C. L. R. had said that he could see the French Revolution in the faces of the fashion models from Paris. For the first time, I understood what he meant. In Haiti, the revolution is on the faces even of the children. There is a dignity, a seriousness, a resilience, and an expectation of winning against almost insuperable odds. Although there are those who trace African roots in the religion and culture generally of modern Haiti, there seems little interest among those who write learned papers in exploring the revolutionary roots of who Haitians are now, the way their revolutionary impertinence has shaped them, and informs their present struggle.

The indomitable spirit that won in 1804 defeated the murderous twentieth-century dictatorships of the Duvaliers (approved by Washington) after thirty years in 1986. It twice elected President Aristide, with 67 percent of the vote in 1990 and 92 percent in 2000—a liberation theology priest who set out to raise Haiti "from destitution to poverty," built schools and hospitals, tried to regenerate agriculture, and raised the minimum wage. It steels the determination of the women I met who carry on fighting for justice against the rapes and murders of the 1991 and 2004 coups. It boycotted election after election when Aristide's Lavalas (flash flood) party was banned from standing (80 percent of the electorate refused to vote at the U.S.-led "selection" that put Michel Martelly in power)—a level of mass organization we almost never see anywhere else. It continues to campaign for withdrawal of the UN troops that have occupied Haiti at the behest of the imperial powers since 2004 and for compensation for the UN-imported cholera that has killed nearly 9,000 people and infected more than 800,000.

Today's Jacobins are fighting today's imperialism: the United States, Canada, France, the multinationals, the Clintons (who "helped" by making a way for sweatshops paying the lowest minimum wage in the Western Hemisphere), and others making deals with the tiny Haitian elite. The "international community" and "civil society"—that conglomerate of nongovernmental organizations which act for governments that have created or coopted and now fund them—has been crucial to reimposing the deification of the market—which the slaves destroyed when they burned down the plantations and won the land to cultivate for their own survival and happiness.

Despite occupation and repression, the murder and disappearance of many grassroots leaders like Lovinsky Pierre-Antoine, the Lavalas movement remains unbowed. Tens of thousands flood the streets to defend the Aristide family every time his freedom is under threat, including every time he is summoned to court on trumped-up charges.

Scandalously, in 2004, at the behest of the United States and just before their coup, heads of state (except Mbeki of South Africa) snubbed Haiti's bicentenary celebrations. Even Latin American countries stayed away, despite their debt to revolutionary Haiti. As C. L. R. points out in his appendix: "Pétion, the ruler of Haiti, nursed back to health the sick and defeated Bolivar, gave him money, arms and a printing press to help in the campaign which ended in the freedom of the Five States."[28]

Only Venezuela and CARICOM (the Caribbean Community) opposed the UN occupation. Even they are now collaborating with Martelly, despite previous objections to electoral fraud and Martelly's attempts to reinstate dictatorship.

As the reader will see from the brief, potent contributions of Mumia Abu-Jamal and Russell "Maroon" Shoatz, two prisoner colleagues, this history book remains integral to present struggle, though this is often missing from commentaries that praise it or its author. It offers an answer to the ultimate question in the mind of every struggler: Can we win, against racism, against every form of slavery, against all the repressive powers that intend to be in charge of us forever? It replies: We did, and we can again.

Notes

1. The cover of this translation had its author as "P.I.R. James"—colonials were often treated carelessly.
2. The theft by nongovernmental organizations ensured that Haitians continue to live with the impact of the earthquake.
3. C. L. R. James, *The Black Jacobins: Toussaint L'Ouverture and the San Domingo Revolution* (London: Penguin, 2001), 71.
4. James, *The Black Jacobins*, xix.
5. James, *The Black Jacobins*, 69.
6. James, *The Black Jacobins*, xvii.
7. Jean Fouchard, *Les Marrons de la Liberté* (Paris: Editions de l'Ecole, 1972), 355.
8. James, *The Black Jacobins*, 16.
9. James, *The Black Jacobins*, 45.
10. Fouchard, *Les Marrons de la Liberté*, 395.
11. Marcus Rediker, *The Slave Ship: A Human History* (London: John Murray, 2007), 264–65.
12. It's worth mentioning that Africans often speak a number of languages because villages and tribes may have their own languages, which their neighbors master, resulting in a general linguistic facility not known in Europe. We don't know if this is true in other parts of the nonindustrialized world.

13. James, *The Black Jacobins*, 196.

14. James, *The Black Jacobins*, 196.

15. He must already have questioned this view: he said that "the German comrades" had told him how wrong he was, that it was state capitalism.

16. James, *The Black Jacobins*, 196.

17. James, *The Black Jacobins*, 307.

18. There were many communal societies on the African continent. Of course they had changed over the years in a variety of ways—they were affected by the slave trade, when many villages were destroyed altogether. Even after European imperialism across the continent, the communalism of African societies had survived, as Tanzania's *ujamaa* demonstrates. See Ralph Ibbott, *Ujamaa: The Hidden Story of Tanzania's Socialist Villages* (London: Crossroads Books, 2014), and Selma James, "Introduction," in Ibbott, *Ujamaa*, 13–39, particularly note 15 for references including Marx's *Ethnological Notebooks* and the perspective of Walter Rodney.

19. James, *The Black Jacobins*, 213.

20. James, *The Black Jacobins*, 233.

21. James, *The Black Jacobins*, 209.

22. James, *The Black Jacobins*, 231.

23. James, *The Black Jacobins*, 215.

24. James, *The Black Jacobins*, 216.

25. But it is not inevitable. It never happened to Fidel Castro, with whom Toussaint is compared in the appendix.

26. C. L. R. James, *Notes on Dialectics: Hegel, Marx, Lenin* (London: Allison and Busby, 1980). For anyone who wants to wrestle with a relevant passage of *Notes*: "We say that this cause seemed to have such a powerful effect because there was an *effect* waiting to be caused. The cause *and* the effect are in the *substance* of the thing."

27. Danny Glover, "Haiti and Venezuela—A Personal View," *Rise* (Summer/Fall 2004): 37.

28. James, *The Black Jacobins*, 321. In fact there were six states: Bolivia, Colombia, Ecuador, Peru, Panama, and Venezuela.

PART II.
THE HAITIAN REVOLUTION
Histories and Philosophies

| | | | |

LAURENT DUBOIS

Like many other readers, I remember well my first encounter with *The Black Jacobins*. The title, whispered to me with a near religious admiration by a teacher, was itself already a lesson: The story of the French Revolution was also the story of a Caribbean revolution. *The Black Jacobins*, published more than seven decades ago, is one of the very few books I have ever read essentially without stopping, stuck to my chair, thrown into a world, propelled onward by a riveting story, angered, exhilarated, confused, and even exhausted by the scope of what James explains and accomplishes in the work. Afterward, something had shifted. The geography and chronology of history looked different to me. After reading *The Black Jacobins*, we find it impossible to look at what we think we know about the past, about the history of democracy and revolution, the history of Europe and the Americas, in quite the same way.

In writing the book, James created a language and a form for his story that was shaped by its content. If it has become a classic work, a touchstone of debate and an inspiration to generations of scholars and activists, it is also because of its form—its combination of hard-nosed narration, political analysis, and philosophical reflection. It is both a narrative of history and a work in the philosophy of history. Like James's book on cricket and colonialism, *Beyond a Boundary*, the work seems inexhaustible, a map of reflections and provocations you can return to again and again. It keeps surprising me. The text changed, too, with additions and changes for the 1963 edition that responded to the decades of transformation that followed its original composition. This new edition also helped make the work much better known to a generation of readers plunged into the process of decolonization, revolution, and dictatorship in Africa, Latin America, and the Caribbean, for whom this old story held remarkable prophesies and lessons.

Many works of history find themselves forgotten, falling away as new narratives revise or refute what has come before. *The Black Jacobins* never has. Thanks to the work of subsequent historians (many inspired by James), we now know much more about the Haitian Revolution. We know that Toussaint Louverture was a freeman, rather than a slave, at the beginning of the revolution. We understand that the "mulattoes," whom James sometimes describes with simplified virulence, were an extremely complicated group with multiple political projects and affiliations. We have a much richer sense of the deep complexities of the political philosophy of the enslaved themselves, who in James's work mostly appear as a relatively undifferentiated mass of rebels. We have gained an understanding of the influences of a variety of African cultures, philosophies, and histories on the course of events in Saint-Domingue. James's work did what any great work of history does: It created descendants and many of them challenged and went beyond their ancestor. It remains the best study written on the Haitian Revolution—indeed, one of the best ever written on revolution itself. It embodies the story of that revolution brilliantly, charging its readers with a sense of drama and direction in a way few works of history do. James essentially got his story right, grasping the core of what the revolution was and what it implied.

Though he didn't use the term to describe what he did, James helped lay the foundation in his work for the field now known as Atlantic history. Along with the work of his onetime student Eric Williams, his book transformed the historiography produced about the Caribbean and Atlantic slavery more broadly in the past decades, particularly in the Anglophone world. James's work was crucial in part simply because it convincingly demanded that historians take the Haitian Revolution seriously as an event of global significance, a touchstone in the political history of Europe and the Americas. It also insisted on seeing the interconnections between events on both sides of the Atlantic, encouraging subsequent historians to think beyond national contexts as they studied the circulation of revolutionary ideals. James's work has inspired historians to write a certain kind of Atlantic history, one that decenters Europe, paying close attention to the ways the central pillar of the Atlantic world—the slave trade and slavery—shaped life and ideas in Europe, Africa, and the Americas. It demands we recall that within this world, the enslaved were never simply workers or victims, but always actors and thinkers. They remade the world in which they lived. Through the Haitian Revolution, enslaved revolutionaries crafted an idea of rights that was truly universal in scope, refusing to accept—as most revolutionaries in the United States and France did—that a human being could be a slave. In this sense the revolution, as James shows, was an epochal and global event, one to which we are all linked, whether or not we know it or accept it.

"The slave-trade and slavery were the economic basis of the French Revolution," James boldly announces early in his book. He quotes Jean Jaurès, one of the few historians of the French Revolution to acknowledge the role of the colonies in the shaping of eighteenth-century France, to buttress his point: "Sad irony of human history . . . The fortunes created at Bordeaux, at Nantes, by the slave-trade, gave to the bourgeoisie that pride which needed liberty and contributed to human emancipation."[1] It is a striking claim, one that intriguingly parallels Eric Williams's claim, in his 1944 *Capitalism and Slavery*, that slavery and the slave trade laid the foundation for the Industrial Revolution in England. Interestingly, however, James's claim has not become a touchstone for debate the way Williams's did in Anglophone historiography, where a generation of historians have argued vociferously about it. In fact, the precise ways the Atlantic plantation economy and the slave trade shaped social life and political thought in France remain curiously understudied, and the provocation issued by James in this passage still awaits a full-fledged response.

Of course, James is also curious about the ways influence traveled in another direction, with the ideas of the French Revolution shaping the course of the uprising in Saint-Domingue. He crystallizes the question in a powerful scene in which he portrays Toussaint Louverture reading a particularly stirring passage from a controversial work compiled by the Abbé Raynal, the *Histoire des Deux Indes*, whose many volumes described and at times harshly critiqued the history of European empire. Drawing directly from the work of Louis Sebastien Mercier, who in his *L'An 2440* imagined a future in which slavery has been abolished thanks to the leadership of a hero whose statue decorates a plaza in Paris, Raynal evoked the coming of a "Black Spartacus" and asked "Where is he?" It was this passage that James imagines Louverture reading. "Over and over again Toussaint read this passage: 'A courageous chief only is wanted. Where is he?'" "Men make their own history," he continues, quoting Karl Marx, "and the black Jacobins of San Domingo were to make history which would alter the fate of millions of men and shift the economic currents of three continents."[2]

Did Louverture truly read Raynal, as James asserts? Scholars have debated the question. In a critique of the Enlightenment's racism, for instance, the French political philosopher Louis Sala-Molins seizes on the image, dismissing the idea as nothing more than a fable, pointing out that for Louverture to be inspired by Raynal, he would have had to read the passages calling for a "black hero" while "systematically skipping" the racist passages of the text. Such an image, he argues, seeks to transform the "black liberators" into "disciples of the Enlightenment." But then the question becomes: How was "the black" able to "succeed in the subtle academic exercise that consists in deducing from a discourse that, occasionally, concerns him, what this discourse does not say or suggest, what it eliminates in with complete serenity and clarity? How does he manage to extract from the Enlightenment what the Enlightenment never dreamed of?" Having emphasized throughout his work that the Enlightenment worked to either openly justify or willfully overlook slavery in the Atlantic, Sala-Molins insists that it had no role in shaping revolution in the Caribbean: "The black, always a slave and still always standing, truly invented his liberty."[3]

In *Tropicopolitans*, meanwhile, Srinivas Aravamudan has argued for the need to gain a better understanding of the responses and interpretation of individuals who were the "accidental, unintended, and indirect addresses" of Enlightenment literature. He approaches the question in one chapter by exploring the assertion (made in *The Black Jacobins*, among other texts) that passages in Raynal's *Histoire Philosophique et Politique* evoking the possibility of a slave revolution helped inspire Louverture. He notes that determining whether this particular literary encounter took place is probably impossible, although he argues that the impact of Raynal's text "can be reconstructed, if somewhat imaginatively, by a literary-critical urge to rush in where historians fear to tread." He does so by inventing a reader designated as "Toussaint's daughter-in-law" and imagining her response to a particular passage from Raynal's text.[4]

James had his own kind of response to the question of how we should think about the impact of Enlightenment thought on the colonies. For him, Louverture not only mastered Enlightenment discourse but ultimately superseded it. "Pericles on democracy, Paine on the Rights of Man, the Declaration of Independence, the Communist Manifesto," James writes in one of my favorite passages. "These are some of the political documents which, whatever the weakness of wisdom of their analysis, have moved men and will always move them." But there was another set of writings that, according to James, had been unjustly excluded from this canon: those of Louverture, who wrote in the midst of war, revolution, and international conflict, without the benefit of a "liberal education," dictating to secretaries "until their devotion and his will had hammered them into adequate shape." Nevertheless, he wrote in "the language and accent" of French philosophers and revolutionaries, all "masters of the spoken and written word." He also "excelled them all," for unlike them he didn't have "to pause, to hesitate, to qualify." "Toussaint could defend the freedom of the blacks without reservation, and this gave to his declaration a strength and a single-mindedness rare in the great documents of the time."[5]

Part of what is so compelling about the story of the Haitian Revolution and James's rendering of it is what David Scott has highlighted as its tragic dimension. James, like many other historians, dwelled at length on the ways Louverture's revolutionary leadership ultimately led him into a role as an autocrat and a dictator, one at odds with much of the population whose liberation he had launched and sustained through his rule. As Scott has shown, James, through a new appendix and a series of edits he made in the 1963 edition, deepened his exploration of the tragedy of Louverture, looking at it from a very different place than he did in 1938, when he first wrote the book.[6] For James himself, the story of *The Black Jacobins* shifted over the decades as the world around him changed. The brilliance of the book is that even as our present transforms how we can read it, it continues to speak to our present.

In the end, Louverture succumbed to Napoleon, surrendering after weeks of fighting French troops sent to take control of the island, and then finding himself shipped off to a dank prison in France, where he died of sickness even as war raged in Saint-Domingue, led by his former generals. As James begins his narrative of the war that brought Haiti its independence in 1804, he notes that what happened in Saint-Domingue after the death of Charles Leclerc, Napoleon's brother-in-law and the general in charge of the French expedition, "is one of those pages in history which every schoolboy should learn, and most certainly will learn, some day." He crystallizes for us what drove and inspired the conflict. The people of Haiti, less than a decade after plantation slavery, "had seen at last that without independence they could not maintain their liberty, and liberty was far more concrete for former slaves than the elusive forms of political democracy in France."[7]

His pages on the war are searing. "Why do you burn everything? asked a French officer to a prisoner. We have a right to burn what we cultivate because a man has a right to dispose of his own labor, was the reply of this unknown anarchist."[8] The story he tells pushes him to make a claim for the present and the future. Just as it was the "masses" of the enslaved in Saint-Domingue who drove the revolution there, he wrote in 1938, so it will be for the future. "Others will arise, and others. From the people heaving in action will come the leaders; not the isolated blacks at Guy's hospitals or the Sorbonne, the dabblers in surréalisme or the lawyers, but the quiet recruits in a black police force, the sergeant in the French native army or British police, familiarizing himself with military tactics and strategy, reading a stray pamphlet of Lenin or Trotsky as Toussaint read the Abbé Raynal."[9]

There is, James insisted through his title and through his book, no way to think of the history of the French Revolution without knowing—and knowing well—the history of the Haitian Revolution. There is no history of France, or of republican democracy, that is not also a history of empire, of those whose lives were shaped by it, and of those who confronted it. This lesson is the challenge posed by *The Black Jacobins*. But the challenge is also larger than that, for James's book is also about trying to grasp how, at rare moments, change becomes possible. "There are periods in human history," he quips at one point, "when money is not enough" to ensure the control of the future.[10] If he and we return to the Haitian Revolution, it is also because it spurs us to imagine the unimaginable.

Notes

1. C. L. R. James, *The Black Jacobins: Toussaint L'Ouverture and the San Domingo Revolution* (New York: Vintage, 1963), 47.

2. James, *The Black Jacobins*, 25. For more on Raynal and Louverture in the context of the Haitian Revolution see Laurent Dubois, *Avengers of the New World: The Story of the Haitian Revolution* (Cambridge, MA: Harvard University Press, 2004).

3. Louis Sala-Molins, *Les Misères des Lumières: Sous la raison, l'outrage* (Paris: Robert Laffont, 1992), 158–60. I discuss Sala-Molins and the broader question of the Enlightenment in the Caribbean in Laurent Dubois, "An Enslaved Enlightenment: Re-Thinking the Intellectual History of the French Atlantic," *Social History* 31, no. 1 (February 2006): 1–14.

4. Srinivas Aravamudan, *Tropicopolitans: Colonialism and Agency, 1688–1804* (Durham, NC: Duke University Press, 1999), 23, 299.

5. James, *The Black Jacobins*, 197–98.

6. David Scott, *Conscripts of Modernity: The Tragedy of Colonial Enlightenment* (Durham, NC: Duke University Press, 2004).

7. James, *The Black Jacobins*, 356–57.

8. James, *The Black Jacobins*, 361.

9. James, *The Black Jacobins*, 377.

10. James, *The Black Jacobins*, 155.

Haiti and Historical Time

BILL SCHWARZ

I want liberty and equality to reign in St-Domingue.
—Toussaint L'Ouverture, August 29, 1791

That is the bitter secret of the apple. The vision of progress is the rational madness of history seen as sequential time, of a dominated future.
—Derek Walcott

Rosa Luxemburg "saw unpredictability lying at the heart of politics. For Luxemburg, we are the makers of a history which exceeds our control, as well it must if we are not to descend into autocracy and terror."
—Jacqueline Rose

All modern political revolutions, while remaining political revolutions, also function as revolutions "in philosophy," enabling new thought to happen. That this was emphatically so in the revolution in Saint-Domingue is the claim I seek to follow in this chapter.[1] The revolt of 1791 and the creation of the black republic that followed defied conventional cognitive possibilities. The idea that free-thinking black Jacobins could arise from the degradation of the slave plantations and a new state be organized by the dark-skinned multitude required that the foundational ideas of civilization be recast. If such things proved historically conceivable—that the wretched of the Earth possessed the right for sovereign lives and the collective desire for its realization lay within their grasp—then the horizons of human life immediately, dramatically expanded.[2]

To make this argument I confine my discussion to C. L. R. James's *The Black Jacobins*, first published in 1938. There is no doubt in my mind that James's book represented and represents a magnificent, singular history, from which we can still learn much. But it never stood alone. It was generated from deep inside an emergent constellation of self-consciously modern or modernist black political, intellectual, and aesthetic practices that coalesced in the diaspora of the 1920s and 1930s and were galvanized by the Italian invasion of Ethiopia in 1935. In their differing idioms, these sought to resurrect the putatively primitive aspirations of early nineteenth-century, insurrectionary Saint-Domingue for the varied Afro-modernisms of mid-twentieth-century diasporic lives. Garveyism, the Harlem Renaissance, Pan-Africanism, *négritude*: all were distinct, yet they represented mobile, shifting networks, sharing at times—if never formal programs or desiderata—common sensibilities in which Haiti frequently constituted a powerful currency. In large part, these memories of Haiti remain ours at the beginning of the twenty-first century. In this respect, James remains a luminous presence.[3]

I'm concerned principally with the question of how historical temporalities can be understood and what political consequences follow. James, in his subsequent ruminations on *The Black Jacobins*, never seemed overly concerned about the question of historical time, despite the innovations his study represents. In important respects it's our problem rather than his, as I'll endeavor to explain later. More particularly I ask about the significance of *The Black Jacobins* for the writing of history today. To think in these terms supposes that the revolution in philosophy associated with the founding of Haiti turns critically on how history itself can be understood.

The answer to my question—What is the significance of *The Black Jacobins* for the writing of history today?—is provided by James himself. In his 1980 preface he invokes his conviction that it was "the slaves who made the revolution."[4] This basic political premise worked as the conceptual premise for his historical narrative. *The Black Jacobins* tells the story of the mass insurrection of black slaves in Saint-Domingue, led by Toussaint Louverture and the consequent foundation of the modern nation-state of Haiti as the first independent black republic. In historical terms it was coterminous with or a constituent of the volcanic revolutions that occurred in the Atlantic world, particularly in North America and France, which drew in their wake Latin America, Spain, parts of Central Europe, Ireland, Wales, and—if one follows E. P. Thompson, as I do on this—England as well. Not so long after the publication of *The Black Jacobins*, it became possible to think of these events as comprising, historically, an identifiable Atlantic Revolution.[5]

It's difficult for contemporary readers familiar with James, a couple of generations after the first publication of *The Black Jacobins*, to keep in focus the enormity—the audacity—of his capacity to give historical agency to the enslaved blacks. James was brought up in a world in which the influence of J. A. Froude, Regius Professor of History at Oxford University who exhibited a masterful, lifelong contempt for "West Indian Negroes," was still an acclaimed figure of public authority.[6] In 1938, James was closer chronologically to Froude than he was to the academic postcolonial common sense of our times. In his own life, when he first arrived in England in 1932, his sympathies seemed to accord as much with the English abolitionists as they did with the rebellious enslaved, which indicates the speed with which he moved from one mental world to another.[7] When he set about researching *The Black Jacobins*, the most authoritative Anglophone historical work on the making of Haiti was still Lothrop Stoddard's *The French Revolution in San Domingo*, which without a blush peddled an unexpurgated audit detailing the primitive proclivities of the nonwhite inhabitants of the island.[8] These historical circumstances make James's determination to tell the story of "the slaves who made the revolution" all the more remarkable.

Although this founding premise can be stated simply enough, its very simplicity, apparently so obvious, works to conceal deeper, more complicated questions. The story of Saint-Domingue stayed with James for all his life. As it first entered his imagination, it was as a literary recounting of Toussaint's biography. As he recalled in 1971: "I had decided—God only knows why, I don't; and I rather doubt if even He would too—that I would write a history of Toussaint L'Ouverture. Why? I don't know . . . I had made up my mind, for no other than a literary reason, that when I reached England I would settle down to write a history of Toussaint L'Ouverture."[9] In 1934, as things turned out, James completed the story of Toussaint as a play, which received its first performance in London in 1936; only after that, in 1938, did the conventional history appear.[10] Thereafter, through the 1960s and continuing up until the 1980s, there appeared a second edition of *The Black Jacobins*, an important historiographical commentary, various reworkings of the drama, and the addition of further introductory material.[11] It thus appears that for half a century, James was compelled to keep returning to the events that created Haiti, experimenting with different generic narrative-forms to marshal his shifting readings. As the world turned, and as his politics entered distinct phases, his telling of the history evolved. Yet wherever his different political investments took him, Saint-Domingue remained a touchstone. Wherever he found himself situated politically, he felt required to retell the story of Toussaint's slave insurrection anew. In James's field of vision, the making of Haiti represented a decisive historical event in the inauguration of the modern world.

Yet when in 1938 James first published his account of the revolution as a formal history, following the conventions of a formal history, what he had to say—for the great majority of his readers—was far from obvious. Today, some generations later, although gesturally acknowledged by a portion of the historical profession, *The Black Jacobins* remains otherwise contentious or of only peripheral interest. Recognition by historians of the significance of the Saint-Domingue revolution has been slow and remains uneven.[12] To some degree, what James wrote in 1938 continues to be what it has always been: *not obvious at all*. Thus those who admire the book are obliged to locate where the creative power of James's narrative lies and ponder why resistance to his interpretation, if that is what it is, might still prevail.

In his original 1938 preface, James acknowledged that "The writing of history becomes ever more difficult."[13] Why should this be so? One might have thought the opposite: that James, as a Trotskyist in the 1930s, was likely to have assumed that as the contradictions of capitalism intensified, the underlying social determinations would have become ever more visible to the naked eye, and thus the job of comprehending history would have become not more difficult but more straightforward.

To approach this problem, I intend to draw out into the open James's conception of the primitive and its various cognates and ask what consequences this had for rethinking the practices of history.

I am persuaded that much hangs on this. The various inscriptions of the primitive have always been historically loaded. Systems of colonial rule, sometimes explicitly, sometimes implicitly, were frequently given justification by recourse to notions of the primitive, which offered a primary vehicle for projecting otherness onto others. "Primitive" functioned as an active, toxic sign of everyday struggle, working (first) to create the figure of the native, or of subalterns more generally, and (second, when that was in train) to naturalize the resulting hierarchies of the social world. And it can still do so in our putatively postcolonial times. Even when spoken sotto voce, or when alluded to rather than stated out loud, "primitive" can work as one of those keywords, to borrow from Raymond Williams, that makes the worlds we inhabit, riven by inequalities and injustice, knowable and familiar.

Moreover, there is good reason to believe that the very project of history itself, as a distinct and privileged intellectual endeavor to comprehend the relations between the past and the present, was born in a conscious bid to outflank all that "the primitive" comprised, in its variant, endless, and perpetually troubling manifestations. Ideas of the primitive have for long haunted historical practice. If, as Nicholas Dirks proposed, history acts as a "sign of the modern," it initially did so by holding to a strict temporality that militantly demarcated the primitive from the modern, such that one could suppose modernity to exist free from any taint of putatively primitive structures of feeling.[14] As history was formed as a discipline, this is what it set out to do: disavow the primitive.[15] Consequently, if the idea of the primitive needs to be recast then out of necessity, so does the idea of history itself and its inherited, given temporalities.

When James left Trinidad for Britain in 1932, he had already been planning to write about Toussaint. But within a year or two a remarkable transition occurred. He had not only crossed the seas, from colony to metropole, but in an accompanying journey he traveled swiftly to Marxism, a transformation animated by his incomparable intellectual curiosity.[16] This in turn required him to revise his ideas of how he would tell the story of Toussaint, forsaking his erstwhile "literary" inclinations. In 1971 he explained what had carried him to Marxism and propelled his reimagining of the revolution in Saint-Domingue. "I became a Marxist through the influence of two books": Oswald Spengler's *The Decline of the West* and Trotsky's *History of the Russian Revolution*.[17] Spengler and Trotsky weren't, and aren't, a conventional pairing. What was it in the early thirties that they promised for James?

The two volumes of Spengler's *Decline of the West*—published in 1918 and 1922, with the first credible translation into English appearing in 1926 and 1928—represent a vast, strange, *Arabian-Nights* compendium of global histories, whose method was ostensibly rooted not in the protocols of formal history but principally in Goethe and to a lesser degree Nietzsche. In its time it was a work of immense influence. The opening pages of the first volume present a brief, stunning broadside against the "meaningless" notion of a programmed historical progression, based on the usual triad of ancient-medieval-modern. This, according to Spengler, "rigs the stage" for "Western Europe," eliminating from the historical record the many civilizations that didn't conform to the given schema. In placing Europe at the center of things, it generated a "phantom" world history, the consequence of an "optical illusion." Spengler believed such a view to be not only "narrow and provincial" but also resulting in the idea of the modern having been "stretched and stretched again to the elastic limit at which it will bear no more." In place of what he perceived to be the delusions of world history, he proposed that the historical imagination should properly take for its object *"the world as history"* manifest (and here Goethe intervenes) not as "the-thing-become" but as "the-thing-becoming."[18]

Even after the torrent of academic writing investigating the postcolonial condition, these are extraordinary pages to encounter. The governing postulate rejects the possibility of a unilinear path for global development, favoring in its place the idea that there exist multiple historical routes to multiple modernities. It was not, Spengler proposed, that the peoples of Asia, Africa, and Latin America occupied a lower level of civilization, nor—in order for them to operate as autonomous, sovereign peoples—was it necessary for them to be inducted into the mysteries of European civilization. Spengler's notion marked a relativist conception of universal history with no fixed center, in which the axiomatic divide between civilized and primitive—although perhaps never quite vanishing—came to be freed from its historical moorings and, in the process, freed from what Derek Walcott identifies as "a dominated future." Although the term was not Spengler's, his was an argument about the constituents of historical time: much that passed as history, he concluded, was no more than phantasmagoric, illusory, or ideological. Invoking the primitive, and conceiving of the primitive to function as the disabled or incomplete precursor of the modern, stipulated exactly the programmed conception of historical evolution that Spengler denounced as myopic, bereft of the capacity to explain the dynamics of the actually existing world.

The case of Trotsky was equally if not more arresting. Max Eastman's translation of the three volumes of Trotsky's *History of the Russian Revolution* first appeared in 1932–33, at the point when James was speeding toward Marxism. When these volumes came James's way, shortly after their first publication in English, James recalls reading them "very hard."[19] They offer a marvelous, breathtaking reconstruction of the role of the Russian masses from April to October 1917 who, in seizing the historical initiative, made a revolution and made it their own. The connections between Trotsky's *History* and James's *Black Jacobins*, in conception and in certain passages, are close. But this isn't merely a matter of sharing a similar theme in a weak or descriptive sense. It's more that Trotsky and James were given to a similar conception of *what politics could do.*

Here it is necessary to make a detour that takes us into a defining controversy in early twentieth-century Marxism. We need to be aware of how the revolution in Russia reordered the intellectual terrain of Marxism and how James chose to position himself on the active, vitalist edge of a revivified Marxist tradition. It's not just that at that moment, he embraced Marxism.

He envisaged *his* Marxism as the politico-intellectual means by which, in the historical present, the capitalist past and the socialist future could be fused into a single political temporality, such that Marxism—for James—signaled an audacious anticipation of a new social realm.

In Trotsky's *History* the narrative proper opens with recounting the end of Lenin's exile in Zurich and his journey in the sealed train across Europe to Petrograd. Lenin's *Letters from Afar*, written between the end of March and the beginning of April (following the Western calendar), chart this moment and allow us to follow his thinking in these crucial days. They represent one of those incendiary interventions that punctuate the history of revolutions. In Trotsky's account, they operate at a strategic juncture, articulating the moment when the spirit of the revolution leaped ahead and when the masses crossed the threshold and entered a new dimension of historical time.

Letters from Afar was driven by this realization that the Russian people were inhabiting "an extraordinary acceleration of world history."[20] The first two letters were addressed to Alexandra Kollantai in Oslo, for forwarding to *Pravda*, envisaged as the means by which Lenin could exert a measure of control over the situation in Russia. Both in *Letters* and on his arrival at the Finland Station, he urged the Bolshevik Party to seize the moment by preparing for an immediate assault on state power. This was perceived by many in his own ranks, and not only by them, as an act of insanity, proof of Lenin's disconnection—his being *very* afar—from the realities of the situation in Russia. The editors of *Pravda*, Lev Kamenev and Joseph Stalin, were aghast. Word got around, reaching the ears of the British ambassador, that Lenin was a "bad" Marxist, succumbing to "syndicalist deviations."[21] Indeed, he was condemned by one of his own party for capitulating to a "primitive anarchism."[22]

Such verdicts derived from the conviction that Russia was a socially primitive society that couldn't possibly leap, in one movement, from peasant backwardness to advanced socialism. To entertain reveries of this temper appeared to deny the founding tenets of Marx's own historical system, which, so it was widely accepted, decreed that socialism could only come about as the necessary culmination of an evolutionary, sequential history, progressing through antiquity, feudalism, capitalism, and thence to socialism. Within this historical reading, capitalism, bequeathing the socialization of the means of production, provided the material precondition for the making of socialism. To disregard such fundamentals was to betray Marxism, failing to appreciate the gravity of the historic disputes—at the time of the First International—

between Marxists and anarchists that had, in effect, given birth to Marxism as a credible collective, political force. In the minds of Lenin's Marxist opponents, the enormity of this error was huge.

In this view of things, socialism should have occurred in Germany, in Europe's most advanced capitalist nation, not in—semi-feudal, barbaric, primitive—Russia.

Trotsky's *History of the Russian Revolution* sought to vindicate Lenin's reading of the situation, in part by elaborating a model of Marxist history freed from the imperatives of a deterministic historical schema. For Trotsky, history itself had made redundant all injunctions that professed to know where or when the next locus of revolution should be. In breaking from the logic of an evolutionary Marxism, the concept of the primitive could take on new meanings and do new work.

The "primitiveness" of Russia's "social forms" and the nation's "long backwardness" are acknowledged from the first page of the first volume. But the argument quickly assumes an unexpected direction. "A backward country assimilates the material and intellectual conquests of the advanced countries." Trotsky continues:

> The privilege of historic backwardness . . . permits, or rather compels, the adoption of whatever is ready in advance of any specified date, skipping a whole series of intermediate stages. . . . The development of historically backward nations leads necessarily to a peculiar combination of different states in the historic process. Their development as a whole acquires a planless, complex, combined character.

In Trotsky's typical way, he determined to demonstrate that contingency, complexity and a state of unschematic lawlessness amounted to a new historical law.

> The laws of history have nothing in common with a pedantic schematism. Unevenness, the most general law of the historic process, reveals itself most sharply and complexly in the destiny of backward countries. Under the whip of external necessity their backward culture is compelled to make leaps. From the universal law of unevenness thus derives another law which . . . we may call the law of *combined development*—by which we mean a drawing together of the different stages of the journey, a combination of separate steps, an amalgam of archaic with more contemporary forms.[23]

These are astonishing words. The force of Trotsky's argument derives from his realization that the primitive can never exist in a pure, abstract form: it can never exist *only* as the primitive. That which is perceived as primitive proves to be the inevitable function of the unevenness that capital accumulation itself generates. From this perspective Trotsky was right to insist that the primitive is always "an amalgam with more contemporary forms," partly on account of the fact that it is indeed *produced* by modern capitalist conditions. After all, the essential conception of the primitive is the creation of modernity itself.

From this vantage one can understand why Spengler and Trotsky were powerful for James. They provided the possibility for mobilizing a historical method that broke with the founding historiographical precepts stipulating the necessary depredations of the primitive. More than that, they offered the prospect that history itself, as an imaginative practice, was not required to disavow all that the primitive represented. They presented James with the analytical means to portray the black slaves of Saint-Domingue as agents of their own history.

"The historian," declared Trotsky at the start of his *History*, "cannot handle revolutionary chronology by mere arithmetic."[24] Nor, I would add, can "arithmetic" grasp the complexities of *any* historical time, underdetermined or overdetermined. The Bolsheviks who were contemptuous of Lenin at the Finland Station felt deep in their bones that Petrograd was the wrong place for Europe's revolution. By the same logic, defying all that history authorized, in an earlier epoch it didn't seem possible for Saint-Domingue—*peripheral* Saint-Domingue, *colonial* Saint-Domingue, *slave* Saint-Domingue, *black* Saint-Domingue, *primitive* Saint-Domingue—to provide the historical conditions for generating the most radical spirit of democracy: for it to be the locale for the making not only of Jacobinism but—the scandal of it—of a *black* Jacobinism.

Such a logic, which assumes that history is the exclusive possession of the "civilized" nations, despite the evidence to the contrary, runs deep. It is essentially a colonial, racial mode of thought. In the late nineteenth century and early twentieth century, it infiltrated many variants of Marxism. It can still be heard today, in different guises. It was against such thought that James, in the wake of Lenin and Trotsky, determined to write *The Black Jacobins*. That this positivist—ideological and racial—assumption still has life today may explain in part the disregard James's study continues to encounter.

Crucially, James "places slavery right at the centre of world history." But in his telling, "slavery did not function as a kind of archaic remnant, belonging to a previous age, which somehow capitalist modernity had not yet got around to abolishing. . . . It is exactly the most archaic social relations which are preserved *in the modern system*. The plantation in the Caribbean was at the advanced front of modern capitalism."[25] He was insistent throughout that what appeared to be backward or primitive—the plantation system; or a slave army, for example, defeating the combined forces of the French, the Spanish and the British—was always an amalgam of the archaic and the modern. In a single passage he could hold together the belief that the slaves of the northern plains "were closer to a modern proletariat" *and* that "voodoo was the medium" of their conspiracy.[26] James compared Toussaint to Pericles, Thomas Paine, Thomas Jefferson, Marx, and Engels, but then went on to say that these "were men of a liberal education, formed in the traditions of ethics, philosophy and history. Toussaint [on the other hand] was a slave, not six years out of slavery . . . dictating his thoughts in the crude words of a broken dialect."[27] He was the archetype of the black Jacobin.

James's Marxism, mediated through Trotsky and Spengler, enabled him to break from the schemata underwriting the mentalities that justified a marxisant historical determinism. What Trotsky's *History* gave to him was the realization that "history possesses a certain movement to it."[28] However, we can see from the first edition of *The Black Jacobins* that the rebellious slaves of Saint-Domingue should never—"by rights"—have improvised an advanced Jacobinism in a backward, black, plantation society. Toussaint's declaration of August 1791—"I want liberty and equality to reign in St-Domingue"— may in retrospect look conventional or even orthodox, but it was nothing of the sort. It was—notwithstanding the "broken dialect" that served as its means of articulation—properly revolutionary, if we understand by this that it encapsulated a new mode of thought which demanded that the received laws of history be jettisoned. A "revolution," James later wrote, "creates disorder and unbalances everything," in thought as much as in social life.[29] Just as the enslaved of Saint-Domingue refused to recognize their rightful place in the global scheme of things, for James they refused to accept their given temporal location, performing their historical role "as if they were in the second half of the twentieth century."[30]

| | | | |

This is the gist of my argument. In *The Black Jacobins* James broke with inherited Marxist conceptions of history that were sequential, stage-ist (or stadial, to employ the term that is often imported from geology), and deterministic, in favor of an approach that recognized the simultaneous coexistence of a plurality of historical times. In this interpretation, the old and the new—the primitive and advanced—were conceived not as fixed entities but as social relations underwritten by a degree of contingency and unpredictability. This significantly expands the domain of politics, giving due weight to the powers of human intervention, and in the process undermines the idea that history is governed by ordained, immutable laws.[31]

For James this opened a way of thinking about history that not only took him back to Hegel but to which he supplied his own particular invocation of politics. As Stuart Hall has observed:

> it was James's particularly Hegelian Marxism that pulled him into the epic moments of historical transformation, the moments when the husk of a whole era is challenged, when it dissolves and breaks up, and when new things come through. His way of thinking about history was formed by his imaginative grasp of the transition from one grand historical moment to another—from the classical age, to the renaissance, to the French revolution, to 1917. These were the big moments for James.[32]

James, in this respect, was aligning himself politically not only with Lenin and Trotsky but with figures such as Luxemburg and Gramsci, in fashioning a Marxism that broke with the intellectual world of late-nineteenth-century positivism. Lenin's arrival at the Finland Station in April 1917 stands in as a necessarily abbreviated dramatization or emblem of this larger, more complex, and multilayered mental and political transformation.[33] This revolution "in philosophy," which functioned as a constituent component of the Russian Revolution of 1917, afforded James the intellectual resources to grasp how the corresponding philosophical revolution worked in Haiti in 1804. The year 1917 stands as the conceptual precondition for James's reconstruction of 1804. In a provocative conceptual orchestration, 1804, 1917, and 1938 (the time of *The Black Jacobins*) are simultaneously articulated in *The Black Jacobins* into an interconnected, *political* temporality.[34]

If I'm right about James's sense of the combined, interactive properties of the coexistence of the past and the present—or of the old and the new or, in this case, of 1804 and 1917—then it is perhaps legitimate to recruit these insights to reflect further on the authorship of *The Black Jacobins*: that is, on the historical position of James himself.

Let's return for a moment to Lenin's *Letters from Afar*. In his opening letter, he took issue with what he took to be the "superficial" historical explanation of the political crisis that was gripping Russia, a view he rightly feared was prevalent within the ranks of his own party. Lenin's contention was that the revolutionary situation had occurred not because the contending forces fell neatly into two opposing camps, in which the underlying class interests, immediately and transparently, determined the domain of politics. On the contrary, the revolutionary moment had only come about, in Lenin's mesmerizing formulation, "as a result of an extremely unique historical situation, *absolutely dissimilar currents, absolutely heterogeneous* class interests, *absolutely contrary* political and social strivings have *merged*, and in a strikingly 'harmonious' manner."[35] Louis Althusser, in his interpretation of this passage, names such a conjunctural situation as "overdetermined." This was a term that had initially been devised by Sigmund Freud to demonstrate how dream life was "differently centred" from the imperatives of wakeful, conscious life. Althusser, in a bold move, transposed Freud's insights concerning the individual psyche to the world of history, to comprehend how a revolutionary situation arose.[36] Inspired though this move was, it can leave us, who have followed after, with an unwieldy dichotomy between the individual subject in Freud, bereft of history, on the one hand, and the historical conjuncture of Althusser, with no acknowledgment of the historical imperatives of subjectivity, on the other.[37] What if the two were conjoined?

Could one understand the historical persona of James himself, due to his status as a colonized, to be "differently centred" from the metropolitan intellectuals of his generation, and—thereby—for him to have experienced his own self as being radically displaced or "out of place"? James wasn't *born* a black Pan-African Marxist. As he says of himself, "I didn't fall from the sky."[38] To become who he became, he was required to relinquish, as far as he was able, the governing ethical and symbolic system in which he had been reared in his colonial family and schooling. He carried within himself, until the end of his days, an undying manful, Victorian sensibility, even as he embraced all that was dynamically and self-consciously modern. The social recognition he received as an accomplished man of letters in the English and European mode counted for much. It was precisely this accomplishment that served as his passport, contingent though it was, out of his natal position as a racialized native. It could not easily be jettisoned. Thus James was never in any simple sense England's or Europe's other, even as he was fierce in his condemnation of the historical record of the metropolitan polities. At no point was his political life composed of simple contraries. Wasn't he, then, in *his own being* constituted by "absolutely dissimilar currents," "absolutely heterogeneous" investments, "absolutely contrary . . . social strivings" which in him "merged . . . in a strikingly 'harmonious' manner"? Who else in the 1930s poured so much of him- or herself into the putative contraries of cricket and Marx, or of Thackeray and Pan-Africanism? In *Beyond a Boundary* he explains that when he was growing up he had "lived in two worlds." In a more graphic formulation, although still attesting to the split within him, he recounted that "Two people lived in me": one, the rebel pitted against the colonial order, as he encountered it in family and school; the other, the intransigent devotee of "the ethics of the game."[39] He later came to realize that such fractured displacements— such instances of living a "double consciousness"—never amounted to a fateful curse. Rather, they conferred a certain intellectual, perceptual privilege. Doesn't this make him, in his own person, not only differently centered but also peculiarly overdetermined? Could this condensation of competing histories, in his own historical-psychic formation, go some way in explaining the singular, historic achievement of *The Black Jacobins*?

I'm content for this to remain an open, speculative suggestion. It may be persuasive, it may not. But it does take us back, finally, to the larger issue of historical method. At the opening of this chapter I raised the question of the relevance of *The Black Jacobins* for imagining history "today." I'll close, briefly, with this.

As I have indicated, the power of *The Black Jacobins* lies in James's appreciation that the agents of the revolution in Saint-Domingue not only failed to obey the given rules of history, they turned them inside out. They were behaving not as the laws of history decreed they should, but as if they were occupying another place and another time, neither of which properly belonged to them. Such a regard for the displaced processes of determinate historical events, for phenomena out of place and out of time, worked against the grain of preconceived philosophies of history, with their concomitant stories of a programmed social evolution. In James's account the historical determinations that organized the making of Haiti were not random, but they never operated as an abstract choreography that could have been mapped out in advance. Theoretically, the space James accords to contingency acts as a significant factor in his historical explanation. Indeed, the determinations that give form to his narrative are, in a word, displaced—in exactly the manner that his own life experience defied orthodox historical expectation. Notwithstanding his commitments to classical Marxism, James's understanding of the unanticipated temporal dynamics of history makes *The Black Jacobins* feel at times—in potential at least—a peculiarly contemporary work.

Through the early decades of the twentieth century, an intellectual reliance on historical laws signaled an unacknowledged debt to the traditions of earlier variants of positivism. It's symptomatic that Trotsky, even as he conceded that history—or at least, that a revolutionary conjuncture—displayed "a planless, complex combined character," nonetheless endeavoured to elevate "planlessness" into a new historical law. Revolutions in thought rarely advance by pure, unsullied epistemological breaks: misapprehensions, wrong turns, doubling back, the temptation to subscribe to contrary views—these are customary. Traces of "old" modes of thought can have long lives. Neither Trotsky's *History of the Russian Revolution* nor indeed James's *The Black Jacobins*, for all their innovation, inaugurated new readings of history that can be appropriated, unworked, as unambiguous prototypes for the future.

The problem is this. The break with a positivist, programmed conception of history, creative though it was, posed—and poses—a new question. What next? All the twentieth-century Marxist figures I've referred to here—Lenin, Trotsky, Luxemburg, Gramsci, James, not to mention the heterodox, startling figure of Walter Benjamin—imagined the political consequences differently, sometimes radically so. Each imagined the break with the older historicisms to involve different degrees of rupture, different qualities of thought, and above all, different political investments. Each arrived at a different resolution. The unresolved question "What next?" continues to be as much our question as theirs.

In part it's likely that the hold of stadial theorizations of history ran deeper than was easily recognized, and perhaps they still do. There is, though, an allied issue. In the 1930s Trotsky and James, while recasting the idea of historical time in important respects, nonetheless still retained much that in their Marxist circles was given and conventional. They were certainly alive to its unexpected dynamics, such that the past, present, and future could simultaneously coexist in a single historical moment. Equally, they recognized the presence of other temporalities—the temporalities of an individual life and of generation; of everyday life, the domestic, and "women's time"; of the mysterious temporal imaginings of the inner world; of the times materialized in the rural and urban landscapes; and of a host of other instances.[40] In other words, they recognized the complex span of conflicting times that inhabit not only a historical moment but also an individual life. But they were resistant to viewing these as if they really mattered, politically or historically. What mattered was a conception of historical time that remained untouched by the impress of other temporalities and demonstrated where history was moving and whom it was carrying in its wake. (Thus, by extension it disclosed where history *was not* happening, and whom it had left behind.) For Trotsky especially, the overriding issues were the temporalities that shaped the vicissitudes of social class. In a grand Hegelian gesture, many of those most won over to a highly charged vision of socialism in the period were sure that the revolution would redeem, along with almost everything, time itself.[41] From this perspective, all else was secondary. This is a species of reductionism. To regard historical time as an absolute in this manner amounts to a temporal reductionism, in which this single dimension of time works to cancel out its varied competitors. It's not that those times deemed nonhistorical were absent: they were just not accredited with social efficacy. As the epigraph from Jacqueline Rose at the start of this chapter indicates, to think in such terms can—in extremity—"descend into autocracy and terror."

What of James? I hope that if I've conveyed one thing, it is his contrariness. By this I don't mean a contrariness in temperament but in terms of the multiple intellectual and historical locations he came to occupy simultaneously. In espousing Marxism, he—with his own predilections uppermost—espoused history as epic. Notwithstanding his appreciation for the manner by which times and places could be turned inside out, James was still drawn to a conception of history that revolved around a dizzying spectacle of absolutes and universals. The imaginative structure of Hegel's *Philosophy of History* was never far away. Like many of his contemporaries who sought to prise Marxism away from its "positivist encrustations," the return to Hegel promised, for his generation, the possibility of resurrecting what they perceived to be the Marxism of Karl Marx.

But alongside James's fondness for absolutes and his restless desire to search out the presence of new, emergent universals, there existed within him a contrary sensibility in which the epic qualities of Hegelian grand narratives gave way to a deeper investment in the local and the particular, driven not by the narratives of modernity but by the "smaller," situated histories of belonging.[42] This proved to be a perpetual tension in his writings. It comes to be visible in James's protracted break with the politics of Trotskyism, not long after *The Black Jacobins* was published. Initially he had become a Marxist as a consequence of reading Trotsky, particularly as a consequence of his engagement with the *History of the Russian Revolution*. Even as he declared himself to be a Trotskyist, and while fulfilling all that was required of him as a renowned Trotskyist cadre, he never dissembled about his misgivings.[43] In the 1940s, and for many years after, he labored hard to break from the founding precepts of Trotskyism and create, out of the resulting prolonged and taxing struggle, new modes of thinking. As he did so, he worked to distance himself from the epic, totalizing Hegelian manner of thought that constituted Trotsky's appropriation of Marxism.[44]

Yet this never represented an unencumbered journey from one habit of thought to another, from A to B. Hall endeavors to catch the complexity of James's commitments to formally contrary ways of thought: "The break from Hegel in the forties brought to the surface elements of James's intellectual life which had always been there. So this isn't something he discovers: it re-surfaces in him."[45] Throughout his life James subscribed, in different moments, to the elusive concept of historical time, with all its accreted conceptual impediments, *and* to its contrary, in which history represented not the phantasmagoria of absolute redemption but, in its place, "the quiet force of the possible."[46] From the 1940s onward, James sought to elaborate the means by which these conflicting ways of understanding history could be brought into dialogue.

For us, today, even as the imperatives of modernity continue apace, the forces of unreason accumulate. On many fronts history—the actual process of history itself—continues to defy our capacities to understand it. The laws that once seemed to govern the passage from the past to the present now appear to be at best threadbare or even obsolete. James in 1938 was right. "The writing of history becomes ever more difficult." Maybe, in fact, this is truer of our own time than it was when James wrote these words. *This* James is our contemporary.

Notes

As ever, thanks to Christian Høgsbjerg, who, on matters of James and much else, continues to teach me a great deal. This essay is for Robert Hill, even though I'm conscious that a James scholar of his imagination, caliber, and grace deserves more.

The first epigraph is cited in Nick Nesbitt, ed., *Toussaint L'Ouverture: The Haitian Revolution*, introduction by Jean-Bertrand Aristide (London: Verso, 2008), 1. The second epigraph is from Derek Walcott, *What the Twilight Says: Essays* (London: Faber, 1998), 41, and his "C.L.R. James" in the same collection; see also Derek Walcott, "A Tribute to C.L.R. James" in *C.L.R. James: His Intellectual Legacies*, edited by Selwyn R. Cudjoe and William E. Cain (Amherst: University of Massachusetts Press, 1995). The third epigraph is from Jacqueline Rose, *Women in Dark Times* (London: Bloomsbury, 2014), 29.

1. I'm conscious that here I enter the slipstream of Susan Buck-Morss's *Hegel, Haiti, and Universal History* (Pittsburgh: University of Pittsburgh Press, 2009). Early on, she insists we recognize "not only the contingency of historical events, but also the indeterminacy of the historical categories by which we grasp them" (11).

2. Indispensable are Robin Blackburn, *The Overthrow of Colonial Slavery, 1776–1848* (London: Verso, 1989); Carolyn E. Fick, *The Making of Haiti: The Making of the Saint Domingue Revolution from Below* (Knoxville: University of Tennessee Press, 1990); Laurent Dubois, *A Colony of Citizens: Revolution and Slave Emancipation in the French Caribbean, 1787–1804* (Chapel Hill: University of North Carolina Press, 2004); and Laurent Dubois, *Avengers of the New World: The Story of the Haitian Revolution* (Cambridge, MA: Harvard University Press, 2004). The centrality accorded to populist reason by Nick Nesbitt is compelling and directly relevant to my argument: *Universal Emancipation: The Haitian Revolution and the Radical Enlightenment* (Charlottesville: University of Virginia Press, 2008).

3. Felix Driver and Bill Schwarz, "Editorial: Haiti Remembered," *History Workshop Journal* 46 (1998). Raphael Dalleo introduces a provocative and perplexing gloss on the place of James in this larger constellation: "'The Independence So Hardly Won Has Been Maintained': C.L.R. James and the Occupation of Haiti," *Cultural Critique* 87 (2014): 38–59.

4. C. L. R. James, *The Black Jacobins: Toussaint L'Ouverture and the San Domingo Revolution* (London: Allison and Busby, 1991), vi. Or as this idea is rendered by George Lamming, in what I regard as his "adaptation" of *The Black Jacobins*, "Caliban Orders History," which is the title he gave to his chapter on Saint-Domingue in *The Pleasures of Exile* (1960; London: Pluto, 2005). There's a touching moment when Lamming notes—toward the end of James's narrative when the political criticisms of Toussaint accumulate—that "James cannot overcome the bond which Toussaint's glory has sealed between the historian and the soldier" (148).

5. R. R. Palmer, *The Age of Democratic Revolution: A Political History of Europe and America, 1760–1800, Vol. I: The Challenge* and *Vol. II: The Struggle* (Princeton, NJ: Princeton University Press, 1959 and 1964). Sandwiched between these volumes, Eric J. Hobsbawm, *The Age of Revolution: Europe, 1789–1848* (London: Weidenfeld and Nicolson, 1962). Gwyn A. Williams's illuminating *Artisans and Sans-Culottes: Popular Movements in France and Britain during the French Revolution* (London: Edward Arnold, 1968) belongs to this same moment. Notwithstanding the power of these histories, conspicuous now is how little Haiti mattered.

6. James Anthony Froude, *The English in the West Indies: Or the Bow of Ulysses* (London: Longmans, Green, 1888).

7. C. L. R. James, "A Century of Freedom," *Listener*, May 31, 1933, and "Slavery Today: A Shocking Exposure," *Tit-Bits*, August 5, 1933; on this see Christian Høgsbjerg,

C. L. R. James in Imperial Britain (Durham, NC: Duke University Press, 2014), 169. C. L. R. James, *The Life of Captain Cipriani: An Account of British Government in the West Indies* (Durham, NC: Duke University Press, 2014), originally published alongside James's *The Case for West-Indian Self Government* (New York: University Place Book Shop/Facing Reality Publishing, 1967) also offers insight into James's political temperament of the time. *Cipriani* was drafted before he left Trinidad and was first published in London in 1932; *The Case for West-Indian Self Government* is largely an extract from *Cipriani*, and first appeared as a separate pamphlet in 1933, published by the Hogarth Press.

8. T. Lothrop Stoddard, *The French Revolution in San Domingo* (New York: Houghton Mifflin, 1914). Stoddard was a journalist-historian who found greatest fame with his *The Rising Tide of Colour against White World-Supremacy* (New York: Scribner, 1920), whose best-known admirer today is the fictional Tom Buchanan in *The Great Gatsby*. Stoddard ended his professional life as a journalist in Nazi Germany, where his accommodation with the regime proved awkwardly intimate.

9. C. L. R. James, "Lectures on *The Black Jacobins*: How I Wrote *The Black Jacobins*," *Small Axe* 8 (2000): 67. See also C. L. R. James, "Lectures on *The Black Jacobins*: *The Black Jacobins* and *Black Reconstruction*: A Comparative Analysis," *Small Axe* 8 (2000), and C. L. R. James, "Lectures on *The Black Jacobins*: How I Would Rewrite *The Black Jacobins*," *Small Axe* 8 (2000). These lectures were delivered at the Institute of the Black World at Atlanta. Elsewhere he explained that the story had been "stuck away in the back of my head for years": C. L. R. James, *Beyond a Boundary* (1963; Durham, NC: Duke University Press, 2013), 119.

10. C. L. R. James, *Toussaint Louverture: The Story of the Only Successful Slave Revolt in History: A Play in Three Acts* (Durham, NC: Duke University Press, 2013). Completed four years before *The Black Jacobins*, in an early stage direction James writes: "They, the Negro slaves, are the most important characters in the play. Toussaint did not make the revolt. It was the revolt that made Toussaint" (54). See C. L. R. James, *The Black Jacobins: Toussaint Louverture and the San Domingo Revolution* (London: Secker and Warburg, 1938).

11. C. L. R. James, *The Black Jacobins: Toussaint L'Ouverture and the San Domingo Revolution* (New York: Vintage, 1963); C. L. R. James, "Lectures on *The Black Jacobins*"; the 1967 recasting of the 1936 play, C. L. R. James, "*The Black Jacobins*," in *The C.L.R. James Reader*, edited by Anna Grimshaw (Oxford: Blackwell, 1992). For a telling discussion of the different historiographical versions, David Scott, *Conscripts of Modernity: The Tragedy of Colonial Enlightenment* (Durham, NC: Duke University Press, 2004), and for the complicated story of the various dramatizations, Christian Høgsbjerg, "Introduction," in C. L. R. James, *Toussaint Louverture: The Story of the Only Successful Slave Revolt* (Durham, NC: Duke University Press, 2013).

12. Michel-Rolph Trouillot, *Silencing the Past: Power and the Production of History* (Boston: Beacon Books, 1995). From an explicitly Atlantic perspective, David P. Geggus (ed.), *The Impact of the Haitian Revolution in the Atlantic World* (Columbia: University of South Carolina Press, 2001); Alyssa Goldstein Sepinwall, "The Specter of Saint-Domingue in American and French Reactions to the Haitian Revolution," in *The World of the Haitian Revolution*, edited by David P. Geggus and Norman Fiering (Bloomington: Indiana University Press, 2009).

13. James, *The Black Jacobins*, x.

14. Nicholas B. Dirks, "History as the Sign of the Modern," *Public Culture* 2, no. 2 (1990): 25–32.

15. The most serious reconsiderations of the historiographical conceptualization of the primitive occur in the *Subaltern Studies* initiatives. This was a vast collaborative intervention, stretching over many years. The core can be tracked in the twelve volumes of *Subaltern Studies*, published between 1982 and 2005. The first six volumes were edited by Ranajit Guha, and all but the last two were published by Oxford University Press (Delhi). Volume 11 appeared from Columbia University Press (New York) and volume 12 from Permanent Black (Delhi). There were numerous accompanying essays and monographs. For my purposes, the most compelling of these is Dipesh Chakrabarty, *Habitations of Modernity: Essays in the Wake of* Subaltern Studies (Chicago: University of Chicago Press, 2002).

16. Høgsbjerg, *C.L.R. James in Imperial Britain*. For James's own record of the communism of the period, first published in 1937, C. L. R. James, *World Revolution, 1917–1936: The Rise and Fall of the Communist International* (Atlantic Highlands, NJ: Humanities Books, 1993).

17. Alan J. Mackenzie and Paul Gilroy, "Interview with C.L.R. James," in *Visions of History*, edited by MAHRO: The Radical Historians Organization (Manchester: Manchester University Press, 1983), 270.

18. Oswald Spengler, *The Decline of the West* (London: George Allen and Unwin, 1934), 16–25.

19. James, "Lectures on *The Black Jacobins*: How I Wrote *The Black Jacobins*," 67.

20. V. I. Lenin, "Letters from Afar," in V. I. Lenin, *Collected Works*, vol. 23 (Moscow: Progress Publishers, 1964), 300. These need to be read alongside V. I. Lenin, *The Development of Capitalism in Russia. Collected Works*, vol. 3 (1899; Moscow: Progress Publishers, 1972), which offers a different emphasis, although not necessarily an incompatible one.

21. Leon Trotsky, *The History of the Russian Revolution* (London: Sphere, 1967), 1:294–95.

22. Cited in Edmund Wilson, *To the Finland Station: A Study in the Writing and Acting of History* (London: Fontana, 1970), 477. This delivers an engagingly energetic account of the relationship between politics and history, from Michelet, through socialism and Marxism, culminating in Lenin's arrival at the Finland Station. It's written in the wake of Max Eastman and throughout is critically sympathetic to the protagonists whom Wilson portrays. James reviewed it when it was first published and, although recognizing the value of Wilson's historical investigations, his final judgment was severe.

"To and from the Finland Station: A Review of *To the Finland Station* by Edmund Wilson," in *C.L.R. James and Revolutionary Marxism: Selected Writings of C.L.R. James, 1939–1949*, edited by Scott McLemee and Paul Le Blanc (Atlantic Highlands, NJ: Humanities Press, 1994).

23. Trotsky, *History of the Russian Revolution*, I:21–23.

24. Trotsky, *History of the Russian Revolution*, I:20.

25. Stuart Hall, "Breaking Bread with History; C.L.R. James and *The Black Jacobins*: An Interview with Bill Schwarz," *History Workshop Journal* 46 (1998): 23.

26. James, *The Black Jacobins*, 86. A few weeks after the revolution broke out, a slave was captured and killed. On his person were discovered revolutionary pamphlets from France; tinder, phosphate, and lime (for firing a gun); and a pouch with herbs and bits of bone, functioning as an amulet; Dubois, *Avengers of the New World*, 102. Fick is persuaded that vodou supplied a crucial "inner force" for the revolution; *The Making of Haiti*, 244.

27. James, *The Black Jacobins*, 197–98.

28. James, "Lectures on *The Black Jacobins*: How I Wrote *The Black Jacobins*," 67.

29. James, "Lectures on *The Black Jacobins*: How I Wrote *The Black Jacobins*," 78.

30. James, *The Black Jacobins*, vii.

31. This determinist, antipolitical strain of historical thought constitutes for Dipesh Chakrabarty "the 'not yet' of historicism," *Provincializing Europe: Postcolonial Thought and Historical Difference* (Princeton, NJ: Princeton University Press, 2000), 8.

32. Hall, "Breaking Bread with History," 20.

33. I'm thinking particularly of Antonio Gramsci's response to the October Revolution as "The Revolution against *Das Kapital*" in Antonio Gramsci, *Selections from Political Writings, 1910–1920*, edited by Quintin Hoare (London: Lawrence and Wishart, 1977). Gramsci understood the Bolsheviks to be freeing themselves from the "positivist and naturalist encrustations" of nineteenth-century Marxism and to be seeking to "live Marxist thought," 34. See, too, in relation to the "primitive" within Italian politics, Antonio Gramsci, "Some Aspects of the Southern Question," in Antonio Gramsci, *Selections from Political Writings, 1921–1926*, edited by Quintin Hoare (London: Lawrence and Wishart, 1978).

34. James in 1938, on his own historical time: "The blacks of Africa are more advanced, nearer ready than the slaves of San Domingo," *The Black Jacobins*, 376. James in 1971: the "obscure creatures"—the active multitude who made the revolution in Saint-Domingue—are resurrected at the end of the twentieth century: "They were not only obscure in San Domingo. They were obscure in Watts, they were obscure in Detroit, they were obscure creatures in Newark, they were obscure creatures in San Francisco, they were obscure creatures in Cleveland, they were obscure creatures in Harlem." "Lectures on *The Black Jacobins*: How I Would Rewrite *The Black Jacobins*," 106.

35. Lenin, "Letters from Afar," 306.

36. Louis Althusser, "Contradiction and Overdetermination," in Louis Althusser, *For Marx* (London: Allen Lane, 1969); "differently centred" comes from Sigmund Freud, *The Standard Edition of the Complete Psychological Works of Sigmund Freud*, vol. 4 (1900), *The Interpretation of Dreams (First Part)* (London: Vintage, 2001), 305.

37. I discuss this in Bill Schwarz, "'Already the past': Memory and Historical Time," in *Regimes of Memory*, edited by Susannah Radstone and Katharine Hodgkin (London: Routledge, 2003).

38. James, "Lectures on *The Black Jacobins*: How I Wrote *The Black Jacobins*," 77.

39. James, *Beyond a Boundary*, 25, 28.

40. Julia Kristeva, "Women's Time," *Signs* 7, no. 1 (1981): 13–35. A terrific reconstruction of the philosophical antecedents of the divide between historical time and everyday time makes up Harry Harootunian, "Shadowing History: National Narratives and the Persistence of the Everyday," *Cultural Studies* 18, nos. 2–3 (2004): 181–200.

41. This returns us to the matter of the primitive. The primitive was frequently invested with contradictory properties, particularly from the 1930s. Aside from being the location of "the old," its intractability also derives from the fact that it is the site where elements of popular life accumulate with peculiar intensity. On the penultimate page of Trotsky's third volume of his *History*, he describes "the historic ascent of humanity" as "a succession of consciousness over blind forces—in nature, in society, in man himself." Parliamentary democracy, he observes, leaves "the blind play of force in the social relations of man untouched." He goes on to note, in a mind-blowing statement, that "It was this deeper sphere of the unconscious that the October Revolution was the first to raise its hand"; Leon Trotsky, *The History of the Russian Revolution*, vol. III (London: Sphere, 1967), 322. This truly did invest the idea of revolution with messianic powers.

42. I draw from the distinction made by Dipesh Chakrabarty between an approach to history characterized by the social sciences and one characterized by hermeneutics: or, in an alternative formulation, between Marx and Heidegger; *Provincializing Europe*, 18. For an indication how these differing systems of thought are worked through Caribbean experience, see Paget Henry, *Caliban's Reason: Introducing Afro-Caribbean Philosophy* (New York: Routledge, 2000).

43. See the discussions between James and Trotsky about "Negro organization" in *Coyoacán*, April 4–11, 1939, reproduced in Leon Trotsky, *On Black Self-Determination* (New York: Pathfinder, 1992), 38–69.

44. As late as 1962–1963, James was complaining to his U.S. comrade Marty Glaberman that we haven't "purged ourselves completely" of Trotskyism: Martin Glaberman (ed.), *Marxism for Our Times: C.L.R. James on Revolutionary Organization* (Jackson: University of Mississippi Press, 1999), 67. I've commented on aspects of this complex trajectory in Bill Schwarz, "C.L.R. James's *American Civilization*," *Atlantic Studies* 2, no. 1 (2005): 15–43; and Bill Schwarz, "Becoming Postcolonial," in *Without Guarantees:*

Essays in Honour of Stuart Hall, edited by Paul Gilroy, Lawrence Grossberg, and Angela McRobbie (Verso, London, 2000).

45. Hall, "Breaking Bread with History," 30.

46. Martin Heidegger, *Being and Time* (Oxford: Blackwell, Oxford, 1962), 446. Later in life, in various moods, James expressed his admiration for Heidegger: particularly C. L. R. James, *Wilson Harris: A Philosophical Approach* (St. Augustine: University of the West Indies, 1965).

8

The Theory of Haiti: *The Black Jacobins*
and the Poetics of Universal History

DAVID SCOTT

What is the contemporary "theory-problem" about Haiti? To phrase it somewhat differently: What is the conceptual conundrum or the ideological problem-space in relation to which Haiti is *made* to appear today as the visible
sign of a predicament, a resolution, a truth? What *theory* of Haiti enables it to
perform this labor? What motivations call it into play? What demand gives
it force and form? What, in short, is the *question* to which Haiti is offered as
an exemplary *answer*?

In posing these general questions, I mean of course to underscore, in a now
somewhat old-fashioned way perhaps, the non-self-evidence, the nontranspar-
ency, of "Haiti" as a figure in the varied discourses, popular and scholarly, in
which it is constructed and through which it circulates. From the fabulous tales
of eighteenth-century colonial prosperity to the images of screaming despair
on international news channels after the catastrophic earthquake of January 12,
2010, Haiti has forever been, in no small part, a fable, less a historicizable geopo-
litical place than a haunting space of vivid, often racialized and sexualized
imagination.[1] Whether under the sign of perverted luxury or disemboweling
violence or impenetrable mystery or irremediable poverty, Haiti has never
ceased to be an overdetermined, overcathected fascination. Where Haiti is
concerned, there seems almost always the pervasive sense of an unnerving
gap between itself and its *otherness.*

Many years ago, in a now famous essay Michel-Rolph Trouillot drew
our attention to some of the ways this apprehension of otherness has functioned to produce the idea of Haiti-as-*exception.* As he put it, a "notion of
Haitian exceptionalism permeates both the academic and popular literature
on Haiti under different guises and with different degrees of candidness."[2]
Haiti, so it appears to many, is "unique"—to foreigners as well as the Haitian
elite. However, it is considered unique not in the obvious ways in which all

historical societies might be said to be distinct cultural-historical formations, but rather in ways that suspiciously render it unintelligible, or at least in need of a sui generis sort of explanation. Trouillot perceived the shadow of a "hidden agenda" lurking behind this idea of Haiti's "special status"—namely, the motivation to obscure the relations of power and knowledge through which Haiti has been historically inscribed in an asymmetrical global structure. Haitian exceptionalism, he wrote,

> has been a shield that masks the negative contribution of the Western powers to the Haitian situation. Haitian exceptionalism functions to obscure Haiti's integration into a world dominated by Christianity, capitalism, and whiteness. The more Haiti appears weird, the easier it is to forget that it represents the longest neocolonial experiment in the history of the West.[3]

I think this is right. In pointing to this exceptionalism, though, Trouillot's critical point, in the end, was to make a plea for a less *isolationist* and more *comparativist* framework within which to set Haiti's cultural history. Again I think this is salutary. Indeed, this style of thinking was in many ways one of the hallmarks of Trouillot's inspiring contribution to Caribbean studies.[4] But from this insight I would want to draw an additional and somewhat different lesson, one not so much connected to better informed or more diverse empirical scholarship, as concerned with cultivating a more acutely reflexive self-consciousness about the conceptual and ideological labors our discursive objects are made to perform. I mean by this that such scholarly objects as "Haiti" are always inscribed in conceptual and ideological problem-spaces: They are theory-problems; they activate *answers*, in other words, to a more or less implicit structure of *questions*. Consequently, in order to make visible the *uses* to which these discursive objects are *being put*—in a certain sense, the ideological motivations they perform—it is necessary to *reconstruct* the questions that organize and give point to the problem-spaces in which they are generated.

Consider Trouillot's discipline, anthropology, American cultural anthropology specifically, in which, at least since Melville J. Herskovits's seminal work, a certain idea of Haiti has been *called on* to help organize a distinctive way of thinking about the cultures of peoples of African descent in the New World. Recall that in the summer of 1934, when Herskovits arrived in Haiti, he was already equipped with a well-articulated theory-problem into which to insert it, namely, the problem of how to demonstrate the cultural continuities between Africa and the African Americas.[5] This was a theory-problem with political-ideological sources in the consequential debates about the African Americas coming out of the Harlem Renaissance years (Herskovits was no negligible observer of the new cultural-politics of black modernism in the 1920s and 1930s), and also with political-ideological implications for the future study of the African Americas.[6] Memorably, Herskovits's theory of acculturation, and in particular his "scale of Africanisms," was to provide the means of measuring the *authentic* presence of African retentions in the former slave societies of the New World, and so to demonstrate conclusively that Africans in the Americas had an identifiable or bona fide cultural heritage. Herskovits had already found the living traces of a deep "Africa" among the maroons of Suriname (the subject of *Rebel Destiny*, published in 1934, and *Suriname Folk-Lore*, published in 1936); and he had subsequently done field research in Dahomey (now Benin) along the old slave coast in order to have an experience of the "real" Africa (the subject of *Dahomey: An Ancient West African Kingdom*, published in 1938).[7] Now, returning to the Americas to close, so to speak, the hermeneutic circle, Herskovits was convinced that he would find a direct cultural connection between Dahomey and Haiti.[8] Famously, the monograph he published in 1937, *Life in a Haitian Valley*, was not merely a keenly observed ethnography but a many-sided *intervention*.[9] It was, for example, a sober professional rebuttal of the sensationalized and lurid images of primitivism and exotic barbarism through which Haiti was constructed for U.S. consumption in the 1920s and 1930s in such travel books as William Seabrook's *The Magic Island* and Richard Loederer's *Voodoo Fire in Haiti*.[10] But perhaps most important, from the point of view I am developing here, *Life in a Haitian Valley* established Haiti as a fundamental *anthropological* theory-object, a *paradigmatic* instance of the theory of New World "culture change" and adaptation—such that Haiti now appeared to be, after Suriname, the *most* African culture in the Americas. And yet, as we know, this particular imagining of Haiti—namely, Haiti as answering an acculturation theory-problem—was not the only "Haiti" potentially available in the 1930s to the observant and engaged Herskovits. Remember that Herskovits had arrived in Haiti in the summer of 1934, literally just as the much-detested U.S. marines were ending their brutal nineteen-year occupation. Taking up the advice of the Haitian scholar Jean Price-Mars, he had spent the twelve weeks of his typically brief research trip in the town of Mirebalais, a center of the 1918–1920 Caco insurgency against the occupation led by Charlemagne Péralte.[11] Curiously though, as controversial as the U.S. presence was, as violently disruptive as it was of Haitian cultural, political, and economic life, it seemed irrelevant, even *invisible*, to Herskovits as an interpretive condition, as a source of Haiti as a theory-problem.[12] In short, Herskovits's Haiti encounter took place in a polyvalent field of varied discursive possibilities and had his questions, his perceived provocations, been different ones, he might well have constructed Haiti as a *political* problem about sovereignty rather than a *cultural* problem about Africa in the Americas.

I do not want to unduly belabor this perhaps not-familiar-enough story about anthropology's Haiti, intriguing though its many directions might be.[13] However, I have a general point that this cursory reflection on the *making* of Haiti as a distinctively anthropological object well demonstrates. I mean to remind ourselves of something we all in fact already know (given the "linguistic turn" and the pervasiveness of the doctrine of "social constructionism" it spawned) but too readily forget (given perhaps the assimilation and normalization of social constructionism), and that is simply that our objects, even philosophical ones, have conceptual histories, and therefore ideological densities, and *consequently*, however seemingly straightforward such objects might appear, however seemingly *given* on the surface of our discourses, they bear a certain reflexive scrutiny regarding the services they perform in the theory-uses to which they are variously put.[14] *Imagining* Haiti, in other words, is never-not a dimension of a theory-problem.

| | | | |

In offering these cautionary remarks concerning the construction of Haiti as a theory-problem, I mean to afford myself some skeptical room in which to come at the recent provocative characterization of the Haitian Revolution in terms of some idea of "universality" or "universal history," or the politics of "universal human rights." It is a characterization that appears to signal—at times in somewhat spectacular language—the arrival of Haiti as a specifically *philosophical* problem.[15] Take, for example, Laurent Dubois, certainly one of the most distinguished contemporary historians of Haiti and its revolution. The transformation of slaves into citizens, he writes, represented "the most radical political transformation of the 'Age of Revolution' that stretched from the 1770s to the 1830s" and constituted

> the most concrete expression of the idea that the rights proclaimed in France's 1789 Declaration of the Rights of Man and Citizen were indeed universal. . . . If we live in a world in which democracy is meant to exclude

no one, it is in no small part because of the actions of those slaves in Saint-Domingue who insisted that human rights were theirs too.[16]

Similarly, Franklin Knight maintains that Haiti played an inaugural and "inordinately important role in the articulation of a version of human rights as it forged the second independent state in modern history."[17] Perhaps most passionately, Nick Nesbitt urges that the Haitian Revolution invented the idea of "universal emancipation." He writes:

> Though individuals had on occasion imagined universal rights as a pure abstraction, no society had ever been constructed in accord with the axiom of universal emancipation. The construction of a society without slavery, one of a universal and unqualified human right to freedom, properly stands as Haiti's unique contribution to humanity.[18]

These are strong claims that are meant, obviously enough, to recuperate the image of Haiti and advance a positive and sympathetic understanding of a much-maligned revolutionary project. Notably, though, they all, in one way or another, treat "universality" as an unexamined regulative ideal or normative horizon in relation to which to stake their claim, on Haiti's behalf, to a privileged—indeed, originary—position. Thus, in a curious way and in a new philosophic key, Haiti returns as exception. Far from being the abject *outside* of universality, Haiti vindicates itself as having the first of righteous claims on it. It may not be hard, therefore, to see what all these formulations unwittingly obscure, namely, the conditions of their own construction of Haiti as a theory-problem. Thus we might ask: What is the contemporary discursive conjuncture of questions in which the Haitian Revolution conceived as universality can be made to appear as the resolution?

I am skeptical, then, but even so my aim here is not to forswear the question of universality. On the contrary, for me, too, there is a pertinent question to be asked about Haiti and the "politics of the universal," specifically a question about the Haitian Revolution conceived through the discursive protocols of universal history. But I think the relevant question ought to be posed in the following way: What is the theory-problem about Haiti that *invites* casting the story of its revolution as a story of universal history? You can see that, so formulated, the question seeks to steer us *away* from any idea of the simple self-presence of a connection between the Haitian Revolution and the problem of universality. And, inevitably you might say, this is a question that leads me back to C. L. R. James's *The Black Jacobins*, since to my mind it is exemplary of books that have accepted this invitation to universal history.[19] As I have said elsewhere, in my response to Buck-Morss's provocation in *Hegel, Haiti, and Universal History*, it is very puzzling to me that *The Black Jacobins*, though admiringly mentioned in such discussions as hers, is taken up merely as one among other informational sources for the study of the Haitian Revolution, a useful introductory text, rather than as itself a *theoretical* intervention, one moreover that precisely casts the story of the Haitian Revolution as a story of universal history.[20] In my view, if we are to adequately think the contemporary question of the Haitian Revolution as a problem about the politics of the universal, James's earlier challenge in *The Black Jacobins* will have to be *reconstructed* and thereby met and engaged, rather than presumed and thereby neglected or disavowed. As we will see, James was not interested in the story of black emancipation in Haiti as a story of universal human rights—as Dubois, Knight, and Nesbitt variously are— but this is clearly not because he was less theory-wise than they are but rather because his *theory-problem* about Haiti was not the same as theirs. The particular post–Cold War ideological problem-space that has redefined human rights as our ultimate horizon, the "last utopia" (as Samuel Moyn puts it),[21] was not his. The problem about eighteenth-century France for James was less as a context for thinking about the universality of rights than for thinking about the universality of *revolution*. Therefore, I want to return to *The Black Jacobins*, now at a somewhat different (though nevertheless connected) angle of preoccupation than that which animated my *Conscripts of Modernity*, and ask the following questions: How are we to understand the incitement to, and the uses of, universal history, in *The Black Jacobins*? How—through what narrative and tropological devices—does James construct Haiti as a theory-problem? What ends are served by his mobilization of an interpretive strategy of universal history to address this theory-problem? In short, what is the question (or complex of questions) in *The Black Jacobins* to which a story of the Haitian Revolution written as universal history is deemed to constitute an answer?[22]

Now, I deliberately frame these questions this way because part of what seems to me worth exploring here is whether or to what degree one can speak of a specifically *narratological* structure and effect of universal history. In other words, is universal history to be understood simply as a *theoretical* (or philosophical) exercise, that is, an exercise in the systematic deployment of concepts to understand the past? Or might it also be considered a *narrative* (or literary) exercise, that is, the *telling* of a story of past-present-future of a certain kind?[23] In drawing this contrast, needless to say, I do not mean to imply that "theory" and "narrative" are mutually exclusive, reciprocally impermeable domains—that what are called concepts, say, don't or can't inhabit identifiable story-forms, or that narrative is devoid of intrinsic propositional or theory purposes.[24] To the contrary: Take Hegel, for example, the acknowledged master of universal history in the tradition of German idealism, and consider for a moment the contrast between the early *Phenomenology of Spirit* (1807) and the later *Lectures on the Philosophy of World History* (1837), both in a certain sense preeminent studies in the project of universal history. Undoubtedly there is a good deal that separates these definitive texts in terms of style and intent—not to mention their contrasting contexts of publication. But one way of marking the contrast I want to foreground here between "narrative" and "theory" is to say that the *Phenomenology* can be described (indeed, has been eloquently described) as a quasi-literary *demonstration* of the difficult spiritual journey of universal freedom, the travail of *Bildung*; whereas the *Lectures* are perhaps best understood more as a didactic *exposition* of the categories and structure of world history (they were "lectures" after all).[25] If the *Lectures* (to which I turn in a moment) tend toward a theoretical or propositional account of universal history, the *Phenomenology* is shaped more by a narrative modeling of its dramatic poetics. The contrast is obviously meant to be *heuristic*, not dogmatic. It is meant to enable me to wonder out loud whether what we call universal history isn't worth describing, in part at least, as a narrative with a distinctive *aesthetic* effect, the outcome of literary devices or a mode of emplotment being *set to work* to tell a story of a certain kind—namely, a story embodying a longing for overcoming and a horizon of expectation, and the rhythm and direction of a persistent if uneven movement carrying the overall purpose into effect. In other words, I want to suggest that, whatever else it is, universal history is also a Romantic art that can be read for the poetics of its narrative drama.[26]

| | | | |

In what remains, then, I want to think of *The Black Jacobins* as putting an idea of universal history to work in its account of the Haitian Revolution. To grasp this idea, however, I have first to sketch in outline—using the account in the *Lectures on the Philosophy of World History*—a fragment of Hegel's idea of universal history as the progressive realization of freedom. I want to think of this Hegelian story as emblematic of a certain Romantic historicism, not least in its figuration of the world-historical individual as the vehicle through which a story of striving and a longing for overcoming can be told. After all, part of the way universal history works in *The Black Jacobins* is through James's heroic figuration of Toussaint Louverture. What is at stake for James in this figuration? What conceptual-political labor does it perform? I think that answering such questions is an important way of trying to grasp the theory-problem of Haiti for James, and why universal history might have seemed to him an appropriate response to it.

Universal History and the Ethos of Vindication

In many respects, of course, it is Hegel's theory of universal history that summarizes, in a philosophical idiom, the historical consciousness of Romanticism, that simultaneously breaks with the abstract Enlightenment constructivism of, say, Vico or Kant, and endows the sense of history with intrinsic movement and direction—that is, with the dynamism of tendency or *telos* that is at least one of the hallmarks of universal history.[27] There is perhaps little need to remind ourselves in any detail of the historicist temper of Romanticism, the "sheer excess and extravagance," as Stephen Bann puts it, "of the Romantic investment in the past."[28] But it may be as well for our purposes here to foreground the distinctive Romantic experience of time because it will help us to grasp the labor of universal history, as Hegel would definitively describe it, and as James would embody it in *The Black Jacobins*. This experience of time, the distinctive Romantic "structure of feeling" of temporality, was one in which time is no longer merely an *object* of extrinsic rational inquiry but an *intrinsic* dimension of virtually every aspect of human thought and activity. Historical time has here acquired its own ethical autonomy, its own self-sufficiency, its own self-movement, its own self-determination. Such that the historical subject is now as much lived *by* history as living *in* it—such that she or he is no longer the merely potential mistress or master of history but also, simultaneously, driven by the force (in Hegel's phrase) of an "internal vital principle."[29] I shall argue, moreover, that the ethos of this internal principle of historical consciousness is that of "vindication" inasmuch as it presents itself as a principle of perpetual longing and striving to *righteously* overcome the obstacles that mark the long road to self-realization. Vindication is also a trope of black radicalism, one that James adopts, and adapts, in *The Black Jacobins*.

Hegel's story of Spirit is famously the story both of its divisions and travails *and* of the metaphysical justice of its eventual triumphs. At the center of his account of the philosophy of world history is, as he puts it, "the simple idea of reason—the idea that reason governs the world, and that world history is therefore a rational process."[30] This is Hegel's historiographical "presupposition." Reason, which is self-originating, self-sufficient, and self-determining, not only brings itself into existence but carries its own purposes into effect. On the one hand, Hegel maintained, reason is

> its own sole precondition, and its end is the absolute and ultimate end of everything; and on the other, it is itself the agent which implements and realises this end, translating it from potentiality into actuality both in the natural universe and in the spiritual world—that is, in world history. (27–28)

In other words, universal history is the working out of the "general design" of reason and of the idea that reveals itself in the world: world history is "the image and enactment of reason" (28). What is of interest from the point of view of universal history, then, are not the "individual situations" of history but the "spiritual principle" or "universal thought" that runs through the whole. This universal element, Hegel argues, "is not to be found in the world of contingent phenomena" but in the "unity behind the multitude of particulars" (30). History is inherently a rational process that articulates itself in a ceaseless principle of change: the melancholy of negation and ruin supplanted by rejuvenation and new life. The intention, the ultimate end that underlies the direction of its movement, is the universal Idea, and more specifically, the universal Idea of human freedom (46). This is the telos of universal history. In the "theater of world history," as Hegel puts it, Spirit as self-sufficient "striving" seeks its realization in the Idea of freedom, the "progress of the consciousness of freedom" (54).

On this account, the universal end of history consists of Spirit's development toward greater and greater self-consciousness (self-consciousness of freedom, self-consciousness of itself as free individuality), or in "its making the world conform to itself," as Hegel puts it in a striking phrase (64). But what is the *means* by which the Idea—or Spirit—realizes itself in history, the means by which "freedom creates a world for itself"? If universal freedom is an "internal concept," belonging to the world of absolute Spirit, it has nevertheless to *enter* the concrete world of contingency, in which, as Hegel says, "the actions of men are governed by their needs, passions, and interests, by the attitudes and aims to which these give rise, and by their own character and abilities" (68). And when the world Spirit or the Spirit of universal freedom converges with the substance of a particular individual will, you have a Hegelian world-historical individual. For Hegel these individuals are those "who seize upon this higher universal and make it their own end. It is they who realize the end appropriate to the higher concept of Spirit" (82–83). He goes on:

> They do not find their aims and vocation in the calm and regular system of the present, in the hallowed order of things as they are. Indeed, their justification does not lie in the prevailing situation, for they draw their inspiration from another source, from that hidden spirit whose hour is near but which still lies beneath the surface and seeks to break out without yet having attained an existence in the present. . . . For this Spirit, in the present world is but a spent shell which contains the wrong kernel. (83)

World-historical individuals are men of action, exertion, and conflict, who, however, never act precipitously but only when the "time is ripe," when the realization of Spirit is immanent. These are men, therefore, unconcerned with personal happiness or satisfaction because far-sighted as they are, they are completely, even blindly, devoted to the coming future, certain that right is on their side (83–84). Their actions, Hegel says, are their "entire being, and their whole nature and character are determined by their ruling passion" (85). But just as there is a time for the world-historical individual, their emergence, and flourishing, there is a time for their decline, when, spent of Spirit, they are cast aside by history. As Hegel puts it: "When their end is attained, they fall aside like empty husks. They may have undergone great difficulties in order to accomplish their purpose, but as soon as they have done so, they die early like Alexander, are murdered like Caesar, or are deported like Napoleon" (85).

In short, Hegel portrays the Romantic story of Spirit's longing to realize itself as the great arc of a temporal movement, uneven but sure, in which the universal Idea embodies itself in the concrete human will of a world-historical hero. And against the odds, and overcoming the near-sighted finitude of the mere mortals crowding the historical stage, the lonely but undaunted hero, lived only by the irrepressible force of his inner vision, imposes the future onto the present. And when at last the work of Spirit is done, when its truth has vindicated itself as the prevailing reason, and when consequently it no longer has need of the hero's services, it casts him aside, indifferent to his righteous pleas for a just accounting. My argument here is that whatever else this is, however authoritative or commanding its propositional virtues, it is also poetry, the *literary* evocation of the present's longing for a certain future.

The Black Jacobins and the Poetics of Universal History

It will not be hard, I think, to map this Hegelian story directly on to the pages of *The Black Jacobins*, to see in the rise and fall of its history's movement the labor of the ceaseless principle of spirit's striving, to recognize in its figuration of Toussaint Louverture the entry of the universal Idea of freedom into a specific conjuncture of self-fashioning and self-determination. Against this background, I want to turn to James's text and put to it the following questions: What is its theory-problem about Haiti? More precisely, what is the theory-problem within which the Haitian Revolution is constructed as the scene of a Hegelian story of the progressive realization of universal Spirit? Finally, how, and through what narrative strategy or literary device, is its *effect* of universal history produced?

Again, I reiterate that my point in raising these questions here is less to put into motion a fully worked-out conceptual history than to oblige us to see the necessity of denaturalizing "Haiti," to attune us to the *connection* between Haiti as the object of a theory-problem, on the one hand, and on the other, of universal history as the *mode* of its literary-theoretical resolution. This is the circumscribed problem at hand.

| | | | |

Speaking somewhat schematically here for the sake of my argument, and thus glossing over a densely complex history, I suggest that the theory-problem about Haiti for *The Black Jacobins* was constituted by a number of intersecting discursive contexts that made the universal history of self-determination and revolution a—perhaps *the*—compelling vindicationist answer to the questions of racial and colonial domination. It scarcely needs rehearsing that the central problem organizing the construction of Africans and peoples of African descent in the context of the scientific racism of the last decades of the nineteenth century and the first decades of the twentieth concerned their fundamental humanity defined in terms of "civilized" achievement: Of what were black people capable? What was their relative level of intelligence? What had they accomplished? What hope was there of progress? The colonial question during these years was of course connected to that of race and humanity, but it centered its attention principally on the capacity of the colonized for self-government, for sovereignty. Were the colonized capable of ruling themselves without supervision, benevolent or otherwise? How would their readiness for self-government be determined? Indeed, could the colonized really ever be entrusted with all the rights and privileges of political responsibility that were taken for granted among civilized states? These were ominous but far-reaching questions in an era in which, as Gerrit Gong has shown, a certain "standard of civilization" governed the very idea of international community.[31] Within the terms of this "standard," Haiti had long been figured as an exemplary signifier—the paradigmatic instance of the horror and failure of black self-determination.

One has only to think (choosing more or less at random) of Hesketh Pritchard's travel memoir, *Where Black Rules White*, published in 1900, to grasp the essential structure of the Haiti-problem to which a vindicationist response might be offered.[32] An adventurer with a familiar late-Victorian taste for racialized travel (James Anthony Froude was only a more accomplished version of the same desire), Pritchard arrived in Haiti in 1899 to "probe" the "mystery and fascination" of the black republic where, as he said, since Dessalines's infamous "wholesale massacre" of the remaining French men, women, and children, the island's interiority had been virtually closed to white eyes. But the real question framing Pritchard's interest was the one that organized his final chapter, significantly titled, "Can the Negro Rule Himself?" This is the question toward which the entire travelogue was oriented; for Pritchard, Haiti provided not only the best but also the "conclusive" answer to it. For in Haiti, as he put it lyrically, the

> negro has had his chance, a fair field and no favour. He has had the most fertile and beautiful of the Caribbees for his own; he has had the advantage of excellent French laws; he inherited a made country, with Cap Haytien for its Paris. . . . Here was a wide land sown with prosperity, a land with wood, water, towns, and plantations, and in the midst of it the Black Man was turned loose to work out his own salvation.[33]

But what has the Negro made of this fair chance?, asked Pritchard rhetorically. The answer is not hard to anticipate: "At the end of a hundred years of trial, how does the black man govern himself? What progress has he made? Absolutely none."[34]

This is an all-too-familiar theory of Haiti. Still, to properly appreciate the discursive context of intervention of *The Black Jacobins*, it is important to remind ourselves that this Haiti idea (Haiti as the instantiation of the incapacity of blacks for sovereignty, of their continuing need of the firm paternal hand of political guidance) was not just an ideologically prominent one in the late nineteenth and early twentieth centuries but also a materially *consequential* one inasmuch as it undergirded the political context in which Woodrow Wilson, in flagrant contradiction of his stated commitment to the self-determination of small states, would invade on July 28, 1915.[35] The thin pretext for the landing of the marines at Port-au-Prince was the chaos that followed the assassination of President Guillaume Sam and the need to protect U.S. interests from the ongoing political instability.[36] But U.S. designs on the Haitian treasury and the strategic territory of Môle-Saint-Nicolas were transparent enough to many observers, and the reduction of Haitians once again to virtual colonial subjugation was carried out with open brutality and undisguised racialized contempt. The occupation offered a virtually unobstructed field for military domination and rampant economic exploitation; but as Michael Dash and Mary Renda have variously shown, once the resistance was subdued, it also provided the controlled occasion for a veritable explosion of writing by white Americans in which Haiti was constructed as a sort of "looking glass"—as the primitivist scene of a racialized and sexualized desire.[37] From Eugene O'Neill's *Emperor Jones* (1920) through marine memoirs such as Captain John Houston Craige's *Black Bagdad* (1933) and *Cannibal Cousins* (1934), and sensationalist histories of Henri Christophe and his citadel such as John Vandecook's *Black Majesty* (1928) to "voodoo" travel books such as Blair Niles's *Black Haiti: A Biography of Africa's Eldest Daughter* (1926), Haiti had become a phantasm in an imperial American imagination. Such historical treatments as Percy Waxman's *The Black Napoleon* (published in 1931), which James dismissed, constituted only a more sober and reflective version of a familiar theme.[38]

Against the direction of this whole body of white writing, there had long been a tradition of vindicationist counterdiscourse in New World black writing in which Haiti was celebrated as the vanguard of black liberation and black self-determination. In a certain sense, *The Black Jacobins* is simply a distinct instance of this black intellectual tradition. The best examples of this vindicationist writing in the nineteenth century were, undoubtedly, the 1857 work of the emigrationist and missionary James Theodore Holly, *A Vindication of the Capacity of the Negro Race for Self-Government, and Civilized Progress, Demonstrated by Historical Events of the Haytian Revolution*; and the lecture given by Frederick Douglass at the Haiti Pavilion of the Chicago World's Fair in January 1893.[39] Less than two decades later, in a conjuncture marked by a rapidly coalescing black internationalism—World War I and its cruel aftermaths for African Americans and West Indians, the rising tide of Pan-Africanism, the growth of Marcus Garvey's Universal Negro Improvement Association and other militant organizations—the U.S. occupation of Haiti became a flash point for black cultural-political consciousness. Already in August 1915, an outraged W. E. B. Du Bois had written in protest to President Wilson seeking assurances and, doubtlessly receiving none, had written a scathing editorial in the October issue of the *Crisis*, denouncing the invasion as a racial violation of the sovereignty of a "sister state."[40] But in the wake of the racial violence of the Red Summer of 1919, nothing would focus the minds of concerned African Americans (and of others, too, including the U.S. government) on Haiti as much as James Weldon Johnson's measured and learned exposé of the abuse of the U.S. Marines, "Self-Determining Haiti," published in 1920.[41] Yet in these years Haiti was still largely the object of a cautious discourse of black accomplishment and outraged solidarity. By the early 1930s, however, a younger, more militant generation of internationalist black writers and artists began to produce a grittier, less appeasing, and on the whole more historical approach to Haiti. Among them were Langston Hughes, Arna Bontemps, and Jacob Lawrence. Also among them was Paul Robeson, who collaborated with James in 1936 in a stage adaptation of the story of Toussaint Louverture. In short, then, by the 1930s the Haitian Revolution had come to be rendered as a crucial site of black inheritance and the claim of black self-determination.

Connected to this problematic of black sovereignty there is at least one other conceptual and ideological context that structures the predicament to which *The Black Jacobins* responds. This is the Marxist context of "world revolution" that animated the interwar years of the early twentieth century. In the 1930s, as Stalin consolidated his position and liquidated the old Bolsheviks one after another, the meaning of revolution was very much in question, and the world revolutionary movement (coalescing around the exiled and beleaguered Trotsky) was seeking to redescribe its history and indeed its world-historical project. As is well known, James was drawn to these circles, becoming himself a center of Marxist discussion. (Remember, too, that the other seminal book that occupied James in these years, which appeared just before *The Black Jacobins*, was his study of the international communist movement, *World Revolution*.)[42] Moreover, George Padmore's break with the Communist International in 1935 over the colonial question and his move from Moscow to London attuned James to the tension between socialist and anticolonial struggles. The U.S. occupation of Haiti had been a live issue for Padmore: in 1930 he had written a critical essay on the December 1929 revolt in Haiti and its bloody repression in the London-based communist periodical *Labour Monthly*; in 1931 he had extended his critique in a short pamphlet, *Haiti, An American Slave Colony*, published in Moscow.[43] In other words, a crucial dimension of the problem-space in which Haiti came to be constructed—or perhaps cathected—as a theory-object for James in the 1930s was the question of placing black emancipation and anticolonial revolution in the wider problematic of world socialist revolution.

On the whole, then, taking these discursive contexts together, the theory-problem or theory-question within which a certain narrative of the Haitian Revolution appears to offer the potential conceptual-ideological resources for an answer might be formulated as follows: How does one tell the vindicationist story of black self-determination as an intrinsic part of the universal history of world revolution? Or to put the critical demand slightly differently: How does one shape a story in which the figure of black humanity, reduced for centuries to the abjection of racialized enslavement, will embody a world-historical longing and the agency that makes possible the realization of universal emancipation? These are large, myth-making questions, but they organize, I think, the challenge *The Black Jacobins* aims to meet.

| | | | |

But how does James produce the *effect* of universal history in *The Black Jacobins*, the dramatic movement from travail to realization that maps the arc of Spirit in History? For if, as I am suggesting, universal history is, partly at least, a narrative or aesthetic effect, we have to inquire into the literary devices—the mode of emplotment, the figuration of character, the tropological strategies—he uses to accomplish this. Readers of *The Black Jacobins* will recall that James was nothing if not profoundly self-conscious of the poetics of writing the past into the present, of shaping the content of the form of historical representation. Indeed, readers will recall the tension James deliberately *stages* in the celebrated preface to the first edition between concept and artifice, between, as he put it, the "science" (that is, the analytic) and the "art" (that is, the story) of history.[44] In some sense, as I have suggested, this was the productive tension between the competing models that were among his principal sources of historiographic inspiration, namely, Jules Michelet's *History of the French Revolution* (1847–1853) and Leon Trotsky's *History of the Russian Revolution* (1932–1933)—both concerned with writing revolution as universal history, the one tending more toward an analytic of historical progress and the other more toward an aesthetics of historical narration.[45] If Michelet and Trotsky aimed to produce their respective revolutions (French and Russian) as realizations of a principle of universality, this I argue is also James's challenge in writing the history of the Haitian Revolution: namely, writing anticolonial revolution—the self-emancipation of the black colonized—as universality. And as with Michelet's and Trotsky's histories, James's principal objective in *The Black Jacobins* is not to recount the basic details of the historical unfolding of the Saint-Domingue insurrection in all their professional completeness (though clearly these details are scarcely unimportant to him). Rather, James's objective is to use these events to emplot a story of the self-emancipation of the slaves as an initiative of universal emancipation and *therefore* as universal history.

Famously, and in striking contrast with Michelet and Trotsky, the principal way James seeks to construct this effect of universal history in the account of the Haitian Revolution is through the device of heroic figuration of his main protagonist, Toussaint Louverture. For James, memorably, Toussaint is not merely a concrete individual with an empirically determinate biography and specifiable career; he is primarily a world-historical figure embodying the progressive self-movement of Spirit from the doomed world of slavery into the coming dispensation of freedom. James's Toussaint embodies the *direction* of Reason in history. The story of the Haitian Revolution in *The Black Jacobins* therefore can be read as the story of Spirit's striving toward a higher self-consciousness, as the movement through which the potentiality of Spirit, the ethical substance of universality, realizes itself as, or is *translated* into, historical actuality. This movement shapes the great arc of the book and the ceaseless principle that drives the momentum of the narrative drama, from the melancholy tyrannies and tortures and debasements and inhumanities of the Middle Passage and plantation enslavement to the joyous opening of the project of freedom as self-determination. Toussaint Louverture, in this respect, is the Hegelian vehicle through which this journey of Spirit comes to self-realization: Toussaint, in other words, is able to seize universality and make it one with himself. Whether or not old Toussaint of Bréda ever read the Abbé Raynal's *Histoire des deux Indes* (1770), the hermeneutic point of that scene of reading in the opening chapter of *The Black Jacobins* when we first meet our protagonist is for James not merely to indicate his hero's induction into the radical Enlightenment (though it is that, too, undoubtedly); it is to show, within that steadily rising curve of his narrative, the moment when universality enters into the concrete particular of Toussaint's historical life and stamps on it the name of his destiny.[46] For James's Toussaint, the inherited slave world of Saint-Domingue was, in Hegel's apt metaphor, a shell containing the wrong kernel. This is the ground of Toussaint's embodied insight. And as James shows it to us (with the deft hand of a novelist), it is not simply that Toussaint recognizes the falseness or irrationality or wrongness of his world; it is that the new world, the future-to-come, is already a faintly glimmering dawn in the abject night of the old. Toussaint inhabits this historical *hinge*—and what he awakens to is the "ripeness" of his moment. Unlike the other leaders of the rapidly unfolding insurrection—Jacques Dessalines, for example, or Henri Christophe—James's Toussaint embodies the inward self-consciousness of this ripening of time and its implications for his destiny and those of his fellows.

This is the Hegelian meaning, then, of that pivotal scene in chapter 4, "The San Domingo Masses Begin," of Toussaint's initial hesitation to join the insurrection in 1791. It is not doubt; it is not fear; it is not servility. Ever "master of himself," as James puts it, this hesitation marks the hero's apprehension of the yet-unripeness of the moment, the yet-*untimeliness* of the time, and his certain conviction that his entry into world history—however seemingly obscure—will be dictated solely by the inner vision of the rightness of the time.[47] Similarly, James has us see that with one exception, Toussaint's various negotiations—with the Spanish, the English, the Americans, the French, the plantocracy, the mulattoes—were never compromises of principle; they were "mere politics," mere *means* to an end that would be larger than the sum of their disparate parts. They were not dictated by his Europhile inclinations, as some would argue (these, anyway, are trivial to James because none of us, the progeny of colonialism, escape them); they were driven by his drive to serve the inner vision, the Idea of the higher truth, planted in him by the design of universal history.

And finally, when the work of Spirit has completed itself in and through Toussaint Louverture, we witness the progressive movement of Reason in history no longer corresponding with his concrete practice—he begins to falter, to busy himself, as James laments, with "sawing off the branch" on which he was sitting.[48] In a slowly gathering alteration of historical forces and conditions, the world now no longer conforms to his indomitable will. There are revolts and subversions on all sides. He has lost touch with the popular pulse; he even feels obliged, out of desperation, to execute his much-beloved Moïse, in whom he senses a rival, the presence of a new Angel of History. Indeed, Toussaint has now been overtaken by the very Spirit of freedom he himself has gifted to the world; and like all world-historical figures at the end of their journey, he will be tossed aside, falling by the way like an empty "husk" (in Hegel's image), leaving the way for others to take up the work left to be done. Writing of the famous battle at the fort of Crête-à-Pierrot in March 1802, one of the deciding battles of the Haitian Revolution when Dessalines proved himself the man of the moment, James is unsentimental in his description of Toussaint's loss of historical direction:

> He seemed still to be hoping that if he defeated Leclerc, Bonaparte would see reason and the valuable connection with France be maintained. But the days for that were over. Dessalines had proclaimed the word independence. . . . Toussaint was still thinking in terms of the decree of February 4th, 1794 [by which the revolutionary French National Convention abolished slavery in the colonies]. The black revolution had passed him by.[49]

Coda

My aim here has not been to set down exhaustively (even nearly so) the whole dramatic labor of James's exercise in writing the Haitian Revolution as universal history in *The Black Jacobins*. What I want us to principally see in my account is not merely this labor in itself, as though it could be disconnected from a historicizable complex of questions. Rather, what I want us to see is the *connection* between the construction of Haiti as a certain kind of conceptual-ideological object, a certain kind of theory-problem (structured around race, colonialism, revolution, and self-determination), and the mobilization of a narrative strategy of universal history that works by *showing* (rather more perhaps than by didactically *explaining*) the unfolding overcoming of the besetting conundrums and the realization of Reason in a specific history. One might call this the literary-political project of universal history that James sets to work through the vindication of his world-historical hero, Toussaint Louverture. Whether or not, in organizing his historical narrative in *this* way, James is writing the Haitian Revolution into a conception of temporality that remains usable in our own time is a question, I suggest, that will have to be *formulated*, not a conclusion that can be assumed a priori, one way or the other. It was precisely an objective of *Conscripts of Modernity* to put this question into critical circulation.

Part of the disfavor, memorably, into which universal history fell during the theory-wars of the 1990s turned, of course, on its grand, often Eurocentric assumption of a metaphysical foundation that propositionally guaranteed the possibility and direction of the general good of universal freedom. And in the political doldrums that marked these years—the end of Bandung, the end of socialism, the reconstitution of the contours of imperial power, and so on—a good deal of postmetaphysical work has gone into dismantling the philosophical hubris of that discourse of freedom. But alas, poststructuralism may indeed have (in its own theory-conceit) thrown the proverbial baby out with the unwanted bath water in the sense that it may have disabled its own poetics of emancipation, its own ability to think imaginatively a future at the limit of the present. But if universal history can be detached from the demand for *propositional* truth—if, that is, we can recognize in the story-form of universal history a normative strategy that secures a *poetic* truth—perhaps we shall feel under less theory-pressure to stifle and dispense with the emancipationist longings into which its mode of emplotment has so earnestly interpellated us as potential subjects of freedom. In any case, offering us this challenge—in Haiti's name—is to my mind one of the unending provocations of *The Black Jacobins*.

Notes

1. See J. Michael Dash, *Haiti and the United States: National Stereotypes and the Literary Imagination*, 2nd edition (London: Macmillan, 1997).
2. See Michel-Rolph Trouillot, "The Odd and the Ordinary: Haiti, the Caribbean, and the World," *Cimarron* 2, no. 3 (1990): 3.
3. Trouillot, "The Odd and the Ordinary," 7.
4. Trouillot, "The Odd and the Ordinary," 9–12. Trouillot suggests that his own work on his native Haiti—for example, *Haiti: State Against the Nation* (New York: Monthly Review Press, 1989)—has been framed by his earlier historical ethnography of Dominica. See Michel-Rolph Trouillot, *Peasants and Capital: Dominica in the World Economy* (Baltimore: Johns Hopkins University Press, 1988). For some reflections on this style of Trouillot's, see David Scott, "The Futures of Michel-Rolph Trouillot: In Memoriam," *Small Axe* no. 39 (November 2012): v–ix.
5. See principally Melville J. Herskovits, "The Negro in the New World: The Statement of a Problem," *American Anthropologist* 32, no. 1 (1930): 145–55, in which he argued that the cultures of peoples of African descent in the New World could be categorized based on their degree of African influence.
6. I have discussed this in David Scott, "That Event, This Memory: Notes on the Anthropology of African Diasporas in the New World," *Diaspora* 1, no. 3 (winter 1991): 261–84.

7. Melville J. Herskovits and Frances S. Herskovits, *Rebel Destiny: Among the Bush Negroes of Dutch Guiana* (New York: Whittlesey House, 1934) and *Suriname Folk-Lore* (New York: Columbia University Press, 1936); Melville J. Herskovits, *Dahomey: An Ancient West African Kingdom*, 2 vols. (New York: J. J. Augustin, 1938). On Herskovits's trajectory, see Jerry Gershenhorn, *Melville J. Herskovits and the Racial Politics of Knowledge* (Lincoln: University of Nebraska Press, 2004), 70–78. See also Richard Price and Sally Price, *The Roots of Roots: Or, How Afro-American Anthropology Got Its Start* (Chicago: Prickly Paradigm Press, 2003).

8. On the decision to study Haiti, see Gershenhorn, *Melville J. Herskovits*, 81.

9. Melville J. Herskovits, *Life in a Haitian Valley* (New York: Knopf, 1937).

10. William B. Seabrook, *The Magic Island* (New York: Harcourt Brace, 1929); Richard Loederer, *Voodoo Fire in Haiti* (New York: Literary Guild, 1935). Herskovits published a review of the latter titled "Voodoo Nonsense" in the *Nation* 141 (September 11, 1935): 308. On Mary Renda's account, the publisher Alfred A. Knopf, seeing the review, solicited from Herskovits a book-length study of Haiti, which resulted in *Life in a Haitian Valley*. See Mary Renda, *Taking Haiti: Military Occupation and the Culture of U.S. Imperialism, 1915–1940* (Chapel Hill: University of North Carolina Press, 2001), 273–74.

11. As Gershenhorn writes in *Melville J. Herskovits*: "Despite the extended presence of American Marines, Herskovits missed their impact on the culture of the Haitian people. In fact, American officials banned the religious practices of Vodun, raided houses of worship, and seized ceremonial objects. Nonetheless, Herskovits found the people friendly toward Americans, an attitude that benefited his work" (81).

12. For a discussion of the period, see Matthew Smith, *Red and Black in Haiti: Radicalism, Conflict, and Political Change, 1934–1957* (Chapel Hill: University of North Carolina Press, 2009).

13. See generally Gérarde Magloire and Kevin Yelvington, "Haiti and the Anthropological Imagination," *Gradhiva* 1 (2005): 127–52.

14. The *locus classicus* of this argument in anthropology is Johannes Fabian, *Time and the Other: How Anthropology Makes Its Object* (New York: Columbia University Press, 1983). See also Arjun Appadurai, "Theory in Anthropology: Center and Periphery," *Comparative Studies in Societies and History* 28, no. 2 (1986): 356–61. Obviously it is in many ways Edward Said's *Orientalism* (New York: Pantheon, 1978) that offered the opening move in redescribing the study of the colonial question in the wake of the linguistic turn. On the question of social constructionism see David Scott, "The Social Construction of Postcolonial Studies" in *Postcolonial Studies and Beyond*, edited by Ania Loomba, Suvir Kaul, Matti Bunzl, Antoinette Burton, and Jed Esty (Durham, NC: Duke University Press, 2005), 385–400.

15. "After two centuries of neglect and disavowal," it has been suggested, "the Haitian Revolution has suddenly become a fundamental reference point for global emancipatory politics, a touchstone for critical philosophers such as Alain Badiou, Slavoj Žižek,

Susan Buck-Morss, Peter Hallward, and Hardt and Negri." This statement comes from the announcement for a conference on "Haiti and the Politics of the Universal" at the Centre for Modern Thought at the University of Aberdeen, Scotland, March 12–13, 2010 (for which this essay was originally written and where it was first delivered). I am not sure myself where Badiou, Žižek, Hardt, or Negri have made the Haitian Revolution a "touchstone" in their philosophy. Peter Hallward has written an important book, less on the revolution itself than on the rise and fall of Jean-Bertrand Aristide: *Damming the Flood: Haiti, Aristide, and the Politics of Containment* (London: Verso, 2008). For Žižek's discussion of it, see "Democracy versus the People," *New Statesman*, August 14, 2008 (http://www.newstatesman.com/books/2008/08/haiti-aristide-lavalas) (accessed October 21, 2010). Susan Buck-Morss is the author of *Hegel, Haiti, and Universal History* (Pittsburgh: University of Pittsburgh Press, 2009).

16. See Laurent Dubois, *Avengers of the New World: The Story of the Haitian Revolution* (Cambridge, MA: Harvard University Press, 2004), 3.

17. See Franklin W. Knight, "The Haitian Revolution and the Notion of Human Rights," *Journal of the Historical Society* 5, no. 3 (fall 2005): 391.

18. See Nick Nesbitt, *Universal Emancipation: The Haitian Revolution and the Radical Enlightenment* (Charlottesville: University of Virginia Press, 2008).

19. C. L. R. James, *The Black Jacobins: Toussaint Louverture and the San Domingo Revolution* (London: Secker and Warburg, 1938). In the years following the publication of *The Black Jacobins*, interestingly, a number of other books authored by Caribbean writers appeared dealing with Toussaint Louverture and the Haitian Revolution, among them perhaps most famously, Stephen Alexis, *Black Liberator: The Life of Toussaint Louverture* (New York: Macmillan, 1949); Aimé Césaire, *Toussaint Louverture: La révolution française et la problème colonial* (Paris: Présence Africaine, 1961); and Edouard Glissant's play *Monsieur Toussaint: A Play*, trans. J. Michael Dash and Edouard Glissant (Boulder, CO: Lynne Rienner, 2005). Each of these books bears witness to the inexhaustible, perhaps inextinguishable semiotic resources of the figure of Toussaint Louverture and his role in the Haitian Revolution, and each of them to some extent draws on Romantic tropes and images. Césaire, for example, draws on the trope of "sacrifice" in picturing Toussaint. Of this book James wrote, in a paragraph added to the bibliography of the 1963 edition of *The Black Jacobins* (New York: Vintage, 1963), 389: "This is a recent biography by the celebrated poet, dramatist and politician of the French West Indian island of Martinique. The book, as could have been expected, is extremely competent and gives a good picture of Toussaint and the San Domingo Revolution. I find, however, that it lacks the fire and constant illumination which distinguish most of the other work of Césaire."

20. See David Scott, "Antinomies of Slavery, Enlightenment, and Universal History," *Small Axe* no. 33 (November 2010): 152–62.

21. The allusion is to Samuel Moyn, *The Last Utopia: Human Rights in History* (Cambridge, MA: Harvard University Press, 2010), in which he reads the post–Cold War rise of human rights (as discourse and project) as a new frontier of utopianism that emerged to occupy the vacuum left by the collapse of communism.

22. David Scott, *Conscripts of Modernity: The Tragedy of Colonial Enlightenment* (Durham, NC: Duke University Press, 2004). I am not, for example, going to be concerned with the adequacy or lack thereof of James's treatment of universal history, and I am not going to be concerned with the poetics of tragedy. Here I am much more concerned with the methodological questions of reading the past in the present.

23. Quite clearly I have Hayden White's work in mind here, especially his idea of the content of narrative form. For a recent and helpful discussion of White's work, see Frank Ankersmit, Ewa Domanska, and Hans Kellner (eds.), *Re-Figuring Hayden White* (Stanford, CA: Stanford University Press, 2009).

24. In her response to me, Susan Buck-Morss ("The Gift of the Past," *Small Axe* no. 33 [November 2010]: 173–85) emphasizes "theory" against "narrative" in a way that suggests a certain hierarchy of value. She urges, for example, that a "narrative rendering of the logic of freedom" ought to yield to a properly "theoretical" one (174). Where in a "literary approach, narration is key," and the "life of the hero" constitutes a "model of the emancipatory idea," in a "philosophical approach, the event is seen as the birthplace of a new conception of freedom that is not embodied in anthropomorphic form. It is a matter of how the present receives the past, or more specifically, how the present is situated in a topology of time and space" (176). More generally, her argument is that universal history is not a "metanarrative" but a "theoretical pragmatics," a "method" not a story nor an "overarching philosophical system": its "goal is to disrupt the intellectual order by exposing the blind spots that hinder conceptual, hence political, imagination" (173).

25. See, for example, Allen Speight, *Hegel, Literature, and the Problem of Agency* (Cambridge: Cambridge University Press, 2001); Donald Philip Verene, *Hegel's Recollection: A Study of the Images in the* Phenomenology of Spirit (Albany: State University of New York Press, 1985). See also Fredric Jameson, *The Hegel Variations* (New York: Verso, 2010).

26. See, helpfully Frederick Beiser, *The Romantic Imperative: The Concept of Early German Romanticism* (Cambridge, MA: Harvard University Press, 2006); Terry Pinkard, *German Philosophy, 1760–1860: The Legacy of Idealism* (Cambridge: Cambridge University Press, 2002).

27. I am obviously thinking here, respectively, of Giambatista Vico, *New Science* (New York: Penguin, 1999), and Immanuel Kant, "Idea for a Universal History with a Cosmopolitan Purpose" (1784) in *Kant: Political Writings*, edited by Hans Reiss (Cambridge: Cambridge University Press, 1991), 41–53.

28. Stephen Bann, *Romanticism and the Rise of History* (New York: Twayne, 1995), 9.

29. Georg Wilhelm Friedrich Hegel, *The Philosophy of History*, trans. J. Sibree (New York: Dover, 1956), 60.

30. Georg Wilhelm Friedrich Hegel, *Lectures on the Philosophy of World History*, trans. H. B. Nesbit, with an introduction by Duncan Forbes (Cambridge: Cambridge University Press, 1975), 27. Hereafter references to this work are given in the text.

31. Gerrit Gong, *The Standard of "Civilization" in International Society* (New York: Oxford University Press, 1984).

32. Hesketh Pritchard, *Where Black Rules White: A Journey across and about Hayti* (Westminster: Archibald Constable, 1900).

33. Pritchard, *Where Black Rules White*, 278.

34. Pritchard, *Where Black Rules White*, 281.

35. On Wilson and self-determination, see Erez Manela, *The Wilsonian Moment: Self-Determination and the International Origins of Anti-Colonial Nationalism* (New York: Oxford University Press, 2007).

36. There had been considerable instability in Haiti from the end of the nineteenth century through the early years of the twentieth, with the presidency changing several times in quick succession. For a discussion of this period in Haiti, see David Nicholls, *From Dessalines to Duvalier: Race, Color, and National Independence in Haiti* (Cambridge: Cambridge University Press, 1979).

37. See Dash, *Haiti and the United*, chapter 2 (the Alice in Wonderland figure is his); Renda, *Taking Haiti*, esp. chapters 5 and 6.

38. See Percy Waxman, *The Black Napoleon: The Story of Toussaint Louverture* (New York: Harcourt Brace, 1931); James, *The Black Jacobins*, 322: "A superficial book," he calls it.

39. See James Theodore Holly, "Vindication of the Capacity of the Negro Race for Self-Government, and Civilized Progress, Demonstrated by Historical Events of the Haytian Revolution," in *Black Separatism in the Caribbean, 1860*, edited by Howard Bell (Ann Arbor: University of Michigan Press, 1970); Frederick Douglass, "Lecture on Haiti," available at http://faculty.webster.edu/corbetre/haiti/history/1844-1915/douglass.htm.

40. W. E. B. Du Bois, "Hayti," *Crisis* 10 (October 1915): 291. Du Bois went on to say: "Here, then is the outrage of uninvited American intervention, the shooting and disarming of peaceful Haytian citizens, the seizure of public funds, the veiled, but deliberate design to alienate Haytian territory at Mole St. Nicholas, and the pushing of the monopoly claims of an American corporation which holds a filched, if not a fraudulent railway charter. SHAME ON AMERICA!"

41. James Weldon Johnson, "Self-Determining Haiti," *Nation* 111 (August 28, 1920). See also his account in *Along This Way: The Autobiography of James Weldon Johnson* (New York: Penguin, 1933), 344–56. After his initial support of the occupation, Johnson became tirelessly devoted to the effort of mobilizing solidarity for Haiti, maintaining intimate contacts with Haitian intellectuals and politicians. He was instrumental, for example, in helping Georges Sylvain organize the opposition political party, l'Union Patriotique, in 1922.

42. C. L. R. James, *World Revolution 1917–1936: The Rise and Fall of the Communist International* (London: Secker and Warburg, 1937).

43. See George Padmore, "The Revolt in Haiti," *Labour Monthly* 12 (June 1930): 356–66; George Padmore, *Haiti, an American Slave Colony* (Moscow: Centrizdat, 1931).

44. See James, *The Black Jacobins*, vii. As he put it: "The analysis is the science and the demonstration the art which is history." "The writer," he had written in the prior paragraph, referring to himself and the distinctive tasks involved in writing about revolution, "has sought not only to analyse, but to demonstrate in their movement, the economic forces of the age; their moulding of society and politics, of men in the mass and individual men; the powerful reaction of these on their environment at one of those rare moments when society is at boiling point and therefore fluid."

45. See Scott, *Conscripts of Modernity*, 65–70.

46. James, *The Black Jacobins*, 16–17.

47. James, *The Black Jacobins*, 70.

48. James, *The Black Jacobins*, 231. "And in those crucial months," James writes, "Toussaint, fully aware of Bonaparte's preparations, was busy sawing off the branch on which he sat."

49. James, *The Black Jacobins*, 366.

9

Fragments of a Universal History:
Global Capital, Mass Revolution, and
the Idea of Equality in *The Black Jacobins*

NICK NESBITT

If anything will emerge from this book, it is not only the strength of principles, but the power of leadership.
—C. L. R. James, *World Revolution, 1917–1936*

What can explain the astonishing success of the Haitian Revolution, the first successful slave revolt in history? Neither mere numbers of revolting slaves, the violence of slavery itself, nor African cultural remnants or even local hygienic conditions in Saint-Domingue played any appreciable role in the unfolding of the Haitian Revolution, according to C. L. R. James. "San Domingo was not the first place where European invaders had met fever. It was the decree of abolition, the bravery of the blacks, and the ability of their leaders, that had done it."[1] In this simple formulation, James summarizes the three heterogeneous causes that, in his view, turned what began as one more slave revolt into a successful mass revolution that overthrew the savage capitalist regime of plantation slavery to show the world how much "power was hidden in a people," as these former slaves went on to create the abolitionist state of Haiti in 1804.[2] These are in turn: the idea of freedom and equality, the idea, in other words, of the French Revolution concretized in the Jacobin abolition decree of February 6, 1794; the concerted struggle of a "mass" (the word James adopts throughout *The Black Jacobins*) of half a million former slaves; and, in what is still the most original and controversial dimension of the book's argument, the guidance of leaders of genius, above all, Toussaint Louverture.

Universal Histories

The Black Jacobins is unabashedly universalist in James's unwavering commitment to tell the story of the Haitian Revolution as a moment or fragment in the universal history of mass revolution against capitalist oppression. The book assembles a series of heterogeneous conceptual fragments to form the structure of the historical conjuncture that is the Haitian Revolution. Radically antihistoricist, James's notion of universality, I argue, lies not in a vision of totality, telos, or essence (whether revolutionary species-being or human essence as production) but in the contingent, open-ended assemblage of revolutionary moments (1789, 1804, 1917) that might prove to his readers that human being is infinite contingency, the always existent possibility to reinvent what he calls a "new race of men."[3]

It is possible to identify three dimensions of this universalism operative in James's argument, each of which I develop in some detail:

1. The Haitian Revolution enacted the localized destruction, on one Caribbean island, of what was by the 1790s a global, universalizing capitalism that strove to reduce all populations it encountered to dependency on the market via the expropriation of their means of production. Slave-based plantation labor such as what James describes in all its savage violence—seizing the African from a traditional social existence to be cast into the Caribbean crucible of ultra-violence and brute labor—was in this view among the primary forms of what Marx famously called the "primitive accumulation" of surplus capital that led to the Industrial Revolution in the next century.[4]

2. The Haitian Revolution is a singular—and singularly important—moment in the universal history of mass revolutions that James wrote in 1938, culminating in the nearly simultaneous publication of three volumes: *The Black Jacobins*, *World Revolution 1917–1938*, and *A History of Pan-African Revolt*. To say that this history is universal is not to claim that it forms a closed or linear totality; instead, James marks out a series of explosive flashes traversing time and space, the blaze of mass uprising hurtling against the violence of capital structured in dominance at sites around the world. He focuses our attention on four moments in particular: France from 1792 to 1794, Saint-Domingue from 1791 to 1804, the Russian Revolution of 1917, and the coming African and Caribbean anticolonial revolutions he foresees in 1938. This history of mass revolution

bears features and tendencies that James repeatedly describes in universal terms independent of their local, situated iterations in any specific case or instance.

3. James argues emphatically that mass revolutions require the focalization and direction of a leader or leaders of genius; his two historical examples are Lenin and Louverture. He describes these leaders in striking, unforgettable terms as figures of global, radical, revolutionary enlightenment. The fundamental and universal form of the successful revolutionary struggles he identifies is thus that of a coalition between the revolutionary masses and sections of the middle classes, but in particular with a radical intellectual leader who successfully articulates and represents the interests of the masses, the terms of their struggle, and the decisions and choices to be made at every turn against the forces of counter-revolution.

Savage Capital and Mass Revolution

Though James spends relatively little time describing the universalist nature of Atlantic capital in the eighteenth century, it is quite clear that he understands plantation production in Saint-Domingue as a local, essential node in an international phenomenon. He describes the enormous profitability of the island from a global perspective: "Never for centuries had the western world known such economic progress."[5] The few lines he devotes to situating the island within an already global economy are nonetheless essential in drawing the horizon for his analysis. If the revolution itself was a phenomenon of universal import, he seems to say, this universality was proceeded by another: that of the spread of primitive capitalism itself, in its expansion across the globe since the Renaissance, resulting in, for example, the annihilation of the Caribbean Amerindian population and their replacement by the immense profitability of slave labor. "On no portion of the globe," he writes, "did its surface in proportion to its dimensions yield so much wealth as the colony of San Domingo."[6]

James makes clear that he views the plantations of Saint-Domingue as the most advanced site of capitalist exploitation prior to 1789. "Working and living together in gangs of hundreds on the huge sugar factories which covered the North Plain, they were closer to a modern proletariat than any group of workers in existence at the time."[7] The specificity of this claim is less than convincing, at least if one takes "proletarian" to mean something more than simply the oppressed and exploited of the world. In fact, the word "proletarian" appears only once in *The Black Jacobins*, and if James says relatively little about it, it is undoubtedly because the focus of his argument is not on a universal history of proletarian but "mass" revolution, a word that appears countless times throughout the volume.

The reason is obvious: If the proletarian is, in classic Marxist usage, a "free" wage laborer forced onto the market by nonpossession of the means of production, James, like Mao in this same period, instead wishes and indeed must refocus hopes for world revolution on a much broader base—that of the colonized masses. If Saint-Domingue formed an essential point in the early development of European capitalism, its slave laborers worked not for a wage, driven into a labor market by the dispossession of the means of production, but were impelled simply by the constant, immediate threat of torture and death. The Haitian Revolution is thus key to demonstrating the viability of this vision of world mass revolution: it offers a successful historical example of the mass-based, anti-imperialist revolutions James hoped for throughout the colonized world.

The Subject of Revolution

James spends relatively little effort in the 1938 edition of *The Black Jacobins* describing the revolutionary masses of Saint-Domingue as anything more than an anonymous, unthinking mass, a neglect he later criticized, beginning with the long footnotes on the historiography of the French Revolution he added for the 1963 edition.[8] In appending this critique of what we might call his own "leader of genius" theory of revolution to the later edition (which he further extended in his 1971 lecture "How I Would Rewrite *The Black Jacobins*"), we must carefully attend to what might be lost even with the addition of a few long, convoluted footnotes. Although it is obvious that James's later self-critique seeks to accommodate *The Black Jacobins* to a model of "history from below," this is not necessarily to the benefit of the argument the book defends. We should not buy into James's own bad faith, his speculation of "what *Black Jacobins* might have been" (if it wasn't what it actually was). I believe it is possible to return to the powerful and original formula of world revolution he articulates in both *The Black Jacobins* and *World Revolution*, to discover elements not of a voluntaristic hagiography of the great leader but of a properly materialist *The Black Jacobins*, even including its seemingly outdated "great leader" theory of revolution. What we find clearly and powerfully demonstrated in the original 1938 volume is a "law" or formula of successful mass revolution: Insurgent Masses + Leader(s) of Genius + Force of the Idea (of equality) yields: World-Historical Revolution.

Might it be possible to understand James's "leader of genius" theory as anything more than a neo-Romantic, heroic, phallocratic individualism that would deservedly be swept away by works of "history from below" (such as Carolyn Fick's celebrated 1990 study *Making Haiti: The Saint-Domingue Revolution from Below*)? Who precisely are these ideal subjects of revolution James presents—Lenin and Louverture? How are they conceptualized by James as *subjects* of revolution? Do they express in concentrated form a universal human essence? Or are these two historical subjects, like all other bodies in a properly materialist reading of *The Black Jacobins*, no more than two singular compositions of forces whose power is expressed in the immediacy of their effects, rather than the interiority of their consciousness?

The answer is not straightforward. The primary contradiction structuring *The Black Jacobins* is surely one to be found in various forms throughout James's oeuvre: the rough admixture of a veritably Shakespearean, idealist hagiography of Louverture inspired by James's literary studies, alongside the radically materialist, Marxist analysis of the dynamics of mass revolution. Without discounting or ignoring the former, it is, I think, eminently possible to read the text from start to finish and to the letter as the purely materialist, deterministic construction of a historical conjuncture, that of the Haitian Revolution understood as a composition of heterogeneous apparatuses and bodies, each with their own powers and effects, rather than as the heroic struggle and conscious intentionality of subjects of freedom. This materialist *Black Jacobins* takes the form of a conjuncture composed of individuals and masses, also including the ideas that are expressed by those bodies, ideas without idealism, existing in pure immanence as the effects of their expression.

This materialist reading of *The Black Jacobins* recognizes not the interiority of conscious intentions (such as that of Toussaint to join the French in 1794) nor the sovereignty of free-floating, self-same ideas existing independently of their localized instantiation (such as the idea of equality), nor even the mere animality of the masses devoid of a revolutionary consciousness to be imputed by those who know. Rather than narrating the textual traces of the archive into a historical expression of one moment in the totality of Western modernity in its forward march to triumph, whether liberal or socialist, this materialist *Black Jacobins* articulates a conjuncture of forces and powers as the historical proof that any composition of apparatuses and bodies, no matter how debased and unequal—including the plantation, the ancien régime, or colonial Africa, India, or the Caribbean in 1938—is radically contingent, subject to decomposition and recomposition at any time, in any place. What James wishes to describe, through his historical investigations, are the universal laws governing the possibility of revolutionary decomposition and recomposition.

The conjuncture of bodies and forces assembled in *The Black Jacobins* includes the repressive apparatus of the plantation, which, decades before Foucault, James describes in the full force of its violent anonymity, creating the subjects of slave labor from captured Africans through the ultra-violence of terror and torture. It includes the temporal, even day-by-day composition, decomposition, and recomposition after 1791 of formerly enslaved bodies into a revolutionary mass of militant Jacobin citizen-soldiers, a mass that, James's history shows us, effectively resisted and eventually destroyed (on one island at least) the terrifying apparatus of plantation slavery. This composition of bodies and forces equal to their effects also includes the immanent, materialist movement, decomposition, and recomposition of ideas, ideas that exist only in the immediacy of their expression in any given time and place, the primary, determinate idea being that which James calls the idea of 1789, the idea of justice as equality.

The force of this idea of the radical Enlightenment entered into composition first with the French masses who overthrew Louis Capet and French feudalism itself and simultaneously traveled overseas, only to be rescored in Saint-Domingue as a potent force entering into this novel configuration James describes, as a power expressed by desiring bodies, bodies that desired to overthrow the plantation slavery apparatus, and who reconfigured the idea of universal equality into a force in the destruction of inequality. Finally, James's work in 1938 entails the recovery and recomposition of the fragments of global revolution, fragments scattered throughout the historical record to be registered not as progress but possibility (*The Black Jacobins*, *World Revolution*, and *A History of Negro Revolt*). These three texts, fragments of a universal history of mass revolution, describe in great detail two revolutionary "subjects of genius," Louverture and Lenin, subjects who remain, judging by the text itself, purely immanent bodies without interiority.

Virtually the entire text of *The Black Jacobins* consists of the description and interpretive analysis of situations, actions, and their effects. On close reading, even the famous passage on Louverture reading Raynal, for example, says literally nothing about Toussaint's psychological interiority but merely registers the repetition of an action: "Over and over, Toussaint read this passage: 'A courageous chief only is wanted. Where is he?'"[9] *The Black Jacobins* is in this sense composed of citations from Toussaint's letters, descriptions of battles and tactics, and, at every moment, James's original and incisive interpretations of the actions he describes. Even and especially the descriptions of Louverture's "decisions" can be read in this materialist fashion, as no more than the actions of bodies and their effects, without any imputed notion of psychological interiority: "Then and only then did Toussaint come to an unalterable decision from which he never wavered and for which he died. Complete liberty for all, to be attained and held by their own strength."[10] This decision is not the unfolding of an interiority but remains strictly equivalent to the change in nature of Louverture's actions from that day forward. Following what James unflinchingly calls the "political treachery" and "abominable betrayal" of the masses in which Toussaint participated with Biassou and Jean-François in 1792, we know of Toussaint's so-called decision to rally to the cause of antislavery and equality not through access to his interior thought process and intentions (which James never imagines or imputes novelistically) but via the sum of his actions, from speeches and letters to the organization of the plantation economy and the direction of military battles that James narrates.

Louverture and Lenin are the two proper names of bodies composed, James shows, with a singular, unequaled power to rearticulate and push forward the revolutionary mass movement. These bodies are, James never ceases to insist, part and parcel of the mass movement itself, simply its most concentrated and powerful points, until, that is, these bodies re- or decompose, separating from the masses, weakening in their effects, whether through isolation and fealty to the idea of France for Toussaint or through illness and precipitous death for Lenin. The human, for this materialist James, is not located in the romantic interiority of a consciousness, that of the Toussaint who "came in the end to believe in himself as the black Spartacus, foretold by Raynal," but in the transient configuration of powers and effects in a singular body—the Toussaint who repeatedly decomposed and recomposed his being. From elite house slave and then free black slave and property owner, Louverture became an obscure militant fighting in the name of the Spanish king for the restoration of the ancien régime, then, following the Jacobin abolition of slavery in 1794, in the years of Thermidor, the Directory, and the

Empire, the most powerful, exemplary, and unyielding Jacobin, the last one standing on the far periphery of the French empire, defending to his death the truth of the abolition of slavery as the most essential, core accomplishment of 1793–1794.

The contradiction between these Romantic and materialist understandings of Louverture is thus concentrated in James's notion of the decision. James locates the primary moment of transformation of the subject Louverture, from faithful house slave to revolutionary subject, in the moment of a choice.

> As the insurrection grew, worn out by the strain of defending the property, his master [Bayon de Libertas] and learning that Madame de Libertas' life was now in danger, *he decided* that the old life was over and a new one had begun. He told Madame de Libertas that the time had come for her to go to Le Cap. . . . He sent his own wife and the two children of the household into a safe spot in Spanish San Domingo. Then he slowly made his way to the camp of the revolted slaves.[11]

These pages show James at his most idealist and humanist: this is the Toussaint "who so deliberately decided to join the revolution," a leader whose actions "would lay the foundations of a Negro State that has lasted to this day." The situation in which Toussaint acted was not of his making (it was, James insists, one of "vast, impersonal forces"): "Men," he famously writes, "make history, and Toussaint made the history that he made because of the man he was."[12]

Before concluding too rapidly as to the irredeemably humanist idealism of such passages, let us pause to consider the tense of the final phrase: "the man that he *was*." What Louverture *was* he will no longer *be*. Toussaint's "nature" transformed repeatedly, to become, time and again, another being. House slave, slave owner, betrayer of the masses, and finally, the subject of the event of 1791, the Jacobin militant of transnational antislavery. The radiant prose of *The Black Jacobins* can be said to tell the story of the infinite contingency of human being, of its plasticity, the historical proof that the invention of a "new human species" is always at hand. It is the story of Louverture's repeated self-reinvention, of a decision that exists only in the immanent immediacy of its effects (he leaves the plantation and joins the revolution), a decision that alters a life course, a story of the struggle to hold and maintain the force of this new composition of bodies—of his own body as Jacobin militant, of that of the masses in their resistance to slavery, and of the ultimate weakening of this power into isolation and blinded refusal to recognize the liquidation of the revolution and draw the necessary conclusions for the maintenance of a slave-free social body in Saint-Domingue: independence. "What should Toussaint have done?," James asks. "He should have declared [in 1802] that a powerful expedition could have no other aim than the restoration of slavery, summoned the population to resist, declared independence, confiscated the property of all who refused to accept and distributed it among his supporters."[13] Only Dessalines, in Louverture's absence, was willing to take such steps.

If Louverture names the site of a series of decisions taken by a former house slave in 1793 (to join the revolt) and 1794 (to join the Jacobin struggle for abolition and justice as equality), James makes clear that this "decision," apparently so sovereign, is the effect of a determinate cause. Louverture the world-historical figure on the order of Thomas Jefferson or Napoleon, James tells us in one of the key passages in the book, was a heroic figure, but one "made" by the revolution of 1789.

> What spirit was it that moved him? Ideas do not fall from heaven. The great revolution had propelled him out of his humble joys and obscure destiny, and the trumpets of its heroic period rang ever in his ears. In him, born a slave and the leader of slaves, the concrete realization of liberty, equality and fraternity was the womb of ideas and the springs of power, which overflowed their narrow environment and embraced the whole of the world. But for the revolution, this extraordinary man and his band of gifted associates would have lived their lives as slaves, serving the commonplace creatures who owned them, standing barefooted and in rags to watch inflated little governors and mediocre officials from Europe pass by, as many a talented African stand in Africa today.[14]

For James, two figures in world history stand out incontestably as great leaders of revolution: Toussaint and Lenin. He makes the comparison explicit in his analysis of Louverture's "mistakes" and the alternate actions he might have taken to ensure the success of the revolution in Saint-Domingue: "Lenin and the Bolsheviks after the October Revolution faced much the same problem as Toussaint [of ensuring the success of the revolution they had begun]." If Lenin, with his superior education, knowledge of Marxism, and revolutionary experience, comes out the superior figure in this analysis, they are remarkably similar figures in this reading. "We can measure Toussaint's gigantic intellect by the fact that, untrained as he was, he attempted to do the same [as the Bolsheviks in their struggle for power]."[15]

Louverture was uniquely prepared for the events of the Saint-Domingue revolution. He had an immense theoretical training, learning the revolutionary military tactics of his own future enemies as a general in the French revolutionary army, combining these with local practices of guerrilla warfare. He read Raynal for a scientific understanding of global colonialism, and above all, his entire life was an investigation (in the Maoist sense of the word) into the reality and functioning of the plantation system and slavery itself, from every position: slave, slave owner, antislavery revolutionary. This investigation allowed him to grasp the entirety of this global system and understand what was necessary to achieve its destruction beyond the futility of mere revolt. This clear understanding of the forces supporting slavery, rather than leading to defeatism or resignation, made him sharp and unyielding, always adjusting and calculating, moving a step forward or retreating to gather forces and strength.

While James's analysis of Toussaint as a creation of the Enlightenment of Raynal and Diderot and its radical actualization in the Jacobinism of the French Revolution are largely familiar, it is worth comparing these with his analysis of the figure of Lenin in one of the key passages in *World Revolution*. For James, Lenin was unquestionably a towering intellectual figure, a genius of enlightenment and insight standing even above Marx thanks to his mastery of theory and practice. James's description is worth citing at length:

> Lenin, first and foremost, knew political economy as few professors in a university did. He was absolute master of political theory and practice. He knew the international working-class movement of the great countries of Europe, not only their history theoretically interpreted by historical materialism, but from years of personal experience in Britain, France, Germany, and Switzerland. He spoke almost faultless German and wrote the language like a second tongue. He was at home in French and English and could read other European languages with ease. Intellectual honesty was with him a fanatical passion, and to his basic conception of allying the highest results of theoretical and practical knowledge in the party to the instinctive movements of millions, honesty before the party and before the masses was for him essential.[16]

James's Lenin, like Toussaint, is first and foremost a great European intellectual, a product of the radical Enlightenment tradition that unites philosophical and theoretical knowledge with an uncompromising will to social justice and equality.[17] As he does in *The Black Jacobins*, James sets the intelligence and insight of the leader of genius in stark contrast to the merely "instinctive movements" of the masses. The effect of this unequaled intellectual and charismatic strength of the leader of genius, in the logic of James's unqualified, eulogistic celebration, is to focus, sustain, and successfully carry forward the struggle of the masses to a degree impossible without such a leader:

> The range and honesty of his intellect, [James continues,] his power of will, the singular selflessness and devotion of his personal character, added to a great knowledge and understanding of men, enabled him to use all types of intellect and character in a way that helped lift the Bolshevik party between 1917 and 1923 to the full height of the stupendous role it was called upon to fulfill. No body of men ever did so much, and how small most of them really were we can realize only by looking at what they became the moment their master left them. . . . No man could ever fill his place.[18]

Unlike the struggle in Saint-Domingue, where in James's analysis Toussaint's hesitancy to declare independence and wage a full struggle against the French actually came to hinder the cause of antislavery, Lenin, in James's anti-Stalinist analysis, carried forward the revolutionary struggle without compromise, struck down only by his incapacitation—but never by lack of correct understanding of the situation, clarity, or resolve—after 1922.

1789: A Headless Revolution?

While James's polemical, uncritical presentation of Lenin stands in stark contrast to his readiness to critique Louverture's failure to sustain the mass revolution of Saint-Domingue, his assertion of the essential role of the leader of genius in the two revolutions (which the former, in this view, fulfilled to perfection and the latter neglected or abandoned) is identical. It is all the more curious to consider, in this light, James's analysis of the French Revolution in both *The Black Jacobins* and *World Revolution*, as it is undoubtedly the weakest link in his general theory of mass revolution. Although there are a number of important facts about the Haitian Revolution that James could not have known but which have been discovered by historians since 1938, few of these actually bear any importance for his analysis. Take for instance the fact that we now know Louverture was not only the house slave of Bayon de Libertas but as of 1776 was a free black who owned a coffee plantation and some dozen slaves.[19] This discovery, although certainly marking a fundamental shift in the understanding of Louverture's life, actually reinforces rather than weakening James's celebration of the historical creation of this "new race of men," former slaves and even enslavers of their fellow blacks who became the radical defenders of the Jacobin struggle for universal human equality. Louverture literally reinvented himself after 1791, from Toussaint Bréda, house slave and then free black property and slave holder to Toussaint Louverture, black Jacobin defender of the rights of man in Saint-Domingue.

The equation of the successful revolution James proposes in his 1938 works is that of mass struggle against an exploiting class, in coalition with a leadership of genius, animated by the idea of equality. In his interpretation of the French Revolution, however, the second element of this combination is notably lacking. Given James's own conclusion based on his analysis of the historical cases of the Haitian and Russian Revolutions that a great leader of the radical intelligentsia is necessary for the success of the mass revolution, one wonders how the French Revolution managed to overthrow the ancien régime and feudalism. Does it follow an alternative logic? Is it simply an exception to the process James identifies? His presentation of the paradigmatic French case, in both *The Black Jacobins* and *World Revolution*, is of a headless revolution, of anonymous French masses pitted against an undifferentiated bourgeoisie, devoid of any notable leadership that would focus and sustain the struggle for revolutionary justice.

Whatever we may make of James's great leader theory, his presentation of the French case, even and already in the 1938 edition, appears anomalous. If his analysis is not universal, but merely holds in the Haitian and Russian cases, he would then have failed to account for the exceptionality of the French case, as well as to have offered a universal model of successful mass revolution. On the other hand, and more simply, one might consider the French Revolution in light of James's logic of mass revolution to reveal a weakness not so much of the equation itself (masses + leader + idea) but of his truncated analysis of the case of 1792. In fact, over a century of leftist interpretations of the French Revolution (from, say, Buonorotti to Mathiez) understood this event in terms quite close to James's: the overthrow of French feudalism was successful because it enacted a tenuous coalition between (1) the militancy of the sans-culottes, (2) the leadership of the Mountain and the "Incorruptible" Robespierre, and (3) the idea of the rights of man. Is not Robespierre precisely this figure of genius structurally equivalent to Louverture and Lenin, the unyielding subject of the rights of man who articulated the goals of the revolution and successfully expressed the desires of the masses for justice?

This revolutionary who for decades after 1789 stood as the embodiment of its egalitarian radicality is reduced in James's reading to the role of a "sinister dictator," a reductive caricature more typical of the Thermidorian reaction and neoliberal historicism.[20] James arrives at this impoverished presentation, I believe, by accepting uncritically the liberal theory of a bourgeois-capitalist French Revolution that Marx and subsequently Marxists had taken on uncritically until the 1970s.[21] Because 1789 did not constitute a crucial problem for Marx, he never closely analyzed the history of the French Revolution—as he did that of the political economy capitalism—to determine whether the bourgeoisie of 1789 was in any sense of the word capitalist. Marx simply and explicitly adopted the idea of a bourgeois-capitalist revolution from Mignet, Guizot, and Thierry, emphasizing in contrast only the violence of class antagonism and economic injustice denied by the idyllic liberal vision. The year 1789, in this view, had as a bourgeois-capitalist revolution prepared the stage for the coming proletarian revolutions against industrial capitalism in Marx's own time. This interpretation of 1789 as bourgeois-capitalist was refined and defended by the Marxist tradition from Jaurès through Lefebvre (the very historian James cites with such praise in his appended footnotes to the 1963 edition) and Albert Soboul, before it was abandoned in the face of its historical untenability in the 1970s.[22]

The essence of the analytical problem is a basic lack of clarity over the nature of the French bourgeoisie.[23] James, like virtually all Marxist historians until the 1970s, simply adopts without question the theory of a bourgeois revolution. At times in *The Black Jacobins*, James equates the French "bourgeois" with *capitalists* ("the political representatives of the bourgeoisie were sober men of business"), while at others, he more correctly identifies the revolutionary leaders of 1789 as being typified by lawyers like Barnave: "Barnave is one of the great figures of the French Revolution. He was bourgeois to the bone, a lawyer with a clear, cold intellect."[24] Robespierre himself was no capitalist but a brilliant young lawyer from Arras. While many of the leading figures of 1789 certainly self-identified as bourgeois, the term emphatically did not imply that they were capitalists, that is, owning the means of production and employing wage labor to extract surplus profits from production under the systemic demands of the process Marx called "the valorization of value." Of the 610 representatives of the Third Estate present at Versailles in 1789, only 10 made their living by industrial production, while fully 500 were lawyers.[25] The word "bourgeois," which was of course applied to these members of a middle class who most often labored for others, in 1789 referred not to capitalists, as the liberal and Marxist traditions would have it, but to a non-noble, professional middle class.[26]

As noted already, James draws on the scholarship of Lefebvre in his appended footnotes to the 1963 edition to invoke the "history from below" that *The Black Jacobins* might have been, that is, the story of a mass revolution given direction and orientation by an anonymous leadership arising from within that mass itself rather than from a coalition with individuals of genius from a separate, radical intellectual class (as were James's Louverture and Lenin, and Robespierre in the French case). This mass-based reading of the French Revolution was already present, however, in the 1938 edition's lack of clarity over the nature of a "bourgeois" revolution, in which an undifferentiated bourgeoisie stands opposed to the aristocracy. This picture is reproduced in even more schematic and reductive form in the opening pages of *World Revolution*. There, James characterizes 1789 as having fully and without qualification accomplished "the emergence of fully-fledged Capitalist society out of the bankruptcy of the feudal regime in France."[27] In these pages, he flatly describes an undifferentiated confrontation between two classes: a "new class, the French bourgeoisie, . . . whose wealth, created in trade and industry, was already greater than that of the aristocracy," pitted in violent struggle against the ancien régime, late-feudal "aristocracy."[28]

Obviously it would be absurd to take James to task in light of research undertaken since 1938. Moreover, one could argue that as for Marx, the exact social nature of the French Revolution is irrelevant to James's analysis of events in Saint-Domingue; he can simply assume without question, as did all Marxist historians of the period, that 1789 had been a "bourgeois revolution."[29] As this liberal interpretation of modern progress readily suited Marx, whose interest was the structure of capitalism and not its genesis, it is enough for James to show that the events in France created the conditions for the successful revolution of 1804—he has no need or even interest in questioning the doxa of a bourgeois revolution, above all because it underscores the modernity of the related revolution in Saint-Domingue.

The importance of this mischaracterization of the French Revolution for our understanding of *The Black Jacobins* is instead that unlike the vast majority of facts surrounding Saint-Domingue recovered from the archives since 1938, James's denial of the leadership role of the radical intellectual class of figures such as St. Just, Petion, Lameth, and Robespierre constitutes a symptomatic contradiction in the logic of *The Black Jacobins* itself: symptomatic insofar as it would reveal James's own growing unease with the great leader theory and his desire, manifest mainly in the notes on Lefebvre, to undermine his own universalist theory of revolution with a hypothetical history of "the San Domingo Revolution from Below."[30] Already in the 1938 edition, with its reduction of Robespierre to the role of "sinister dictator," and even more so with the addition of footnotes on Lefebvre in 1963, *The Black Jacobins* possesses not one but two logics of universal mass revolution. The first, the one James openly analyzes and endorses, is that a leader of genius is necessary to focus the anonymous and even unthinking passion of the masses, or more simply, a Leninist vanguard theory that James finds operative, though certainly not identically so, in the Haitian and Russian Revolutions. At the same time, analysis of the French Revolution in *The Black Jacobins* follows an entirely different logic, untheorized in the 1938 edition, then supported by the citations from Lefebvre in 1963 ("It is therefore," James cites Lefebvre, "in the popular mentality [and not the actions of a leader such as Robespierre] . . . that we must seek the explanation of what took place").[31] Rather than the vanguardism that is one of the principal features of *The Black Jacobins'* explicit argument, the French Revolution seems to have proceeded as a leftist, spontaneous uprising, one in which popular leaders freely arose like mushrooms in the forest as the masses heroically overthrew feudalism. This reading, which James affirmed in retrospect as proper for the Haitian Revolution as well, enacts the gesture of theoretical simplification of such leftist thought: the reduction of social conflict to the binary opposition of a shapeless mass and an oppressive state apparatus, a conflict and struggle devoid of mediating resources (leaders, parties, ideas) that would modulate and focus this conflict.[32] In 1938, James knew better; in place of this theory of leftist spontaneity, the first edition of *The Black Jacobins* offers a masterful analysis of the political struggles in Saint-Domingue (if not those in France) in all their enormous complexity.

The problem with James's leftist reading is not simply the total contradiction between these two logics but that his initial coalition theory, and not that of an anonymous, reductive, and spontaneous leftism, appears to be the correct one, judging from the historical record. Certainly, we may legitimately critique the neo-Romantic and phallocratic aspects of James's overwhelming focus on a single, male leader who carried on his shoulders the burden of the struggle. James himself was an early critic of the party form of organization, and this critique in no way weakens his original analysis of the Haitian Revolution, where there was no vanguard party organization. We may wish to enlarge the scope of our focus to encompass a range of various figures of leadership, including Louverture, Dessalines, Sans Souci, Hyacinthe, Moïse, and others who led the struggle against the French in Saint-Domingue.

That said, James goes to enormous lengths in *The Black Jacobins* and *World Revolution* to show that Louverture and Lenin were in fact exceptional figures in the revolutionary alliances they formed. Although he may devote less attention to them, he certainly does not ignore the roles played by those he sees as secondary leaders, such as Moïse and Dessalines or Trotsky. The historical record of successful mass revolutions since 1789 shows, however, that only by forming alliances with radical elements of the middle classes and elites has radical reform or revolution been achieved.[33] Again and again, the exploited have been defeated when standing alone against their exploiters, and the theory of successful, spontaneous leftist revolution without coalitions appears unsupported by any actual historical instance.[34]

James himself places particular emphasis on this fact in *A History of Pan-African Revolt*. When slaves throughout the Americas revolted in isolation, no matter how bravely they fought, they inevitably met defeat. "That is a theme," James writes, "on which the variations were played in state after state in America as in island after island in the West Indies. The slaves gained nothing by these revolts. No attempt is made to treat them more kindly. Instead revolts are savagely repressed and the severity of slave legislation increased."[35] One of the indispensable factors in the success of the revolution in Saint-Domingue and the American Civil War is this alliance between former slaves, willing to fight to the death to avoid returning to slavery, and a shifting and complex, yet real and substantial, alliance with various radical sectors of the nonslave population.

To paraphrase *The Black Jacobins* itself, what should James have done? Quite simply, he should have shown that the basic, universal logic of successful mass revolution is identical in the French, Haitian, and Russian cases alike. James had available in 1938 ample historical material to build a case every bit as strong for the French Revolution as an alliance between the masses and a radical left intellectual leadership as for the Haitian and Russian cases. In the French case, as in the other two, a revolutionary sans-culottes mass entered into alliance with elements of a radical intellectual middle and elite class (the Jacobins of 1792–1794), and moreover, in each case one exceptional figure in particular (Robespierre in France) focalized and articulated that struggle with unparalleled clarity and effectiveness.

Rather than the leftist logic of Lefebvre, James should have marshaled the decades of work on Robespierre's decisive contribution to the French Revolution undertaken prior to 1938 by the holder of the Sorbonne Chair in French Revolutionary Studies, Albert Mathiez (whom James mentions in his 1963 annotated bibliography of sources).[36] Mathiez destroyed the myth of a bloodthirsty, dictatorial Robespierre, drawing on a lifetime of research to show that the latter was in fact the voice of the oppressed and most ardent, eloquent, and steadfast defender of the ideals of popular sovereignty and justice as equality from 1789 to 1794.[37] Such a reading of the French Revolution would have resulted in James writing a truly universal history of successful mass revolution, a history supported by the concrete analysis of its three most essential cases through 1938: 1789, 1804, and 1917.

Universal History

C. L. R. James was not an academic historian but a Marxist revolutionary, in 1938 perhaps the most prominent Anglophone Trotskyist critic of Stalinism and a precocious militant for the destruction of global colonialism. *The Black Jacobins*, correspondingly, is not a work of academic historiography, seeking to locate the events in Saint-Domingue within the teleological continuum of the progress of modernity, where it would safely take its place between the fall of Louis XVI and the rise of the Napoleonic empire, as a peripheral, exotic outcropping of the Jacobin *dérapage*. The book instead seizes the Haitian Revolution from the oblivion of this liberal-modern continuum (in which it had no place or importance in any case) to name it as the paradigmatic moment in a universal history of mass (and not merely proletarian) revolution.

The Black Jacobins was emphatically not a defense of the power of cultural resistance to capital, a thesis familiar in many writings of postcolonial theory from Édouard Glissant's concept of the resistant "opacity" of local culture to Dipesh Chakrabarty's theory of local histories and cultural practices that resist and disrupt the globalization of capital.[38] The success of the Haitian Revolution, James implicitly argues, had nothing to do with the African cultural remnants of the slaves, nor with vodou or Kreyol, or any other local feature of the culture of Saint-Domingue. Virtually the only evocations of local culture in the book are the brief mention of Boukman the vodou priest's (failed) revolt and a brief allusion to Toussaint's banning of "voodoo."[39] James's history, I wish to argue in conclusion, is of another school and time than today's postcolonial celebrations of local cultural politics and their inherent resistance to capital: not so much *post*colonial (though it certainly looks forward in 1938 as in 1963 to a time after decolonization) as it is *anti*colonial. The singularities of local culture, for James, play no appreciable role in this process, and rightly so, for if mass revolution is truly a universal potentiality, the particularities of this or that human culture are simply irrelevant. In James's analysis, it is not intransigent cultural difference that disrupts the globalization of capitalism and colonial imperialism, as a certain postcolonial theory would have it, but revolutionary mass resistance latent "in all populations when deeply stirred and given a clear perspective by a strong and trusted leadership."[40]

> At the same time as the French, the half-savage slaves of San Domingo were showing themselves subject to the same historical laws as the advanced workers of revolutionary Paris; and over a century later the Russian masses were to prove once more that this innate power will display itself in all populations when deeply stirred and given a clear perspective by a strong and trusted leadership.[41]

These "universal laws" are those of a history of a very particular sort. James is not attempting to convince academic or armchair historians of the existence of universal laws that hold in every time and place across human history. He is concerned with only one aspect of historical development: the possibility of the revolutionary destruction of global, imperial capitalism. The universality he envisions is of a very particular sort, concerned only with the historical nature of successful mass revolution, but as a universal human possibility proven by the three historical cases he considers. This is history as fragment rather than totality, as seemingly impossible events rather than the implacable movement of absolute spirit, the exposition of a handful of isolated eruptions arising against the monotonous continuity of exploitation and injustice. This is a universality of human potentiality. If in these three cases, humans, no matter how violated and debased, have successfully risen up to overthrow their oppressors and, in the process, reinvented themselves to the core of their very being, then, James tells us, this can and will happen again, as did in fact occur—in China, Cuba, Algeria, the Belgian Congo, and Vietnam.

"The Revolution Had Created a New Race of Men"

To escape the exhausted impasse of leftism versus Leninism, a contradiction internal to both editions of *The Black Jacobins*, we need only recognize three heterogeneous historical structures that come together in singular fashion in

1791–1804: (1) a theory of the structure, that of a savage, slave-based capitalism functioning on the plantations of Saint-Domingue; which preexists (2) the initial, organized, and successful mass revolt, the aims of which were negative: to burn down the plantations and end slave-labor; along with (3) a theory of the subject, of the "new man" and "new race" that came into being in the years in which this initial revolt becomes a true revolution.

James's theory of the revolutionary subject is by no means limited to the story of a single individual: "Toussaint was no phenomenon, no Negro freak. The same forces which molded his genius had helped to create his black and Mulatto generals and officials."[42] These various subjects did not preexist the uprising of September 29, 1791, but came into being in the ensuing years as they asserted their commitment to defend and articulate what had been the inchoate and merely negative goals of that night, as they became "black Jacobins." James's subject is not a heroic individual but those singular groupings or bodies that composed the revolution, aggregates ranging in number from the half-million-strong mass of former slaves to the handful of revolutionary black Jacobin leaders including Dessalines, Christophe, Moïse, Belair, and Maurepas, to the absolutely singular subject James identifies in Louverture.[43] These subjects, literally inexistent prior to 1791, struggled together to produce in the present the effective conditions of a postabolition world unimagined in their time by holding tenaciously, at the risk of their lives, to this single point of dispute: would Saint-Domingue be a world with or without slavery after 1791?

The Black Jacobins is the political analysis of the multiple subjects of the uprising of 1791 in Saint-Domingue, in their various orientations to that initial event: those who affirmed the truth of general equality as universal emancipation; others who continued to affirm in contrast the universal rights of property, including the possession of other humans as absolute, dehumanized labor power; others still who looked back to reaffirm the structural inequality of the monarchy. It is the story of the shifting allegiances, betrayals, decisions, and mistakes of the various elites and classes in conflict, and, in James's leftist analysis, the always sure sense of the masses to hold fast to their own interests.

James concludes of these singular black Jacobin subjects,

All the French blacks [in Saint-Domingue], from the laborers at Port-de-Paix demanding equality, to the officers in the army, were filled with an immense pride at being citizens of the French Republic "one and indivisible" that had brought liberty and equality into the world . . . Five years of revolution had wrought these astonishing changes. . . . The population had been transformed.[44]

The story of the Haitian Revolution is for James the proof of an absolute, universal human contingency. The change he identifies can truly be called ontological, extending to the very being or nature of these revolutionaries, "a new race of men," they were a "people created by the revolution."[45] This infinite, unpredictable contingency is the promise *The Black Jacobins* continues to offer its readers in these postcolonial times of resignation, depoliticization, and global inequality.

Notes

1. C. L. R. James, *The Black Jacobins: Toussaint L'Ouverture and the San Domingo Revolution* (New York: Vintage, 1963), 214.

2. James, *The Black Jacobins*, 356.

3. James, *The Black Jacobins*, 242.

4. "The capital-relation presupposes a complete separation between the workers and the ownership of the conditions for the realization of their labor. . . . These newly-freed men [wage-laborers] became sellers of themselves only after they had been robbed of all their own means of production, and all the guarantees of existence afforded by the old feudal arrangements. And this history, the history of expropriation, is written in the annals of mankind in letters of blood and fire." Karl Marx, *Capital*, vol. 1 (Harmondsworth: Penguin Books, 1976), 874–75.

5. James, *The Black Jacobins*, 45.

6. James, *The Black Jacobins*, 46.

7. James, *The Black Jacobins*, 86.

8. In the long footnotes added to pages 276 and 338, James marshals Georges Lefebvre's analysis (James cites the mimeographed Sorbonne lectures of Lefebvre rather than his classic 1951 history of the revolution or other published works) to argue against overemphasizing the role of leaders such as Louverture or Robespierre: "It is wrong to attach too much importance," writes Lefebvre, "to any opinion that the Girondins or Robespierre might have on what needed to be done. . . . We must pay more attention to the obscure leaders and the people who listened to them." Cited in James, *The Black Jacobins*, 338. I analyze James's shifting analysis of the militant "rationality" of the Saint-Domingue masses in section two of my book *Caribbean Critique* (Liverpool: Liverpool University Press, 2013).

9. James, *The Black Jacobins*, 25.

10. James, *The Black Jacobins*, 107.

11. James, *The Black Jacobins*, 90; emphasis added.

12. James, *The Black Jacobins*, 90–91.

13. James, *The Black Jacobins*, 282, 284.

14. James, *The Black Jacobins*, 265.

15. James, *The Black Jacobins*, 282–83.

16. C. L. R. James, *World Revolution, 1917–36: The Rise and Fall of the Communist International* (Atlantic Highlands, NJ: Humanities Press, 1994), 142.

17. Anthony Bogues sees James's Lenin in contrast "as a personality deeply rooted in the intellectual tradition of Russian society." See Anthony Bogues, *Caliban's Freedom: The Early Political Thought of C.L.R. James* (Chicago: Pluto Press, 1997), 35.

18. James, *World Revolution*, 142.

19. Jacques de Cauna, *Toussaint Louverture et l'indépendance d'Haïti* (Paris: Karthala Cauna, 2004).

20. James, *The Black Jacobins*, 177. Unlike Louverture, Robespierre never actually possessed "dictatorial" powers other than those of his own rhetoric, and he stood even during the Terror only on the elected and revocable Committee for Public Safety, while all legislation continued to be passed by the National Assembly (Mazauric). I argue for the centrality of Robespierre in the struggle for justice as equality in the 1790s and beyond in the first chapter of *Caribbean Critique*.

21. This was the theory of a "bourgeois" revolution invented by François Mignet, Augustin Thierry, Henri de Saint-Simon, and François Guizot in the 1830s and 1840s. This theory took the revolutionary bourgeoisie to constitute the legitimate representative of the French nation, founding the tradition of representational, parliamentary democracy that would characterize the Third, Fourth, and Fifth French Republics, a representationalism called into question by events such as the Commune of 1871 and May 1968. See George C. Comninel, *Rethinking the French Revolution: Marxism and the Revisionist Challenge* (London: Verso, 1987); Lionel Gossman, "Augustin Thierry and Liberal Historiography," *History and Theory* 14, no. 4 (December 1976): 3–83.

22. See Comninel, *Rethinking the French Revolution*.

23. For a recent discussion of this problem in relation to postcolonial theory, see Vivek Chibber, *Postcolonial Theory and the Specter of Capital* (London: Verso, 2013), 70.

24. James, *The Black Jacobins*, 71.

25. See William H. Sewall Jr., *A Rhetoric of Bourgeois Revolution: The Abbé Sieyès and What Is the Third Estate?* (Durham, NC: Duke University Press, 1994).

26. See Albert Soboul, *The French Revolution 1787–1799* (London: NLB, 1974), 44–46. Comninel concludes: "The [French] bourgeoisie [of 1789] certainly was not a capitalist class. Lawyers and owners of non-noble state offices—notaries, bailiffs, lower-ranking magistrates, etc.—along with far less numerous private professionals, together formed the largest group within the bourgeoisie. They may have been as much as 60 percent of the whole. . . . The next largest group, at about one-third of the total, lived off the income from their property. Of the remainder who were engaged in commerce or industry at all, the overwhelming majority were merchants. . . . There simply were no capitalist relations—no appropriation of *surplus-value*, as opposed to mere commercial

profit making—that can be attributed to the [French] bourgeoisie." See Comninel, *Rethinking the French Revolution*, 180.

27. James, *World Revolution*, 22.

28. James, *World Revolution*, 24.

29. Of course, Marx's penetrating critique of the liberal celebration of 1789 and the rights of man—that it only "freed" the oppressed, reduced to the status of a proletariat, to sell their labor power to a now-dominant capitalist class—entirely depends on this logic of a bourgeois-capitalist revolution.

30. James, *The Black Jacobins*, 276, 338.

31. James, *The Black Jacobins*, 338.

32. See Bruno Bosteels, "The Leftist Hypothesis: Communism in the Age of Terror," in *The Idea of Communism*, edited by Costas Douzinas and Slavoj Žižek (New York: Verso, 2010), 40–41.

33. Among the most compelling examples of this is surely the case of the Algerian Revolution, in which the coalition of a mass uprising with the National Liberation Front (FLN) and dissident French intellectuals sustained and focused the Algerian struggle, while the intellectual class in France ensured through the public knowledge of the French use of torture that the military remained unable to assert the full extent of its superiority. In alliance with the National Liberation Front and articulating with extraordinary rhetorical power the contradiction between French democratic ideals inherited from 1789 and the use of torture, French intellectuals such as Frantz Fanon, Henri Alleg, Francis Jeanson, and Jean-Paul Sartre played a key role in the defeat of France in this colonial revolution. A similar analysis can be applied to the U.S. defeat in Vietnam. See Gil Merom, *How Democracies Lose Small Wars: State, Society, and the Failures of France in Algeria, Israel in Lebanon, and the United States in Vietnam* (Cambridge: Cambridge University Press, 2003).

34. See Chibber, *Postcolonial Theory and the Specter of Capital*; Dietrich Rueschemeyer, Evelyne Huber Stephens, and John D. Stephens, *Capitalist Development and Democracy* (Chicago: University of Chicago Press, 1992).

35. C. L. R. James, *A History of Pan-African Revolt* (Oakland, CA: PM Press, 2012), 52. James goes on to note the corresponding importance of a 1795 revolt in Louisiana where, for the first time, "there were whites in alliance with the Negroes from the very beginning."

36. Oddly, in the 1938 edition, James tells readers that "a good general volume on the French Revolution is that by Mathiez which ends with the fall of Robespierre." C. L. R. James, *The Black Jacobins: Toussaint Louverture and the San Domingo Revolution* (London: Secker and Warburg, 1938), 319. This early reading of Mathiez does not seem to have affected James's analysis of Robespierre, which is identical to what we find in the 1963 edition: "Robespierre and the Mountain gave France a strong [revolutionary] government" in 1793. Though "he was not a Communist" (a strange anachronism, given that the words *communist* and *communism* in their modern sense were not invented until 1797 by Rétif de la Bretonne), James judges the period of the Terror, "Paris between

March 1793 and July 1794 . . . one of the supreme epochs in political history." James, *The Black Jacobins* (1938), 111. James's Robespierre is seemingly identical to his portrayal of Toussaint: each a world-historical figure of revolutionary politics and, at the end, a "dictator" who "was now lagging behind his own masses." James, *The Black Jacobins* (1938), 144. "It was," James writes of Toussaint's period in power, "a dictatorship, but not for base personal ends or the narrow interests of one class oppressing another." James, *The Black Jacobins*, 247. Despite these nearly identical profiles, James's Toussaint is judged to possess "that electrifying effect characteristic of great men of action," whereas Robespierre, in both editions, is melodramatically and without evidence caricatured as a "sinister dictator." James, *The Black Jacobins* (1938), 144.

37. Albert Mathiez, *The French Revolution* (New York: Knopf, 1928).

38. Édouard Glissant, *Le Discours antillais* (Paris: Seuil, 1981), 11; Dipesh Chakrabarty, *Provincializing Europe* (Princeton, NJ: Princeton University Press, 2000).

39. James, *The Black Jacobins*, 309. James's celebration of various forms of cultural resistance of the colonized all occur instead in the 1963 appendix to *Black Jacobins*, "From Toussaint Louverture to Fidel Castro," rather than in the text itself (including in its second edition).

40. This conceit of cultural difference as resistant and even disruptive to the globalization of capitalism takes its most fully articulated form in Chakrabarty's *Provincializing Europe*. The particularities of local cultures are an entirely independent variable to capitalism's spread, however, as Vivek Chibber has argued in a powerful critique of the subaltern studies movement. If capital can successfully manipulate local cultural differences to increase the dependency of labor to market demands, it will do so. If it cannot, it will seek to undermine those cultural differences. James's theory of universal mass revolution, most powerfully articulated in *The Black Jacobins*, and not that of any postcolonial difference, enacts a true provincializing of Europe, making Paris a mere moment in a global process that has no center, liable to arise in any time or place across the planet.

41. James, *The Black Jacobins*, 243.

42. James, *The Black Jacobins*, 256.

43. James, *The Black Jacobins*, 256.

44. James, *The Black Jacobins*, 154, 356.

45. James, *The Black Jacobins*, 242, 244.

10

"We Are Slaves and Slaves Believe in Freedom":
The Problematizing of Revolutionary
Emancipationism in *The Black Jacobins*

CLAUDIUS FERGUS

One of the salient features in the invalidation of colonialism as a civilizing mission was the debunking of the long-standing, patriotic historiography of the abolition of Britain's Atlantic slave trade and its slave-labor system. To Seymour Drescher, the "emblematic work" that informed this antithesis was Eric Williams's *Capitalism and Slavery*.[1] No less emblematic, however, was C. L. R. James's *The Black Jacobins*, without which Williams could not have conceived *Capitalism and Slavery*.[2] Although Williams wished his work to remain "strictly an economic study,"[3] James purposefully wrote *The Black Jacobins* to inspire African nationalists to hasten the emancipation of Africa.[4] With the consummate skill of the experienced teacher, James coded this objective within his preface: to explain why and how a colony of terrified "slaves, trembling in hundreds before a single white man," dramatically transformed themselves "into a people able to defeat the most powerful European nations of their day."[5] He explicitly states the political significance of the work early in the first chapter when he infers that the Anansi intelligence of the enslaved Haitians that "frightened the colonists" was the same that "frightens the whites in Africa today."[6]

Jacob Carruthers emblematizes the Haitian revolution as the alpha of "intellectual warfare," too enigmatic for European historiography and thus conveniently buried in the "corners of history" for over a century.[7] This contrived amnesia was functional to the continuance of the myth of racial superiority in postslave colonies and the advancement of European imperialism in Africa. Published at the height of British militarism in Africa, William Fortescue's seminal acknowledgment of Britain's ill-fated Haitian campaign pragmatically avoided heroizing the "Black Jacobins."[8] Accordingly, up to the 1930s, the history of the colonial Caribbean remained irrefutably British and European.

More emphatically than any previous work, *The Black Jacobins* reconfigured the historiography of enslaved Africans as insensitive, unintelligent, and subservient chattels with a narrative showcasing only their humanity, military prowess, and commitment to revolutionary emancipation. James's 1934 play, *Toussaint Louverture*, tactically forewarned academia of a comprehensive subversion of the imperial orthodoxy of Quashie subservience and emancipation from above. One of the most eloquent affirmations of revolutionary emancipation in the revised play, *The Black Jacobins*, was Toussaint's response to a "Spanish General" shortly after the news of France's emancipation decree of 1794. The officer deceptively tried to convince Toussaint to betray the French republic and embrace the Spanish monarchy, because "Africans believe in a King." Dissecting frills from substance, Toussaint replied philosophically, "We are slaves and slaves believe in freedom."[9] Toussaint as chief protagonist of the revolution was reinscribed in the subtitle of *The Black Jacobins*. He remains James's chief mouthpiece for explicating freedom from an African and enslaved perspective, different from bourgeois moral philosophy. In one memorable exposition on the subject, Toussaint declared in a speech denouncing special agent General Hédouville's treachery in deposing Moïse, Toussaint's nephew: "Hédouville says that I am against liberty, that I want to surrender to the English, that I wish to make myself independent; who ought to love liberty more, Toussaint L'Ouverture, slave of Breda, or General Hédouville, former Marquis and Chevalier de Saint-Louis?"[10] These and similar dialogues in the play and the monograph attest to James's early mastery of Hegelian dialectics.

Notwithstanding his commitment to a new subaltern historiography, James demonstrated with scientific detachment that not all believers of freedom were potential martyrs: with equal fervor he detailed several examples of *nouveaux libres'* backsliding to embrace slavery, if only for survival; the most painful example was Toussaint's early involvement in a conspiracy to betray the revolution to save his own skin.[11] This chapter reexamines James's treatment of the enslaved as emancipators and the implication of his nearly absolute deracination of the revolution for the historiography of subaltern abolitionism.

The Pedagogical Framework of *The Black Jacobins*

The Black Jacobins is at once revisionist history, creative literature, political agitation, and a handbook of dialectical materialism. Its rich dialectical tapestry spans the complexity of enslavement in the colony. The burden of slavery did not fall equally on the enslaved population of Saint-Domingue; even the privileged few played some of the most critical leadership roles in the revolution, a phenomenon James continually explores in interpreting a core principle of dialectical materialism.

James was unquestionably an independent thinker, and the very title of the book was a daring challenge to conventional Marxist historiography. Throughout the narrative he deceptively flirts with racial and religious etiology but always methodically insulates himself from Marxist inquisitors who condemned these subjects as "distractions" to the serious application of historical materialism.[12] Not infrequently resorting to conjecture and poetics more suitable to literature than history, James remains faithful to his promise of presenting The Black Jacobins as the "history of a revolution" in which the chaotic entanglements of race, religion, political ideologies, and class were merely "the unfolding of the economic forces of the age."[13] Interestingly, Williams's mind-set was similarly wired to economic determinism in attempting to explain the genesis of the 1831–1832 "Baptist War" in Jamaica, arguably the most decisive moment in the dismantling of British colonial slavery. Applying classic Marxist dialectics, Williams concludes, "The Negroes had been stimulated to freedom by the development of the very wealth which their labour had created."[14] Thus, despite their seminal effects, both works reflect the limitations of classic Marxist methodology in interpreting the history of subaltern emancipationism.

The Jamesian Frame of Freedom

Historians are challenged to authenticate the Haitian Revolution as a manifestation of enslaved African consciousness independent of the French Revolution. James not only postulated that "the slaves had revolted because they wanted to be free";[15] he also iterated their intellectual independence, affirming: "One does not need education or encouragement to cherish a dream of freedom."[16] Contemporaries, however, blamed everyone else for the uprising in August 1791. If anything, James is also culpable of sending mixed signals about whether the leaders of the enslaved insurgents had formulated the right to freedom from their own revolutionary consciousness or whether it was the French Revolution that had sown the seeds of this ideal.

Boukman is James's primary evidence of an enslaved "proletarian" consciousness at the commencement of the revolution. The Black Jacobins accredits him the role of convincing the enslaved masses that their "primary identity" lay with other enslaved groups.[17] Without comparing Boukman with Toussaint, James nonetheless shows that Toussaint only experienced this revolutionary consciousness several months after Bois Caïman, when he made an about-face from sacrificing the revolution for self-preservation.[18]

Not surprisingly, the emphasis on Haitian revolutionaries' dependence on metropolitan French militarism and ideology dominates the historiography of the Haitian Revolution. In this regard, *The Black Jacobins* is sacred literature. Although unquestionably committed to showcasing black militarism and the individual heroism of Toussaint, James does not fall prey to political sentimentality. Of the three principal black Jacobins "to lead their brothers to freedom"— Jean-Jacques Dessalines, Henri Christophe, and Toussaint Louverture—only Toussaint had any "constructive ideas" of the rights of man before 1789; James had no doubt that his hero "did not make the revolution. It was the revolution that made Toussaint. And even that was not the whole truth."[19] James is adamant that Toussaint cannot be fully understood outside the context of French Enlightenment philosophy and Jacobinism; the Abbé Raynal planted the germ of freedom and revolutionary destiny in Toussaint: "Toussaint alone read his Raynal. 'A courageous chief only is wanted.' "[20]

We do not know enough about Boukman to make a final judgment on the source of his inspiration for revolutionary emancipation. James does not impute foreign influence, except that the political wrangling in the colony provoked by the metropolitan revolution provided an opportune moment for a successful strike against slavery. If the account of Boukman's transfer from Jamaica is correct, one must objectively take into account that island's long tradition in revolutionary struggle. The only insight James offers into Boukman's philosophy of revolution comes from his status as "Papaloi or High Priest" of Voodoo. Unlike classical Marxists, James recognizes that African cosmology, often expressed through song, dance, and sacred rituals, could not be the mere "sighs of the oppressed"; thus, he emphatically inscribes Voodoo as "the medium of the conspiracy,"[21] which underscores the ideology of Boukman's leadership as decidedly African and creole. Having completed his address to the war party at Bois Caïman, Boukman announced "that the loas (deities) had agreed to his plans."[22] If Toussaint did not make the revolution, Boukman certainly did: The *loas* did not instruct Boukman; rather, they ratified his plan, thus making him the ultimate master of the situation. James's acknowledgment that Boukman's plan of insurgency "was conceived on a massive scale"[23] evidences the enslaved's discovery of military advantage in their superior numbers as the crucial turning point to revolution in

Saint-Domingue.[24] Although Boukman was killed in the early phase of the uprising, he was succeeded by able leaders also schooled in African martial spiritualism.

Notwithstanding his privileging of metropolitan France, James was well aware of the slaves' independent commitment to liberty. Indeed, long before La Marseillaise and "Ça Ira," they had sung their "favourite" song, "Eh! Eh! Bomba." James must have been fascinated with the revolutionary encryption in the song: he began his 1967 play with it and reproduced it twice in *The Black Jacobins*, the second occasion as the epigraph to the chapter "The San Domingo Masses Begin." He acknowledges that the slaves collectively chanted "Eh! Eh! Bomba!" as "a dream of freedom" for "over two hundred years," the same "as the Jews in Babylon sang of Zion, and the Bantu today sing in secret the national anthem of Africa."[25] The song did not go unnoticed by whites, who recognized its subversive potential, but they were unequal to stamping it out. James's resurrection of this song contradicts his more emphatic assertion that the slaves were awakened by the slogans of the French Revolution to a consciousness of their revolutionary potential.

Not without some merit, James might be indicted with creating his own contradictions, even to the extent of espousing colonial prejudices he stridently debunks. To arrive at this simple conclusion, however, might be erroneous. Any serious critic of the work must be aware that James is continually engaging the reader didactically with dialectical materialism, because "in true dialectical fashion, we establish a category only to break it up. . . . You no longer have it fixed than you must at once crack it wide open."[26]

In *A History of Pan-African Revolt*, James explicitly relegates the Saint-Domingue revolutionaries and the African "arm" in the American Civil War to "unconscious but potent levers in two great propulsions forward of modern civilization."[27] The concept of levers implies that the enslaved were merely puppet-soldiers subject to the machination of more intelligent beings. James is not disparaging the military competence of the Haitian insurgents. He admits, "Many had fought well before and have fought well since." The credit for their success, however, was that "they had not only received inspiration from France" but that the course of the French Revolution had afforded them "time to organize themselves as soldiers."[28]

Typically, James immediately attempts self-redemption by astutely recognizing Jean François and Georges Biassou as "men born to command." Like many leaders of the revolution, Jean François, a maroon, had learned martial arts.[29] James might not have considered that many others were war veterans before their capture by slave traders. Recent scholarship has shown that tens of thousands of African soldiers were imported into Saint-Domingue between 1780 and 1791, fresh from wars in west and west-central Africa. Most of the millions of firearms imported into west Africa were absorbed into armies within the areas most ravaged by slave traders and thus were a known technology to combatants in the Saint-Domingue revolution.[30]

James's portrait of the slaves of Saint-Domingue as the most advanced in proletarian consciousness anywhere in the world[31] is in striking contradiction to their subordination to metropolitan proletarians. Yet he brilliantly balances the mutual effects of both revolutions: "The slaves by their insurrection had shown revolutionary France that they could fight and die for freedom; and the logical development of the revolution in France had brought to the front of the stage masses who, when they said abolition, meant it in theory and practice."[32] However, he gives us no insight into the position of the Parisian masses when the decision was made to reimpose slavery. The case for *sans-culottes* alliance demands that the reader knows. Without this enlightenment, James proceeds to underscore the liberalism of the sans-culottes: "The great gesture of the French working people towards the black slaves, against their own white ruling class, had helped to save their revolution from reactionary Europe."[33] He did not reckon with the majesty of revolutionary insurgency by the "black san culottes" in the eastern Caribbean, including the Fédon rebellion; the brigand wars in Guadeloupe, Dominica, and St. Lucia; and the Black Carib offensives in St. Vincent.[34]

Race-Class Dichotomy

One of the greatest challenges in writing a history of the Haitian Revolution is the pervasive intrusion of race, which James conceives as "the most irrational of all prejudices." In Caribbean plantation colonies, class was intricately interwoven with ethnicity and race. In prerevolutionary Haiti, the 128 ethnic categories, each with its own description, read "like a cross between a nightmare and a bad dream."[35] All slaves had African ancestry, but not all colonial Africans were enslaved. Enslaved or free, all persons with African blood were lesser mortals than whites, even to the *petits blancs* among whom were some of the most decrepit of humanity.[36] Not until James has sidestepped every racial confrontation does he explain why, despite its irrationality, race must remain a major consideration in colonial history: "The race question is subsidiary to the class question in politics, and to think of imperialism in terms of race is disastrous. But to neglect the racial factor as merely incidental is an error only less grave than to make it fundamental."[37]

In colonial Saint-Domingue, as in other sugar colonies, race defined caste from which only a small minority escaped. Even among the petits blancs, "race prejudice was more important than even the possession of slaves."[38] James succinctly affirms, "The advantages of being white were so obvious that race prejudice against the Negroes permeated the minds of the Mulattoes who so bitterly resented the same thing from the whites. . . . The Mulatto, rather than be a slave to a black, would have killed himself."[39] These acknowledgments pose significant challenges for the treatment of the revolution as class conflict.

Imbued with the racial nuances of early twentieth-century Trinidad, James implicitly pursued social respectability through racial lines. Despite the early influence of Marcus Garvey, his self-definition as "dark" rather than "black" might have delayed his political education for years,[40] but it certainly influenced his apostleship of Marxism. Scott McLemee tells us that it was only after an unforgettably frightening racial encounter in the southern United States that James became "aware of himself . . . as black."[41] Although this self-realization further convinced him that the black struggle for liberty and justice was unique, it did not fundamentally affect his interpretation of class conflict as the engine of historical change. Not even James could escape the drama of race in the Haitian Revolution. In doing so, he makes a seminal contribution to neo-Marxist historiography.

At every opportunity, James reminds the reader that he is aware of the prerogatives of racism but is obliged to escape its snares. It is James's voice we hear, not Toussaint's, in the fatal face-off between the latter and Colonel Vincent over the publication of the constitution in 1801. James muses, "Vincent was a white man. He could never dread slavery as a black man could, never have that unsleeping fear of white treachery so strong in that generation of San Domingo."[42] Although racism defined the utter degradation of the enslaved, to James it was not race but the "method of production" that created and nourished the "vicious society"[43] in which civilization lost its conventional meaning. To exorcise racism from the plethora of police laws in Caribbean slave colonies, James presents Greco-Roman slavery as evidence that "severe legislation against slaves and freedmen have nothing to do with the race question."[44]

The reader cannot be faulted for concluding that Boukman had unleashed a race war at the Bois Caïman congress of August 1791. He did not simply seek to destroy slavery but "aimed at exterminating the whites."[45] On the fateful night of August 21 in the forests of Morne-Rouge, Boukman issued his declaration of emancipation, not in mimicry of the French revolutionary principles but in the name of African gods of war and thunder. As holy war, the insurrection was also a clash of civilizations, each with its clearly racialized cosmology: only whites were targets of bloody retribution, although the enslaved suffered just as much under mulatto enslavers.[46] In describing the scenes of destruction, James intones, "For two centuries the higher civilization had shown them that power was used for wreaking your will on those whom you controlled. Now that they held power they did as they had been taught." Conjuring a clear picture of a race war, he reiterates, "In the frenzy of the first encounters they killed all [the whites]," except the priests and surgeons.[47] However, James interprets the moment as a prototype of a modern proletarian revolution. To him this early phase of the revolution was simply "a thoroughly prepared and organised mass movement."[48]

The contemporary translation of "Eh! Eh! Bomba!" spoke of unmitigated violence, sweeping away all obstacles to liberty: "We swear to destroy the whites and all that they possess; let us die rather than fail to keep this vow."[49] The lyrics were clearly articulated as a race war. Linguists have retranslated the song as a creolized Kikongo praise song. One of the many revised translations interprets it as an appeal to Mbumba, a Kongolese deity, to terminate the evils perpetrated by whites and blacks alike, that is, the enemies of liberty.[50] This translation supports James's primary interpretation of the revolution as a class war.

Even without this translation, James critically pierced the racial veil in recognizing the existence of "a small privileged caste" of enslaved persons located mainly in domestic occupations and including the "foremen of the gangs." Intoxicated with the vices of their masters they despised the field slaves. Yet in his inimitable, didactic style, James did not rule them out from the revolution, a device that readily conforms to Marxist dialectics; he theorizes: "The leaders of a revolution are usually those who have been able to profit by the cultural advantages of the system they are attacking, and the San Domingo revolution was no exception to this rule." James brilliantly demonstrates that even the "privileged caste" among the enslaved, who "danced minuets and quadrilles, and bowed and courtseyed in the fashion of Versailles," and generally "profited by the cultural advantages of the system," actively contributed to the revolution.[51] This privileged caste included Boukman, Biassou, Christophe, and Toussaint.

James also challenges the reader not to conceive the mulatto war as a race war. In the early stages of the civil war, mulatto alliances remained fluid and included free and enslaved blacks as well as poor and elite whites. James does not shroud the fact that "the Mulattoes hated the black slaves because they were black." Hate and prejudice, however, were not sufficient to maintain aloofness when they threatened self-interest. As James states, "when they actually saw the slaves taking action on such a grand scale, numbers of young Mulattoes from Le Cap and round about rushed to join the hitherto despised blacks and fight against the common enemy."[52]

Despite crossing military lines for political expediency, the mulattoes were fighting for their own sovereignty in Saint-Domingue. As James saw it, once they perceived the whites were no longer a force to be reckoned with, they reset their goal of dominating the colony as "theirs by right."[53] On several occasions they betrayed Toussaint by intriguing with the British to recapture lost ground.[54] Toussaint had become the main enemy of the mulatto conspirators as well as the mulatto republicans.[55] Yet with a combination of personal disdain and typical Marxist-Leninist dogmatism, James concludes, "This was no question of colour, but crudely a question of class, for those blacks who were formerly free stuck to the Mulattoes. Persons of some substance and standing under the old regime, they looked upon the ex-slaves as essentially persons to be governed."[56] It is not that these facts do not support a credible case for class conflict, but as Henry Beecher states, "Whatever is only almost true is quite false, and among the most dangerous of errors, because being so near truth, it is more likely to lead astray."[57] The alliance of a small minority of "blacks" with the mulattoes does not vindicate the latter from a racial agenda. Oppressors have always co-opted members of the class they oppress. James does not qualify these formerly free "black" allies in relation to the 128 divisions of color and caste in the colony and thus leaves the case for class conflict open. To what extent did they develop familial ties with the mulattoes? How far to the left or right of center of the melanin race continuum were they? Left unanswered, such questions expose fundamental flaws in treating with the revolution purely from a basis of historical materialism.

Interestingly, the reader does not wait in vain for a compromise on the race-class dichotomy. James ultimately concedes that Leclerc's deliberate drowning of more than one thousand Africans in the harbour of Le Cap "in one stroke" in 1802 "started the race war"; exasperated by his sickly troops and the indomitable spirit of the blacks, Leclerc opted for a "war of extermination." What he began, Rochambeau sought to complete "by attempting to exterminate blacks and Mulattoes as well."[58] This admission was not a case of better late than never; indeed, the revolution was ending the way it had begun.

The Black Jacobins and the "New Master Narrative" of Emancipation

Neo-imperialist historians have recently reacted to revolutionary emancipationism with the argument that it does not conform to the definition of antislavery because "Abolition means the will to put an end to slavery as a system, wherever it exists."[59] The alleged incapacity of enslaved Africans to bear this contrived burden of total emancipation is the justification for their portrayal as intellectual parasites of white, Euro-American antislavery ideologues. Paradoxically, the Haitian Revolution is the benchmark for this pedagogy.

A significant aspect of this "new master narrative" pivots round João Pedro Marques's essay "Slave Revolts and the Abolition of Slavery: An Overinterpretation."[60] Despite Marques's explicit acknowledgment that the primary objective of slave insurgencies was "to reconquer freedom, kill the whites, destroy the sugar mills and other facilities, and . . . escape or subjugate the region," he concludes that "as a general rule, the rebels' aim was not to suppress slavery, which they often were to perpetuate, albeit with a reversal of roles."[61] His best case in point is Toussaint's labor policy, which he interprets as backsliding from principles of revolutionary freedom. Although he admits that under Toussaint "flogging was abolished" and "workers received a small part of their production," to underscore the stereotype of African incapacity for unconditional freedom, Marques asserts that the new laborers were still "punished in many ways."[62] Most contributors to the collection of essays responding to Marques explicitly or implicitly support his basic interpretations.

Ironically, the "new narrative" draws inspiration from The Black Jacobins. Mainly for this reason James has been less of an enigma to neo-imperialist historians than is Williams for his Capitalism and Slavery. Whereas Williams subordinates the insurgency called the Baptist War to economic forces, consistent with his main thesis of economic change from mercantilism to free trade and from a declining West Indies to a rising India as the key explanation for British abolition of her slave trade and colonial slavery, James subordinates his black Jacobins to "agents of economic necessities" and to disciples of white Jacobinism and French liberal ideology.[63] Notwithstanding his privileging of French Enlightenment for Toussaint's education of the rights of man, James convincingly demonstrates that the historian who measures Toussaint's political pragmatism with the idealism of France's Declaration of the Rights of Man is in grave error. To Toussaint the only distinction between "men" was between good and evil.[64] James engages Toussaint's war economy to reveal an astute statesman, conscious of the imperative of bridging multiple worlds with multiple options. Although Toussaint maintained the plantations and compelled the noveaux libres to work, he wished to see them "civilized and advanced in culture," toward which end he built schools and laid the foundation for "racial equality."[65] He tried to convince the workers that it was their duty and responsibility as good citizens to obey the law. Preempting a charge of condescension, James admits that this posturing was "the propaganda of a dictatorship"; however, it was "not for base personal ends or the narrow interest of one class oppressing another."[66] Under Toussaint, "race prejudice, the curse of San Domingo for two hundred years, was vanishing fast." To underscore this revolutionary dispensation, James highlights the fact that the newly built Hotel de la République was "frequented by blacks, local whites, and Americans, all on equal footing"; even Toussaint, who frequently dined there, would take his place "in any vacant seat like any of the rest."[67] James concludes that despite its many compromises, Toussaint's form of governance was "the best";[68] to add "in the Atlantic world" would not be an exaggeration.

The pedagogy of legislated emancipation as the end to servile and forced labor in European colonies is fictive. Robin Blackburn acknowledges that white abolitionists at best opted for "half measures"; he also exposed other myths of white abolitionism, including free-womb laws, statutory emancipation in many liberal northern states of the United States, and the widespread resort to forced labor disguised under legal pseudonyms.[69] British emancipation, for example, was followed by numerous legislative and regulative strategies to deny genuine freedom and create a landless peonage under penalties reminiscent of Toussaint's Haiti; furthermore, chattel slavery was followed by forced labor systems of indentured immigrants recruited from a wide geographical net. The same European powers that abolished slavery in the Caribbean and other maritime colonies reimposed it on Africans at home during the establishment of the colonial economy. France's emancipation decree of 1794 was not applied to their empire in the Indian Ocean. Even today, slavery contributes to industrial production in some of the most advanced economies of the North Atlantic.

Conclusion

For a long time *The Black Jacobins* will continue to provide pedagogical fodder in the "intellectual warfare" between neo-imperialists and postcolonial historians of Caribbean antislavery. We have seen that liberty did not have the same meaning in France and the colonies. The so-called black Jacobins of Saint-Domingue were not the equivalent of the white Jacobins of France. As Robespierre stated to the National Assembly, "You urge without ceasing the Rights of Man, but you believe in them so little yourselves that you have sanctified slavery constitutionally."[70] On the other hand, Toussaint expresses the uncompromising resolve of the black revolutionaries: "We confronted dangers in order to gain our liberty, and we will be able to confront death in order to keep it."[71] If the slaves of Saint-Domingue were so moved by clichés from Paris, it is reasonable to question whether they would not have had equal knowledge of the duplicity of French liberals.

The philosophy of liberty espoused by the enslaved was certainly different from that of the Enlightenment; the latter, constrained by economies dependent on trading in and the enslavement of Africans could not become truly universal in its application. In the wake of Boukman's campaigns, Thomas Clarkson had argued that the French Revolution merely offered a rare opportunity for the revolutionaries of Saint-Domingue "to vindicate for themselves the unalterable Rights of man."[72] True, Clarkson was on the defensive against charges that his abolition movement had instigated the revolt. Nevertheless, James suggests that there was a connection; Clarkson had visited the fledgling French antislavery society Les amis des noirs and distributed propaganda and money.[73] Still, as Clarkson contended, the British anti–slave trade society had been established only in 1787; thus, it could not have had any serious impact on enslaved peoples of Saint-Domingue. Clarkson also intimated that the motive for revolt should be sought within the experiences of the enslaved; in doing so, he cited a long build-up to Bois Caïman: the Tacky revolt in Jamaica, "various insurrections" in many other islands, including "a bloody one at St. Domingo" prior to Boukman.[74]

Even though William Fortescue reintroduced European students of British military history to the debacle of the Haitian campaign, he did not unduly disturb this colonialist portrait. On the contrary, James was determined to change this pedagogy and present Africans as historically conscious who "would themselves be taking action on a grand scale and shaping other people to their own needs." In this regard, *The Black Jacobins* is a monumental success. Yet the narrative of the revolution is too narrowly focused on Haiti, the implication of which might best be perceived through a Jamesian paradox: "What does he know of cricket who only cricket knows?"[75] The Haitian Revolution was not the only mass revolt against slavery in the Caribbean in the mid-1790s; it was also not the first such revolt and certainly not the last. Thus *The Black Jacobins* is an incomplete narrative of the "only successful revolt in history." However, to have opened the vista to include other emancipation wars before Boukman would have negated the central role of the French Revolution; for James, this would be self-defeating: removing the "Jacobins" from the emancipation wars would emasculate the narrative into a history of a "black" revolution—an unpardonable heresy, too radical even for James to contemplate.

Notes

1. Seymour Drescher, "Civilizing Insurgency: Two Variants of Slave Revolts in the Age of Revolution," in *Who Abolished Slavery? Slave Revolts and Abolitionism, A Debate with João Pedro Marques*, edited by Seymour Drescher and Pieter C. Emmer (New York: Berghahn Books, 2010), 122, 130.

2. Williams explicitly acknowledged James as the inspiration for his work, stating, "On pages 38–41 [of *The Black Jacobins*] the thesis advanced in this book is stated clearly and concisely and, as far as I know, for the first time in English"; see Eric Williams, *Capitalism and Slavery* (London: Andre Deutsch, 1964), 268.

3. Williams, *Capitalism and Slavery*, vii.

4. C. L. R. James, *The Black Jacobins: Toussaint L'Ouverture and the San Domingo Revolution* (New York: Random House, 1963), 402; also in B. W. Higman, *Writing West Indian Histories* (London: Macmillan Education, 1999), 94.

5. James, *The Black Jacobins*, ix.

6. James, *The Black Jacobins*, 18. To James, the daily life of the enslaved was a grand lesson in dialectics conveniently alternating "fatalistic stupidity" with a "remarkable liveliness of intellect and vivacity" and "a feeling of superiority to their masters."

7. Jacob H. Carruthers, *Intellectual Warfare* (Chicago: Third World Press, 1999), 3–4.

8. James, *The Black Jacobins*, 214.

9. Anna Grimshaw (ed.), *The C. L. R. James Reader* (Oxford: Blackwell, 1992), 77. For the original play, see C. L. R. James, *Toussaint Louverture: The Story of the Only Successful Slave Revolt in History: A Play in Three Parts* (Durham, NC: Duke University Press, 2013).

10. James, *The Black Jacobins*, 220.

11. James, *The Black Jacobins*, 103–9.

12. Robin D. G. Kelley, "The World the Diaspora Made: C.L.R. James and the Politics of History," in *Rethinking C. L. R. James*, edited by Grant Farred (Oxford: Blackwell, 1996), 113.

13. James, *The Black Jacobins*, x–xi.

14. Williams, *Capitalism and Slavery*, 208.

15. James, *The Black Jacobins*, 95.

16. James, *The Black Jacobins*, 18.

17. Laurent Dubois and John D. Garrigus, *Slave Revolution in the Caribbean, 1789–1804: A Brief History with Documents* (Boston: Bedford/St. Martin's, 2006), 183, 186–87. Bois Caïman was "the moment of revolution." For an explanation of this Hegelian interpretation of the birth of revolutionary consciousness, see Moira Ferguson,"Introduction to the Revised Edition," in *The History of Mary Prince: A West Indian Slave (Related by Herself)*, edited by Moira Ferguson (Ann Arbor: University of Michigan Press, 1997), 17–18. Bois Caïman is now embroiled in controversy over its authenticity as a historical event; see for example, David Geggus, "The Bois Caiman Ceremony," *Journal of Caribbean History* 25, nos. 1 and 2 (1991): 41–57.

18. James, *The Black Jacobins*, 103–9.

19. James, *The Black Jacobins*, x.

20. James, *The Black Jacobins*, 82.

21. James, *The Black Jacobins*, 86.

22. Michel S. Laguerre, *Voodoo and Politics in Haiti* (New York: St. Martin Press, 1989), 62–63.

23. James, *The Black Jacobins*, 86.

24. See Dubois and Garrigus, *Slave Revolution in the Caribbean*, 183.

25. James, *The Black Jacobins*, 18.

26. C. L. R. James, *Notes on Dialectics: Hegel, Marx, Lenin* (London: Allison and Busby, 1980), 47.

27. C. L. R. James, *The History of Pan-African Revolt* (Washington, DC: Drum and Spear Press, 1969), 25–29.

28. James, *The History of Pan-African Revolt*, 15.

29. James, *The Black Jacobins*, 94.

30. See J. E. Inikori, "The Import of Firearms into West Africa 1750–1807: A Quantitative Analysis," *Journal of African History* 18, no. 3 (1977): 339–68; W. A. Richards, "The Import of Firearms into West Africa in the Eighteenth Century," *Journal of African History* 21, no. 1 (1980): 43–59; Robin Law, "Horses, Firearms, and Political Power in Pre-Colonial West Africa," *Past & Present* 72 (August 1976): 122–23.

31. James, *The Black Jacobins*, 86.

32. James, *The Black Jacobins*, 120.

33. James, *The Black Jacobins*, 214.

34. See Claudius Fergus, "War, Revolution and Abolitionism," in *Capitalism and Slavery: Fifty Years Later: Eric Eustace Williams—A Reassessment of the Man and His*

Work, edited by Heather Cateau and Selwyn Carrington (New York: Lang, 2000), 173–91; also Claudius K. Fergus, *Revolutionary Emancipation: Slavery and Abolitionism in the British West Indies* (Baton Rouge: Louisiana State University Press, 2013), 79–81, 85–88.

35. James, *The Black Jacobins,* 38.

36. James, *The Black Jacobins,* 33.

37. James, *The Black Jacobins,* 283.

38. James, *The Black Jacobins,* 34.

39. James, *The Black Jacobins,* 42–43.

40. C. L. R. James, *Beyond a Boundary* (London: Stanley Paul, 1963), 53.

41. Scott McLemee, *C.L.R. James on the 'Negro Question'* (Jackson: University Press of Mississippi, 1996), xvii.

42. James, *The Black Jacobins,* 268.

43. James, *The Black Jacobins,* 27, 33.

44. James, *The Black Jacobins,* 38.

45. James, *The Black Jacobins,* 86.

46. See James, *The Black Jacobins,* 87.

47. James, *The Black Jacobins,* 88.

48. James, *The Black Jacobins,* 86.

49. James, *The Black Jacobins,* 18, 85.

50. Hein Vanlee, "Central African Popular Christianity and the Making of Haitian Vodou Religion," in *Central Africans and Cultural Transformations in the American Diaspora,* edited by Linda M. Heywood (Cambridge: Cambridge University Press, 2002), 248–49.

51. James, *The Black Jacobins,* 19.

52. James, *The Black Jacobins,* 89.

53. James, *The Black Jacobins,* 162.

54. James, *The Black Jacobins,* 164.

55. James, *The Black Jacobins,* 165.

56. James, *The Black Jacobins,* 166.

57. Available at www.tentmaker.org/quotes/truthquotes.htm.

58. James, *The Black Jacobins,* 371.

59. Olivier Pétrié-Grenouilleau, "Slave Resistance and Abolitionism: A Multi-Faceted Issue," in *Who Abolished Slavery: Slave Revolts and Abolitionism: A Debate with João Pedro Marques,* edited by Seymour Drescher and Pieter Emmer (New York: Berghahn Books, 2010), 160.

60. Drescher, "Civilizing Insurgency," 120.

61. João Pedro Marques, "Slave Revolts and the Abolition of Slavery: An Overinterpretation," translated by Richard Wall, in *Who Abolished Slavery: Slave Revolts and Abolitionism: A Debate with João Pedro Marques,* edited by Seymour Drescher and Pieter Emmer (New York: Berghahn Books, 2010), 13.

62. Marques, "Slave Revolts and the Abolition of Slavery," 23.

63. For James's explicit qualification of *The Black Jacobins*, see James, *The History of Pan-African Revolt*, 24.

64. Laurent Dubois, *Avengers of the New World: The Story of the Haitian Revolution* (Cambridge, MA: Harvard University Press, 2005), 210.

65. James, *The Black Jacobins*, 246–47.

66. James, *The Black Jacobins*, 247.

67. James, *The Black Jacobins*, 247–48.

68. James, *The Black Jacobins*, 247.

69. Robin Blackburn, "The Role of Slave Resistance in Slave Emancipation," in *Who Abolished Slavery: Slave Revolts and Abolitionism: A Debate with João Pedro Marques*, edited by Seymour Drescher and Pieter Emmer (New York: Berghahn Books, 2010), 172–73.

70. James, *The Black Jacobins*, 76.

71. Dubois, *Avengers of the New World*, 209.

72. Thomas Clarkson, *True State of the Case Respecting the Insurrection at St. Domingo* (London, 1792), 114.

73. James, *The Black Jacobins*, 54.

74. Clarkson, *True State of the Case*, 113.

75. James, *Beyond a Boundary*.

11

"To Place Ourselves in History": The Haitian
Revolution in British West Indian Thought
before *The Black Jacobins*

MATTHEW J. SMITH

As you will have seen from my book, the revolutionary and creative power of untaught slaves is what interests me about the revolution in San Domingo more than
anything else.

—C. L. R. James

The book was written in 1938 and still has a validity today . . . because I came originally from the kind of territory which produced René Maran, Marcus Garvey,
George Padmore, Aimé Césaire, and Frantz Fanon.

—C. L. R. James

In 1838, precisely one century before C. L. R. James published the greatest
of all histories of the Haitian Revolution, the enslaved people in his native
Trinidad and across the British Caribbean colonies received general emancipation. The colonies then joined neighboring Haiti as postslavery societies.
The struggle for emancipation was, however, radically different in both situations. The revolutionary war in Saint-Domingue was an unprecedented annihilation of slavery in France's premier sugar colony that in many ways influenced the direction of abolitionism in the British islands, which received "full
freedom" after a long and gradual process. Yet the Haitian Revolution was far
more than a prelude to 1838; for many it was a powerful example of what was
achievable in the Caribbean. Planters feared its export, hearing stories of what
happened in Saint-Domingue from thousands of their French counterparts arriving in their islands. Others took a different view of the Haitian Revolution.
For the recently freed, the revolution and in particular the leadership of Toussaint Louverture were received more positively. In 1838 an anonymous writer
from Jamaica published in a local newspaper a long essay titled "Toussaint

Louverture" that celebrated Toussaint and linked him to the British islands just after emancipation: "While society is waiting for evidence of what the negro race, at large, can do and become, it seems to be rational to build high hopes upon such a character as that of the man. . . . the model upon which Napoleon formed himself." Toussaint was, for that writer, "among a very few individuals of the African race who have distinguished themselves by intellectual achievements."[1]

As the scholars in this volume and others have shown, a similar sense of elevation of Toussaint motivated James a century later. *The Black Jacobins* is connected to this longer tradition of West Indian identification with the Haitian Revolution and especially the figure of Toussaint. Toussaint's achievements were attractive to generations of West Indians since the nineteenth century for several reasons, significant among them that Toussaint and the Haitian Revolution were products of the West Indies. James made the point plainly in a retrospective lecture on the writing of *The Black Jacobins*: "Toussaint was not only a black man, he was also a West Indian."[2] He never lost sight of this fact throughout the book's narrative and in lectures on Toussaint given over the four decades after the book's first appearance.

James had multiple purposes for writing *The Black Jacobins*. His own explanations over the years ranged from a clearly thought-out political intention to the following admission more than thirty years later: "I had long made up my mind to write a book about Toussaint L'Ouverture. Why, I couldn't tell you. Something was in the atmosphere and I responded to it."[3] The book's interpreters have expanded on these reasons through fine-grain study of James's life and work. The most sustained discussions of *The Black Jacobins*, in fact, have treated with many of the book's nuances and subtle inconsistencies, analyzing how it fits into and goes beyond traditions of racial vindicationism, postcolonialism, modernity, Marxism, African liberation, and Caribbean and specifically Haitian historiography.[4] That there can be sophisticated theoretical discussions on these elements speaks to the incredible staying power of James's achievement. This chapter attempts a different type of exploration of *The Black Jacobins*, one that moves away from the book and its arguments, shortcomings, and achievements to consider the context within which the preliminary idea for the book was created. One of James's most consistent claims was that he had the plan to write a book about Toussaint Louverture and the Haitian Revolution before he left Trinidad for England early in 1932. What was it about his intellectual environment in Trinidad that drove his conviction to pursue a study of the Haitian Revolution so passionately? What was his knowledge about that event at that point in his life, and what purpose did that history serve for him?

This chapter argues that the answers to these questions can be found by looking outside of *The Black Jacobins* and its author and exploring a wider intellectual tradition in the colonial British West Indies to which James was connected long before he left Trinidad. It is often assumed that *The Black Jacobins* brought the "silenced" story of the Haitian Revolution to the attention of James's contemporaries in the British colonies.[5] On the contrary, the Haitian Revolution, and especially its leadership, had a central place in British West Indian thought in the nineteenth and early twentieth centuries. This was not unique to the Caribbean islands that surrounded Haiti. As Ifeoma Kiddoe Nwankwo has argued, "Whites' fear of the revolution and its presumably contagious nature forced people of African descent throughout the Americas, particularly those in the public and published eye, to name a relationship to the Haitian Revolution, in particular, and to a transnational idea of Black community in general."[6] This idea was clearly present at the moment of "full freedom" as the anonymous 1838 quotation indicates. Throughout the rest of the century, British West Indian views on the Haitian Revolution tended to reflect intellectual aspirations and a burgeoning sense of West Indian identity. The most pervasive element of these approaches are also found in James's narrative—that Toussaint was the first iconic West Indian hero and his tragic demise put Haiti on a course of political confusion. Indeed, surprisingly few black British West Indians (James included) ever wrote extensively about Dessalines or postrevolutionary Haiti, preferring to focus on the monumental achievements of Toussaint in the Haitian Revolution.[7]

In a path-breaking essay, Michel-Rolph Trouillot has argued that the Haitian Revolution was an "unthinkable" event, particularly for European powers.[8] In the British West Indies, as this essay argues, it was quite the opposite: the Haitian Revolution was a Caribbean revolution that shook the world. Many of its elements were found in the other islands. The plantocracy feared its imitation in the British colonies. For black middle classes, it held an even stronger presence. The revolution was a frequent referent in writings and public speeches about the past and future of the Caribbean. No one in the British colonies attempted the detailed exploration of the revolution that James later undertook. This was partially attributed to opportunity and timing. Few had the linguistic skills he had or the opportunity to do the necessary archival work.[9] Furthermore, the rise in West Indian nationalism in the 1930s infused James with an unparalleled sense of mission in how he went about telling a story that had long been familiar to British West Indians. Notwithstanding this, the generations before James generally accepted the importance of the revolution as a global *and* West Indian event. In one of his most brilliant commentaries on this subject, James perceptively captured this feature of West Indian intellectualism:

> I have long believed that there is something in the West Indian past, something in the West Indian environment, something in the West Indian historical development, which compels the West Indian intellectual when he gets involved with subjects of the kind, to deal with them from a fundamental point of view, *to place ourselves in history*.[10]

Through a discussion of disparate and fragmentary record of views on the Haitian Revolution and Toussaint by black British West Indians in the period from the 1830s to the 1930s, this chapter presents glimpses of how they placed themselves in the history of the Haitian Revolution and how that process shaped James's early interests in Toussaint while he was still an aspiring writer and teacher in Port of Spain.

Haiti's revolutionary history drew varied responses among British West Indians as they emerged from slavery. The 1838 perspective on Haiti and Toussaint that many held in the euphoric early days after emancipation remained strong. But as the century progressed and Haiti's political realities of coups and overthrows became more frequent, this view was tempered by references to the present. Toussaint and the Haitian Revolution appeared glorious and the postrevolutionary course the antithesis of the liberty and equality Toussaint staked his life on. British West Indian commentators who referenced Haiti in the postemancipation period exhibited the duality of their class concerns in their interpretations of Haiti: On the one hand Toussaint Louverture and the revolution were to be universally celebrated; on the other, perpetually troubled Haiti was to be distanced. It was also a looming threat for the elites in power especially after the 1865 Morant Bay rebellion in Jamaica. That event was the most important rising in the postemancipation British Caribbean and was falsely regarded as being inspired by the Haitian Revolution. After the rebellion and with the establishment of Crown rule in all the colonies, Haiti was less a threat to the British islands than an example to be avoided.

In the following decades, what Haiti represented most of all for black West Indians was an independent black state in the West Indies whose origins and existence was proof of black achievement. Imperial investigators loudly challenged the notion that "troubled" Haiti could represent something worthwhile for British West Indians. Most notorious of all such commentators was James Anthony Froude. As is well known, Froude's survey of the British islands, published in his notorious *The English in the West Indies* in 1888, concluded that the islands were far from suited for self-government based on racial factors. James later dismissed Froude's assessments, particularly of the Haitian Revolution, as "lies and nonsense from the first word to the last," but it was the generation before James that made the first defense of the "enlightened" Caribbean.[11]

Haiti and the Haitian Revolution was the basis of Froude's critique and had a substantive place in the responses of his critics as well. Viewed from the late nineteenth century, Froude argued, the Haitian Revolution was a total failure: "Republics which begin with murder and plunder do not come to much good in this world."[12] Toussaint Louverture was not spared responsibility for Haiti's state in the late nineteenth century. "The republic of Toussaint L'Ouverture, the idol of all believers in the new gospel of liberty, had, after ninety years of independence, become a land where cannibalism could be practiced with impunity."[13]

In British West Indian responses to Froude, the dual views of Haiti are clearly visible. They also provide a hint of the type of context that shaped the British West Indian middle class—the setting in which James grew up—and its views on Haiti. Apart from newspaper editorials, one of the earliest rebuttals of Froude came from Grenadian N. Darnell Davis, who took issue with Froude's blatant stereotyping of middle-class British West Indians but reinforced his prejudices about Haiti. "The bulk of the people of the infantile Republic of Hayti were revolted slaves of unmixed barbarism. . . . On the other hand, during the past 95 years, the Africans in the British West Indies have remained under English influence and control."[14]

Another of Froude's prominent detractors was C. S. Salmon, former president of Nevis. In his 1888 book-length rejoinder to Froude, Salmon included a chapter titled "The Foreign West Indies—The Haytian Mystery Explained." He defended Haiti against Froude's attacks and illustrated a vision of an inclusive Caribbean that acknowledged the Haitian Revolution as central to West Indian development. This supported his argument of a Caribbean confederation. Salmon, nonetheless, was also of the view that even though the Haitian Revolution was a success for the region, it produced no great achievement for the Haitians themselves. This was because in 1804 Haiti lacked the civilizing tools needed for progress in his estimation. "This Haytian question being put on its true footing, it is nevertheless obvious the people have gained nothing by absolute independence."[15]

The most celebrated response to Froude, *Froudacity*, written by Trinidadian J. J. Thomas—who significantly was an educator like the young James—raised similar questions about Haiti.

> [Froude] calls upon us to believe that, in spite of being free, educated, progressive, and at peace with all men, we West Indian Blacks, were we ever to become constitutionally dominant in our native lands, would emulate in savagery our Haytien fellow-Blacks who at the time of retaliating upon their actual masters, were tortured slaves.[16]

It is instructive that James, in a later essay on Thomas, recognized his "mistakes and misconceptions" but claimed they were irrelevant to the book's larger contribution, which was how Thomas engaged with the Caribbean. In James's words, it was a "particular type of social and intellectual activity which we can definitely call West Indian."[17]

Jamaican medical doctor Theophilus Scholes in his opus *Glimpses of the Ages* took a similar approach. Scholes recognized Toussaint Louverture as "the greatest Negro born in the Western Hemisphere, and one of the greatest of the greatest men whom the three races have produced."[18] To prove his point, he quoted at length U.S. abolitionist Wendell Phillips's famous 1861 speech on Toussaint. Phillips's brilliant speech was immensely popular in the West Indies in the nineteenth and early twentieth centuries, as it had been among abolitionists in the United States. For black West Indians, however, there was added significance because it was foreign validation of the greatness of Toussaint, an icon of the race and a man from the region. Often quoted at length, the speech was found in books, newspaper columns, and public orations. Scholes himself offered but a few words of comment, preferring instead to quote Phillips at length. Phillips's speech in fact had become a popular reference in the West Indian celebration of Toussaint.

The intention for Scholes, as it was for Salmon and Thomas, was to implicitly present black West Indians as descendants of Toussaint. By drawing on Phillips, Scholes and others emphasized that respected white commentators shared West Indian views about Toussaint's mythology. More to the point, Toussaint's example confirmed that black West Indians, contrary to the falsehoods of Froude and his followers in the Colonial Office, were capable of "civilization." If all these men were negative on the postrevolutionary trajectory of Haiti, it was because they firmly believed it was the antithesis of Toussaint's vision of universal liberty. They separated Toussaint from Haiti's independent history and treated that history as retrogressive. Betraying an acceptance of popular generalizations of the revolution, they lay responsibility on Toussaint's successors—especially Dessalines—for making Haiti into what Salmon called "a disorganized society."[19]

Thus Toussaint remained idealized in British West Indian thought, an ever-present hero unto whom people could project their own interpretations of the West Indian past and expectations of its future. At the turn of the twentieth century, that future was more uncertain than ever. Everywhere the world was gripped by tension: the political upheavals in Europe that would lead to world war, segregation and racial violence in the U.S. South, and the intensity of U.S. imperialism in Cuba and its encroaching presence in Haiti that eventually led to occupation (1915–1934). All of this was closely followed in the British colonies. For British colonists, the convergence of these issues raised new questions about imperialism. What would become of the Caribbean islands in the new century? The options ranged from a form of Caribbean federation to acceptance of the inevitability of U.S. domination. The march of global forces and presumptions of great power reinforced external presumptions of racial inferiority. Some black West Indians looked toward the Haitian Revolution and Toussaint as reminders of a past when other West Indians like themselves were able to resist the great powers. Toussaint's importance began to widen, and he was regarded not only as a hero of the race with his superior intelligence but as a victor against foreign imperialists.

Joseph Robert Love, a Bahamian medical doctor who had spent several years living in Haiti before settling in Jamaica in the 1890s, was one such champion of Toussaint Louverture's example. A powerful orator and unrelenting activist for black political rights, he was also renowned for his public lectures, one of the most celebrated being "A Lecture on Toussaint L'Ouverture: The Lessons and Result of His Life."[20] These lectures were notable affairs. They were held in public venues in Kingston and Spanish Town in the evenings and drew large crowds from across the island. Love, it appears, never published these lectures on Toussaint. But the public delivery suggests the popularity of the subject among all classes of Jamaicans. The example of Toussaint, "one of those pure spirits who was born to live for others," was held up to black Jamaicans at the turn of the century, as it was in 1838, as an example of what the black race, particularly black West Indians, could achieve. The *Daily Gleaner,* in a review of Love's lectures, crystallized the point with a line from Wordsworth: "What one is why may not millions be?"[21]

The importance of these modes of circulation of ideas about Haiti and Toussaint should not be underestimated. The colonial education, which black middle-class students like James received, did not include the Haitian Revolution in its curriculum. It was a classical British public school model that took root in the Caribbean in the late nineteenth century. James later included himself as a pioneer in the teaching of West Indian history in Trinidad.[22] Yet in the years prior to the expansion of West Indian nationalism, the memory of Toussaint Louverture and the revolution was kept alive in public conscience and transferred through the writings of men like Scholes, Thomas, Salmon, journalists in the local papers who referenced "the great Toussaint," and the public speeches of charismatic orators like Love. By the 1930s public gatherings, special meetings, and secondary school elocution competitions in Jamaica often included renditions of Phillips's lecture on Toussaint as a matter of course.[23] In short, Toussaint was the only West Indian icon on a frequently referenced list of heroes of the black race that affirmed the deep association black West Indians in particular had for him.

The power of public expressions of Toussaint in the colonial West Indies was perhaps most profoundly exemplified in the reflections of Marcus Garvey and the United Negro Improvement Association, the largest of all movements to emerge from the British West Indies in the twentieth century. Garvey's writings are peculiarly silent on the history of the Haitian Revolution, although Toussaint often featured prominently in his discussions of the pantheon of black leaders. There is, however, some indication of Garvey's views on Toussaint and Haiti in a speech he delivered in Kingston not long after his return to Jamaica in 1929 following deportation from the United States. The occasion was a massive rally to mark the Sixth International Convention of the Negro Peoples of the World. Over fifteen thousand people turned out to hear Garvey deliver the main address. At one point he compared the Haitian Revolution with emancipation in the British West Indies and invoked the spirit of Toussaint.

> The agitation for the abolition of slavery was a success to the extent that in 1838 English sentiment forced Queen Victoria of England and her Parliament to emancipate the blacks of the Dominion—the blacks of the colonies of the West. Other countries of the world fought independently for their freedom and first among them was that great but now sorrowing

Republic which is a stone's throw from us—a neighbour known as Hayti or Santo Domingo. There the abolitionists did not agitate or the white philanthropists did not contribute to the cause of emancipating the people of that country. But there to the honour of their country and our race a black man fought for the liberty of his people—Toussaint L'Ouverture— the greatest Negro to ever come out of the West; because he was success- ful in leading in Santo Domingo an army which beat the trained soldiers of France and the trained soldiers of England.[24]

In this way, West Indians learned about, honored, and mythologized Tous- saint. Always above reproach, the revolutionary hero—treated as the com- posite of the entire revolution itself for British West Indians—fitted into their imaginary of the West Indies, a region in which Haiti was always included. In "now sorrowing" Haiti, "a stone's throw from us," according to Garvey, Tous- saint had achieved the incredible and in so doing tied Jamaica, Trinidad, and the entire Caribbean together with the entire black race in the memory of that historic struggle against oppression.

This sense of Caribbean inclusiveness shaped James in early twentieth- century Trinidad and it was an element that he believed strengthened him when he left for England. His comments on this point in an interview with Stuart Hall are revealing:

> I brought this with me from the Caribbean—I was aware of the ordinary man who wasn't able to read and had not studied very much in the Ca- ribbean but he was a highly civilized person, highly developed. Many of them were more developed than the average English worker, who lived in a certain narrow sphere. But in Trinidad and Jamaica, you knew who the lawyer was, you knew who the doctor was, you knew who the parson was, you knew who was the Member of Council, you read every day in the paper what they were doing; life was small and you had a small con- spectus of society there. . . . But we brought that—at least I brought that with me, Padmore had it too—we kept on seeing the whole thing as a whole.[25]

But if black West Indians saw their history and that of the Haitian Revolu- tion as part of the whole, they were in constant contention with an outside world that challenged their firmly held convictions. The substance of the ra- cial element in the debate between Froude and his West Indian critics in the late nineteenth century remained no less inflamed in early 1930s Trinidad as it had been in the late nineteenth century. In 1931 two debates raged in the pages of the literary magazine *The Beacon*, organized by a group of prominent Trinidadian writers including James. In each debate Toussaint's and Haiti's past and present were featured. In July, the paper's founder, Albert Gomes, wrote a short prose piece, "Black Man," that criticized discrimination in the United States. The article raised a call for black resistance: "Back to back, Black Man. You have to fight the white man's fury." The essay and ensuing debate, which stretched for several issues—and prompted a police investigation of Gomes—drew on Toussaint's example as evidence of black achievement. "There have been Toussaint L'Ouvertures, but these have always been received with a great deal of skepticism by their people. . . . Shoulder to Shoulder Black Man. Stop having no confidence in your folks."[26] In a counterargument, Fred West challenged the view that Toussaint still held relevance for black people in the 1930s Caribbean or, for that matter, in occupied Haiti. "Toussaint L'Ouverture . . . yes . . . he's been dead some time hasn't he? The overture to the black opera is finished . . . is there any more of the same . . . we are still listening? . . . If Hayti is happy, it is made so chiefly by American discipline and dollars."[27]

West's comments indicate a weariness and cynicism on his part of the frequent celebration of Toussaint and Haitian independence in the face of mounting political tensions in the Caribbean and across the globe. More important, it indicated that among certain sectors of the black middle class, the Haitian present was viewed as more relevant than the revolutionary past. Even Gomes's comments suggested that some distance between the nineteenth and twentieth centuries was beginning to set in. The sentiment was found in the views of other activists of the same generation. "Today," wrote New York–based Jamaican champion for self-government W. A. Domingo, "these Haitians who welcomed Americans into their country, believing all the democratic fairy tales written about the United States, are praying for another Toussaint L'Ouverture to rid them of their new masters."[28]

This controversial position on Toussaint among middle-class writers in the British Caribbean paled in comparison to the other debate that took place in the pages of *The Beacon* earlier in 1931 and involving James. Dr. Sidney Harland, a British "geneticist" working at the Imperial College of Tropical Agriculture, published an essay that reinforced racist arguments of black inferiority. The article drew a famous response from James and has been the subject of several analyses of his early political thought and views on the Haitian Revolution. Indeed, in this article James revealed for the first time in print his thoughts about Toussaint. Using a highly questionable categorization scale, Harland ranked Toussaint as being of "the lowest of the superior classes." In his rejoinder, James took apart each of Harland's claims. Yet Harland's judgment of Toussaint is what most irritated James; it was a "monstrous blunder," the greatest of all of Harland's mistakes. Considered within the history of British West Indian reverence for Toussaint, James's response is all the more significant. In a trenchant riposte, James evoked the sentiments of black middle-class West Indians since the nineteenth century who lionized Toussaint for his brilliance. This brilliance could not be explained by Harland's flawed schema which meant, James facetiously suggested, that there were "about 80" Toussaints in "Trinidad to-day."[29] These frustrations, faced by Thomas over Froude and James over Harland, strengthened James's commitment to write a history of Toussaint Louverture.

The arguments of British West Indians in the three generations after emancipation who wrote positively about the Haitian Revolution had strong resonances with the intellectual work of their Haitian contemporaries. Indeed, this was a struggle that Haitian intellectuals had long been engaged in having to combat more hostile and personal indictments from foreign writers. In his response to Harland, James opened his essay by linking him with nineteenth-century progenitors of biological determinism—"Gobineau at once springs to mind," he wrote. He was correct in pointing to the way "scientific racism" had relied on Haiti's past and present to justify its skewed claims. The celebrated challenge to Gobineau, however, had come in the late nineteenth century with Haitian intellectual Anténor Firmin's classic *De l'égalité des races humaines*. Firmin's 1885 demolition of Gobineau's racist theories relied on Toussaint, the "most striking example of the astonishing and rapid evolution which Africans have undergone in Haiti," to disprove notions of black inferiority.[30] Similar to his British West Indian counterparts, Firmin quoted Phillips's essay on Toussaint at length and used it as evidence of the universal recognition of his greatness. From the classic nineteenth-century histories of Thomas Madiou's multivolume *Histoire d'Haïti* and Beaubrun Ardouin's equally expansive *Études sur l'histoire d'Haïti* to H. Pauléus Sannon's three-volume *Histoire de Toussaint Louverture* (1920–1933)—another major influence on James—Haitian intellectuals had developed more complex interpretations of the revolution than did their British West Indian allies.[31] Both traditions nonetheless shared the emphasis on the centrality of the revolution to Caribbean history.

These two intellectual currents intersected in Paris sometime between 1934 and 1935 when James, firmly committed to research and writing his history of Toussaint Louverture, met Haitian General (called colonel in France) Alfred Nemours. Nemours was a military historian, Haitian delegate to the League of Nations, and diplomat in France in the 1920s and 1930s. He had earlier published a study on Toussaint Louverture.[32] James heard about Nemours while working in the archives and sought him out. Quite soon afterward they were having discussions about the Haitian Revolution over coffee and tea. It was probably James's first encounter with a Haitian intellectual, and from Nemours he learned a lot about Haitian history, geography, and the organization of the principal battles of the revolution. One can imagine both men staring intently at a mock strategy board of "books and coffee cups upon a large table," mapping with great enthusiasm the military operations of Toussaint, Dessalines, and Christophe.[33] Both James and Nemours understood that the history they excitedly discussed in Paris belonged to them both. Of two different Caribbean backgrounds, they anchored their identities to the series of events that erupted in the French colony of Saint-Domingue in the late eighteenth century. "These are my ancestors, these are my people," James later mused.[34]

Both men understood the responsibility and importance of the research they were doing on the Haitian Revolution as an instructive model of resistance and Caribbean leadership through which they could explain the urgent transformations already in motion in their native lands. In Trinidad in 1934, Captain Cipriani, the subject of James's first publication in England, had formed the Trinidad Labour Party, an important step toward self-government. Also that year the U.S. Marine occupiers finally withdrew from Haiti. Caribbean nationalism of the 1920s gained new power, and so did the study of the past. According to Trouillot in a comment on Haitian history-writing of the period, "the instructional value of the past" made history "more than ever, patriotic duty."[35] James's perspective on Haitian history was enlarged by his work on the play *Toussaint Louverture*, frenzied political activity in England, rapid absorption of Marxism, intensely wide reading, and careful observation of the genesis of decolonization movements in Africa. But it was his Caribbean background—appreciated by Nemours—and a conscious awareness of the intellectual spheres that molded him, that he drew on in formulating his approach to the book. "I was therefore specially prepared," he later asserted, "to write *The Black Jacobins* not the least of my qualifications being the fact that

I had spent most of my life in a West Indian island not, in fact, too unlike the territory of Haiti."[36]

The year James and Nemours met, another Haitian writer and lawyer, Joseph Charles, issued a call for a new history of the Haitian Revolution that would remind West Indians that it was the foundation of their own history.

> It is my hope that [West Indians] will appreciate the fact that not only Haitians but all and sundry who belong to the Black Race ought to be proud of Toussaint L'Ouverture, and of Christophe, and to feel themselves debtors of Haiti, the country which gave these heroes immortal fame and glory in exchange for their best.[37]

Charles had in mind Nemours's current project, expected to be published under the title *Christophe, the Magnificent*. That book never materialized. But three years later, in the centennial year of "full freedom," James, transformed in his perspective of Toussaint and the Haitian Revolution, delivered an explosive answer to that call with a masterpiece study that would transcend all that came before it.

Notes

The first epigraph is from C. L. R. James to Étienne Charlier (General Secretary of the Parti Socialiste Populaire [Haitian Socialist Party]), London, August 24, 1955, "C.L.R. James Collection," University of the West Indies, St. Augustine, Box 7, file 190. The second epigraph is from C. L. R. James, "The Old World and the New," in *At the Rendezvous of Victory: Selected Writings* (London: Allison and Busby, 1984), 3:211.

1. *The Jamaica Standard and Royal Gazette*, December 1, 1838.
2. C. L. R. James, "Lectures on *The Black Jacobins*: How I Wrote *The Black Jacobins*," *Small Axe* 8 (September 2000): 74. James held the same opinion of Fidel Castro. "From Toussaint L'Ouverture to Fidel Castro," he later wrote, "our people who have written pages on the book of history, whoever and whatever they have been, are West Indian, a particular social product." C. L. R. James, "The West Indian Intellectual," in John Jacob Thomas, *Froudacity: West Indian Fables by James Anthony Froude* (London: New Beacon Books, 1969), 27.
3. James, "The Old World and the New," 211.
4. For discussions of the book along these varied lines see, for example, Robert A. Hill, "C.L.R. James: The Myth of Western Civilization," in *Enterprise of the Indies*, edited by George Lamming (Port of Spain: Trinidad and Tobago Institute of the West Indies, 1999), 255–59. Hill makes a powerful and influential argument that the book should be regarded as part of a tradition of African vindicationism. See also David

Geggus, *Haitian Revolutionary Studies* (Bloomington: Indiana University Press, 2002), 33–36; Brian Meeks, "Re-Reading *The Black Jacobins*: James, The Dialectic and the Revolutionary Conjuncture," *Social and Economic Studies* 43, no. 3 (1994): 75–13; Kent Worcester, *C.L.R. James: A Political Biography* (New York: State University of New York Press, 1996), 34–40; David Scott, *Conscripts of Modernity: The Tragedy of Colonial Enlightenment* (Durham, NC: Duke University Press, 2004), offers a penetrating new reading of the book and its arguments.

5. In a spirited reappraisal of *The Black Jacobins*, Archibald Singham argued that prior to its publication, Toussaint and Dessalines were unimportant to James's generation (and presumably preceding generations), which instead uncritically accepted imperial narratives of Haitian backwardness. See A. W. Singham, "C.L.R. James on the Black Jacobin Revolution in San Domingo: Notes toward a Theory of Black Politics," *Savacou* 1, no. 1 (1970): 83.

6. Ifeoma Kiddoe Nwankwo, *Black Cosmopolitanism: Racial Consciousness and Transnational Identity in the Nineteenth-Century Americas* (Philadelphia: University of Pennsylvania Press, 2005), 7.

7. To be sure, James did pen short surveys of postrevolutionary Haiti in the appendix to the 1963 reissue of *The Black Jacobins* and in a brief 1964 essay, "Black Sansculottes," in *At the Rendezvous of Victory: Selected Writings* (London: Allison and Busby, 1984), 3:159–62.

8. Michel-Rolph Trouillot, "An Unthinkable History: The Haitian Revolution as a Non-Event," in *Silencing the Past: Power and the Production of History* (Boston: Beacon Press, 1995), 70–107. For an illuminating and thoughtful critique of this argument using the work of Victor Schoelcher, see Dale Tomich, "Thinking the 'Unthinkable': Victor Schoelcher and Haiti," *Review* 31, no. 3 (2008): 401–31.

9. On this point, see Bernard Moitt, "Transcending Linguistic and Cultural Frontiers in Caribbean Historiography: C.L.R. James, French Sources, and Slavery in San Domingo," in *C.L.R. James: His Intellectual Legacies*, edited by Selwyn Cudjoe and William E. Cain (Amherst: University of Massachussetts Press, 1995), 136–37.

10. James, "The West Indian Intellectual," 45; emphasis in original.

11. James, "The West Indian Intellectual," 43.

12. James Anthony Froude, *The English in the West Indies. Or the Bow of Ulysses* (London: Longmans, Green, 1888), 341.

13. Froude, *The English in the West Indies*, 126. The stir produced by this book and its responses can only be briefly treated here. For more extensive discussion, see the excellent analysis in Faith Smith, *Creole Recitations: John Jacob Thomas and Colonial Formation in the Late Nineteenth-Century Caribbean* (Charlottesville: University of Virginia Press, 2002), 128–72, and Selwyn R. Cudjoe, *Beyond Boundaries: The Intellectual Tradition of Trinidad and Tobago in the Nineteenth Century* (Amherst: University of Massachusetts Press, 2003).

14. N. Darnell Davis, *Mr. Froude's Negrophobia or Don Quixote as a Cook's Tourist* (Demerara: "Argosy" Press, 1888), 38–39.

15. C. S. Salmon, *The Caribbean Confederation* (London: Cassell, 1888), 94.

16. John Jacob Thomas, *Froudacity: West Indian Fables by James Anthony Froude* (London: T. Fisher Unwin, 1889), 17.

17. James, "The West Indian Intellectual," 27. This comment could be applied to *The Black Jacobins*.

18. Theophilus Scholes, *Glimpses of the Ages* (London: J. Long, 1905), 264.

19. Salmon, *Caribbean Confederation*, 95.

20. *Daily Gleaner*, October 10, 1893; W. Adolphe Roberts, *Six Great Jamaicans* (Kingston: Pioneer Press, 1957), 77.

21. *Daily Gleaner*, October 12, 1893.

22. See Stuart Hall, "A Conversation with C.L.R. James," in *Rethinking C.L.R. James*, edited by Grant Farred (Oxford: Blackwell, 1996), 16. See also C. L. R. James, *Beyond a Boundary* (Durham: Duke University Press, 1993), 37–39; Howard Johnson, "Decolonising the History Curriculum in the Anglophone Caribbean," *Journal of Imperial and Commonwealth History* 30, no. 1 (2002): 27–60. I thank Carl Campbell and Michael Dash for their suggestions on this point. It is interesting to note that even after *The Black Jacobins* was published—and before the 1963 reissue—it registered little impact and was not included in the secondary school curriculum and apparently was not widely read, no doubt a consequence of the Marxist analysis that shapes the book, which was likely discouraged in the islands. Evidence of the book's reception in the British islands in the first two decades of its appearance can only be anecdotal. For example, in 1955, Jamaican track star Gilbert McGregor visited Haiti and publicly claimed his interest in seeing the land where Toussaint Louverture had come from. McGregor's knowledge of Toussaint, he claimed, was based on his readings in Jamaica. This did not include *The Black Jacobins*, but the work of Haitian writer Stephen Alexis, *Black Liberator: The Life of Toussaint Louverture* (London: Ernest Benn, 1949). See *Haiti Sun*, August 14, 1955. Also in the early 1950s, Haitian intellectuals and writers such as Jean Brierre visited Jamaica and gave public lectures on Toussaint at the University College of the West Indies. See, for example, *Daily Gleaner*, January 15, 1953.

23. See, for example, the reports in *Daily Gleaner*, December 6, 1932, July 31, 1934, and April 24, 1935.

24. *Daily Gleaner*, August 2, 1929. A subsidiary point worth mentioning here relates to how Toussaint served as a personal model for black West Indian intellectuals of the period. Garvey was once referred to as the "L'Ouverture of West Indian America," in the Panamanian paper *Workman*. See Robert A. Hill, ed., *The Marcus Garvey and UNIA Papers*, vol. XI (Durham, NC: Duke University Press, 2011), 531. Louise Cripps, who worked closely with James during his writing of *The Black Jacobins*, made a similar comment in the 1930s: "I think James very much identified himself with Toussaint L'Ouverture." Louise Cripps, *C.L.R. James: Memories and Commentaries* (New York: Cornwall Books, 1997), 20.

25. "A Conversation with C.L.R. James," 22.

26. Albert Gomes, "Black Man," *Beacon* 1, no. 4 (July 1931): 2.

27. Fred West, "You Are Right, Black Man, But How . . . ?: A Reply to Albert Gomes' 'Black Man,'" *Beacon* 1, no. 7 (October 1931): 11. For more on this debate and the activities of the *Beacon* group in Trinidad more generally, see Reinhard Sander, "The Trinidad Awakening: West Indian Literature of the Nineteen-Thirties," Ph.D. diss., University of Texas, Austin (1979), 54–74.

28. Taken from Domingo's letter to the editor in *The Daily Gleaner*, May 21, 1924.

29. C. L. R. James, "The Intelligence of the Negro: A Few Words with Dr. Harland," *The Beacon*, 1, no. 5 (August 1931): 9. In his response to James, in which he reiterated his belief in "the mental inferiority of the negro to the white," Harland pointed out that his calculation "in which a man of the culture of Toussaint l'Ouverture is predicted to occur alludes to the expectation in the white race, not in the coloured." See Sidney C. Harland, "Magna Est Veritas Et Praevalebit: A Reply to Mr. C.L.R. James," *The Beacon* 1, no. 7 (October 1931): 18, 20.

30. Anténor Firmin, *The Equality of the Human Races*, translated by Asselin Charles (New York: Garland, 2000), 369.

31. For an excellent discussion of this literature, see Michel-Rolph Trouillot, "Historiography of Haiti," in *General History of the Caribbean vol. VI: Methodology and Historiography of the Caribbean*, edited by B. W. Higman (London: UNESCO/Macmillan, 1999), 451–77.

32. Alfred Nemours, *Histoire de la captivité et de la mort de Toussaint Louverture. Notre pèlerinage au Fort de Joux* (Paris: Berger-Levrault, 1929), which James called a "thorough and well-documented study"; James, *The Black Jacobins*, 336. In 1938 Nemours also published a short book of reflections on Toussaint. See Nemours, *Quelques jugements sur Toussaint-Louverture* (Cap-Haïtien: Valcin, 1938). For James's comments on this meeting see C. L. R. James, "Interviews with Ken Ramchand," San Fernando, Trinidad and Tobago, September 5, 1980, http://www.marxists.org/archive/james-clr/works/1980/09/banyan.htm (accessed April 28, 2013).

33. James, *The Black Jacobins*, xvi.

34. C. L. R. James, "The Making of the Caribbean People (1966)," *Radical America* 4, no. 4 (1970): 44.

35. Trouillot, "Historiography of Haiti," 461.

36. James, *The Black Jacobins*, xvi.

37. *The Daily Gleaner*, October 31, 1935.

PART III.
THE BLACK JACOBINS

Texts and Contexts

| | | | |

The Black Jacobins and the Long Haitian Revolution: Archives, History, and the Writing of Revolution

ANTHONY BOGUES

The transformation of slaves, trembling in hundreds before a single white man, into a people able to organize themselves and defeat the most powerful nations of their day, is one of the great epics of revolutionary struggle and achievement.
—C. L. R. James

The Black Jacobins is a seminal twentieth-century radical historiographical text. Like all such texts—for example, E. P. Thompson's *The Making of the English Working Class* or the book that was in part a model for *The Black Jacobins*, Leon Trotsky's *History of the Russian Revolution* and the text published three years before, W. E. B. Du Bois's *Black Reconstruction*—*The Black Jacobins* has become a historical marker. It is a text to be studied, critiqued, and deployed as a probe into our present while engaging with the historical past. *The Black Jacobins* is still considered as the single most important English-language text on the Haitian Revolution, in spite of the plethora of texts on the topic. Thus *The Black Jacobins* remains a distinctive text, one to be read and reread not so much for its historical portrayal and narrative of the Haitian slave revolution but for its grappling with the "fever and fret" of *revolution itself* as a political and social phenomenon and what it means to write about such historical moments.

Sometimes in the recent past there has been a strange kind of probing and studying of *The Black Jacobins* that elides the complex conundrum of writing about revolution. Perhaps it is the times we inhabit when the word, concept, and practices of revolution seems lost in the mist of the past and where for many the angel of history has turned her head firmly against such a past for a "progress" that negates this possibility. We are, it seems at least for some writers and scholars, in a conjuncture where history is sublimated and defeated. In such a situation it seems as if Ulysses listens to the story of his life and turns away. But here one is reminded, as Hannah Arendt astutely notes, that to understand tragedy in that way is to say that history becomes the need to "save human deeds from futility that comes from oblivion."[1]

It is time and the times that hold us in its grasp, and so, making a contrapuntal move, I want to recall and think about *The Black Jacobins* not so much as a book of its times but as a marker of a historical moment of the twentieth century and one that was pregnant with the possibilities of the new. Thus, I want to think about *The Black Jacobins* not so much as a book about anticolonialism or even of slave revolution (and it is both) but primarily as one about the possibility of revolution in general. Here I am not deploying the book to talk about those possibilities. Instead, I wish to think with the book about temporality and the writing of revolution. In doing this, I end the chapter with a few remarks about how it might be productive to think about the Haitian Revolution if one were to take seriously C. L. R. James's statement at the 1971 lectures he delivered at the Institute of the Black World (IBW). In the third and final lecture he says: "I don't want today to be writing and say that's what *they* said about how *we* were being treated. . . . I would want to say what we had to say about how we were being treated and I know that information exists in all the material."[2] I suggest that in thinking through this statement, we are forced to confront the question: What would such a stance mean for the archive, radical historiography, and the narrative of the Haitian Revolution today? To begin the discussion, we start with the historical conditions for the writing of *The Black Jacobins*.

The Historical Conditions for Writing *The Black Jacobins*

It is March 1937 and a group of West Indians and Africans have come together to form a radical anticolonial political organization—the International African Service Bureau (IASB). The antecedents of this formation reside within a couple of groups; the International African Friends of Abyssinia formed before the outbreak of the second imperial war, with James as chairman and including individuals like Peter Milliard, T. Albert Marryshow, and Amy Ashwood Garvey as treasurer. This group morphed into the Pan African Federation with George Padmore and Wallace Johnson becoming deeply involved. In 1937 when the IASB was formed, its executive committee included James, Amy Ashwood Garvey, Jomo Kenyatta, Ras Makonnen, George Padmore, Wallace Johnson, N. Azikiwe, and G. Kouyate, among others.[3] Padmore describes the group as a "non party organization . . . which owed no affiliation or allegiance to any political party, organization or group in Europe."[4] The formation of this group in London was another instance of the radical anticolonial black diasporic tradition which had by then emerged in various European capitals.[5] The IASB became a dynamic political organization. James, reflecting on the group, noted, "But what I think was even more important was that we allowed no opportunity of our case to pass us by [for] the 'Colonial Question' we were always there."[6] Alongside this political practice, for several months the group published a journal, *International African Opinion*.[7] Four things galvanized the IASB: the Italian invasion of Ethiopia in 1935; the emergence of what Padmore later called "colonial fascism"; and the political turn of the Comintern toward a politics of the Popular Front, for which one result was a political practice that made the anticolonial struggle secondary to the fight against fascism. The fourth was the IASB radical commitment to global anticolonial struggles. Importantly for our current discussion was that the group set itself an extraordinary writing program in which books, pamphlets, and articles became central to its political practice. Why this writing program, and how did writing for the IASB constitute itself as a radical political act on equal footing with political organizing?

The radical politics of anticolonialism requires a process of historical reclamation. The noted African revolutionary thinker Amilcar Cabral notes what colonialism was about: "The colonists usually say that it was they who brought us into history . . . that is not so. They made us leave history . . . to follow the progress of their history."[8] Writing the colonized back into history became a critical practice of anticolonial politics. But there were two kinds of historical writing of reclamation. The first was a narrative form of history that sought to detail the history of the colony prior to colonialism and then recounted the stories of resistance to colonial domination. In this kind of history, the issues of social structures and the forms of economic and political structures were key. Often this kind of history attempted to vindicate the forms of societies (particularly in Africa) before colonial conquest.[9] The preoccupation with this kind of history was with a notion of temporality and whether it was possible to re-create connections to a historical past in which historical flows and time were ruptured through colonial conquest. The other kind of historical reclamation practiced by radical anticolonial thinkers was a form of historical writing in which the writer, while taking into account the past, was intent in opening what Walter Benjamin would call the "open sky of history."[10] Such a form of writing was typically about revolution and was primarily about using the past as an index for possible ruptures of the present. To paraphrase and extend Benjamin, it was about taking control of a memory as it flashes and presents itself not in moments of danger but within futures of possibilities. It is this form of historical writing, I would submit, that James was practicing when he wrote *The Black Jacobins*.

For the IASB there was another reason for a preoccupation with writing: it had to do with understanding writing as criticism, as a way to expose the wrongs of colonial power. For this kind of writing, Padmore was the exemplar. If one puts together the requirement of historical reclamation and the need for critique and exposure of colonial power, then the reasons for the IASB writing and publishing program become clear. James himself in reflecting on the political achievements of the IASB notes that as far as political organizations in England were concerned, the black intellectuals had not only arrived, but "were significant arrivals."[11]

The first historical condition for the writing of *The Black Jacobins* was thus the political anticolonial work James and his political colleagues were involved in at the time. Put simply the book was partly a result of collective political work. Robert Hill confirms this when, in an article on James's life in England in the 1930s, he notes that *The Black Jacobins* was probably the most important factor in the emergence of the group's perspective on "armed struggle and African Independence."[12] The second condition was James's own work as a writer. Before leaving the Caribbean in March 1932, he had published in the magazine the *Beacon* an essay that identified Toussaint Louverture as a "great individual." In the article, he used the achievement of Toussaint to illustrate and destroy the racist arguments posited by Sidney Harland, an Englishman teaching in colonial Trinidad in the early twentieth century.[13] In *The Black Jacobins*, Toussaint became an epic figure transformed from a revolutionary slave leader to a universal revolutionary, a "world-historical figure" in the pantheon of revolutionaries that would include Lenin and Trotsky. In the IBW lectures, James notes that before he arrived in London he wanted to write a history of Toussaint Louverture. He further comments that by then he had "a good knowledge of history, historical writing and biography."[14] He continues that on his arrival in Nelson, "I began to import books from France on the history of black Jacobins."[15] Two things are noteworthy here. First, James uses the phrase "black Jacobins," suggesting that he may have already made up his mind that the slave revolutionaries of Saint-Domingue belonged to the left wing of the French Revolution. Second, he felt that the genre of his historical writing on the revolution would be that of biography. My view is that the biographical form allowed him to think deeply about the complicated relationship between an individual and society. In addition, a biographical focus would limit attention on the other social actors in the revolution except in their specific engagement with Toussaint. Finally this genre would facilitate James developing a notion of the great individual, a preoccupation that followed him throughout his intellectual and political life. To think about *The Black Jacobins* as a biography allows us to see in clearer terms its literary achievements and the possible ways the narrative structure of the work unfolds. It seems James initially had a literary reason for writing *The Black Jacobins*. By the late 1930s, this initial literary reason becomes entangled with the politics of the IASB and his own Marxist theoretical formation.

Arriving in London, James quickly gravitated toward revolutionary Marxism, specifically Trotskyism, and by 1937 he was considered a leading Marxist theoretician; his book *World Revolution* an important text. To write *World Revolution,* James made a thorough study of Marxism. In the preface he writes that the text is "a survey of the revolutionary Socialist movement since the War— the antecedents, foundations and development of the Third International—its collapse as a revolutionary force."[16] *World Revolution* was a text in which James the Marxist theoretician was concerned with telling the story of how the European revolutionary movement had stalled.[17] The book was written in political conversation with the Marxist movement and was part of a radical political praxis at the time. In the text James argued that the stalling of the European revolutionary movement was temporary as he notes that "statesmen and publicists [are] frightened at the steady rise of the revolutionary wave."[18] James's idea of the live possibility of revolution found its way into *The Black Jacobins*. During his early years in England, he had carefully read Trotsky's three-volume *History of the Russian Revolution*. Reflecting on his reading, he observed that "this is a tremendous book and is filled with historical development and the role of the masses and the role of the party, and so on."[19] It would therefore seem that this text would be influential on James's historical theory. One final condition that went into the writing of *The Black Jacobins* was James's 1936 play about the life of Toussaint, performed at Westminster Theatre. In this play Paul Robeson acted the lead.[20] In summary we can say that the following historical and discursive conditions went into the writing of *Black Jacobins*: a literary ambition, James's absorption of Marxism, and his political work with the IASB for African political independence along with writing the play on Toussaint's life. These conditions combined to create a text that, as I have argued elsewhere, was one of historical intervention and radical political ideas.[21]

The Writing of Revolution

The Black Jacobins was published a year after *World Revolution*. If the latter was a survey of revolutionary movements in the early twentieth century littered with the Marxist revolutionary figures of the period, the former was about a single event. The Haitian thinker Michel-Rolph Trouillot has written that the Haitian Revolution entered "history with the peculiar characteristic of being unthinkable even as it happened."[22] Frankly, unthinkability is not uncommon in the making of revolutions. However, in this case what Trouillot points us to is an epistemological understanding about what and who were the slaves. Citing the colonist La Barre, who wrote, "there is no movement amongst our Negroes . . . they are very tranquil and obedient. A revolt among them is impossible,"[23] Trouillot draws our attention to two things. First, within the framework of Western thought at the time, slaves were nonhuman and therefore capable only of passive obedience under the duress of slavery.

Second, he wants to suggest that for many years in Western historiography the revolution was elided. I would suggest, however, that what happened was not elision but the creation of a counterarchive on the revolution, one in which horror and chaos were the evoking imaginaries. The creation of this counterarchive was an attempt to consolidate a dominant nineteenth-century idea of black incapacity for self-government. This counterarchive included novels, paintings, engravings, and newspaper articles. Within the early twentieth-century popular imagination, the consolidation of this counterarchive was achieved with the publication of William Seabrook's book *The Magic Island* and the first zombie film made in 1931, *White Zombie*.[24] Alongside this archive was the publication in 1914 of T. Lothrop Stoddard's book, *The French Revolution in San Domingo*. Outside of this archive was the publication in 1914 of the remarkable book written by the African American intellectual Thomas Steward, *The Haitian Revolution, 1791–1804*. James makes no reference to these texts, but his North American audience would read *The Black Jacobins* against the backdrop of the Stoddard text, as one of the reviewers of the book did.[25]

So when James wrote *The Black Jacobins* he was intervening into a growing debate within the context of colonialism about the possibilities of black self-government and sovereignty. It is why the book ends with the possibility of African political independence. In other words, it ends with a note about possible futures. Within the American context, Haiti had already been discursively painted as a strange island dominated by a superstitious other. Thus from within the dominant political view in the imperial West, the unthinkability of a black-led revolution which had now become a historical reality had to be rolled back and defeated.[26] In writing the story of the Haitian Revolution, James was grappling with a revolution that was not only unthinkable in dominant political terms but was seen at the time as impossible in ontological ones. It was a deep conundrum. Marxist that he was, he turned to Trotsky's history and radical French historiography and the writings of Jules Michelet. Let us spend some time with Trotsky's text. In the preface to *History of the Russian Revolution*, Trotsky writes the following:

> The history of a revolution, like every other history, ought first of all to tell what happened and how. . . . Events can neither be regarded as a series of adventures, nor strung on the thread of a preconceived moral. They must obey their own laws. *The discovery of these laws is the author's task.* The most indubitable feature of a revolution is the direct interference of the masses in historical events . . . the history of a revolution is for us first of all a history of the forcible entrance of the masses into the realm of rulership over their own destiny.[27]

A few things here. Trotsky's description of revolution is about mass entrance into political life and the creation of a new ground for social and political life. Second, for him the task of the historian was to "discover the laws" by which this intervention occurs. This idea was a consistent reading of the practices of historical materialism, and James would have deployed this reading fairly often. However, if in 1937 he was deploying this rendition of historical materialism in other writings, in *The Black Jacobins* the writing of history, revolution, and the biography of Toussaint became more nuanced as the story unfolds and James posits a distinctive theory of radical historiography.

At first blush the structure of *The Black Jacobins* with its preface seems to follow the conventional historical materialist approach with the obvious influence of Trotsky. For example, James begins with the dates the Haitian Revolution breaks out. In Trotsky's book there is the same attention to periodization, and it begins with the first months of 1917. For James the revolution in the colony of Saint-Domingue was connected to the French Revolution of 1789. He positions the colony as the "greatest colony in the world . . . the envy of every other imperialist nation. The whole structure rested on the labor of half-a-million slaves." He then summarizes the revolution and collapses it into a single event, making the independence of Saint-Domingue a secondary event to the revolt of the slaves, "the only successful slave revolt in history."[28] Similar to Trotsky, James states that *The Black Jacobins* is about this "epic revolutionary struggle and achievement" and why and how it happened. At this point there is nothing unusual about the rendering of what the author is doing, as he is following the conventional protocols of historical materialism. However James moves quickly in the preface and confronts the problem that he grapples with throughout the entire text—the political personality of Toussaint Louverture (recall here he is writing biography as well); there we begin to see his distinctive theory of historical writing emerging.

James posits that Toussaint was one of the most remarkable men of the period, that he was a gifted figure, and "yet Toussaint did not make the revolution. It was the revolution that made Toussaint. And even that is not the whole truth."[29] Obviously James is thinking through Marx's adage in the *Eighteenth Brumaire* that men determine history but in conditions they themselves do not necessarily create. But Saint-Domingue is a slave revolution and a successful one at that, so there are some unique features to contend with. For James the revolution was the moment when the "slow accumulation of centuries bursts into volcanic eruption." In such circumstances of revolution, I suggest that historical time is compressed and historical flows quicken. In such a moment for James, although "Great men make history . . . their freedom of achievement is limited by the necessities of their environment. To portray the limits of the necessities and the realization, complete or partial of all possibilities, that is the true business of the historian."[30] For James, therefore, historical writing was not about the "discovery of laws" as Trotsky had suggested; rather, it was about the play within the interstices between "freedom of achievement" and the necessities of environment. I suggest that this play is at work in its profoundest form during the course of revolution, that moment James argues when "society is at boiling point and therefore fluid." In his formulation, historical writing becomes the art of demonstrating this play while the analysis of the various social forces that constitute this "boiling point" is a science.

Here James is making a fine distinction between the writing of history and the political analysis of a moment. In this distinction he recognizes the centrality of the imagination in historical writing; the way that although the archive functions as an anchor, the telling of the story is an imaginative exercise since historical flows of a moment, what Benjamin calls its "consequences of eventualities," shapes the story. By reading the preface this way, is it not safe to say that James was positing a different theory of history in which there was active agency particularly in moments of revolution? Is it not safe to say that for James it is within the play of the events that we see glimpses of possibilities? Put another way, was James in *The Black Jacobins* not positing a theory of the subject? I turn to this matter now.

Revolution as an Event

As was stated already, James describes revolutions as a "ceaseless slow accumulation of centuries [which] bursts into volcanic eruption."[31] I have come to understand revolution as a ruptural moment, one that opens the passages for new questions about the possibilities of different forms of human life in a society. But I would argue as well that it is more than a series of actions that open the grounds for a set of practices in which the new questions are only posed. It is a moment when these questions can actually be acted on. Hannah Arendt has noted that in the "modern age . . . the idea of freedom and the experience of a new beginning should coincide."[32] She goes on to make the point that revolution is the only political event with the idea of a new beginning at its core. She writes, "The modern concept of revolution, inextricably bound up with the notion that the course of history suddenly begins anew, that an entirely new story, a story never known or told before is about to unfold."[33] Central to this new story, this new history that is about to begin, is a conception of possibilities. Because this new beginning ruptures historical time, I want to suggest that the revolution is an *event*. Here I am defining *event* not just in Badiouian terms, thinking of an event as a historical moment/opening in which epiphanies emerge but suggesting that these openings occur alongside the old because there are no fixed predicates within the "flux of history," particularly at the moment of revolution. Much current thinking about the event and history from Althusser to Deleuze and Derrida circles around Marx's remarkable text, the *Eighteenth Brumaire of Louis Bonaparte*. Deleuze in particular develops the idea of the "time out of joint" and a notion of repetition. About the latter he writes:

> Marx's theory of historical repetition, as it appears notably in *The Eighteenth Brumaire of Louis Bonaparte* turns on the following principle . . . historical repetition is neither a matter of analogy nor a concept produced

by the reflection of the historians, but above all by the condition of historical action itself.[34]

What Deleuze calls repetition is to my mind the ways in which the *Event*, the rupture, presents itself in contradictory forms in which the old and the new, while in contestation, fleetingly embrace each other. With regard to the Haitian Revolution, we may understand this notion clearer when we think on the words of Macaya, the guerrilla leader, who in 1793 was asked to join the French forces and fight against the Spanish at a moment when the French Commissioners have abolished slavery in the colony of Saint-Domingue. This is what he says: "I am the subject of three Kings: of the Kongo, master of all Blacks: of the King of France who represents my father; of the King of Spain who represents my mother. Those three kings are the descendants of those who led by a star came to adore God made man."[35] What do we make of such a remarkable statement? First, this is a statement by a revolutionary slave who is engaging in a struggle against slavery. Second, in terms of the ways of ruling and notions of sovereign power, Macaya recognizes various kings but note that one king, the king of Congo, rules all blacks. In other words, while he recognizes other kings, they do not rule him; hence I would suggest that the recognition is tactical. Finally the statement follows elements of the narrative Christian story of the birth of Christ. Yet in all of this Macaya remains a revolutionary slave. It is a complex set of juxtapositions of the past with the present.

Deleuze's formulation of "time out of joint" as an attempt to think about a radical moment is important. First I want to suggest that history is about a human engagement with time. Put another way, the making of history as an active human process involves an engagement with time, which is why narrative form becomes so central to historical writing. When revolution disrupts that time what Benjamin calls the "exploding of the continuum of history," then how to write that explosion, this disruption in time, becomes a critical issue.

James was very aware of this and decided that he would attempt to do writing with a focus on a great man of history—that he would use the personality of Toussaint Louverture to explicate and explore the revolution. The resultant structure of that decision meant that *The Black Jacobins* could only tell one version of the history of the revolution. It meant that unlike his other major works, throughout his long life James in *The Black Jacobins* did not pay attention to the practices of the ordinary slave and his or her drive for

freedom. When the masses make their entrance in the book through the figure of Moïse, James writes one of the most complex and layered passages of
the text. Describing the political situation in the north, which had emerged
after Toussaint had been in power for a while, and noting the fact of growing
disaffection with his leadership, James describes the revolutionary ex-slaves
who were disaffected thus:

> Revolutionaries through and through, those bold men, own brothers of
> the Cordeliers in Paris and the Vyborg workers in Petrograd, organized
> another insurrection. Their aim was to massacre the whites, overthrow
> Toussaint's government and, some hoped, put Moise in his place. . . .
> The insurrection [the slave revolt] proved that they were following him
> because he represented that complete emancipation from their former
> degradation which was their chief goal. As soon they saw that he was no
> longer going to this end, they were ready to throw him over.[36]

In this passage James puts into historical conversation a number of revolutionary moments with the Haitian slave revolution, those of Paris and
the workers of Petrograd. In doing this he opened both the revolutionary
canon of events and revolutionary history. Moïse was eventually executed,
and James asks what could Toussaint have done differently and why were
the revolutionaries now disaffected? His answer was to recount Toussaint's
policy of plantation labor and his attitudes toward the former white planters.
He writes:

> Criticism is not enough. What should Toussaint have done? A hundred
> and fifty years of history and the scientific study of revolution began by
> Marx and Engels, and amplified by Lenin and Trotsky, justify us in point-
> ing to an alternative course. . . . The whole theory of the Bolshevik policy
> was that the victories of the new regime would gradually win over those
> who had been constrained to accept by force. Toussaint hoped for the
> same. If he failed it was for the same reason that the Russian Revolution
> failed, even after all its achievements—the defeat of the revolution in Eu-
> rope. Had the Jacobins been able to consolidate the democratic republic
> in 1794, Haiti would have remained a French colony, but an attempt to
> restore slavery would have been most unlikely.[37]

These are telling passages. James's study of the Russian Revolution and
the state of the European Marxist movement led him to examine Toussaint's
leadership failures as partly externally driven. At the core of his description

was a comparison that the Russian socialist revolution could not be fully successful until it became a world or at least a European revolution. The Haitian Revolution was not a socialist one, but the revolutionary principle for success was the same—common struggle in this case between the revolutionaries in the colony and those in the metropole. In foregrounding this perspective, James, although paying some attention to the ways in which Toussaint related to the ex-slaves, elided two notions of freedom that collided in Saint-Domingue during Toussaint's tenure.

In this regard it might be useful to review a letter by Toussaint about an episode that occurred during the revolution, perhaps one of many such incidents. In February 1796, there were reports of revolts by ex-slaves working on a plantation. As was his habit, Toussaint rode to deal with the matter. In a letter to Laveaux he wrote:

> I mounted my horse and entered the circle where after having condemned the murders they had committed. I told them that if they wished to preserve their liberty they would have to submit to the laws of the Republic, and be *docile and work, that it was only in this way that they could benefit from their freedom.*[38]

In response the ex-slaves said they wanted "equality."

There are two conceptions of freedom operating and colliding here. For Toussaint, freedom for the ex-slave was about work and a labor regime that included forms of respectability. For the ex-slave on the other hand, freedom included a notion of radical equality. What are we to make of this? The first is that the historical writing of the *Black Jacobins* elides what the slaves desired and thought about freedom and a new beginning. Second, by focusing on Toussaint, James misses the layered complexities of the revolution. Included in this elision were the ways the revolutionary army was structured; the role of Maroonage, of religion, and the conflicts between creole slaves and the African-born slaves.

James later recognizes some of these elisions, and in the preface to Jean Fouchard's *The Haitian Maroons: Liberty or Death*, he writes that "one begins to write about history when one writes about the great untutored mass of the population." He continues, "any great revolution in historical thought has as its origins a revolutionary recognition of the concrete events, hitherto unsuspected, in the historical concatenation of the epoch in which the writer lives."[39] Recognizing that he has missed the centrality of Maroonage to the revolution, James states that Fouchard's work fills gaps. My point is that

James's elisions allow him to grapple with the event of the Haitian Revolution as a slave revolution in which the personality of Toussaint becomes the glue that holds the book's narrative structure. But this most complex of revolutions requires a more layered approach. Like all revolutions, there existed currents and conflicts; there was the old and the new colliding. How to tell that story takes us back to James's historical insight and the play within the interstices of the circumstances faced by the different engagements of subjects in the making of the revolution.

When *The Black Jacobins* was published, George Novack, the Marxist American philosopher, wrote that:

> One of the singular merits of James's work is that he avoids . . . forms of narrowness . . . he traces the parallel and interpenetrating phases of the revolution on the colony and the mother country. . . . This book provides irrefutable answers to the reactionary prejudices concerning the inherent inferiority of the Negro Race . . . the *Black Jacobins* demonstrates how indestructible is the link between the liberation struggle in the enslaved colonials and the revolutionary mass movements in the metropolis.[40]

For Novack and others who operated with a theory of the relationship between the anticolonial struggles and socialist revolution, the book was a historical illustration about these forms of revolutions with the mass movement in the "metropolis" serving as the catalyst.[41] Another review in the *Hispanic American Historical Review* compared the text with that of T. Lothrop Stoddard, stating that *The Black Jacobins* "explores ground surveyed by T. Lothrop Stoddard twenty five years ago." The reviewer continues, "It may be doubted whether any man could write with complete detachment of so passionate an affair" and ends by saying "on the whole the book is an illuminating study, provocative if not definitive."[42] *The Black Jacobins* was of course seminal— the complexities of the archive he worked through and its singular focus on Toussaint would make this a seminal work, but one which did not grapple completely with the revolution from within the frame of the "traditions of the oppressed."

The Long Haitian Revolution

Perhaps the most important English-language text that has attempted to contend with the Haitian Revolution from below is Carolyn Fick's *Making of Haiti*. In it she argues that the revolution "that began in 1791 and ended in

Haitian Independence in 1804 constituted one of the great revolutions of the modern world."[43] I agree with Fick that the revolution therefore becomes an event that shaped the modern world. From this perspective, it would seem that one might begin to think about the ways this revolution was distinctive from the other revolutions in the so-called Age of Revolution. Arendt reminds us that with the French Revolution the social became a central element of the modern revolution. This intervention of the social terrified many and led to Edmund Burke's *Reflections on the Revolution in France*. If the social in the French Revolution meant that the peasant and the Parisian masses had to struggle for forms of social equality, then in a slave colony where slavery pervaded the social, the overthrow of such a system by the slaves themselves was an extraordinary radical act. A review of the history of major revolutions in which the social intervenes and is acted on shows that there is a period of working out of the new—often incomplete and halting but very much a working out—because there are no precedents to draw on. In this case the Haitian revolution had two logics to it: a logic to end racial slavery and one to create a new independent state. At each moment a formal constitution recognized each: Toussaint's constitution in 1801 and then Dessalines's in 1805. With these two logics in operation we can perhaps describe the Haitian Revolution as the *Long Haitian Revolution*. This frame might allow us to begin to pay attention to the leads in Fick's book. It may allow us to grapple with the Kingdom of Platons in the south, the women's struggles for equal pay in the north, and what she calls the "independent attitude towards land and the implacable resistance to forced labor expressed in diverse ways."[44]

James had noted in *The Black Jacobins* the attitude of the ex-slaves to land and forced labor but did not tease out what it meant at the level of ideology, political, and social ideas. Here I argue that we need to discern the "traditions of the oppressed." We are at a moment in the historiography of the revolution in both English and French scholarship where one key issue is about the political ideas that played themselves out in the long Haitian Revolution. It is what James means when he says in the IBW lectures that "Today, we now realize, however, that the ideas that people have, the songs that they sing, the stories they tell one another, these are historical things that matter greatly in history."[45] In making this statement James was of course comparing *The Black Jacobins* to Du Bois's *Black Reconstruction*, but the point is clear. We need a new archive to begin to write about the political ideas of the revolutionary slaves. Such a form of historical writing is an intellectual/political history from below. In the end, that is where *The Black Jacobins* takes us.

In 1939 in a letter to Constance Webb James writes that in making a study of Marx's volumes of *Capital* he was looking for a "method of thinking, of looking at history." *The Black Jacobins* opened that process for him. Within his writings there are two turning points: 1948 and his work *Notes on Dialectics* and his 1963 semi-autobiography, *Beyond a Boundary*. In the first his historical thinking developed the political philosophical idea of the end of the Leninist party as the active agent of revolution. In the second he posed a different historical question not so much about revolution but "What did men want?" These two moments, I suggest, have a gestation period that begins with thinking about the agency of Toussaint in *The Black Jacobins*.

The Haitian Revolution was a pivotal moment in world history. A group of revolutionary slaves did the impossible—they formed a revolutionary army as an instrument of their liberation and went to war. Writing at a moment in the twentieth century when the hope for revolution was pronounced, James explored the possibilities of profound political changes in colonial Africa. *The Black Jacobins* was not just the exemplar of an anticolonial text, it was about revolution and how an individual had been pitched onto the world stage by this revolution. We read and reread *Black Jacobins* because the "fever and fret" of revolution keeps alive the pages as the narrative weaves us in to the social structures of Saint-Domingue and the French Revolution.

Unlike Marx's *Eighteenth Brumaire*, which seeks to tell us how reaction consolidated itself after the French Revolution, *The Black Jacobins* was about hope and possibility. Hence there is no room for repetition. This is a historical text that generates a memory of a past possibility as a hope for the future. This is why it is a text about revolution not as failure but as one form of possible historical action.

Notes

The epigraph is from C. L. R. James, *The Black Jacobins: Toussaint L'Ouverture and the San Domingo Revolution* (New York: Vintage, 1963), ix.

1. For a discussion of the role of tragedy and its relationship to action see Hannah Arendt, *The Human Condition* (Chicago: University of Chicago Press, 1958), 175–247.
2. C. L. R. James, "Lectures on *The Black Jacobins*: How I Would Rewrite *The Black Jacobins*," *Small Axe* 8 (2000): 99.
3. For a detailed description of members of this group and a discussion of the groups at the time, see Jonathan Derrick, *Africa's "Agitators": Militant Anti-Colonialism in Africa and the West, 1918–1939* (New York: Columbia University Press, 2008).

4. George Padmore, *Pan Africanism or Communism?* (New York: Anchor Books, 1972), 125.

5. For a discussion of this, see Brent Hayes Edwards, *The Practice of Diaspora: Literature, Translation and the Rise of Black Internationalism* (Cambridge, MA: Harvard University Press, 2003), as well as Derrick, *Africa's "Agitators."*

6. C. L. R. James, "Black Intellectuals in Britain," in *Color, Class and Consciousness,* edited by Bhikhu Parekh (London: Allen and Unwin, 1974), 16.

7. For a discussion of the journal, see Matthew Quest, "George Padmore's and C.L.R. James's *International African Opinion,*" in *George Padmore: Pan African Revolutionary,* edited by Rupert Lewis and Fitzroy Baptiste (Kingston: Ian Randall Press, 2009), 105–32.

8. Amilcar Cabral, *Selected Speeches: Return to the Source* (London: PAIGC Information Committee, n.d.).

9. Vindication was also practiced by telling of great men. Commentators have already noted that James's writing of *The Black Jacobins* was within a strain of black vindicationism; however, I do not think this current subsumes this book.

10. Walter Benjamin, "Theses on the Philosophy of History," in *Illuminations* (New York: Harcourt Brace, 1968), 261.

11. James, "Black Intellectuals in Britain."

12. Robert Hill, "In England, 1932–1938," in *C.L.R. James: His Life and Work,* edited by Paul Buhle (London: Allison and Busby, 1986), 61–80.

13. C.L.R. James, "The Intelligence of the Negro: A Few Words with Dr. Harland," *Beacon* 1, no. 5 (August 1931).

14. C. L. R. James, "Lectures on *The Black Jacobins*: How I Wrote *The Black Jacobins,*" *Small Axe* 8 (2000): 67.

15. James, "Lectures on *The Black Jacobins*: How I Wrote *The Black Jacobins,*" 67.

16. C. L. R. James, *World Revolution, 1917–1936: The Rise and Fall of the Communist International* (Westport, CT: Hyperion Press, 1973), xi.

17. I would note here that another Marxist at the time, Antonio Gramsci, pondered this movement as well and asked himself not about the stalling of the revolution but why the European revolution had been defeated. From his studies and thinking around this question, Gramsci developed the idea of hegemony.

18. James, *World Revolution,* xi.

19. James, "Lectures on the *Black Jacobins*: How I Wrote *The Black Jacobins,*" 68.

20. For a good discussion of the play and its context, see C. L. R. James, *Toussaint Louverture: The Story of the Only Successful Slave Revolt in History: A Play in Three Acts* (Durham, NC: Duke University Press, 2013).

21. For a discussion of this, see Anthony Bogues, *Black Heretics, Black Prophets: Radical Political Intellectuals* (New York: Routledge, 2003), chapter 3.

22. Michel-Rolph Trouillot, *Silencing the Past: Power and the Production of History* (Boston: Beacon Press, 1995), 73.

23. Trouillot, *Silencing the Past*, 72.

24. For a discussion of this historical discursive process and its significance, see Anthony Bogues, "Haiti as an Idea," in *The Haitian Revolution and the Early United States: Histories, Textualities, and Geographies*, edited by Elizabeth Dillon and Michael Drexler, 314–25 (Philadelphia: University of Pennsylvania Press, 2016).

25. It is crucial to note that in 1938, the African American artist Jacob Lawrence created a series of paintings about Toussaint Louverture continuing an explicit African American tradition and concern with Haiti. For a discussion of this tradition see Maurice Jackson and Jacqueline Bacon, eds., *African Americans and the Haitian Revolution* (New York: Routledge, 2010).

26. It is one of the strangest elisions in *The Black Jacobins* that James writes the book without any reference to the U.S. occupation of Haiti, which had lasted from 1915 to 1934. Living in Europe, James did not seem to be aware of the ways an archive was being created in the Americas about the meanings and significances of Haitian independence.

27. Leon Trotsky, *History of the Russian Revolution* (Chicago: Haymarket Books, 2008), xv; emphasis added.

28. James, *The Black Jacobins*, preface.

29. James, *The Black Jacobins*, x.

30. James, *The Black Jacobins*, x.

31. James, *The Black Jacobins*, x.

32. Arendt, *On Revolution*, 29.

33. Arendt, *On Revolution*, 28.

34. Gilles Deleuze, "Difference & Repetition," in *French Philosophy since 1945: Problems Concepts and Inventions*, edited by Etienne Balibar and John Rajchman (New York: New Press, 2011), 176.

35. John Thornton, "'I Am the Subject of the King of the Congo': African Political Ideology and the Haitian Revolution," *Journal of World History* (fall 1995): 181–214.

36. James, *The Black Jacobins*, 276.

37. James, *The Black Jacobins*, 282–83.

38. "Letter to Laveaux" (May 23, 1797), in *Toussaint L'Ouverture: The Haitian Revolution*, edited by Nick Nesbitt (London: Verso, 2008), 22; emphasis added.

39. C. L. R. James, introduction to Jean Fouchard, *The Haitian Maroons: Liberty or Death* (New York: Blyden Press, 1983).

40. George Novack, "Revolution, Black and White," *New International* 5, no. 5 (May 1939): 155.

41. It is accurate to say that *The Black Jacobins* can be read that way, and what might be interesting is to see how ten years later in 1948, James in his work on the "Negro question" develops a position in which the African American struggle becomes the catalyst for the struggle for socialism in America. See *C.L.R. James on the 'Negro Question*,' edited by Scott McLemee (Mississippi: University of Mississippi Press, 1996).

42. Ludwell Lee Montague, "*The Black Jacobins*," *Hispanic American Historical Review* 20, no. 1 (February 1940): 129–30.

43. Carolyn E. Fick, *The Making of Haiti: The Saint Domingue Revolution from Below* (Knoxville: University of Tennessee Press, 1990), 1. It is interesting to note that in her acknowledgments, Fick makes the point that James proposed to George Rudé that she do her dissertation on the Haitian Revolution. She followed this advice. See chapter 3 in this volume.

44. Fick, *The Making of Haiti*, 180.

45. C. L. R. James, "Lectures on the *Black Jacobins*: *The Black Jacobins* and *Black Reconstruction*: A Comparative Analysis," *Small Axe* 8 (2000): 95.

CHARLES FORSDICK

In every island and every slave state [. . .], there were hundreds of slave revolts which prove, as Haitian historians say, that the French Revolution did not spread from France to the West Indies but from the West Indies to France. Negro revolt under the Maroons culminated in Haiti where Britain, France and Spain were worsted and the United States was frightened into stopping the slave trade.
—W. E. B. Du Bois

This opening quotation from W. E. B. Du Bois—extracted from a 1955 piece not on Haiti or the resistance of the enslaved, but on segregated schools in the United States—encapsulates several key issues that are explored in this chapter. In his article, Du Bois mentions directly the work of his mentee, Herbert Aptheker, to evoke the shifts in mid-twentieth-century historiography that had begun to foreground the place of the popular resistance of the enslaved in narratives of the history of the Americas. More important, developing a thesis already explored by C. L. R. James in *The Black Jacobins*, Du Bois endeavors to write this resistance back into Atlantic history, making it clear that at certain points in the 1790s, far from being an exotic sideshow, the Haitian Revolution may be understood as the driver of change in the development of its French counterpart—and, indeed, in the Atlantic world more generally. Du Bois alludes to the contestatory work of unnamed "Haitian historians" (including, I suggest, the Marxist Étienne Charlier, whose *Aperçu sur la formation historique de la nation haïtienne* had just appeared in 1954),[1] while suggesting that French and North American accounts of the revolutionary period had continued to privilege alternative interpretations that systematically underplayed the active role of the enslaved in their own emancipation. In a text that remains an article on African American education, Du Bois's core argument is that continued policing of physical resistance had led to other forms of organization against white supremacism—that is, a determination "to achieve freedom by brain if not by muscle." As such, he begs questions about continuities and discontinuities within histories of rebellion, relating to not only the links between physical revolt and forms of intellectual resistance but also the extent to which the exemplum of the Haitian Revolution has had a continued impact within histories of African American struggle.[2]

As the title of this chapter suggests, this study focuses on the ways (1) in historiography, but more notably in a range of other cultural representations, the legacies of the Haitian Revolution have been personified, singularized, and associated with individual leaders (most notably Toussaint Louverture, to whom Du Bois himself devoted several studies);[3] and (2) in these representations, accounts of popular resistance have been to some extent downplayed and obscured. Associated with this reliance on revolutionary heroism is a questioning of the extent to which an emphasis on the Haitian Revolution, and the clear-cut judgments of "success" and "failure" to which this historical process often seems to lend itself, has not only eclipsed other instances of resistance but also encouraged the development of a one-dimensional focus on autonomy and rebellion that denies the complexity of those various sites seen by Anthony Kaye as dynamic "terrains of struggle" that characterize the everyday culture and geography of slave societies.[4]

Black Resistance, White Philanthropy

This chapter is situated at the point of convergence of several projects in which I have been involved for a number of years. The first is a wide-ranging study of representations of Toussaint Louverture, itself triggered by an interest in how a specific version of the Haitian revolutionary was conscripted to the French republican project of commemorating, in 1998, the sesquicentenary of the definitive abolition of slavery in the French empire.[5] Tracking representations of Louverture has proved to be a project of nearly encyclopedic proportions, encompassing over two centuries of refigurings in a variety of genres, a range of historical and geographical locations, and a number of often contradictory ideological niches. Related to this overarching project is, second, a more focused interest in C. L. R James and the proliferation of material (drama and history, of course, but also essays, lectures, correspondence, and other texts) through which, over the course of nearly sixty years, James's engagement with the Haitian Revolution may be tracked and via which its evolution may be observed. Finally, in a more general context of public history, I have a long-standing interest in the commemoration and specific memorialization of slavery and abolition, especially in France and Britain, most notably in Liverpool, where the International Slavery Museum (ISM) has become a beacon of museological practice for those seeking to present a narrative of slavery that challenges European emphases on abolition and privileges the historical phenomenon of the resistance of the enslaved.[6] As the ISM was developed for inauguration in 2007, the year of the bicentenary of the abolition of the slave trade in the British empire, the curators actively sought to elaborate such a narrative, implicitly challenging the transformation of the bicentenary—through repeated emphasis on abolitionism as a legislative and philanthropic process—into what some critics dubbed at the time a "Wilberfest" or even a "Wilberfarce."[7] The bicentenary of abolition led, perhaps to the first time in the United Kingdom, to public debates about what Diana Paton has called "the individuality of enslaved people, naming them and giving voice to their stories, [. . .] and presenting the full complexity and difficulty of their lives."[8] What was striking in 2007 was the way reflection on the importance, both historical and symbolic, of the Haitian Revolution—and of its spectral presence in debates around slavery in Britain—provided the means to address this question.

The mayor of London at the time, Ken Livingstone, proved to be a rare dissident voice as he claimed in a public intervention in March 2007 that the state failure to issue an official apology for a "crime as monstrous as the slave trade" had the effect of diminishing Britain in the eyes of the world. In a piece titled "Why I Am Saying Sorry for London's Role in This Horror," Livingstone emphasized the importance of an account of slavery and its abolition that foregrounds continual resistance and the assertion of the historical agency of the enslaved.[9] Actively focusing on James's *The Black Jacobins* (acknowledged by him as an enduringly important text for the British Left), Livingstone cited the examples of Jamaica in 1760, Saint-Domingue in 1791, Barbados in 1816, Demerara in 1823, and Jamaica again in 1831. Following James and Eric Williams, he concluded: "No one denigrates William Wilberforce, but it was black resistance and economic development that destroyed slavery, not white philanthropy." In this reference to Wilberforce and the relationship of black resistance to white philanthropy, it is possible to encapsulate those debates relating to history and historiography that characterized various public exchanges regarding the meanings of 2007—exchanges that were equally apparent but with different emphases in France in 1998, when commemorations of the sesquicentenary of (the second) French abolition, regularly drawing on Louverture as an honorary French republican hero, were complicated by questions over where in 1848 history had actually taken place.[10]

What follows falls into two principal sections. The first addresses the foregrounding of Toussaint Louverture in cultural representations of the Haitian Revolution and seeks to ask whether the development of (what may be seen as) Louverture's global iconicity has rendered more challenging the recovery of alternative accounts of the resistance of the enslaved. The second, focusing on the specific engagement by James with Louverture across more than half a century, suggests a gradual evolution in patterns of representation from the individual to the collective. As such, my focus is on the narrative afterlives—historiographic and fictional—of the forms of resistance of the enslaved and on the implications for those afterlives of the foregrounding of figures such as Toussaint Louverture, the extent and limits of whose resistance are to be understood in a framework of what John Walsh has recently described—in a telling comparative study of Louverture and Aimé Césaire—as "loyal opposition" to France.[11]

Toussaint Louverture as Global Icon

It is significant that Livingstone focused in his comments on the work of James. He made it clear that despite the continued amnesia regarding the 1794–1798 expedition to Saint-Domingue,[12] *The Black Jacobins* remains a key reference to the Haitian Revolution in British debates, both public and academic, on the resistance of the enslaved, especially at a time when there is a resurgence of interest across a range of fields in the wider oeuvre of its author. James's 1938 history of the Haitian Revolution is central to a cluster of historical representations of Haiti that appeared in the interwar period. This engagement with the Caribbean republic and its revolution was genuinely transnational, and there is clear evidence of the entanglement of refigurings of Toussaint Louverture in sites as distant as Moscow, Paris, London, and New York. Immediately after the occupation, the hemispheric connections between Haiti and North America evident during the Harlem Renaissance were also developed more intensively for a brief period into a "Haiti-mania," a phenomenon exemplified perhaps by Orson Welles's extravagant 1936 Federal Theatre Project production in Harlem of the *Voodoo Macbeth*.[13]

The specific niche of the 1930s constituted a particularly concentrated moment in the ongoing (and certainly unfinished) transformation of Haiti into an (African) American *lieu de mémoire*.[14] This process began in the ante-bellum period (as scholars Alfred Hunt and more recently Matt Clavin have made clear),[15] continued at key postbellum sites such as the Haytian Pavil-ion at the 1893 Chicago World's Fair,[16] and remains visible in the work of popular authors, artists, and musicians from Ntozake Shange to Jean-Michel Basquiat, from Edwidge Danticat to Wyclef Jean. As has been suggested al-ready, the interwar period also represents an especially fruitful moment for international engagement with Haiti, in particular with its revolution. This was not only because of the renewed visibility of the Caribbean nation-state as its occupation by the United States was subject to increasing criticism. At the same time, Haiti's by-then-over-a-century-long tradition of independent postcoloniality, complemented by neocolonial intervention, was beginning to irradiate and resonate, with increasing clarity, with twentieth-century situations elsewhere. James's *Black Jacobins*—both the 1938 history and the 1936 play (of which Christian Høgsbjerg's recent edition for Duke University Press is attracting increasing attention)—remains central to such processes of recognition, and this book is to be read in the context of its dialogue with other engagements with the revolution with which it is contemporary. In retrospect, it is evident that this network of representations was genuinely transnational and firmly "black Atlantic," connecting, for example, Britain and the Anglophone Caribbean with African American activism through the figure of Paul Robeson (who played the lead in James's play), but also linking the Francophone and Anglophone Caribbeans, often via the detour of Paris, through resonances between James's work and that of Césaire.

The links within this bundle of representations are at times tenuous and rarely direct. They provide evidence of linking Haiti to what might be seen as more of an international "structure of feeling" in the interwar period, relating in particular to emerging anticolonial sentiment and the quest for a genu-inely Pan-African identity, rather than any orchestrated transnational re-sponse. Networks are apparent, however, linking négritude with the Harlem Renaissance and creating intercontinental alliances through Pan-Africanism, although the connections I have identified were at times fortuitous. As the introduction to this volume makes clear, James's impact in North America postdated the publication *The Black Jacobins* and reflected a major evolution in his own political journey; connections between James and Césaire only became strongly evident in the 1960s, especially in the former's comments on the *Cahier* in the appendix to the 1963 edition of *The Black Jacobins*, published four years before their actual meeting in Cuba in 1967. The specific example of the 1930s—to which James's work remains central—nevertheless represents a particularly useful means of interrogating the unwieldly, baroque corpus of representations that act as vehicles for the international impact of the Haitian Revolution in the two centuries following it.

Focusing on the privileged figure of Toussaint Louverture—by no means a metonym for the revolution but the character often conscripted to act as its representative—it is possible to ask whether interpretations of the revolution have always been localized, shaped by the clear national contexts in which they occur, or whether it is possible (and indeed constructive) to evoke a type of global iconicity that sees the revolutionary leader transformed into a cipher or individual vehicle for wider understandings of Haiti in a global frame. Underlying this analysis is a comparison that is often made but rarely scrutinized—that between Louverture and Che Guevara. The Haitian and Cuban revolutionaries are frequently united in anthological approaches to anticolonial revolution. Both are included, for instance, among the twenty-four "liberation struggle heroes" proposed for inclusion in March 2009 in the South African Freedom Park in Pretoria, a memorial site that aims at fostering a sense of national identity but has been associated by its critics more with a sense of political pageantry (Louverture and Guevara are celebrated alongside figures of national resistance such as Steve Biko and Oliver Tambo, as well as international leaders such as Amilcar Cabral and Fidel Castro);[17] at the same time, Louverture and Guevara reflect the recurrent sense of a Haiti–Cuba axis, evident historically in events such as the 1812 Aponte Rebellion, for which images of the Haitian revolutionary leaders apparently served as a trigger, and present in the revolutionary processes that have shaped the modern Caribbean.[18] These are links that are also central to James's 1963 appendix to *The Black Jacobins*, in which the connection of Haiti and Cuba brings the impact of the 1791–1804 revolution to the present day, creating an all-encompassing narrative summed up in Susan Gillman's equation: "from Columbus to Toussaint + from Toussaint to Castro = from Columbus to Castro."[19]

Che Guevara is now indisputably recognized as a global icon, situated recently by the art historian Martin Kemp—in his book *Christ to Coke: How Image Becomes Icon*—in the company of a range of prominent historical and contemporary examples such as those indicated in his title.[20] Louverture's place in such a process is more ambiguous. The world historical significance of the Haitian Revolution, to which Du Bois alludes in the epigraph, has attracted increasing attention in recent years, with the pioneering historiographic work of scholars such as David Geggus complemented by the reflections of Susan Buck-Morss and Nick Nesbitt on the revolution's philosophical radicalism. Nesbitt's focus on what he calls the "idea of 1804," moreover, reveals the ways the modernizing project of the age of revolutions was forced to address its own inadequacies as it failed to deliver the logical outcome of universal emancipation.[21] Underlying such recent analyses are responses to the forms of policing and domestication summed up by Michel-Rolph Trouillot in his important discussion of the historiographic "silencing" of the Haitian Revolution (through processes of banalization and erasure) and by Sibylle Fischer in her complementary analysis of its disavowal.[22]

Beyond Control and Containment: Representing Louverture

Such mechanisms of control and containment serve to attenuate any claims of international, and especially global reach, although the context of my own interest in Louverture is that of rapidly renewed attention devoted to him in recent years, especially increased visibility in the decade since the bicentenary of his death in 2003. The implications of this renewed attention are twofold, enhancing Louverture's role as "exemplary" icon but also, through recovery of a historical figure, challenging the mythologization that such iconicity may be seen to betoken. Such a challenge can at times be part of an active recognition and celebration of the agency of the enslaved, but it may also lead to debunking hagiography whose motivation lacks any such historiographic radicalism. Philippe Girard's study of the Haitian War of Independence tends to reduce its protagonist Louverture in ways reminiscent of the 1989 biography by Pierre Pluchon, suggesting not least that Louverture's principal motivation was not ideology but greed. "The simple and sad truth," Girard concludes, "is that Louverture died forgotten, of cold, old age, and sorrow, a month before his estimated sixtieth birthday."[23] Emphasis on the historical Louverture inevitably contributes to the reductive and often denigrating processes of demythologization of the revolutionary, but this does not take away from the importance of exploring the complexities and ambiguities, contradictions and paradoxes, of the processes of mythologization that now extend over two centuries. Not only are increasing amounts of historical source material relating to these processes becoming available,[24] we now have access to Louverture's own memoirs, evidence of his own awareness of his potentially totemic power for future generations;[25] and the corpus of this material continues to expand, not least cinematically (Danny Glover's long-promised biopic of Louverture is yet to appear, but 2012 saw the release of Philippe Niang's television mini-series that has attracted considerable international attention).[26]

In a 2012 study of "black heroism in the transatlantic imagination," *Characters of Blood*, Celeste-Marie Bernier privileges Louverture in her exploration of "six iconic African, African American and African Caribbean men and women [who] have played a key role in the construction and theorizing of an alternative visual and textual archive."[27] Bernier's focus is on "malleable symbolism," and she distances herself from "any quest to penetrate beneath obfuscations within the archive to recover an essential or even historically verifiable heroic figure," a quest that she sees as "not only illusory but ultimately doomed to failure" (7). She is interested instead in reimagination and reuse of individuals such as Louverture in the transatlantic imagination to cater for "differing agendas, audiences, and movements" (11). Central to her argument is the notion of iconicity, associated not only with recognition of the various forms of exceptionalism, exemplarity, and surrogacy to which figures such as Louverture, Nat Turner, Frederick Douglass, and Harriet Tubman are related, but also with their persistent circulation—in radical, transformative, and transgressive ways—as icons that turn them into controversial "sites of contestation" (25).

Bernier does not dwell on the meanings of the word *icon*, a term that may be seen to privilege visual representation; she brings with it overtones of an enduring blend of exceptionalism and exemplarity, at times associated with reverence and the curiosity created by notoriety. Clearly iconicity betokens a degree of ubiquity, either chronological or geographical, although often a combination of both. It is clear that Guevara—representations of whom, based most consistently on Alberto Korda's chance image from March 1960, have proliferated in the five decades since its subject's death—fits such an understanding well. From posters and book covers produced in the immediate aftermath of Guevara's death, the image shifted rapidly in the 1970s to T-shirts and other consumer products to ensure the immortality evident today as icon morphs into brand. Michael Casey, in a book called *Che's Afterlife*, has tracked the evolution of the image and illustrated its versatility in a range of cultural contexts.[28] He stresses the diversification on which the construction of such an icon depends and concludes that "since Che is one of the most contested and politicized of all popular icons, the range of ideas contained within it is very broad indeed" (15). Although, in numerous contexts (and especially Latin America), the political power of the image persists, at the same time (as Martin Kemp notes) "Che sells,"[29] and he may even be seen as the "quintessential capitalist brand." The countercultural icon is conscripted to the cause of globalized consumer capitalism, simultaneously granted—and then at risk of being robbed of—an afterlife.

There are many reasons Louverture does not stand comparison with the unique iconicity of Guevara, not least because—as discussions of the visual representation of the Haitian revolutionary repeatedly state—there is no definitive likeness of him extant. As a result, the Haitian revolutionary does not enjoy the same degree of ubiquity and mass familiarity, although the images of him to have the greatest visibility are, like those of Guevara, associated with defiant martial prowess or linked to the tragic circumstances of death, which—in both cases and in certain interpretations—grants the victim Christ-like characteristics. In one of the most useful anthologies of Louverture's textual afterlives, George Tyson states: "he has been all things to all men, from bloodthirsty black savage to 'the greatest black man in history.'"[30] What is of interest is precisely the malleable, often contradictory complexity of this mythologization or instrumentalization, that is, the ways the context of production of images of Louverture affect these posthumous refigurings, creating often unexpected connections between the Haitian revolutionary and other distinct historico-political moments and cultural settings.

The corpus of visual images of Louverture is wide and varied, beginning with those that began to circulate—as frontispieces to books and pamphlets, as newspaper illustrations, as engravings—from before his death.[31] Posthumous processes of representation led to a real proliferation of images whose inherent ephemerality makes an exhaustive catalog extremely unlikely.[32] The Maurin lithograph, first appearing in 1832, is perhaps one of the most influential and is arguably the closest we have to the Korda portrait of Guevara. Although the genuflecting black body, passive, vulnerable, and mute, was a formulaic element in the representation of the black slave, used even in abolitionist images, the majority of Louverture's images from the earlier nineteenth century present him instead, as does Maurin's, before capture and humiliation, with the exceptionalist detail of his French officer's uniform exploited as a marker of the artists' admiration of (or indignation at) the perceived mismatch between black body and a French general's insignia.[33] Very different from a number of its antecedents in its overt racialization, it portrays its subject's features in a way that either reflects in its jutting jaw the marked prognathism on which a number of those who met Louverture commented or is inspired by early nineteenth-century phrenological and physiognomic assumptions regarding the reflection of intellectual hierarchies in the contours of the face and skull. As some contemporary critics have pointed out, the risk remains that a modern interpreter miscasts as derision a portrayal (through high forehead and pronounced cranium) of strength and determination, superior intelligence and moral fortitude. It is undeniable that Maurin's profile was adopted in other representations, most notably in the work of Jacob Lawrence in the 1930s, a key element of the interwar cluster of representations of Haiti and its revolution to which *The Black Jacobins* remains central.

Lawrence's work is to be read, in part at least, in the context of the transcultural abstraction of Louverture from his local, Haitian context into a North American one to which I have already alluded.[34] His forty-one panels of Louverture's life are accordingly part of a long tradition of U.S. reinterpretations of the revolution and its principal revolutionary, reinterpretations that reached a peak in the abolitionist and postabolitionist debates of the later nineteenth century (in which the revolutionary played an important and strategic role in vindicationist discourse), but at the same time achieved a particular intensity in the interwar years. For Lawrence, Louverture's role in the emergence of a black separatist movement has clear allegorical implications for the stirrings of the civil rights movement in the 1930s United States. The internationalization of Louverture has not, however, prevented a continued exploration of his iconicity in the culture within which he came to prominence. Twentieth- and twenty-first-century Haitian artists—history painters, magical realists, and those who, like Édouard Duval-Carrié, defy critics insisting on any such division—have continually returned to him in their work, often challenging former emphases in their refiguring of his life and person.

Over the past decade, the status of Louverture as a revolutionary icon in a global frame has acquired renewed intensity, but at the same time—I suggest—it has taken a new turn as the specific implications of this iconicity for anticolonial struggle and postcolonial reflection have risked becoming diluted into generality. Whether as the subject of early nineteenth-century Parisian lithographs or of a later nineteenth-century British folk artist's papier-mâché figurine, Louverture has long figured in popular culture. However, a number of recent manifestations—the Louverture character in the video game expansion pack Age of Empires III: The War Chiefs (in which the Haitian revolutionary is available to serve the French or the British); the Louverture T-shirts, hoodies, and aprons available at the Social Justice Store; Toussaint Louverture liqueur (mix with brandy to make a "Napoléon noir")—suggest that any strategic substance left in Louverture is progressively being eroded and replaced by the ubiquity, recognizability, and ultimate ambivalence that characterize the few genuinely globalized icons. Louverture has indeed long been the one revolutionary figure whose transcontinental visibility seems to rival that of Guevara. Both Louverture and Guevara often float free of their actual revolutionary contexts, and in the process risk becoming detached from their initial, incendiary impact. There is therefore a drift toward a commercialized global iconicity that elevates the Haitian revolutionary to rival Guevara and sees him progressively emptied of specific meaning. Nevertheless, in particular with the work of Nick Nesbitt on "universal emancipation," echoed in fictional work such as Jean-Claude Fignolé's novel *Moi, Toussaint Louverture*,[35] we are witnessing a regrounding, an acknowledgment of the importance of Louverture as the figure who embodies pushing the American and French revolutions to unimaginable limits whose implications have not yet been fully realized. Such recognition nevertheless implies a singularization that through residual processes of mythologization or hagiography tends more toward exceptionalism than exemplarity—this is the dilemma with which James engaged in his evolving struggle with the representation of Louverture, and I turn to this in conclusion.

"The Revolutionary and Creative Power of Untaught Slaves"

As I suggested in the previous section, in the complex archive of representations—visual, textual, musical, and other—that constitute the afterlives of Toussaint Louverture, James's *Black Jacobins* plays an essential role. The book made available, for the first time for an Anglophone readership, much French-language material on Haiti largely (if not entirely) ignored within French revolutionary historiography. It also provided a clear focus for the eclectic range of interwar representations of Louverture—primarily European, North American, and Soviet—that emerged from the entangled contexts of the U.S. occupation of Haiti, the growth of négritude and the Harlem Renaissance, and the consolidation of a modern Pan-Africanism. Finally, the progressive transformations of *The Black Jacobins* in the now three-quarters of a century since its publication permit an understanding of evolving responses to Toussaint Louverture, historiographic, literary, and ideological, not only in James's own thinking but also more generally. Central to the reflection with which this chapter concludes is one of the key paradoxes of *The Black Jacobins* (i.e., the volume), produced initially in the very specific sociopolitical niche of the 1930s, is that it has not only traveled to a variety of different contexts but also been transformed at a variety of different moments.

"This book is not an accident," James stated in 1971, "It didn't just fall from a tree."[36] The observation is supported by the earlier reference (in the 1938 preface) to Franco, Stalin, and the "fierce, shrill turmoil of the revolutionary movement striving for clarity and influence": "Such is our age," continued James, "and this book is of it, with something of the fever and the fret. [...] Written under different circumstances it would have been a different but not necessarily a better book."[37] This work's niche is therefore associated with global politics in the 1930s (especially postrevolutionary power struggles in the Soviet Union), as well as with nascent anticolonialism (in particular the Italian invasion of Ethiopia).[38] The project's origins are, however, located in the Caribbean. As James made clear on several occasions, on arrival in Plymouth in 1932, the manuscripts in his trunk were accompanied by notes relating to his plans to work on the Haitian Revolution. "Stuck away in the back of my head for years," he comments in *Beyond a Boundary*, "was the project of writing a biography of Toussaint Louverture."[39] The exact roots of this project are unclear. Dave Renton, in his study of James, discusses "Revolution," the last short story written before departure from Trinidad, a reflection on failed insurrection and forms of revolutionary leadership in which references to the Haitian case might be seen as implicit;[40] James was also influenced at an early stage by the work of J. J. Thomas, whose 1889 rebuttal to J. A. Froude's *The English in the West Indies* was one of the first assertions that Caribbean people had a legitimate claim to govern themselves.[41] More important, arguably, was James's retort in *The Beacon* in 1931, a year before his departure, to the pseudo-scientific taxonomies of IQ outlined by Sidney Harland in "Racial Admixture," a work in the same racist lineage as Froude's.[42] Dismissing Harland's article as "antiquated," naïve, and characterized by "monstrous blunder[s]," James was particularly critical of the "arrant nonsense" about Louverture, to whom he himself devotes a long paragraph. In an exasperated final section, reflecting on the racial and educational implications of Harland's piece, James concludes: "I think I have written enough. I would have far preferred to write on Toussaint Louverture, for instance."[43] Already embryonic here are issues that characterized the history seven years later, not least the question of Louverture as exception or exemplum (or both). At the same time, by referring to Percy Waxman's *Black Napoleon*—a

1931 biography dismissed curtly in the bibliography of *The Black Jacobins* as a "superficial book"—James reveals how his own refigurings of Louverture represent a series of implicit and usually highly critical dialogues with other interpreters of the revolutionary, and result from what he describes (in the 1971 Atlanta lectures at the Institute of the Black World [IBW] on the genesis of *The Black Jacobins*) as a genuine dissatisfaction with the existing literature.

In these evolving dialogues and as a result of this dissatisfaction, *The Black Jacobins* evolves, with redraftings of the text, with the addition of new material (textual and paratextual) and with the development of an extensive self-critical apparatus (notably in correspondence, lectures, and interviews). James's Louverture becomes a mobile figure, evolving over the final five decades of his life. In his 1971 interview with Studs Terkel, James underscores the ways *The Black Jacobins* reasserted the importance of Louverture, whose role had by this stage been downplayed in Haitian historiography, leading him to claim that—through engagement with the French translation of *The Black Jacobins*—Haitians had discovered "a new conception of the role of Toussaint in the revolution"; but James's own evolving engagement with the Haitian Revolution reveals a progressive attenuation of that initial engagement. Such evolution is a result of James's changing responses to social, political, and personal events; it reflects at the same time his reactions to the readings of the revolutionary in the thought and writings of others, as well as to the emergence of new historical details (not least the claim by Debien, Fouchard, and Ménier, that Louverture was himself by 1791 a slave-owner who had been freed fifteen years previously).[44] The encounter with Aimé Césaire—on the page of the *Cahier d'un retour au pays natal* (1939) rather than in person—was instrumental in steering *The Black Jacobins* back to its Caribbean context, a shift made clear in the 1963 appendix.[45] Other variants in the 1963 edition, especially the paragraphs added to the final chapter, have allowed David Scott to enlist James in what has been read as a highly pessimistic narrative of postcolonial politics.[46]

As Frank Rosengarten has convincingly suggested, it is questionable whether Scott tells the full story that the progressive rewritings of *The Black Jacobins* imply.[47] Study of the manuscript variants of the 1967 rewriting of the dramatic version of the Haitian Revolution reveal, for instance, a gradual writing out of Louverture; a shift of emphasis to new characters (including Moïse, not included in the 1936 London production, and the peasant Samedi Smith), who become the means of articulating a critique of Louverture and Dessalines; and the insistent, more pluralistic focus, foregrounding the role of the enslaved. Already in the 1950s James had corresponded with the Haitian Marxist historian Étienne Charlier, whose *Aperçu sur la formation historique de la nation haitienne* had challenged the predominantly hagiographic tendencies of Haitian historiography—that is, the emphases on what Maryse Condé subsequently dismissed, in a reflection inspired in part by the overt gendering of such narratives, as "conventional revolutionary bric à brac."[48] Charlier presents Louverture as an ancien régime figure and, for the first time, gestures toward a more popular history of the Haitian Revolution, along the lines that Michel-Rolph Trouillot and Carolyn Fick subsequently developed. A 1955 letter from James to Charlier is illuminating. Rejecting the ancien régime thesis, James nevertheless acknowledged the importance of his correspondent's new emphases:

> Toussaint was a revolutionary who had gone a long way but could not continue to what the situation actually demanded, the independence of the island. Revolution exhausts different layers of men and Toussaint had reached the end of his tether before the revolution was concluded. However, that is a question more of the biographical analysis of Toussaint than of the fundamental analysis of the classes and forces in conflict. And there I have learnt much from you! [T]he revolutionary and creative power of untaught slaves is what interests me about the revolution in San Domingo more than anything else.[49]

These observations also resonated in James's engagement with Jean Fouchard's *Les Marrons de la Liberté* (1972), for whose 1981 English translation he provided an introduction where he celebrates the transformation of those previously sidelined as "accessories" in historical process into privileged participants. Fouchard's innovation, he claims, is not (only) about sources and historical method but illustrates the "expansion of the knowledge of, and insight into, the great majority of human beings."[50]

In 1938, the risks of hagiography and hero worship that characterize certain strands of Haitian revolutionary historiography had—it is important to stress—already been apparent as James negotiated a path between a materialist analysis of history and more conventional portraiture: "Great men make history," he wrote, "but only such history as it is possible for them to make."[51] The 1955 exchange with Charlier is an early statement of what became apparent in the third of the IBW lectures in 1971 and in the introduction to Fouchard—James's realization that the 1938 *Black Jacobins* does not constitute a history of the Haitian Revolution genuinely, for want of a better expression, "from below." In the Atlanta lectures, James stated that if he were to completely overhaul his history, he would "write descriptions in which the black slaves themselves, or people very close to them describe what they are doing and how they felt about the work that they were forced to carry on."[52] By the early 1970s, his disillusionment over postcolonial nationhood (and the questions of leadership with which this is associated) was growing, not least as a result of the case of Trinidad. "The seats of power," he stated in 1971, "are very warm and very comfortable." At the same time, he was increasingly aware of ongoing shifts in French historiography, in particular new attention being given by researchers such as Albert Soboul to the *sansculottes*. These shifts in James's thinking are crystallized in his attention to a detail in Pamphile de Lacroix, French general and member of Leclerc's 1802 expedition, whose two-volume eyewitness account of the revolution and its final stages (published 1819) he had consulted four decades earlier in Paris (and described then in his bibliography as "indispensable").[53] What interests James is Lacroix's prescient reference to the "obscure creatures" who, more than the Haitian generals themselves, maintained the impetus of the unfinished revolution. It seems clear that in a redrafted *Black Jacobins*, Louverture's predominance would have been replaced by a multiplicity of voices, perhaps similar to that attempted by Madison Smartt Bell in his recent trilogy of novels on the revolution—and this shift that would undoubtedly have foregrounded Moïse, increasingly central to James's reflections, more importantly and as we have seen more recently in the work of Carolyn Fick, Marcus Rediker, and others, while allowing the recovery of the voices of the enslaved themselves.

Conclusion

Louverture may still be read, as he was in the work of Jacob Lawrence, as "an iconic signifier of historical resistance, but also as a lens through which to debate contemporary injustices" and "anonymized histories of suffering"—not least those relating to ongoing economic and social persecution in contemporary Haiti itself.[54] What such a reading ignores, however, are the implications of such iconicity for recognition of a wider historiography of resistance as well as of the ways the focus on an "acceptable," portable, translatable figure such as Louverture might still have much to teach us about the reluctance of white audiences to see popular representations of black figures engaged in acts of resistance to white authority. Without being able to develop this observation in the current context, I suggest that these debates are particularly evident in the domain of film, where Quentin Tarantino's *Django Unchained* has at least provided a new frame for debating these questions. Nevertheless, certain relevant projects (such as Sergei Eisenstein's *Black Consul*, Danny Glover's *Toussaint Louverture* and also *The Black Jacobins* itself, the cinematic rights to which James attempted to sell) remain unmade,[55] and others (such as Gillo Pontecorvo's *Quemada/Burn!* [1969] and Tomàs Gutiérrez Alea's *The Last Supper* [1976]) have not attracted the attention (and audiences) they merit. As Natalie Zemon Davis notes, cinema nevertheless has the potential to provide a privileged means of representing "flesh-and-blood human beings with some agency, shaped by the distinctive circumstances and values of their time, sometimes accommodating, sometimes resisting, sometimes suffering, sometimes escaping, sometimes changing things and trying something new."[56] Along the lines of this argument, films like those I have mentioned provide clear material for exploration of Nicholas Mirzoeff's notion of countervisuality, in whose elaboration Louverture is one of the key examples on which he draws.[57] Focusing on the representation of the revolutionary hero, Mirzoeff sees such a figure as the "condensation of the popular movements" that has the potential to grant "the enslaved everywhere a new weapon" (104), but also, through the mechanisms of iconicity and hagiography, the "means to contain" those same movements. It is possible, of course, that a focus on representations of Dessalines or Christophe may provide slightly different conclusions—but the evolving, contradictory, and unfinished refigurings of Louverture continue to provide a compelling illustration of these unresolved tensions between the individual hero and collective resistance, between the struggle for liberation and its continued containment.

Notes

Epigraph is from W. E. B. Du Bois, "200 Years of Segregated Schools," *Jewish Life* (February 1955): 7.

1. Étienne Charlier, *Aperçu sur la formation historique de la nation haïtienne* (Port-au-Prince: Presses libres, 1954).
2. See Maurice Jackson and Jacqueline Bacon, "Fever and Fret: The Haitian Revolution and African American Responses," in *African Americans and the Haitian Revolution*, edited by Maurice Jackson and Jacqueline Bacon (New York: Routledge, 2010), 7–24.
3. See, for example, the sections devoted to Haiti in *The Negro* (London: Williams and Norgate, 1915).

4. Anthony Kaye, *Joining Places: Slave Neighborhoods in the Old South* (Chapel Hill: University of North Carolina Press, 2007).

5. See, for instance, Charles Forsdick, "The Travelling Revolutionary: Translations of Toussaint Louverture," in *Re-interpreting the Haitian Revolution and Its Cultural Aftershocks*, edited by Martin Munro and Elizabeth Hackett-Walcott (St. Augustine: University of the West Indies Press, 2006), 150–67, and "Postcolonial Toussaint," in *Echoes of the Haitian Revolution, 1804–2004*, edited by Martin Munro and Elizabeth Hackett-Walcott (St Augustine: University of the West Indies Press, 2008), 41–60.

6. On the development of the Liverpool museum, see Renaud Hourcade, "Un musée d'histoire face à la question raciale: l'International Slavery Museum de Liverpool," *Genèses* 92 (2013): 6–27.

7. On 2007, see Cora Kaplan and John Oldfield (eds.), *Imagining Transatlantic Slavery* (Basingstoke: Palgrave, 2010).

8. Diana Paton, "Telling Stories about Slavery," *History Workshop Journal* 59 (2005): 252.

9. See Ken Livingstone, "Why I Am Saying Sorry for London's Role in This Horror," *Guardian*, March 21, 2007, http://www.guardian.co.uk/commentisfree/2007/mar/21/comment.society.

10. On the 1998 commemoration, see Emmanuel de Roux, "La discrète célébration du 150e anniversaire de l'abolition de l'esclavage," *Le Monde*, April 5, 1998; Madeleine Dobie, *Trading Places: Colonization and Slavery in Eighteenth-Century French Culture* (Ithaca, NY: Cornell University Press, 2010), 287–94.

11. See John Patrick Walsh, *Free and French in the Caribbean: Toussaint Louverture, Aimé Césaire and Narratives of Loyal Opposition* (Bloomington: Indiana University Press, 2013).

12. On this expedition, see David Geggus, *Slavery, War and Revolution: The British Occupation of Saint Domingue, 1793–1798* (Oxford: Oxford University Press, 1982).

13. See Nick Moschovakis, "Reading *Macbeth* in Texts by and about African Americans, 1903–1944: Race and the Problematics of Allusive Identification," in *Weyward Macbeth: Intersections of Race and Performance*, edited by Scott L. Newstok and Ayanna Thompson (New York: Palgrave Macmillan, 2010), 65–75. The following section develops material initially explored in the following short article: Charles Forsdick, "Toussaint Louverture in a Globalized Frame: Reading the Revolutionary as Icon," *Contemporary French & Francophone Studies/SITES*, 19, no. 2 (2015): 325–34.

14. Elizabeth Rauh Bethel, "Images of Hayti: The Construction of an Afro-American *lieu de mémoire*," *Callaloo* 15, no. 3 (1992): 827–41.

15. Alfred N. Hunt, *Haiti's Influence on Antebellum America: Slumbering Volcano in the Caribbean* (Baton Rouge: Louisiana State University Press, 1988); Matthew Clavin, *Toussaint Louverture and the American Civil War: The Promise and Peril of a Second Haitian Revolution* (Philadelphia: University of Pennsylvania Press, 2010).

16. See Charles Forsdick, "Exhibiting Haiti: Questioning Race at the World's Columbian Exhibition, 1893," in *The Invention of Race: Scientific and Popular Representations*, edited by Nicolas Bancel, Thomas David, and Dominic Thomas (New York: Routledge, 2014), 233–46.

17. Robyn Autry, "Doing Memory in Public: Postapartheid Memorial Space as an Activist Project," in *Memory and Postwar Memorials: Confronting the Violence of the Past*, edited by Marc Silberman and Florence Vatan (New York: Palgrave Macmillan, 2013), 137–54.

18. For a recent discussion of the links between Haiti and Cuba, see Ada Ferrer, *Freedom's Mirror: Cuba and Haiti in the Age of Revolution* (Cambridge: Cambridge University Press, 2014). It is significant that Ferrer concludes with an epilogue in which Alejo Carpentier's *Kingdom of This World* and James's *Black Jacobins* are read together in relation to a consideration of antislavery and the afterlives of revolution. Focusing on James's 1971 lecture "How I Would Rewrite *The Black Jacobins*," Ferrer links Carpentier's protagonist Ti-Noël to the "obscure creatures" largely sidelined by James in the 1938 history and reflects on the perception of Haiti as a beacon of freedom and the everyday existence in the postindependent country: "Revolution abroad is not always the same thing as revolution at home. The stories of how new forms of domination emerge out of a process of revolution is, however, another one. Indeed, it is the central question of Haiti's history in the nineteenth century, and of Cuba's in the twentieth" (346).

19. Susan Gillman, "Black Jacobins and New World Mediterraneans," in *Surveying the American Tropics: A Literary Geography from New York to Rio*, edited by Maria Cristina Fumagalli, Peter Hulme, Owen Robinson, and Lesley Wylie (Liverpool: Liverpool University Press, 2013), 174.

20. Martin Kemp, *Christ to Coke: How Image Becomes Icon* (Oxford: Oxford University Press, 2012). For a recent reflection on representations of Guevara, see Maria-Carolina Cambre, *The Semiotics of Che Guevara* (London: Bloomsbury Academic, 2015).

21. Nick Nesbitt, "The Idea of 1804," *Yale French Studies* 107 (2005): 6–38.

22. Michel-Rolph Trouillot, *Silencing the Past: Power and the Production of History* (Boston: Beacon Press, 1995); Sibylle Fischer, *Modernity Disavowed: Haiti and the Cultures of Slavery in the Age of Revolution* (Durham, NC: Duke University Press, 2004).

23. Philippe Girard, *The Slaves Who Defeated Napoleon: Toussaint Louverture and the Haitian War of Independence, 1801–1804* (Tuscaloosa: University of Alabama Press, 2011), 279.

24. See, for example, Philippe Girard and Jean-Louis Donnadieu, "Toussaint before Louverture: New Archival Findings on the Early Life of Toussaint Louverture," *William and Mary Quarterly* 70, no. 1 (2013): 41–78.

25. See *Mémoires du général Toussaint-Louverture*, edited by Jacques de Cauna (Guitalens-l'Albarède: Editions la Girandole, 2009); *Mémoires du général Toussaint Louverture*, edited by Daniel Désormeaux (Paris: Classiques Garnier, 2011); and *The Memoir of General Toussaint Louverture*, edited by Philippe Girard (Oxford: Oxford University Press, 2014).

26. On this, see Alyssa Goldstein Sepinwall, "Happy as a Slave: The *Toussaint Louverture* Miniseries," *Fiction and Film for French Historians: A Cultural Bulletin* 4, no. 1 (2013), http://h-france.net/fffh/maybe-missed/happy-as-a-slave-the-toussaint-louverture-miniseries/.

27. Celeste-Marie Bernier, *Characters of Blood: Black Heroism in the Transatlantic Imagination* (Charlottesville: University of Virginia Press, 2012), xiii.

28. Michael Casey, *Che's Afterlife: The Legacy of an Image* (New York: Vintage Books, 2009).

29. Kemp, *Christ to Coke*, 192.

30. George Tyson, *Toussaint L'Ouverture* (Englewood Cliffs, NJ: Prentice Hall, 1973), 2–3.

31. It is suggestive to reflect on the ways this iconography has been reflected in cover illustrations of *The Black Jacobins*. For an illuminating blog post on this subject, see Josh MacPhee, "68: *The Black Jacobins*," *Just Seeds*, Judging Books by Their Covers 68 (July 21, 2011), http://justseeds.org/jbbtc-68-the-black-jacobins/. To take some examples, the cover of the 1963 Vintage paperback edition has a design by Loren Eutemy, inspired it seems by Jacob Lawrence, who in turn drew on the Maurin lithograph; the original 1949 French edition included a version of Jean's equestrian portrait of Louverture, and a colour version of this has been used for the cover of the new 2008 edition produced by Editions d'Amsterdam; and the cover of the most recent (Penguin) English-language edition (2001) shows not Louverture but Anne-Louis Girodet de Roussy-Trioson's 1797 portrait of Convention member Jean-Baptiste Belley.

32. On the iconography of Louverture, see Fritz Daguillard, *Mystérieux dans la Gloire: Toussaint Louverture (1743–1803)* (Port-au-Prince: MIPANAH, 2003); Helen Weston, "The Many Faces of Toussaint Louverture," in *Slave Portraiture in the Atlantic World*, edited by Agnes I. Lugo-Ortiz and Angela Rosenthal (Cambridge: Cambridge University Press, 2013), 345–73.

33. On this subject, see Srinivas Aravamudan, *Tropicopolitans: Colonialism and Agency, 1688–1804* (Durham, NC: Duke University Press, 1999), 303.

34. On Lawrence's work, see Carolyn Williams, "The Haitian Revolution and a North American Griot: The Life of Toussaint L'Ouverture by Jacob Lawrence," in *Echoes of the Haitian Revolution, 1804–2004*, edited by Martin Munro and Elizabeth Walcott-Hackshaw (Kingston: University of the West Indies Press, 2008), 61–85.

35. Jean-Claude Fignolé, *Moi, Toussaint Louverture* (Mont-Royal, Québec: Plume et encre, 2004).

36. C. L. R. James, "Lectures on *The Black Jacobins*: How I Wrote *The Black Jacobins*," *Small Axe* 8 (2000): 71.

37. C. L. R. James, *The Black Jacobins* (London: Penguin, 2001), xx.

38. *The Black Jacobins* was written, James makes clear, "with the African revolution in mind," but also with one eye on Trotsky's *History of the Russian Revolution*.

39. C. L. R. James, *Beyond a Boundary* (London: Hutchinson, 1969), 122.

40. Dave Renton, *C.L.R. James: Cricket's Philosopher King* (London: Haus, 2007).

41. See Selwyn R. Cudjoe, "The Audacity of It All: C.L.R. James's Trinidadian Background," in *C.L.R. James's Caribbean*, edited by Paget Henry and Paul Buhle (Durham, NC: Duke University Press, 1992), 46–50.

42. For a full discussion of this exchange, see Aldon Lynn Nielsen, *C.L.R. James: A Critical Introduction* (Jackson: University Press of Mississippi, 1997), 8–12.

43. C. L. R. James, "The Intelligence of the Negro: A Few Words with Dr. Harland," *Beacon*, 1, no. 5 (August 1931).

44. See Gabriel Debien, Jean Fouchard, and Marie-Antoinette Menier, "Toussaint Louverture avant 1789, légendes et réalités," *Conjonction: revue franco-haitienne* 134 (1977): 65–80.

45. Césaire and James met at last in Cuba in 1967. See Andrew Salkey, *Havana Journal* (Harmondsworth: Penguin, 1971), 91.

46. David Scott, *Conscripts of Modernity: The Tragedy of Colonial Enlightenment* (Durham, NC: Duke University Press, 2004). James's correspondence with his editor at Random House, Morris Philipson, reveals negotiation over other changes, not least a reduction of detail on military encounters and a removal of explicitly Marxist terminology.

47. Frank Rosengarten, *Urbane Revolutionary: C.L.R. James and the Struggle for a New Society* (Jackson: University Press of Mississippi, 2007).

48. See Maryse Condé, "Order, Disorder, Freedom and the West Indian Writer," *Yale French Studies* 83, no. 2 (1993): 133.

49. C. L. R. James, letter to Étienne Charlier, August 24, 1955, UWI, Box 7, folder 190.

50. See James's introduction to Jean Fouchard, *The Haitian Maroons: Liberty or Death* (New York: E.W. Blyden Press, 1981).

51. James, *The Black Jacobins*, x.

52. C. L. R. James, "Lectures on *The Black Jacobins*: How I Would Rewrite *The Black Jacobins*," *Small Axe* 8 (2000): 99–112.

53. James, *The Black Jacobins*, 329.

54. Bernier, *Characters of Blood*, 67, 69.

55. On Eisenstein's project, see Charles Forsdick and Christian Høgsbjerg, "'The Confrontation between Black and White Explodes into Red': Sergei Eisenstein and the Haitian Revolution," *History Workshop Journal* 78 (2014): 157–85.

56. Natalie Zemon Davis, *Slaves on Screen: Film and Historical Vision* (Cambridge, MA: Harvard University Press, 2000).

57. See Nicholas Mirzoeff, *The Right to Look: A Counterhistory of Visuality* (Durham, NC: Duke University Press, 2011).

14

On "Both Sides" of the Haitian Revolution?:
Rethinking Direct Democracy and
National Liberation in *The Black Jacobins*

MATTHEW QUEST

C. L. R. James, in his 1971 lectures on *The Black Jacobins* at the Institute for the Black World in Atlanta, Georgia, made a profound assertion. Writing a history of a social revolution necessitates rejection of being fair to "both sides." One can either be on the side of insurgent proceedings or oppose them. He added that those who oppose insurrectionary acts often, despite their contempt and fear for crucial events, illuminate their radical character.[1] This is an ironic criterion for reconsidering this classic account of the Haitian Revolution.

Paradoxically, James, the radical historian, in certain respects wrote on both sides of this national liberation struggle. Rarely could it be said that he was moderate or reformist in his anticolonial politics. Certainly, in opposition to white supremacy and empire, James was overwhelmingly militant. Yet his postcolonial thought was awkward and unresolved at best in his role as historian. James has often been understood as seeking to capture the changing forms of thought and action, spontaneity and organization, in the Haitian revolutionary movement. Was black autonomy secured by the nation-state or the self-emancipation of the slaves themselves?

The Black Jacobins: A History from Below?

Rethinking *The Black Jacobins* requires questioning this heralded history from below that we have come to know by reputation. Aspects equally appear of an authoritarian administrative vista animated by centering emerging postcolonial state power. Not always Toussaint Louverture's deficient optics, a vision from above society was, far more than we realize, James's own way of seeing. We must reconsider how he speaks of aspiring rulers and the self-organization of the ordinary slave. Alex Dupuy, in a reassessment of *The Black Jacobins*, argues our capacity to reevaluate James's reading of the Haitian Revolution is partially indebted to his own methodology of writing history, as well as his self-critical evaluation of his intellectual legacies.[2] In the 1963 edition of *The Black Jacobins*, which revised the original work in concise but significant ways, and his 1971 lectures on how he wrote and might rewrite the story of the Haitian Revolution, James suggested modified meanings of these events based on comparative and contemporary considerations. In conversation with the French and Russian revolutions, Haiti was a cautionary tale for more contemporary black freedom struggles.

Especially through his later lectures and added footnotes in the second edition, James suggested that *The Black Jacobins* in its original form was not sufficiently animated by a direct democratic perspective. At times, he imagined a class struggle of "the Black Sans-culottes" in Haiti, and moved beyond the influence of Jules Michelet to mirror Daniel Guérin's and Peter Kropotkin's reading of the French Revolution.[3] One wonders if "the Black Sans-culottes" would be the title of the proposed rewritten account.

Reminding his audience that to rewrite *The Black Jacobins* in the fashion he desired in 1971 could make it a fundamentally different book, James reflected on himself in the third person: "poor James" is now "confined to the footnotes" for making new interventions.[4] But even as we reconsider his original purpose and shifting intentions, we see a permanent tension.

From the French to the Russian Revolutions

In *The Black Jacobins*, there is a discourse that compares Toussaint to Lenin. Similarly, the rebellion led by Moïse against Toussaint's regime was shaped by James's peculiar understanding of Trotsky, the famous 1921 Kronstadt rebellion against the Bolshevik state, and to a lesser extent, the Petrograd Soviet.[5] There is no evidence that James was prepared to rethink his interpretation of the Russian Revolution, which despite being an anti-Stalinist vision, had authoritarian implications. His mature outlook on the French Revolution viewed it not through the Jacobins but through the *sans-culottes* and their spokesmen, the Enragés' Jean-François Varlet and Jacques Roux.[6] The revolt against the aspiring revolutionary government of Robespierre and the capacity of the obscure local leaders became the final mirror for James's rereading of the Haitian Revolution.

James's comparative readings of the Haitian/French revolutions and the Haitian/Russian revolutions have conflicting implications for direct democracy and national liberation.[7] However, this is obscured if we read *The Black Jacobins* primarily as a vindication narrative or a discourse on the tragedy of Toussaint's leadership. Crucial in a proper understanding of the Haitian Revolution is transcending preoccupation with how Western civilization misread the slaves' humanity and the limited choices the new national bourgeoisie faced in economic terms.[8]

To better understand how James's reading is problematic, we must examine his treatment of the self-activity of everyday Haitians under slavery and wage labor more closely. How does he contextualize their potential for direct self-government before and after the Moïse revolt? In comparative revolutions of the Atlantic world, the modernity that has been disavowed by most scholars has not been France's and Haiti's equal potential to establish a nation-state or republic as the meaning of independence. Rather, far more ignored and neglected has been the French and Haitian working people's (unwaged and waged) capacity for self-emancipation. Thus the masses' self-organization in the Haitian Revolution rarely is made central to comparative scholarly discourse on modernity or the Atlantic world.

Carolyn Fick contributes to clarifying this historical problem when she explains: "if the [Haitian] Constitution of 1801 left little authority for the French on the one end, it left none at all, at the other end for the political and economic participation of the masses in the new social order." Furthermore, Haitian ex-slaves, who became "salaried workers," clashed with Toussaint's social and economic programs and policies.[9] Far from appearing to be the forerunner of bourgeois democracy or the nation-state ignored by the silences of Hegel, the Haitian modernity disavowed may be a perspective of class struggle decades before Marx's *Communist Manifesto*.[10]

Haitian Activity: "The Property" Comes Alive

James meticulously documented the sadistic brutality to which the Haitian slaves were subjected and the false portraits of their contentment by white supremacist historians sympathetic to the slave masters. The Africans on one level accommodated themselves to their institutionalized oppression by displaying false public masks.[11] But their relationship to their workplace and social conditions was something else entirely. Out of their master's sight, these oppressed toilers, deemed inferior, illustrated remarkable self-governing capacities for economic planning, moral philosophy, health care, military, and judicial affairs. James's insights are the origins of later projects of sketching direct democratic possibilities in slavery studies.[12]

Black autonomy among slaves in Haiti could be difficult to fathom with a rational gaze that valued nonviolence and human self-preservation at all costs in the face of white supremacy and empire. The Africans' lives were subjected to so much random and irrational assault that self-government began with schemes to take back the terms on which they would live and work from their slave masters.

The slaves' bodies, property, and the means of production of the plantation economy, in James's depiction, became the site of rebellions of their own invention. When carried out not as individuals but in groups, these rebellions approached a status of dual power, where in certain respects a new society existed within the shell of the plantation order. James chronicled how many Africans placed knowledge of plants for medicinal purposes into strategies of self-governance—often carried out by use of poison. The historian thus began to illustrate an incipient understanding of slavery's relationship to political economy.

The chattel poisoned the master's younger children to influence the line of succession and thereby the management of their workplaces in the future. This often had implications for protecting their own families from being divided for sale on the market. Slave children were killed by their parents and nurses to save another generation from degradation. In addition, the adults desired to avoid an increase in workplace production associated with a larger workforce capacity. Where pregnancies were often a product of rape and otherwise unplanned save by the slave master, a jaw sickness induced by black midwives ensured that many newly born babies could not eat and would die off quickly. Black nurses who worked at hospitals poisoned colonial soldiers who brutally policed their community's labor. Horses, cows, and mules were killed by this means to throw disorder into production, and the possibility that they could be transported away from their family for sale.[13]

Following Trotsky's doctrine of combined and uneven development and the conception of the workplace and labor process found in Marx's *Capital* volume 1, James argued that the slaves, who worked together in gangs of hundreds on huge sugar plantations, experienced a type of factory life where they struggled to politically control their workplace. They had an experience equivalent to the modern proletariat, and through economic production the tasks of governance were instinctively learned. Significantly, this experience of modernity was owned by the slaves, and it suggested their direct capacity to govern.[14]

Following the example of Jules Michelet's *The People*, James contested that the intellectual level of the Africans, in contrast to the planters' image of them (as subhuman, irrational, and beyond ethics, morality, and merit) was quite vibrant away from the master's gaze.[15] A sense of intellectual and cultural superiority to their masters and willingness toward animated storytelling and opinionated discussion could be found away from their workplace. Religious practices, African-derived linguistic expression, and song, which the colonizers attempted to ban, animated a moral philosophy of an emerging independent nation or people.[16]

In the mountains, liberated zones of free maroons (often seen by historians as runaway slaves) took direct action to raid the colonizer's plantations in an effort to establish dual power in a military sense. At its best this resistance, led by François Mackandal, an orator who was said to have spiritual revelations, returned to plantations not only to pillage and massacre whites but to propagandize, make converts to the movement for self-government, and spread a vision of the destruction of white supremacy in Haiti. James explained that the Mackandal movement did not ultimately succeed, perhaps because of his personal lack of discipline that led to his capture and lynching.[17]

The Origins of the Vanguard and the National Bourgeoisie

All the slaves, despite great demeaning hardship, did not undergo an instinctive conversion to nationalist values. A "small privileged caste" emerged, including the plantation foreman, coachmen, cooks, waiters, butlers, maids, nurses, female companions, and other house servants. James noted that earlier historians focused on this caste and imagined a paternal and colonial trusteeship between master and slave. He noted that house slaves generally assimilated to the culture of their masters. In contrast, this social layer did not attempt to fool their masters through masking as much as the field slaves did. Still, since they were positioned closer to the Europeans' more vulnerable private lives, they could better orient themselves for subversive action if so inclined.[18] Out of this sector, Toussaint surfaced.

For Toussaint, managing livestock on the estate where he himself was still property, and where such a job was usually held by white men, gave him opportunities to learn concrete administrative abilities. He was able to approach whites informally in a type of peer relationship.[19] He was depicted by James as coming to the Haitian Revolution later and yet still better prepared than the average slave. We must be alert, subsequently, to the criteria by which such a dubious evaluation was made.

In the closing of his chapter on "the property," James suggested that the tragedy of mass movements was their difficulty in locating adequate leadership. "Opportunity could be seized but could not be created."[20] But Toussaint appeared more prepared than the ordinary rebellious field slave in some respects. It was proper to see Toussaint as central to military victory against the slave masters and imperialists bent on suppressing the Haitian Revolution. But those victories were not of his making alone. They were mirrored by independent triumphs in other parts of the country, not beholden to Toussaint. In reality Toussaint was one of the many who could plan and strategize. The ordinary slaves also were depicted by James as having those skills, even if our historian did not initially appreciate their full implications.

Toussaint had certain capacities that most slaves, who James characterized elsewhere as intellectually "dulled" and morally "degraded," did not possess.[21] This appraisal of slave character is remarkable coming after crisp vistas of slaves' capacities for self-emancipation. With the training of his mental faculties, Toussaint, through reading and writing (with assistance) appeared to reconcile mental and manual labor in his identity like no other Haitian ex-slave.

Where Toussaint had previous managerial experience, a position of authority, even where he was held as property, James's rank-and-file slaves instinctively held some of this self-managing experience through association with the economic processes of their workplaces. Despite the concrete strategic ingenuity among ordinary toilers, which James depicted and intermittently minimized, Toussaint was elevated as extraordinary for what appeared to be his progressive bureaucratic capacities.

Toussaint was extremely efficient, rational, and careful of details—it seemed at first. He took pride in his labor partially out of a latent desire for racial vindication, showing that the false hierarchy of merit based on white supremacy was a sham. He also developed a physical mastery of his body through exercise, diet, and an increasing modest and conservative disposition toward sexual and family life. Having an ascetic personality, Toussaint slowly started to develop a cadre fighting force in which mistakes and technical weaknesses in warfare were corrected.

The Need for Leadership: Political Treachery and the Proper Political Program

James asked readers to witness Toussaint first compared with ordinary people and then compared to other "leaders" to the former's advantage. Recall that Mackandal, the best of his generation, was creative but without discipline in contrast to Toussaint. Boukman was recognized as a prophetic African theologian who propagandized revolt. It was clear that James believed Toussaint to be a superior thinker. After a comparative discourse on Toussaint, Jean-François Papillon, and Georges Biassou, where James argued that other leaders embodied as well "a sense of order, discipline, and a capacity to govern" and could motivate the masses toward both powerful strikes and keeping order, he reminded us that no one but Toussaint had any idea what was to be subsequently initiated in terms of economic planning.

James took this opportunity to highlight a principle of revolutionary political philosophy.

> Political treachery is not a monopoly of the white race, and this abominable betrayal so soon after the insurrections show that political leadership is a matter of program, strategy and tactics and not the color of those who lead it, their oneness of origin with their people, nor the services they have rendered.[22]

With this philosophical pivot, James anticipated the postcolonial condition. Yet his bifocal narrative continued to be loyal to "both sides" at the postcolonial moment. He defined a perspective from below as what aspiring rulers should possess. He sensed that Toussaint's understanding of the possible terms of independent political economy were superior to that of other leaders of the Haitian events. Yet James was also aware that Toussaint could not accommodate popular self-government. The historian recognized that the slaves revolted because they "wanted total freedom," which no aspiring ruler above society, however progressive, "can ever admit."[23]

A Populist Autocrat's Way of Seeing

James acknowledged that Toussaint Louverture led an autocracy. His populism idolized the degree of popular resistance and the inevitability of African suffering. Toussaint subtly lectured the masses. Apparently desiring to minimize bloodshed, Toussaint, with a centralized and yet dialogic leadership style toward his fellow Africans (or, as he imagined them, French citizens), underscored limits to how much everyday people could directly govern.

James attributed the rise of Toussaint to his ability to listen to the concerns of ordinary people. He was largely not depicted by James as having great insights into governing at the grassroots. Rather, Toussaint steered the "ignorant, starving, badgering, and nervous" to gain their confidence.[24] James's Haitian did not always appear to have creative capacities. This was the context in which he situated Toussaint. This was satisfactory to the extent that individuals of all economic stations in life can be found to be bereft of political acumen, unstable, and unpredictable as a result.

Nevertheless Toussaint, rather than enhancing the legitimate popular self-activity he observed, sometimes blunted it into an emerging administrative order. Aware that the freedom and social equality the slaves had been fighting for appeared lost, direct action for self-emancipation bubbled up among the rank and file. Toussaint was merely able to affirm that this sentiment was justifiable. Who and what does this affirmation serve?

At the first hint of insurrection in any part of the country, Toussaint traveled by horseback to gather Africans to lecture them on how to conduct themselves. In the districts of the Northern Province (Limbé, Plaisance, Marmelade, Port-de-Paix), the early centers of the revolt, Toussaint had particular difficulty putting his own stamp on regional politics. Assassinations against whites continued even as blacks began to hold the reins, however tenuously, of representative government. Toussaint counseled that retribution was not the way to redress racial grievances. This was valid in certain respects. Yet expressions of white discrimination were still pervasive. Furthermore, such counseling to blacks was how Toussaint's own state responded to those who persisted questioning his authority.

The former slave masters continued to own substantially the political economy even as slavery was abolished. Satisfactory prices for the ex-slaves' agricultural products were elusive through the market, which they could not control. Toussaint appeared to suggest in response only an ethic of obedience and hard work. At a rally in Port-de-Paix, he raised the slogans of liberty and equality as he appointed a military commander over the population. Though Toussaint was cheered and left, soon after there was another local tribunal not beholden to him. His appointed leader and twelve associates were shot. James underscored that Toussaint returned "without firing a shot," "arrested no one," and talked to the masses to encourage them to go back to work.

But the shadow of his ability to militarily conquer, if need be, informed the reception of his dialogic stance. Toussaint's humble disposition, of which James was so fond, could come across as arrogance to a courageous direct democratic mind or a competing local warlord.

Toussaint wasn't always successful at mediating conflicts and was once shot at, conjuring later revolutionary history when Lenin and Nkrumah were shot at by dissidents with legitimate grievances. James argued that it was difficult to evaluate the authoritarianism of Toussaint's efforts at the intersection of an emerging state power in the midst of conditions of dual power, imperialist intrigue, and civil war. Yet James saw Toussaint's evolving legitimacy as a national leader of all the regions of Haiti as consistent with aspirations to consolidate a growing centralized army and maintain the loyalty of black labor under duress.

Restoring Agriculture and Establishing "Free Labor" under Feudal Capitalism

In James's account, Toussaint had a certain vision of the quality of self-government from the first days of his command. Political power was a means to a good life based on alienated work redefined in virtuous terms. Freedom could not function in a type of permanent Luddism, perpetually burning down the plantation workplaces. But a more decentralized federation of independent self-governing producers was never considered. The agricultural economy, Toussaint insisted, had to be restored and built back up on new centralized terms.

For Toussaint, in a context of civil war, compulsory and militarized plantation workplaces were seen as liberated zones. The coercion was carried out by a black military loyal to Toussaint. The ex-slaves were impressed at first. Work hours were limited and their wages guaranteed by the white former masters, now workplace owners. If the wages were not remunerated by whites, their property (land) would be confiscated. But Toussaint could be read as favoring the former slave master. Their class had "knowledge, education, and experience" and "culture," which Toussaint perceived a few mulattoes had and none of the African ex-slaves had. Collaboration with the white plantation owners appeared necessary to make Haiti's political economy functional, which aimed to minimize total external dependency.

James was enamored that Toussaint's program for the country was often presented in distinguished oratory and "framed like a philosopher" to blacks and whites alike. Toussaint lectured: "Learn to appreciate the glory of your new political status . . . do not forget the duties it imposes on you." "The age of fanaticism is over. The reign of law has succeeded to that of anarchy."[25] Toussaint suggested that freedom for labor is tied to the soil or economic production, rather than any special role in direct governance. He attempted over time to work out a satisfactory relationship with France, while acknowledging the uneven historical development of the colonizer and its former enslaved population. James favorably viewed Toussaint's belief that there should be "no distinctions of rank outside the public service."[26] This claimed the peculiar importance of social equality under what is in fact a hierarchal bureaucracy. Scholars enamored with the Haitian constitutional republic, as a peer modernity with the French Jacobin state, understand "democracy" to mean minority rule by professional elites. The James who saw aspects of direct democracy in the French Revolution knew better.

James was so captivated with his philosophical capacity that he only unevenly perceived Toussaint's restrictive conception of the new citizenship for blacks as "free labor," or coerced feudal wage earner. His criticisms of Toussaint as cultivator of the popular will would not suffice. The "dreadful mistake" of Toussaint, for James, was not negotiating with the French, for he acknowledged Toussaint did not trust the "liberties" of the ex-slaves to the "promises" of the imperialists. Rather, Toussaint declined in his patience to "explain" what he was attempting in policy to "his own people."[27] James portrayed Toussaint, animated by Rousseau's ideas of the social contract, as having refined the popular will and personified its lack of clarity. Toussaint's disposition was pretentious. He was of the belief that if he merely spoke, the Haitian masses desired to follow. At the same time, it was dangerous to explain to insurgent masses the dependent relations of global political economy. It was hazardous to examine in public why the promises of national liberation seemed to be unfulfilled.

Toussaint's administration erected schools, fine buildings, and monuments. In proclamations, laws, and decrees, he uplifted religious toleration, free trade, and racial equality. He publicly illustrated the duties and responsibilities of citizenship animated by moral rhetoric and law and order. His state had to genuinely combat the crime that was a legacy of the instability of the insurrection, and that could not always be considered motivated by social injustices of past and present. He also defined radical democratic rebellion as sedition. For James, Toussaint's personal example and leadership now and again modeled a psychological liberation that had taken hold among the Haitian masses. But he argued something else about the approach of Toussaint's state.

> It was the propaganda of a dictatorship, but not for base personal ends or the narrow interests of one class oppressing another. His government, like the absolute monarchy in its progressive days, balanced between the classes, but it was rooted in the preservation of the interests of the laboring poor. With the growth of a black ruling class, complications were already arising. But for this period his form of government was the best.[28]

This might seem like a peculiar revolutionary Marxist perspective. It is unclear where Toussaint, as equivalent to Lenin and Robespierre began, and where Toussaint as "a Black Stalin" or "a Black Napoleon" ended. Of course Bonaparte's historical contribution was to crush aspects of direct democracy that had overtaken the Jacobin regime in France during "the terror." Yet where Stalinism and Trotskyism ended and "Bonapartism" began has always been a gray area of revolutionary Marxism. A ruling class that functioned like a monarchy, James knew at his best, should not be deemed progressive and acting in the interests of the working class.

Toussaint's postcolonial regime truly mirrored Stalin's Russia in important regards, and James was silent about it. According to Carolyn Fick:

> Not only did [Haitian] workers no longer have the option of changing plantations at the end of their contracts, they were also forbidden to change occupations. That is, in order to stabilize the agricultural labor force, only those individuals who held domestic positions or trades prior to emancipation were allowed to exercise these functions.[29]

This militarized abuse of Haitian wage labor, their restriction of freedom of movement, and freedom to choose their own terms of work in the name of stabilizing national production anticipated exactly the agricultural policy of both Lenin's and Stalin's Soviet Union. James was familiar with their policies in the early 1930s, as a result of translating Boris Souvarine's *Stalin* (1939).[30]

That Toussaint's militarized labor regime was not immediately assessed as a disaster and the rightful subject of a campaign to be toppled was a product of a few peculiarities. James the anti-Stalinist uncritically supported aspects of authoritarian politics. Second, the consolidation of the consciousness of an alternative form of revolutionary government, based on popular self-management, has always been present and possessed an insurgent quality, but was partial. The potential for total emancipation or direct self-government most often doesn't develop in stages but expresses itself spontaneously. As other aspects of James's story illustrate, there were present all along self-governing instincts among everyday people and the capacity for an alternative form of government where ordinary Haitians held the reins. This consciousness was at its height, not after the law and order of the new black government was firmly established, but while it was constructed under the dual pressures of the still-burning self-mobilization of the masses and imperialist intrigue.

James portrayed Toussaint's exploitative regime as a success based on its aspirations to a state-planned economy, not by the quality of self-government of the Haitian toilers.

> No doubt the poor sweated and were backward so that the new ruling class might thrive. But at least they too were better off than they had been. While on the one hand the authority, social ease and culture of those who, a dozen years before, had been slaves, amazed all observers, the success of Toussaint's administration can be judged by the fact that in a year and a half he had restored cultivation to two thirds of what it had been in the most flourishing days of the old regime.[31]

Through the force of his personality, Toussaint was given overwhelming credit for the consolidated advancement of the social forces of the slaves as represented by their cultural and economic "progress." James's view was that Toussaint's new state was the administrative vehicle for that consolidation. Nowhere else in this narrative was James's orthodox Trotskyist view more present and at its ethical worst, in the defense of a degenerate regime, as progressive and embodying black labor's social revolution. But within Toussaint's centralized bureaucracy, there arose differences in how to manage "free labor," those who were actually submitted to a forced plantation regimen, under a shortened (or now established) work week. The Haitian slaves fought the former masters to establish the working day. It was not granted benevolently by Toussaint.

James had not yet arrived at the emphasis he would in later years. Toilers, be their payment high or low, did not revolt for a little more culture and material gain. Rather, labor revolted to directly manage their workplaces. There was no separation of economic production and governance. Workers' self-emancipation was a revolt against value production itself.[32]

But James's assessment of Haitian labor was subordinated to the national liberation struggle's aspiring rulers' need to retain state power. Since James revised and reinterpreted his Haitian narrative partially in 1963 and 1971, these critical ideas on colonized and enslaved labor's relationship to state power should be placed in conversation with how he might have rewritten *The Black Jacobins*.

James fell back on attempting to justify an ugly reality—that rebel Haitian workers were whipped by black military leaders for not working to specification under their "free status." The new black regime had an apparent proto-socialist or state capitalist nature. That is, the ex-slaves were paid not merely wages but a percentage of their produce under farming arrangements where the plantations were substantially owned by the former white slave masters and partially owned by the new state. Toussaint militarized economic production to prepare for a final military battle with Napoleon Bonaparte.

The Meaning of the Moïse Revolt

In the irrepressible cauldron of the Northern Province, the first major uprising of the second liberation of the Haitian Revolution took place. It is interesting that James later labeled these forces, from places like Plaisance, Limbé, and Dondon, "the vanguard of the revolution . . . not satisfied with [the] new regime."[33] James attributed Toussaint's failure to the decline of his ability to organize the popular will of the nation, and these forces in particular.

Despite this disconnect, throughout most of *The Black Jacobins*, Toussaint was characterized as the vanguard of the Haitian Revolution. Yet James's measurement of Toussaint—while in preparation for war with Bonaparte he was "busy sawing off the branch on which he sat"—was mistaken.[34] It is not clear what he did to earn this base in the northern provinces. In fact, he rarely had this region's loyalty.

At this instant James appeared to make a leap in his narrative interpretation. Toussaint and all educated observers, he argued, may believe that he owned the undying loyalty of black labor. But when Toussaint's policies consistently created disillusion, he was discarded for another leader. Moïse, who commanded the northern regional military, although adopted by Toussaint as his nephew, openly disdained Toussaint's authoritarian labor regime. The only way to maintain some semblance of order in that province was for the letter of the law not to be imposed. The rising popular forces would not stand for its abuse and coercion. Moïse articulated this discontent and thus, the masses rebelled in his name: "Long live Moïse!"

The Haitians in the Northern Province resented working for the whites, who still owned the plantations. They desired land reform, where they could work their own plot of land without producing a surplus for the state. Moïse appeared to represent these desires and acquired a strong reputation as sympathetic to labor and opposed to continuing white power after the movement to abolish slavery took hold. James argued that these revolutionaries for a second liberation wanted to massacre the whites and overthrow Toussaint's government, and "some hoped to put Moïse in his place." The historian, in telling this account, suggested a comparison of these insurgent forces to the Cordeliers of revolutionary France and the Vyborg workers of Petrograd in revolutionary Russia.[35] Before we examine James's analysis of comparative revolution, let us look again at how he reinforces Toussaint's leadership qualities.

Anticipating his later essay, "Lenin and the Problem," in which he suggested how Nkrumah's Ghana declined and Julius Nyerere's Tanzania might prosper, James argued that Toussaint needed to explain to the Haitian masses why the whites were excluded from political power but were retained for assistance and collaboration in economic reconstruction of the nation. White capitalists, elites, and specialists would have to be used until ordinary black workers developed the full cultural capacity to maintain an independent government within the relations of the global economy.

In James's narrative, like his view of Lenin's approach to the New Economic Policy, Toussaint should have patiently explained each step of collaboration and the exact position of the ex–slave masters' role in his would-be revolutionary regime. Instead, he made a grave mistake in shooting Moïse and putting down the rebellion that resented white property and privilege's place in the postcolonial regime. Toussaint implemented in response a most fierce police state in the Northern Province.

Toussaint and the Problem

The problem with the way James evaluated Toussaint at this juncture of the Moïse revolt, even as he shifted the reader's awareness to social forces that now took the lead of the revolution, was that he justified the suppression of the direct democratic forces. Behind James's discourse of Toussaint taking his eyes and ears off what the masses think and do, and not just the machinations of the imperialists, was an awkward framework. Toussaint crushed "his own" left wing and sealed his "own" fate.[36] There was a tension between James's portrayal of Toussaint as "needing" the black sans-culottes, and a sense that Toussaint had ownership of them—specifically their political meaning and destiny. "*After* Toussaint himself, Moise symbolized the revolution"[37] was a formulation less than precise.

James argued there was no fundamental difference in aim between the social forces of the Moïse revolt and Toussaint. But this was as absurd as his recommendation that Toussaint should have covered the country "not" with "reprisals" but with his past "homely" way of talking to the masses.[38] Like Lenin in Russia, Toussaint consolidated state power in Haiti by a most ruthless dictatorship. Partially successful because of its populism, Toussaint's regime crushed other sincere revolutionaries, however obscure in name, who saw direct control of their workplaces as synonymous with emancipation from slavery and colonial freedom. He was even shot at previously, and his minions in the Northern Province were overthrown by popular forces. Yet James continued to partially defend Toussaint as a representative personality.

James persisted to write on both sides of the direct democratic revolt. On one hand, Toussaint should have brought these social forces closer to him, and James labeled them "to his left." On the other, Toussaint "crushed the revolt as he was *bound* to do."[39] His focus here was not that Toussaint likely or inevitably would do this. Rather, that Toussaint *must* do this. Burdened by the philosophical shackles of his Leninism, James invested the sovereignty of the Haitian Revolution in the postcolonial ruling elite who wished to centralize state power. This new class above society, acting in the interests of labor by in fact subordinating it to a state plan, represented the consolidation of freedom. There was a certain authoritarian high modernism that James's Leninism/Jacobinism shared with all visions of the modern nation-state.

Toussaint and Lenin: Moïse and Kronstadt

James compared Toussaint's dilemmas with Lenin's. The Moïse revolt he likened to another aspect of the Russian Revolution: the Vyborg workers of the Petrograd Soviet, who from a questionable Trotskyist outlook anticipated with their own direct democracy, the Bolshevik consolidation of state power. The crushing of the Moïse revolt is compared more sensibly to the Kronstadt rebellion of 1921.[40]

Lenin, despite a pretense to workers' participation in economic planning, outlawed and brutally suppressed all independent political self-organization not loyal to the Bolsheviks. He did this under the pretext of national unity in a time of civil war and imperialist war, and an economic plan, "War Communism," that militarized society. He attempted to eliminate the market price for peasants' grain and destroyed the economy of the country under the dictates of the assumed demands of modern production in a presumed backward culture. This created a civil war, not with "counter-revolutionaries" but with direct democratic political forces to Lenin's left. These radical forces animated the very soviets his state suppressed and hijacked their identity as luster. In James's eyes, Toussaint was heroic by anticipating these dilemmas of statecraft, modern politics, and economics, with far less education than Lenin. He arrived on his own authority and embodied an embryonic black radical tradition in political thought.

Yet it is a confusing analogy to suggest that Toussaint shooting Moïse was the equivalent of Lenin shooting Trotsky, in James's outlook, for how it bewildered militant Haitian labor.[41] Trotsky, later seen as a dissident in exile, in contrast to Stalin actually led the military repression of the Kronstadt sailors. Moïse, the Haitian military commander, not unlike the Kronstadt sailors' relationship to wildcat strikes in Petrograd, came to personify the direct democratic revolt among independent black labor.

James explained: "It was in method, and not in principle, that Toussaint failed."[42] This stance was irreconcilable with the historian who, as political thinker, more fully advocated a direct democracy later. For this implied popular self-management existed merely to legitimate a populist state that subordinated or murdered it. James's enhanced reading, comparing the French and Haitian revolutions, in some respect clarifies the Haiti/Russia discourse.

The Meaning of the Black Sans-Culottes

The Haitian Revolution's Moïse revolt would be rewritten with greater significance if James had taken up the task, as he proposed, of rewriting *The Black Jacobins*. In doing so, he may have addressed a historical problem summed up in Toussaint's last words to Moïse before executing him. In Laurent Dubois's translation: "Could I a former slave, work toward the re-establishment of servitude?"[43] When exchanging one hierarchal form of governance for another, with a reengineered representation, the reconstruction of servitude is inevitable.

In James's initial narrative, the Haitian rebels of the Northern Province are mirrored by "the Paris masses." There were a series of ruptures of popular assemblies and committees. These both make and break Robespierre's Jacobins, whom James initially labeled "the extreme left wing." The sans-culottes, through a process of instant recall, discard the Girondins, who did not wish to implement from state power aspects of their desired public policies, and replaced them at first with the Jacobins.[44]

James argued that the radical reforms of Robespierre in state power were imposed on his faction by the popular forces below them, whose politics, for our historian, "anticipated communism." Jean-François Varlet and Jacques Roux, leaders of the Enragés, spoke for the sans-culottes as a class—the independent artisans and laborers who, in James's view, prefigured the modern proletariat's potential.

This could lead to a misreading if one interpreted this as the sans-culottes' desire for a new kind of freedom called totalitarianism. Instead, James underscored that through trial and error and their desire for direct self-government, the Parisian sans-culottes brought about a regime with new contradictions, which needed to be resolved.

Most orthodox Marxists view the Jacobins as ancestors of the Leninist vision. But James at times has a peculiar libertarian Leninism that approaches syndicalism. Capitalism had not yet been consolidated to be opposed in France. But state restrictions on the profiteering of the new ruling elite and provisional aspects of a welfare state surfaced during the so-called terror, which discarded and killed Robespierre, who feared his left wing's growing power and took steps to repress them. As James clarified in *Notes on Dialectics*, the French sans-culottes desire to be directly self-governing made "state capitalism" appear for a time in Robespierre's Jacobin state. This was consistent with his initial view in *The Black Jacobins*.[45] As a doctrine and program, state capitalism was a compromised aspect of the sans-culottes' own will to power more than a century before it was a basic staple of modern statecraft in the twentieth century. James attributed the progressive quality of the Robespierre-led Jacobin state, even while it suppressed the sans-culottes, to the self-activity of ordinary people and not the middle classes. This suggested pregnant possibilities for the comparative meaning of the Moïse revolt in Haiti.

In his new footnotes in the second edition of *The Black Jacobins*, James went further by quoting the lectures of George Lefebvre, the historian of the French Revolution.

The Jacobins, furthermore, were authoritarian in outlook. Consciously or not, they wished to act with the people and for them, but they claimed the right of leadership, and when they arrived at the head of affairs they ceased to consult the people, did away with elections, proscribed the Herbertistes and the Enragés. They can be described as enlightened despots. The sans-culottes on the contrary were extreme democrats: they wanted direct government of the people by the people; if they demanded a dictatorship against the aristocrats they wished to exercise it themselves and to make their leaders do what they wanted.[46]

Through Lefebvre, James appeared to condemn Toussaint, the personification of the black Jacobin, by proxy. James added that the Paris sans-culottes saw very vividly "what was required at each stage of the revolution at least until it reached its highest peak. Their difficulty was that they had neither the education, experience, nor the resources to organize a modern state, if only temporarily." He did not make clear here if he means the revolutionary state should be provisional and quickly wither away, or if he was skeptical that this class, animated by a nearly anarchist vision of direct democracy, could organize a regime with the necessary centralization to consolidate its desires in a transitional period. Nevertheless, James clearly felt this was "pretty much" the same situation the revolutionaries of the Northern Province of Haiti found themselves in relation to Toussaint.[47] Except for the matter of James's inference that as ex-slaves they and their aspiring leaders had less formal political education than the French Revolution's masses and leaders.

Still, James cannot escape the judgment that although it is correct to vindicate Toussaint as an intelligent person, he also implied Toussaint had neither special knowledge to fulfill the demand for direct democracy, nor did the Jacobins in France. The Jacobins, regardless of race, were simply opposed to the direct self-government of everyday people. The question remained: Which class led the national liberation struggle? The black Jacobins or black sans-culottes? At the postcolonial moment, James, as historian and political philosopher, could not convincingly speak for both. Just as the program of the Moïse revolt cannot be known for certain, the direct democratic potential of the Haitian Revolution can only remain speculation. But James insisted that if you study history, merely diagnosing the past without speculating about the future, it is of no use to practical political thought. This is a valid premise for reconsidering the state, political economy, and popular democracy in the Haitian Revolution.

Notes

1. C. L. R. James, "Lectures on *The Black Jacobins*: How I Wrote *The Black Jacobins*," *Small Axe* 8 (2000): 78.
2. Alex Dupuy, "Toussaint L'Ouverture and the Haitian Revolution: A Reassessment of C.L.R. James's Interpretation," in *C.L.R. James: His Intellectual Legacies,* edited by Selwyn R. Cudjoe and William E. Cain (Amherst: University of Massachusetts Press, 1995), 106–17.
3. Daniel Guérin, *Class Struggles in the First French Republic,* trans. Ian Patterson (London, Pluto Press, 1977); Peter Kropotkin, *The Great French Revolution* (Montreal: Black Rose, 1989). James illustrates his debt to Guérin in "Lectures on *The Black Jacobins*: How I Wrote *The Black Jacobins*," 77. In his bibliography to *The Black Jacobins*, he states "the best general book in English is still Kropotkin's brief history of over fifty years ago. Kropotkin thought the Revolution was a wonderful event, and was neither afraid nor embarrassed to say so." C. L. R. James, *The Black Jacobins: Toussaint L'Ouverture and the San Domingo Revolution* (New York: Vintage, 1963), 384–85. In the late 1940s and early 1950s, James worked on translating Guérin's study into English but never completed this task.
4. C. L. R. James, "Lectures on *The Black Jacobins*: How I Would Re-Write *The Black Jacobins*," *Small Axe* 8 (2000): 103–6.
5. James, *The Black Jacobins,* 282–85.
6. James, *The Black Jacobins,* 177. See Michael Sonenscher, *Sans-Culottes* (Princeton, NJ: Princeton University Press, 2008); Murray Bookchin, *Third Revolution,* vol. 1 (London: Cassell, 1996); Morris Slavin, *The Making of an Insurrection* (Cambridge, MA: Harvard University Press, 1986); Morris Slavin, *The French Revolution in Miniature* (Princeton, NJ: Princeton University Press, 1984); R. B. Rose, *The Making of the Sansculottes* (Manchester: Manchester University Press, 1983); R. B. Rose, *The Enragés* (Melbourne: Melbourne University Press, 1965).
7. I have comprehensively established for the first time in scholarly literature James's affinity for direct democracy and workers' self-management. I have also pursued the contours of direct democracy and national liberation struggles (and the tension between direct democracy and Leninism) in James's life and work. See Matthew Quest, "Every Cook Can Govern: Direct Democracy, Workers' Self-Management, and the Creative Foundations of C.L.R. James's Political Thought," *C.L.R. James Journal* 19, nos. 1–2 (Fall 2013): 374–91; "Silences on the Suppression of Workers' Self-Emancipation: Historical Problems with C.L.R. James's Interpretation of V.I. Lenin," *Insurgent Notes* 10 (October 2012); "The 'Not So Bright Protégées' and the Comrades that 'Never Quarreled': C.L.R. James's Disputes on Labor's Self-Emancipation and the Political Economy of Colonial Freedom," *Insurgent Notes* 11 (October 2013).
8. For two recent books about the Haitian Revolution that engage and frame James's interpretation in this fashion, see Sibylle Fischer, *Modernity Disavowed* (Durham, NC: Duke University Press, 2004); David Scott, *Conscripts of Modernity* (Durham, NC: Duke University Press, 2004).

9. Carolyn E. Fick, *The Making of Haiti: The Saint Domingue Revolution from Below* (Knoxville: University of Tennessee Press, 1990), 207–10.

10. For discussions of Hegel, Haiti, and the Third World that have been partially inspired by James, see Susan Buck-Morss, *Hegel, Haiti and Universal History* (Pittsburgh, PA: University of Pittsburgh Press, 2009); Teshale Tibebu, *Hegel and the Third World* (Syracuse, NY: Syracuse University Press, 2010).

11. James, *The Black Jacobins*, 15.

12. One in particular is worth mentioning here. Animated by these principles, James's comrade George Rawick wrote *From Sundown to Sunup*, which introduced a project of multiple volumes reconstructing U.S. slave narratives as autobiography. Transforming the field of slavery studies, it was a fundamental blow against the notion that African Americans were psychologically and culturally "damaged" and "debased" by this monumental experience of oppression. Africans in America did not become the Sambo stereotypes the mythology of white supremacy (and some black nationalists) persisted in imagining. See George P. Rawick, *From Sundown to Sunup: The Making of the Black Community* (Westport, CT: Greenwood, 1972).

13. James *The Black Jacobins*, 16–17.

14. James, *The Black Jacobins*, 85–86.

15. James, *The Black Jacobins*, 17.

16. James, *The Black Jacobins*, 17–18.

17. James, *The Black Jacobins*, 20–21.

18. James, *The Black Jacobins*, 19–20.

19. James, *The Black Jacobins*, 24–25.

20. James, *The Black Jacobins*, 25.

21. James, *The Black Jacobins*, 91.

22. James, *The Black Jacobins*, 106.

23. James, *The Black Jacobins*, 95.

24. James, *The Black Jacobins*, 153–54.

25. James, *The Black Jacobins*, 206.

26. James, *The Black Jacobins*, 248.

27. James, *The Black Jacobins*, 240.

28. James, *The Black Jacobins*, 247.

29. Fick, *The Making of Haiti*, 208.

30. Boris Souvarine, *Stalin: A Critical Survey of Bolshevism*, trans. C. L. R. James (New York: Alliance Book, 1939), 522–27.

31. James, *The Black Jacobins*, 248.

32. C. L. R. James, Raya Dunayevskaya, and Grace Lee, *The Invading Socialist Society* (Detroit: Bewick, 1972), 13; C. L. R. James, "Marx's *Capital*, the Working-Day and Capitalist Production," in *You Don't Play with Revolution: The Montreal Lectures of C.L.R. James*, edited by David Austin (San Francisco: AK Press, 2009), 141–60.

33. James, *The Black Jacobins*, 275.

34. James, *The Black Jacobins*, 275.

35. James, *The Black Jacobins*, 276.

36. James, *The Black Jacobins*, 286.

37. James, *The Black Jacobins*, 278; emphasis added.

38. James, *The Black Jacobins*, 285.

39. James, *The Black Jacobins*, 286; emphasis added.

40. James, *The Black Jacobins*, 285.

41. James, *The Black Jacobins*, 284.

42. James, *The Black Jacobins*, 238.

43. Laurent Dubois, *Avengers of the New World: The Story of the Haitian Revolution* (Cambridge, MA: Harvard University Press, 2004), 247.

44. James, *The Black Jacobins*, 138.

45. C. L. R. James, *Notes on Dialectics* (Detroit: Friends of Facing Reality, 1971), 207–10; James, *The Black Jacobins*, 138.

46. James, *The Black Jacobins*, 276n6.

47. James, *The Black Jacobins*, 276n6.

15

The Black Jacobins: A Revolutionary Study
of Revolution, and of a Caribbean Revolution

DAVID AUSTIN

On January 11, 1970, Robert Hill wrote a letter to his friend and political associate, Franklyn Harvey of Grenada. Three years before, Hill had returned
home from Canada to play an active part in the "coming struggle"[1] in Jamaica
after completing a political science degree at the University of Toronto. By
1970 Hill was known for what Jamaica author Andrew Salkey described as his
"objectively inquiring mind" and his active study of revolutions.[2] He was also
a cofounder of Abeng, a popular political group that, among other things, produced a newspaper by the same name. Abeng came into being in the aftermath
of the political protest that erupted in Kingston when the University of West
Indies historian and popular intellectual Walter Rodney was barred from returning to Jamaica following his participation in the Congress of Black Writers in Montreal. Hill, who also participated in the Congress, and Rodney had
issued a joint statement on the Jamaican political scene during the Montreal
meeting, and Hill was among those who mobilized people in Jamaica and
Canada following Rodney's expulsion, leading to the founding of Abeng.[3]

In his letter Hill reflected on the accomplishments of the C.L.R. James
Study Circle (CLRJSC), of which he, Harvey, Tim Hector, Anne Cools, and
Alfie Roberts—a young band of "maroon intellectuals," to borrow a term
from W. F. Santiago-Valles[4]—had been core members. Centered in Montreal,
the Canada-based group not only studied and disseminated James's work but
also published *Notes on Dialectics*[5] in collaboration with the Detroit-based
political organization that James cofounded, Facing Reality. The CLRJSC also
assisted in the publication of James's *Perspectives and Proposals*, a series of
lectures on political organization and leadership,[6] and anticipated publishing
a multivolume collection of James's work.[7]

In the same letter, Hill also mentioned a "review" (his quotation marks)
by A. W. Singham and noted that he had been "forced to write a rejoinder,"

which was now in Alfie Roberts's possession, "to put the record straight."[8] Hill does not explain why he was compelled to write his rejoinder, but it is obvious he felt the need to clear up any misconceptions about *The Black Jacobins* appearing in Singham's review—which was eventually published in the first issue of the Caribbean literary journal *Savacou.*[9] The rejoinder was written in the midst of ongoing problems with Jamaican authorities as a result of his political commitments, but Hill and other members of the CLRJSC situated themselves within the same revolutionary tradition as James—a tradition embodied in *The Black Jacobins.* The group developed a close political-intellectual and personal relationship with James, in essence becoming his prodigious sons; or, in the case of Barbadian-born Anne Cools, one of his prodigious daughters whose experience as the sole woman to play an active role in the circle perhaps exemplified the gendered nature of left politics of the time.[10] (It's interesting to note that Cools was charged with the mission of negotiating a Spanish translation of *The Black Jacobins* during a 1966 visit to Cuba.)[11]

Despite his personal troubles, Hill clearly felt that he needed to defend James's intellectual and political integrity against Singham's musings, which, among other things, queried James's motivation for writing *The Black Jacobins*, a source of confusion that partly lies in the fact that James's own position on the issue was often ambiguous or contradictory. In a series of lectures delivered at the Institute of the Black World in June 1971, James mentioned Trotsky's *History of the Russian Revolution* and his subsequent study of the debates between Trotsky, Lenin, and Stalin—all of which led him to Marx and, more significantly, toward the Marxist methodology, ultimately influencing the form and content of *The Black Jacobins.*[12] Although it is true that James later became an active Trotskyist, he insisted that it was as a result of his independent reading that he came to appreciate Lenin and Trotsky and arrived at the conclusion that the "Stalinists are the greatest historical liars in the world at the present time."[13] He recounted how he had turned to the great French historians of the French Revolution, including Jules Michelet, who gave him a sense of historical development which, along with Marxism, influenced the structure and tone of *The Black Jacobins.*[14] He also recalled how his work with George Padmore and the International African Service Bureau (IASB) in England gave him "a conception of black people" that he did not have in the Caribbean, but for which he was prepared "because people in the Caribbean are not deficient in any way that one can see."[15] Having read and been dissatisfied with accounts of the Haitian Revolution while still in the

Caribbean, he decided that he would write a satisfactory one, but then suggests that he decided to do this "for no other reason than a *literary* reason."[16] In other words, he conceded that he had conceived of writing a book about the Haitian Revolution prior to leaving the Caribbean for the first time in 1932 to become a fiction writer, but not that he eventually wrote the book with the Caribbean in mind.

Furthermore, it is not clear what he means by "a literary reason." Did he imagine writing a literary account of the Haitian Revolution? As I speculate, literature certainly played a role in the book's formation, as did Marxism, international socialism, and African politics, which clearly shaped how he conceived and wrote the book. But the place of the Caribbean in his conception of *The Black Jacobins* remains ambiguous in his lecture. He acknowledged that he left the Caribbean with an understanding of Western civilization and this facilitated his understanding of European socialist history, contemporary politics, and his understanding of French history insofar as it all related to Saint-Domingue. But again, he did not specifically claim a Caribbean influence on the book.[17] In fact, he explicitly stated that the book "wasn't written about the Caribbean" and references Hill's view, apparently referring to the rejoinder, that "the book has something else in mind than Caribbean emancipation."[18]

Despite James's and Hill's perspectives, the Singham-Hill debate demonstrates the extent to which historical memory can be a slippery slope,[19] and how writing—in this case the writing of history—is as much about the present as it is about the past and is as much an unconscious process as it is a conscious one. Drawing on this debate, I would like to suggest that the Caribbean was central to James's early conception of the book. True, James argued in his 1963 appendix to *The Black Jacobins* that Aimé Césaire, like Marcus Garvey and George Padmore before him, had discovered "that salvation for the West Indies lies in Africa, the original home and ancestry of the West Indian people,"[20] and that "The road to West Indian national identity lay through Africa."[21] But the Haitian Revolution was a peculiarly Caribbean historical event in a colony whose transplanted population was essentially a composite island of African nationalities. This would suggest that part of the road to Caribbean emancipation passed through Haiti and embracing the Haitian Revolution was part of the process of coming to terms with the Caribbean's regional identity and acknowledging the ability of Caribbean people to make their own history and shape their own destinies. As David Scott has argued, for James *The Black Jacobins* represented "a *revolutionary* history of that remarkable revolution," "a revolutionary account of a seminal revolution," and a "*revolutionary* study of revolution" in general.[22] But to state the obvious, the Haitian Revolution was a *Caribbean* revolution, and in this spirit the book represents a revolutionary study of a *Caribbean* revolution. This point is often, quite remarkably, overshadowed in James's accounts of why he wrote *The Black Jacobins* and in studies of the book that have emphasized his ambition to serve African liberation, examine the history of the Russian Revolution and international socialism, or focus on his 1963 revisions in which the issue of revolution and tragedy is raised.[23] In addition to James's analysis of Toussaint's "tragic dilemma," Scott acknowledges the importance of the 1963 appendix, which situates the Caribbean within modernity.[24] But the Caribbean context that shaped James and *The Black Jacobins* is somewhat understated in *Conscripts of Modernity*. Considering and not withstanding Scott's warning about reading the book outside of the context in which it was written,[25] I suggest that it must be situated within the specific body of literature that James produced prior to writing the book and within the Trinidadian context that nurtured him just six years before it was published. The issue here is both the motivation behind the book and whom it was intended to motivate. Consciously acknowledging the Haitian Revolution as a Caribbean revolution and *The Black Jacobins* as a book partly inspired by the Caribbean enables us to read it with renewed interest in relation to the Caribbean's immediate political reality at the time that the book was written and its new reality today.

In 1970 A. W. Singham was a senior lecturer in government at the University of the West Indies' Mona campus in Kingston, Jamaica, and author of *The Hero and the Crowd in a Colonial Polity*, a classic study in politics and the human personality that anticipated Eric Gairy's dictatorship in Grenada. To fully appreciate Singham's review, it is important to understand that it was written in the context of the Black Power movement in the Caribbean and the resurgence of the Caribbean left. Singham clearly was not enamored with its Caribbean advocates, whom he somewhat disdainfully dismissed as "fadists with their Afro-hairdos and daishikis."[26] In another instance he argued that "symbols, even though they may be as potent as that of Black Power, are not enough to sustain a social movement unless they are part of a wider ideology for developing new types of relations between members of the society."[27] If Black consciousness "is to truly liberate the black man"—and we might perhaps assume that he also meant Black women—it "must act as a new type of humanizing social movement in the twentieth century" and "unless its positive aspects predominate it will reduce itself to another form of barbarism, similar to those produced by the white states, whether capitalist or communist."[28] Paraphrasing James and Eldridge Cleaver—two names rarely found in the same company—he wrote: "it is a fatal mistake to subordinate the restructuring of institutions and social relations in the society to the racial struggle. What is needed is an ideology designed to transform the nature of society and man's relation to man, rather than replacing white oppressors with black oppressor."[29]

Clearly, Singham was responding to what he interpreted as the more chauvinistic tendencies in the Black Power movement in the Caribbean in which class and internationalism were at times absolutely subordinated to race. In the face of this, he read *The Black Jacobins* as a counterweight to this tendency, referring to what he describes as the "more humane concept of Black Power," a humanism "which is yet to be realized in Third World Societies."[30] *The Black Jacobins* anticipated what he understood to be the best of Black Power, a movement in which the particular and universal come together as Haiti's slaves take the center stage in world history. For him, *The Black Jacobins*, like almost all of James's nonfiction work, was the result of his "burning desire to understand and explain the phenomenon of revolution in the world around him."[31] In this sense, it is James the international socialist that is central to the book.

In his rejoinder Hill acknowledged Singham's appreciation of the importance of *The Black Jacobins* as a book written outside the boundaries of academia and not shaped by the requirements of graduate studies or a research fellowship. Despite, or perhaps as a result of, being ensconced in Jamaica's Black Power/New Left movement he demonstrated no objections to Singham's remarks on Black Power in general, or with the idea that *The Black Jacobins* anticipated the Black Power movement. He did, however, disapprove of the book being too closely associated with Black Power advocates and detached from academia.[32] For Hill, James demonstrated the self-activity of the slaves and the colonized in Haiti, their creative resistance to slavery, which was carried out on their own terms. Like James's *History of Negro Revolt*, *The Black Jacobins* anticipated a new generation of scholarship, including Hebert Aptheker's *American Negro Slave Revolts* (1943), Shepperson and Price's study of John Chilembwe and the Nyasaland Native uprising of 1915, among other monographs, and including the work of Walter Rodney.[33]

These issues aside, there are two main themes in Singham's review with which Hill took issue: First, the claim that *The Black Jacobins* was written to demonstrate that West Indians could take their destinies into their own hands and did not need to be prepared for self-government by the British. Second, he also strongly objected to what Singham described as the other purpose of the book: to address socialist debates that were being waged in Europe in the 1930s. We begin with the second issue before turning to the first.

Hill categorically denied Singham's claim that *The Black Jacobins* was concerned with central issues within international socialism, arguing instead that James addressed these debates in *World Revolution 1917–1936: The Rise and Fall of the Communist International*. *World Revolution* was conceived as the scourge of fascism emerged in Germany and Italy and against the backdrop of what Denis Benn describes as "the short-lived socialist triumphs in Spain, and the formation of the *Front Populaire* in France" and represents an attack on Stalin's domestic and international policies and the idea of "socialism in one country."[34] James's publisher, Fredric Warburg, later described the book as an important statement on the disintegration of the revolution in the Soviet Union under Stalin and "a kind of Bible of Trotskyism."[35] Trotsky himself described it is as "a very good book" despite suffering from "a lack of dialectical approach, Anglo-Saxon empiricism, and formalism which is only the reverse of empiricism."[36] Arguably its most remarkable feature, however, is its critique of Trotsky, who, as one of the chief architects of the Russian Revolution and the former leader of the Red Army, was beyond reproach for most of his supporters. James reminded us that Trotsky had warned against the "'replacement of the dictatorship of the proletariat by the dictatorship over the proletariat'"[37] and "'political rule of the class by the organisational rule over the class,'"[38] both developments that characterized the Soviet Union at the time James penned *World Revolution*. He also praised Trotsky for his brilliance and personal appeal, suggesting that he was Russia's most brilliant figure.[39] Despite the accolades he showered on him, James was audacious enough to criticize Trotsky for his "imperiousness," what he described as "a certain inability to function easily with men his equal in status but obviously inferior in quality,"[40] and his lack of "Lenin's comprehensive good-nature and homeliness."[41]

Moreover, perhaps as a result of his profound study of history, Trotsky "seems to have accepted with too much fatalism this emergence of bureaucratic corruption [in the Soviet Union] in a period of revolutionary ebb," according to James.[42] To support this claim, he cited Lenin's criticism of Trotsky for being "'far too much attracted to the purely administrative side of affairs,' that is to say control from above, leading consciously or unconsciously to the suppressing of individual initiative."[43] This is precisely the criticism that James would make of Toussaint as he consolidated his power in Saint-Domingue, and particularly in relation to his nephew, Moïse, the popular North commandant whom Toussaint eventually had executed for treason.[44] James's criticisms of Trotsky no doubt alarmed many of his socialist associates. But future developments showed that he was not far from breaking with Trotskyism altogether at this stage, a fact that in hindsight was obvious in James's ultimate critique of Trotsky in *World Revolution*. Stalin's and Trotsky's perspectives on the future of socialism were wholly incompatible. Whereas Stalin professed that socialism in one country was possible, Trotsky championed the idea of world revolution. Yet, rather than mobilize "his considerable support to do what Lenin had said, and remove Stalin, Trotsky tried to collaborate with Stalin," only to be eventually outfoxed and exiled by him.[45]

Hill's hostility to Singham's claim that *The Black Jacobins* was shaped by socialist debates in Europe seems to have been premised on the idea that *World Revolution* and *The Black Jacobins* were at cross-purposes, written for distinct audiences and with divergent objectives. Although he acknowledged that *The Black Jacobins* was influenced by Lenin's ideas on nationalism,[46] Hill strongly objected to the book being dragged into what he described—referring to the notion of socialism in one country—as "the ridiculousness of that whole debate."[47] Yet James clearly broached the issue of internationalism in *The Black Jacobins* when he emphasized the symbiotic relationship between the Haitian and French revolutions and in reference to Toussaint Louverture's ambition to not simply put an end to slavery in Haiti but to sail to Africa to put an end to the European slave trade of Africans in general.[48] Toussaint dithered when he needed to be decisive with Napoleon, who outwitted him when he attempted to placate Napoleon and who clearly harbored contempt for him and intended all along to discipline and punish the Haitian general and restore slavery. We may very well read Toussaint's dilemma as a reflection of Trotsky's attempts to cooperate with Stalin, only to be outmaneuvered, exiled, and eventually killed by one of Stalin's agents, as Toussaint was exiled in France where he unceremoniously died in prison.

Beyond any other consideration, for Hill, *The Black Jacobins* represented James's contribution to debates within the IASB. Of course, the book is littered with references to Africa, and James acknowledged that it was animated by the African liberation struggle. The IASB emerged out of the International African Friends of Abyssinia (IAFA), which was established by James and others in the mid-1930s to mobilize against the fascist Italian invasion of Ethiopia. Despite its small size, the IAFA played a pivotal role in disseminating information on fascist Italy's invasion of Ethiopia.[49] The IAFA's work resulted in public outcry against the invasion and the boycotting of Italian products.[50] Like many people of African descent—in Ghana, South Africa, St. Lucia, Jamaica, Dominica, Barbados, Trinidad, Antigua, and other parts of the Caribbean, as well as in Britain and the United States[51]—James offered to enlist in the Ethiopian army "to make contact not only with the masses of the Abyssinians and other Africans, but in the ranks with them I would have had the best possible opportunity of putting across"—note this—"the International Socialist case." At the time, he surmised "that two or three years there, given the fact that I am a Negro and am especially interested in the African revolution, was well worth the attempt."[52] By the time he had made his decision, the Ethiopian armed forces had been defeated on the battlefield.[53] James wrote extensively on Ethiopia and the struggle against imperialism in general during this period. He also wrote the play *Toussaint Louverture: The Story of the Only Successful Slave Revolt in History*, which was first performed with Paul Robeson, the extraordinary American actor, singer, and political figure. Clearly, then, the political fortunes of the African continent were an abiding preoccupation for him as he conceived *The Black Jacobins*.

By 1937 the IAFA had evolved into the IASB, led by James's childhood friend George Padmore (born Malcolm Ivan Meredith Nurse), the distinguished Trinidadian and a former prominent figure in the Comintern. James served as editor of the organization's paper, *International African Opinion*, and the organization included many of the IAFA former members. Leading up to the Fifth Pan-African Congress in 1945, the IASB was one of the most important groups concerned with African liberation outside of Africa and included Jomo Kenyatta and Kwame Nkrumah. Prior to World War II, the group engaged in an internal debate about the method of African liberation struggle. According to Hill, James successfully argued a position in favor of armed struggle against imperialism which, after considerable debate, was adopted by the group up until the end of World War II, when "the change in the balance of world forces" occurred.[54]

According to James, "Nkrumah and other revolutionaries absorbed" *The Black Jacobins*.[55] In his 1980 foreword to the book, James tells the remarkable story of its impact in South Africa. It's a fascinating passage that vividly captures what Nelson Mandela has described as the "unbreakable umbilical cord"[56] that has historically tied the fates of South Africans with the Black diaspora. James recalled that he met two South African Pan-Africanists when he attended Ghana's independence celebrations in 1957. They had discovered *The Black Jacobins* in what he describes as the "Black University" and found the passages in the book related to Black–mulatto relations very useful in terms of understanding the complexities of race in South Africa. As James recalled, he "could not help thinking that revolution moves in a mysterious way its wonders to perform."[57] That *The Black Jacobins* should influence South Africans in much the same way that Marcus Garvey's *Negro World* newspaper once influenced early members of the African National Congress gives us some indication of how important the book must have been for those who read it as they contemplated and struggled to liberate themselves from colonialism. It is also intriguing to note that according to Tim Hector, James slept with a map of Africa in front of his bed in the latter years of his life with the state of South Africa emphasized. For James, a postapartheid South Africa augured the prospect of an African state with advanced development in modern technology in the hands of an African population, and this prospect presented tremendous possibilities for the African continent on the whole.[58] We are left to speculate what James would think of today's South Africa.

James made frequent references to contemporary Africa in the book. For example, in the opening chapter he referred to the intelligence of the slaves of Haiti "which refused to be crushed, these latent possibilities, that frightened the colonists, as it frightens the whites in Africa to-day." Referring to a chant in which Haitian slaves swore to fight to the death to destroy their white colonizers, he wrote: "For over two hundred years the slaves sang it at their meetings, as the Jews in Babylon sang of Zion, and the Bantu to-day sing in secret the national anthem of Africa."[59] Elsewhere, referring to Toussaint's sense of destiny, he writes: "he and his brother slaves only watched their masters destroy one another, as Africans watched them in 1914–1918, and will watch them again before long."[60] He also referred to South Africa's social and political inequality[61] and, as we have seen, Toussaint's long-term plan to sail to Africa and put an end to the slave trade.[62] There is then little doubt that *The Black Jacobins* was written with the African struggle in mind and with the intention of inspiring the continent's liberation struggle. In fact, in his 1980 foreword to the book, James said he wanted "to write a book in which Africans or people of African descent instead of constantly being the object of other peoples' exploitation and ferocity would themselves be taking action on a grand scale and shaping other people to their own needs."[63] Despite the insistence that the book was written with Africa in mind—and notwithstanding the fact that the Haitian Revolution might, in part, be understood as an African revolution in the Caribbean, which may have accounted for some of its appeal to Africa in James's eyes—his use of the phrase "people of African descent" implies not only continental Africans but also members of the African diaspora, including in the Caribbean. Yet James adds that he was working closely with Padmore and the IASB when he wrote the book and that "As will be seen all over and particularly in the last three pages, the book was written not with the Caribbean but with Africa in mind."[64] On the last page of the book James wrote:

> Imperialism vaunts its exploitation of the wealth of Africa for the benefit of civilisation. In reality, from the very nature of its system of production for profit it strangles the real wealth of the continent—the creative capacity of the African people. The African faces a long and difficult road and he will need guidance. But he will tread it fast because he will walk upright.[65]

The guidance to which James refers is likely another allusion to internationalism and workers' solidarity, the idea, or the hope, that Europe's "advanced" working class would lend support, even guide Africa as it embarks on freedom's road. Elsewhere, I have discussed this problematic formulation in relation to James's later musings on the African continent and the relationship between Africa, and particularly African culture, and the Caribbean.[66] Again, we can only imagine how these passages and others like it resonated with those Africans who read them.

Despite the numerous references to Africa, it is hard to imagine that both the debates related to European socialism and Caribbean politics in the 1930s—particularly the labor revolts that swept the Anglophone Caribbean at the time—did not influence James's thinking on rebellion and revolution as he wrote *The Black Jacobins*, that he simply put aside those concerns after publishing *The Case for West Indian Self-Government* (1933) and *World Revolution* in order to exclusively immerse himself in the African liberation struggle. Hill acknowledged that *The Black Jacobins* may well have inspired West Indians who read it as a means of resisting colonialism in the Caribbean, but ultimately, for him, this was the primary objective of *The Case for West Indian Self-Government*, not *The Black Jacobins*.[67] Citing James's *Beyond a Boundary*, Hill argued that *The Case for West Indian Self-Government* helped those involved in the protests that swept across the Anglophone Caribbean in the 1930s "make the mental and moral transition which the new circumstances required."[68]

Hill and his "circle of associates" in the CLRJSC also concluded that *The Case for West Indian Self-Government* anticipated James's Marxism.[69] Certainly it is not difficult to see how they would arrive at this conclusion. Like his sole novel, *Minty Alley*, *The Case for West Indian Self-Government* was written in Trinidad, before James left for England in 1932. Whereas *Minty Alley* captured the spirit and possibilities embodied in the lives of so-called ordinary Trinidadians, *The Case for West Indian Self-Government* explicitly laid claim to Western civilization as an integral part of West Indian culture, the inference being that West Indians had all the necessary cultural and political prerequisites for self-rule.[70] James went further, arguing that the people of the Caribbean are "indeed, far more advanced in Western culture than many a European community."[71] The cultural assumptions on which James's analysis rests deserve more critical attention, but as Hill and other CLRJSC members deduced, by exposing the exploitation of what he described as the Caribbean's "wage-slaves"[72]—a term that certainly contains Marxian echoes—James wrote in a manner that anticipated the political road that he would later travel.

The Case for West Indian Self-Government is not *The Black Jacobins*, in which James focused on the self-activity of Saint-Domingue's slaves. Instead he appealed to the British authorities to grant self-government, conscious that if necessary, Britain would use its cruisers and airplanes to maintain its hold on power as it later did in Guyana in 1953. " 'Self-government when fit for it,' " he writes, "That has always been the promise. Britain can well afford to keep it in this case, where evidence in favour is so overwhelming and she loses so little by keeping her word."[73] James would later learn enough about imperialism to know that logic and reason often defy those who believe that the reach of their power is limitless and their superiority incontrovertible. But he learned that lesson in Britain as a member of the IAFA and IASB and in the archives in France as he researched for *The Black Jacobins*—a lesson that, once discovered, shaped his writing from that point onward.

Clearly, then, James's previous writing haunted *The Black Jacobins*. We see these resonances in the followings passages:

Always the West Indian of any ambition or sensibility has to see positions of honour and power in his own country filled by itinerant demi-gods who sit at their desks, ears cocked for the happy news of a retirement in Nigeria or a death in Hong Kong.[74]

But for the revolution, this extraordinary man [Toussaint] and his band of gifted associates would have lived their lives as slaves, serving the common place creatures who own them, standing bare-footed and in rags to watch inflated little Governors and mediocre officials of Europe pass by, as many talented Africans stand in Africa to-day.[75]

The similarities between the first passage, taken from *The Case for West Indian Self-Government*, and the second, from *The Black Jacobins*, are obvious. Both speak to the inadequacies of colonial administrators and the stifled possibilities their rule represented for colonial subjects. Clearly the same spirit that animated *The Case for West Indian Self-Government* also found a home in *The Black Jacobins*.

We know that James was delivering talks on the Caribbean as late as 1938, several years after *The Case for West Indian Self-Government* was published.[76] It is not too much of a stretch to argue that some of the inspiration for *The Black Jacobins* came from the same source as his earlier work on Caribbean self-government. Cedric Robinson has tied the book to James's quest for African liberation, an expression of Trotsky's theory of permanent revolution and critique of Stalinism, Lenin's notion of the dictatorship of the proletariat, and Marx's "imperialist accumulation of capital."[77] In naming African liberation and James's Trotskyism and Marxism, Robinson recalls the fact that Blacks joined the International Brigades to fight against fascism in Ethiopia and Spain. But he does not stop there, recalling the protests and strikes in the Caribbean in the 1930s; as James observed these developments from afar, he bore witness to "the capacities for resistance of ordinary Black people" and "the transformation of peasants and workers into liberation forces," all of which convinced him that "successful armed rebellion among Black people was possible."[78] For Robinson, then, acts of rebellion and resistance in the Caribbean significantly shaped the contours and content of *The Black Jacobins*. His account brings us closer to a more rounded understanding of the political and historical context in which *The Black Jacobins* was forged, tipping the balance of the debate between Singham and Hill in Singham's favor.

The Black Jacobins's compelling literary narrative also harkens back to James's *Minty Alley* (1936). Said to be the first major Caribbean novel published in Britain, the book is unique in its characterization of "barrack-yard life," the day-to-day existence of Trinidad's underclass. James's keen eye for the life of "people down below" and his ability to not only capture that life but recognize it as a source of resilience and strength is artistically displayed.

This acute sense of the possibilities of "everyday people" would become a hallmark trait in his later writing, including *Notes on Dialectics, Mariners, Renegades, and Castaways,* and *Beyond a Boundary* with his depiction of Matthew Bondman.[79] But we might also read the book's chief protagonist, Mr. Haynes, as a kind of Toussaint-like figure insofar as he is, like Toussaint, allied with but a social class above the other tenants who live at number two Minty Alley. Like James who as a child observed the world from his bedroom window facing a cricket pitch, Haynes takes a keen interest in the household gossip and goings on, but essentially as an outsider peering in.

In his 1986 essay on James's work in England in the 1930s, Hill argues that *The Case for West Indian Self-Government* represented the completion of James's "West Indian period" and, having published *Minty Alley* during this period, also signaled his transition from literature to politics.[80] I am suggesting that *The Black Jacobins* was both part of James's West Indian period and can be read as both a literary and political work. In other words, its dramatic tone and structure and at times lyrical prose make it as much a literary achievement as it is a historical and political one. It would be difficult to pinpoint exactly how *Minty Alley* affected *The Black Jacobins* literarily and, to my knowledge, there is nothing to indicate that James suggested that it did. Art works in mysterious ways, tapping into our subconscious mind and creatively inspiring us to think and act—or in this case, write—in imperceptible ways. Poet and novelist Dionne Brand would perhaps agree. As a child growing up in Trinidad, she followed James as he contested Eric Williams, then prime minister, in the political arena. Comparing James's seminal work with Williams's *Capitalism and Slavery*, she writes, "I was to read C.L.R.'s *Black Jacobins* and his novel *Minty Alley.* . . . Maybe the difference was that C.L.R. recovered the resistance that people mounted against colonialism and slavery, and Williams spoke about the overwhelming nature of colonialism."[81] By linking the two books, Brand hints at a connection between them in much the same way I have suggested. The point here is not so much that *Minty Alley* influenced *The Black Jacobins* in some kind of causal relationship—that would be very difficult to prove—but that, as Brand implies, the same creative energies that fueled *Minty Alley* also shaped and animated *The Black Jacobins.*

Minty Alley is not the only work of fiction that touched *The Black Jacobins.* I would also argue that *The Black Jacobins* contains echoes of one of James's favorite books, William Makepeace Thackeray's *Vanity Fair.* Beginning in Trinidad as a child, James would read *Vanity Fair* repeatedly throughout the course of his life, laughing "without satiety at Thackeray's constant jokes and sneers and gibes at the aristocracy and at people in high places."[82] The novel had such a lasting effect on him that he could unequivocally claim, "Thackeray, not Marx, bears the heaviest responsibility for me."[83] Weaving through the pages of Thackeray's classic work, it is not difficult to recognize aspects of his narrative style and penetrating insights in *The Black Jacobins*. Thackeray refers to Napoleon's exploits in Europe and other worldly events, demonstrating his knowledge of history and current affairs in a way that we also recognize in James's writing. Despite its Victorian setting, *Vanity Fair* also makes a number of allusions to Blacks—"a little black porter," the specter of "mahogany grandchildren," a "black footman"; Miss Swartz, the "mulatto," "woolly-haired young heiress from St Kitts," and so on, as well as the "Negro Emancipation question" and speeches at the Quashimaboo-Aid Society in England, presumably an abolitionist group. Sambo, a Black servant, also lurks behind the scenes in the novel, entering the stage at opportune moments to jest and make timely remarks. It is not too much of a stretch to suggest that Thackeray's references to the Black population in England, slavery, and the West Indies might have, however unconsciously, had an important impact on James, adding to his resolve to remove Blacks from the background of history and bring them into the foreground.

Yet to acknowledge the importance of *Vanity Fair* to *The Black Jacobins* is to acknowledge a part of James's childhood in the Caribbean—where he repeatedly read the book—as an important part of the making of his study of the Haitian Revolution. James often said that, growing up in the Caribbean, he grew tired of hearing that Black people had no history and were merely the hapless objects of forces beyond their control. In his lectures on *The Black Jacobins* he argued that although he did not know a great deal about the history of Black people when he left Trinidad for England, he nonetheless did not believe the argument "that black people are a lowly people, that we came to the Caribbean as slaves, and that it was a benefit to us to have come rather than to have stayed in backward Africa."[84] In recounting this story, James was perhaps unconsciously referring to a particular incident that sharpened his resolve to write about Black people and turn conventional history on its head. *The Beacon* was a Trinidadian literary and cultural magazine to which James regularly contributed essays, reviews, and fiction as one of the magazine's inner circle of writers, critics, and intellectuals. In one issue, British scientist Sidney C. Harland, a resident of Trinidad's Imperial College of Tropical Agriculture, argued that Blacks were inferior to Whites and therefore unfit for self-rule.[85] James responded to Harland's remarks in a lengthy polemic that was published in *The Beacon*. He applied logic to counter the doctor's arguments, describing Harland as a scientist who nonetheless adopted unscientific methods to posit the idea of Black intellectual inferiority, including a "disregard of essential facts, large conclusions drawn from small premises, random statements of a patent absurdity; in fact, taking it for all in all, the very negation of the scientific temper, the very antithesis of the scientific attitude." He then posed the question: "If the high priests of the temple cannot apply the doctrine, what hope is there for the multitude without!"[86] As we know from *The Black Jacobins*, James later came to the realization that the "multitude" often sees reason most clearly, not the "high priests." Having dismissed Harland's spurious argument, he made another point that turned out to have a tremendous bearing on the course of his life. He invoked the memory of Toussaint Louverture, recounting his exploits as a general, his military genius, and his remarkable diplomatic skills before concluding: "I think I have written enough. I would have preferred to write on Toussaint L'Ouverture for instance. But I have thought it necessary to reply to Dr. Harland's view of the negro."[87] James, then, was not only aware of the history of the Haitian Revolution long before he left Trinidad for England, but Harland's theatrics appeared to have strengthened his resolve to embark on his study of the Haitian Revolution as a means of "vindicating" Black people in the Caribbean as intellectual and historical subjects.[88]

James mentions in his 1980 foreword to *The Black Jacobins* that he had written about Toussaint Louverture before leaving Trinidad for England in 1932 (he is likely referring to his allusion to Toussaint in his essay on Harland), reiterating a point made in *Beyond a Boundary* where he wrote, "Stuck away in the back of my head for years was the project of writing a biography of Toussaint L'Ouverture—the leader of the revolt of the slaves in the French colony of San Domingo . . . the most outstanding event in the history of the West Indies." He added—and this is key—"I had not been long in Nelson before I began to import from France the books that I would need to prepare a biography of Toussaint."[89] Here he acknowledges that he began sending for books from France while still living in Nelson, Lancashire, which meant that he began preparing to write *The Black Jacobins* before he became immersed in socialist and African politics. But without describing the context that prompted him to write about Toussaint while still living in Trinidad, we are left with the impression—and James himself frequently contributes to this view—that the book was essentially written without any consideration for the Caribbean. His polemic against Harland tells us otherwise and, in this sense, appears to substantiate Singham's view that much of what we read in *The Black Jacobins* was inspired by the peculiar circumstances in the Caribbean in the 1930s.

There is yet another reason to take the presence of the Caribbean in *The Black Jacobins* beyond the realm of conjecture, and again it comes in the form of an admission from James. In a 1967 Canadian Broadcasting Corporation interview conducted by Hill—part of an entire program on the Caribbean that included writer-poets Jan Carew and Derek Walcott—James reflected on his work over the previous thirty-five years. He insisted that the slaves of Saint-Domingue served as a model and a kind of moral incentive for African liberation. But in a moment of introspection, he also admitted that, like Césaire who published *Notebook of a Return to My Native Land* one year after *The Black Jacobins* was released, and despite the range of subjects he had covered in his own writing, the Caribbean permeated all of his work. He attributed this to the fact that he left Trinidad as a mature adult who had been nurtured on Caribbean soil.[90] James does not specifically mention *The Black Jacobins* in this statement, but of all of the books he wrote, it would be difficult to exclude it from the list of his Caribbean-inflected intellectual and literary achievements.

For James, *The Black Jacobins* was an important part of the Caribbean road to self-discovery. It was and remains a revolutionary study of revolution, and a revolutionary study of a *Caribbean* revolution. Sixteen years after writing his rejoinder to Singham's review, Hill wrote an essay in which he cited a passage from *Beyond a Boundary* in which James described the Haitian Revolution as "the most outstanding event in the history of the West Indies." Hill then argued that the Caribbean served as James's "basis or point of departure" in relation to his work in the 1930s.[91] Brian Meeks has suggested that the idea of West Indians playing a role in world history is subliminally reflected in *The Black Jacobins* and then highlights the book's 1963 appendix, which situates the Haitian Revolution within the political and intellectual history of the Caribbean leading up to and including the Cuban Revolution as evidence of this.[92] But as the following passage from the original 1938 edition suggests, James's revolutionary study of this Caribbean revolution was more than a point of departure or a subliminal occurrence in the book:

> It all reads like a cross between a nightmare and a bad joke. But these distinctions still exercise their influence in the West Indies to-day. While whites in Britain dislike the half-caste more than the full-blooded Negro,

whites in the West Indies favour the half-caste against the blacks. These, however, are matters of social prestige. But the racial discriminations in Africa to-day are, as they were in San Domingo, matters of Government policy, enforced by bullets and bayonets, and, and we have lived to see the rulers of a European nation make the Aryan grandmother as precious for their fellow-countrymen as the Carib ancestor was to the Mulatto. The cause in each case is the same—the justification of plunder by any obvious differentiation from those holding power. It is as well to remind the reader that a trained observer travelling in the West Indies in 1935 says of the coloured man there, "A few at the top, judges, barristers, doctors, whatever shade of colour, could hold their own in any circle. A great many more are the intellectual equals or superiors of their own white contemporaries."[93]

As James later wrote in a note to this passage, this is "Still true in 1961."[94] Clearly, in the late 1930s as he wrote the book and in 1961 as he revised it, James was thinking about this Caribbean revolution in relation to the Caribbean. Perhaps we can say that *The Black Jacobins* is part of a Caribbean political-historical and literary journey that passed through international socialism en route to African liberation, only to return to the Caribbean as the above note and 1963 appendix suggest. In much the way James intended, Hill and other members of the CLRJSC read *The Black Jacobins* with the Caribbean in mind, thinking about the emergent postcolonial order as they attempted to chart a course toward Caribbean liberation in the 1960s and 1970s.

Notes

1. "The Coming Struggle" was the title of an unpublished essay by Robert Hill in which he examined the prospects for revolutionary struggle and change in Jamaica following his involvement in the country's Young Socialist League in the mid-1960s. See Robert A. Hill, "The Coming Struggle for Liberation" (unpublished), n.d., Alfie Roberts Collection (ARC).
2. Andrew Salkey, *Havana Journal* (Harmondsworth: Penguin Books, 1971), 34.
3. Rodney and Hill participated in political-historical discussions among Jamaica's downtrodden in the months preceding the Congress of Black Writers. It was Rodney's role as a non-Jamaican in these "groundings" that led to his expulsion by the Jamaican authorities in October 1968.
4. Santiago-Valles uses this concept of maroon intellectuals to describe "small research groups" that drew on the Caribbean's history of rebellion and resistance between the sixteenth and nineteenth centuries to chart a new political and intellectual course in

the region. See W. F. Santiago-Valles, "The Caribbean Intellectual Tradition that Produced C.L.R. James and Walter Rodney," *Race and Class* 42, no. 2 (2000): 53.

5. C. L. R. James, *Notes on Dialectics* (Detroit: ARC, 1966).

6. See C. L. R. James, *Perspectives and Proposals* (Detroit: Facing Reality, 1966).

7. I have discussed the role of this small but important group elsewhere. See David Austin, *Fear of a Black Nation: Race, Sex, and Security in Sixties Montreal* (Toronto: Between the Lines, 2013), 73–93.

It is not insignificant that this current collection of essays on *The Black Jacobins* is part of an anticipated multivolume collection of James's work that, published under Hill's stewardship, was anticipated in 1970.

8. Robert Hill to Franklyn Harvey, January 11, 1970, in author's possession.

9. *Savacou* 1, no. 1 (1970). The journal was published by Edward (now Kamau) Brathwaite who served as its early editor, along with Andrew Salkey and Ken Ramchand. Between 1970 and 1979 *Savacou* was one of the most important literary journals in the Americas. This essay draws on a prepublished draft of Singham's review and Hill's draft rejoinder in the ARC. Both the review and the rejoinder were published in *C.L.R. James Symposium*, Doc. No. 2, published by the Guild of Undergraduates (Mona) for the C. L. R. James Symposium, n.d.

10. For more on Anne Cools's role within the group and the gendered nature of politics within it, see Austin, *Fear of a Black Nation*, 81–84. See also David Austin, "Anne Cools: Radical Feminist and Trailblazer?," *MaComère*, 12, no. 2 (2010).

11. Robert Hill to Marty and Jessie Glaberman, August 5, 1966. A Cuban edition of James's classic study of the Haitian Revolution was not published until 2010. See *Los Jacobins Negros: Toussaint L'Ouverture y la Revolución de Saint-Domingue* (La Habana: Casa de las Americas, 2010).

12. C. L. R. James, "Lectures on *The Black Jacobins*: How I Wrote *The Black Jacobins*," *Small Axe* 8 (2000): 67–69, 70.

13. James, "Lectures on *The Black Jacobins*: How I Wrote *The Black Jacobins*," 68–69.

14. James, "Lectures on *The Black Jacobins*: How I Wrote *The Black Jacobins*," 76–77.

15. James, "Lectures on *The Black Jacobins*: How I Wrote *The Black Jacobins*," 69.

16. James, "Lectures on *The Black Jacobins*: How I Wrote *The Black Jacobins*," 67; emphasis added.

17. James, "Lectures on *The Black Jacobins*: How I Wrote *The Black Jacobins*," 71.

18. James, "Lectures on *The Black Jacobins*: How I Wrote *The Black Jacobins*," 73.

19. Austin, *Fear of a Black Nation*, 138–39.

20. C. L. R. James, *The Black Jacobins: Toussaint L'Ouverture and the San Domingo Revolution* (London: Allison and Busby, 1984), 399.

21. James, *The Black Jacobins*, 402.

22. David Scott, *Conscripts of Modernity: The Tragedy of Colonial Enlightenment* (Durham, NC: Duke University Press, 2004), 58, 71, 88; emphasis in original.

23. Scott discusses how James deploys Aristotle's notion of harmartia, or "tragic flaw" and Hegel's notion of tragic "collision," in his 1963 revisions of *The Black Jacobins* to highlight the tragic nature of Toussaint's rise and fall (Scott, *Conscripts of Modernity*, 167). We might also see tragedy as a precursor to enlightenment in much the same way we think of "moments of vision" emerging from moments of dread.

24. Scott, *Conscripts of Modernity*, 125.

25. Scott, *Conscripts of Modernity*, 29–30.

26. A. W. Singham, "C.L.R. James on the Black Jacobin Revolution in San Domingo: Notes toward a Theory of Black Polities," *Savacou* 1, no. 1 (1970): 1. See also George Shepperson and Thomas Price, *Independent African: John Chilembwe and the Origins, Setting, and Significance of the Nyasaland Native Rising of 1915* (Edinburgh: Edinburgh University Press, 1958).

27. Singham, "C.L.R. James on the Black Jacobin Revolution in San Domingo," 17.

28. Singham, "C.L.R. James on the Black Jacobin Revolution in San Domingo," 21.

29. Singham, "C.L.R. James on the Black Jacobin Revolution in San Domingo," 21.

30. Singham, "C.L.R. James on the Black Jacobin Revolution in San Domingo," 1.

31. Singham, "C.L.R. James on the Black Jacobin Revolution in San Domingo," 1.

32. Robert A. Hill, "Rejoinder," unpublished, 1969.

33. Hill, "Rejoinder," 1–2.

34. Denis Benn, *The Caribbean: An Intellectual History, 1774–2003* (Kingston: Ian Randle, 2004), 154.

35. Fredric Warburg, *An Occupation for a Gentleman* (London: Hutchinson, 1959), 211.

36. C. L. R. James, *At the Rendezvous of Victory: Selected Writings* (London: Allison and Busby, 1984), 3:60.

37. C. L. R. James, *World Revolution, 1917–1936: The Rise and Fall of the Communist International* (Atlantic Highlands, NJ: Humanities Press, 1993), 51.

38. James, *World Revolution*, 51.

39. James, *World Revolution*, 145.

40. James, *World Revolution*, 145.

41. James, *World Revolution*, 145–46.

42. James, *World Revolution*, 154.

43. James, *World Revolution*, 190.

44. James, *The Black Jacobins*, 275–78.

45. James, *World Revolution*, 160.

46. Hill, "Rejoinder," 4.

47. Hill, "Rejoinder," 7.

48. James, *The Black Jacobins*, 265.

49. IAFA members Jomo Kenyatta and Arthur Lewis went on to play significant roles in their respective parts of the world. Kenyatta became Kenya's first independent head of state, and Lewis did brief stints in both Africa and Asia before becoming the Caribbean's Nobel Prize–winning economist. In *Beyond a Boundary* (258), James later described IAFA member Amy Ashwood Garvey—along with cricketer Frank Worrell, Leon Trotsky, and to a certain extent Arthur Lewis—as having "a unique capacity to concentrate all the forces available and needed for the matter at hand, usually conversation, but, I suspect, applicable in other fields." IAFA member Ras Makonnen (formerly George T. N. Griffith of Guyana) along with George Padmore, worked with Kwame Nkrumah in Ghana.

50. Tim Hector, interview by David Austin, May 23, 1999.

51. James was not alone among Caribbean women and men who dedicated themselves to African liberation in one form or another. This phenomenon is captured in Horace Campbell, *Rasta and Resistance: From Marcus Garvey to Walter Rodney* (Trenton: Africa World Press, 1987). In much the same way they would later do during the struggle against South African apartheid, people of African descent in diverse ways demonstrated their solidarity with Ethiopia during the Italian invasion. In addition to those from across the Pan-African world who offered to fight alongside Ethiopians (some of whom actually did), Blacks in New York rioted and fought in the streets against Italians over the invasion (73). A massive demonstration in support of the Abyssinians was held in Jamaica on October 15, 1935, and Amy Jacques Garvey spoke to a packed house in Ward Theatre on October 13, 1935, after which the Kingston division of the United Negro Improvement Association called on the British to permit ex-servicemen to fight alongside the Ethiopian army (74). And "in South Africa, black workers who were organised under the ideas of Garveyism began a march up the continent to assist their African brothers in Abyssinia. They were turned back [after] a few hundred miles by the British, who disarmed them" (74). From Barbados, Arnold Ford, an old Garveyite who had established a sect of Black Jews in the United States and "determined that the real Jews were the *Falashas* of Ethiopia," moved to Ethiopia with his wife. They are credited with establishing the first coeducational secondary school in Ethiopia. Herbert Julian of Trinidad joined and served in the Ethiopian armed forces and rose to the rank of colonel (157). On the other hand, Marcus Garvey criticized Haile Selassie for not being as well prepared for battle as he could have been. Cited from *The Blackman* (July/August 1936), in Campbell, *Rasta and Resistance*. Garvey stated: "If Haile Selassie had educated thousands of his countrymen and women, and raised them to the status of culture and general knowledge necessary to civilisation, the Italians never could have dared an offensive against Abyssinia, because Abyssinia could have found leaders on the spot competent and ready to throw back the invader. But that is not all. If Haile Selassie had negotiated the proper relationship with the hundreds of millions of Africans outside Abyssinia, in South and Central America, in the United States, in Canada, in the West Indies, in Australia, he could have had an organisation of men and women ready for service, not only in the development of Abyssinia as a great Negro nation, but on the spur of the moment to protect it from any foreign foe" (75). Perhaps heeding Garvey's advice, in 1937 Selassie sent his cousin, Malaku Bayen, to New York City to help consolidate support for the Ethiopian cause, particularly among people of African descent. The result was the formation of the Ethiopian World Federation, which ultimately set up branches throughout the United States and the Caribbean.

52. Cited from C. L. R. James, "Fighting for the Abyssinian Empire," *New Leader*, June 5, 1936, in Kent Worcester, *C.L.R. James: A Political Biography* (Albany: State University of New York Press, 1996), 32.

53. James, "Fighting for the Abyssinian Empire," in Worcester, *C.L.R. James*, 32.

54. Hill, "Rejoinder," 5.

55. C. L. R. James, *Nkrumah and the Ghana Revolution* (Westport, CT: Lawrence Hill, 1977), 66.

56. In his autobiography, *Long Walk to Freedom* (Boston: Back Bay Books, 1995), Nelson Mandela writes of what he describes as "an unbreakable umbilical cord" that "connected black South Africans and black Americans, for we were together children of Africa. There was a kinship between the two . . . that had been inspired by such great Americans as W.E.B. Du Bois, Marcus Garvey, and Martin Luther King Jr." (583). Mandela, a boxer in his own right, also mentions the legendary Joe Louis, whose career he followed with great interest.

57. James, *The Black Jacobins*, vii.

58. Hector interview.

59. James, *The Black Jacobins*, 18.

60. James, *The Black Jacobins*, 82.

61. James, *The Black Jacobins*, 141.

62. James, *The Black Jacobins*, 265.

63. James, *The Black Jacobins*, v.

64. James, *The Black Jacobins*, vi.

65. James, *The Black Jacobins*, 377.

66. David Austin, "Introduction: In Search of a National Identity: C.L.R. James and the Promise of the Caribbean," in *You Don't Play with Revolution: The Montreal Lectures of C.L.R. James*, edited by David Austin (Oakland: AK Press, 2009); David Austin, "Class Struggle: Cabral, Rodney, and the Complexities of Culture in Africa," in *Claim No Easy Victory: The Legacy of Amilcar Cabral*, edited by Firoze Manji and Bill Fletcher (Dakar: Codesria/Dajara Press, 2013); and David Austin, "Searching within the Boundaries: Modernism, Africanism, and the Worldview of C.L.R. James," paper delivered at *Beyond a Boundary* at 50 conference, University of Glasgow, May 9–11, 2013.

67. Originally published as *The Life of Captain Cipriani* in 1932, the book was abridged as *The Case for West Indian Self-Government* a year later. Captain Arthur Cipriani was a Trinidadian trade union leader, mayor of Port of Spain, and a staunch opponent of British Crown colony rule. James had been associated with Cipriani in Trinidad.

68. James in Hill, "Rejoinder," 3.

69. Hill, "Rejoinder," 3.

70. C. L. R. James, *The Case for West Indian Self-Government* (New York: University Place Book Shop/Facing Reality Publishing, 1967), 5.

71. James, *The Case for West Indian Self-Government*, 5–6.

72. James, *The Case for West Indian Self-Government*, 31.

73. James, *The Case for West Indian Self-Government*, 32.

74. James, *The Case for West Indian Self-Government*, 32.

75. James, *The Black Jacobins*, 265.

76. James R. Hooker, *Black Revolutionary: George Padmore's Path from Communism to Pan-Africanism* (New York: Praeger, 1967), 53.

77. Cedric Robinson, *Black Marxism: The Making of the Black Radical Tradition* (1983; Chapel Hill: University of North Carolina Press, 2000), 265.

78. Robinson, *Black Marxism*, 273.

79. C. L. R. James, *Beyond a Boundary* (Durham, NC: Duke University Press, 1993), 4.

80. Robert Hill, "In England, 1932–1938," in *C.L.R. James: His Life and Work*, edited by Paul Buhle (London: Allison and Busby, 1986), 66.

81. Dionne Brand, *Bread Out of Stone: Recollections, Sex, Recognitions, Race, Dreaming, Politics* (Toronto: Coach House Press, 1994), 93.

82. James, *Beyond a Boundary*, 39.

83. James, *Beyond a Boundary*, 47.

84. James, "Lectures on *The Black Jacobins*: How I Wrote *The Black Jacobins*," 66.

85. For a discussion on the context in which this debate took place, see Robert A. Hill, "C.L.R. James: The Myth of Western Civilization," in *Enterprise of the Indies*, edited by George Lamming (Port of Spain: Trinidad and Tobago Institute of the West Indies, 1999); Scott, *Conscripts of Modernity*, 79–81.

86. C. L. R. James, "The Intelligence of the Negro," in *From Trinidad: An Anthology of Early West Indian Writing*, edited by Reinhard Sander (New York: Africana, 1978), 237.

87. James, "The Intelligence of the Negro," 236.

88. The term *vindicationism* was used by St. Claire Drake in *Black Folk Here and There* (Los Angeles: Center for Afro-American Studies, University of California, 1987) to describe the intellectual tradition in which Black women and men countered ideas of inferiority (xvii, xviii). Partly drawing on Hill's essay, "C.L.R. James: The Myth of Western Civilization," David Scott argues that *The Black Jacobins* is essentially a vindicationist study, what he calls a "romantic" or "indignant" vindication of the humanity or achievements of Blacks. See Scott, *Conscripts of Modernity*, 63–64, 79, 81, 83–87, 131.

89. James, *Beyond a Boundary*, 119.

90. Robert Hill interview with C. L. R. James on CBC Tuesday Night, the Canadian Broadcasting Corporation, February 13, 1967.

91. Hill, "In England, 1932–1938," 66.

92. Brian Meeks, "Re-Reading *The Black Jacobins*: James, the Dialectic and the Revolutionary Conjuncture," in *Radical Caribbean: From Black Power to Abu Bakr* (Kingston: Press of the University of the West Indies, 1996), 103, 119n6.

93. James, *The Black Jacobins*, 43.

94. James, *The Black Jacobins*, 43.

16

Making Drama out of the Haitian Revolution
from Below: C. L. R. James's *The Black Jacobins* Play

RACHEL DOUGLAS

Famed as the classic history of the Haitian revolution, C. L. R. James's *The Black Jacobins* is widely credited with having transformed colonial historiography. One little-known fact about *The Black Jacobins* is that it both begins and ends life as a play. Both plays have a crucial importance because they bookend the first and last editions of the history: the 1936 performance of the first play *Toussaint Louverture* antedates the initial 1938 publication of *The Black Jacobins* history by two years, while the second 1967 *The Black Jacobins* play comes more than four years after the revision of the history for its second 1963 edition. The remaking of *The Black Jacobins* as James's second 1967 play will be the chief focus of this essay. Its predecessor of more than thirty years, the first play *Toussaint Louverture: The Story of the Only Successful Slave Revolt in History* was performed only twice in London at the Westminster Hall on March 15 and 16, and its script—previously feared to be lost for good—was only recently published and made widely available, thanks to Christian Høgsbjerg's excellent 2013 critical edition.[1] Surprisingly, less seems to be known about the second *Black Jacobins* play than would be expected, despite the script appearing twice in print and being performed across a number of countries over the decades since its December 14–16, 1967, premiere by the Arts Theatre Group, University of Ibadan, Nigeria.[2]

Making drama out of history, it will be argued, enables James to go furthest in rewriting the Haitian Revolution from below. Changes to protagonists will be explored as spotlighting "from below" historical and political perspectives, which become crucial in the intervening years between the 1930s and 1960s moments of James's work on the Haitian revolution. Reshaped, *The Black Jacobins* 1967 play will be shown to bear strong imprints of history from below approaches of Marxist historiography and ideas developed during James's most intensive political collaboration and theorization in the United States in the 1940s as part of the Johnson-Forest tendency concerning self-activity, self-organization, mobilization of the masses from below, and rejection of the orthodox Marxist-Leninist concept of the vanguard party.[3] Turning to drama again, I argue, enables James to tell a different story of the Haitian revolution and change the protagonists by shifting the spotlight downward during the rewriting of *The Black Jacobins* as a play in 1966–1967.[4] Explored as a corrective to top person's history, and as a version of the Haitian revolution seen from below, the play is analyzed particularly from the viewpoint of its demythologization of revolutionary leaders Toussaint, Dessalines, and Christophe, simultaneously bringing into view crowds, peasants, ordinary soldiers, and popular alternative leaders.[5]

A 1971 lecture tantalizingly titled "How I Would Rewrite *The Black Jacobins*" spells out the influence of "history from below" perspectives on James's rethinking of his classic history of the Haitian Revolution.[6] Were he to rewrite this history again, he would base his analyses on a completely different type of source. Instead of building on descriptions of foreign white observers, he would look for ones written by slaves themselves or those closest to them. Rewriting the history along these lines would necessitate altering "the whole movement of the thing," and interstitial changes of the revised 1963 history edition made in footnotes, beginnings/endings of chapters, appendix, and bibliography would instead become important parts of the body of the work itself, taking up page after page of this hypothetical rewritten history.[7] Nowhere does James indicate that he is actually proposing to redo his archival research from scratch in order to seek out and incorporate these alternative source materials of which he speaks, meaning he remains "poor James, condemned to footnotes."[8]

Rewriting *The Black Jacobins* as a play is, however, a different matter, as turning to drama liberates James from the need for the scholarly apparatuses of textual history-writing to gloss existing historiography and refer to sources: footnotes and bibliographies. A further advantage of drama as means for representing the past is that its "multivoicedness" enables alternative characters, of whom there is little archival trace, to speak more audibly.[9] This chapter argues that James goes far toward actually making changes outlined hypothetically in the 1971 "How I Would Rewrite" lecture when remaking drama out of the Haitian Revolution for a second time in 1966–1967.[10]

Haitian Revolutionary Crowds

What emerges clearly is James's attempt to represent the unrepresented by bringing crowds of ordinary slaves more sharply into view, so that they function as a chorus. Here is added in the entry of the classical chorus as envisaged by James in his lecture on "How I Would Rewrite *The Black Jacobins*," where the crowd represents the wider population of ex-slaves, and further highlights tensions between leaders and masses.[11] Crowds are written in by stage directions that portray these slaves as alternative collective protagonists, bearing heroic characteristics: "Crowds say little but their presence is felt powerfully at all critical moments. This is the key point of the play and comments cannot, must not, be written. It must be felt dramatically, and be projected as essential to action in the downstage areas."[12] Problematically, however, this crowd-as-protagonist nevertheless remains largely silent, with limited and unscripted dramatic roles.[13] Tellingly, while reworking representations of such rank-and-file characters, the playwright poses a revealing handwritten question in the margins: "Should they speak?"[14] What is at stake in James's marginal insertions is confrontation with a question not unlike the one orienting the title of Gayatri Chakravorty Spivak's later influential essay and idea "Can the Subaltern Speak?";[15] an intervention theorizing a kind of reading responsive to the aporias and silences of history.[16] Exposed throughout the play is the mechanism of imperial acts of silencing to which this group of Caribbean slaves has been subjected. James brings us back to the act of writing the silences of history, which need to be supplemented and transcended by the playwright. Drama is used as a means of "giving voice" to those who have none, or next to none, in the imperial archive and of making such crowds of slaves more audible and visible. Nevertheless, even in *The Black Jacobins* play where lower ranking ex-slaves are supposed to become protagonists, decentering top-ranking revolutionary generals, these subalterns still do not speak much. Here James runs into the same difficulties of portraying a "positive" crowd faced by other radical playwrights who have often failed to achieve goals of shining the spotlight sympathetically on "the people," and making crowds play a significant role in the action.[17] Marxist playwrights may be all too happy to agree that their true protagonist is "the people," yet readers/viewers would be harder pushed to agree with such assessments, given that the crowd's actual role points to the contrary.[18] Despite new emphasis, crowds remain problematically rather silent and faceless.

James does take pioneering "from below" studies of European crowds by Albert Soboul, George Rudé, E. P. Thompson, and Eric Hobsbawm in new directions by widening the focus to Haitian revolutionary crowds, and from *sans-culottes*, *bras-nus*, and *enragés* to the *menu peuple* mass of ordinary black ex-slaves.[19] This crowd, representing the great mass of slaves, functions as a chorus, operating as organizing tool for theater from below, as in the type of radical Marxist theater theorized by Augusto Boal, where crowds do not meekly toe the line or speak dutifully in chorus but function as dissenting choruses that challenge and answer back.[20] Crowd scenes are used increasingly toward the end to highlight fundamental divisions between official generals and the great mass of ex-slaves, showing that they are fighting for different political goals, with leaders actually fighting *against* the masses. Nowhere is this made clearer than in the scenes where particularly Dessalines but also Toussaint and Christophe suppress ordinary revolutionaries.

This widespread repression meted out by revolutionary leaders against popular masses emerges when Dessalines barks orders that the singing of their own popular anthem "To the Attack, Grenadier" must be halted forthwith.[21] This anthem is used to contrast the masses' political goals and capacities with those of the main leaders—a stark contrast writ large when Dessalines contemptuously mocks this song of the rank-and-file revolutionaries,[22] while Christophe professes not even to know it, showing the extent to which out-of-touch leaders are alienated from the masses. Generals are portrayed carrying out (on French orders) widespread repression against popular forces who continue to fight against the French.[23] Increasingly, this crowd voices opposition, expressing discontent and what, according to Boal, are the fundamental principles of the chorus in radical theater: conflict, contradiction, clash, and combat.[24] At the end of the scene, Dessalines flings open the window and shouts down dictatorially to the crowd below what they must chant: "Dessalines, Emperor of Haiti!"[25] First responding as prescribed, this crowd-chorus then begins to express mass protest through their own revolutionary anthem. As the scene ends, there is confrontation between the expression of popular resistance and the minuet which Dessalines orders to drown out the protest song. At news of Toussaint's death, the popular protest becomes a mournful chant, through which the crowd directs resentment at Dessalines. Hard-nosed in his own pursuit of power, Dessalines very forcibly orders his music and dancing to recommence as the crowd flees.

Samedi Smith, Peasants, Brigands, and Barefooted Men

Called the "Samedi Smith" song throughout the play, the revolutionary fighting/protest anthem of the masses takes its name from an alternative popular leader described as "a black peasant" and "barefooted and in rags," but "undoubtedly a man of authority."[26] Singled out of the crowd as peasant leader of an insurrectionary band, Samedi Smith represents one of the many thousands of obscure leaders organizing popular resistance about whom James says he would like to know more about in the "How I Would Rewrite" lecture.[27] Disparagingly, generals repeatedly use "name-calling" to denigrate Samedi Smith and the mass of ordinary soldiers and peasants as brigands, rebels, insurgents, bandits, robbers, gangsters, and, most tellingly, enemies, creating an adversarial situation in which grassroots rebels are pitted against the triumvirate of top generals, who are working with French colonial troops to crush popular resistance.[28] Divisions between leadership and masses are made clear when Samedi Smith "speaks with a certain restraint looking at Toussaint out of the corner of his eye,"[29] distrusting leaders who go back on their word by conceding peace and relinquishing weapons to the French. Samedi Smith presents ever-multiplying bands as nuclei of effective political rebellion, with military strata drawn from the ordinary peasantry portrayed as leading spontaneous, but well-organized forms of guerrilla war against the old French enemy. Their tactics are described here in a manner reminiscent of Johnson-Forest ideas regarding self-activity of the masses and rejection of the vanguard. Capable of autonomous political organization, these bands fight en masse as a well-organized collective of fighting men. They, and not the top leadership, are presented as the true revolutionaries.

Samedi Smith is the only representative of these bands who actually speaks, but Dessalines and Toussaint note popular leaders are everywhere, singling out Macaya, Sylla, Sans Souci, and Jean Panier, who represent a more popular leadership stratum, able to guide the people's own autonomous action simultaneously against French troops and forces of Haitian generals.[30] Throughout Samedi Smith's interventions, the pronoun "we" predominates to indicate a collective function, where exploits depend less on any single leader, belonging instead to "a socially recognized collection of heroes," much like Hobsbawm's bandits.[31] As collective protagonists, the relationship of these "men of the people" is presented as one of total solidarity with the peasantry, as symbolized by the fact that this "champion of the barefooted man" is himself a barefoot ordinary peasant.[32]

Representations of Lower Ranking Soldiers

Parallel "writing in" of ordinary soldiers means that they open three scenes: Act I, Scene 2; Act III, Scene 1; and Act III, Scene 2. In the first of these scenes, three rank-and-file soldiers choose new names—Max, Marat, and Orleans—renaming themselves after French revolutionaries and symbolically throwing off their slave names, foisted on them by old masters. A main part of these characters' function is to lug heavy furniture, enabling symbolic prop changes: "removing the remaining signs of French colonial gentility from the central area," and replacing them with "severely functional furniture." Slaves express discontent that slave-like labor continues and freedom remains abstract, not appearing to correlate to any substantive change for ex-slaves. All three scenes show ordinary ex-slaves trying to make sense of the latest political developments, translating the French Revolution into their own terms: "The white slaves in France heard that the black slaves in San Domingo had killed their masters and taken over the houses and the property. They heard that we did it and they follow us."[33] Likewise, these soldiers work out their own understandings of key slogans adapted from the French revolutionary idiom—liberty, equality, fraternity—and such talk shows how receptive these former slaves are to revolutionary ideas, which each interprets in his own way.[34]

By Act III, Marat and Orleans are now higher ranking soldiers, promoted to the ranks of sergeant and corporal, respectively, and correspondingly more elegantly dressed than their previous "semblance of a uniform."[35] Again, soldiers are "doing the work," arranging furniture, trying to make sense of recent developments, and offering their own assessments about things looking "pretty bad" in the wake of Toussaint's sentencing to death of Moïse and close aides, including their comrade Max.[36] They reflect on the ramifications of these shootings, try to make sense of happenings in France—the "terror" and parallel killings of their namesakes—and lament Toussaint's surrender to the French and retirement. Similarly opening the final scene, Act III, Scene 2, Orleans and Marat enter with a "huge throne-like chair,"[37] a visual symbol that Dessalines is taking over the reins of power. Now Orleans offers a more positive assessment of the current situation "looking pretty good," as the final push of the war of independence is debated. Sure that Dessalines will be next governor of San Domingo, even his closest aide Marat does not foresee that Dessalines will aim for even higher power. When Dessalines declares himself emperor from his throne-like chair, Marat plays rabble-rouser, directing the uncertain crowd to join in the chant: "Dessalines! Emperor of Haiti! Emperor!"[38] As the last soldier to abandon Dessalines on stage, Marat points to Dessalines's alienation of those closest to him as the final scene closes.[39]

Certainly, James comes closest in *The Black Jacobins* play to doing what he said he would like to do in 1971: rewriting the history to give Toussaint Louverture only a walk-on part by foregrounding other obscure, popular leaders instead. Even in the 1967 play, Toussaint's role remains more important than that of a walk-on part, but representational shifts have taken place with the top black Jacobin leadership of Toussaint, Dessalines, and Christophe now challenged by popular alternative leaders Samedi Smith, Panier, Sylla, Sans Souci, and the most important challenger: Moïse.

Enter Moïse, Alternative Protagonist, Stage Left

Writing out initial arch-protagonist Toussaint Louverture during the making of *The Black Jacobins* of *The Black Jacobins* play, James progressively "writes in" an alternative "hero of the masses": Moïse. Here, Moïse takes center stage, and his showdown with Toussaint forms the epicenter of the entire play. Moïse had long been on James's mind, as revealed in a 1955 letter: "I notice that there is still very little precise to put one's hands upon in the history of Moyse. He is the man of the minor figures who interests me most. I hope that one day something will turn up."[40] Rewriting *The Black Jacobins* as a play specifically enables James to develop this "minor" figure of Moïse into main protagonist. Three scenes are crucial for understanding his role: Act I, Scene 2, Act I, Scene 3, and Act II, Scene 4 (Act I, Scene 7 in early drafts).

Moïse rushes onto the stage in Act I, Scene 2, excitedly waving a copy of French newspaper *Le Moniteur* and shouting "News, citizens! News!"[41] Taking center stage, he conveys to crowds of ordinary soldiers that the French Convention in Paris has officially abolished slavery in every French colony by dramatically reading the news aloud from the newspaper. Translator and interpreter is a major part of Moïse's role of communicating effectively with crowds of ordinary people. He is translating the written word for them because they are illiterate and cannot read or write—the reason telling their history "from below" is difficult because these ex-slaves left no written records of their own.[42] Moïse's translations mediate between revolutions in France and San Domingo, between leaders and masses, between written and spoken words, and between elite and common languages in the colony. Through such translation, the people quickly grasp ramifications of political developments, including why Toussaint makes a startling *volte-face*, suddenly switching sides from the Spanish to the French Republic now that France has abolished slavery. Moïse's deployment of literacy for effective communication with the great mass of the population contrasts with Toussaint's aloof and cerebral uncommunicativeness about his strategies.

Conspicuously dabbing a handkerchief to his right eye as he enters the next scene (Act I, Scene 3), Moïse declares that he has "lost an eye in the service of liberty"[43] with bravery depicted visually through use of props as well as bold words. The spotlight turns on the contrasting leadership styles of Moïse, Dessalines, Christophe, and Toussaint, pitting them against one another to reveal different attitudes to freedom and independence in response to the British offer to make Toussaint king. Moïse's clear-sighted vision for San Domingo's future can be summed up in a single word: independence. As James wrote in 1955: "Toussaint was a revolutionary who had gone a long way but could not continue to what the situation actually demanded, the independence of the island."[44] Toussaint cannot continue to independence, whereas in stark contrast, Moïse stands clearly for independence throughout—positions that also contrast with those of Dessalines and Christophe. On the British offer of king, Dessalines also declares himself for independence but has no qualms about accepting this offer, not seeing the threat of binding the island to another slave-holding power. As for Christophe, his lines depict him as weak and wavering. Juxtaposing Moïse and Christophe shows just how much the former's decisiveness and clear-sighted vision contrasts with Christophe's lack of any position whatsoever. Moïse also acts as a differentiating incorruptible foil by deriding this pair for being duped by high-sounding aristocratic titles.

At the crux of the play is the showdown (Act II, Scene 4; Act I, Scene 7 in early drafts) where Moïse acts as defiant foil and challenger to Toussaint, directly calling into question his alienating leadership methods.[45] Here, prisoner Moïse has just been court-martialed and sentenced to death for treason, accused of leading rebellions against Toussaint's rule. Upon entering the scene, stage directions indicate that Moïse's black eye patch should be immediately and prominently visible, speaking to the true meaning of words like liberty, freedom, and independence; causes for which he will not only lose an eye but ultimately sacrifice his life. Presented here as political organizer with mass popular support, Moïse helps translate slaves' political consciousness into an active collective movement against "big leaders" and acts as alternative to increasingly unpopular and isolated Toussaint. Advocating independence, Moïse makes it clear that this is what is needed to safeguard the ex-slaves' freedom, demands reinforced by his parting shot which calls for ties to all symbols of colonialism and slavery to be severed, making San Domingo truly independent.[46] As foil, Moïse acts to show up major flaws in "pitiful old" Toussaint's leadership style, especially uncommunicativeness about strategies and his continued allegiance to the French despite the threat of slavery restoration.[47] Clear-sighted as ever, Moïse sees through French assurances that slavery will not be restored.

Labor and land reforms are the main bone of contention. Moïse voices the widespread opposition to Toussaint's rural code, which forces ex-slaves to work on the plantations and regiments their labor. Such freedom, Moïse points out, is nothing but an abstraction, devoid of any real meaning, as draconian regimentation of labor carries on as before. As chief agricultural inspector, Moïse articulates the people's personal attachment to the land and their perception that slavery is being restored in all but name because generals have been quick to take control of many sequestered plantations, flogging laborers as if they were slaves. While Toussaint preserves old plantations, handing them out to black generals to maintain production, Moïse vehemently opposes this alienating policy, advocating instead the parceling off of the large plantations and redistribution of land to ordinary soldiers, not just the top leadership.[48]

On behalf of the masses, Moïse opposes another Louverturian agrarian policy—inviting émigré white planters back to take charge of plantations—and is particularly contemptuous of Madame Bullet, the white plantation mistress.[49] Stage directions have him cast "a withering sweep of his one good eye" very pointedly in her direction, while challenging Toussaint to cut San Domingo completely from all "symbols of colonialism and slavery" and make the country independent once and for all.[50] Much of the scene opening portrays close relations between Toussaint and his white mistress, Madame Bullet, and her character indicates that Toussaint is courting white émigré planters, enticing them to return, instead of concentrating on his own people. Significantly, Toussaint describes Madame Bullet as the only one on whom he can rely, so alienated is he from the black masses.

Familial ties linking Toussaint and his adopted nephew Moïse are stressed, always presenting them as father and son, and Moïse's death sentence is tantamount to Toussaint killing his own son. Drama has a way of compressing relationships, as Lindenberger argues, and here Moïse usurps the role of son, which compresses father-son-type family bonds as tightly as possible.[51]

Consequently, Toussaint's sentencing to death of his adopted nephew/son is presented as the most outrageous violation of their bond, magnifying divergences between the worlds they represent—the people and the top brass—previously held together by their closest of relationships.

Moïse's sentencing forms the structural and thematic center of the play, but even after death his popular and principled alternative leadership style and ideas continue to loom large, with Dessalines underscoring that killing Moïse was pivotal in Toussaint's own downfall, but now Moïse's ideas are flourishing in new soil through thousands of Samedi Smiths.[52] The specter of what Moïse represented is again raised when news of Toussaint's death is announced: "DESSALINES: Moïse told [Toussaint] exactly what to do, but he killed Moïse."[53] Right at the end, clear-sighted Moïse is invoked as the one who could have charted the path toward true independence. What hope is there at the end of this final bleak scene? Answer: very little. Ideals of the Haitian revolution are symbolized above all by Moïse, and Moïse is dead.

Changing the Ending: The Epilogue

In the unperformed and unpublished epilogue, however, Moïse is not dead but reincarnated as modern-day political organizer: Speaker D. Clearly bringing the play "up to date," this epilogue fast-forwards in time from the declaration of Haitian independence to the present day—a "time travel" indicated visibly by costume changes to modern clothes. As for the setting of this scene, it too is clearly in the present day, taking place in "a private room in a hotel somewhere in an underdeveloped country" at the end of a conference. Unlike the rest of the play, epilogue characters have no names, although stage directions stipulate they should be easily recognizable from parts played before, and Speakers A, B, and C display similar characteristics to their opposite numbers: Toussaint, Christophe, and Dessalines respectively. This namelessness also presents Speakers A, B, and C as modern-day political "types." Almost two whole pages of this three-page epilogue sketch out a political skit, dramatizing a startling neocolonial situation where "independence" becomes an empty word bandied about by this new political elite. Costume changes also expose the hypocrisy of this "independence" situation when actors doff the "native dress" of all previous scenes, only to don "Western clothes," reminiscent of similar costume changes in Ousmane Sembène's film *Xala*. There, three-piece suits and briefcases, filled with wads of cash bankrolled by the returning/departing neo/colonial white masters, act as status symbols and shorthand for postindependence aping of foreign power.[54] In James's epilogue, suits donned by the three speakers are symbols of this hollow independence because they metonymically identify their wearers as postindependence bureaucrat-type leaders, vying to prop up their power with foreign capital. Against this new "top" leadership who compromise newly acquired independence with continuing dependence on foreign capital and a bureaucratic, top-down approach stands archetypal revolutionary alternative: Speaker D, a.k.a. Moïse.

Reincarnated as the twentieth-century equivalent of Haitian revolutionary forebear Moïse, Speaker D's popular leadership is buoyed up by the masses, unlike Speakers A, B, and C, whose struggle is *against* the people. Now that Moïse has morphed into a principled political organizer, Speaker D concludes the epilogue by delivering a rousing speech to an audience offstage. At the outset, suspense is created by positioning him "three-quarters turned away" from the real audience, with most of his face still hidden. Only when the speech ends and he half-turns toward the audience is his true identity as Moïse revealed because now can be seen that symbol of revolutionary struggle for independence: the black patch over the sacrificed eye. Turning to face the real audience, Moïse also deliberately wipes his face with a handkerchief, a gesture that recalls mopping blood from the lost eye and thereby all the sacrifices for true independence.

This closing speech presents Speaker D, like his Haitian revolutionary counterpart Moïse, as clear and viable political alternative to the hollow "age of independence" leadership styles represented by Speakers A, B, and C. Words and substance delivered change and, as a prime function of the epilogue is to act as reconfiguration tool, it is also essential to consider James's own reworking of this epilogue in its three different versions. The earliest draft from a specifically Caribbean vantage point makes explicit reference to the West Indies, Caribbean politics, and especially the failed West Indian Federation project.[55] Caribbean references are then removed from the two subsequent versions where the epilogue is rewritten to make it less localized. In so doing, the epilogue loses its situatedness and immediate context, particularly at the end of the second version of Speaker D's "present-day" speech: "Fighting means taking risks. You have to learn to risk your liberty, your property, even your life."[56] Here, Speaker D's closing words appear just as platitudinous as those of Speakers A–C, whose alternative he is supposed to represent. Similar charges were also given by director Dexter Lyndersay when he cut the epilogue ahead of the play's Nigerian premiere.[57]

A third alternative version of the epilogue's final page turns attention to the true meaning of independence.[58] Interrogating the current so-called independence, Speaker D asks: "Independence. What is independence? How can you be independent if the very ground on which you walk belongs to people in London, New York, and Paris?" Independence symbols—new flag, new national anthem, new prime minister, and new parliament—are presented by Speaker D as empty status symbols if true power still resides in foreign hands. A refrain punctuating this version repeats like a mantra "we must get the land back." References to getting back the land recall the platform of the Trinidad Workers' and Farmers' Party (WFP), cofounded by James in 1965, which called for redistribution of land and tighter controls over foreign ownership of land and investment.[59]

A confident optimistic note characterizes all three speech versions, ending with the upbeat Samedi Smith resistance anthem, and one constant throughout all the reworkings is the impact of the closing speech on the crowds. Punctuating Speaker D's speech are bursts of euphoric applause, indicating mass support. Is this representational inscription of Speaker D/ Moïse as vehicle of such united popular support wishful thinking on James's part? Certainly, the epilogue does end by inscribing an ideal(ized) response from large crowds. This could be read as a rather utopian representation of the ideal mass popular support James would have liked during his own bruising foray into West Indian politics, particularly the WFP's election failure in November 1966.

Despite this model of active mass participation set up by the epilogue, where popular leader Moïse functions as spokesman for the masses and key Johnson-Forest ideas, including self-activity, self-organization, mobilization from below, and the rejection of vanguardist leadership, this short epilogue scene revolving around Speaker D/Moïse could represent a kind of one-man vanguard or yet another scion of a long postcolonial tradition of "big man" politics and trade unionism, towering head and shoulders above the rest.[60] Despite inflections of "from below" approaches, James nevertheless retains a marked preference for exceptionally superlative, larger-than-life, heroic revolutionary figures, singled out for extraordinary capacities and energy.[61] Even with these shortcomings, however, the alternative version of the epilogue ending does give Speaker D/Moïse a positive proposal that is clearest when the focus turns to the true meaning of independence.

Ultimately, no version of the epilogue has ever been performed or published, and without it the entire play ends very differently. The whole raison d'être for the epilogue is to be usable for other situations—ever-shiftable/updatable qualities, which are further stressed when reworked by James, so that the epilogue can itself be reconfigured and extrapolated as the play travels to different times and places. Indeed, stage directions stipulate that contemporary parallels should always be stressed, and that top priority for staging or filming should be making this epilogue "completely adaptable to the circumstances and environs of the production" so that it "may be altered as necessary." These three pages of epilogue in their various states constitute a hybrid document between play, political pamphlet/speech, and paratext, which reconfigures and reframes the whole play.

Paratexts—all the prefaces, appendices, and epilogues that multiply in new editions—always function as crucial sites and privileged modes of expression in James's work. To conclude, I consider what the epilogue form enables James to *do*, arguing that epilogues—and by extension other paratextual near-equivalents, including prefaces and appendices—offer advantages over other modes of writing. Generically, this epilogue form compels maximum use of directness and clarity, and yields the strongest ideological and political insights of the whole play. Compressed into only three pages, this epilogue has a strikingly condensed quality within the architecture of the play as a whole. Use of such concise forms enables James to magnify, concentrate, illuminate, reinforce, make more accessible, and bring to new contexts the crucial points of the preceding main play, around which these paratextual elements are positioned. As mode of expression, the epilogue most resembles that of a direct political speech, pamphlet, or interview because it consists of clear understandable messages—an updatable statement for changing times, summing up, and pointing out implications for the future.

Reaching its political climax in Speaker D/Moïse's closing speech, the epilogue ending is where there is clearest exposition of political ideas and of how one actually organizes to change society. Containing the most direct call to action of the entire play, the epilogue also most explicitly represents political activities in the present. Designed specifically with a view to being opened up through extrapolation and reconfiguration to new chronotopes, the epilogue is inscribed with the idea of "traveling" because its whole raison d'être is to allow the dramatic text of *The Black Jacobins* to travel as widely as possible, presenting a way of radically reframing themes from the play proper through reconfiguration of relations among new pasts, presents, and futures.[62]

Ironically, this epilogue never did permit *The Black Jacobins* play to travel anywhere through time/space because it was discarded on director Lyndersay's orders long before the play was first performed or appeared in print. Endings are key sites of plays, as the very last thing an audience sees performed and ultimately takes away with them when leaving the theater.[63] Minus the epilogue, the play as performed and published ends in a fundamentally different key and another register entirely with Act III, Scene 2 (1803) (Act II, Scene 2 of earlier drafts). Unlike the declaration of Haitian independence scene, from which embodiment of revolutionary qualities Moïse is absent, the epilogue actually ends with his rousing, optimistic words looking to the future. Without the epilogue, the play ends instead with Dessalines portrayed in the act of crowning himself "emperor of Haiti," hollowing out new symbols of independence as they are being created, violently suppressing ordinary people and their popular revolutionary anthem.

Notes

This chapter, based on research conducted in Trinidad and New York funded by a British Academy Small Research Grant, was written while its author was in receipt of an Arts and Humanities Research Council Fellowship. The support of the British Academy and AHRC is gratefully acknowledged.

1. C. L. R. James, *Toussaint Louverture: The Story of the Only Successful Slave Revolt in History* (Durham, NC: Duke University Press, 2013).

2. There are two nearly identical published playtexts in *A Time and a Season: Eight Caribbean Plays*, edited by Errol Hill (Port-of-Spain: University of the West Indies, Trinidad, Extramural Studies Unit, 1976), 382–450; *The C.L.R. James Reader*, edited by Anna Grimshaw (Oxford: Blackwell, 1992), 67–111. The Black Jacobins play has also been produced by BBC Radio in 1971 and for the stage by (among others) Dexter Lyndersay, the Arts Theatre, University of Ibadan, Nigeria, December 14–16, 1967; Rawle Gibbons and University Players at Mona, Jamaica, in 1975; Rawle Gibbons and the Yard Theatre in Trinidad in 1979; by Eugene Williams and the Graduate Theatre Company of the Jamaica School of Drama in Kingston in 1982; by Yvonne Brewster for Talawa Theatre Company's maiden production at the Riverside Studios in London in 1986; by Rawle Gibbons and Danielle Lyndersay at the Theatre Arts Faculty, University of the West Indies, St. Augustine, Trinidad, in 1993; and by Harclyde Walcott at the University of the West Indies, Cave Hill Campus, Barbados, in 2004. For want of the *Toussaint Louverture* 1936 playtext until 2013, this 1967 play has understandably often been read *as* the 1936 play, and even billed as such when published in Grimshaw, *The C.L.R. James Reader*. See Nicole King, *C.L.R. James and Creolization: Circles of Influence* (Jackson: University of Mississippi Press, 2001), 30–51; Nicole King, "C.L.R. James, Genre and Cultural Politics," in *Beyond Boundaries: C.L.R. James and Postnational Studies*, edited by Christopher Gair (London: Pluto, 2006), 13–38; Reinhard

Sander, "C.L.R. James and the Haitian Revolution," *World Literature Written in English* 26, no. 2 (1986): 277–90; Reinhard Sander, *The Trinidad Awakening: West Indian Literature of the Nineteen-Thirties* (New York: Greenwood, 1988). Confusion has also reigned over whether *Toussaint Louverture* (1936) and *The Black Jacobins* (1967) are the same play, slightly altered versions of the same play, or indeed two different plays with different titles. In his correspondence, James always maintained that they were, in fact, two very different plays, and that the 1967 *The Black Jacobins* drama was the one he infinitely preferred, and would always describe as the better play. Letter from C. L. R. James to "My dear Marina," October 29, 1967, Alma Jordan Library, University of the West Indies, St. Augustine, Trinidad, C. L. R. James Collection (henceforth UWI), Box 7, folder 190; letter from Anna Grimshaw to Joseph B. Boromé, dated June 6, 1986, UWI, Box 7, folder 191.

3. On the Johnson-Forest tendency, see James D. Young, *The World of C.L.R. James: His Unfragmented Vision* (Glasgow: Clydeside Press, 1999), 162–79; Frank Rosengarten, *Urbane Revolutionary: C.L.R. James and the Struggle for a New Society* (Jackson: University Press of Mississippi, 2008), 61–84; Scott McLemee and Paul Le Blanc (eds.), *C.L.R. James and Revolutionary Marxism: Selected Writings of C.L.R. James, 1939–1949* (Atlantic Highlands, NJ: Humanities Press, 1994), 8–18, 48–51. On Haitian history from below, see the James-mentored study by Carolyn Fick, *The Making of Haiti: The Saint Domingue Revolution from Below* (Knoxville: University of Tennessee Press, 1990); Jean Fouchard, *The Haitian Maroons: Liberty or Death* (New York: Blyden, 1981), which has a preface by James. Generally, see Jim Sharpe, "History from Below," in *New Perspectives on Historical Writing*, edited by Peter Burke (Cambridge: Polity Press, 1991), 24–41; Frederick Krantz (ed.), *History from Below: Studies in Popular Protest and Popular Ideology* (Oxford: Blackwell, 1988). On Marxist French revolutionary historiography, see C. L. R. James, "Rousseau and the Idea of General Will," in *You Don't Play with Revolution: The Montreal Lectures of C.L.R. James*, edited by David Austin (Oakland, CA: AK Press, 2009), 114; C. L. R. James, "Lectures on *The Black Jacobins*: How I Would Rewrite *The Black Jacobins*," *Small Axe* 8 (2000): 104–9; Robert A. Hill, "Literary Executor's Afterword," in C. L. R. James, *American Civilization* (Oxford: Blackwell, 1993), 338–45.

4. I am working with unpublished playscripts for *The Black Jacobins* play from the following sources: Alma Jordan Library, UWI (SC82, Box 9, folders 230, 229, and 228; Box 12, folder 280); Schomburg Center for Research in Black Culture, New York Public Library, Manuscripts, Archives and Rare Books Division [SG MG 53] (henceforth Schomburg); Rare Books and Manuscripts, Special Collections Library, Pennsylvania State University, State College, Charles L. Blockson Collection of African Americana and the African Diaspora (uncataloged) (henceforth Penn State I); Rare Books and Manuscripts, Special Collections Library, Pennsylvania State University, State College (0581/VF LIT) (henceforth Penn State II); Dartmouth College, Rauner Special Collections Library, Hanover, New Hampshire, Papers of Errol G. Hill (ML–77, Box 70) (henceforth Dartmouth); Columbia University, Rare Books and Manuscripts Library, C. L. R. James Papers (henceforth Columbia) (MS #1529 Box 5, Folders 14, 15, and 17); Wayne State University, Walter P. Reuther Library, Archives of Labor and Urban Affairs, Martin Glaberman Collection (Box 21, file 6); performance script of director Dexter Lyndersay, private collection; performance script of Harold Preston who played Maitland in the 1967 production, soon to be deposited at the Brotherton Library, University of Leeds. Many thanks to Danielle Lyndersay and Martin Banham for lending me these last two scripts.

5. On the perspective of top person's history, to which history from below acts as a corrective, see Sharpe, "History from Below," 25, 32, 34.

6. James, "Lectures on *The Black Jacobins*: How I Would Rewrite *The Black Jacobins*," 99–112.

7. James, "Lectures on *The Black Jacobins*: How I Would Rewrite *The Black Jacobins*," 103.

8. James, "Lectures on *The Black Jacobins*: How I Would Rewrite *The Black Jacobins*," 106.

9. On alternative modes of historical expression, see Alun Munslow, *Narrative and History* (Basingstoke: Palgrave Macmillan, 2007), 67, 84; Paul Breslin, " 'The First Epic of the New World': But How Shall It Be Written?," in *Tree of Liberty: Cultural Legacies of the Haitian Revolution in the Atlantic World*, edited by Doris Lorraine Garraway (Charlottesville: University of Virginia Press, 2008), 241.

10. James's role in this play has sometimes been seen as minimal. See Selwyn Cudjoe, "C.L.R. James Misbound," *Transition* 58 (1992): 127; Scott McLemee, "Afterword: American Civilization and World Revolution; C.L.R. James in the United States, 1938–1953 and Beyond," in *C.L.R. James and Revolutionary Marxism*, edited by Paul Le Blanc and Scott McLemee (Atlantic Highlands, NJ: Humanities Press, 1994), 239, n9; Mary Lou Emery, *Modernism, the Visual and Caribbean Literature* (Cambridge: Cambridge University Press, 2007), 259n63, but his own contributions were far from negligible. I address the roles played by James and collaboration at length in forthcoming work.

11. James, "Lectures on *The Black Jacobins*: How I Would Rewrite *The Black Jacobins*," 111.

12. C. L. R. James, "The Black Jacobins," in *A Time and a Season: Eight Caribbean Plays*, edited by Errol Hill (Port-of-Spain: University of the West Indies, Trinidad, Extramural Studies Unit, 1976), 384.

13. On the top-heaviness of *The Black Jacobins* history, see Paul B. Miller, *Elusive Origins: The Enlightenment in the Modern Caribbean Historical Imagination* (Charlottesville: University of Virginia Press, 2010), 57–83; Kara M. Rabbitt, "C.L.R. James's Figuring of Toussaint Louverture: The Black Jacobins and the Literary Hero," in *C.L.R. James: His Intellectual Legacies*, edited by Selwyn Cudjoe and William Cain (Amherst: University of Massachusetts Press, 1994), 128–30; Nana Wilson-Tagoe, *Historical Thought and Literary Representation in West Indian Literature* (Gainesville: University Press of Florida, 1998), 27–28; Fick, *The Making of Haiti*, 4.

14. UWI, Box 9, folder 230.

15. Gayatri Chakravorty Spivak, "Can the Subaltern Speak?," in *Colonial Discourse and Post-Colonial Theory: A Reader*, edited by Patrick Williams and Laura Chrisman

(Hemel Hempstead: Harvester Wheatsheaf, 1994), 66–111; see also Rosalind C. Morris, ed., *Can the Subaltern Speak? Reflections on the History of an Idea* (New York: Columbia University Press, 2010).

16. See Rosalind C. Morris, ed., *Can the Subaltern Speak? Reflections on the History of an Idea* (New York: Columbia University Press, 2010), 1–18.

17. See Herbert Lindenberger, *Historical Drama: The Relation of Literature and Reality* (Chicago: University of Chicago Press, 1975), 150–52.

18. Lindenberger, *Historical Drama*, 148.

19. As this is a study of the rewriting of *The Black Jacobins* 1967 play, I am especially stressing significant changes. However, it is also crucial to recognize the strong dynamic of continuity that runs from his first to last writings on this subject. James also already envisioned the black ex-slaves functioning as a Greek chorus in his first play, and his 1938 history already constitutes a pioneering Marxist "history from below" avant la lettre of 1960s work by Soboul, Rudé, Thompson, Hobsbawm, and others. Ideas already pioneered by James in his 1930s work are crystallized, inspiring him to combine new "from below" historical and political perspectives from the intervening period between the moments of his first *Toussaint Louverture* play and the second one, applying them to new contexts. These include (1) the influential "history from below" approach of English and French Marxist historiography of the French revolution; (2) James's most important political theories, developed during his years in the United States (1940s–early 1950s), as part of the Johnson-Forest tendency. Too little credit has been given for James's decisive contribution to perspectives on the making of the Haitian Revolution from below, and this is because his remaking of the play in the 1960s could be taken further into account, even by his protégés more associated with the "history from below" tendency. See, for example, the assessments made by Fick, *The Making of Haiti*, 3.

20. Augusto Boal, *Theater of the Oppressed*, trans. Charles A. McBride, Maria-Odilia Leal McBride, and Emily Fryer (London: Pluto, 2000), xix, 33, 41, 183.

21. James refers to the version/commentary found in Jean-Baptiste Lemonnier-Delafosse, *Souvenirs historiques et succincts de la première campagne* (Havre: H. Brindeau, 1846–1850), 84–86. C. L. R. James, "The Making of the Caribbean People," in *You Don't Play with Revolution: The Montreal Lectures of C.L.R. James*, edited by David Austin (Oakland, CA: AK Press, 2009), 44–45; C. L. R. James, "The Haitian Revolution in the Making of the Modern World," in *You Don't Play with Revolution: The Montreal Lectures of C.L.R. James*, edited by David Austin (Oakland, CA: AK Press, 2009), 58. On this song's complex history, see Jean-Pierre Le Glaunec, "*Tant qu'il resterait un nègre.*" *La bataille de Vertières ou l'histoire d'Haïti* (Montreal: Lux, forthcoming). Recent uses include Michel "Sweet Micky" Martelly, musician and current Haitian president's song, "Grenadier," and calls to support the Haitian football team.

22. James, "The Black Jacobins," 436.

23. See similar emphasis in Fick, *The Making of Haiti*, 228, 231, 248.

24. Boal, *Theater of the Oppressed*, 58.

25. James, "The Black Jacobins," 449–50.

26. James, "The Black Jacobins," 433. Historically, "Grenadiers" is associated with François Capois/Capoix-la-mort, not Samedi Smith. See Le Glaunec, *"Tant qu'il resterait un nègre."*

27. Samedi Smith's name has been read as James invoking Vodou *lwa* Baron Samedi (see, for example, King, *C.L.R. James and Creolization*, 40). Samedi Smith, however mythologized, did exist as an identifiable individual and is not just a construct of James's literary imagination. See Fick, *The Making of Haiti*, 225–26, 231.

28. See Eric Hobsbawm, *Bandits* (London: Abacus, 2001), 10, 20; Fick, *The Making of Haiti*, 111–12, 216, 242.

29. James, "The Black Jacobins," 434.

30. On these leaders, see Fick, *The Making of Haiti*, 59, 222–23, 226.

31. Hobsbawm, *Bandits*, 82.

32. Like Captain Cipriani, whose political biography James published in 1932 on the question of West Indian self-government, Samedi Smith is a self-professed "champion of the barefooted man."

33. James, "The Black Jacobins," 393. See James, "The Haitian Revolution," 54.

34. See Fick, *The Making of Haiti*, 75, 86.

35. James, "The Black Jacobins," 391, 432.

36. James, "The Black Jacobins," 432–33.

37. James, "The Black Jacobins," 443.

38. James, "The Black Jacobins," 445–49.

39. James, "The Black Jacobins," 450.

40. Letter from C. L. R. James to Haitian historian Étienne Charlier, August 24, 1955, UWI, Box 7, folder 190.

41. James, "The Black Jacobins," 395.

42. On gaps and silences in historical records relating to Haiti and the Caribbean, see Michel-Rolph Trouillot, *Silencing the Past: Power and the Production of History* (Boston: Beacon Press, 1995); Sibylle Fischer, *Modernity Disavowed* (Durham, NC: Duke University Press); B. W. Higman, *Writing West Indian Histories* (London: Macmillan Education, 1999); and Wilson-Tagoe, *Historical Thought and Literary Representation*.

43. James, "The Black Jacobins," 403.

44. Letter from James to Charlier, August 24, 1955.

45. James produced at least two alternative versions for this most reworked scene, including an introductory commentary outlining his decision to rewrite it entirely, and proposing to print as appendixes all alternative versions in an afterword to the published playtext, in which he planned to "discuss how the play was arrived at." UWI, Box 9, folders 228 and 229.

46. James, "The Black Jacobins," 428.

47. On Toussaint's flaws in the revised 1963 history edition, see David Scott, *Conscripts of Modernity: The Tragedy of Colonial Enlightenment* (Durham, NC: Duke University Press, 2004).

48. See Fick, *The Making of Haiti*, 209–10.

49. On this policy, see Fick, *The Making of Haiti*, 209, 247.

50. James, "The Black Jacobins," 428.

51. Lindenberger, *Historical Drama*, 156–57.

52. James, "The Black Jacobins," 440.

53. James, "The Black Jacobins," 450.

54. David Murphy, *Sembene: Imagining Alternatives in Film and Fiction* (Oxford: James Currey, 2000), 105, 110–13, 117, 120.

55. This more Caribbean epilogue version can be found in UWI, Box 9, folder 230.

56. See UWI, Box 9, folders 228 and 229, Schomburg, Columbia, and Penn State I and II for this epilogue version.

57. Letter from Lyndersay to James, October 8, 1967, UWI, Box 10, folder 240.

58. Copies of "Alternative to p. 46 of Epilogue" can be found in UWI, Box 9, folders 228 and 229.

59. See Robert A. Hill, "Preface," in *You Don't Play with Revolution: The Montreal Lectures of C.L.R. James*, edited by David Austin (Oakland, CA: AK Press, 2009), xv; David Austin, "Introduction: In Search of a National Identity: C.L.R. James and the Promise of the Caribbean," in *You Don't Play with Revolution: The Montreal Lectures of C.L.R. James*, edited by David Austin (Oakland, CA: AK Press, 2009), 14–15; Rosengarten, *Urbane Revolutionary*, 110, 118, 124, 128–31.

60. On this tradition, see Biodun Jeyifo, *Wole Soyinka: Politics, Poetics and Postcolonialism* (Cambridge: Cambridge University Press, 2004), xvi–xx, 58, 97–99, 285.

61. On James's foregrounding of Toussaint's exceptionalism, see Robert A. Hill, "C.L.R. James: The Myth of Western Civilization," in *Enterprise of the Indies*, edited by George Lamming (Port of Spain: Trinidad and Tobago Institute of the West Indies, 1999), 256–57.

62. See Biodun Jeyifo, "Whose Theatre, Whose Africa?: Wole Soyinka's *The Road* on the Road," *Modern Drama* 45, no. 3 (2002): 449–50.

63. My argument here diverges from Genette's dismissal of the postface/epilogue as capable of "only a curative or corrective function" because of its position at the end. Gérard Genette, *Paratexts: Thresholds of Interpretation*, trans. Jane E. Lewin (Cambridge: Cambridge University Press, 1997), 237–39.

ALDON LYNN NIELSEN

The Wings of Atalanta are the coming universities of the South.
—W. E. B. Du Bois

One of the frequent criticisms leveled against the Harlem Renaissance by intellectuals and artists of the Black Power and Black Arts Movements was that the earlier era of activist thinkers and creators failed to establish institutions that might serve their communities after the initial flush of New Negro enthusiasm had given way to the economic pressures of the Depression and the renewed, never really quiescent forces of racism. If there was some merit to those critiques, it was also the case that most efforts of the 1960s and 1970s to form such lasting institutions also gave way in their turn to the rampages of political repression, the shifting stages of economic devastation, and the occasional infighting that struck so many organizations, with and without the help of J. Edgar Hoover's COINTELPRO minions. While we still have such organizations as Haki Madhubuti's Third World Press, other efforts, including the Black Repertory Theater of Washington, DC, *First World* journal, and the Howard Theater Foundation, floundered following their initial successes. This record should induce humility in any of us who might be on the point of condemning our elders, but it is also a record of local histories marked by stunning and sustaining accomplishments. The Institute of the Black World, founded in Atlanta in 1969, was just such a short-lived but sustaining story.

Vincent Harding, founding director of the Institute, recalls that the original impetus was to create the Institute of the Black World based on the idea that "the whole study of the Black experience . . . ought to be essentially defined by Black people," and that intellectual work should be "carried on in the service of continuing struggle."[1] That history is important to recollect in our present moment, as progressives increasingly turn their attention to seeking ways to counter the extraordinarily well-funded and politically powerful archipelago of right-wing think tanks stretching from the Hoover Institution in the American West to the Heritage Foundation, American Enterprise Institute, and Cato Institute on the East Coast. Where the pressure to create institutional support for conservative intellectual activities has always come from a carefully calculating circle of wealth and power, black studies had its origins in the organizing and demands of masses of students and activists. The intellectuals who formed the Institute of the Black World were not, like the Dinesh D'Souzas of this world, plucked by power from anonymity to do its bidding, but were people who sought to put their scholarly abilities in the service of the movements growing out of black people's struggles to forge their own powers into more effective instruments of action.

In retrospect, the Institute of the Black World appears to be a breathtaking crossroads of people who would continue to make crucial contributions as scholar-activists for decades to come. Howard Dodson, longtime director of the Schomburg Center for Research in Black Culture and recently called out of retirement to do the same for Howard University's Moorland-Spingarn Collection, was executive director from 1974 through 1979. Abdul Alkalimat was one of the Institute's cofounders. Robert A. Hill, longtime director of UCLA's Marcus Garvey Papers Project and C. L. R. James's literary executor, was on the staff. St. Clair Drake, Sylvia Winter, Patricia Daly, Kamau Brathwaite, Tran Van Dinh, George Beckford, and Joyce Ladner all spent time at the Institute. Margaret Walker gave a memorable seminar there in 1972. Lerone Bennet was a senior fellow in 1969 and 1970 and worked with Institute colleague William Strickland on the steering committee for the first National Black Political Convention in Gary, Indiana. The Institute had its origins as a part of the Martin Luther King Memorial Center, but separated from the Center over ideological differences and took on an independent life in the summer of 1970. Perhaps one of the most far-reaching organizational efforts mounted at the Institute was the first national gathering of black studies directors.

The Institute's work has always been diasporic in scope, and one of its most enduring publications has been *Walter Rodney Speaks*.[2] In 1974, Robert Hill and Howard Dodson arranged for Rodney, author of *How Europe Underdeveloped Africa* and *The Groundings with My Brothers*, to spend the summer between his departure from Tanzania, where he had been teaching, and his return to Guyana working in Atlanta as codirector of a research symposium on "African Peoples and the International Political Economy." The book that was eventually edited by Hill and published with an introduction by Dodson grew out of subsequent meetings the Institute's leadership held with Rodney in spring 1975 in Massachusetts. The colloquies with Rodney came at an especially reflective moment in the short history of the Institute. Immediately following the summer symposium that featured Rodney, the staff and board of the Institute held a retreat in Pennsylvania to meet with leading proponents of several tendencies that had found their feet in the era of Black Power and then were roiling the intellectual community. These debates have continued to trouble the agendas to this day.

On one hand, there was an emerging struggle over the understanding of the interlocking roles of race and class. These debates cut in several directions at once. Simultaneous with the erosion of the explanatory powers of cultural nationalist perspectives, this period saw the beginnings of what was soon recognized as neoconservative sociopolitical views. Just a year prior to Rodney's visit, William Julius Wilson had published his textbook *Power, Racism and Privilege*, and only four years after the Institute's retreat, Wilson published *The Declining Significance of Race*. The latter volume was slow to gain attention among the general audience of educated white readers but was immediately recognized among black activist intellectuals as an argument that found favor among the powerful, especially the powerful who were already seeking euphemisms by which to carry out racism by other means than the Lester Maddox ax handle. At the same time, many African American intellectuals who had grown dissatisfied with cultural nationalism were seeking their own class-based analyses that would produce a more radical agenda than the more ameliorative politics of Wilson or Sowell. Most notably, a fair portion of the leadership of the Congress of African Peoples were working with Amiri Baraka on the elaboration of a black Marxist approach that horrified the remaining adherents of cultural nationalism, a debate perhaps most memorably expressed in the attacks from Haki Madhubuti (that rift didn't really begin to heal until both Madhubuti and Baraka had grown older). Then, too, there were always interventions from the several secret police services of the 1970s. Shortly after the Institute retreat, the Atlanta offices were burglarized. Tapes and memoranda from the retreat were stolen, as were significant organizational files. The offices were broken into twice more, and the staff began receiving almost daily bomb threats and hate mail at the offices and at home. It would seem that the interest in the future directions of black activism went far beyond the intellectuals of the Atlanta Institute.

The Rodney symposium was a sign of the Institute's interest in a research and discussion agenda that was diasporic in reach, that would link anticolonial struggles abroad with the struggles within a war-torn United States, and that would offer a serious and radical class analysis in opposition to a class-based argument that had the chief effect of turning off debate about racism. Three years prior to the Rodney symposium, there was another that had done the initial spade work that was carried on by Rodney: this was a visit from the international Marxist philosopher and historian C. L. R. James, whose memorial tribute and critique of Rodney, published later as *Walter Rodney and the Question of Power*, made a significant observation about the changing imperatives and possibilities facing different generations. "As we grew up and went along," James argued then:

> we had to fight the doctrines of the imperialist powers in order to establish some Caribbean foundation or foundations for the underdeveloped peoples. *Walter did not have to do that.* . . . Walter grew up in an atmosphere where for the first time a generation of West Indian intellectuals was able, not only to study the revolutionary and creative works that had been created in Europe, but also to benefit from and be master of what had been done in the same tradition in direct reference to the Caribbean.[3]

James went on to criticize Rodney for an insufficient study of the actual taking of power, but his eulogy demonstrates an incisive understanding of what had been accomplished and what remained to be done. This is what made James's earlier visit to the Institute of the Black World, just one year after the institute had set out on a course apart from the King Memorial Center, such a powerful preparation for the challenges faced in the mid-1970s.

The James symposium also marked a significant stage of James's life and career. He had been forced to leave the United States at the high-water mark of the McCarthyite and McCarran persecutions of U.S. leftists. He had been in the country illegally for more than fifteen years and had married a U.S. citizen with whom he'd had a U.S. child. These facts, however, afforded him no protection when the attorney general's office sought to expel him, largely on the basis of his career (often under pseudonyms) as an author of radical texts. Following imprisonment on Ellis Island and a drawn-out legal proceeding, in the end James departed voluntarily, in hopes that such departure might allow him to return one day. It was fourteen years before he was allowed back into the country legally. He was initially granted a visa when he was given a formal offer to come to Northwestern University. In the course of his June 17,

1971, lecture at the Institute, he commented in passing, "I went to Northwestern for a semester. I will never again go anywhere for a semester."[4] The Northwestern invitation had been instigated by black intellectuals there as a means of permitting James reentry into the United States, and although he no doubt faced enormous difficulties at the close of that interlude, he eventually found a position at the newly created Federal City College. This was an urban land grant college making the Liberal Arts available to the people of the nation's capital, which attracted an idealistic cadre of scholars and activists in its early years before they were nearly all driven away by the crippling budgets and the corruption that marked its successor, the University of the District of Columbia, in a pattern long familiar to those of us in the only population in the continental United States that is entirely subject to the whims of Congress. James was as new to the position of professor as Federal City College was to the community of higher learning, and both were finding their way to a liberatory education model that could serve in the struggles of the final decades of the twentieth century.

So it came to pass that in the summer of 1971, James, Trinidad-born author, activist, and teacher, arrived in Atlanta to begin a series of well-attended lectures at the Institute of the Black World running from June 15 through June 19. For many years, these lectures were only available in the form of audio tapes, part of a series the Institute made available, which were collected by many libraries at the time. In 2000, the Caribbean studies journal *Small Axe* transcribed and published three of the six lectures. The partial publication of the symposium is a signal event in the recovery of James's widely scattered and largely unknown corpus, an event for which scholars and general readers alike can be grateful. But there are numerous errors of transcription in the published versions, and there is much to be gleaned from listening to the original tapes that were circulated by the Institute. For one thing, the published versions omit the voices of the moderators and the discussants. Furthermore, those too young to have heard James will find that these tapes present his characteristic presentation style from the later years of his life. Still to be heard amid the ambient Atlanta traffic sounds leaking in through the window, and underneath the dulling surface of early 1970s audio technology, is the exciting and engaging voice that had been sharpened through years of public speaking. At that age, he always spoke sitting down, but here he still sounds like the vibrant young orator who used to practice by pacing back and forth in front of a window, reciting his speeches until he could do them apparently effortlessly. The scholar heard holding forth on these tapes is still the man who used to inveigh against the evils of colonialism in the public squares of Britain, and offer the most spirited and exacting analyses of U.S. racial politics in church basements and union halls across the United States. Here as well we can witness the humor that characterized James even in his darkest moments. In the discussion following one of the lectures, the questioner makes reference to a specific page. James responds, "Ah, I like a question that mentions a page."[5] In discussing George Padmore, author of such landmark works as *Pan-Africanism or Communism* and *Africa and World Peace*, James recalls that the preface to one of Padmore's books thanks James for reading the proofs. "It is always good to get somebody else to read your proofs," James observes wryly. Then, indicating the nearby Robert Hill, who had provided the introduction for James's lecture that day, he adds that he sometimes asks Hill to read his proofs, "continuing the great intellectual tradition."

At the heart of the 1971 James symposium is the invaluable series of three lectures having to do with his book *The Black Jacobins*, which have been published now in *Small Axe*. But it was a lecture delivered on June 16 that proved to be especially important to the subsequent symposium involving Rodney and the Institute's work on the emerging debates over race and class. The subject of James's meditations was Oliver Cromwell Cox's *Caste, Class and Race*. This was considered sufficiently important that this lecture was the very first one released in the Institute's series titled *New Concepts for the New Man*, a series that was released in the same year that saw Rodney's visit to the Institute. Cox's book was well known among black intellectuals in past years; it even figures prominently in the notes of poet Melvin B. Tolson, where Tolson opposes it to T. S. Eliot's "Class and the Elite," arguing that Eliot could never have written his essay if he had read Cox's work. Today, however, it is probably not well known outside circles of social scientists who work on the history of race and class. There is a recent study published by Chris McAuley which may help restore Cox to broader attention.[6] As it happens, McAuley once studied with Martin Glaberman, a central figure in the circle of political activists advancing James's thought in the Detroit area. Though Cox was a Trinidadian by birth, James argues for the Americanness of Cox's book. (He also argues that Gunnar Myrdal's *An American Dilemma* is "a very American book.") James remembers that he had been in the United States at the time of the publication of Cox's *Caste, Class and Race*. "I had been in the United States for eight or ten years," he recalls. "And the book created a sensation, because for the first time a black man had made a scholarly and highly political" intervention in the debates about the nature of class and caste and what each had to say about the peculiar institution of race in the United States.[7] But James argues that his own experience of working early in his career in the European political context had given him an advantage. "In 1937 I had already gone way beyond where Cox has," claims James. "And that was not because I was smart. It was because I was working in Europe." By this he simply means that "the immense accumulation of materials" and the political discussions available to him as he wrote *World Revolution* gave him a grounding that later proved invaluable as he turned his attention to the U.S. scene. Cox, in James's view, "was working virtually alone in the United States." In contrast, James had succeeded in assembling around himself a remarkable group of political workers and intellectuals whose collaborations produced such works as *American Civilization* and *State Capitalism and World Revolution.* By 1947, James says, while Cox "was struggling with this I was already working on the Hegelian dialectic and its relation to Marxism." In short, James and his comrades at mid-century, working through many of the questions addressed so ably by Cox, were already confronting the very questions of race and class that Rodney and the Institute of the Black World grappled with in the early 1970s.

Also clearly setting a framework for the internationalist and activist agendas of the Institute were James's lectures on June 17 and 18. On June 17, his topic was "Nkrumah, Padmore and the Ghanaian Revolution." Fortunately, his long-awaited work *Nkrumah and the Ghana Revolution* was finally published in 1977, and readers today, as long as they can find a library copy, can study much of what James had to say on the subject when he spoke in Atlanta in 1971. (Visitors to the Nkrumah museum and park in Accra can see the furniture on which Nkrumah and James sat during their first encounters in Pennsylvania.) Of special note is James's lengthy reminiscence of his early days in London working with George and Dorothy Padmore and the comrades of the International African Service Bureau, an anticolonial grouping whose political influence extended far beyond what might have been expected given their small numbers in the 1930s. On June 18, James gave two addresses, one of which was "The Role of the Black Scholar in the Struggles of the Black Community," a topic at the very heart of debates among the scholars at the newly formed Federal City College and at the center of the Institute's own concerns. Here James speaks of Du Bois, Lincoln, the Arusha Declaration (a favorite topic of his Federal City courses in the 1970s), the Depression and Democratic politics, and the documents James and his group worked out in the 1940s for the Socialist Workers Party on the subject of the independent black struggle.

The Black Jacobins, the one book of James's that has remained in print in the United States across a span of decades, formed the subject of his major lectures, those given on June 14, 15, and 18, and these are available in the journal *Small Axe*. The first of these is titled "How I Wrote *The Black Jacobins*" and, like the speech on Nkrumah and Padmore, is indispensable for its insights on the small radical political groups of the 1930s. James's characteristic humor is evident here. Knowing that he was addressing an audience that included a fair number of cultural nationalists, he recollected the significant role that Englishman Harry Spencer had played in making it possible for James to conduct his research. Then he adds in a mischievous aside, "Anybody who calls Harry Spencer 'Whitey' will find that I am not pleased about it at all."[8] Most important to this first lecture, though, is the internationalist perspective James takes from beginning to end. "I wrote my book with the African revolution in mind," he insists. "Those who come from a very small island always think of the revolution in world-wide terms," precisely the perspective Walter Rodney was to bring to the Institute just three years later.

"Now," begins James (though that opening word has gone missing from the published transcripts), "*The Black Jacobins*—how I came to write this book and what is in the book, what did I think was in the book when I wrote it and what do I find in the book now—all these are very interesting questions not only to you but to me."[9] He opens with autobiographical musings that afford the grounding context for what he was to do in that monumental study. He presents himself as the product of a sound colonial education, a veritable British intellectual. ("We didn't bother with the United States then," he notes impishly.)[10] He arrived in England with what he calls "a certain attitude" that he holds distinguishes people from the Caribbean, an attitude he promises to describe at another time, yet we can glean much of what he is hinting at from a passage that has been omitted from the transcripts, in which he invokes Garvey, Fanon, and Padmore and their importance to the evolution of that "certain attitude." That attitude probably accounts for much of James's dissatisfaction with the extant accounts of the revolution in Saint-Domingue. This is something that he presents to his Atlanta audience as having been a crucial issue of writing itself. "I had made up my mind," he insists, "for no other reason than a *literary* reason, that when I reached England I would settle down to write a history of Toussaint L'Ouverture."[11] It is another deleted passage of the lecture that makes that literary reason more compelling and explicit. James comments on white people's ideas about black people, ideas that dominated the published literature on the subject, and underscores the need for a book on the subject written by a black writer.

By 1934 James had read the major texts of Marxism and, as he notes in the lectures, was "meeting a lot of black people and African people in London," among them Padmore, Kenyatta, Ras Makonnen, Louis Mbanefo, Adegboyega Ademola, J. B. Danquah, Amy Ashwood Garvey, and Paul Robeson.[12] The first step toward the work on Louverture was the play in which Robeson appeared in 1936, the text of which has now been published in an edition prepared by Christian Høgsbjerg. The work on Haiti is put on hold for a year while James writes *World Revolution* (and here one has to take note of the breathtaking rate of production he is keeping up in the 1930s), but is then published by Warburg in 1938. Few among James's Atlanta audience would have seen that first edition; most were carrying with them the 1963 revision, and James referred to that later edition when he called out page numbers so his listeners could follow along. He goes on to emphasize something that should have been evident to any reader of *The Black Jacobins* but was missed by some who came to the book in later years. "It was written about Africa. It wasn't written about the Caribbean." One of the things that gave James great satisfaction was the African reception of his work. "I am glad to say that many in Africa read it, and it passed about among them and it contributed towards helping those who were taking part in the African revolution to understand what the movement of the masses was, how a revolution went."[13]

I can testify to the assurance James took as he talked with his college students about the uprisings in Soweto, from the fact that his book, published prior to the 1948 assumption of full power by South Africa's Reunited National Party with the attendant turn toward apartheid and greater censorship, circulated widely among activists of the African National Congress and other groups. Comparing his outlook to Fanon, Castro, Césaire, Padmore, and Toussaint himself, James asserts that his directing his book toward Africa was in keeping with a distinctly West Indian way of thinking. "It seems that those who come from a very small island always think of revolution in very wide terms."[14] It could not have escaped his notice that the English had themselves been people from an island (not small) who had developed a certain attitude and way of thinking in very wide terms indeed. It was the task of those established on the smaller islands of the Caribbean to think the revolution that would liberate them from the dominance of that larger island. The hard work of research made James's achievement possible, but that West

Indian outlook gave the work its revolutionary internationalist perspective. In a speech on the character of the Caribbean, James had made the point that diasporic Africans had not arrived in the New World with nothing, they had *themselves*. In the lecture in Atlanta, James tells his largely American audience: "I didn't fall from the sky. I didn't go up like Moses and come back with documents."[15] Just as the Africans surviving the terror of Middle Passage to life in the New World had brought with them a cosmology and philosophy from which evolved a revolutionary perspective and that "certain attitude," so had James come to his task as a revolutionary historian with not only the deep learning acquired from his colonial education but an intrinsically radical view of the history he was to study. Similarly, the mostly young people sitting in front of him in Atlanta did not enter the room with nothing. The civil rights movement had not fallen from the sky, much less been the product of mythical "outside agitators," and neither had these young people come into the room with empty heads to be filled by visiting lecturers. They had a certain attitude of their own. (In the United States of the 1970s, young people were forever "copping an attitude.") That attitude was forged in the revolutionary experience of the mass movements of mid-century, was in touch with the revolutionary movements on the African continent, and was informed by a Jamesian dialectic.

On June 18, James's topic was "How I Would Rewrite *The Black Jacobins*," though curiously he does not fully address the changes that were made in the final passages of his book when it was reprinted in the 1960s. (In the course of the lecture on Du Bois, James says of the 1963 edition only: "I made very few changes, about eight pages at most.")[16] He does suggest that the material addressed in footnotes to the second edition would be incorporated into the text if he could do it again, but more significant, he remarks that the descriptions of slaves at work in Saint-Domingue that he gleaned from contemporary accounts of travelers would be replaced with statements from the former slaves themselves. Furthermore, he tells his audience that today he would present "the actual statements where the rank and file in France and the ordinary people were saying what they were thinking about slavery."[17] In fact, even in the first edition of *The Black Jacobins*, the emphasis is already on the role that the Africans themselves played in their own liberation. It is, after all, the *black* Jacobins who were James's subject. Nonetheless, his work in the intervening decades took him still further in the direction of looking to the thoughts and actions of the masses of the population as he sought to understand the currents of history.

Recalling the matter of his lecture on June 15, James brings these realizations into contact with his readings of Du Bois. There is a long passage missing from the published transcripts in which James discusses slavery in the United States, the point of which is summed up for his audience when he declares:

> The black slaves in W.E.B. Du Bois's *Black Reconstruction*, they were the ones who saw what should happen. But it's very hard for you all to understand that because you have been taught the exact opposite every day, on television and in the press, and hence you lose sight of the fact of the people down below and what the people down below are capable of doing.[18]

James's lifelong resistance to vanguardism and his perpetual trust in the abilities of the masses of the people to see where they have to go are here in full evidence. He may have written *The Black Jacobins* with Africa in mind, he may have gone to England in the 1930s with little thought of the United States, but in his lectures in the 1970s and in *The Black Jacobins*, he assures us, had he been writing it in the 1970s, those understandings would have been pointing to the very recent history of the United States in much the same way that his 1960s revisions of the book had used Cuba as a ground for discussing the continuing revolutionary ferment in the wake of colonialism. In Haiti, James observes, it was not the great men but the "obscure creatures" who gave the signal for revolt. Likewise:

> They were not only in San Domingo obscure. They were obscure in Watts, they were obscure in Detroit, they were obscure in Newark, they were obscure creatures in San Francisco, they were obscure creatures in Cleveland, they were obscure creatures in Harlem.[19]

In each instance, the revolutionary impetus was seen to come from *below*, and James outlines for his audience historic precedents for the rebellions they had all so recently witnessed and participated in. It was the movement from below, literally in the case of the Underground Railroad, that had made it impossible for the North to abide the slavery of the South and made the American Civil War inevitable even though it was Southern military action that began the war itself. Just as James had urged members of his U.S. political group to make an effective study of the social forces of the abolitionist movement and the legacies of the Civil War, an event that James held to be as significant as the French Revolution, one reason he made the journey to Atlanta to deliver these lectures was to urge newer work upon those in attendance. What the black scholar should do, according to James, was "to find out who are the obscure people who did what they did in Detroit, in Cleveland, in Watts, etcetera."[20]

Much as James had drawn these lessons from a life of revolutionary struggle and study, he confesses that he had not entirely understood Toussaint's failures until he read Du Bois. The great mistake Toussaint had made, the mistake of growing away from the masses and substituting his judgment for theirs, had been the mistake of many great revolutions. This insight was clarified for James by Du Bois, one he was to anatomize most clearly in his later work on Kwame Nkrumah. In his reflections on this, and on the psychology of Toussaint, we also get a glimpse of one of James's own failures. As he closes his lecture on an imagined rewrite of *Black Jacobins*, he promises to undertake an analysis of Eric Williams. He suggests that he may do this in his autobiography. Keep in mind that these lectures were delivered in 1971. In 1977 James was still making such promises about a potential autobiography. He often commented in the course of discussing Shakespeare that he intended to address the Bard in a chapter of his autobiography. As the volumes of Solzhenitsyn's *Gulag Archipelago* appeared in English translation—volumes James held to be of greatest importance—he frequently told his college students that he would include a chapter on Solzhenitsyn in his memoirs, at which I was probably not the only listener to despair of him ever completing an autobiography. That he did not in the end, though, is not something to complain about given the mass of manuscripts and lectures, including these, that he left for us to work through.

Easily the key lecture to James's entire Institute residency, though, was the one on June 15 titled "*The Black Jacobins* and *Black Reconstruction*: A Comparative Analysis." James credits himself with ending *The Black Jacobins* by talking about what was to happen in Africa, something he says Du Bois did not do. But, and here it is crucial to remember that Du Bois's *Black Reconstruction* appears just three short years prior to *The Black Jacobins* (the same number of years, as it happens, that separate the visits of James and Rodney to Atlanta's Institute of the Black World), James says of Du Bois that:

> He had opened out the historical perspective in a manner I didn't know. He had been at it for many years. He was a very profound and learned historian, but he was always driven by the need of expanding and making clear to black people in what way they were involved in world history.[21]

James subsequently adds, "he taught me to think in those terms." The fact is that James and Du Bois are even now so seldom studied side by side that it is easy to lose sight of just how unprecedented their books were in the 1930s. Each author makes the argument, not only that African peoples of the diaspora were truly the first modern peoples, but that Africans and the slave trade became the very condition of possibility of modernity per se. This, James tells his audience, is what the West chooses to blind itself to, making possible such travesties as William Styron's *Confessions of Nat Turner*, which James dismisses as Styron's attempt to say that black men "made their revolution in order to get closer to white women." For James and Du Bois, blacks in the Americas were the most truly revolutionary force on the world stage. This is why James quotes a passage from *Black Reconstruction* that resonated powerfully with his listeners in the 1970s as they confronted their own struggles with race, class, and political oppression. It is a passage James calls us to attend to even today, as we hear callow cries from those who have never fought imploring us to a battle of civilizations, as we face a new dusk of dawn in our confrontation with the withering values of the burnt out Bush:

> Such mental frustration cannot indefinitely continue. Some day it may burst in fire and blood. Who will be to blame? And where the greater cost? This the American black man knows: his fight here is to the finish. . . . He will enter modern civilization as a black man on terms of perfect and unlimited equality with any white man, or he will not enter at all. Either extermination root and branch, or absolute equality. There can be no compromise. This is the last great battle of the West.[22]

Notes

1. Hazel Carby and Don Edwards, "Vincent Harding," in *Visions of History*, edited by MAHRO: The Radical Historians Organization (Manchester: Manchester University Press, 1983), 232.
2. Walter Rodney, *Walter Rodney Speaks: The Making of an African Intellectual* (New York: Africa World Press, 1990).
3. C. L. R. James, *Walter Rodney and the Question of Power* (London: Race Today, 1983), 4.
4. C. L. R. James, *The C.L.R. James Lectures* (Atlanta: Institute of the Black World, 1971), audio tape.
5. James, *The C.L.R. James Lectures*.
6. Christopher McAuley, *The Mind of Oliver C. Cox* (South Bend, IN: University of Notre Dame Press, 2004).

7. James, *The C.L.R. James Lectures.* James's lecture on Cox has now been published in *New Politics.* See Derrick White and Paul Ortiz, "Introduction to C.L.R. James on Oliver Cox's *Caste, Class, and Race,*" *New Politics* 60 (Winter 2016), and C. L. R. James, "The Class Basis of the Race Question in the United States," *New Politics* 60 (Winter 2016).

8. James, *The C.L.R. James Lectures.*

9. C. L. R. James, "Lectures on *The Black Jacobins*: How I Wrote *The Black Jacobins,*" *Small Axe* 8 (2000): 65.

10. James, "Lectures on *The Black Jacobins*: How I Wrote *The Black Jacobins,*" 66.

11. James, "Lectures on *The Black Jacobins*: How I Wrote *The Black Jacobins,*" 67.

12. James, "Lectures on *The Black Jacobins*: How I Wrote *The Black Jacobins,*" 69.

13. James, "Lectures on *The Black Jacobins*: How I Wrote *The Black Jacobins,*" 73.

14. James, "Lectures on *The Black Jacobins*: How I Wrote *The Black Jacobins,*" 74.

15. James, "Lectures on *The Black Jacobins*: How I Wrote *The Black Jacobins,*" 77.

16. C. L. R. James, "Lectures on *The Black Jacobins*: *The Black Jacobins* and *Black Reconstruction*: A Comparative Analysis," *Small Axe* 8 (2000): 90.

17. C. L. R. James, "Lectures on *The Black Jacobins*: How I Would Rewrite *The Black Jacobins,*" *Small Axe* 8 (2000): 100.

18. James, "Lectures on *The Black Jacobins*: How I Would Rewrite *The Black Jacobins,*" 105.

19. James, "Lectures on *The Black Jacobins*: How I Would Rewrite *The Black Jacobins,*" 106.

20. James, "Lectures on *The Black Jacobins*: How I Would Rewrite *The Black Jacobins,*" 106.

21. James, *The C.L.R. James Lectures.*

22. James, "Lectures on *The Black Jacobins*: *The Black Jacobins* and *Black Reconstruction,*" 98; W. E. B. Du Bois, *Black Reconstruction in America: 1860–1880* (New York: Free Press, 1998), 628.

PART IV.
FINAL REFLECTIONS

| | | | |

MADISON SMARTT BELL

For purposes of *disclosure* (that loaded American term), I will reveal that *The Black Jacobins* was the second book I read about Toussaint Louverture (the first being *Citizen Toussaint*, by Ralph Korngold), and that C. L. R. James's definitive work was the main platform I used to begin writing a series of novels about Toussaint Louverture and the Haitian Revolution. The first novel in my trilogy, *All Souls' Rising*, is especially dependent upon James—even too much so. And yet everyone told me that *The Black Jacobins* was far and away the best work on the subject in the English language. Everyone was right. Even now, when a vogue for "post-colonial studies" in U.S. universities has stimulated powerful new waves of research and writing on the Haitian Revolution, there is really only one other work in English—*Avengers of the New World* by Laurent Dubois—which can stand up to James on his own comprehensive ground. Until Dubois appeared on the scene a few years ago, James really was the only Anglophone writer to have given the Haitian Revolution a sufficiently broad *and* deep treatment to do justice to the subject while still remaining accessible, even seductive, to the general reader.

I read *The Black Jacobins* for the first time circa 1984 and continued studying it and rereading it for the next five years, until I had practically worn it out. Then, for another fifteen years, I turned to other sources, some of which were more recent and more up to date than James—yet many of my "new" sources, more than half of them, were first indicated to me by James's amazingly thorough notes and bibliography. The last volume of my trilogy of novels appeared in 2004. I found, however, that I could not quite let go of Toussaint Louverture, so I began to write a short biography of the Haitian hero—with very little reference to *The Black Jacobins* this time. Having just completed a revision of the biography, I now reread James's work cover to cover for the first time in about fifteen years. Let it be understood that I return to the book and its author infected by Bloomian anxiety of influence, along with the usual Oedipal striving.

James and I share (with a few other people), an enduring, even incurable, fascination with Toussaint Louverture. For a novelist, this kind of engagement isn't a problem—on the contrary, it is unambiguously desirable. But James's undeniable attraction to Toussaint's unique and extraordinary personal qualities must have been something of a problem for him. The subtitle of *The Black Jacobins: Toussaint L'Ouverture and the San Domingo Revolution*, suggests that James's interest in the individual career of the man and the larger story in which it is embedded were more or less equal. But when James first engaged the topic in the 1930s, he was not only a firmly convinced Marxist but also a Trotskyite activist. Therefore, he was ideologically prohibited from believing in the influence of "great men" upon history. The preface to the 1938 edition lays out this inner conflict:

> Beauchamp in the *Biographie Universelle* calls Toussaint L'Ouverture one of the most remarkable men of a period rich in remarkable men. He dominated from his entry until circumstances removed him from the scene. The writer believes, and is confident circumstances will prove, that between 1789 and 1815, with the single exception of Bonaparte himself, no single figure appeared on the historical stage more greatly gifted than this Negro, a slave till he was 45. Yet Toussaint did not make the revolution. It was the revolution that made Toussaint.[1]

James's need to prove the last statement above introduces a considerable tension into the work which follows. Certainly it is true that Toussaint did not make the Haitian Revolution all by himself. In the final phase of it, when Toussaint left the scene in 1802, his individual leadership no longer made any difference at all to the final outcome—which is perhaps the main point that both Toussaint himself and C. L. R. James are out to prove. But without Toussaint's catalytic role in the middle 1790s, the Haitian Revolution very likely would have remained a mere rebellion—a rebellion on a terrifyingly vast scale but still a revolt, not a revolution. James feels this truth, throughout his work, though he is ideologically inhibited from saying it outright.

In the 1930s, when James was at work on the book, the respectable, idealistic left in Britain and the U.S. and Western Europe was communist in some form or other. The Communist International was still expected to bring about the reform of the entire world. Some very substantial forces of history had yet to reveal themselves completely. It was still possible for some devout leftists to make themselves believe that the Soviet Union under Stalin was a Marxist-Leninist utopia (though James, by this time, was no longer one of them). The scariest thing on the horizon was not Stalinist totalitarianism, but fascism as expressed by Franco, Mussolini, and Hitler.

Times have changed considerably since then, and James's periodic insistence on a purely Marxist interpretation of the Haitian Revolution is one aspect of *The Black Jacobins* that has not aged tremendously well. In the twenty-first century, to say that "Lenin and the Bolsheviks after the October Revolution faced much the same problem as Toussaint"[2] seems a little strained. Of Toussaint's execution of his lieutenant Moïse, James writes, "It was almost as if Lenin had had Trotsky shot for taking the side of the proletariat against the bourgeoisie."[3] To have published this line just two years before Trotsky's savage assassination in Mexico is a truly unfortunate accident of history.

Like many theories of its author's day, dogmatic Marxism expects human behavior to follow mechanically predictable rules. This, human behavior often and obstinately refuses to do. James is at his least convincing when he tries to hammer the Haitian Revolution into the Marxist mold. However, James's intermittent spasms of dogmatic Marxism are as easy to bypass as Tolstoy's considerably longer and more painful disquisitions on historical inevitability in *War and Peace*.

There is no difficulty in reading the French Revolution in Marxist terms, since Marx did so himself, analyzing the event as the paradigmatic bourgeois revolution, in which the medieval class structure was finally overthrown by capitalism. But the classes and races of colonial Saint-Domingue don't fit this equation perfectly (as the white Jacobins themselves had to learn, at great cost). Within its borders, France had none of the excruciatingly complicated racial issues of the colony, and Saint-Domingue really had no class analogous to the late eighteenth-century French bourgeoisie. It makes sense for James to refer to the black slaves of the colony, who so vastly outnumbered the other half-dozen identifiable groups, as "the masses," but to regard them as a proper Marxist proletariat risks considerable distortion.

There were three races in colonial Saint-Domingue—the white, the black, and the colored—but each had its internal divisions. The white plantation owners were inclined to be royalist; the less prosperous whites joined the Jacobin clubs. The term *affranchis*—freedmen—was often used interchangeably with "colored people" or mulattoes, yet [a] small, significant group of these people were of pure African blood, and class-wise they had little in common with their colored cousins, though their legal status was the same. The majority of slaves had been born in Africa—*bossales*—and the colony-born, creole minority of slaves constituted a very different social group. All the discriminatory measures of the years running up to the revolution were expressed along racial lines, yet affected the different subdivisions of the racial groups differently. After 1804 and Haitian independence, the majority of James's liberated masses reverted to an African way of life which had next to nothing to do with any European social model, Marxist or otherwise.

What you see depends very much on the lens that you look through. In the 1990s, the scholarly trend has been toward multiculturalism, ethnocentrism, and finally the worst kind of identity politics (which James, if he were here to see it, would probably recognize as a prelude to fascism). Still, the current intellectual habit of analyzing conflict in terms of culture more than those of race or class does focus on some areas of the Haitian Revolution—the creole-bossale split among slaves and the class/color division that persisted among the freedmen—more clearly than James's lens was able to do. However, it is safe to predict that eventually the ideological reflexes of our time will seem at least as antiquated as James's Marxist extremes do now.

James's saving grace is (though he might not have thought so himself) that he was a novelist first and a political theorist only second. He was steeped in the nineteenth-century English novel, particularly the socially panoramic works of Thackeray, and published novels of his own in the 1920s. The first finished product of his study of the Haitian Revolution was a play, *Toussaint Louverture*, designed among other things to provide a heroic part for Paul Robeson. Artistic insight is what leads James to grasp the Haitian Revolution as a human story first—spread on a canvas as vast as that of Thackeray's *Vanity Fair*.

James's gift for pure storytelling is what gives *The Black Jacobins* its enduring greatness. Much of the time he doesn't even bother to strain the story through the Marxist filter but simply tells it the way it was. Here his broad, deep study of earlier writers and the intimidating mass of archival material delivers a tremendous return. He has a great gift for dramatizing the key scenes, and a very sharp eye for the novelistic details which animate the historical figures and make them knowable as people. In his hands the purely dramatic qualities of the tale really do become irresistible.

As for Toussaint the man—James is close to the first writer to see and report him clearly. Observers of Toussaint's own time either demonized or sanctified him—his political volatility was such that no one could afford to treat him in his full human complexity. As Wendell Phillips (himself a Toussaint hagiographer) resoundingly put it, "All the materials from his biography are from the lips of his enemies." The claim was not entirely true—roughly half of the whites who reported on Toussaint during his own time saw him positively—recognizing his great gifts and large achievements and also using him as proof of arguments for abolition of slavery and equality among the races. His enemies, meanwhile, reviled him in the most vicious terms. Among contemporary observers, the French general Pamphile de Lacroix comes closest to an objective view (one which James exploits to the maximum).

The nineteenth-century Haitian historians (Saint-Rémy and Beaubrun Ardouin, whom James cites, and Thomas Madiou, whom he does not) built up an impressive edifice of narrative about their revolution and its protagonists, Toussaint eminently among them, but were inevitably too close to the subject to take an entirely nonpartisan view. Outside of Haiti, the nineteenth-century trend was to treat Toussaint as a classic tragic hero. Holmes did this to a degree, the French abolitionist Victor Schoelcher even more so. Thus Toussaint becomes the hero of a verse tragedy by Lamartine, and of a sonnet by William Wordsworth:

> Toussaint, the most unhappy Man of Men!
> Whether the whistling Rustic tend his plough
> Within thy hearing, or thy head be now
> Pillowed in some deep dungeon's earless den—
> O miserable Chieftain! Where and when
> Wilt thou find patience? Yet die not, do thou
> Wear rather in thy bonds a cheerful brow;
> Though fallen Thyself, never to rise again,
> Live and take comfort. Thou has left behind
> Powers that will work for thee; air, earth and skie;
> There's not a breathing of the common wind
> That will forget thee; thou has great allies;
> Thy friends are exultations, agonies,
> And love, and Man's unconquerable mind.

James was a great admirer of Shakespeare as well as of Thackeray, and the elements of classical tragedy in Toussaint's story have a hold on him. In James's version, Toussaint's tragic flaw is his reluctance to commit, overtly and completely, to Haitian independence, the "magic word" that would have rallied the masses back to him in the end. It was Dessalines who picked up the standard of independence where Toussaint had—inexplicably—dropped it. At the time of James's writing he was preoccupied with other independence struggles simmering all over the crumbling colonial empire, especially in Africa. But treating Toussaint as a hero with this tragic defect is also a handy way of completing the dramatic arc of his story.

Before *The Black Jacobins*, the only lucid and objective full-length study of Toussaint was the biography by the Haitian writer Pauléus Sannon, which appeared in three volumes between 1920 and 1933, and which James succinctly acknowledges as "the best biography yet written of Toussaint."[4] In 1960, another contender emerged: *Toussaint Louverture: La Révolution française et le problème colonial* by Aimé Césaire. This work is extremely competent, James comments, somewhat grudgingly. "I find, however, that it lacks the fire and constant illumination which distinguish most of the other work of Césaire."[5] In fact James, a native of Trinidad, and Césaire, both a writer and a politician in his native Martinique, were looking at Toussaint from about the same degree of separation—with plenty of direct interest in the subject but just enough distance to allow a balanced view of it. James, though generally an admirer of Césaire, may have been moved to belittle this work on Toussaint by the suspicion that it was the only book that could give *The Black Jacobins* a run for its money.

And yet these books by Sannon, Césaire, and James (along with every other work on Toussaint to appear before the last quarter of the twentieth century) are *all* founded on a colossal error of fact: that Toussaint was a slave, though an unusually privileged one, until 1791. He was not. In 1970s, documents came to light that prove, indubitably, that Toussaint was not only a free man by 1776 but also that he owned land and slaves himself.

That changes everything. Or does it?

One of the most curious things about the fact of Toussaint's freedom is that, although it obviously must have been a matter of public information, *none* of his contemporary observers ever mentions it. Another factor, somewhat easier to understand, is that Toussaint did his level best to conceal or at any rate minimize the point that he had not only been a free man well before the Revolution, but also a prosperous land and slave-owner. That means among other things that James, though in error on this important fact, is telling Toussaint's story *the way Toussaint wanted it to be told.*

The vast majority of freedmen in the colony were *gens de couleur*. They benefited from connections with their European families—these relations were often troublesome but they did at least exist. Many of these colored freedmen were fully as prosperous in the slave-driven plantation system as the whites. That situation caused terrible friction between the two groups but at the same time it did give land- and slave-owning mulattos a considerable common interest with land- and slave-owning whites.

The full-blooded African freedmen were a much smaller group. Some, but fewer, were as successful in the slavery-based colonial economy as either the whites or the free mulattoes—Toussaint was one of these, it now appears. But the black freedmen were racially and socially a quite separate group from the colored freedmen. Black freedmen had no white fathers, and lacked the advantage of education in France which many colored freedmen did enjoy, despite their privation of political rights. But for Toussaint the critical problem was that the all-African freedmen, the group to which he properly belonged, was far too small to provide him any sort of adequate power base. Power was with the masses, as James and Toussaint would certainly have agreed, the five to eight hundred thousand *nouveaux libres* who had fought their way out of slavery beginning in 1791.

Therefore, Toussaint did his utmost to identify himself with the *nouveaux libres*, to place himself at their head, while at the same sweeping away all traces of his previous career as a landed, slave-owning proprietor. His success in doing that let him ride the wave of the Revolution to a peak of personal power. He never made any public mention of the fact that he had been free for fifteen years before 1791. He did, with some frequency, remind his fellow citizens that he had suffered the experience of slavery from the inside (like most of them)—which was true as far as it went, since Toussaint did not obtain his freedom until 1776, when he would have been in his middle thirties.

The image he wanted to project was that of a slave who—like all the rest of them—won freedom through revolutionary struggle in the years after 1791. He convinced everyone so successfully with this version of the tale that all evidence to the contrary vanished for nearly two hundred years. James, and the other biographers working before the 1970s, accepted the image that Toussaint had so carefully fashioned at face value. (I must admit that with no real excuse I did the same thing; the first volume of my trilogy proceeds from the idea that Toussaint was still a slave until the risings of 1791—that is to say, I too have done my part to tell the story as Toussaint chose for it to be told—not as it really was.)

James's class analysis ought to be derailed once the salient fact of Toussaint's freedom is introduced into it. And yes, there is a bump, but not a full-fledged train wreck. What keeps James's analysis wobbling down the right track is the fact that Toussaint consistently played the part of a slave made free in 1791, even though it was a fiction. When he addressed the black masses, he would sidestep the question of slavery by invoking his race—*Am I not black, like you*? Race, blackness rather, was to be the universal solvent, resolving differences among the blacks and between the blacks and the other two races— James lovingly reports the various stage devices Toussaint used to demonstrate the absorption of all other races into the African, which he thought was the inevitable future of the island.

But there were divisions among the blacks, though James does not much notice them. Perhaps the group of pure-black freedmen was too small to matter much. But a division between colony-born creole blacks and African-born bossales split the largest population in the colony on a line close to the middle, leaving the bossales (sometimes called "Africans") in majority by 10 or 15 percent. Most of the leaders who carried on the struggle through guerrilla warfare after the surrender of Toussaint and most of his officers were bossales. Toussaint, and most of his surrendering officers, were creoles. They had adapted to the situation in the colony from birth and had adopted many of the manners and mores of their masters.

James thinks in terms of "Black Jacobins" and is inclined to interpret Toussaint as a black Napoleon. James himself wrote the book at a time where the struggle of blacks for equal rights meant matching the Europeans in their own cultural practices—meeting or exceeding the standards whites claimed to set for themselves—beating them at their own game. James's Toussaint behaves in this way, forging himself into a military commander and political machinator who can defeat and outmaneuver the best that the great powers of Europe can throw against him . . . on their own terms. That much is true of the "real" Toussaint, but it is not the only thing true of him. At least from 1796 on, Toussaint was well aware of the divisive risk of the split between creoles and Africans, and did all he could to bridge and seal that gap. Though it left less trace in the written record, his African side was at least as powerful in him as the European face he used to confront and deal with his various European allies and adversaries. In fusing these two cultures together within his own being, Toussaint becomes 100 percent Haitian.

There are certain warts on Toussaint that he didn't want seen and that James does not show. In an appendix added to *Black Jacobins* in 1963, James compares the Haitian to the Cuban Revolution, and Toussaint to Fidel Castro. Perhaps it would have made more sense to compare Toussaint to "Papa Doc" Duvalier in Haiti. There are some disquieting resemblances between the Louverturian and the Duvalierist state—military dictatorship, rulership for life. . . . Today, in the mid-2000s, most Haitians look rather wistfully at Cuba, which though by no means a free society does have essential security and a functioning infrastructure, with roads, electricity, telephones, plumbing, a reasonable health care system and enough doctors to export them in significant numbers across the windward passage to Haiti. Possibly, if Toussaint had been able to complete his course in Saint-Domingue, he would have also achieved these goods—if he had not fallen victim to the treachery of his enemies and of those that should have been his friends. If he had not fallen victim to his own infrequent but fatal misjudgments and personal weaknesses . . . the idea of Toussaint Louverture as a tragic hero is hard to shake, not only for James but for later observers.

James's central thesis holds up well enough in the end. The slave revolt of 1791 could not have evolved into a full-fledged revolution without being shaped by some leader of Toussaint's unique . . . greatness. But Toussaint would not have become what he finally was without the wave of the revolution to ride. Their relationship was catalytic, symbiotic . . . and temporary. In the end, the Haitian Revolution no longer needed Toussaint, but it wouldn't have happened without him.

Notes

This chapter is from *I Giacobini neri: La prima rivolta contro l'uomo bianco*, "Postfazione alla nuova edizione Italiana" (Rome: Derive Approdi, 2006).

1. C. L. R. James, *The Black Jacobins: Toussaint L'Ouverture and the San Domingo Revolution* (London: Allison and Busby, 1984), 8.
2. James, *The Black Jacobins*, 282.
3. James, *The Black Jacobins*, 284.
4. James, *The Black Jacobins*, 383.
5. James, *The Black Jacobins*, 389.

Introduction to the Cuban Edition
of *The Black Jacobins*

JOHN H. BRACEY

The response to the earthquake that struck Haiti in January, 2010, and the often patronizing, denigrating, and grossly inaccurate portrayals of the country, its history and its people, make the appearance of a Cuban edition of *The Black Jacobins* quite timely and relevant. Even the most generous North American and European donors of relief to Haiti too often couch it in terms of the need to help a country that is devoid of any resources: political, social, economic, cultural, and whose entire history since its founding is one of misery, superstition, violence, and corruption. Many liberals also see the need to assert a strong but benevolent military presence to help Haiti move toward some version of democracy. Rightists who still hold on to the myths of white supremacy talk of a country populated with practitioners of voodoo and other primitive, that is, non-European Christian, religious beliefs and practices. One prominent Christian evangelist asserted that the earthquake was just one of the many disasters that have afflicted Haitians since they made a pact with the devil to secure satanic support for their struggle against the French. The implication that Satan was an abolitionist and that the Christian church in Haiti was proslavery was lost on the benighted reverend.

Few commentators have mentioned the unique struggle of the enslaved Africans in Haiti in establishing the first and only independent nation founded as a result of a slave uprising. Even fewer commentators mention that the United States, as with Cuba after 1959, refused to extend diplomatic recognition to the island for the first sixty years of its existence. Also left unsaid was that a significant factor in Haiti's economic troubles was the agreement of European countries and the U.S. that Haiti owed the French the value of the liberated slaves. That the United States has invaded and occupied Haiti is more often mentioned humanitarian gestures gone for naught rather than as typical examples of the treatment of Latin American and Caribbean countries by U.S. economic and political interests. Few have mentioned the role of the Haitian Revolution as an inspiration for the Bolivarian struggles that resulted in the political independence of many Latin American countries during the first half of the nineteenth century, or that the outpouring of assistance to Haiti from countries such as Cuba and Venezuela is an acknowledgment of a tradition of solidarity that goes back two hundred years. To comprehend the reality of Haiti today we need some understanding of how Haiti came into existence through armed insurrection against their slave masters and their allies and the consequences visited upon the Haitian people as a result of the success of their efforts.

C. L. R. James's *The Black Jacobins* is an indispensable starting point both for those who know something of the contribution of Haiti to the development of the Western Hemisphere—north and south, and those who do not. It is one of the finest studies of a revolution and the revolutionary process ever written from a Marxist, or any other perspective. James gives a masterful reading of the relationship between the goals and actions of individuals and their class/status backgrounds that avoids reducing complex historical events to either the whims of leaders and elites, or the result of the blind unfolding of social forces. Toussaint Louverture's name appears in the subtitle of James's book, but the significance of the thoughts and actions of the masses of slaves in Saint-Domingue and of the Parisian masses is made clear throughout.

James was born in Trinidad on January 4, 1901. He attended the leading schools on the island, receiving a British education that would prepare him for a lifelong career as a civil servant or as a schoolteacher. James's interest in sports, especially cricket, led him to London where he worked as a reporter on cricket matches for the *Manchester Guardian* newspaper and collaborated in the writings of Learie Constantine, a fellow Trinidadian widely recognized as an outstanding cricket batsman. Acknowledging the unlikelihood of pursuing a successful career as a cricket bowler, James concentrated on his writing. In 1936 he published *Minty Alley*, a fine novel about life among the lower classes of Trinidad and the relationship of the island's educated elite to their plight.

While in London, James became involved in radical politics, and was attracted to the views of Leon Trotsky and the Fourth International. James maintained a complex relationship with Trotsky and with various Trotskyist splinter groups for the rest of his life. James first came to the United States in the late 1930s, was deported in 1953, returned in the late 1960s and was an influential figure among many younger members of left and minority movements in the United States. After the death of W. E. B. Du Bois in 1963, for many, James was viewed successor to Du Bois as the elder statesman of radical anticolonialism and Pan-Africanism. For the next quarter century James traveled widely lecturing, teaching, advising, and analyzing the movements of the time. James died in London on May 31, 1989. Since his death, James's life and works has generated substantial interest on the part of younger scholars and activists.

Despite his own political affiliations, James maintained friendships and deep respect for individuals of African descent who supported the Bolshevik revolution and the politics of various communist parties and the Comintern. James has written of his interactions with Paul Robeson, George Padmore, and Richard Wright. When he turned his attention in later years to African American women writers, he expressed his admiration for Angela Davis. And of course James steadfastly laid claim to the legacy and achievements of W. E. B. Du Bois. My copy of the Longman's edition of *The Souls of Black Folk* (1965), which contains an introduction by James, was inscribed by James to me as follows: "For J.B. from C.L.R. you will make good use of our ancestor." The "you" and the "our" are underlined. James's view expressed in that introduction, and on numerous occasions elsewhere, was that *"Black Reconstruction* is and is likely to continue to be one of the finest history books ever written." To James, *Black Reconstruction* was indispensable for gaining an understanding of the history of the United States and of the role of people of African descent within that history. One could make the claim that *The Black Jacobins* does for the entirety of the Western Hemisphere what *Black Reconstruction* does for the United States.

During a time when many European Marxists placed little emphasis on the impact of political initiatives of non-Europeans, James's study of the Saint-Domingue revolution and its significance for the development of capitalism in Europe and North America was a tremendous breakthrough. Two decades later, James saw in the Cuban Revolution further confirmation of his earlier conclusions, and his epilogue to the 1962 edition of *The Black Jacobins* gave him an opportunity to reaffirm them. *The Black Jacobins* like many of James's historical works is written in such a way as to address multiple issues and multiple audiences. In this Cuban edition of *The Black Jacobins* I would like to point out some of the issues that James was attempting to address. Some of this will be obvious to even the casual reader. Some of the less obvious of my assertions will be based on a combination of my reading of James's other writings and of the nature of his political work. In addition I was most fortunate to have had the opportunity to engage in lengthy discussions with James during his stay in the United States during the late 1960s and early 1970s. James had the ability to engage people easily and respectfully across a range of political points of view and levels of understanding. I discovered early in our encounters that the more you knew of his writings, and of the thinkers and artists that he attached great importance to, and the more you questioned him about possible interpretations and implications of his own writing, then the more engaged and forthcoming he was. When James's voice got a certain edge to it, or if he directed you to reread a particular work that he felt you had not understood properly, or to go read a work that obviously you had not read, then you could experience James's mind at its best. Some of my comments here are a result of several specific discussions about *The Black Jacobins*.

At its most elemental level *The Black Jacobins* is a magnificent portrayal of the life of Toussaint Louverture and of the events known as the Haitian Revolution. As pure narrative history it ranks with such works as Du Bois's *Black Reconstruction* or E. P. Thompson's *The Making of the English Working Class*. Despite the recent outpouring of scholarship on the Haitian Revolution, James's work is the place to begin. Echoing the structure of *Black Reconstruction*, *The Black Jacobins* lays out with great care and sophistication the various social groupings that would carry forward the dramatic events that are the subject of his study. In addition however James blends in the life and actions of Toussaint Louverture so that unlike in Du Bois's work we get an analysis of the complex relationship of individual leaders and structures to a larger mass movement. James relates Toussaint's rise to leadership of the enslaved population, narrates the complex and often bewildering shifting of alliances and tactics that constituted the reality of the Haitian Revolution. He relates the tragic end of Toussaint, and the rise of Dessalines and the consequences that these two events had for the future success of the Revolution. The story of Toussaint and the Haitian Revolution alone justifies making *The Black Jacobins* available to the widest possible readership.

But there is more to *The Black Jacobins* than this. James had other fish to fry that had as much to do with the state of politics and world affairs during the 1930s, as with events in San Domingo at the beginning of the nineteenth century. James was concerned with the failure of many Marxists in Europe and North America to comprehend the impact of events and movements among peoples of African descent on the flow of world events. The labeling of Haitian revolutionaries as Jacobins, and the meticulous linking of events in France and San Domingo makes it impossible not to see the revolutionary breaks with feudalism and the onset of capitalism as truly a worldwide phenomenon.

James's sympathetic but critical analysis of Toussaint's leadership is directed at the Marxist political parties and leaders who were the heirs of the Bolshevik Revolution. James is cognizant of the tremendous challenges involved in leading a revolution to a successful conclusion, and in building a new society. James was optimistic about the potential of the masses of humanity to run their own lives, but he was not naïve. The most poignant warnings in *The Black Jacobins* are those on the ever present possibility of counter-revolution, of stagnation and of betrayal. History to James was not a straight-line lockstep movement upward and onward. Struggles can be won, and struggles can be lost.

The Black Jacobins also can be read as a reflection on the reciprocal (dialectical) relationship between the masses of a people in motion to transform their society and their leaders. James's careful delineation of the complex and shifting interactions between Toussaint and the Haitian masses can be read as a critique of the vanguardist and antidemocratic tendencies that have characterized too much of the European Left and of anticolonial leadership in the twentieth century. That James was active in the International African Service Bureau and in the intense politics of the Fourth International gives his assessments about Haitian leadership a sense of urgency and immediacy not often found in the works of academics. In the year prior to the publication of *The Black Jacobins*, James published a lengthy history of the Third International titled *World Revolution, 1917–1936*. Clearly these issues were very much on his mind. In *The Black Jacobins* James demonstrates that Toussaint was at his best and was most effective when he was most in tune with the aspirations of the Haitian masses. James details how Toussaint falters and is ultimately defeated when he separates himself from the counsel and protection of the masses and puts too much trust in his former adversaries.

But James is too sophisticated a thinker to view Toussaint's actions totally at the level of personal behavior. Another unstated but easily grasped aspect of James's history of the Haitian Revolution is the difficulty if not the impossibility of carrying through a revolution limited to one country. Without links to broader movements that share the same goals, survival as a political entity is possible, but the more substantive efforts at social transformations will be extremely difficult to sustain. Without some principled allies and external support some compromises will be inevitable. This is the world in which Toussaint had to navigate. In the wake of the Haitian Revolution Latin America experienced a number of successful efforts to overthrow European political domination. But Simón Bolívar for all his achievements, was not Toussaint Louverture. And most tellingly, the Latin American leaders of the early nineteenth century draped themselves in the mantle of Bolívar, not of Toussaint. In addition, within three decades of the Haitian Revolution the British had abandoned chattel slavery in their possessions in the Western Hemisphere and shifted to what we now see as the more modern forms of colonialism and imperialist exploitation.

The caveat that James raised, i.e., that one cannot understand imperialism without understanding racism, and vice versa, a theme that runs throughout *The Black Jacobins*, remains valid to this day. The significance of the question of how to address the specific concerns of those peoples who are descended from Africans brought to the Western Hemisphere as slaves, and who have yet to get their just share from societies based upon the expropriation of their unpaid labor has not diminished with the passage of time. Wherever you look in the Western Hemisphere black peoples are on the lowest rungs of society or share those rungs with indigenous peoples.

C. L. R. James died two decades ago after a long and productive life. We are fortunate that he has left us such a rich and fruitful body of writings to help us make sense of the world in which we live. The issues that James devoted his life to are still very much with us. We have yet to come to grips with the reality of the continuing strength of white supremacist ideologies and practices, with the complex legacies or slavery and colonialism, with how to organize for and bring into being a world where all human beings can realize their full potential and live in peace. The bulk of James's writings still are worthy of serious and critical consideration. The place to begin is *The Black Jacobins*.

Note

This chapter is from *Los Jacobinos Negros: Toussaint Lóuverture y la Revolución de Saint-Domingue* (Havana: Casa de las Américas, 2010).

C. L. R. James and Studs Terkel Discuss
The Black Jacobins on WFMT Radio
(Chicago), 1970

JAMES: [*Reading*] "Christopher Columbus landed first in the New World at the island of San Salvador, and after praising God he inquired urgently for gold. The natives, Red Indians, were peaceable and friendly and directed him to Haiti, a large island (nearly as large as Ireland), rich, they said, in the yellow metal. He sailed to Haiti. One of his ships being wrecked, the Haitian Indians helped him so willingly that very little was lost and of the articles which they brought on shore not one was stolen. The Spaniards, the most advanced Europeans of their day, annexed the island, called it Hispaniola, and took the backward natives under their protection. They introduced Christianity, forced labor in mines, murder, rape, bloodhounds, strange diseases and artificial famine (by the destruction of cultivation to starve the rebellious). These and other requirements of the higher civilization reduced the native population from an estimated half-a-million, perhaps a million, to 60,000 in 15 years."

TERKEL: And thus it is that Dr. C. L. R. James, a distinguished scholar, reads the first two paragraphs of his prologue. A remarkable book, a classic, *The Black Jacobins*, which deals with the Toussaint Louverture–led Black slave rebellion in San Domingo two years after the French Revolution. In these two paragraphs Dr. James, your style of writing of course is a very salubrious one indeed, but the bite, the irony, and the truth, you might say of white man and all these years of Western civilization so-called, in these two paragraphs you've almost essentialized it.

JAMES: Yes I think so, and I wrote it quite naturally. I didn't have to search, but I am a West Indian, and we in the West Indies are very much aware of the contrast between what the white man says and what he does because we are Western-civilized in our orientation so we are aware of all the things he's saying much more than people who speak a different language or live a different type of civilization.

TERKEL: This very point you make, we should point out Professor James now visiting professor at the Northwestern University. Ah, the fact that you're West Indian. This has always been a fascinating historical point, isn't it?

JAMES: It is.

TERKEL: We think among the leaders and the whole Black liberation movement through the years have been West Indians.

JAMES: Yes we have had a whole lot of them. We have had Marcus Garvey. We have had Aimé Césaire the poet, with that magnificent poem on Africa in which he stated the question of Negritude. We have had René Maran, who won the Prix Goncourt with the book *Batouala* on Africa. We have had, ah,—

TERKEL: George Padmore.

JAMES: —George Padmore, Marcus Garvey, as I said, and we have had, there is no doubt about it that Malcolm X's mother was a West Indian and that had something to do with it; and Stokely Carmichael was born and grew up there as a boy. I also took some part, I believe this is something that is worthwhile, and I know and feel myself as a West Indian as Padmore was.

TERKEL: It's as though two, two cultures are fused, in a sense.

JAMES: Yes, we are not admitted completely into the Western culture but we have all the possibilities of developing it. So [in?] being kept back at home, we went abroad and made the best use of both the opportunities of education and the impulse towards freedom which we felt in the islands. That is the reason why the West Indians have done so well. And I would like to add this. Yet [that?] Fidel Castro and the Cubans are not [of all?] Black people, Fidel isn't Black at all, but the attitude of the revolution and what they're doing is essentially a West Indian revolution, similar to what Toussaint Louverture did.

TERKEL: Yes, so we come in fact you have a, an appendix to your book, ah an epilogue. You wrote the book in 1938 how remarkably prescient and prophetic, ah, Professor James's book is. Because he dealt with the nature of Africa and the possible independence movements back then; but the, the epilogue is from Toussaint Louverture to Castro. Now Toussaint Louverture, and it's, it's imperative of course that white people know this. Ah, more Blacks do, well we know that younger Blacks are aware of this. I had difficulty finding this book, by the way, in white bookstores, I found at the [Ellis?] Bookshop on South Cottage. Which is significant in itself, I think.

JAMES: I think the book now is being sold and read everywhere.

TERKEL: Yes.

JAMES: I think [in] the movement on the whole,—

TERKEL: Yes.

JAMES: —it is being read and studied in universities, predominantly white in the United States.

TERKEL: Yes.

JAMES: That is a fact. Although it's the Black movement that has given it great impetus.

TERKEL: Perhaps we should dwell upon the, ah, nature of this book and it's a terribly important one. It's, the subt—, *The Black Jacobins*, the subtitle: *Toussaint Louverture and The San Domingo Revolution*. Now here, you, you describe a scene. Ah, the ah Spaniards came, the French, the British. They found a great deal of profit to be made in the West Indies; San Domingo and Haiti. And now—

JAMES: It was the wealthiest colony in the world at the time, not only in the West Indies.

TERKEL: And so, th—, but it could only be done, you describe of course the slave trade and the nature of the slave ships, and the—

JAMES: Yes.

TERKEL: —incredible brutishness. So the question is, how could a people, the Black people in this case, the Africans, and this, well I'll ask about the mulattos in a moment, the Creoles. How could they survive is the question. This is the key.

JAMES: The question is this. Number one: they were a people obviously who had basically a very fine physique. Otherwise they would have been wiped away by the sheer objective circumstances of the Middle Passage and their lives. They have a fine physique and secondly, which is a most important point, they obviously were a highly civilized people. Otherwise they wouldn't have been able to be integrated into this sla—, into the sugar production in the way that they were, and learn as rapidly as they did the language and all the b—, ah, techniques of Western civilization. There were civilized people in Africa, and today people are p—, are more and more recognizing that even when there were slaves in Africa, they were slaves of a certain organized society. That is what must be remembered about the West Indian. And he was more fortunate than he was in the United States because the islands were small. Immensely concentrated, the sugar plantation had many of them living together. So they were closely connected. And this backbone of civilization in Africa and African physical strength, and then having to learn the elements of Western civilization made them what they did and what they have become.

TERKEL: Ah, so we come to several points Dr. James raises and again the question of submerged history or suppressed history; that there was a highly developed, I know Basil Davidson among others points this out.

JAMES: Basil Davidson is doing a lot of that work, and that work is very important and I'm very glad that Basil Davidson is doing it because I have to say there is a tendency to critic- criticism, sharp criticism of people who are whites because they are white. And Basil Davidson is a white man who would be an adornment to any Black university.

TERKEL: But in his books, whether it be *The Lost Cities of Africa*, others, he speaks, and indeed many anthropologists now are discovering, there was a highly developed civilization before the slave ships came.

JAMES: Yes. Not only that, the man who I know has carried that to the highest point is Professor George Rawick. He used to be at Rochester and he's now professor of sociology at Washington University in St. Louis. And he's doing some work on that subject which is the very finest and most developed that I know. I myself am writing something and most of my work is based not only on previous knowledge, but on what he and I have worked out together.

TERKEL: Before I ask you further about the book, move on to the book, we should point out to the audience that Professor James is a historic figure. I hope you don't mind my saying this, [*unintelligible*]. Professor James was an acquaintance of Nkrumah, ah, he had met him, you discovered him when he was going to University of Pennsylvania; he was a friend of Dr. Du Bois; was a friend of George Padmore, a remarkable too little known, too—

JAMES: [Well now?] a close ally of George Padmore. I used to know Marcus Garvey too.

TERKEL: Knew [who?], oh you knew Marcus Garvey?

JAMES: [I knew?] Marcus Garvey. Marcus Garvey came to Trinidad sometime about 1928. He had already been sent away from the United States and I was a reporter, and I went and interviewed him and followed him around where he spoke. He was a tremendous man.

TERKEL: You probably are one of the few living people I would guess, who knew Marcus Garvey personally.

JAMES: Yes, I knew Marcus Garvey. And I interviewed somewhere about 1928.

TERKEL: Perhaps this is worth dwelling on. The role of Marcus Garvey. Here's a man who's been ridiculed to great extent and yet he made people aware, did he not, this West Indian?

JAMES: I believe the intellectual origin of the Black movement must rest with Dr. Du Bois. A man with a range of scholarship, practical activity, and ambition for the development of humanity which is not exceeded by anybody in the twentieth century. But his chief concern was to appeal to and get in contact with intellectuals, historians, organizers, et cetera. When Du Bois was finished, Garvey began so—

TERKEL: Yeah.

JAMES: —to speak, and Garvey made Black emancipation something popular, which it had never been before. So both of them, although they may have had conflict,—

TERKEL: [*unintelligible*]

JAMES: —they fill political roles. Du Bois made it an intellectual, ah, discussion, posed the question; Garvey made it a popular question. When Garvey was finished, everybody knew there was a Black question; both white people knew and Black people all over the world knew. And that is what Garvey did. Despite the mistakes that he made, that is to his great credit.

TERKEL: And Garvey's name was known throughout the Black world; in Africa too, they knew of Marcus Garvey.

JAMES: And also throughout the white world.

TERKEL: Yes.

JAMES: Garvey had made everybody, Black and white,—

TERKEL: Yes, yes.

JAMES: —understand that the Black man was sleeping no longer; he was on his way. That is his great contribution.

TERKEL: Here again, a West Indian. And so we return to this moment that that with which your book begins. Ah, here was a colony, profitable to the colonist, the absentee landlords, the powers. Ah, people being used, abused, yet surviving. Now something happened in France, now. In 1789 was a French revolution. Therefore it had a certain impact. How did word come to San Domingo?

JAMES: For one reason, people used to go up and down. But the French whites discussed the doctrines of the French Revolution with the utmost freedom; and there were white people from France who ask them, "Aren't you worried a bit that you should discuss these things before these Black people?" But they paid no attention to the Blacks; they looked upon them as some sort of animal. A white woman used to undress before the Black slaves as if they were a horse or a dog. They looked upon them as nothing. And they discussed these things very freely. And people from France asked them, "But aren't you [nervous?] talking?" They didn't bother. But the Blacks were listening.

TERKEL: Now what is interesting about this, what makes Professor James's book so contemporary is this very point you just made. Often there is a woman, working as a domestic, in the home of white mistress, you know, and she's talked about; many tell me this, friends of mine who've worked as domestics, elderly women who say that, ah, they know everything about this person and the person knows nothing about her—

JAMES: Yes.

TERKEL: —because they talk in front of her as though she were furniture.

JAMES: That is a fact. That is a fact, that is a fact. You see [and?] a great deal of that is due to the fact that the Black man is looked upon as a barbarous African [nature?], but he has had to learn the language. That is very important. He has had to learn the European language. So today in the Caribbean he speaks English, French, or Spanish; and he's equally a master of all of those languages.

TERKEL: And he's learned these languages, he's learned far more indeed than the white master knew, to survive. And so we come to many other aspects in your book; the nature of survival itself. Sometimes it's clowning, sometimes it's pretending not to know in order to survive. And behavior different wha—Black people among Blacks different than say in front of the white [*unintelligible*].

JAMES: That is quite true but the thing that I emphasize in regard to the Caribbean Islands and regard to the San Domingo Revolution and the Cuban Revolution is this: the islands are rather small, judging on a world scale; the population is immensely concentrated; the type of industry where there is some is sugar, or scraps of modern industry, which develop a highly civilized population; and in for example Trinidad, the island I come from, Barbados and Jamaica, we have the extraordinarily advantage of having newspapers, telev—papers, radio, et cetera from Britain, from the United States and from Canada. The opportunity of being in touch with the advanced centers of civilization is very great.

TERKEL: So then the people are au courant with all aspects of life.

JAMES: The people are aware. They just have to pay two or three dollars a month, and they get a radio and they hear everything that's going on.

TERKEL: Now going back to this time. Something was happening when, at this moment, in France, a revolution. Two years later something broke out in San Domingo and we soon we learn of a man named Toussaint [L']Ouverture. But before that, now, was an attempt by the colonists to split the people? After all, there were mulattoes, there were Creoles, and there were the Blacks.

JAMES: Yes, the San Domingo revolution began the Black revolution because of the fierce struggle that was carried on between the San Domingo whites and the mulattoes who owned property, and some of them were educated. And, after seeing the ferocity of that violence, the Blacks themselves entered. They entered as a result of the conflict between San Domingo whites and San Domingo mulattoes; in the same way as the masses of France intervened because of the conflict between the nobles, the aristocracy, and the bourgeoisie. This went on and then the masses came in. The same thing happened in San Domingo.

TERKEL: So a parallel was working both ways.

JAMES: Parallel was working.

TERKEL: Remarkable.

JAMES: As a matter of fact I'm very much struck by the tremendous parallels between the development in San Domingo and the developments in France. Much of my book pays careful attention to that, and I believe there are more parallels to be found later as we study both the French Revolution and the San Domingo Revolution.

TERKEL: So there was a question of paradox involved, a question of contradiction involved. You point out the French Revolution was, in a sense, bourgeois.

JAMES: It was.

TERKEL: Taking over, knocking off the nob—. At the same time slave trade—

JAMES: Yes.

TERKEL: —was part of their—

JAMES: Yes.

TERKEL: —life.

JAMES: They, the money that the bourgeoisie got, that made them what they were, and as Jaurès says, gave them the feeling for liberty, that came from the slave trade. It's a very sharp contradiction.

TERKEL: A paradox.

JAMES: Now the second paradox that I am concerned with is that this sugar plantation was a very severe and demanding mode of labor but it also concentrated the b—the Blacks and gave them some element of social civilization, some feeling of unity, and even then to learn fundamentally many aspects of Western civilization.

TERKEL: So—

JAMES: So that this sugar plantation was at the same time the most degrading and at the same time a very civilizing effort on the part of the Black people.

TERKEL: Again, paradox. The degrading nature of the work, the exploitation; at the same time communication.

JAMES: Communication.

TERKEL: Because the constant contact.

JAMES: Of constant contact, and also the sugar plantation produced sugar and the food that they ate came from abroad. The sugar was sent abroad and so forth so that they had education not only in what was going on around them and a close relation with their masters, but the sugar plantation was intimately connected with foreign developments and finance and so forth, and all that the slaves learned.

TERKEL: So the window now was being opened. The window, awareness was occurring and once that happens, people can no longer be the same.

JAMES: They and the moment the French Revolution began, because what is important about the San Domingo Revolution, which has made it the most successful, the only successful slave revolt in history, is the fact that they were slaves that had these elements of civilization in them; but they were able to use the doctrines and ideas of the French Revolution, and apply them, these ideas, to their own situation. So they had not only a physical basis, contact with society, but they had a new ideology. That's what they were—liberty, equality, fraternity: all that meant to them. The Republic, and so on.

TERKEL: So again, perhaps the crowning paradox is the fact that it was the bourgeoisie that would factors in the French Revolution, and also profiting from slave trade, but because of what they did. The window was now open to the Black slaves, as well as the colored slaves, [in, in?]

JAMES: And they learned it, they learned, oh they it took it over and made it something for themselves.

TERKEL: And so the time was right then for a certain figure, or group of figures,—

JAMES: Yes.

TERKEL: —and so we come—

JAMES: On, on the basis of that objective development and the spread of ideas, there emerges this remarkable man. It's difficult to say that the revolution made him, but he made the revolution, but the interplay between them is such that it's difficult to distinguish.

TERKEL: And here we come to a man who's been a slave for forty-five years.

JAMES: Yeah.

TERKEL: Toussaint Louverture.

JAMES: Yes.

TERKEL: And he comes at this moment, about 1791 or so.

JAMES: Yes. However, more important is the fact that the Abbé Raynal had written a famous book on the situation in the East and the West Indies; and he had said in that book, eh, magnificent gesture, that the time was coming when some revolutionary person would relieve the slaves of the burdens from which they were suffering. And what is most fantastic, that book came into the hands of Toussaint Louverture. And he read repeatedly this passage in which the Abbé Raynal, I'm sure he was just a revolutionary intellectual; he just said, "Someday somebody would arise." And Toussaint kept on saying, "Someday somebody should arise"; and he kept on thinking that someday somebody should arise. And the moment the revolt started in San Domingo he said, "This is—I am the person now." That is a very strange business.

TERKEL: The reading that which, now something was happening in France; you mention that Diderot—there were writings against slavery.

JAMES: That is before the revolution.

TERKEL: Yeah, yeah.

JAMES: The *Encyclopedia*, yes.

TERKEL: [They're?] writing, but very often, I think you point this out in the case of Robespierre, that it was the word rather than the deed that was being attacked.

JAMES: Yes, because to abolish slavery meant a revolution, a tremendous revolution; not only in San Domingo but in France. And they had reached 1793, and the days of May 1793, and they had reached this, mmm, this spring of '94 before they abolished slavery.

TERKEL: So now the word had come. The man had come and his colleagues, now the word. Were they, and, for twelve years now the battle raged, the revolution, with, with pressures back and forth. Were the colonists [holy?] now we come to the question of awareness or lack of awareness of the absentee landlords or the colonists themselves.

JAMES: Now the colonists began by joining the revolution because the ancient monarchy had what is called the "exclusif," and by that means they dominated the economy; so the colonists began by joining the revolution. But afterwards they saw that the revolution in France was assisting the Black people and saying, "At any rate if you are fighting for freedom we should have it, et cetera." Whereupon the colonists to a large majority offered the colony to the British.

TERKEL: [*Laughter*]

JAMES: [That?] they offered it to the British.

TERKEL: [*Laughing*] I see [*unintelligible*].

JAMES: They were ready, they were ready to get rid of king and all this loyalty. They told them if slavery was not matter to them.

TERKEL: Yeah.

JAMES: And so they offered it to the British and the British came to get it, but they were defeated by Toussaint Louverture and the Black army.

TERKEL: So we have here again, we come back to your very opening two paragraphs read the prologue, the question of the coin.

JAMES: Yes, the question of the property.

TERKEL: The question of the gold, the question of property.

JAMES: The wealth, the production, the control of it.

TERKEL: So, I think what's bone-deeply powerful about ah, Dr. James's book, *The Black Jacobins*, is it deals with the reality of today too. Though you deal with a time 100 and almost 200 years ago, and you would say that there are, there's lip service very often offered but until the reality faced that may concern property itself, then a shift occurs in the case of the colonists.

JAMES: I was able to write this book because I was taking part, in London and thereabouts, with George Padmore, Jomo Kenyatta, and various others,

I had been friendly. I got to know Nkrumah. And we were living this life. In other words the French Revolution, the revolution of San Domingo, was to us a forecast of what would take place in Africa. So this book is closely the result of the kind of activity we were carrying on; both of the Marxist movement, with the Black movement, and with the Labour Party and various others in Europe. The book is the result of a collabor—collaboration of a lot of people.

TERKEL: So it really is a fusion of past and present.

JAMES: It's a—

TERKEL: So you wrote about the past writing about present and future.

JAMES: [I? nnn-?] if you read the book carefully, as you will, you will see that all through I am concerned with the effect of what I am writing on Africa.

TERKEL: Yes.

JAMES: Yes.

TERKEL: Even have, if we come to another aspect and this connects with the revolution itself, Toussaint Louverture. Vodouism, for instance. The very fact that this had to be done secret too because how could Black people be Christians or [to?] would make them such equal to the white, the colonists.

JAMES: They stuck to their vodouism because it formed a secret means of communication. But when the revolution actually took place, Toussaint and ah, his officers were very severe against vodouism. They thought it was a backward [means?]. But undoubtedly, I have no doubt as time goes on that vodouism, not only before 1791 but afterwards, was a secret means of communication—

TERKEL: Ah.

JAMES: —between the Haitian—

TERKEL: Just like with slaves in America, the spiritual had a double meaning,—

JAMES: Yes.

TERKEL: —and so the gatherings—

JAMES: We were very close to Africa, so you see, because many of the slaves who made the revolution had made the Middle Passage; so they had their vodouism, well they had—

TERKEL: Now, now a question because your book raised these questions, which makes it so fascinating a work, too. The role of the French working people, masses now, at the time the French Revolution and after, what effect this was having on the revolt elsewhere. We naturally think of today—America and, ah, Vietnam, in a sense, you see.

JAMES: No, I think this much. First of all the French Revolution was a bourgeois revolution in that it resulted in the displacement of the feudal elements by the bourgeoisie and the bourgeoisie took over, but the fact remains that the bourgeoisie would not have been able to carry that revolution to its success—

TERKEL: Mm hm.

JAMES: —unless the masses of the French people, the *sans-culottes*, had done it for them. The sans-culottes didn't win the revolution, but they were so hostile to the regime that they carried the bourgeois revolution to its complete end. [*Paper rustling? Pages turning?*] And also in San Domingo, the revolt there meant that the Black soldiers were able to defend that wealthy colony against the British, Spaniards,—

TERKEL: Yeah.

JAMES: —and the rest of them.

TERKEL: Yeah.

JAMES: So that they help one another.

TERKEL: Yes.

JAMES: And, in, at the high peak of the revolution in France, that was the time when the French revolutionary forces declared freedom for Blacks everywhere.

TERKEL: Yeah.

JAMES: So the two of them were working together.

TERKEL: Yeah. Now where there are attempts, I think you point this out in your books too, there was a great ambivalence on the part of mulattoes, the many, many cases [who themselves were?]

JAMES: Yes, the mulattoes were an intermediate class. It has nothing to do with this color or their blood or their mixture of blood. It is that they were not clo—closely allied with rich whites but they were rich people and they were allied in a way with the Blacks; they were partially racial Black. So in between there, they were a typical intermediate class and wobbled both sides; now they would go with this one, [then?] the other. And the ultimate victory in San Domingo was won when the mulattoes joined completely with the Blacks to finish up—

TERKEL: Yes.

JAMES: —with the French invasion.

TERKEL: Now we come to several people invo—in Toussaint's life. You mentioned Abbé Raynal, and a remarkable name, man named Sonthonax.

JAMES: Sonthonax was a Jacobin. He was [*thoughtful sound*] a right-wing Jacobin. But there was something about him, he came out of Fra—to San Domingo being sent by the government more than once; and although he made mistakes and things and so forth, he was a man completely devoted to the emancipation of the Black people. And he taught them literacy. He taught them revolutionary songs. He taught them Latin and Greek stories and education, the doctrines of the revolution, and he told them, "You have your guns, keep them. If at any time anybody does tell you to give up your guns they mean to restore slavery." Sonthonax was a bit uncertain as to what was taking place in France, but when he got to San Domingo to, ah, fifty years after, Black slaves still remembered him.

TERKEL: Yeah.

JAMES: Because he had devoted himself completely to Black emancipation.

TERKEL: But there was always this memory and this knowledge that there'll be an attempt to restore slavery.

JAMES: He had that and he warned them: anybody tells you to give up your guns, that means the restoration of slavery.

TERKEL: And so we come to, ah, many documents you have, writings of Toussaint and others. Perhaps, ah, I remember you reading the first part, the prologue. I've underlined something here of your writings, Toussaint's writings. The underlining, the question is, ah, are the colonists aware now that the Black people will never, will never return to that [*unintelligible*].

JAMES: Toussaint is writing to the French government—

TERKEL: Yeah.

JAMES: —and he's warning them that the colonists are plotting to restore slavery, and he's telling the French government, "I am somewhat uncertain as to what you intend to do." So he's telling them, "Well I don't think you will." It is a very fine passage. [*Reading or reciting, quoting Toussaint Louverture*] "Do they think that men who have been able to enjoy the blessing of liberty will kindly see it snatched away? They supported their chains only so long as they did not know any condition of life more happy than that of slavery; but today when they have left it, if they had a thousand lives they would sacrifice them all rather than then be forced into slavery again." And then he speaks here to the French government: [*continues to quote Louverture*] "But no, the same hand which has broken our chains will not enslave us anew. France will not revoke her principles, she will not withdraw from us the greatest of her benefits." He is telling the French government you wouldn't do it, but I am telling you not to do it. [*Continues to quote Louverture*] "She will protect us against all our enemies; she will not permit her sublime morality to be perverted, those principles which are most honored to be destroyed, her most beautiful achievement to be degraded. But if to reestablish slavery in San Domingo, this was done, then I declare to you it would be to attempt the impossible: we have known how to face dangers to obtain our liberty, we shall know how to brave death to maintain it." And then he ends up like [*unintelligible*]. [*Continues to quote Louverture*] "This, Citizens Directors, is the morale of the people of San Domingo, these [*sic*] are the principles that they transmit to you by me." [Awfully?] was beautiful.

TERKEL: The power and the eloquence.

JAMES: Oh yes.

TERKEL: And yet wasn't this the one flaw in Toussaint, his faith in France? [*Recording stops and restarts*] I come to Toussaint Louverture's, possibly his one flaw. Dr. C.L.R. James, Professor James, our guest scholar, particularly on Black African West Indian history. A reading talking about his book. It's a classic called *The Black Jacobins*, beginning with Toussaint Louverture revolt, beginning in 1791 in San Domingo, and he was just reading one of the letters Toussaint wrote to France. In a moment we return to the theme and to Professor James. [*Recording stops and restarts*] We return to Professor James his book *The Black Jacobins*. He has just been reading a letter that Toussaint Louverture wrote to the French government, and, we continue.

JAMES: The flaw. I admit that it was a flaw, but to see it only as a flaw is a mistake because that enabled him—

TERKEL: Yeah.

JAMES: —to lay the foundation in San Domingo that Dessalines and these others were able to use. That he, he had a limit, but it was this limitation that enabled him to establish something which the others could use.

TERKEL: I withdraw that word *flaw* because this again is part of the power of your book. The nature of paradox, the nature of limitation, the nature of human possibilities.

JAMES: I would like—

TERKEL: This is Toussaint.

JAMES: I would like to tell you something. For a hundred years or more, Toussaint was somewhat ignored in the history of San Domingo. People looked upon Toussaint as having made mistakes and Dessalines as the man who carried the revolution to success, which undoubtedly he did. My book was translated into French. It went to Haiti, and I have been told by many Haitians that today in Haiti there is a new conception of the role of Toussaint in the revolution due to the, the, what my book has said.

TERKEL: So because even though, as you say, ah, he was tied, France very much—

JAMES: Yes.

TERKEL: This, the nature of this enabled one of his colleagues, Dessalines, to go further—

JAMES: To go further, but enabled—

TERKEL: —and fight for independence.

JAMES: —Toussaint to lay the foundation and to establish certain principles. The real mischief-maker in that business was Bonaparte.

TERKEL: Ah, so now we come to, Bonaparte misusing—

JAMES: Mis—and mis—Bonaparte who sent this tremendous expedition, mo—, perhaps the greatest expedition that had ever left Europe to conquer the Haitians, the Blacks in San Domingo. And they failed.

TERKEL: You know this is incredible, and again the book, and its 1969, '70 counterparts. The greatest expedition to conquer an island, we think naturally of ourselves in Vietnam at the moment, but here it was Leclerc led this incredible—something happened to him, this French general, and his letters, his agony.

JAMES: Yes.

TERKEL: Something, he thought was easy [*sound of a snap or clap*], was a cinch—

JAMES: Yeah, na—

TERKEL: —and then something happened to him to [*unintelligible*].

JAMES: And in the end he says [*quoting Leclerc, possibly with slight changes*], "We in France have a false idea of the country in which we fight and the kind of men we fight against." That was wrung out of him at the end. He realized that the Blacks of San Domingo were not people whom you could just drive into slavery. He said we don't understand these people. I remember many passages of his letters but I remember this passage in particular: "It is not enough to have taken away Toussaint. There are two thousand leaders in San Domingo to be taken away."

TERKEL: And right there even though Toussaint was betrayed; he returned to France, he was imprisoned and died in prison. He said so, yeah, that eh, there were still others.

JAMES: Yes, he said, you have in getting rid of me you have taken away only the trunk of the tree, but its roots are deep and slavery will never be restored in San Domingo. That must be remembered. Toussaint could take the chances that he did and tie himself to French civilization because he was absolutely certain that the slavery could never be restored.

TERKEL: And so it was twelve years or so.

JAMES: Yes they had—

TERKEL: The French lost thousands, of course the Black—

JAMES: They lost some sixty thousand men and more than that. The historian of the British army says that the British army was destroyed in the Caribbean. Totally destroyed. He says that is why when the war began in '93 they made little attempt or could do little in regard to France in regard to the army, in to, in regard to military invasion of France. The reason was because they were attempting to capture the West Indian territories of France, and the Black armies destroyed the British army completely. Fortescue, the historian of the British army, says that 1798 is the most disgraceful year in the history of the British army because those Blacks in the San Domingo did what they did.

TERKEL: You know your book has ev—a never-ending possibilities because it occurs to me, the Black Jacobins, and of course the phrase deals with the French Revolutionary Party, the Jacobin Party, but also the role that the Toussaint Louverture revolution played in the American Civil War.

JAMES: Now not only that, I would prefer to say this: it is in regard to the independence of the Latin American countries; because this all, America independent, good they accepted that. But then they saw these Black slaves not only win the independence but keep it! Whereupon a lot of them in Latin America began to say well if they could win the independence and keep it, it isn't only America and a big country like. So we can. And Pétion was beaten from Latin America, was welcomed in Haiti.[1] He was given food, he was made better; doctors attended him, and then they gave him men.

TERKEL: This was a Latin American?

JAMES: Latin America. They gave him men they gave him b—, ah, arms, they gave him money, they gave them a printing press, and it is from there he went back to Latin America to win the independence of the five states. So they took a tremendous part in the development of Latin America.

TERKEL: Latin America and then of course here. We come to the United States.

JAMES: Because, ah, they, they people, them people in the United States refused to recognize Haiti until after 1865. Because the Southern slave owners were always upon that as somewhere where they could expand their territorial, ah, development of cotton number one, and number two: San Domingo and Haiti had given an example to the French, to the Blacks in, bu—, the United States which they knew very well, and which these Southern plantation owners were mightily afraid of. That was a tremendous role.

TERKEL: You know again, the contemporary aspects of your book, toward the latter part of the War of Independence, the last chapter, you speak of the pride of, in three years! People ask, "How could this happen in three years?" This, any part of your home, your own writing there and I'm thinking about the—

JAMES: Yes. [*Reading*] "If in 1788 anyone had told the Comte de Lauzerne, the minister; the Comte de Peynier, the governor; General Rochambeau, the soldier; Moreau de Saint-Mery, the historian; Barbé de Marbois, the bureaucrat, that the thousands of dumb brutes who were whipped to labor at dawn and whipped back at midnight, who submitted to their mutilations, burnings, and other savageries, some of whom would not even move unless they were whipped. If these fine gentlemen had been told that in three years the Blacks would shake off their chains and face extermination rather than put them on again, they would have thought the speaker mad. While if today, one were to suggest to any white colonial potentate that among those Blacks whom they rule, a man so infinitely their superior in ability, energy, range of vision, and tenacity of purpose; that 100 years' time these whites would be remembered only because of their contact with the Blacks, one would get some idea of what the counts, marquises, and other colonial magnates of the day thought of Jean François, Toussaint, and Rigaud when the revolt first began."

TERKEL: Thus again we came to the question of awareness and the lack of awareness on the other side.

JAMES: Yes.

TERKEL: [While it was?] happening, what is about to happen.

JAMES: Yes, they—

TERKEL: Which again has this prophetic quality. It's 1938 first written [*unintelligible*].

JAMES: And many of these things have al—, are written. In 1938 I didn't write them and I made one or two changes, but and introduced one or two new points. But essentially 98 percent of the book is as it was. [*Pages turning*] Now I would like, if you don't mind, to read this. This is one of my favorite passages in the—

TERKEL: Please.

JAMES: —in the book. Yes. You must remember that this was written in 1938. [*Reading; may not precisely follow written text*] "He had sent millions of francs to America to wait for the day when he would be ready to invade Africa, put an end to the slave-trade and make millions of Blacks free and French; as the French Revolution had made the blacks of San Domingo . . . The great revolution had propelled him out of his humble joys and obscure destiny and the trumpets of its heroic period rang ever in his ears. In him, born a slave and the leader of slaves, the concrete realization of liberty, equality and fraternity was the womb of ideas and the springs of power, which overflowed their narrow environment and embraced the whole of the world. But for the revolution, this extraordinary man and his band of gifted associates would have lived their lives as slaves, serving the commonplace creatures who owned them, standing barefooted and in rags to watch inflated little governors and mediocre officials from Europe pass by, as many a talented African stands in Africa today." I wrote that in 1938 and today I'm very proud of it because I knew what was taking place. They were standing there in rags and having to wave when these fellows pass.

TERKEL: Yes.

JAMES: And they only needed a few years for them to be driving past, in charge, whatever they did. And these fellows became the [*unintelligible*].

TERKEL: It is amazing, your passage, that, as well as your book, Professor James, the fact that you described this and toward the end of it you, you speak of a, a letter from a Rhodesian Black—

JAMES: Yes.

TERKEL: —that speaks to this particular aspect of it. Your writing of course, the style, ah, the power, but also the truth. That in this one man, then you saw the development of a people, too.

JAMES: Yes.

TERKEL: And you spoke of, ah, the West Indians earlier of course the great poet Aimé Césaire whom you know.

JAMES: Yes I know Césaire, and he is a man I admire very much. And in the course of this appendix in which I deal with the history of the West Indies from the Toussaint Louverture to Fidel Castro, I referred to Césaire's great poem, "Cahier d'un retour au pays natal," "Statement of a return to the country where I was born," and I've translated some of it because it's in this poem that is first stated the poetic conception of Negritude. He says [*reading or citing his own translation*] "My negritude is not a stone; it's deafness a sounding board for the noises of the day. My negritude is not a mere spot of dead water on the dead eye of the earth. My negritude is no tower, no cathedral. It cleaves to the red flesh of the teeming earth. It cleaves into the glowing flesh of the heavens. It penetrates the seamless bondage of my unending patience." And then he makes a tremendous statement on behalf of African civilization. "Hoorah for those who never invented anything, for those who never explored anything, for those who never mastered anything; but who, possessed, give themselves up to the essence of each thing, ignorant of the coverings but possessed by the pulse of things, indifferent to mastering but taking the chances of the world." And then he launches an attack on white civilization. In 1938 you see me, I wrote this book. And today with all these [missiles?] about, he says, "Listen to the white world. Its horrible exhaustion from its immense labels. Its rebellious joints, cracking under the pitiless stars. Its blue steel rigidities, cutting through the mysteries of the flesh. Listen to their vainglorious conquests trumpeting their defeats. Listen to the grandiose alibis of their pitiful floundering. But he says, "I must not be hate; I must not have hate." He says, "For it is not true that the work of man is finished; that man has nothing more to do in the world but to be a parasite in the world; that all we now need is to keep in step with the world. But the work of man is only just beginning and it remains to man to conquer all the violence entrenched in the recesses of his passion, and no race possesses the monopoly of beauty, of intelligence, or force; and there is a place for all at the rendezvous of victory." It is a magnificent poem, oh yes. It is the finest poem ever written on Africa.

TERKEL: You know, has, has, has—

JAMES: He's a West Indian too, I want to say.

TERKEL: [*chuckles*] Professor C. L. R. James, that you just read these excerpts from the Césaire poem, I couldn't help but think of the power of the humanity of it and of course of your book and your scholarship. The book, by the way, if, if ah listeners will be inquiring, it's a Vintage. It's a paperback; it's a Vintage. It's definitely available; it's a classic. And it's ah, it should be read it seems to me, by anyone who wants to know about the open window and what is going on in the world, and what will continue and perhaps it's just one, as sort of a postscript, your own courses—the way you teach, mana—. All literature is used as your base in speaking of liberation; and it's used in one of your courses, "Origin of Western Civilization," ah, mmm, the Bible of the Hebrews, revolt of colonial people: Exodus; or women against second-class citizenship: Esther. And you go on to speak of Greek, use Greek, ah, classics.

JAMES: Yes.

TERKEL: You go on as—

JAMES: I use the Greek classics because the basis of Western civilization is the work of the Hebrews and of the Greeks. Everybody understands that. So in studying the [risk?] and the radicalism of race, I take the examples of the radicalism of the Hebrews and the radicalism of the Greeks. I am happy to do the story of Moses because he was the first that we know of who led a suppressed people to freedom. So if you're talking about freedom and the release of a suppressed people, I begin with Moses. That is what we are rooted in particularly in the United States and in the Caribbean; we are rooted in Western civilization. So we cannot ignore African civilization; we do the best we can to be in contact with it. That series of talks I deal with Mau Mau, I deal with ah, Nkrumah, et cetera, the emergence of Africa. But I say we have to be aware of where we have come from. We cannot, ah, deny the roots of Western civilization and the radicalism that we find in it we absorb and take it to ourselves. So that I think we have a lot to learn because we both Western and African civilization, we of the Black people in the Caribbean and in the United States, we touch civilization at two points, and all my work I try to be aware of that.

TERKEL: Yes indeed, as ah, also what Dr. Du Bois has said, "The soul of—"

JAMES: Dr. Du Bois, Dr. Du Bois is one of the greatest men of the twentieth century. I have been very hostile to people who talk about the Du Bois as one of the great Black leaders and even Black people say, "Well he was one of our best." I say by do that, by you doing that you denigrate him. He was one of the most distinguished citizens of the twentieth century—Black, white, yellow, or anything. A remarkable man.

TERKEL: So in Dr. James we have a scholar. At the same time not the academician; not the removed, detached. Very much the advocate-scholar.

JAMES: Yes, I'm the advocate and wherever possible I participate in the struggles of the people. I know on my courses end up proving that without the conscious intervention or even the unconscious intervention of the mass of the people there can be no real progress towards liberation. The intellectual may express, make clear, what is really taking place in the majority of the people.

That is what my course is seeking to [put?] and that is what my book *The Black Jacobins* expresses both for France and for the colonies [in?] San Domingo.

TERKEL: Just as there are two cultures, just as you find the fusion of the two, and the contributions of the Black man to both tremendous. So you'll see knowledge, you'll see activity from the scholar, but from the street as well. The book and the street: you see it going both ways.

JAMES: Both together and one expresses the other. And the, the work of the book is of no serious value unless it is supplemented and stimulated by the work of the street. That is a view I have.

TERKEL: *The Black Jacobins* is the book. It's my privilege indeed to have been here with Professor C.L.R. James, now visiting professor at Northwestern University. It's a Vintage, and thank you very much indeed.

JAMES: Much obliged to you, sir. Much obliged to you. [*Recording stops and restarts*]

TERKEL: This particular conversation took place on, during Dr. James's last day in America. He was returning to his home in London. He'll be returning to America soon to lecture at Princeton, at Yale, and at Columbia. We trust at Northwestern again where he'd like to talk about the various literatures of history and liberation: Old Testament, New Testament, the Greeks. Ah, that's was part of a series, too, at Northwestern, so we trust in the not-too-distant future once more Dr. James will be our guest. The book is *The Black Jacobins*. Paperback. Vintage, the publishers. We thought perhaps some music that might be appropriate now in the time remaining. They're ah, songs, slave songs and code songs sung in the islands. San Domingo then, and no doubt many of them found their way in in America itself, in the states in the pre–Civil War days. "Vodou [Voodoo?] American" is such a song. It is code as ah, Black spirituals are code. It's a funeral song, [Via Va Luco?]; at the same time it speaks of freedom and though it speaks of that body of water when the burden of life becomes too much for he, for the man who has died, there's a deep body of water separating him from freedom so we could say this could be the River Jordan, and also could be that river separating slave from free state, or slave state from Canada, and these are songs that are commonly found today in the sea islands off the coast of Florida, Georgia, and South Carolina. They could be traced there, but I imagine could go back to, ah, the Caribbeans as well. This one, "Vodou [Voodoo?] American." [*Music*]

TERKEL: This song that began as a "Vodou [Voodoo?] American," ah, became an uptempo blues, ah, [Michelle à Rose?] sang it; ah, was mixing several forms here in the song itself, a sort of ah, meant as sort of a postscript to the conversation with Dr. James.

Notes

This appendix is the audio transcript of "C.L.R. James talks with Studs Terkel: on WFMT; 1970," https://www.popuparchive.com/collections/938/items/12764. Transcript prepared by Grace Q. Radkins. The Studs Terkel: Radio Archive is managed by the WFMT Radio Network along with the Studs Terkel Center for Oral History of the Chicago History Museum. The rights to the recording are owned by the Chicago History Museum.

1. Ed. note: James is referring to Simón Bolívar, not Pétion.

The Revolution in Theory

C. L. R. JAMES

The Ghana revolutionaries, including Nkrumah himself, take a great and natural pride in recalling that the national movement for independence was not born with Nkrumah and the Convention People's Party, but has a long and honourable ancestry, beginning with the Fanti Confederation in 1871. That is undoubtedly true. Writers in the West, on the other hand, are apt to stress Nkrumah's experiences in the revolutionary and socialist movements in Britain, where he is supposed to have learnt the principles of what they call "party organisation." But both these views are superficial and do not touch the heart of the question.

The first and ever-to-be-remembered name in the history of the body of political ideas which went to the making of Nkrumah is that of George Padmore, an extraordinary man and a Trinidadian known to me from my youth up. He was a journalist in the West Indies and in the twenties went to the United States. As usual with the young West Indians of that day, he had ideas of qualifying for a profession, but he was drawn to the ideas of communism and, while at Howard University, threw a bunch of revolutionary leaflets into the face of Sir Esme Howard, the British Ambassador, at some university function, and finally joined the Communist Party. He worked with the Communist Party in the United States and ultimately became head of the Negro Department of the Profintern, the Communist Trade Union International, with an office in the Kremlin. In the course of this work he was constantly in contact with African nationalist revolutionaries all over the world and himself visited and helped to organise revolutionary activities in various parts of Africa, acquiring an immense practical and theoretical experience. In his relations with Stalin, Manuilsky and the other leading figures in the Comintern, he devoted himself to African and Negro problems and studiously avoided being involved in the great conflicts of Russian politics.

In strict theory it was a mistake. You cannot divide the colonial struggle and the metropolitan struggle into separate compartments. In actual fact it turned out well, for it almost certainly saved Padmore's life, and in addition to his own unique personal qualities enabled him to preserve for future use much that was valuable in the Comintern of those days. The inevitable break came in 1935. In that year Stalin, seeking the alliance of the democracies against fascism, decreed that henceforth the colonial peoples of Africa and elsewhere should support the democracies. But it was the democracies and not the fascists who held the greater part of Africa. The international policies of the Stalinist regime had caught up with him at last, and Padmore broke decisively with the Comintern. He came to live in London permanently in 1935, and to continue his work for the freedom of colonial peoples there upon a new basis: he would collaborate with any or all of the metropolitan revolutionary or socialist movements, but he would never again submit himself to any of them.

At that time in London the leading African politicians were Jomo Kenyatta and Wallace-Johnson, afterwards collaborator with [Nnamdi] Azikiwe, the Premier of Eastern Nigeria, in the publication of the first revolutionary paper in West Africa, and now a member of the Legislative Council in Sierra Leone. Both Kenyatta and Johnson had had experience with Stalinism and had revolted against it. I was at that time a Trotskyist, and though I looked askance at the practical separation of the colonial movement from the struggle for the socialist revolution in Europe, I was able to work with them without friction. What united us was not only the cause of political freedom for the colonies but our common repudiation of Stalinist policies in the colonies. Padmore (in *Pan-Africanism [or Communism? The Coming Struggle for Africa]*) gave an accurate, though condensed, account of the Ghana revolution. The theory as developed and carried out by Nkrumah in my opinion is of immense importance for political theory in general, and will play a great role not only in the colonies but throughout the world in the twentieth century. It is not only that Nkrumah carried it to the Gold Coast, it is that the people of the Gold Coast accepted it so completely that gives it international significance.

The first move in London in 1935 was the formation of the International African Friends of Ethiopia in response to the Italian invasion of Ethiopia. It was a body formed to educate British and international opinion and to agitate against the imperialist plans for Africa. Padmore had not been very long in Britain at the time and I was therefore the chairman of that body, Padmore serving with Kenyatta and others as members of the committee.

The International African Friends of Ethiopia fulfilled its purpose, and when for the moment the Ethiopian question was over, the question arose as to what next was to be done. Padmore now formed the International African [Service] Bureau, an organisation that devoted itself to the study of the colonial question and the spread of propaganda and agitation all over Britain, in Africa and in the territories inhabited by people of African descent. Of this new organisation Padmore was the chairman. I was the editor of the paper and was responsible for the most part for its literary publications. Padmore himself carried on an unceasing correspondence with people all over the world. He made a precarious living by being correspondent for a great number of papers in the United States, in the West Indies, in West Africa, in East Africa, everywhere, and, though limited by the political opinions of his employers, he gave his readers a steady stream of information about European matters that affected them. The Bureau published a journal in which it was free to say what it pleased and this was sent over the world. We carried on agitation and propaganda in England whenever we got the opportunity, speaking in Hyde Park regularly and addressing meetings of the Independent Labour Party, the Labour Party, attending all the front organisations that the communists organised. Articles and letters were written for papers that would publish. Members of parliament were kept informed on questions that would be or might be raised in parliament.

The basis of that work and the development of ideas was Padmore's encyclopaedic knowledge of Africa, of African politics and African personalities, his tireless correspondence with Africans in all parts of the continent, the unceasing stream of Africans who made the Bureau and its chairman their political headquarters when in London. Revolutionaries and bourgeois nationalists all came, and not only programme and tactics for the revolutionary nationalist movement in Africa but many a tactical approach to the Colonial Office by bourgeois African politicians were worked out with Padmore's advice and not infrequently under his direct inspiration. He kept a strict eye on all colonial struggles, maintaining contacts with movements, organisations and individuals in the Far East. At the same time he published for general reading *How Britain Rules Africa* and *Africa and World Peace*, for which Sir Stafford Cripps wrote an introduction.

My own approach was different, and although I was immersed in the British revolutionary movement I worked on the application of Marxist and Leninist ideas to the coming African revolution, and for this purpose wrote *The Black Jacobins*, a full-scale study of the only successful revolution of people of African descent that the world had yet seen—the revolt of the slaves in the French colony of San Domingo during the French revolution, which ended in the establishment of the state of Haiti. Nkrumah and other revolutionaries read and absorbed the book. In the French edition it has been studied and referred to in the French press of the left, for the light which it throws on the relations of French imperialist policy and North Africa. It is treasured by most African nationalists and is widely known among Negro leaders in the United States. Historical in form, it drew its contemporaneousness, as all such books must, from the living struggle around us, and particularly from the daily activity that centred around Padmore and the African Bureau. It represented in a specific form the general ideas that we held at the time, and it is still the only book of its kind, perhaps the most direct attack on the [colonialist] myth that has yet appeared in England.

The theoretical basis of the book, amply demonstrated, is that in a period of world-wide revolutionary change, such as that of 1789–1815 and our period which began with 1917, the revolutionary crisis lifts backward peoples over centuries and projects them into the very forefront of the advanced movement of the day. The slaves in San Domingo were two-thirds raw Africans from the Guinea Coast in a strange country, many of them not knowing the language. Yet with the example and slogans of the French revolution, these for the most part illiterate blacks organised themselves in a manner fully comparable to the great achievements of the same movement in France, produced a body of great leaders in politics and administration, differentiated among themselves in clear alignments of right, left and centre, and all in all showed themselves immensely superior in every human quality to the highly educated colonial officials and ministers in France who ruled them. The final conclusion must be given here:

> These black Haitian labourers and the mulattoes have given us an example to study. Despite the temporary reaction of fascism, the prevailing standards of human liberty and equality are infinitely more advanced and more profound than those current in 1789. Judged relatively by these standards, the millions of blacks in Africa and the few of them who are educated are as much pariahs in that vast prison as the blacks and mulattoes of San Domingo in the eighteenth century. The imperialists envisage an eternity of African exploitation: the African is backward, ignorant ... They dream dreams. If in 1788 anyone had told the Comte de Lauserne, the Minister; the Comte de Peynier, the Governor; General Rochambeau, the soldier;

Moreau de Saint-Mary [*sic*], the historian; Barbe de Marbois, the bureaucrat, that the thousands of dumb brutes who were whipped to labour at dawn and whipped back at midnight, who submitted to their mutilations, burnings and other savageries, some of whom would not even move unless they were whipped, if these fine gentlemen had been told that in three years the blacks would shake off their chains and face extermination rather than put them on again, they would have thought the speaker mad. While if today one were to suggest to any white colonial potentate that among those blacks whom they rule are men so infinitely their superior in ability, energy, range of vision, and tenacity of purpose that in a hundred years' time these whites would be remembered only because of their contact with the blacks, one would get some idea of what the Counts, Marquises, and other colonial magnates of the day thought of Jean-Francois, Toussaint, and Rigaud when the revolt first began.

If I show scant respect for the British colonial ministers, governors and other officials, it is because I have met them before and have unimpeachable knowledge of how they think and act.

The book concludes:

The blacks of Africa are more advanced, nearer ready than were the slaves of San Domingo . . . Imperialism vaunts its exploitation of the wealth of Africa for the benefit of civilisation. In reality, from the very nature of its system of production for profit it strangles the real wealth of the continent— the creative capacity of the African people. The African faces a long and difficult road and he will need guidance. But he will tread it fast because he will walk upright.

This was not directed only against the imperialists. We had learnt from hard experience that, in those days in particular, not only socialists of the right and of the left needed to have this placed before them in unambiguous terms. The Communists of the metropolitan countries were all for the African revolution (until the Kremlin changed the line), but they continually wrote and spoke in terms of "giving" freedom to Africans. In time I was to learn that the Trotskyists also saw revolutionary politics as the giving of leadership to masses who were otherwise helpless without it, and the Africans (and American Negroes) being the most backward, of necessity needed the most leadership. But the reader is asked to note the complete confidence in the self-emancipation of the African people from imperialism as a contemporary political issue that imbued everything we did, and if he is interested, to compare it with the dreary repetition of percentages of literacy, centuries of barbarism, centuries of training, and all the rubbish now in the dustbins that characterised the official attitudes and pronouncements of the time. Colonial politics is not a parlour game, and it is a duty not to give but to remind all concerned of the blindness and folly of many of our present-day colonial pundits and their immediate ancestors.

But the book had other premises, raising urgent questions which had to be readily revised and are by no means settled. It took armed rebellion for granted as the only road to metropolitan and colonial freedom, and from this premise flowed certain theoretical perspectives. The San Domingo revolution had been directly inspired by the French revolution, had developed side by side with it, and had had an enormous influence upon the course of that revolution. The book therefore constantly implied that the African revolution would be similarly contingent upon the socialist revolution in Europe. It did not envisage an independent movement of Africans as being able to succeed in the face of the enormous military power that a stable imperialist government would be able to bring to bear. This has been apparently contradicted by the experience of the Ghana revolution, but conversely reinforced during the same period by the experience of the revolt in Kenya. If a British government had been unable to send assistance to Kenya, or a revolutionary British government had been in a position where the success of the Kenya revolt against the counter-revolution was necessary for its own preservation (this is what happened during the French revolution) the revolt in Kenya, though made by the same people, would have been entirely different. It would have had socialist allies and would have been made under socialist slogans, representatives of the British government would have taken part in it and guided it, and the result, particularly in the modern world, would have been an African government under which (of this there can be no question to any who have studied the San Domingo revolution) white settlers, once they saw no other way out, would have fraternised, male and female, with General Kimathi, General China and their associates and successors. This has happened before and will happen again, and we must not be too surprised if from limbo querulous voices assure us that this too was the settled policy of the government. Whatever the future of tropical Africa will be, one thing is certain, that it will not be what the colonial powers are trying to make of it. It will be violent and strange, with the most abrupt and unpredictable changes in economic relations, race relations, territorial boundaries and everything else.

The work of the Bureau continued all through the war and in 1945 there came a sharp break with the theory outlined above. The Bureau changed its position from the achievement of independence by armed rebellion to the achievement of independence by non-violent mass action. But to say that is one thing, to carry it out in practice is another. The problem has never been treated fully even in the publications of the Bureau, and it is time that this was done.

No serious politician is unalterably opposed to a policy of armed rebellion. The question is always armed rebellion by whom, against whom and for what. A great number of people in the world were for the armed rebellion of the Germans against Hitler, especially during the war. It is a significant testimony to where our society has reached that thousands of dyed-in-the-wool conservatives found themselves urging on and cheering the rebellion led by Hungarian workers under the leadership of workers' councils against a totalitarian government. Against a revolutionary dictatorship in Britain, the supporters of the Establishment would most certainly plot an armed rebellion. Against a fascist dictatorship the workers of Britain most certainly would do the same. Political thought today is in no sphere lower, and nowhere more than in the United States, than when it seeks the condemnation of armed rebellion in the fact that the rebels' forces have only forty-nine per cent of the votes.

When the revolution and the counter-revolution in any country are approaching an ultimate crisis, it is usually the supporters of the existing regime who raise the question of armed rebellion by constituting themselves into all sorts of military or semi-military organisations which enjoy the protection of the government. Central Europe was full of these before Hitler came to power. In the United States today, in the Southern states, the defenders of segregation have formed themselves into White Citizens' Councils. In response to these, the revolutionary forces—especially if the military forces of the counter-revolution begin to attack them, break up their meetings and murder their leaders, and feel that the government in power has no firm foundation—in their turn begin to form extra-legal organisations. Thus both sides move to the ultimate climax, and the question of forty-nine or fifty-one per cent of the votes fades into insignificance except as propaganda. Elections then become merely a means whereby each side can draw its own conclusions as to its own strength and the strength of the opposing side. Under these circumstances public warning of the necessity for armed struggle and open and secret military preparations are taking place on both sides.

In a colonial country and especially in tropical Africa, these moves and counter-moves are impossible. The colonial government in power can call upon the power of the metropolitan country as soon as it is aware of any dangerous movement against it. To stake independence upon armed rebellion was therefore to have as a precondition the collapse or military paralysis of the metropolitan government. It was in other words to place the initiative for African struggle upon the European proletariat. In *The Black Jacobins* are the words: "Let the blacks but hear from Europe the slogans of Revolution, and the Internationale, in the same concrete manner that the slaves of San Domingo heard Liberty and Equality and the Marseillaise, and from the mass uprising will emerge the Toussaints, the Christophes, and the Dessalines. They will hear." Those were exactly the ideas that we had had.

But by the end of the war the proletariat of Britain and France had not spoken. Imperialism still held sway at home. Only a radical alteration in theory could form a basis for action. The perspective of armed rebellion was abandoned (though held in reserve) and non-violent mass action was substituted.

Both the advocates of armed rebellion and of militant non-violence follow the same road up to a certain point, and that point is the general strike. A Marxist revolutionist uses the same means as the militant advocate of non-violence to mobilise the population. He uses all grievances, demonstrations, mass rallies, an unceasing attack upon the government, exposure and denunciation of the timid or reactionary elements in the mass movements whose vacillations might weaken the will and sense of solidarity of the masses; and ultimately, when the movement is ripe and the occasion presents itself calls the population out in a general strike and faces the government with the unified opposition of the people. It is here, however, that the problem begins. Lenin, and after him Trotsky, summing up the lessons of their own tremendous experiences and studies, laid it down categorically that it is adventurism of the worst kind to lead (or sometimes to follow) a population to the stage of the general strike against a government without at the same time openly warning the people and making armed preparation for the fact that you cannot stop at a general strike. It is the ultimate challenge to the ruling powers. Either you go on, and that means taking the power from them by force, or you retreat. And if, after having taken the people so far, you retreat, it is certain that the ruling powers will recognise your weakness, recognise the demoralisation that is likely to set in within the revolutionary forces, and most certainly counter-attack with all the armed force at their disposal and crush the movement for a long time to come. This does not mean to say that there are not general strikes for a brief period, say, twenty-four hours or even for less, one day, which do not immediately involve the movement towards the seizure of power by force or the immediate resort to arms by the government. But these brief general strikes are merely stages in the mobilisation of the people for the ultimate challenge to the government. The general strike poses the question: "Who is to be master in the house?" Furthermore, the great Marxists denounced social democracy for playing with the general strike, hoping to bring down the government by the mere threat of force. By this means one reactionary government might be replaced by another. But they considered it criminal not to be prepared for the fact that ultimately the decision would be made with arms.

But the situation was not quite the same in the colonies. The colonial government forces consisted of soldiers and police who were able to deal with a riot or a demonstration of a few thousand people. They could easily shoot down demonstrators, very often they would provoke them in order to put a quick end to a movement which threatened to involve large masses. But colonial governments had neither the forces nor the experience to deal with a general strike of the great body of the people who refused to be provoked.

It was calculated that the organisation of the masses, in trade unions, cooperatives, political organisations, those that existed and new ones, in whatever form they presented themselves, strikes in industry, political demonstrations, etc. were all constitutional, and therefore, in theory at least, could be carried out with a fair chance of being able to avoid cruel reprisals. By the time the masses were organised, it would be possible then to challenge the government. This also was constitutional in that it did not involve armed rebellion.

But it was just here that the theory was skating on very thin ice indeed, because a general strike and an economic boycott which threatened or could actually bring the whole social and economic life of a colony to a standstill could not stay there. Either the government would have to give way or it would be compelled to mobilise forces at its disposal or send to the home government for larger forces, in order to intimidate or to crush the total disruption of society with which it was faced. Risk though it was, a colonial territory, particularly a territory where the government had a very slender basis in the population, was a territory where the risk could be taken. It required that the organisation of the masses should be complete, a gigantic task, and that further, the control of the leadership should be such as to prevent sporadic or partial violence, particularly at an early stage which would give the government an excuse or an opportunity to act.

Changes in political strategy are often motivated by appreciations of deep social changes which have not been fully formulated but of which all involved are very much aware. The war had seen, in Britain in particular, an immense objective growth of the power of the proletariat in the social structure. On the other hand, as a result of the war, of revolutions and crises which had shaken contemporary society to its foundations for almost forty consecutive years, the bourgeoisie had lost its self-confidence in the face of a united mass movement. It had lost the confidence of large sections of the population on whom formerly it could rely. It had been accepted on all sides in the period previous to the war that in the face of a Labour government with a substantial majority which attempted to put its hands upon the sources of economic power, the bourgeoisie would most certainly reply with an attempt at armed rebellion. Lenin and Trotsky believed this and John Maynard Keynes also believed it. It was an axiom in the revolutionary movement in all branches that India could not gain its freedom except by armed rebellion, and this rebellion would have to be led by the proletariat.

By 1945 it was clear that the bourgeoisie in Britain could not attempt extra-legal action against a legally elected Labour government; it was fairly clear in 1945 that it would never be able to carry out military action against India in revolt. The relation of forces had changed and changed decisively to the increase in energy and audacity of any colonial people determined to revolt. Undoubtedly the influence of Gandhi's non-violent campaigns played a great role. But in 1945 when the change was made, India was not yet free.

Marxism is a guide to action in a specific system of social relations which takes into account the always changing relationship of forces in an always changing world situation. But political analysis and political directive can only go thus far. They are a guide, not a blueprint. It took the revolution in the Gold Coast itself to make possible a true evaluation of this policy elaborated in 1945. So it always is with a theory. What is written here does not embrace all that is involved and it is certain that it could not have been written at the time nor was there any need to do so. But when all is said and done the new political directive, breaking with the well-established ideas of the pre-war period, is one of the great theoretical achievements of the present age, perhaps the first real break towards what the Marxist movement requires today, the application of the traditional principles of Marxism in complete independence of the Stalinist perversion. It is to be noted that the theory did not reject armed rebellion, but held it in reserve in the event that the political and moral pressure envisaged failed to influence British imperialism.

Where the new theory comes from is only less important than the theory itself and in fact you cannot separate the two. First of all, there was the work of Padmore and the Bureau he founded, as I have described it over the ten years that followed his break with the Comintern in 1935. The second influence was the work of another man of African descent, this time from America, the celebrated Dr. W. E. B. Du Bois. Du Bois was writing authoritatively on the American Negro in the Home University Series even before World War I. By 1945 he had taken always a prominent and often a leading part in all types of efforts in the United States to bring home to the American people the need to cut out the national cancer of racial segregation. Before Padmore organised the Bureau with its concentration on day to day problems, Du Bois had educated a whole generation in the more literary and historical manner that was characteristic of the period, and he reached the climax of his theoretical work in 1935 with *Black Reconstruction*, a history of the American Civil War written from the point of view of the Negro slaves and the Negro people as a whole. Though limited in scope, he approached his subject broadly, and this book is still incomparably the best account of that great event in the development of the American people. Despite his preoccupation with the Negro question in the United States, Du Bois had for many years devoted immense time and energy to the problems of Africa, its past history, its present problems and its future emancipation. He organised a series of world conferences to bring together the peoples of Africa and the people of African descent with the aim of organising a united movement for the emancipation of Africa as an indispensable step in the achievement of freedom and equality for people of the coloured race everywhere. To this movement he gave the name Pan-Africanism. His actual political programme was a programme of militant non-violence. In 1945 Du Bois and Padmore merged their ideas and influence to hold the fifth Pan-African conference in Manchester, and it was at this conference that the resolution analysed above was produced. Du Bois, then seventy-three years of age, flew from America to attend.

This conference, however, was unlike all other previous conferences of the kind. It was attended by over two hundred delegates from all over the world, the great majority of them engaged in trade union work or other type of work connected with the organisation of the masses of workers and farmers in Africa. Nkrumah had landed in Britain in June 1945. By October he was joint political secretary of the conference with Padmore and he made the report on the problems of the West African colonies and European domination. The merging of the two currents represented by Padmore and Du Bois and the entry of Nkrumah signalised the ending of one period and the beginning of another.

Until Nkrumah came, it is true to say that despite the faithful work of some Africans and a few Negro workers, the moving spirits in this work were West Indian intellectuals living in England. The Bureau needed money and organisation in order to live a material existence at all. This had been supplied in the first case by [Ras T.] Makonnen, another West Indian, a man of fantastic energy and organisational gifts who found the money, found the premises, kept them in order not only as an office but as a sort of free hostel for Africans and people of African descent and their friends who were in any way connected with the Bureau or needed assistance, organised meetings, interested people and did his share as propagandist and agitator. When during the war he was able to run a successful restaurant business in Manchester, he devoted most of the money he made into furthering the interests of the work and helping to finance the fifth Pan-African Conference. Chairman of the conference was another West Indian, this time from British Guiana, Dr. Peter Milliard, who had had experience in the United States and had practised for many years in Manchester. Many gifted young West Indians, though not organisationally connected with the Bureau, were under its influence and shared its emphasis on the importance for all peoples of African descent of the emancipation of Africa. It would be beyond the scope of this book to explain why West Indians devoted themselves with so much energy and single-mindedness to the African question. But they did so. They had had the benefit of the excellent, if rather academic, system of secondary education which existed in the islands. Having no native culture, no native language, no native religion and being raised entirely in the British tradition, they mixed easily in English intellectual and left-wing political circles. In the political thirties they participated fully in the intense discussions and activities of the time, and few in England, except European refugees, had had more actual inside experience of revolutionary politics than Padmore. It was to this circle with its accumulated knowledge, experience and wide contacts that Nkrumah was introduced in June 1945. Nowhere in the world could he have found a better school. For two years and a half he worked and lived in the very closest association with Padmore.

Nkrumah not only took. He gave. This large body of active workers in Africa who attended the Manchester conference symbolised a new stage of the work in England. Nkrumah brought to this work what had never been done before. To theoretical study, propaganda and agitation, the building and maintaining of contacts abroad, he added the organisation politically of Africans and people of African descent in London. He helped to found a West African National Secretariat in London for the purpose of organising the struggle in West Africa. The leading members of this were Africans, and thus Africans with roots in Africa began to take over from the West Indians who had hitherto been the leaders. Most important of all, he was the leading spirit in the formation of the Coloured Workers' Association of Great Britain. Through this organisation he linked together the students and the workers from Africa and the people of African descent living in England, organised them and carried on political work among them. The Bureau had never done anything like this.

It is now possible to form some estimate of what Nkrumah represents. An African whose mother was a petty trader, he received his early education in the Gold Coast. But at the age of twenty-five or thereabouts he went to the United States and lived there for ten years. His academic education and his reading should not be allowed to take a preponderant place in this development. This African had lived an intensely active life among all classes of the coloured people in the United States, and that life is the life of a very advanced and highly civilised community, sharpened and broadened by its incessant conflict against the domination and persecution of official society. Not only in books but in his contact with people and his very active intellectual and political life, he was the inheritor of the centuries of material struggle and intellectual thought which the Negro people in the United States had developed from all sources in order to help them in their effort to emancipate themselves. Nkrumah had an astonishing capacity to learn, and there was much to learn in the United States that has not yet found its place in books. At the University of Pennsylvania he worked with students who were for the most part white.

After this shaping experience, in London he found himself at the centre of the highly political consciousness of post-war Europe within which had grown ideas and organisations for years specifically devoted to the cause which had always been the centre of his life. Thus the man who landed at Takoradi in December 1947 was, in the most precise sense of the term, a unique individual. In his elemental African consciousness of centuries of wrong and an unquenchable desire for freedom, there had met and fused, by theory and practice, some of the most diverse, powerful and highly developed currents in the modern world. He was a man strong enough to embrace them and be expanded by them, yet always keeping them disciplined and subordinate to his particular purpose. To this day the Colonial Office and the government have no idea of what hit them, and if they haven't now, it can be imagined how blank they were in 1947. While they were meditating on how to restore order after the economic boycott and the shooting of the ex-servicemen, Nkrumah sat alone and wrote out his precise plans for what they would have considered stark insanity, their final and irrevocable ejection from Ghana.

Note

Extract from C. L. R. James, *Nkrumah and the Ghana Revolution* (London: Allison and Busby, 1977), 61–78.

Translator's Foreword by Pierre Naville
to the 1949 / 1983 French Editions

Translator's Foreword (1949)

I believe that this work—written in 1938—will be a real revelation for many French readers: that is because, in its underlying dynamics and even in its specific details, the history of the Saint-Domingue Revolution heralds almost exactly the current drama that we have successively dubbed *colonial territory, Empire, Overseas France*, and most recently the *French Union*.

I could undoubtedly be challenged with the observation that history never repeats itself, that 150 years separate us from the contemporaries of Toussaint Louverture, that living conditions both internationally and of Black societies have altered significantly . . . That is to a large extent true, especially if the various aspects of the two situations are considered separately, as free-standing phenomena and as it were quantitatively. But if the general structure of the events and the conflicts that served as a driver for them are taken into account, the similarities quickly become apparent, as does the recurrence of such a huge drama on an extended basis. Because this time, in repeating itself, history did not go from tragedy to farce . . . On the contrary. There are in fact cases—and this is one of those cases—in which, for a sufficiently brief period (at least on a certain scale, as it can run to one or two centuries or more), history does not simply repeat itself, but boils itself down terribly so that what was originally experienced as tragedy recurs as inevitability. The present crisis of the French colonial system is not a caricature of its previous developments, upheavals and disasters—it is, on the contrary, their exaggeration and logical conclusion, and a form of being crushed by fate.

It is undoubtedly for this reason that the history of the Haitian Revolution, with its Black, colored and white actors, has been hardly at all evoked in the French public consciousness over the past 150 years, and has in a way been so discreetly concealed that no major book has been devoted to it in France. Neither the 150th anniversary of the 1789 Revolution, nor even the 100th anniversary of the 1848 Revolution and the definitive judicial abolition of slavery that accompanied it, have brought the historical facts into the foreground.

This major event, which was the first successful slave revolt in history, has left its mark on the bourgeois imagination as an impossible conflict, and often as well, by extension, on the working-class and popular imagination too. The circumstances of the Revolution, its brutal events and ultimate triumph reminded the French on a daily basis of too many live issues, of too many problems that have remained deeply challenging, of bloody reality and of short-term threats—as if they were the fatal conclusion of its imperial history; everything that was necessary done for the memory of the event to fade.

To no avail, by the way! Today nobody in France can fail to be struck by the extraordinary topicality of the racial and social struggles which took place in the Caribbean Sea 150 years ago. There is nobody who—in my view—can fail to understand in the light of those struggles the deeper meaning of what is currently happening before our eyes, stretching from that same Caribbean Sea to the South China Sea, and nobody who cannot use them as a means of reflecting thoughtfully on the very evident current crisis in the French colonial system, now dubbed (with this appellation perhaps adopted too late) the "French Union."

Mr James, a native of Jamaica [sic], wrote—and purposefully wrote—the history of the Haitian Revolution and of the War of Independence which led to the Constitution of the Republic of Haiti, without losing from sight subsequent developments in the world. This is implicit throughout the book. But he knew that what happened there—in the sugar and coffee paradise—was a form of anticipation of what would emerge later in all the colonies of the major powers, undoubtedly as a result of the particular effects of subsequent developments, in much more complex and fearsome local and more general circumstances, but ultimately as a result of similar social circumstances.

That is why his book, although it is primarily a history book, is also a "history lesson"—and a lesson to which we should pay attention. Not to avoid the repetition of events which—I say it again—have been inevitable, but because colonial policies and all the economic, social, cultural and even strategic problems that have resulted from them have reached a stage of maturation at which change is becoming apparent—and at which, as a result, what was for several centuries seen as the fate and systematic impoverishment that are characteristic of a thriving capitalist system can once again become freedom, a new structure for the relationship between classes, races and nations, in such a way that History could then set off again in the direction of another story, one that would be much less ominous, much more intelligent, unexpected and even a happy one.

| | | | |

What then is so implacably modern behind the masks of these white colonists and black Jacobins? Oh, it is not only cruelty, blood liberally spilled, the brutal release of forces that are, until the present day, vital to the evolution of human societies! It is also the structure of relationships of dependency as well as of contributions of specific racial groups, quarrelsome conflicts of interest, political intrigue, the logic of engagement on battlefields, the spirit of emancipation, hope in the face of a moment that is at once painful, hated, fanatical, and insatiable. It is everything that we still experience every day, and that exercises the sharp tongues of journalists, novelists and poets. It is all of these conflicts whose astonishing and now wearily familiar mechanisms the author demonstrates before our very eyes—just as it is also our responsibility to explain carefully, rigorously and vigilantly the expanding conflicts that are now the substance of our own reality.

When the French people, in 1789, rose up against the monarchy and its sense of having a divine right, those in power hardly possessed a single colony, although it is true that the one it had was the most precious and the richest in the world at the time. It counterbalanced the British, Spanish, Portuguese and Dutch colonies. Louis XV had lost nearly all the rest. And it was the French Revolution that would transform this island—Saint-Domingue—for a decade into the theatre of a series of entangled and superimposed conflicts of which only today can we understand the extent to which they in a way epitomized the blueprint of the antagonisms that would later be reproduced in all the parts of the world on a volcanic scale. Let us list only the main outlines of these antagonisms.

First, the framework of a *racial struggle* in which a *class struggle* was inscribed. Black people are objects of trade, like any other livestock; their status is much lower than that of serfs. But it is they who have to cultivate the white men's land. By bowing to the commands of color, they therefore obey at the same time the commands of economics. The struggle for civil and economic rights is therefore simultaneously a struggle of the workers against the property owners, and indirectly against the Atlantic trade: a class struggle.

This struggle is complicated by the specific situation of the colored population, and by the divisions between white Royalists, colonists, minor republican bourgeois civil servants, "poor whites," etc. Class struggles in the colonies are much more complicated than in the metropolitan centre, but there is also a need to untangle these strands by constantly resorting to consideration of the social interests involved, as well as of the political trends and the ideologies of the various ethnic groups who interpret them in their own way. This class struggle was driven to the extremes of violence, civil war and of war itself. Unfortunately its acuteness exceeded the possibilities afforded by economic development at the time: the stubborn refusal of the whites and colonists to give anything up caused the whole country to collapse for a long period into a state of destitution.

Then, the struggle took a *national* turn. The enslaved Black population had been imported from Africa, but Saint-Domingue had become their land. Americans and Australians are today also immigrant "nationals," whites who have come from Europe. A hardworking, established majority population, the Blacks represented the future nation in Saint-Domingue: the struggle for racial and class-related emancipation inevitably became a struggle for independence, a national struggle. This is what guaranteed its definitive success, after Toussaint had exhausted all the opportunities for agreement with the French bourgeoisie.

Thirdly, at the very core of the black and coloured nation, there emerged *a division between landowners and workers*, between young members of the bourgeoisie and the working classes, and this itself gave rise to conflicts, even though these conflicts often appeared at the time as nothing more than disagreements. There were members of the Black population, and especially of the coloured population, for whom the Revolution and independence also signified the consolidation of privileges recently wrenched from the whites. This seriously influenced the behaviour of certain of Toussaint's generals, and perhaps of Toussaint himself.

Fourthly, these struggles that are internal to the systems of the French Revolution are to be inscribed in turn in the context of a *major imperial rivalry, on a global scale, between France, Britain and Spain*. This rivalry played a major role in the development of the struggle in Saint-Domingue, at times obscuring and misrepresenting its meanings, at times accelerating it, illuminating it and providing it with a real sense of sharpness. The government in London attempted to exploit France's difficulties to guarantee its own influence over an island just next to the British possessions in the

Caribbean. By his whole approach, Toussaint revealed great perspicacity in this area.

The four characteristics that we have just outlined underpin every detail of the events, and all the particular forms they assumed. In other words, the principles, tactics and methods of struggle deployed by both sides in this theatre of conflict received their particular form from these four principal characteristics of French colonial history in the late eighteenth century. Yet these characteristics have remained present in the subsequent development of French colonial history, which experienced a new leap forward under the July Monarchy with the conquest of Algeria, and developed into an imperial-ist policy on a global scale that has today reached a period of general crisis. This also means that the methods of struggle tried out in Saint-Domingue by the various classes, populations and social groups involved in the struggle have been transferred into a much larger arena where they have been enhanced by entirely new experiences. Let us take a look then at this general history of the colonial policies of the French bourgeoisie.

| | | | |

It can be said that France has had three colonial empires, the succession of which coincides with the major shifts in its internal politics. The first was conquered under Louis XIV and Louis XV, with Colbert serving as its first organizer and bringing a minimum of system to the role. Almost entirely lost by the end of Louis XV's reign, it was reduced to nothing under the Revolution and Empire, even though Bonaparte took his troops as far as the pyramids. The Saint-Domingue revolt had sealed the fate of this first empire.

The second was born with the conquest of Algeria after 1830. At its roots were Louis-Philippe and the new industrial and commercial bourgeoisie. Kabylie was the bridgehead of an African empire that stretched first from Tunisia to the march of Morocco, then to the colonial establishments of Senegal, Guinea and Gabon, and which almost reached Egypt around 1880. But once again, the Empire—Napoleon III's France—had replaced longer term hopes generated by the colonial market with a European and American policy that then had a more immediate importance for an industrial sector in a fully expansive mode.

The third colonial empire, which was that of the Third Republic, fixed itself to the previously conquered imperial sphere, and was established after 1871, as a form of retaliation for defeat in Europe, and as an unavoidable requirement of financial capital then reaching its peak. The first phase consisted of the takeover of the Indochinese peninsula from bases in Cochinchine, the conquest of Madagascar and deep penetration into East and West Africa. The second phase consisted of the progressive conquest of the whole of Morocco and the Syrian "mandate" acquired after 1918.

Around the peripheries of the major zones of expansion that are associated with these three colonial empires, France had since the beginnings of its world power maintained settlements—and these had progressively multiplied, such as with Guadeloupe and Martinique, New Caledonia, Tahiti and Reunion Island, French Guiana and trading posts in India. And now, look how the whole colonial realm has been shaken to its very foundations, despite the lethargy of a Parliament which is seeking to perpetuate the tradition of a "smothered" colonialism: silence and action! Yet it is too late—because once more, as was the case at the time of Toussaint Louverture, things have been ignited already.

Throughout the development of France's three colonial empires, the sequence of which I have outlined above, there are to be found concerns, tendencies and approaches which became more complex, but nevertheless scarcely vary at all. These aspects were of course more or less evident in the colonial development of all the major European capitalist centres, most notably in that of Great Britain, the Netherlands and Belgium.

The elements common to the major world imperial systems are due to the fact that—despite rivalries between them—they are all functions of a single set of dynamics and of a single world market: the shared need for global expansion leads to antagonism between particular countries. But in the individual behaviour of each of these nations there is an original element that must be examined carefully if you wish to write the history of it and foresee its new developments. Just like Britain and France, for example, Russia was drawn in the nineteenth century into a policy of extensive imperialist expansion: however, the country was not in concrete terms pulled in this direction in the same way; its "interests" were located elsewhere than those of France and Britain, and must be studied according to their distinctive features.

At first sight, it appears that geographical location, climate and demographics play a key role in determining the distinctive aspects of colonial development. And these factors are indeed far from being negligible, and can on occasion—on a particular point, or in relation to a particular question—be a determining factor. For example, there is no doubt that Turkestan or Siberia were geographically more suited to colonization by Russia than by Britain. But was Britain more predisposed in terms of geography than Russia or France to subjugate Hindustan? It is difficult to say with certainty. The point is that beneath determining factors relating to geography or climate, there are economic mechanisms that regulate with a much more exclusive authority the forms of imperialist expansion on earth. This expansion depends much more on the specific forms of economic development present in the colonizing center than on the geographical or climatic circumstances in the territories that are themselves being colonized. The great European states seized with a frenzy of equal intensity deserts, human anthills, impenetrable forests, open coastlines, islands and seas, tropical countries and cold regions. But in all of these cases, the penetration and conquest of territories apparently very dissimilar from a geographical, climatic or demographic viewpoint conformed to analogous motives, followed comparable methods and led to similar outcomes.

First came the traveller, the pirate, the trader, the missionary; big companies then followed; fleets and armies finally came with administrators and scientists at the same time as the tide of capital initiated the establishment of structures in which the fruit of the ready-made labour of the indigenous populations would be harnessed to allow the accumulation of huge profits. People and economic systems from the colonial centre had to adapt to geography and climate, and not vice versa. Whence the development of the political ecology, health, scientific research of all kinds—including military tactics—which went hand in hand with the extension of exploitation.

Yet in line with this singular mechanism, France had to give its colonial empire a very specific hallmark—and it is this that today represents its weakness. Commercially, it was unable to escape from the principles of the "colonial pact" established at the time of Colbert; financially and economically, it had no real desire to establish a significant infrastructure in the colonized territory, to create a large consumer market, to invest and reinvest production capital; politically, it could neither definitively defeat former local leaders, nor populate the territories with its own people, nor fully "assimilate" the indigenous population to its own nationals. And on top of that, it spread— willy nilly—the ideas of its heraldic trinity: Liberty, Equality, Fraternity, presenting to the oppressed colonial populations the whole gamut of general statements that not could be distorted even by history lessons in which the kings of the jungle were called descendants of the Gauls.

Saint-Domingue was already familiar with all of this, on a reduced scale and in conditions specific to the period: its trade was bound up with Nantes,

Bordeaux or Le Havre; there was a lack of local attention to industrial equipment used for processing agricultural products, which remained a monopoly for those same French ports; there were rapid and extraordinary profits; there were slavery and forced labour; and there was the creation, under the auspices of Catholicism, of a tiny Black "elite," sometimes raised to this rank on the whim of a mistress. And in this mix there was the seed sowed by Enlightenment philosophy, which would grow in these East Indies with the force of the tropics. Bonaparte himself was unable to dominate this complex situation.

Yet France no longer has either Bonaparte or Napoleon, and its fate has been established along similar lines in its new colonial empires—and will perhaps come undone in the same way too. But this time, on a stage which encompasses the complete circumference of a tropical line of latitude, in the complex context of international conflicts that have reached their breaking point, and without the means of founding one day a fourth colonial empire. This time it is international socialism that will benefit from the legacy.

What then is the value of this last-minute attempt called the "Union française?" Is it really the swan song of a colonial centre about to experience the same fate as Spain and Portugal—or rather is it the way of establishing an unexpected renewal and a lasting form of solidarity? Is it not the rather shaky evidence of a sort of Late Empire, in which the exarchs of the final days of Byzantium must yield to the growing protests of the freed populations, to forces only controlled with great difficulty—of a Byzantium which might have the opportunity to avoid fading away when faced with Barbarians, but not when faced with the power of real progress? And is it not that the peoples of Asia, Africa and the Americas are rising up today against a relatively recent yoke, against antiquated institutions and customs, against a fate inscribed with perpetual disaster? That the Vietnamese, the Moroccans, the Tunisians, the Senegalese, the Congolese, the people of the Caribbean are straining against their loathed straitjacket in the name of social emancipation enhanced with a socialist hope, making more progress in a single movement than other peoples similarly subdued but too subtly bound to be able boldly to untie their bonds? Is it not like a form of dialectical revenge, like the explanation in the eyes of history, if such a thing exists, of the imperial conduct of the tricoloured Byzantium?

In fact, the general demands of populations colonized by France inevitably challenge all the current structures of the "Union française," derived from the traditional colonial system; far from requiring partial or local solutions, they must rely on principles with a more general significance. It is in this way that *a genuinely socialist solution to the crisis in the "Union française"* is being conceived.

The capitalist solution to this crisis—if capitalism can for some time provide any solution—consists on the other hand of fragmenting the situations as much as possible, and looking for a different solution for each case, so that there can be proliferation on a global scale of the classic policy based on the principle of divide and rule. This policy is all the more deceptive since it presents itself as a unitary solution.

Indeed, the Constitution of the Fourth Republic has created bodies such as the Conseil de la République and the Assemblée de l'Union française which centralize the business and representation of the overseas territories in a much more wide-ranging way than was ever the case under the Third Republic; the President of the Republic is at the same time president of the Union française, meaning that the new constitution has granted the arbiter of French capitalism a role that he would never have dreamed of adopting in the context of the 1875 constitution. But this policy of "unity" among the organizations running the Union conceals tactics of division in the territories themselves, the goal of which is always to guarantee as strict a domination as possible over the financial, industrial and commercial interests of the metropolitan centre. The French Caribbean, for example, was departmentalized at the same time as Algeria—which already answered to the Ministry of the Interior—was permitted the beginnings of autonomy; while yielding to Vietnam certain rights of self-government, France tightened in the same proportion its links with Cambodia and Laos; French West Africa and French Equatorial Africa were granted enhanced direct representation at the same time as their links with the authorities in Paris were becoming increasingly strained; Morocco remains deprived of political rights at the same time as there are attempts to involve its ruling classes in economic development, etc.

In all of these cases, partial solutions—inspired by the policy of the moment, as well as by fear of more unified anticolonial demands—have been attempted since 1945, without any real success. However, the moment has come when the general consciousness of subject peoples is, through demands specific to their circumstances, formulating more general solutions. And these solutions presuppose a complete reform of the colonial system, the principal characteristics of which have been outlined above—and this reform can only be durable if it abandons the ways of capitalism and leads to a federation based on genuine equality. In this case, it is of course linked to a social revolution in the metropolitan centre itself. But it needs to be recognized that, until now, colonized peoples seem to have had a much clearer awareness of these requirements than socialist movements in France itself. Through their struggle against imperialist stranglehold, in their desire for independence and national revival, these people were able to maintain a sense of social and anti-oppressive solidarity with the workers in France. They were fully aware that, without the strong support of European socialists, they were at risk of falling into new imperialist clutches, those located now in the U.S.A.

It is not superfluous to say a few words here about the attempted "redevelopment" of "backward countries" via which the U.S.A. is currently attempting to replace France and Britain, whose decline remains uneven. For its part, the British Commonwealth has very specific features, which—as far as it is concerned—make the new American policy much more difficult. Most of its principal elements have in effect acquired dominion status, even political independence (Canada, Australia, New Zealand, South Africa, Pakistan, India, Burma) on the basis of enhanced autonomy, so that each of these countries finds in itself reasons to resist in some way or other American proposals and pressures.

But this is not the case in the Union française. The flaws of colonization have suddenly been revealed in the failings of the "mother country," incapable now—as a result of its impoverishment in its own domestic context—to undertake the effort of modernization that might have linked it more firmly to local "elites," or at least to the nascent local middle classes. And in the face of increasingly clear and general demands made by the working-class populations of the former colonies, the United States comes up with extensive capital resources, as if this were the system already and inevitably designated to take things over.

It is perfectly clear today that one of the main war aims of the U.S.A. has indeed been to reconstruct a global policy on the backs of Britain and France. Whence the "anti-colonialist" attitude of the U.S.A., always hostile to the direct domination of colonized territories, always in favour of an "open door" policy—a door by which American capital, technicians and administrators can strive to penetrate the private hunting grounds of other imperial powers. This concern was the central (and barely disguised) impulse of Franklin Roosevelt's policy, of his squabbles with Churchill during the war, and of his willingness to enter into an agreement with the U.S.S.R. in Europe. Roosevelt made no secret of this to his advisers. His son Elliott—a fairly brutal wheeler-dealer—repeats this at length in the little book he devoted to the subject of his father: "Churchill told me, Roosevelt recounted on one occasion, that he was not Her Majesty's Prime Minister for the sole purpose of overseeing the dissolution of the British Empire [...]. I think I speak as would the U.S. President in claiming that America will not help Britain in this war for the sole purpose of allowing it to continue the brutal domination of colonial peoples [...]."

"As far as France was concerned, Roosevelt said another day, its former colonies should be placed under its guardianship. As part of its responsibility for this guardianship, the country would report on its management of each of these situations, indicating the decline of illiteracy, the reduction of death rates, progress in the struggle against illness [...]." Franklin D. Roosevelt had a predilection to return to this subject, calculating already everything that the U.S.A. could do with Africa, Asia (and the rest of the world ...) if it had a free hand, and could deploy moreover a creative enthusiasm that had previously been revealed by European capitalism. "We talked, said his son, of the salt pans in the south of Tunisia, which are probably the remains of a huge inland sea, of great rivers whose source is in the Atlas Mountains and which disappear into the Sahara [...]. It would be enough, my father said, to reroute the course of these rivers for the purposes of irrigation, and this region would become so fertile that Imperial Valley in California would look in comparison like a cabbage patch [...]. The Sahara would be in bloom for hundreds of kilometres!" And here he is, already discussing the matter with the Sultan of Morocco: "My father continued to develop the idea as he toyed with his glass. He said that the sultan could easily request the assistance of American businesses which, in return for a lump sum or percentage of profits, would help him to carry out a programme of work. Such a scheme, he stressed, would have the advantage of allowing the sovereign government of Morocco to control the country's resources to a large extent, to benefit from them, and sooner or later to take the country's economy in hand."

It is understandable then why Franklin D. Roosevelt went on to exclaim: "You see, beyond the fact that the allies must maintain military control of the French colonies in North Africa for a period of months, if not for several years, I am not at all sure, in my heart of hearts, that it would be generally wise ever to return these colonies to France without first having received a sort of guarantee, a commitment for each colony in particular, setting out what it planned to do for the administration of each of them." To this, Roosevelt Junior commented that these colonies "belonged, after all, to France ... ," prompting Roosevelt's response: "What does it mean that they belong to France? On what grounds could Morocco, inhabited by Moroccans, belong to France? Or let's consider Indochina. This colony is now under Japanese authority. Why was Japan so confident in its conquest of this country? The indigenous population was so oppressed that they said to each other: anything is better than living under the French colonial regime. Can a country belong to France? On the grounds of what logic, which tradition and which historical law?"

It is thanks to clear messages along these lines that the U.S.A. won the friendship of people who wished, above all, to escape their former subjugation, now stagnant and without hope. But the problem faced now by these people is that of knowing whether they are not risking replacing one master with another one—undoubtedly a richer and better equipped one, whose tips might be more generous—but essentially still a master whose primary wish remains that of receiving profits from its capital.

In the face of such a serious situation, the reflections provided by a work such as C. L. R. James's assume their full importance. As will become apparent, the book is inspired by an extraordinarily current experience of struggle and negotiation. And its great advantage over so much of the gossip and superficial ranting that fills newspapers and meetings is that it poses these problems in all their raw reality. Some readers might think that he would have been better advised to reduce the vividness of his account. But those who are capable of studying the real state of the former colonial world in its current turmoil—as opposed to its representation in official discourses and diplomatic formulae—will think, on the contrary, that such a vigorous analysis is the only real means of shedding light faithfully on problems which cannot much longer remain without resolution.

Pierre Naville (1 February 1949)

[From *Les Jacobins Noirs: Toussaint Louverture et la révolution de Saint Domingue* (Paris: Gallimard, 1949).]

Translator's Foreword (1983)

I translated *The Black Jacobins*, a work by C. L. R. James, during the years 1943 and 1944, i.e., at the time of the French occupation by Nazi Germany. I reckoned then that if France managed to restore its national sovereignty—with the support of Anglo-American forces—its first duty would be to grant freedom to its colonial empire as it had existed before 1939. I thought that this hope would be served by the publication of James's book, that I had first discovered before the war, with its account of the liberation struggle of the "Haitians" on Saint-Domingue during the first French Revolution.

However, when the text was ready for publication in 1949, the French government had taken a totally different path, along which General de Gaulle had led it and to which he had committed it. His intention was to restore France's domination over its former colonies, not of course in the form it took before the war, but nevertheless in the same vein, i.e., as a territorial power that could only be exercised through force. Whence the combination of new institutional projects with traditional military expeditions.

The preface to James's book that I wrote at that time charts unreservedly this new episode in the politics of colonization. I think it is still necessary to reproduce that text today, nearly thirty-five years later, just as it is still important to reread today the history of the revolt led by Toussaint Louverture against Bonaparte. At the same time, the reader will understand everything that colonized peoples were suffering before 1939.

Indeed the most profound revolution since that date, and the richest in terms of the new perspectives it provides, has not been the collapse of Hitler's ventures, nor the consolidation of the Stalinist regimes, nor the development of large-scale technical innovations—it has been the global emancipation of colonized peoples. Two whole continents, Africa and Asia, have been the main theatres of this struggle. And this emancipation has not been the fruit of a late developing generosity on the part of the European metropoles, but that of struggles and uprisings whose most famous example had been given a century earlier by the populations led by Toussaint Louverture.

As a result, the attempts at setting up the Union française, or the British Commonwealth, both of which there were efforts to revive immediately following the Second World War, now look like the last gasps of a dreadful imbalance seeking in vain its own survival and perpetuation. Africa and Asia are at last made up of independent nations recognized under international law, even if some of them still feel as if they are subject to the supervision of the European powers that established in them an imprescriptible heritage of domination. A sequence of struggles, of bush-fights and wars, and of popular rebellions—everything that Toussaint Louverture's revolt had prefigured—paved the way for developments that have reached all factors of civilization. But this shift of balance has not been without cost: how much blood spilt, how many victims created, how much havoc wrought, with all of this mixed in with the rush of rapidly expanding populations, with major regeneration in terms of technology and productivity!

Some observers may have feared, however, that the independence gained by colonized peoples is only the prelude to new forms of enslavement, somewhat in the same way as Dessalines and King Christophe squandered the hopes created by Toussaint's revolt. But they ruined those hopes while ensuring nevertheless that they retained a status without which any restoration of past abuses could not be possible: the abolition of racial and economic slavery, the independence of plans, the autonomy of a people who were at that time—in the islands of the Caribbean—only the resurgence of an enslaved population exported from Africa.

It is no longer the time when the demand for previously unknown freedom merely paved the way for forms of utopian happiness. From now on, liberated colonies face for themselves and by themselves situations which also involve misfortunes and difficulties that it is no longer possible to ascribe exclusively to the former imperialist powers. Certain countries like India and China soon revealed to their new leaders that the control of the independent state not only allowed them to dispense justice to their indigenous populations, but also to suppress harshly internal rebellion and dissidence. Africa has in turn shown itself to be the theatre of national rivalries and of internal conflicts just as harmful as the forms of oppression emerging from Europe. The drama of this Third World (as some people have chosen to dub it) is to have inherited these transformations and substitutions—in certain cases, for example, of local languages with European ones—which pose to the whole of humanity problems of a previously unknown scale.

In addition to so much hope, this new situation entails grave dangers, not only for the newly emancipated peoples, but for Europe itself. Neither party has an interest in setting themselves up as opposing movements. The history of the former revolutionary colony of Saint-Domingue—transformed into Haiti, which lacked the quality of its previous manifestation—shows that the riskiest of transformations is the one that replaces a depleted oppression with a domination that draws its strength from the very impulse by which it was permitted. In other words, the most demanding challenge that history addresses to oppressed people who have become independent is that of organizing new structures of power.

If it is accepted that history can provide useful lessons, then the one that C. L. R. James recounts ought to be seen as exemplary. This is why this book's current distribution is both urgent and welcome. May it be granted the success that its powerful force of conviction deserves.

Pierre Naville (1 February 1983)

[From *Les Jacobins Noirs: Toussaint Louverture et la révolution de Saint-Domingue* (Paris: Éditions Caribéennes, 1983).]

Note

Translations by Charles Forsdick.

BIBLIOGRAPHY

Unpublished Primary Sources

Dunayevskaya, Raya. Letter to C. L. R. James, July 29, 1947. Raya Dunayevskaya Collection at Wayne State University Archives of Labor and Urban Affairs, Detroit, MI.

Genovese, Eugene. Letter to C. L. R. James, November 29, 1979, Box 1, File 11, C. L. R. James Collection, Quinton O'Connor Library, Oilfield Workers' Trade Union, San Fernando, Trinidad and Tobago.

Grimshaw, Anna. Letter to Joseph B. Boromé, June 6, 1986. C. L. R. James Collection, Alma Jordan Library, University of the West Indies, St Augustine, Trinidad and Tobago (UWI), Box 7, folder 191.

Hill, Robert A. Interview with C. L. R. James on CBC Tuesday Night, the Canadian Broadcasting Corporation, February 13, 1967.

———. "The Coming Struggle for Liberation" (unpublished), n.d., Alfie Roberts Collection.

———. "Rejoinder" (unpublished), 1969.

James, C. L. R. "Autobiography, Section 4, 1932–38." UWI, Box 14, folder 309.

———. "Eric Williams." UWI, Box 16, folder 338.

———. Letter to Jean Brierre, March 1, 1958. UWI, Box 7, folder 190.

———. Letter to Étienne Charlier, August 24, 1955. UWI, Box 7, folder 190.

———. Letter to Basil Davidson, March 15, 1964. UWI, Box 7, folder 190.

———. Letter to George Lamming, March 15, 1964. UWI, Box 7, folder 190.

———. Letter to Colin Legum, March 15, 1964. UWI, Box 7, folder 190.

———. Letter to Marina Maxwell, October 29, 1967. UWI, Box 7, folder 190.

———. Letter to John G. Pattisson at Secker and Warburg, February 9, 1961. UWI, box 7, folder 179.

———. Letters to Morris Philipson, December 10, 1960, and June 23, 1961. UWI, Box 7, folder 181.

———. Letter to Fredric Warburg, September 1, 1960. UWI, Box 7, folder 179.

———. Letter to Fredric Warburg, January 10, 1969. George Padmore Institute, Box 429, folder 4.

————. *The Black Jacobins* play typescripts. UWI, Box 9, folders 228, 229, 230; Box 12, folder 280; Schomburg Center for Research in Black Culture, New York Public Library, Manuscripts, Archives and Rare Books Division (SC MG 53); Rare Books and Manuscripts, Special Collections Library, Pennsylvania State University, State College, PA, Charles L. Blockson Collection of African Americana and the African Diaspora (uncataloged); Rare Books and Manuscripts, Special Collections Library, Pennsylvania State University (0581/VF LIT); Dartmouth College, Hanover, NH, Rauner Special Collections Library, Papers of Errol G. Hill, ML-77, Box 48, folder 47; performance script of director Dexter Lyndersay, private collection. Columbia University, Rare Books and Manuscripts Library, C. L. R. James Papers (MS#1529 Box 5, folders 14, 15, and 17); Wayne State University, Walter P. Reuther Library, Archives of Labor and Urban Affairs, Martin Glaberman Collection, Box 21, file 6.

————. *The C.L.R. James Lectures.* Atlanta: Institute of the Black World, 1971. Audio tape.

Lamartinière Honorat, Michel. Letter to Félix Morisseau-Leroy. April 16, 1958. UWI, Box 7, folder 190.

Lyndersay, Dexter. Letter to C. L. R. James, October 8, 1967. UWI, Box 10, folder 240.

Ministère de la Culture, *Bibliotheque Fonds Frantz Fanon.*

National Archives, London, KV/2/1824/13a.

Naville, Pierre. Letter to Franklin Rosemont, June 20, 1989. Franklin and Penelope Rosemont Papers, Joseph A. Labadie Collection, University of Michigan Library, Ann Arbor.

Philipson, Morris. Letters to C. L. R. James, November 7, 1960, February 24, 1961, and December 21, 1961. UWI, Box 7, folder 181.

Public Record Office, London, CO 318/427/11.

Published Primary Sources

Mémoires du général Toussaint-Louverture, edited by Jacques de Cauna. Guitalens-l'Albarède: Editions la Girandole, 2009.

Mémoires du général Toussaint Louverture, edited by Daniel Désormeaux. Paris: Classiques Garnier, 2011.

The Memoir of General Toussaint Louverture, edited by Philippe Girard. Oxford: Oxford University Press, 2014.

The Negro. London: Williams and Norgate, 1915.

Alexis, Stephen. *Black Liberator: The Life of Toussaint Louverture.* New York: Macmillan, 1949.

Arendt, Hannah. *On Revolution.* New York: Penguin, 1990.

Austin, David. "Introduction: In Search of a National Identity: C.L.R. James and the Promise of the Caribbean." In *You Don't Play with Revolution: The Montreal Lectures of C.L.R. James,* edited by David Austin. Oakland, CA: AK Press, 2009.

Austin, David, ed. *You Don't Play with Revolution: The Montreal Lectures of C.L.R. James*. Oakland, CA: AK Press, 2009.

Ballard, Arthur. "The Greatest Slave Revolt in History." *New Leader*, December 9, 1938.

Blake, David, and Anthony Ward. *Toussaint, or The Aristocracy of the Skin: Opera in Three Acts*. Sevenoaks: Novello, 1977.

Carby, Hazel, and Don Edwards. "Vincent Harding." In *Visions of History*, edited by MAHRO: The Radical Historians Organization, 217–44. Manchester: Manchester University Press, 1983.

Carmichael, Stokely, and Michael Ekwueme Thelwell. *Ready for Revolution: The Life and Struggles of Stokely Carmichael (Kwame Ture)*. New York: Scribner, 2005.

Carson, Claybourne, Susan Carson, Adrienne Clay, Virginia Shadron, and Kieran Taylor, eds. *The Martin Luther King Jr. Papers Project: Vol. IV: Symbol of the Movement*. Berkeley: University of California Press, 2000.

Césaire, Aimé. *Toussaint Louverture: La révolution française et la problème colonial*. Paris: Présence Africaine, 1961.

Charlier, Étienne. *Aperçu sur la formation historique de la nation haïtienne*. Port-au-Prince: Presses libres, 1954.

Clarkson, Thomas. *True State of the Case Respecting the Insurrection at St. Domingo*. London, 1792.

Cooper, Anna J. *Slavery and the French Revolutionists (1788–1805)*. New York: Edwin Mellen Press, 1988.

Courlander, Harold. "Revolt in Haiti." *Saturday Review of Literature*, January 7, 1939.

Cripps, Louise. *C.L.R. James: Memories and Commentaries*. London: Cornwall Books, 1997.

Davis, N. Darnell. *Mr. Froude's Negrophobia or Don Quixote as a Cook's Tourist*. Demerara: "Argosy" Press, 1888.

Debien, Gabriel. "Les travaux d'histoire sur Saint-Domingue (1938–1946): essai de mise au point," *Revue d'Histoire des Colonies* 34 (1947): 31–86.

Douglass, Frederick. "Lecture on Haiti." Available at http://faculty.webster.edu/corbetre /haiti/history/1844-1915/douglass.htm (accessed November 6, 2010).

Du Bois, W. E. B. *Black Reconstruction in America: 1860–1880*. 1935; New York: Free Press, 1998.

———. "Hayti." *Crisis*, 10 (1915): 291.

———. "200 Years of Segregated Schools." *Jewish Life* (February 1955): 7–9.

———. "Two Hundred Years of Segregated Schools." In *W.E.B. Du Bois Speaks: Speeches and Addresses 1920–1963*, edited by Philip S. Foner, 304–10. New York: Pathfinder, 2000.

Ferguson, Moira. "Introduction to the Revised Edition." *The History of Mary Prince: A West Indian Slave (Related by Herself)*. Ann Arbor: University of Michigan Press, 1997.

Foot, Michael. "C.L.R. James." In *C.L.R. James: His Intellectual Legacies*, edited by Selwyn R. Cudjoe and William E. Cain, 98–105. Amherst: University of Massachusetts Press, 1995.

Freud, Sigmund. *The Standard Edition of the Complete Psychological Works of Sigmund Freud. Vol. 4. (1900). The Interpretation of Dreams (First Part)*. London: Vintage, 2001.

Froude, James, Anthony. *The English in the West Indies. Or the Bow of Ulysses*. London: Longmans, Green, 1888.

Gambino, Ferrucio. "Only Connect." In *C.L.R. James: His Life and Work*, edited by Paul Buhle, 195–99. London: Allison and Busby, 1986.

Georgakas, Dan. "Young Detroit Radicals, 1955–1965." In *C. L. R. James: His Life and Work*, edited by Paul Buhle, 185–94. London: Allison and Busby, 1986.

Glaberman, Martin, ed. *Marxism for Our Times: C.L.R. James on Revolutionary Organization*. Jackson: University of Mississippi Press, 1999.

Glissant, Édouard. *Le Discours antillais*. Paris: Seuil, 1981.

———. *Monsieur Toussaint: A Play*. Trans. J. Michael Dash. Boulder, CO: Lynne Rienner, 2005.

Gomes, Albert. "Black Man." *Beacon* 1, no. 4 (July 1931): 1–2.

Gramsci, Antonio. "Some Aspects of the Southern Question." In *Antonio Gramsci, Selections from Political Writings, 1921–1926*, edited by Quintin Hoare. London: Lawrence and Wishart, 1978.

———. "The Revolution against *Das Kapital*." In *Antonio Gramsci, Selections from Political Writings, 1910–1920*, edited by Quintin Hoare. London: Lawrence and Wishart, 1977.

Grimshaw, Anna, ed. *The C. L. R. James Reader*. Oxford: Blackwell, 1992.

Guérin, Daniel. *La Lutte de classes sous la première république. Bourgeois et "bras nus," 1793–1797*. Paris: Gallimard, 1946.

———. *Class Struggles in the First French Republic*. Trans. Ian Patterson. London: Pluto Press, 1977.

Hall, Stuart. "A Conversation with C.L.R. James." In *Rethinking C.L.R. James*, edited by Grant Farred, 15–44. Oxford: Blackwell, 1996.

Harland, Sidney C. "Magna Est Veritas Et Praevalebit: A Reply to Mr. C.L.R. James." *Beacon* 1, no. 7 (October 1931): 18–20.

———. "Race Admixture." *Beacon* 1, no. 4 (July 1931): 25–29.

Hegel, Georg Wilhelm Friedrich. *Lectures on the Philosophy of World History*. Trans. H. B. Nesbit, with an introduction by Duncan Forbes. Cambridge: Cambridge University Press, 1975.

———. *The Philosophy of History*. Trans. J. Sibree. New York Dover, 1956.

Herskovits, Melville J. *Dahomey: An Ancient West African Kingdom*, 2 vols. New York: J. J. Augustin, 1938.

———. *Life in a Haitian Valley*. New York: Knopf, 1937.

———. "The Negro in the New World: The Statement of a Problem." *American Anthropologist* 32, no. 1 (1930): 145–55.

Herskovits, Melville J., and Frances S. Herskovits. *Rebel Destiny: Among the Bush Negroes of Dutch Guiana*. New York: Whittlesey House, 1934.

———. *Suriname Folk-Lore*. New York: Columbia University Press, 1936.

Hill, Robert A., ed. *The Marcus Garvey and UNIA Papers*, vol. XI. Durham, NC: Duke University Press, 2011.

Holly, James Theodore. "Vindication of the Capacity of the Negro Race for Self-Government, and Civilized Progress, Demonstrated by Historical Events of the Haytian Revolution." In *Black Separatism in the Caribbean, 1860*, edited by Howard Bell. Ann Arbor: University of Michigan Press, 1970.

Isaacs, Harold. *The Tragedy of the Chinese Revolution*. Stanford, CA: Stanford University Press, 1961.

James, C. L. R. *Beyond a Boundary*. London: Stanley Paul, 1963.

———. *Beyond a Boundary*. London: Hutchinson, 1969.

———. *Beyond a Boundary*. Durham, NC: Duke University Press, 1993.

———. *Beyond a Boundary*. Durham, NC: Duke University Press, 2013.

———. "Black Intellectuals in Britain." In *Color, Class and Consciousness*, edited by Bhikhu Parekh. London: Allen and Unwin, 1974.

———. "The Black Jacobins." In *A Time and a Season, 8 Caribbean Plays*, edited by Errol Hill, 382–450. Port-of-Spain: University of the West Indies, Trinidad, Extramural Studies Unit, 1976.

———. "The Black Jacobins." In *The C.L.R. James Reader*, edited by Anna Grimshaw, 67–111. Oxford: Blackwell, 1992.

———. *The Black Jacobins: Toussaint Louverture and the San Domingo Revolution*. London: Secker and Warburg, 1938.

———. *The Black Jacobins: Toussaint L'Ouverture and the San Domingo Revolution*. New York: Vintage, 1963.

———. *The Black Jacobins: Toussaint L'Ouverture and the San Domingo Revolution*. London: Allison and Busby, 1984.

———. *The Black Jacobins: Toussaint L'Ouverture and the San Domingo Revolution*. London: New York: Vintage, 1989.

———. *The Black Jacobins: Toussaint L'Ouverture and the San Domingo Revolution*. London: Allison and Busby, 1991.

———. *The Black Jacobins: Toussaint L'Ouverture and the San Domingo Revolution*. London: Penguin, 2001.

———. "Black Sansculottes." In *At the Rendezvous of Victory: Selected Writings*, vol. 3, 159–62. London: Allison and Busby, 1984.

———. *The Case for West Indian Self-Government*. New York: University Place Book Shop/Facing Reality Publishing, 1967.

———. "A Century of Freedom." *Listener*, May 31, 1933.

———. "The Class Basis of the Race Question in the United States." *New Politics* 60 (Winter 2016).

———. "A Convention Appraisal: Dr. Eric Williams, First Premier of Trinidad and Tobago; A Biographical Sketch [1960]." In *Eric E. Williams Speaks*, edited by Selwyn R. Cudjoe, 327–51. Wellesley, MA: Calaloux, 1993.

———. "Correspondence [27 February 1950]." *Les Temps Modernes* 56 (June 1950).

———. "Fanon and the Caribbean." In *International Tribute to Frantz Fanon: Record of the Special Meeting of the United Nations Special Committee Against Apartheid, 3 November 1978*, 43–46. New York: United Nations Centre Against Apartheid, 1979.

———. "The Haitian Revolution in the Making of the Modern World." In *You Don't Play with Revolution: The Montreal Lectures of C.L.R. James*, edited by David Austin, 51–70. Oakland, CA: AK Press, 2009.

———. *A History of Negro Revolt*. London: F.A.C.T., 1938.

———. *The History of Pan-African Revolt*. Washington DC: Drum and Spear Press, 1969.

———. *A History of Pan-African Revolt*. Oakland, CA: PM Press, 2012.

———. *I Giacobini neri: La prima rivolta contro l'uomo bianco*. Rome: Derive Approdi, 2006.

———. "The Intelligence of the Negro: A Few Words with Dr. Harland." *Beacon* 1, no. 5 (August 1931): 6–10.

———. "The Intelligence of the Negro." In *From Trinidad: An Anthology of Early West Indian Writing*, edited by Reinhard Sander. New York: Africana, 1978.

———. "Interview [1972]." In *Kas-Kas; Interviews with Three Caribbean Writers in Texas: George Lamming, C.L.R. James, Wilson Harris*, edited by Ian Munro and Reinhard Sander, 22–41. Austin: University of Texas Press, 1972.

———. "Interviews with Ken Ramchand." San Fernando, Trinidad and Tobago, September 5, 1980. http://www.marxists.org/archive/james-clr/works/1980/09/banyan.htm (accessed April 28, 2013).

———. Introduction to Jean Fouchard, *The Haitian Maroons: Liberty or Death*. New York: Blyden Press, 1981.

———. "L'actualité de la Révolution française." *Perspectives socialistes: revue bimensuelle de l'Union de la Gauche Socialiste*, February 15, 1958, 20–21.

———. "Lectures on *The Black Jacobins*: *The Black Jacobins* and *Black Reconstruction*: A Comparative Analysis." *Small Axe* 8 (2000): 83–98.

———. "Lectures on *The Black Jacobins*: How I Would Rewrite *The Black Jacobins*." *Small Axe* 8 (2000): 99–112.

———. "Lectures on *The Black Jacobins*: How I Wrote *The Black Jacobins*." *Small Axe* 8 (2000): 65–82.

———. "Letters on Politics: III. 20 March 1957." In *The C.L.R. James Reader*, edited by Anna Grimshaw, 269. Oxford: Blackwell, 1992.

———. *The Life of Captain Cipriani: An Account of British Government in the West Indies*. Durham, NC: Duke University Press, 2014.

———. *Los Jacobins Negros: Toussaint L'Ouverture y la Revolución de Saint-Domingue*. Havana: Casa de las Americas, 2010.

———. "The Making of the Caribbean People." *Radical America* 4, no. 4 (1970).

———. "The Making of the Caribbean People." In *You Don't Play with Revolution: The Montreal Lectures of C.L.R. James,* edited by David Austin, 29–49. Oakland, CA: AK Press, 2009.

———. "Marx's *Capital,* the Working-Day and Capitalist Production." In *You Don't Play with Revolution: The Montreal Lectures of C.L.R. James,* edited by David Austin, 141–60. Oakland, CA: AK Press, 2009.

———. *Minty Alley.* London: Secker and Warburg, 1936.

———. "My Knowledge of Damas Is Unique." In *Leon-Gontran Damas, 1912–1978: Father of Negritude: A Memorial Casebook,* edited by Daniel L. Racine, 131–34. Washington, DC: University Press of America, 1979.

———. *Nkrumah and the Ghana Revolution.* London: Allison and Busby, 1977.

———. *Nkrumah and the Ghana Revolution.* Westport: Lawrence Hill, 1977.

———. *Notes on Dialectics.* Detroit: ARC, 1966.

———. *Notes on Dialectics.* Detroit: Friends of Facing Reality, 1971.

———. *Notes on Dialectics: Hegel, Marx, Lenin.* London: Allison and Busby, 1980.

———. "The Old World and the New." In *At the Rendezvous of Victory: Selected Writings,* vol. 3, 202–17. London: Allison and Busby, 1984.

———. *Party Politics in the West Indies: Formerly PNM Go Forward.* San Juan, Trinidad: Vedic Enterprises, 1962.

———. *Perspectives and Proposals.* Detroit: Facing Reality, 1966.

———. *At the Rendezvous of Victory: Selected Writings,* vol. 3. London: Allison and Busby, 1984.

———. "A Revolution Ignored." *Third World Book Review* 1, no. 1 (1984): 36–37.

———. "Romanticising History." *New Society,* February 15, 1979.

———. "Rousseau and the Idea of General Will." In *You Don't Play with Revolution: The Montreal Lectures of C.L.R. James,* edited by David Austin, 105–20. Oakland, CA: AK Press, 2009.

———. "Slavery Today: A Shocking Exposure." *Tit-Bits,* August 5, 1933.

———. "To and from the Finland Station: A Review of *To the Finland Station* by Edmund Wilson." In *C.L.R. James and Revolutionary Marxism: Selected Writings of C.L.R. James, 1939–1949,* edited by Scott McLemee and Paul Le Blanc. Atlantic Highlands, NJ: Humanities Press, 1994.

———. *Toussaint Louverture: The Story of the Only Successful Slave Revolt in History: A Play in Three Acts.* Durham, NC: Duke University Press, 2013.

———. "Trotsky's Place in History." In *C.L.R. James and Revolutionary Marxism: Selected Writings of C.L.R. James, 1939–1949,* edited by Scott McLemee and Paul Le Blanc, 92–130. Atlantic Highlands, NJ: Humanities Press, 1994.

———. *Walter Rodney and the Question of Power.* London: Race Today, 1983.

———. "The West Indian Intellectual." In John Jacob Thomas, *Froudacity: West Indian Fables Explained,* 23–49. London: New Beacon, 1969.

———. "W.E.B. Du Bois [1964]." In *The Future in the Present; Selected Writings*, vol. 1, 202–12. London: Allison and Busby, 1977.

———. *Wilson Harris: A Philosophical Approach*. St. Augustine: University of the West Indies, 1965.

———. *World Revolution 1917–1936: The Rise and Fall of the Communist International*. London: Secker and Warburg, 1937.

———. *World Revolution, 1917–1936: The Rise and Fall of the Communist International* Westport, CT: Hyperion Press, 1973.

———. *World Revolution, 1917–1936: The Rise and Fall of the Communist International*. Atlantic Highlands, NJ: Humanities Press, 1994.

———. *You Don't Play with Revolution: The Montreal Lectures of C.L.R. James*. Edited by David Austin. Oakland, CA: AK Press, 2009.

James, C. L. R., Raya Dunayevskaya, and Grace Lee. *The Invading Socialist Society*. Detroit: Bewick, 1972.

James, C. L. R., and Martin Glaberman. "Letters." In *C.L.R. James: His Life and Work*, edited by Paul Buhle, 153–63. London: Allison and Busby, 1986.

James, Selma. "Striving for Clarity and Influence: The Political Legacy of C.L.R. James (2001–2012)." In Selma James, *Sex, Race and Class: The Perspective of Winning: A Selection of Writings 1952–2011*. Oakland, CA: PM Press, 2012. 283–96.

Johnson, James Weldon. *Along This Way: The Autobiography of James Weldon Johnson*. New York: Penguin, 1933.

Kant, Immanuel. "Idea for a Universal History with a Cosmopolitan Purpose." In *Kant: Political Writings*, edited by Hans Reiss, 41–53. Cambridge: Cambridge University Press, 1991.

Kropotkin, Peter. *The Great French Revolution*. Montreal: Black Rose, 1989.

La Rose, John. "C.L.R. James—The Revolutionary as Artist." In John La Rose, *Unending Journey: Selected Writings*. London: New Beacon Books/George Padmore Institute, 2014.

Lamming, George. *The Pleasures of Exile*. 1960; London: Pluto, 2005.

Lefebvre, Georges. "La Fuite du Roi." In *Les Cours de Sorbonne, 1947*. Paris: Centre de documentation universitaire, 1951.

Lemonnier-Delafosse, Jean-Baptiste. *Souvenirs historiques et succincts de la première campagne*. Havre: H. Brindeau, 1846–1850.

Lenin, V. I. "Letters from Afar." In V. I. Lenin, *Collected Works*, vol. 23. Moscow: Progress Publishers, 1964.

———. *The Development of Capitalism in Russia. Collected Works, vol. 3*. Moscow, Progress Publishers, 1972.

Loederer, Richard, *Voodoo Fire in Haiti*. New York: Literary Guild, 1935.

Logan, Rayford W. "Reviews—Caribbean History." *Opportunity: Journal of Negro Life* 17, no. 2 (1939).

Mackenzie, Alan. "Radical Pan-Africanism in the 1930s: A Discussion with C.L.R. James." *Radical History Review*, 24 (1980).

Mackenzie, Alan, and Gilroy, Paul. "Interview with C.L.R. James." In *Visions of History*, edited by MAHRO: The Radical Historians Organization. Manchester: Manchester University Press, 1983.

Marx, Karl. *Capital*, vol. 1. Middlesex: Penguin Books, 1976.

Mathiez, Albert. *The French Revolution*. New York: Knopf, 1928.

McLemee, Scott, ed. *C.L.R. James on the 'Negro Question.'* Jackson: University Press of Mississippi, 1996.

McLemee, Scott, and Paul Le Blanc, eds. *C.L.R. James and Revolutionary Marxism. Selected Writings of C.L.R. James, 1939–1949*. Atlantic Highlands, NJ: Humanities Press, 1994.

Ménard, Louis. "*Les Jacobins noirs.*" *Les Temps Modernes* 52 (February 1950).

Montague, Ludwell Lee. "*The Black Jacobins.*" *Hispanic American Historical Review* 20, no. 1 (1940): 129–30.

Munro, Ian, and Reinhard Sander, eds. *Kas-Kas: Interviews with Three Caribbean Writers in Texas: George Lamming, C.L.R. James, Wilson Harris*. Austin: University of Texas at Austin, 1972.

Naville, Pierre. "Avant-propos." In C. L. R. James, *Les Jacobins Noirs: Toussaint Louverture et la révolution de Saint Domingue*. Paris: Gallimard, 1949.

———. "Avant-propos." C. L. R. James, *Les Jacobins noirs: Toussaint L'Ouverture et la Révolution de Saint-Domingue*. Paris: Éditions Caribéennes, 1983.

Nemours, Alfred. *Histoire de la captivité et de la mort de Toussaint Louverture. Notre pèlerinage au Fort de Joux*. Paris: Berger-Levrault, 1929.

———. *Quelques jugements sur Toussaint-Louverture*. Cap-Haïtien: Valcin, 1938.

Nesbitt, Nick, ed. *Toussaint L'Ouverture: The Haitian Revolution*. Introduction by Jean-Bertrand Aristide. London: Verso, 2008.

Novack, George. "Revolution, Black and White." *New International* 5, no. 5 (May 1939).

Padmore, George. *Haiti: An American Slave Colony*. Moscow: Centrizdat, 1931.

———. *Pan Africanism or Communism*. NYL Anchor Books, 1972.

———. "The Revolt in Haiti." *Labour Monthly* 12 (June 1930): 356–66.

———. "Toussaint, the Black Liberator." *People* (Trinidad), November 12 and 19, 1938.

Paul, Emmanuel C. *Questions d'histoire*. Port-au-Prince: Imprimerie de l'Etat, 1955.

Pizer, Dorothy. "A Lesson in Revolution." *Controversy* 28 (January 1939).

Pritchard, Hesketh. *Where Black Rules White: A Journey across and about Hayti*. Westminster: Archibald Constable, 1900.

Report of the Commission appointed to enquire into the Disturbances in the Copperbelt, Northern Rhodesia. Cmd. 5009. London, 1935.

Richardson, Al, Clarence Chrysotum, and Anna Grimshaw. *C.L.R. James and British Trotskyism: An Interview*. London: Socialist Platform, 1987.

Rodney, Walter. "The African Revolution." In *C.L.R. James: His Life and Work*, edited by Paul Buhle, 30–48. London: Allison and Busby, 1986.

———. *Walter Rodney Speaks: The Making of an African Intellectual*. New York: Africa World Press, 1990.

Salkey, Andrew. *Havana Journal*. Harmondsworth: Penguin Books, 1971.

Salmon, C. S. *The Caribbean Confederation*. London: Cassell, 1888.

Scholes, Theophilus. *Glimpses of the Ages*. London: J. Long, 1905.

Seabrook, William, B. *"The Black Jacobins." Journal of Negro History* 24, no. 1 (January 1939).

———. *The Magic Island*. New York: Harcourt Brace, 1929.

Souvarine, Boris. *Stalin: A Critical Survey of Bolshevism*. Trans. C. L. R. James. New York: Alliance Book, 1939.

Spengler, Oswald. *The Decline of the West*. London: George Allen and Unwin, 1934.

Stoddard, T. Lothrop. *The French Revolution in San Domingo*. New York: Houghton Mifflin, 1914.

———. *The Rising Tide of Colour against White World-Supremacy*. New York: Scribner, 1920.

Thomas, John Jacob. *Froudacity: West Indian Fables by James Anthony Froude*. London: T. Fisher Unwin, 1889.

Trotsky, Leon. *"Fontamara." New International* 1, no. 5 (December 1934).

———. *The History of the Russian Revolution. Vol. I*. London: Sphere, 1967.

———. *The History of the Russian Revolution. Vol. III*. London: Sphere, 1967.

———. *The History of the Russian Revolution*. London: Pluto, 1977.

———. *The History of the Russian Revolution*. Chicago: Haymarket Books, 2008.

———. *How the Revolution Armed: The Military Writings and Speeches of Leon Trotsky*, vol. 1. London: New Park, 1979.

———. *On Black Self-Determination*. New York: Pathfinder, 1992.

Vico, Giambatista. *New Science*. New York: Penguin, 1999.

Warburg, Fredric. *An Occupation for a Gentleman*. London: Hutchinson, 1959.

Waxman, Percy. *The Black Napoleon: The Story of Toussaint Louverture*. New York: Harcourt Brace, 1931.

West, Fred. "You Are Right, Black Man, But How . . . ?: A Reply to Albert Gomes' 'Black Man.'" *Beacon* 1, no. 7 (October 1931): 11.

Williams, Eric. *British Historians and the West Indies*. New York: A and B, 1994.

———. *Capitalism and Slavery*. London: Andre Deutsch, 1964.

———. *Inward Hunger: The Education of a Prime Minister*. London: Deutsch, 1969.

Wilson, Edmund. *To the Finland Station: A Study in the Writing and Acting of History*. London: Fontana, 1970.

Newspapers and Periodicals

African Sentinel
Beacon
Crisis

Daily Gleaner
Fight
Haiti Sun
International African Opinion
Jamaica Standard and Royal Gazette
Manchester Guardian
Nation
New Leader
New Statesman
Port of Spain Gazette
Time

Secondary Sources

Adi, Hakim, and Marika Sherwood. *The 1945 Manchester Pan-African Congress Revisited*. London: New Beacon Books, 1995.

Adolphe Roberts, W. *Six Great Jamaicans*. Kingston: Pioneer Press, 1957.

Agozino, Onwubiko. "The Revolutionary Sociology of C.L.R. James: An Interview with Manning Marable." *Transition* 106 (2011): 127–38.

Althusser, Louis. "Contradiction and Overdetermination." In Louis Althusser, *For Marx*. London: Allen Lane, 1969.

Anderson, Benedict. *Imagined Communities*. London: Verso, 1983.

Ankersmit, Frank, Ewa Domanska, and Hans Kellner, eds. *Re-Figuring Hayden White*. Stanford, CA: Stanford University Press, 2009.

Appadurai, Arjun. "Theory in Anthropology: Center and Periphery." *Comparative Studies in Societies and History* 28, no. 2 (1986): 356–61.

Aravamudan, Srinivas. *Tropicopolitans: Colonialism and Agency, 1688–1804*. Durham, NC: Duke University Press, 1999.

Asante, S. K. B. *Pan-African Protest: West Africa and the Italo-Ethiopian Crisis, 1934–1941*. London: Longman, 1977.

Austin, David. "Anne Cools: Radical Feminist and Trailblazer?" *MaComère*, 12, no. 2 (2010).

———. *The Black Jacobin*. Canadian Broadcasting Corporation, 2006.

———. "Class Struggle: Cabral, Rodney, and the Complexities of Culture in Africa." In *Claim No Easy Victory: The Legacy of Amilcar Cabral*, edited by Firoze Manji and Bill Fletcher. Dakar: Codesria/Dajara Press, 2013.

———. *Fear of a Black Nation: Race, Sex, and Security in Sixties Montreal*. Toronto: Between the Lines, 2013.

———. "Introduction: In Search of a National Identity: C.L.R. James and the Promise of the Caribbean." In *You Don't Play with Revolution: The Montreal Lectures of C.L.R. James*, edited by David Austin, 1–26. Oakland, CA: AK Press, 2009.

Autry, Robyn. "Doing Memory in Public: Postapartheid Memorial Space as an Activist Project." In *Memory and Postwar Memorials: Confronting the Violence of the Past*, edited by Marc Silberman and Florence Vatan, 137–54. New York: Palgrave Macmillan, 2013.

Bann, Stephen. *Romanticism and the Rise of History*. New York: Twayne, 1995.

Baumann, Gerd. "Interview: Eric Wolf: How Ideological Involvement Actually Operates." *European Association of Social Anthropologists Newsletter* 25 (March 1999): 8–12.

Beiser, Frederick. *The Romantic Imperative: The Concept of Early German Romanticism*. Cambridge, MA: Harvard University Press, 2006.

Bell, David A. "Renewing the Comparative Study of Revolutions," *AHA Today* (a blog of the American Historical Association), December 7, 2015, http://blog.historians .org/2015/12/comparative-study-of-revolutions/.

Benn, Denis. *The Caribbean: An Intellectual History, 1774–2003*. Kingston: Ian Randle, 2004.

Bernier, Celeste-Marie. *Characters of Blood: Black Heroism in the Transatlantic Imagination*. Charlottesville: University of Virginia Press, 2012.

Bethel, Elizabeth Rauh. "Images of Hayti: The Construction of an Afro-American *lieu de mémoire*." *Callaloo* 15, no. 3 (1992): 827–41.

Biondi, Martha. *The Black Revolution on Campus*. Berkeley: University of California Press, 2012.

Blackburn, Robin. "Haiti, Slavery and the Age of the Democratic Revolution." *William and Mary Quarterly* 63, no. 4 (2006).

———. "*The Black Jacobins* and New World Slavery." In *C.L.R. James: His Intellectual Legacies*, edited by Selwyn R. Cudjoe and William E. Cain. Amherst: University of Massachusetts Press, 1995.

———. *The Overthrow of Colonial Slavery, 1776–1848*. London: Verso, 1988.

———. "The Role of Slave Resistance in Slave Emancipation." In *Who Abolished Slavery: Slave Revolts and Abolitionism: A Debate with João Pedro Marques*, edited by Seymour Drescher and Pieter Emmer, 169–78. New York: Berghahn, 2010.

Boal, Augusto. *Theater of the Oppressed*. Trans. Charles A. McBride, Maria-Odilia Leal McBride, and Emily Fryer. London: Pluto, 2000.

Bogues, Anthony. "Afterword." *Small Axe* 8 (2000): 113–17.

———. *Black Heretics, Black Prophets: Radical Political Intellectuals*. New York: Routledge, 2003.

———. *Caliban's Freedom: The Early Political Thought of C.L.R. James*. Chicago: Pluto Press, 1997.

———. "Haiti as an Idea." In *The Haitian Revolution and the Early United States: Histories, Textualities, and Geographies*, edited by Elizabeth Dillon and Michael Drexler, 314–25. Philadelphia: University of Pennsylvania Press, 2016.

Bookchin, Murray. *Third Revolution*. London: Cassell, 1996.

Bosteels, Bruno. "The Leftist Hypothesis: Communism in the Age of Terror." In *The Idea of Communism*, edited by Costas Douzinas and Slavoj Žižek. New York: Verso 2010.

Brand, Dionne. *Bread Out of Stone: Recollections, Sex, Recognitions, Race, Dreaming, Politics.* Toronto: Coach House Press, 1994.

Breslin, Paul. " 'The First Epic of the New World': But How Shall It Be Written?" In *Tree of Liberty: Cultural Legacies of the Haitian Revolution in the Atlantic World*, edited by Doris Lorraine Garraway, 223–48. Charlottesville: University of Virginia Press, 2008.

Broué, Pierre. *The German Revolution.* Leiden: Brill, 2004.

Broué, Pierre, and Emile Témime. *The Revolution and the Civil War in Spain.* London: Faber and Faber, 1972.

Buck-Morss, Susan. *Hegel, Haiti and Universal History.* Pittsburgh, PA: University of Pittsburgh Press, 2009.

———. "The Gift of the Past." *Small Axe* 33 (2010): 173–85.

Buhle, Paul, ed. *C.L.R. James: His Life and Work.* London: Allison and Busby, 1986.

———. *C.L.R. James: The Artist as Revolutionary.* London: Verso, 1989.

———. *Tim Hector: A Caribbean Radical's Story.* Kingston: Ian Randle, 2006.

Cabral, Amicar. *Selected Speeches: Return to the Source.* London: PAIGC Information Committee, n.d.

Callinicos, Alex. "The Drama of Revolution and Reaction: Marxist History and the Twentieth Century." In *Marxist History-Writing for the Twenty-first Century*, edited by Chris Wickham, 158–79. Oxford: Oxford University Press, 2008.

Cambre, Maria-Carolina. *The Semiotics of Che Guevara.* London: Bloomsbury Academic, 2015.

Campbell, Horace. *Rasta and Resistance: From Marcus Garvey to Walter Rodney.* Trenton: Africa World Press, 1987.

Carlin, Norah. "Daniel Guérin and the Working Class in the French Revolution." *International Socialism* 47 (1990): 197–223.

Carruthers, Jacob H. *Intellectual Warfare.* Chicago: Third World Press, 1999.

Casey, Michael. *Che's Afterlife: The Legacy of an Image.* New York: Vintage Books, 2009.

Chakrabarty, Dipesh. *Habitations of Modernity: Essays in the Wake of Subaltern Studies.* Chicago: University of Chicago Press, 2002.

———. *Provincializing Europe: Postcolonial Thought and Historical Difference.* Princeton, NJ: Princeton University Press, 2000.

Chibber, Vivek. *Postcolonial Theory and the Specter of Capital.* London: Verso, 2013.

Chu, Patricia E. *Race, Nationalism and the State in British and American Modernism.* Cambridge: Cambridge University Press, 2006.

Clavin, Matthew. *Toussaint Louverture and the American Civil War: The Promise and Peril of a Second Haitian Revolution.* Philadelphia: University of Pennsylvania Press, 2010.

C.L.R. James Symposium. Doc. No. 2. Published by the Guild of Undergraduates (Mona) for the C.L.R. James Symposium, n.d.

Cobb, Richard. *The Police and the People: French Popular Protest, 1789–1820.* New York: Oxford University Press, 1970.

Collier, Ruth Berns. *Paths toward Democracy: The Working Class and Elites in Western Europe and South America.* Cambridge: Cambridge University Press, 1999.

Collin, Paul. "The Tragedy of the Chinese Revolution: An Essay in the Different Editions of That Work." *Revolutionary History* 2, no. 4 (1990).

Comer, James P., Paula J. Giddings, Richard A. Goldsby, William Chester Jordan, Randall Kennedy, David Levering Lewis, Albert J. Raboteau, and Ronald Waters. "Books That Changed the Lives of Black Scholars." *Journal of Blacks in Higher Education* 19 (1998).

Comninel, George C. *Rethinking the French Revolution: Marxism and the Revisionist Challenge.* London: Verso, 1987.

Condé, Maryse. "Order, Disorder, Freedom and the West Indian Writer." *Yale French Studies* 83, no. 2 (1993): 121–35.

Cooper, Frederick. *Decolonization and African Society: The Labor Question in French and British Africa.* Cambridge: Cambridge University Press, 1996.

Cudjoe, Selwyn R. "The Audacity of It All: C.L.R. James's Trinidadian Background." In *C.L.R. James's Caribbean,* edited by Paget Henry and Paul Buhle, 39–55. Durham, NC: Duke University Press, 1992.

———. *Beyond Boundaries: The Intellectual Tradition of Trinidad and Tobago in the Nineteenth Century.* Amherst: University of Massachusetts Press, 2003.

———. "C.L.R. James Misbound." *Transition* 58 (1992): 124–36.

Daguillard, Fritz. *Mystérieux dans la Gloire: Toussaint Louverture (1743–1803).* Port-au-Prince: MIPANAH, 2003.

Dalleo, Raphael. "'The Independence so hardly won has been maintained': C.L.R. James and the U.S. Occupation of Haiti." *Cultural Critique* 87 (spring 2014): 38–59.

Dash, J. Michael. *Haiti and the United States: National Stereotypes and the Literary Imagination.* London: Macmillan, 1997.

Davis, Natalie Zemon. *Slaves on Screen: Film and Historical Vision.* Cambridge, MA: Harvard University Press, 2000.

de Cauna, Jacques. *Toussaint Louverture et l'indépendance d'Haïti.* Paris: Karthala Cauna, 2004.

de Roux, Emmanuel. "La discrète célébration du 150e anniversaire de l'abolition de l'esclavage." *Le Monde,* April 5, 1998.

Debien, Gabriel, Jean Fouchard, and Marie-Antoinette Menier. "Toussaint Louverture avant 1789, légendes et réalités." *Conjonction: revue franco-haïtienne* 134 (1977): 65–80.

Deleuze, Gilles. "Difference & Repetition." In *French Philosophy since 1945: Problems Concepts and Inventions*, edited by Etienne Balibar and John Rajchman. New York: New Press, 2011.

Denzer, LaRay. "Wallace-Johnson and the Sierra Leone Labor Crisis of 1939." *African Studies Review* 25, nos. 2/3 (1982): 159–84.

Derrick, Jonathan. *"Africa's Agitators": Militant Anti-Colonialism in Africa and the West, 1918–1939*. New York: Columbia University Press, 2008.

Dirks, Nicholas B. "History as the Sign of the Modern." *Public Culture* 2, no. 2 (1990): 25–32.

Dobie, Madeleine. *Trading Places: Colonization and Slavery in Eighteenth-Century French Culture*. Ithaca, NY: Cornell University Press, 2010.

Drake, St. Clair. *Black Folk Here and There*. Los Angeles: Center for Afro-American Studies, University of California, 1987.

Drescher, Seymour. "Civilizing Insurgency: Two Variants of Slave Revolts in the Age of Revolution." In *Who Abolished Slavery? Slave Revolts and Abolitionism: A Debate with João Pedro Marques*, edited by Seymour Drescher and Pieter C. Emmer. New York: Berghahn Books, 2010.

Drescher, Seymour, and Pieter Emmer, eds. *Who Abolished Slavery: Slave Revolts and Abolitionism: A Debate with João Pedro Marques*. New York: Berghahn Books, 2010.

Driver, Felix, and Bill Schwarz. "Editorial: Haiti Remembered." *History Workshop Journal* 46 (1998).

Dubois, Laurent. *Avengers of the New World: The Story of the Haitian Revolution*. Cambridge, MA: Harvard University Press, 2004.

———. *A Colony of Citizens: Revolution and Slave Emancipation in the French Caribbean, 1787–1804*. Chapel Hill: University of North Carolina Press, 2004.

———. "An Enslaved Enlightenment: Re-Thinking the Intellectual History of the French Atlantic." *Social History* 31, no. 1 (February 2006): 1–14.

———. "Foreword." In C.L.R. James, *Toussaint Louverture: The Story of the Only Successful Slave Revolt in History*, vii–x. Durham, NC: Duke University Press, 2013.

Dubois, Laurent, and John D. Garrigus. *Slave Revolution in the Caribbean, 1789–1804: A Brief History with Documents*. Boston: Bedford/St. Martin's, 2006.

Dupuy, Alex. "Toussaint L'Ouverture and the Haitian Revolution: A Reassessment of C.L.R. James's Interpretation." In *C.L.R. James: His Intellectual Legacies*, edited by Selwyn R. Cudjoe and William E. Cain, 106–17. Amherst: University of Massachusetts Press, 1995.

Edwards, Brent Hayes. *The Practice of Diaspora: Literature, Translation and the Rise of Black Internationalism*. Cambridge, MA: Harvard University Press, 2003.

Emery, Mary Lou. *Modernism, the Visual, and Caribbean Literature*. Cambridge: Cambridge University Press, 2007.

Fabian, Johannes. *Time and the Other: How Anthropology Makes Its Object*. New York: Columbia University Press, 1983.

Farred, Grant, ed. *Rethinking C. L. R. James.* Oxford: Blackwell, 1996.

Featherstone, David. *Resistance, Space and Political Identities: The Making of Counter-Global Networks.* Chichester: Wiley-Blackwell, 2008.

Fergus, Claudius, K. *Revolutionary Emancipation: Slavery and Abolitionism in the British West Indies.* Baton Rouge: Louisiana State University Press, 2013.

———. "War, Revolution and Abolitionism." In *Capitalism and Slavery: Fifty Years Later: Eric Eustace Williams—A Reassessment of the Man and His Work,* edited by Heather Cateau and Selwyn Carrington, 173–91. New York: Lang, 2000.

Ferrer, Ada. *Freedom's Mirror: Cuba and Haiti in the Age of Revolution.* Cambridge: Cambridge University Press, 2014.

Fick, Carolyn E. *The Making of Haiti: The Saint Domingue Revolution from Below.* Knoxville: University of Tennessee Press, 1990.

———. "The Saint Domingue Slave Revolution and the Unfolding of Independence, 1971–1804." In *The World of the Haitian Revolution,* edited by David P. Geggus and Norman Fiering, 177–95. Bloomington: Indiana University Press, 2009.

Fignolé, Jean-Claude. *Moi, Toussaint Louverture.* Mont-Royal, Quebec: Plume et encre, 2004.

Firmin, Anténor. *The Equality of the Human Races.* Trans. Asselin Charles. New York: Garland, 2000.

Fischer, Sibylle. *Modernity Disavowed: Haiti and the Cultures of Slavery in the Age of Revolution.* Durham, NC: Duke University Press, 2004.

Foot, Paul. "Black Jacobin." *New Statesman,* February 2, 1979.

Forman, James. *The Political Thought of James Forman.* Detroit: Black Star, 1970.

Forsdick, Charles. "The Black Jacobin in Paris." *Journal of Romance Studies* 5, no. 3 (2005): 9–24.

———. "Exhibiting Haiti: Questioning Race at the World's Columbian Exhibition, 1893." In *The Invention of Race: Scientific and Popular Representations,* edited by Nicolas Bancel, Thomas David, and Dominic Thomas, 233–46. New York: Routledge, 2014.

———. "Postcolonial Toussaint." In *Echoes of the Haitian Revolution, 1804–2004,* edited by Martin Munro and Elizabeth Hackett-Walcott, 41–60. St. Augustine: University of the West Indies Press, 2008.

———. "Toussaint Louverture in a Globalized Frame: Reading the Revolutionary as Icon." *Contemporary French & Francophone Studies / SITES* 19, no. 2 (2015): 325–34.

———. "The Travelling Revolutionary: Translations of Toussaint Louverture." In *Reinterpreting the Haitian Revolution and Its Cultural Aftershocks,* edited by Martin Munro and Elizabeth Hackett-Walcott, 150–67. St. Augustine: University of the West Indies Press, 2006.

Forsdick, Charles, and Christian Høgsbjerg. " 'The Confrontation between Black and White Explodes into Red': Sergei Eisenstein and the Haitian Revolution." *History Workshop Journal* 78 (2014): 157–85.

Fouchard, Jean. *Les Marrons de la Liberté*. Paris: Editions de l'Ecole, 1972.

———. *The Haitian Maroons: Liberty or Death*. Trans. A. Faulkner Watts with a preface by C. L. R. James. New York: Blyden, 1981.

Fryer, Peter. *Staying Power: The History of Black People in Britain*. London: Pluto Press, 1987.

Gaines, Kevin K. *American Africans in Ghana: Black Expatriates and the Civil Rights Era*. Chapel Hill: University of North Carolina Press, 2006.

Geggus, David Patrick. "The Bois Caiman Ceremony." *Journal of Caribbean History* 25, nos. 1 and 2 (1991): 41–57.

———. *Haitian Revolutionary Studies*. Bloomington: Indiana University Press, 2002.

———, ed. *The Impact of the Haitian Revolution in the Atlantic World*. Columbia: University of South Carolina Press, 2001.

———. *Slavery, War and Revolution: The British Occupation of Saint Domingue, 1793–1798*. Oxford: Oxford University Press, 1982.

Genette, Gérard. *Paratexts: Thresholds of Interpretation*. Trans. Jane E. Lewin. Cambridge: Cambridge University Press, 1997.

Genovese, Eugene D. *From Rebellion to Revolution: Afro-American Slave Revolts in the Making of the Modern World*. Baton Rouge: Louisiana State University Press, 1979.

———. *In Red and Black: Marxian Explorations in Southern and Afro-American History*. London: Allen Lane, 1971.

Georgakas, Dan, and Marvin Surkin. *Detroit: I Do Mind Dying: A Study in Urban Revolution*. London: Redwords, 1998.

Gershenhorn, Jerry. *Melville J. Herskovits and the Racial Politics of Knowledge*. Lincoln: University of Nebraska Press, 2004.

Gillman, Susan. "Black Jacobins and New World Mediterraneans." In *Surveying the American Tropics: A Literary Geography from New York to Rio*, edited by Maria Cristina Fumagalli, Peter Hulme, Owen Robinson, and Lesley Wylie, 159–82. Liverpool: Liverpool University Press, 2013.

Gilly, Adolfo. *The Mexican Revolution*. London: Verso, 1983.

Girard, Philippe. *The Slaves Who Defeated Napoleon: Toussaint Louverture and the Haitian War of Independence, 1801–1804*. Tuscaloosa: University of Alabama Press, 2011.

Girard, Philippe, and Jean-Louis Donnadieu. "Toussaint before Louverture: New Archival Findings on the Early Life of Toussaint Louverture." *William and Mary Quarterly* 70, no. 1 (2013): 41–78.

Glick, Jeremy Matthew. *The Black Radical Tragic: Performance, Aesthetics, and the Unfinished Haitian Revolution*. New York: New York University Press, 2016.

Glover, Danny. "Haiti and Venezuela—A Personal View." *Rise* (summer/fall 2004).

Gong, Gerrit. *The Standard of "Civilization" in International Society*. New York: Oxford University Press, 1984.

Gorelick, Nathan. "Extimate Revolt: Mesmerism, Haiti, and the Origin of Psychoanalysis." *New Centennial Review* 13, no. 3 (2013): 115–38.

Gossman, Lionel. "Augustin Thierry and Liberal Historiography." *History and Theory* 14, no. 4 (1976): 3–83.

Hall, Catherine, and Keith McClelland. "Introduction." In *Race, Nation and Empire: Making Histories, 1750 to the Present*, edited by Catherine Hall and Keith McClelland. Manchester: Manchester University Press, 2010.

Hall, Catherine, Keith McClelland, Nick Draper, Kate Donington, and Rachel Lang. *Legacies of British Slave-Ownership: Colonial Slavery and the Formation of Victorian Britain*. Cambridge: Cambridge University Press, 2014.

Hall, Stuart. "Breaking Bread with History; C.L.R. James and *The Black Jacobins*: Stuart Hall Interviewed by Bill Schwarz." *History Workshop Journal* 46 (1998): 17–32.

Hallward, Peter. *Damming the Flood: Haiti, Aristide, and the Politics of Containment*. London: Verso, 2008.

Harootunian, Harry. "Shadowing History: National Narratives and the Persistence of the Everyday." *Cultural Studies* 18, nos. 2–3 (2004): 181–200.

Heidegger, Martin. *Being and Time*. Oxford: Blackwell, Oxford, 1962.

Henry, Paget. *Caliban's Reason: Introducing Afro-Caribbean Philosophy*. New York: Routledge, 2000.

Henry, Paget, and Paul Buhle, eds. *C.L.R. James's Caribbean*. Durham, NC: Duke University Press, 1992.

Higman, B. W. *Writing West Indian Histories*. London: Macmillan Education, 1999.

Hill, Robert A. "C.L.R. James: The Myth of Western Civilization." In *Enterprise of the Indies*, edited by George Lamming, 255–59. Port of Spain: Trinidad and Tobago Institute of the West Indies, 1999.

———. "In England, 1932–1938." In *C.L.R. James: His Life and Work*, edited by Paul Buhle, 61–80. London: Allison and Busby, 1986.

———. "Literary Executor's Afterword." In C. L. R. James, *American Civilization*, 293–366. Oxford: Blackwell, 1993.

———. "Preface." In *You Don't Play with Revolution: The Montreal Lectures of C.L.R. James*, edited by David Austin, xiii–xvi. Oakland, CA: AK Press, 2009.

Hobsbawm, Eric J. *The Age of Revolution: Europe, 1789–1848*. London: Abacus, 2002.

———. *Bandits*. London: Abacus, 2001.

———. "The Historians Group of the Communist Party." In *Rebels and Their Causes: Essays in Honour of A. L. Morton*, edited by Maurice Cornforth. London: Lawrence and Wishart, 1978.

Høgsbjerg, Christian. *Mariner, Renegade and Castaway: Chris Braithwaite: Seamen's Organiser, Socialist and Militant Pan-Africanist*. London: Socialist History Society and Redwords, 2014.

———. *C. L. R. James in Imperial Britain*. Durham, NC: Duke University Press, 2014.

———. "'The Fever and the Fret': C.L.R. James, the Spanish Civil War and the Writing of *The Black Jacobins*." *Critique* 44, nos. 1–2 (2016): 161–77.

———. "Introduction." In C. L. R. James, *Toussaint Louverture: The Story of the Only Successful Slave Revolt in History*, 1–39. Durham, NC: Duke University Press, 2013.

———. "'A Thorn in the Side of Great Britain': C.L.R. James and the Caribbean Labour Rebellions of the 1930s." *Small Axe* 35 (2011): 24–42.

Hooker, James R. *Black Revolutionary: George Padmore's Path from Communism to Pan-Africanism*. New York: Praeger, 1967.

Horne, Gerald. *Confronting Black Jacobins: The United States, the Haitian Revolution, and the Origins of the Dominican Republic*. New York: Monthly Review Press, 2015.

Hourcade, Renaud. "Un musée d'histoire face à la question raciale: l'International Slavery Museum de Liverpool." *Genèses* 92 (2013): 6–27.

Hunt, Alfred N. *Haiti's Influence on Antebellum America: Slumbering Volcano in the Caribbean*. Baton Rouge: Louisiana State University Press, 1988.

Ibbott, Ralph. *Ujamaa: The Hidden Story of Tanzania's Socialist Villages*. London: Crossroads Books, 2014.

Inikori, J. E. "The Import of Firearms into West Africa, 1750–1807: A Quantitative Analysis." *Journal of African History* 18, no. 3 (1977): 339–68.

Ivy, James W. "Break the Image of the White God . . ." *Crisis* 46, no. 8 (August 1939).

Jackson, Maurice, and Jacqueline Bacon, eds. *African Americans and the Haitian Revolution*. New York: Routledge: 2010.

———. "Fever and Fret: The Haitian Revolution and African American Responses." In *African Americans and the Haitian Revolution*, edited by Maurice Jackson and Jacqueline Bacon, 7–24. New York: Routledge, 2010.

James, Leslie. *George Padmore and Decolonization from Below: Pan-Africanism, the Cold War, and the End of Empire*. Houndmills: Palgrave Macmillan, 2015.

James, Selma. "Introduction." In Ralph Ibbott, *Ujamaa: The Hidden Story of Tanzania's Socialist Villages*, 13–39. London: Crossroads Books, 2014.

Jameson, Fredric. *The Hegel Variations*. New York: Verso, 2010.

Jeyifo, Biodun. "Whose Theatre, Whose Africa?: Wole Soyinka's *The Road on the Road*." *Modern Drama* 45, no. 3 (2002).

———. *Wole Soyinka: Politics, Poetics and Postcolonialism*. Cambridge: Cambridge University Press, 2004.

Johnson, Howard. "Decolonising the History Curriculum in the Anglophone Caribbean." *Journal of Imperial and Commonwealth History* 30, no. 1 (2002): 27–60.

Johnson, James Weldon. "Self-Determining Haiti." *Nation* 111 (August 28, 1920).

Kadalie, Modibo M. "Introduction." In *Organization and Spontaneity*, edited by Kimathi Mohammed, 11–30. Atlanta: On Our Own Authority!, 2012.

Kamugisha, Aaron. "C. L. R. James's *The Black Jacobins* and the Making of the Modern Atlantic World." In *Ten Books that Shaped the British Empire: Creating an Imperial Commons*, edited by Antoinette Burton and Isabel Hofmeyr, 190–215. Durham, NC: Duke University Press, 2014.

Kaplan, Cora, and John Oldfield, eds. *Imagining Transatlantic Slavery*. Basingstoke: Palgrave, 2010.

Kaye, Anthony. *Joining Places: Slave Neighborhoods in the Old South*. Chapel Hill: University of North Carolina Press, 2007.

Kelley, Robin D. G. "The World the Diaspora Made: C.L.R. James and the Politics of History." In *Rethinking C. L. R. James*, edited by Grant Farred, 103–30. Oxford: Blackwell, 1996.

Kemp, Martin. *Christ to Coke: How Image Becomes Icon*. Oxford: Oxford University Press, 2012.

King, Nicole. *C.L.R. James and Creolization: Circles of Influence*. Jackson: University of Mississippi Press, 2001.

———. "C.L.R. James, Genre and Cultural Politics." In *Beyond Boundaries: C.L.R. James and Postnational Studies*, edited by Christopher Gair, 13–38. London: Pluto, 2006.

Knight, Franklin W. "The Haitian Revolution and the Notion of Human Rights." *Journal of the Historical Society* 5, no. 3 (2005).

———. "Toussaint, the Revolution and Haiti." *Reviews in American History* 2, no. 2 (1974).

Krantz, Frederick, ed. *History from Below: Studies in Popular Protest and Popular Ideology*. Oxford: Blackwell, 1988.

Kristeva, Julia. "Women's Time." *Signs* 7, no. 1 (1981): 13–35.

Laguerre, Michel S. *Voodoo and Politics in Haiti*. New York: St. Martin Press, 1989.

Law, Robin. "Horses, Firearms, and Political Power in Pre-Colonial West Africa." *Past & Present* 72 (1976).

Le Glaunec, Jean-Pierre. *"Tant qu'il resterait un nègre." La bataille de Vertières ou l'histoire d'Haïti*. Montreal: Lux, forthcoming.

Lindenberger, Herbert. *Historical Drama: The Relation of Literature and Reality*. Chicago: University of Chicago Press, 1975.

Livingstone, Ken. "Why I am saying sorry for London's role in this horror." *Guardian*, March 21, 2007. http://www.guardian.co.uk/commentisfree/2007/mar/21/comment.society.

Löwy, Michael. *Morning Star: Surrealism, Marxism, Anarchism, Situtationism, Utopia*. Austin: University of Texas Press, 2009.

Macmillan, W. M. *Warning from the West Indies: A Tract for Africa and the Empire*. London: Books for Libraries Press, 1936.

MacPhee, Josh. "68: The Black Jacobins." *Just Seeds*, Judging Books by Their Covers, 68 (July 21, 2011). http://justseeds.org/jbbtc-68-the-black-jacobins/.

MARHO (Radical Historians' Organization), ed. *Visions of History*. Manchester: Manchester University Press, 1983.

McAuley, Christopher. *The Mind of Oliver C. Cox*. South Bend, IN: University of Notre Dame Press, 2004.

Magloire, Gérarde, and Kevin Yelvington. "Haiti and the Anthropological Imagination." *Gradhiva* 1 (2005): 127–52.

Maingot, Anthony P. "Politics and Populist Historiography in the Caribbean: Juan Bosch and Eric Williams." In *Intellectuals in the Twentieth-Century Caribbean: Volume II, Unity in Variety: The Hispanic and Francophone Caribbean,* edited by Alistair Hennessy. London: Macmillan Caribbean, 1992.

Mandela, Nelson. *Long Walk to Freedom.* Boston: Back Bay Books, 1995.

Manela, Erez. *The Wilsonian Moment: Self-Determination and the International Origins of Anti-Colonial Nationalism.* New York: Oxford University Press, 2007.

Marable, Manning. "Black Studies and the Racial Mountain." *Souls: Black Politics, Culture, and Society* 2, no. 3 (2000): 17–36.

Marques, João Pedro. "Slave Revolts and the Abolition of Slavery: An Overinterpretation." Trans. Richard Wall. In *Who Abolished Slavery: Slave Revolts and Abolitionism: A Debate with João Pedro Marques,* edited by Seymour Drescher and Pieter Emmer, 1–89. New York: Berghahn, 2010.

May, Vivian M. "'It Is Never a Question of the Slaves': Anna Julia Cooper's Challenge to History's Silences in Her 1925 Sorbonne Thesis." *Callaloo* 31, no. 3 (2008): 903–18.

Maza, Sarah. *The Myth of the French Bourgeoisie: An Essay on the Social Imaginary, 1750–1850.* Cambridge, MA: Harvard University Press, 2003.

McLemee, Scott. "Afterword: American Civilization and World Revolution; C.L.R. James in the United States, 1938–1953 and Beyond." In *C.L.R. James and Revolutionary Marxism,* edited by Paul Le Blanc and Scott McLemee, 209–38. Atlantic Highlands, NJ: Humanities Press, 1994.

———. "C.L.R. James: A Biographical Introduction." *American Visions* (1996).

McLemee, Scott, and Paul Le Blanc, eds. *C.L.R. James and Revolutionary Marxism: Selected Writings of C.L.R. James, 1939–1949.* Amherst, NY: Humanity, 1994.

Meeks, Brian. "Re-Reading *The Black Jacobins:* James, the Dialectic and the Revolutionary Conjuncture." *Social and Economic Studies* 43, no. 3 (1994).

———. "Re-Reading *The Black Jacobins:* James, the Dialectic and the Revolutionary Conjuncture." In Brian Meeks, *Radical Caribbean: From Black Power to Abu Bakr.* Kingston: Press of the University of the West Indies, 1996.

Merom, Gil. *How Democracies Lose Small Wars: State, Society, and the Failures of France in Algeria, Israel in Lebanon, and the United States in Vietnam.* Cambridge: Cambridge University Press, 2003.

Miller, Paul B. *Elusive Origins: The Enlightenment in the Modern Caribbean Historical Imagination.* Charlottesville: University of Virginia Press, 2010.

Mirzoeff, Nicholas. *The Right to Look: A Counterhistory of Visuality.* Durham, NC: Duke University Press, 2011.

Mohammed, Kimathi. *Organization and Spontaneity.* Atlanta: On Our Own Authority!, 2012.

Moitt, Bernard. "Transcending Linguistic and Cultural Frontiers in Caribbean Historiography: C.L.R. James, French Sources, and Slavery in San Domingo." In *C.L.R. James: His Intellectual Legacies*, edited by Selwyn Cudjoe and William E. Cain. Amherst: University of Massachusetts Press, 1995.

Morris, Rosalind C., ed. *Can the Subaltern Speak? Reflections on the History of an Idea*. New York: Columbia University Press, 2010.

Moschovakis, Nick. "Reading *Macbeth* in Texts by and about African Americans, 1903–1944: Race and the Problematics of Allusive Identification." In *Weyward Macbeth: Intersections of Race and Performance*, edited by Scott L. Newstok and Ayanna Thompson, 65–75. New York: Palgrave Macmillan, 2010.

Moyn, Samuel. *The Last Utopia: Human Rights in History*. Cambridge, MA: Harvard University Press, 2010.

Munslow, Alun. *Narrative and History*. Basingstoke: Palgrave Macmillan, 2007.

Murphy, David. *Sembene: Imagining Alternatives in Film and Fiction*. Oxford: James Currey, 2000.

Nesbitt, Nick. *Caribbean Critique*. Liverpool: Liverpool University Press, 2013.

———. "The Idea of 1804." *Yale French Studies* 107 (2005): 6–38.

———. *Universal Emancipation: The Haitian Revolution and the Radical Enlightenment*. Charlottesville: University of Virginia Press, 2008.

Nicholls, David. *From Dessalines to Duvalier: Race, Color, and National Independence in Haiti*. Cambridge: Cambridge University Press, 1979.

Nielsen, Aldon Lynn. *C.L.R. James: A Critical Introduction*. Jackson: University Press of Mississippi, 1997.

Nwankwo, Ifeoma Kiddoe. *Black Cosmopolitanism: Racial Consciousness and Transnational Identity in the Nineteenth-Century Americas*. Philadelphia: University of Pennsylvania Press, 2005.

Oehser, Paul H. "Louis Jean Pierre Vieillot (1748–1831)." *Auk* 65, no. 4 (1948): 568–76.

Ott, Thomas O. *The Haitian Revolution 1789–1804*. Knoxville: University of Tennessee Press, 1973.

Palmer, R. R. *1789: les révolutions de la liberté et de l'égalité*. Paris: Calmann-Lévy, 1967.

———. *The Age of the Democratic Revolution: A Political History of Europe and America, 1760–1800. Volume I: The Challenge*. Princeton, NJ: Princeton University Press, 1959.

———. *The Age of the Democratic Revolution: A Political History of Europe and America, 1760–1800. Volume II: The Struggle*. Princeton, NJ: Princeton University Press, 1964.

———. *The World of the French Revolution*. New York: Harper and Row, 1971.

Paton, Diana. "Telling Stories about Slavery." *History Workshop Journal* 59 (2005): 251–62.

Pétrié-Grenouilleau, Olivier. "Slave Resistance and Abolitionism: A Multi-Faceted Issue." In *Who Abolished Slavery: Slave Revolts and Abolitionism: A Debate with*

João Pedro Marques, edited by Seymour Drescher and Pieter Emmer. New York: Berghahn Books, 2010.

Pettinger, Alasdair. "'Eh! eh! Bomba, hen! hen!': Making Sense of a Vodou Chant." In *Obeah and Other Powers: The Politics of Caribbean Religion and Healing*, edited by Diana Paton and Maarit Forde, 80–102. Durham, NC: Duke University Press, 2012.

Pinkard, Terry. *German Philosophy, 1760–1860: The Legacy of Idealism*. Cambridge: Cambridge University Press, 2002.

Price, Richard, and Sally Price. *The Roots of Roots: Or, How Afro-American Anthropology Got Its Start*. Chicago: Prickly Paradigm, 2003.

Przeworski, Adam. "Conquered or Granted? A History of Suffrage Extensions." *British Journal of Political Science* 39, no. 2 (2009): 291–321.

Quest, Matthew. "Afterword: C.L.R. James and Kimathi Mohammed's Circle of Black Power Activists in Michigan." In *Organization and Spontaneity*, edited by Kimathi Mohammed, 105–32. Atlanta: On Our Own Authority!, 2012.

———. "Every Cook Can Govern: Direct Democracy, Workers' Self-Management, and the Creative Foundations of C.L.R. James's Political Thought," *The C.L.R. James Journal* 19, nos. 1–2 (Fall 2013): 374–91.

———. "George Padmore and C.L.R. James's *International African Opinion*." In *George Padmore: Pan African Revolutionary*, edited by Rupert Lewis and Fitzroy Baptiste, 97–132. Kingston: Ian Randall Press, 2009.

———. "Silences on the Suppression of Workers' Self-Emancipation: Historical Problems with C.L.R. James's Interpretation of V.I. Lenin," *Insurgent Notes* 10 (October 2012).

———. "The 'Not So Bright Protégées' and the Comrades that 'Never Quarreled': C.L.R. James's Disputes on Labor's Self-Emancipation and the Political Economy of Colonial Freedom," *Insurgent Notes* 11 (October 2013).

Quinn, Kate, ed. *Black Power in the Caribbean*. Gainesville: University Press of Florida, 2014.

Rabbit, Kara. "C.L.R. James's Figuring of Toussaint Louverture: *The Black Jacobins* and the Literary Hero." In *C.L.R. James: His Intellectual Legacies*, edited by Selwyn Cudjoe and William Cain, 118–35. Amherst: University of Massachusetts Press, 1994.

Rawick, George, P. *From Sundown to Sunup: The Making of the Black Community*. Westport, CT: Greenwood, 1972.

Rediker, Marcus. *The Slave Ship: A Human History*. London: John Murray, 2007.

Renault, Matthieu. *C. L. R. James: la vie révolutionnaire d'un 'Platon noir.'* Paris: La Découverte, 2016.

Renda, Mary. *Taking Haiti: Military Occupation and the Culture of U.S. Imperialism, 1915–1940*. Chapel Hill: University of North Carolina Press, 2001.

Renton, Dave. *C.L.R. James: Cricket's Philosopher King*. London: Haus, 2007.

Richards, W. A. "The Import of Firearms into West Africa in the Eighteenth Century." *Journal of African History* 21, no. 1 (1980): 43–59.

Robinson, Cedric. *Black Marxism: The Making of the Black Radical Tradition.* 1983; Chapel Hill: University of North Carolina Press, 2000.

Roediger, David, and Martin Smith, eds. *Listening to Revolt: The Selected Writings of George Rawick.* Chicago: Charles H. Kerr, 2010.

Rose, Jacqueline. *Women in Dark Times.* London: Bloomsbury, 2014.

Rose, R. B. *The Enragés.* Melbourne: Melbourne University Press, 1965.

———. *The Making of the Sansculottes.* Manchester: Manchester University Press, 1983.

Rosengarten, Frank. *Urbane Revolutionary: C.L.R. James and the Struggle for a New Society.* Jackson: University Press of Mississippi, 2008.

Rudé, George. *The Crowd in the French Revolution.* Oxford: Clarendon, 1959.

———. *The Crowd in the French Revolution.* London: Oxford University Press, 1969.

Rueschemeyer, Dietrich, Evelyne Huber Stephens, and John D. Stephens. *Capitalist Development and Democracy.* Chicago: University of Chicago Press, 1992.

Said, Edward W. *Culture and Imperialism.* London: Chatto and Windus, 1993.

———. *Orientalism.* New York: Pantheon, 1978.

———. "Travelling Theory." In Edward W. Said, *The World, the Text and the Critic,* 226–47. 1983; London: Vintage, 1991.

———. "Travelling Theory Reconsidered." In *Critical Reconstructions: The Relationship of Fiction and Life,* edited by R. Polhemus and R. Henke, 251–65. Stanford, CA: Stanford University Press, 1994.

Sala-Molins, Louis. *Les Misères des Lumières: Sous la raison, l'outrage.* Paris: Robert Laffont, 1992.

Salvemini, Gaetano. *The French Revolution: 1788–1792.* Trans. I. M. Rawson. London: Jonathan Cape, 1969.

Sander, Reinhard W. "C.L.R. James and the Haitian Revolution." *World Literature Written in English* 26, no. 2 (1986): 277–90.

———. "The Trinidad Awakening: West Indian Literature of the Nineteen-Thirties." Ph.D. diss., University of Texas, Austin, 1979.

———. *The Trinidad Awakening: West Indian Literature of the Nineteen-Thirties.* New York: Greenwood, 1988.

Sannon, H. Pauléus. *Histoire de Toussaint-Louverture,* 3 vols. Port-au-Prince: A.A. Héraux, 1920–1933.

Santiago-Valles, W. F. "The Caribbean Intellectual Tradition that Produced C.L.R. James and Walter Rodney." *Race and Class* 42, no. 2 (2000).

Schama, Simon. *Citizens: A Chronicle of the French Revolution.* London: Random House, 1989.

Schwarz, Bill. "'Already the Past': Memory and Historical Time." In *Regimes of Memory,* edited by Susannah Radstone and Katharine Hodgkin. London: Routledge, 2003.

———. "Becoming Postcolonial." In *Without Guarantees: Essays in Honour of Stuart Hall*, edited by Paul Gilroy, Lawrence Grossberg, and Angela McRobbie. Verso, London, 2000.

———. "C.L.R. James's *American Civilization*." *Atlantic Studies* 2, no. 1 (2005): 15–43.

———. "C.L.R. James and George Lamming: The Measure of Historical Time." *Small Axe* 14 (2003).

———. "Crossing the Seas." In *West Indian Intellectuals in Britain*, edited by Bill Schwarz. Manchester: Manchester University Press, 2003.

———. "Not Even Past Yet." *History Workshop Journal* 57 (2004).

Scott, David. "Antinomies of Slavery, Enlightenment, and Universal History." *Small Axe* 33 (2010): 152–62.

———. *Conscripts of Modernity: The Tragedy of Colonial Enlightenment*. Durham, NC: Duke University Press, 2004.

———. "That Event, This Memory: Notes on the Anthropology of African Diasporas in the New World." *Diaspora* 1, no. 3 (1991): 261–84.

———. "The Futures of Michel-Rolph Trouillot: In Memoriam." *Small Axe* 39 (2012): v–ix.

———. "The Social Construction of Postcolonial Studies." In *Postcolonial Studies and Beyond*, edited by Ania Loomba, Suvir Kaul, Matti Bunzl, Antoinette Burton, and Jed Esty, 385–400. Durham, NC: Duke University Press, 2005.

Seidman, Derek. "An Interview with Paul Buhle." *Counterpunch*, March 8, 2004.

Sepinwall, Alyssa Goldstein. *Haitian History: New Perspectives*. New York: Routledge, 2013.

———. "Happy as a Slave: The Toussaint Louverture Miniseries." *Fiction and Film for French Historians: A Cultural Bulletin* 4, no. 1 (2013). http://h-france.net/fffh/maybe-missed/happy-as-a-slave-the-toussaint-louverture-miniseries/.

———. "The Specter of Saint-Domingue in American and French Reactions to the Haitian Revolution." In *The World of the Haitian Revolution*, edited by David P. Geggus and Norman Fiering. Bloomington: Indiana University Press, 2009.

Sewall, William H. Jr. *A Rhetoric of Bourgeois Revolution: The Abbé Sieyès and* What Is the Third Estate? Durham, NC: Duke University Press, 1994.

Sharpe, Jim, "History from Below." In *New Perspectives on Historical Writing*, edited by Peter Burke, 24–41. Cambridge: Polity, 1991.

Shepperson, George, and Thomas Price. *Independent African: John Chilembwe and the Origins, Setting and Significance of the Nyasaland Native Rising of 1915*. Edinburgh: Edinburgh University Press, 1958.

Singham, A. W. "C.L.R. James on the Black Jacobin Revolution in San Domingo: Notes toward a Theory of Black Politics." *Savacou* 1, no. 1 (1970).

Slavin, Morris. *The French Revolution in Miniature*. Princeton, NJ: Princeton University Press, 1984.

———. *The Making of an Insurrection*. Cambridge, MA: Harvard University Press, 1986.

Smith, Faith. *Creole Recitations: John Jacob Thomas and Colonial Formation in the Late Nineteenth-Century Caribbean*. Charlottesville: University of Virginia Press, 2002.

Smith, Matthew. *Red and Black in Haiti: Radicalism, Conflict, and Political Change, 1934–1957*. Chapel Hill: University of North Carolina Press, 2009.

Soboul, Albert. *The French Revolution 1787–1799*. London: NLB, 1974.

———. *The Parisian Sans-Culottes and the French Revolution, 1793–4*. London: Oxford University Press, 1964.

———. *Les Sans-culottes parisiens en l'an II. Mouvement populaire et gouvernement révolutionnaire, 2 juin 1973–1979 Thermidor an II*. Paris: Clavereuil, 1958. Translated as *The Sans-Culottes: The Popular Movement and Revolutionary Government, 1793–1794*. Oxford: Clarendon, 1964.

———. *Les sans-culottes parisiens en l'An II: mouvement populaire et gouvernement révolutionnaire, 2 juin 1793–9 thermidor An 11*. Paris: Librairie Clavereuil, 1962.

Sonenscher, Michael. *Sans-Culottes*. Princeton, NJ: Princeton University Press, 2008.

Speight, Allen. *Hegel, Literature, and the Problem of Agency*. Cambridge: Cambridge University Press, 2001.

Spivak, Gayatri Chakravorty. "Can the Subaltern Speak?" In *Colonal Discourse and Post-Colonial Theory: A Reader*, edited by Patrick Williams and Laura Chrisman, 66–111. Hemel Hempstead: Harvester Wheatsheaf, 1994.

Stoler, Ann Laura, and Frederick Cooper. "Between Metropole and Colony: Rethinking a Research Agenda." In *Tensions of Empire: Colonial Cultures in a Bourgeois World*, edited by Frederick Cooper and Ann Laura Stoler, 1–56. Berkeley: University of California Press, 1997.

Thompson, E. P. *The Making of the English Working Class*. London: Gollancz, 1963.

Thornton, John. "'I Am the Subject of the King of the Congo': African Political Ideology and the Haitian Revolution." *Journal of World History* 4, no. 2 (1995): 181–214.

Tibebu, Teshale. *Hegel and the Third World*. Syracuse, NY: Syracuse University Press, 2010.

Tomich, Dale. "Thinking the 'Unthinkable': Victor Schoelcher and Haiti." *Review* 31, no. 3 (2008): 401–31.

Trouillot, Michel-Rolph. *Haiti: State against the Nation*. New York: Monthly Review Press, 1989.

———. "Historiography of Haiti." In *General History of the Caribbean Vol. VI: Methodology and Historiography of the Caribbean*, edited by B. W. Higman, 451–77. London: UNESCO/Macmillan, 1999.

———. "The Odd and the Ordinary: Haiti, the Caribbean, and the World." *Cimarron* 2, no. 3 (1990).

———. *Peasants and Capital: Dominica in the World Economy*. Baltimore: Johns Hopkins University Press, 1988.

———. *Silencing the Past: Power and the Production of History*. Boston: Beacon Press, 1995.

———. "An Unthinkable History: The Haitian Revolution as a Non-Event." In Michel-Rolph Trouillot, *Silencing the Past: Power and the Production of History*, 70–107. Boston: Beacon, 1995.

Tyson, George. *Toussaint L'Ouverture*. Englewood Cliffs, NJ: Prentice Hall, 1973.

Vanlee, Hein. "Central African Popular Christianity and the Making of Haitian Vodou Religion." In *Central Africans and Cultural Transformations in the American Diaspora*, edited by Linda M. Heywood. Cambridge: Cambridge University Press, 2002.

Verene, Donald Philip. *Hegel's Recollection: A Study of the Images in the Phenomenology of Spirit*. Albany: State University of New York Press, 1985.

Walcott, Derek. "A Tribute to C.L.R. James." In *C.L.R. James: His Intellectual Legacies*, edited by Selwyn R. Cudjoe and William E. Cain. Amherst: University of Massachusetts Press, 1995.

———. *What the Twilight Says: Essays*. London: Faber, 1998.

Walsh, John Patrick. *Free and French in the Caribbean: Toussaint Louverture, Aimé Césaire and Narratives of Loyal Opposition*. Bloomington: Indiana University Press, 2013.

Weston, Helen. "The Many Faces of Toussaint Louverture." In *Slave Portraiture in the Atlantic World*, edited by Agnes I. Lugo-Ortiz and Angela Rosenthal, 345–73. Cambridge: Cambridge University Press, 2013.

White, Derrick, and Paul Ortiz. "Introduction to C.L.R. James on Oliver Cox's *Caste, Class, and Race*." *New Politics* 60 (Winter 2016).

White, Sarah, Roxy Harris, and Sharmilla Beezmohun, eds. *A Meeting of the Continents: The International Book Fair of Radical Black and Third World Books – Revisited*. London: New Beacon Books, 2005.

Williams, Carolyn. "The Haitian Revolution and a North American Griot: The Life of Toussaint L'Ouverture by Jacob Lawrence." In *Echoes of the Haitian Revolution, 1804–2004*, edited by Martin Munro and Elizabeth Walcott-Hackshaw, 61–85. Kingston, Jamaica: University of the West Indies Press, 2008.

Williams, Gwyn A. *Artisans and Sans-Culottes: Popular Movements in France and Britain during the French Revolution*. London: Edward Arnold, 1968.

Williams, Patrick. *Ngugi wa Thiong'o*. Manchester: Manchester University Press, 1999.

Wilson-Tagoe, Nana. *Historical Thought and Literary Representation in West Indian Literature*. Gainesville: University Press of Florida, 1998.

Wolf, Eric R. "Encounter with Norbert Elias." In *Human Figurations: Essays for Norbert Elias*, edited by Peter Gleichmann, Johan Goudsblom, and Hermann Korte. Amsterdam: Amsterdams Sociologisch Tijdschrift, 1977.

———. *Pathways of Power: Building an Anthropology of the Modern World*. Berkeley: University of California Press, 2001.

Worcester, Kent. *C.L.R. James: A Political Biography*. New York: State University of New York Press, 1996.

Young, James D. *The World of C.L.R. James: His Unfragmented Vision*. Glasgow: Clydeside Press, 1999.

Žižek, Slavoj. "Democracy versus the People." *New Statesman*, August 14, 2008. http://www.newstatesman.com/books/2008/08/haiti-aristide-lavalas (accessed October 21, 2010).

CONTRIBUTORS

MUMIA ABU-JAMAL is an award-winning journalist and author of several works, including his best-selling *Live from Death Row*, which brilliantly portrays the deep impact of death row on individual prisoners, *Death Blossoms: Reflections from a Prisoner of Conscience*, *We Want Freedom: A Life in the Black Panther Party*, and *Jailhouse Lawyers: Prisoners Defending Prisoners v. the U.S.A.*, about the inspiring resistance of prisoners to the prison system from the inside. In 1981 he was elected president of the Philadelphia chapter of the Association of Black Journalists. His 1982 trial and conviction for murder have been widely condemned for constitutional violations as well as blatant racism. Throughout the more than three decades he has spent in prison, almost all of it in solitary confinement on Pennsylvania's death row, he has consistently fought against injustice and for his freedom. He holds a BA from Goddard College and an MA from California State University, Dominguez Hills.

DAVID AUSTIN is the editor of *You Don't Play with Revolution: The Montreal Lectures of C.L.R. James* and author of *Fear of a Black Nation: Race, Sex, and Security in Sixties Montreal*. He teaches in the Humanities, Philosophy, and Religion Department at John Abbott College, Montreal.

MADISON SMARTT BELL is winner of the Strauss Living Award from the American Academy of Arts and Letters and holds the Chair for Distinguished Achievement (with his wife, poet Elizabeth Spires) at Goucher College where he is Professor in the English Department and Co-Director of the Kratz Center for Creative Writing. Among his many writings, he is the author of an epic novelized trilogy of the Haitian Revolution: *All Souls Rising*, *Master of the Crossroads*, and *The Stone That the Builder Refused*.

ANTHONY BOGUES is the Asa Messer Professor of Humanities and Critical Theory and Director of the Center for the Study of Slavery and Justice at Brown University where he is also a professor of Africana Studies and affiliated professor of History of Art and Architecture. His latest book is *From Revolution in the Tropics to*

Imagined Landscapes: The Art of Edouard Duval-Carrié (2014). His edited volume *From Slave Petitions to Black Lives Matter and Rhodes Must Fall: A History of Black Radical Thought* is forthcoming. He is currently working on a Reader on the history of Haitian Art and a major exhibition on Haitian and Caribbean art in 2018.

JOHN H. BRACEY JR. has taught in the W. E. B. Du Bois Department of Afro-American Studies at the University of Massachusetts, Amherst, since 1972. During the 1960s, he was active in the civil rights, black liberation, and other radical movements in Chicago. His publications include several coedited volumes, including *Black Nationalism in America, African-American Women and the Vote: 1837–1965, Strangers and Neighbors: Relations between Blacks and Jews in the United States,* and *African American Mosaic: A Documentary History from the Slave Trade to the Present.*

RACHEL DOUGLAS is Lecturer in French at the University of Glasgow and author of *Frankétienne and Rewriting: A Work in Progress.*

LAURENT DUBOIS is Marcello Lotti Professor of Romance Studies and History at Duke University. He is the author of *Avengers of the New World: The Story of the Haitian Revolution* and *Haiti: The Aftershocks of History.*

CLAUDIUS K. FERGUS is Senior Lecturer in the Department of History at the University of the West Indies at St. Augustine and visiting scholar at the University of Ghana, Legon. He is the author of *Revolutionary Emancipation: Slavery and Abolitionism in the British West Indies.*

CAROLYN E. FICK is Associate Professor in the Department of History at Concordia University. She is the author of many articles on the Haitian Revolution and the book *The Making of Haiti: The Saint Domingue Revolution from Below.*

CHARLES FORSDICK is James Barrow Professor of French at the University of Liverpool, and AHRC Theme Leadership Fellow for "Translating Cultures." His publications include *Travel in Twentieth-Century French and Francophone Cultures,* and he has edited and coedited a number of volumes, including *Francophone Postcolonial Studies: A Critical Introduction, Human Zoos: Science and Spectacle in the Age of Colonial Empire,* and *Postcolonial Thought in the French-Speaking World.* He was President of the Society for French Studies, 2012–14, and Co-Director of the Centre for the Study of International Slavery, 2010–13.

DAN GEORGAKAS is coauthor of *Detroit: I Do Mind Dying* and author of *My Detroit: Growing Up Greek and American in Motor City.*

ROBERT A. HILL is Professor of History and editor-in-chief of the Marcus Garvey and Universal Negro Improvement Association Papers Project at the University of California, Los Angeles. He is the literary executor of the C. L. R. James Estate.

CHRISTIAN HØGSBJERG is Teaching Fellow in Caribbean History at UCL Institute of the Americas. He is the author of *C.L.R. James in Imperial Britain* and *Chris Braithwaite: Mariner, Renegade and Castaway*, the editor of *Toussaint Louverture: The Story of the Only Successful Slave Revolt in History* by C.L.R. James, and the coeditor of *Celebrating C.L.R. James in Hackney, London*.

SELMA JAMES is founder of the International Wages for Housework Campaign and author of *The Power of Women and the Subversion of the Community*, and *Sex, Race, and Class—The Perspective of Winning*.

PIERRE NAVILLE (1903–1993) was a significant figure in postwar French social science and a prominent poet, writer, artist, and activist in both the Surrealist and Trotskyist movements.

NICK NESBITT is Professor of French at Princeton University. He is the author of *Caribbean Critique: Antillean Critical Theory from Toussaint to Glissant, Universal Emancipation: The Haitian Revolution and the Radical Enlightenment*, and *Voicing Memory: History and Subjectivity in French Caribbean Literature* and the editor of *Toussaint Louverture: The Haitian Revolution*.

ALDON LYNN NIELSEN is the George and Barbara Kelly Professor of American Literature at Pennsylvania State University. He is the author of *C.L.R. James: A Critical Introduction* and *Integral Music: Languages of African American Innovation*.

MATTHEW QUEST is Lecturer in African American Studies at Georgia State University in Atlanta. He has published widely on C. L. R. James, particularly on the themes of direct democracy and national liberation, for publications such as the *C.L.R. James Journal, Science & Society, Insurgent Notes*, and *Classical Receptions Journal*. He has also written scholarly introductions to Ida B. Wells's *Lynch Law in Georgia & Other Writings* and Joseph Edwards's *Workers Self-Management in the Caribbean*.

DAVID MICHAEL RUDDER is a singer songwriter from Trinidad and Tobago and the former United National Development Programme Goodwill Ambassador for the Caribbean. He is holder of the Hummingbird Medal (Silver) for service to Trinidad and Tobago and an Honorary Doctor of Letters from the University of the West Indies.

BILL SCHWARZ is Professor in the Department of English, Queen Mary, University of London, and an editor of *History Workshop Journal*. He is the editor of *West Indian Intellectuals in Britain, Caribbean Literature after Independence: The Case of Earl Lovelace*, and *The Locations of George Lamming*. His most recent book, *The White Man's World*, the first volume in his Memories of Empire series, won Book of the Year at the Longman/History Today Awards.

DAVID SCOTT is Professor of Anthropology at Columbia University. He is the author of *Conscripts of Modernity: The Tragedy of Colonial Enlightenment* and *Omens of Adversity: Tragedy, Time, Memory, Justice* and the editor of *Small Axe: A Caribbean Journal of Criticism*.

RUSSELL MAROON SHOATZ is a dedicated community activist, founding member of the Black Unity Council, former member of the Black Panther Party, and soldier in the Black Liberation Army. He is serving multiple life sentences as a U.S.-held prisoner of war. He is the author of *Maroon the Implacable: The Collected Writings of Russell Maroon Shoatz*.

MATTHEW J. SMITH is Professor of History at the University of the West Indies. He has published several articles and book chapters on various aspects of Haitian history and politics, and more recently a book, *Red and Black in Haiti: Radicalism, Conflict, and Political Change, 1934–1957*.

STUDS TERKEL (1912–2008) was an American Pulitzer Prize–winning author and radio broadcasting personality. He is best remembered for his oral histories of working-class Americans, in works such as *Working, Hard Times,* and *Race*. He hosted a daily radio show from 1952–1997 in Chicago on WLMT during which he conducted over five thousand interviews.

Abeng, 256
abolition, 21, 89, 167, 307; of British slavery, 7, 8, 162, 171–72, 327; commemorations of, 217–18; in French colonies, 132, 145–46, 216, 284–85, 338, 368; historiography of, 162; of slave trade, 11, 44n71, 162
Abu-Jamal, Mumia, 58, 411
Abyssinia, 7, 8, 263, 275n51. *See also* Ethiopia; IAFA
Ademola, Adegboyega, 305
Adorno, Theodor W., 38
Africa: *The Black Jacobins* and, xviii, 16, 18, 29, 87, 179, 265, 304, 305, 330; civilization and, 98, 332, 349, 350; communalism in, 83n18; Communism and, 354, 357–58; Copperbelt in, 10; France and, 375; labor movement in, 10; national independent movements in, 23–24, 73, 140, 275n51; revolutionary leaders in, 147; West Indies and, 258. *See also names of African regions and countries*
African Americans: activism of, 219; journals of, 19; in prison, 70–72; in radical labor movement, 55–56. *See also* Blacks
African diaspora, 23, 94, 199, 264, 265, 309; IBW and, 298, 300, 306; liberation struggles and, 8

African National Congress, 264, 305
Africans: *The Black Jacobins* and, 20, 162; cultural survivals of, in Caribbean, 12, 88, 169, 239, 306; creative capacity of, 357; dancing and, 6; European language acquisition of, xv–xvi, 334–35; Herskovits's theories on, 117; impressiveness of, 70–72; as intellectuals, 33; in revolutionary Haiti, 67, 76–77, 78, 167, 237–38, 316, 331–32, 340, 356; scale of Africanisms and, 117; as speakers at British labor protests, 8
African Standard, 16
agency, 129, 205, 230; of enslaved, 217, 221; of Haitian blacks, 12, 35; of Louverture, 211
Alexis, Stephen, 135n19, 192n22
Algeria, 156, 160n33, 371, 375
Alkalimat, Abdul, 298
Allison and Busby, as publisher of *The Black Jacobins*, 5, 34
Althusser, Louis, 104, 205
American Enterprise Institute, 298
Anderson, Benedict, *Imagined Communities* (1983), xv
anthropology, anthropologists, 18–20, 116; Haiti and, 117–18
anticolonialism, 22, 140–41, 156, 198, 219, 224, 226, 300, 326, 375, 376; activism for, 7, 27, 65, 199, 355; of Haitian

anticolonialism (*continued*)
Revolution, 65, 130; James and, 13,
155–56, 200, 235, 303; radical, 198, 199,
324; revolution and, 140, 211, 220;
romanticism of, 28; socialism and,
128, 129, 209
Antonius, George, *The Arab Awakening*
(1938), 13
apartheid, 23–24, 33, 73, 74, 264, 275n51,
305. *See also* South Africa
Aptheker, Herbert, 215; *American Negro
Slave Revolts* (1943), 260
Aravamudan, Srinivas, *Tropicopolitans*,
90
archives: counter-, 202; in France, 5, 7,
62, 64, 66, 189; slave sources in, xviii
Arendt, Hannah, 198, 205, 210
Aristide, Jean-Bertrand, 74, 80, 81, 135n15
Armstrong, Louis, 25
Armstrong, Lucille, 25
Arusha Declaration, 303
Asia, 98; 374, 377, 379. *See also names
of countries*
Atlantic history, 37, 88, 94, 215, 237; of
slavery and slave trade, 11, 22, 77, 83n18
Austin, David, 30, 411; on *The Black
Jacobins*, 256–72
Azikiwe, Nnamdi, 198, 354

Badiou, Alain, 134–35, 205
Baker, General, 56, 57
Ballard, Arthur, reviews *The Black
Jacobins*, 16
Bann, Stephen, 122
Baraka, Amiri, 299
Barbados, 8, 26, 51, 52n158, 217, 257, 263,
275n51, 291, 335
Barbé de Marbois, François, 347, 357
Barnave, Antoine Pierre Joseph Marie,
65, 151
Beacon, The, race debates in (1931), 2–3,
187–88, 193n29, 200, 226, 269–70

Beaubrun Ardouin, Alexis, 5, 317; *Études
sur l'histoire d'Haïti*, 188
Beckford, George, 298
Beecher, Henry, 170
Belair, 157
Bell, David A., xvii
Bell, Madison Smartt, 36, 229, 313–21, 411
Benjamin, Walter, 106, 199–200, 204–5,
206
Benn, Denis, 261
Bennet, Lerone, 298
Bernier, Celeste-Marie, *Characters of
Blood* (2012), 222
Beyond a Boundary (James, 1963), 105,
211, 265, 268, 274–75n49; concep-
tion of culture in, xvi–xvii; James on
origins of *The Black Jacobins* in, 2, 5,
226, 270, 271; James's "voyage in" in,
3; preface to, xvii; Naipaul reviews,
48n119
Biassou, Georges, 145, 166, 169, 241
Biko, Steve, 220
Black Arts Movement, 297
Blackburn, Robin, 37
*Black Jacobins, The: Toussaint L'Ouverture
and the San Domingo Revolution*
(C. L. R. James): African activists
influenced by, 20, 162; art inspired
by, 37, 51–52n158; chapter 4, "The San
Domingo Masses Begin," 131; cinematic
rights to, 230; as classic, 37, 87, 197;
as collaborative work, 7; in contemporary frame, 37–39; in context
of James's writings, 4–11; contradictions in, 156–57; cover illustrations of,
233n31; Hall on origins of, 7; internationalism in, 262; James on how he
would rewrite, 35–36; literary quality
of, 268; narrative of, 17, 171–73; Ott
on, 36–37; paratexts of, 290; pedagogical framework of, 163–64; persistent
presence of, 19–26; postcolonial

engagement with, 38; as prophecy, 23; research for, 5; rethinking of, 33–37; reviews of, 17–18; revolutionary emancipationism in, 162–74; revolution in, 142–49; Said on, 13; as seminal radical historiographical text, 197, 217; as "text-network," 4; as theoretical intervention, 120; as underground text, 19, 23–24, 33; vindicationism of, 277n88; West Indies and, xviii, 26–27, 306; Williams's contributions to, 7; Wolf on, 19, 20. *See also under separate editions*

Black Jacobins, The: Toussaint Louverture and the San Domingo Revolution (1938 ed.), 49n138, 67, 140, 278, 347–48; activists and, 15, 263, 356; ad for, 14; Africa and, 29, 65, 305, 355–56; anticolonial romanticism in, 28; bourgeois revolution in, 152; Caribbean and, 258; Caribbean revolution in, 271–72; contemporary historiography and, 3, 11–15; contemporary response to, 15–19; dust jacket of, 1, 39n2; emergence of, 1–4; as first major English-language study of Haitian Revolution, 1; global politics and, 226; goes out of print, 73; historical context of, 93–94, 198–201; IASB and, 262–63; James on genesis of, 2, 24, 35, 179, 304; James on limitations of, 34; Marxist language in, 28, 192n22; mass revolution in, 143; *Minty Alley* and, 267–68; as pioneering cultural study of revolution, xvii; preface to, xiii, xiv–xv, xvi, xvii, 15, 58, 68, 96, 162, 205, 314; publisher of, 1, 305; reception of, 17–19; reviews of, 15–16, 209; rewriting of, 25, 26–33; *Vanity Fair* and, 268–69; white sources of, 3

Black Jacobins, The: Toussaint L'Ouverture and the San Domingo Revolution

(1963 ed.), 26–33, 62, 95; Africans and language in, xv–xvi; appendix to ("From Toussaint L'Ouverture to Fidel Castro"), xviii–xix, 29, 30, 48n119, 82, 83n25, 91, 161n39, 191n7, 220, 227, 258, 259, 271, 279, 320–21, 330–31, 348; bibliography of, 135n19, 155, 227, 279; black activists and, 31, 55–57, 339–40; *The Black Jacobins* play and, 278; changes in, 28–29, 30, 62–63, 87, 135n19, 142, 151, 153, 158n8, 227, 236, 251–52, 259, 272, 273–74n23, 279, 306, 347; chapter 13, "The War of Independence," in, 28; cover illustration of, 233n31; Hall on, 32; as handbook of revolution, 36; introduction to, 29; James on success of, 31, 34; Palmer on, 30; political context of, 87; postcolonial tragedy in, 28; prologue to, 329; published by Random House, 30; U.S. civil rights movement and, 27, 331

Black Jacobins, The: Toussaint L'Ouverture and the San Domingo Revolution (1980 ed.): James's foreword to, 5, 34, 35, 76, 94, 263, 270

Black Jacobins, The: Toussaint L'Ouverture and the San Domingo Revolution (2001 ed.), 36, 233n31

Black Jacobins, The: Toussaint L'Ouverture and the San Domingo Revolution (C. L. R. James), translations and foreign editions of, 36; Caribbean edition, 47n111; Cuban edition, 36, 273n11, 322–27; German translation, 49n136, 51n157; Haitian edition, 26; Italian translation, 31–32, 34, 36, 313–21; James encourages, 49n136; Japanese translation, 49n136, 50n151; *Les Jacobins noirs* (Naville's French translation, 1949), 20–21, 22–23, 34, 36, 73, 227, 233n31, 356, 367–81; Portuguese

Black Jacobins, The (continued)
   translation, 50n151; Spanish
   translation, 47n111, 49n136, 50n151,
   257
Black Power movement, 27, 297, 299,
   340; *The Black Jacobins* and, 36, 56;
   Black Panthers and, 32; in Caribbean,
   30, 31, 259–60
blacks: agency of, 12, 277n88; *The Black
   Jacobins* and activism of, 31, 55–57,
   339–40; black modernism and, 117;
   communist revolution and, 10; as
   historians, 18; internationalism of,
   128, 267; as Jews, 275n51; liberation
   of, 330; as Marxists, 299; in Paris, 6;
   pigmentocracy and, 6, 22; as radicals
   and revolutionaries, 31, 56, 122, 309;
   U.S. civil rights movement and, 25, 27,
   31, 73, 224, 306, 331. *See also* Africans;
   African Americans
black studies, 298; *The Black Jacobins*
   and, 31
Boal, Augusto, 282
Boggs, Grace Lee, 55
Boggs, James, 55
Bogues, Anthony, 10–11, 159n17, 411–12;
   afterword of, in *Small Axe*, 36; on
   The Black Jacobins and writing and
   researching Haitian Revolution,
   197–211
Bolívar, Simón, 82, 323, 327
Bolsheviks, 99, 101, 112n33, 147, 207,
   249–50, 324; James and, 326;
   Kronstadt and, 236, 249–50; Lenin
   and, 149, 315; Stalin and, 128
Bonaparte, Napoleon, 36, 79, 91, 132, 147,
   245, 314, 374, 379; in Egypt, 371; exile
   of, 124; Haitians defeat armies of, 73,
   344; Louverture vs., xiii, 247; plans
   to restore slavery in Saint-Domingue,
   xviii, 63, 67, 138n48; tomb of, 7
Bontemps, Arna, 128

Boukman, Dutty, 65, 173, 174, 241; death
   of, 166; failed revolt of, 155, 166; James
   on, 164–65; rituals of, 20, 165
bourgeoisie: British, 8, 11–12, 362;
   French, 11, 151–52, 159n20, 159–60n26,
   341, 370, 371; Haitian Revolution and,
   21, 315, 336; moral philosophy of, 163;
   national, 239–40. *See also* middle class
Bracey, John, 36, 322–27, 412
Braithwaite, Chris (pseud. "Chris
   Jones"), 8
Brand, Dionne, 268
Brathwaite, Kamau, 46n97, 298, 273n9
Bréda, Toussaint, 130, 150, 163. *See also*
   Louverture, Toussaint
Brierre, Jean-Fernand, James and, 26,
   192n22
Brissot, Jacques Pierre (de Warville),
   65
Brockway, Fenner, 17, 44n69
Broué, Pierre, 15
Buck-Morss, Susan, 135n15, 136n24, 221;
   Hegel, Haiti, and Universal History
   (2009), 109n1, 120
Buhle, Paul, 37, 51n156
Burke, Edmund, *Reflections on the Revo-
   lution in France*, 210

Cabral, Amilcar, 199, 220
Caesar, Julius, xvi, 124
Callinicos, Alex, 15
Cambodia, 375
Canada, 30, 31, 81, 256, 271, 275n51, 335,
   351, 376; Montreal, 30, 61, 256
capital, capitalism, xv, 16, 74, 78, 116,
   159n26, 161n40, 223, 377; feudal,
   243–47; Haitian Revolution and,
   324, 326; imperialism and, 102, 156,
   372–73, 375; Marxists on, 12, 96, 99,
   140, 151–52, 160n29, 251, 303; primitive,
   141–42, 157; state, 83n15, 251
Carew, Jan, 46n97, 271

Caribbean, xv, xviii, 87, 102, 219, 256, 269, 288, 322, 380; African liberation and, 275n51; attitude of, 304, 306; *The Black Jacobins* and, 20, 258, 304; Black Power and New Left in, 30, 259–60; British and, 371; CARICOM and, 82; cultural revolution in, xix; eastern, 167; Francophone, 27, 73, 374, 375; history of, 18, 162, 173; labor rebellions in, 7–8; national identity and independent movements in, xviii–xix, 23–24, 140, 189; revolution in, 87; self-government in, 2, 5; studies, 116; writers of, 135n19. *See also* West Indies; *and names of individual islands*

Caribs, 8, 167, 272

Carmichael, Stokely, 31, 330

Carruthers Jacob, 162

Casey, Michael, *Che's Afterlife*, 222–23

Castro, Fidel, xviii 28, 30, 83n25, 220, 305, 348; James on, 190n2, 320, 330, 348; Louverture compared to, 320–21

Cato Institute, 298

Central America, 68, 275. *See also* Latin America

Césaire, Aimé, 34, 51n158, 135n19, 330, 349; *The Black Jacobins* and, 73; James and, 135n19, 218, 219–20, 227, 234n45, 258, 305, 348–49; *Notebook of a Return to My Native Land*, 271; *Toussaint Louverture*, 318

Chakrabarty, Dipesh, 111n15, 112n31, 113n42, 155, 161n40

Charlier, Étienne: *Aperçu sur la formation historique de la nation haïtienne* (1954), 22, 34, 215, 228; James and, 22–23, 64, 228

China, 20, 156, 380; Chinese Revolution (1925–27) and, 15, 24, 156

Churchill, Winston, 376–77

cinema and film, xvi, 49n136, 230

Cipriani, Arthur Andrew, 5, 189, 276n67, 295n32

Clarkson, Thomas, 173

class, classes, 18, 32, 181, 251, 252, 268; analysis of, 299, 300, 319; antagonism between, 151; characteristics of, 80; definition of, 76; formation of, 32; interests and concerns of, 104, 181, 245; intermediate, 341, 342; James on, 161n36, 164, 172, 261, 319, 323; Marx on, 160n29; medieval, 315; nexus of race and, xiv, 6, 11, 22, 167–71, 260, 299, 302–3, 309, 316, 369; pigmentocracy and, 22; Trotsky on, 15, 107. *See also* class struggle; *and names of social classes*

class struggle, 31; *The Black Jacobins* and, 18; Haitian Revolution and, 11, 169, 236, 237, 369–70

Cleaver, Eldridge, 260

CLRJSC (C.L.R. James Study Circle) (Montreal), 30, 256–57, 266

Cobb, Richard, *The Police and the People* (1970), 60

Cockrel, Ken, 56

Colbert, Jean-Baptiste, 371, 373

colonialism, 19, 29, 37, 87, 131, 132, 148, 162, 307, 327, 372; James and, 155, 202, 302; liberation from and resistance to, 264, 265, 268; post-, 26, 38, 156, 173, 179, 219, 241; slavery and, 286, 327. *See also* anticolonialism

Coloured Workers' Association, 365

Columbia University, 19, 351

Columbus, Christopher, 22, 30, 220, 329

Communism, Communists, 16, 17, 128, 136n21, 160n36, 250, 251, 260, 314, 324, 353, 357–58

Communist (Third) International (Comintern), 17, 128, 199, 201, 263, 314, 324, 326; Padmore and, 353–54, 363

Communist Party Historians' Group, 17, 44n71

Communist Party of Great Britain, 17, 129, 353

Communist Party (US), 353

Condé, Maryse, 228

Congo, 27, 156, 206

Congress of African Peoples, 299

Congress of Black Writers, 256, 272n3

Constantine, Learie, 323

Cools, Anne, 30, 256, 257

Cooper, Anna J., *Slavery and the French Revolutionists (1788–1805)* (1988), 42n52

Cooper, Frederick, 10

counterrevolution, 21, 141, 250, 326, 358, 359; Stalinist, 1, 10

Courlander, Harold, reviews *The Black Jacobins*, 18

Cox, Oliver Cromwell, 35; *Caste, Class, and Race*, 50n149, 302; James on, 302–3

cricket, 174, 268, 274n49; in *Beyond a Boundary*, xvi, 87, 105; James as reporter of, 5, 8, 323

Cripps, Louise, 6–7, 40n26, 192n24

Cripps, Stafford, 355

Crisis, The, 19, 128

Cuba, Cubans, 29, 57; *The Black Jacobins* and, 36, 47n111, 257, 273n11, 307, 322, 324; Haiti and, 220, 232n18, 321, 323; James in, 219, 234n45; James on, 324, 330, 335; Revolution of, xviii–xix, 27, 28, 37, 156, 220, 271, 320, 324, 335; United States and, 184, 322

Cudjoe, Selwyn R., 2

Dahomey (Benin), 117

Daily Gleaner, 184

Daly, Patricia, 298

Damas, Léon-Gontran, 40; James and, 5

Danquah, J. B., 305

Davidson, Basil, 29, 332

Davis, Angela, 324

Davis, Natalie Zemon, 230

Davis, N. Darnell, 182

Declaration of the Rights of Man and Citizen (1789), 118, 172

decolonization, 24, 30, 36, 87, 156, 189

de Gaulle, Charles, 379

Deleuze, Gilles, 205–6

Demerara, 217

Derrida, Jacques, 205

Dessalines, Jean-Jacques, 10, 132, 154, 157, 165, 180, 227, 230, 285, 317–18, 380; constitution of 1805 and, 210; creates disorganized society, 184; demythologization of, 279; generalship of, 189; Haitian independence and, 147; James on, 344; in James's play, 281, 283–84, 291; rise of, 325; whites massacred by, 40n21

Detroit, 55, 256, 302; *The Black Jacobins* in, 31, 55–57; James on, 112n34, 307, 308

dialectics, 261, 374; Hegelian, 163, 303; James on, xiii–xiv, 163–64, 166, 169, 174n6, 251, 306, 326. *See also* James, C. L. R., works of: *Notes on Dialectics*

Dial Press, as publisher of *The Black Jacobins*, 17

Diderot, Denis, 148, 338

Dirks, Nicholas, 97

Dodson, Howard, 298, 299

Domingo, W. A., 187

Douglas, Rachel, 30, 412; on *The Black Jacobins* play, 278–91

Douglass, Frederick, 127, 222

Drake, St. Clair, 277n88, 298

Drescher, Seymour, 162

DRUM (Dodge Revolutionary Union Movement), 56

Dubois, Laurent, 36, 120, 250, 412; *Avengers of the New World*, 313; on Haitian slaves becoming citizens, 118–19; on reading *The Black Jacobins*, 87–92

Du Bois, W. E. B., 215, 220, 303, 306, 308, 324; *Black Reconstruction in America* (1935), 12, 35, 37, 42n49, 197, 210, 307, 308, 309, 324, 325, 363; in *The Crisis*, 128, 137n40; Garvey and, 333; on Haitian Revolution, 22; James on, 308, 324, 350, 363; on Louverture, 216; Mandela on, 276n56; *The Souls of Black Folk*, 324

Dunayevskaya, Raya, 19, 20, 55

Dupuy, Alex, on *The Black Jacobins*, 235–36

Duval-Carrié, Edouard, 224

Duvalier, François "Papa Doc," 26, 320

Duvalierism, 27, 321

East Africa, 372

Eisenstein, Sergei, 230

Eliot, T. S., 302

elites, 70, 181, 323; Black, 374; of France, 154, 244, 251; of Haiti, 80, 81, 115, 157, 170; language of, 284; postcolonial, 249, 287, 376; as white, 248. *See also* ruling class

emancipation, 133, 369, 370, 374, 379; of Africa, 162, 363, 364; Black, 333, 342; bourgeoisie and, 89; British, 178–79, 181, 185, 188, 269; Caribbean, 258; Haitian Revolution and, 10, 120, 129, 207, 246, 249; revolutionary, 162–74; self-, 130, 215, 235, 237, 240, 242, 357; universal, 119, 129, 130, 157, 221, 225

Engels, Friedrich, 102, 207

English language, 1, 15, 73, 197, 209, 313

Enlightenment, 374; constructivism of, 122; French Revolution and, 144; impact of, in colonies, 90–91; liberty and, 173; Louverture and, 130, 148,

165, 172, 244; racism of, 89; rationality of, xv

Ethiopia: invaded by Italy, 6, 7, 94, 199, 226, 263, 267, 275n51, 354; James and, 8, 10, 263; Pan-Africanism and, 7; support for, 8, 9. *See also* Abyssinia

Ethiopian World Federation, 275n51

Europe, 3, 199; civilization and, 97–98; communist revolution in, 10, 207; fascism in, 4. *See also names of European cities and countries*

Faber, Seymour, 55

Facing Reality (Detroit), 55, 256

Fanon, Frantz, 22, 34, 38, 46n97, 160n33, 304; *The Black Jacobins* and, 45n91, 73; James and, 305

fascism, fascists, 18, 67, 261, 353, 359; anti-, 17; colonial, 199; Ethiopian invasion and, 10, 263, 267; as greater threat than Stalinism, 315; refugees from, 19. *See also* Germany; Italy

Federal City College (University of the District of Columbia), James teaches at, 31, 301, 303

Fergus, Claudius K., 412; on revolutionary emancipationism in *The Black Jacobins*, 162–74

Fick, Carolyn, 36, 37, 60–68, 214n43, 228, 229, 237, 245; doctoral thesis of, 34, 64; James meets with, 60, 61–62; *The Making of Haiti: The Saint Domingue Revolution from Below* (1990), 34, 60, 62, 64, 66, 68, 112n26, 143, 209–10

Fignolé, Jean-Claude, *Moi, Toussaint Louverture*, 225

Firmin, Anténor, *De l'égalité des races humaines* (1885), 188

Fischer, Sibylle, 221

Foot, Michael, 17, 44n70

Foot, Paul, 44n70

Ford, Arnold, 275n51

Forsdick, Charles, 381, 412; on Louverture's cultural afterlife, 215–30
Fortescue, William, 162, 173, 346
Foucault, Michel, 144
Fouchard, Jean, 36, 76, 227; James and, 34, 77, 208–9, 228; *Les Marrons de la liberté* (1972), 34, 66, 69n17, 77, 228
Fourth International, 323, 326. *See also* Trotskyism, Trotskyists
Fox-Genovese, Elizabeth, 44n66
France, 140, 159n21, 370; colonies and colonialism of, 27, 89, 172, 367, 377–78, 379; commemorates abolition, 217–18; Fourth Republic, 375; Front Populaire in, 261; Haiti and, 81; James's research in, 5, 188; North Africa and, 356; restoration of slavery by, xiv; Third Republic, 371, 375; Trotskyists in, 20–21; in World War II, 376–77, 378–79. *See also* French Revolution
Franco, Francisco, 15, 226, 315
French Guiana, 5, 372
French Revolution, 24, 118, 144, 210; Enragés in, 236, 251, 252, 281; February 4, 1794, abolition decree and, 132, 139, 145–46, 163, 172; Haitian Revolution's relationship to, 1, 10, 13, 22, 32, 36–37, 51n154, 87, 92, 236–37, 283, 334, 336, 358; historiography of, 5, 23, 28, 35–36, 60, 142, 150–51, 203, 225, 229, 236, 257, 294n19; James on, 149; Marxist scholarship on, 61; Parisian models and, 81; 1789 in, 149–55; slavery and slave trade and, 89; slogans and anthems of, 10, 283, 356, 360; Terror in, 159n20, 160n36, 245, 251, 283; Third Estate in, 151
French Union (Union française), 367, 368, 374–75, 379
Freud, Sigmund, xix, 104
Froude, James Anthony, 126, 188; dismissed by James, 182; *The English in the West Indies* (1887), 11, 182, 226; racism of, 95, 186–87; rebutted by Thomas, 2, 183
Fryer, Peter, 17

Gairy, Eric, 259
Gambino, Ferrucio, on *The Black Jacobins*, 31–32
Gandhi, Mahatma, 80, 362
Garvey, Amy Ashwood, 7, 46n97, 198, 274n49, 275n51, 305; on *The Black Jacobins*, 16, 43n60
Garvey, Marcus, 34, 192n24, 304; James meets, 333; James on, 258; on Louverture, 185–86; Mandela on, 276n56; Marxism and, 168; *Negro World* and, 264; papers of, 298; on Selassie, 275n51; Universal Negro Improvement Association and, 128, 185
Garveyism, Garveyites, 94, 275n51
Geggus, David Patrick, 221; on *The Black Jacobins*, 15, 21, 30, 36, 445n88
Genovese, Eugene, 37; on *The Black Jacobins*, 17, 44n66
Georgakas, Dan, 31, 55–57, 412
Germany, 148, fascism in, 261, 378; France and, 378; revolution in, 15, 100
Ghana: Independence Day celebrations of (March 6, 1957), 23–24, 264; James on, 24, 26; Nkrumah and, 20, 23, 70, 248, 353; revolution in, 353, 354, 358; West Indians in, 46n97
Gillman, Susan, 4, 30, 220
Gilly, Adolfo, 15, 43n55
Girard, Philippe, 221
Girondins, 63, 158n8, 251
Glaberman, Jessie, 55
Glaberman, Martin, 55–56, 113n44, 302
Glissant, Édouard, 27, 135n19, 155
Glover, Danny, 80, 221–22, 230

Gobineau, Joseph Arthur, comte de, 188
Goethe, Johann Wolfgang von, 97, 98
Gold Coast, 354, 362, 365
Goldmann, Lucien, 38
Gomes, Albert, 187
Gong, Gerrit, 126
Gramsci, Antonio, 103, 106, 112n33, 211n17
Great Britain: abolition and, 7, 8, 21, 95, 162, 171–72, 327; Alien Internment Camps in, 19; *The Black Jacobins* in, 32; Black Panthers in, 32–33; British Commonwealth and, 376, 379; British Empire and, 7, 44n71, 377; Communist Party in, 17, 129, 353; former colonies of, 27; Haitian Revolution and, 73, 285, 339, 345–46, 370–71; imperialism of, 327; Industrial Revolution in, 89; James in, xviii, 1, 2, 4, 15, 24, 31, 33, 95, 97, 226, 304; Kenya and, 358; labor movement in, 17; Labour Party in, 17, 340, 355, 362; Marxism in, 73, 340; Pan-Africanist movement in, 7, 8, 20; Public Record Office, 66; Rhodesia and, 10; security services of, 8; socialist movement in, 353; Trotskyist movement in, 1; West Indians and, xvii, 32; in World War II, 376–77. *See also* West Indians; West Indies; *and names of British cities*
Great Depression, 4
Grenada, 182, 256, 259
Grierson, Flora, reviews *The Black Jacobins*, 16
Guadeloupe, 27, 67, 167, 372
Guérin, Daniel, 23, 236, 253n3
Guevara, Che, 57, 220; as global icon, 220–21, 222–23, 225
Guiana, 5, 27, 364, 372
Guizot, François, 151, 159n20
Gutiérrez Alea, Tomàs, *The Last Supper* (1976), 230
Guyana, 32, 266, 275n49, 298

Haiti (Hayti), 36, 75, 80–81, 320, 323, 380; as abolitionist state, 139; *The Black Jacobins* in, 22–23; Caco insurgency in, 117–18; as cautionary tale, 236; at Chicago's World Fair, 127, 219; Columbus and, 329; constitutions of, 210, 237; Cuba and, 321; diplomats of, 6, 26, 189; Duvalierism in, 27, 68; earthquakes in, 74, 82n2, 322; ethnicity in, 167; exceptionalism of, 115–16; as fable, 115; as France's premier sugar colony, 178, 369; Herskovits and, 116–18; historians and historiography of, 5, 18, 22, 179, 188, 215–30, 228; historical time and, 93–108; as independent black republic, 10, 21, 73, 91, 132, 147, 181–82, 289, 322, 368; instability in, 137n36; James and, 25–26; League of Nations and, 5, 189; mania for, 218; North Plain of, 75, 102, 141; self-rule in, 126; Southern Province of, 66–67; theory of, 115–33; United States and, 57, 80–81, 82; U.S. occupation of, 7, 17, 18, 117, 127, 128–29, 134n11, 137n40, 184, 189, 213n26, 225. *See also* Haitian Revolution; Saint-Domingue; San Domingo
Haitian Revolution, 208; from below, 61–68, 297–309; bicentennial of, 82; Black Power and, 27; Bois Caïman and, 165, 168–69, 173, 175n17; Bolivarian struggles and, 323, 326–27, 346; Boukman and, 20, 164–66, 168–69; bourgeoisie and, 21; British West Indians and, 2, 178–90; as Caribbean revolution, 259; creoles in, 75, 76, 79, 165, 208, 320, 331, 335; Crête-à-Pierrot battle in, 132; Cuban Revolution and, xviii; as cultural revolution, xvii, xix; equality in, 244; French Revolution's relationship to, 1, 10, 13, 21, 22, 36–37, 51n154, 73, 87, 92, 236–37, 283, 334, 336,

Haitian Revolution (*continued*) 358; future African revolution and, 10; guerrilla warfare in, 8, 10; Haitian children and, 81; historiography and historians of, 11–15, 25, 34, 36, 37, 42n45, 51n154, 60, 88, 134–35n15, 189, 190, 315, 317; imaginative geography of, 51n154; James on, 21–22, 150, 153–54; in James's plays, 278–91; James's travel to Britain and, 4; long, 209–11; Louverture and, 314; maroons in, 22, 76–77, 166–67, 239; as Marxist revolution, 13, 315–16; Moïse and, 63, 79, 237, 247–48; neglected in France, 367–68; new man and, 157–58; Northern Province in, 63, 242, 247, 248, 249, 251, 252; as phenomenon, xiii; popular movements in, 66; as savage race war, 11; scholars of, 36; slaves as leaders of, xvii–xviii, 34, 282; songs and anthems of, 166, 169, 281, 282, 289; as subject discussed by success of, 139; tragic dimension of, 91; universality and, 119, 132; vanguard and, 153, 239–40, 247, 279; as world historical event, 3, 13, 88–89, 101–2, 180, 220–21. *See also* Louverture, Toussaint; Saint-Domingue: revolution and revolutionary culture in; San Domingo: slave revolution in

Hall, Catherine, 37

Hall, Stuart: on James and *The Black Jacobins*, 3–4, 7, 32, 39; death of, 39; interviews James, 186; on James's Hegelian Marxism, 103, 108

Hallward, Peter, 135n15

Hamlin, Mike, 56

Harding, Vincent, 297

Harland, Sidney C., 2–3, 187–88, 193n29, 200, 226, 269–70

Harlem Renaissance, 94, 117, 218, 219, 225, 297

Hart, Richard, on *The Black Jacobins*, 50n148

Harvey, Franklyn, 30, 256

Hector, Tim, 30, 256, 264

Hegel, Georg Wilhelm Friedrich, 237, 273n23; dialectics of, 163, 303; James's study of, 80, 103, 107; *Philosophy of History*, 107; on reason, 123; Spirit and, 122–24, 125, 131; Trotsky and, 107–8; universal history and, 121, 122–24, 130

Heidegger, Martin, 113n42, 114n46

Heiger, Esther, accompanies James to Paris, 6–7

Henri Christophe, 10, 13, 127, 131, 157, 165, 230, 360, 380; books on, 190; demythologization of, 279; generalship of, 189; in James's play, 281, 284, 285, 287; in privileged caste, 169

Heritage Foundation, 298

Herskovits, Melville J., 133n5, 134nn10–11; on African culture in Haiti, 116–18; *Life in a Haitian Village* (1937), 117

Hill, Robert A., 108n, 190n4, 200, 265, 272n3, 412; on *The Black Jacobins*, xiii–xix; "C.L.R. James: The Myth of Western Civilization," 277n88; C.L.R. James Study Circle and, 30, 256–57; IBW and, 298; interviews James, 271; as James's literary executor, xix, 298; meets with James, xix; Jamaica's Young Socialist League and, 272n1; proofreads for James, 302; published collection of James's works, 273n7; Singham vs., 256–57, 258, 260–61, 262, 267, 273n9; *Walter Rodney Speaks*, 298–99

Hispanic American Historical Review, 209

Hispaniola, 329

history and historiography: cultural studies and, xv, xvi, xvii; of French Revolution, 5, 23, 28, 35–36, 60, 142, 150–51, 203, 225, 229, 236, 257, 294n19;

of Haitian Revolution, 11–15, 25, 34, 36, 37, 42n45, 51n154, 60, 88, 134–35n15, 189, 190, 315, 317; historical truth and, xix; historicism and, 106, 112n31, 121, 151; Marxist, 17; modern and, 97; movement in, 102; new social, xv, 30; people's 17; philosophy of, 87; radical, 5; science and art of, 129, 138n44; Spengler and, 97; universal, 120, 122–25, 130, 133, 136n22, 136n24, 140–41, 155–56. *See also* history from below

history from below, 17; *The Black Jacobins* and, 142, 152, 153, 228–29, 235–36; European crowds and, 281; Fick's *The Making of Haiti* and, 34, 60–68, 143; James's plays and. 278–91, 294n19; Thompson's *The Making of the English Working Class* and, xv

Hitler, Adolf, 73, 315, 359, 379

Hobsbawm, Eric, 281, 282, 294n19; on *The Black Jacobins*, 17

Hogarth Press, 5, 110n7

Høgsbjerg, Christian, 108n; James's 1936 play and, 110n10, 219, 278, 305

Hoover Institution, 298

Howard University, 18, 298, 353

Howe, Darcus, 49n138

Hughes, Langston, 128

human rights, 13, 118, 119, 120, 135–36n21

Hungarian Revolution, 24, 359

Hyacinthe, 154

IAFA (International African Friends of Abyssinia), 198, 274–75n49; IASB and, 198–99, 262; James and, 7, 8, 9, 10, 262–63

IASB (International African Service Bureau), 16, 201, 359, 363; *The Black Jacobins* and, 262–63; creation of, 198, 355; IAFA and, 198–99, 262; James and, 8, 65, 257, 265, 303, 326, 355

IBW (Institute of the Black World) (Atlanta), 297–309; founding of, 297–98; James's lectures at (1971), 35–36, 64, 198, 200, 227, 228–29, 301–9; *New Concepts for the New Man*, 302; personnel of, 298; Rodney symposium at, 299–300, 302

imperialism, 32, 156; anti-, 73, 263; British, 327, 363; European, 83n18, 162, 372–73; Haiti fights, 81; James on, xiv, 167–68, 357; postwar, 360; U.S., 184. *See also* colonialism

Independent Labour Party, 3, 17, 355

India, 171, 362, 372, 376, 380

Indochina, 372, 378. *See also* Vietnam

intellectual class, 152, 160n33

International African Friends of Ethiopia, 354–55

International African Opinion, 199; James as editor of, 263

Internationale, 10, 360

ISM (International Slavery Museum), 217

Isaacs, Harold, 15; James and, 43n55; *Tragedy of the Chinese Revolution* (1938), 43n55

Italy, 10, 32; fascism of, 261, 263; invades Ethiopia, 6, 7, 10, 94, 199, 226, 263, 275n51, 354

Jacobinism, Jacobins, 63, 101, 154, 172, 173, 207, 245, 249, 346; as authoritarian, 252; in Paris, 13, 251

Jamaica, Jamaicans, 48n123, 50n148, 178, 184, 186, 335; Baptist War and, 164, 171; Boukman and, 165; Amy Jacques Garvey and, 275n51; Marcus Garvey and, 185; Hall and, 32; Hill and, 256, 272n1; Morant Bay rebellion and, 181; resistance and, 217; Singham and, 259; Tacky revolt and, 173

James, C. L. R.: as academician, 31, 155, 330; as actor, 263; as anticolonial

James, C. L. R. (*continued*)
  activist, 7, 20, 324; as black Pan-African
  Marxist, 104; as black Trinidadian,
  1; as chair of IAFA, 198; child of, 300;
  death and funeral of, xxi, 51n158, 324;
  education of, 3; evasiveness of, 2;
  as hard reader, 5; Hill and, xix, 271,
  273n7, 277n88, 298, 302; humor of,
  302, 304; imprisonment of, 300; interviews of, 271, 277n90, 329–52; Italy's
  Ethiopian invasion and, 8, 10, 263;
  newspapers and, 56; Nkrumah and,
  23, 24–25; as orator, 301–2; on organization of slave masses, 62; photos of,
  iii, 9; on primitive, 96–97; radicaliza-
  tion of, 4; Rudé and, 61–62; Victorian
  sensibility of, 104; as West Indian,
  xvii–xviii, 190, 239–30; Williams and,
  7, 26, 47n107; wives of, 211
James, C. L. R., correspondence of,
  24–25; with Brierre, 26; with Charlier,
  64, 228; with Davidson, 29; with King,
  25; with Lamming, 29; with Legum,
  29; with Maxwell, 30; with Naipaul,
  47–48n119; with Patisson, 28; with
  Philipson, 28, 29, 47n111, 234n46; with
  Warburg, 31; with Webb, 211
James, C. L. R., lectures by, 64, 351;
  "*The Black Jacobins* and *Black Reconstruction*: A Comparative Analysis,"
  35, 306, 308–9; "How I Would Rewrite
  The Black Jacobins," 35, 142, 232, 279,
  280, 282, 306; "How I Wrote *The Black
  Jacobins*," 35, 304; "Lectures on *The
  Black Jacobins*" (IBW, 1971), 35–36, 64,
  142, 198, 200, 210, 227, 228–29, 232n18,
  236, 257, 279, 280, 282, 301–9; "Nkrumah, Padmore and the Ghanaian
  Revolution," 303; "The Old World and
  the New" (1971), 2, 33–34; *Perspectives and Proposals*, 256; publication
  of, 35, 36, 303; "The Role of the Black
  Scholar in the Struggles of the Black
  Community," 303; speeches and, 8, 64
James, C. L. R., as Marxist, xvii, 1, 4,
  5, 11, 102, 105, 170, 201, 257, 266, 314;
  anti-Stalinism of, 245; readings in
  Marxism by, 12, 97, 98, 305; reflected
  in *The Black Jacobins*, 28, 36–37,
  37–38, 44n66, 143; Trotskyism of,
  1, 6, 17, 73, 78, 80, 96, 107–8, 155, 201,
  236, 246, 249, 314, 354; Williams on,
  47n107
James, C. L. R., plays by, 163, 278–91;
  costumes and settings of, 287; Duke
  University Press edition (2013),
  110n10, 219, 278, 305; epilogue to,
  287–91; film based on, 49n136; lower
  ranks in, 283–84; *Toussaint Louverture: The Story of the Only Successful
  Slave Revolt in History* (1936 ed.), 4,
  7, 41n29, 95, 128, 201, 227, 263, 278,
  305; 1963 Nigerian production of,
  29–30, 278, 288, 294n19; paratexts of,
  290; playtexts and scripts of, 291n2,
  292–93n4; *The Black Jacobins* (1967
  ed.), 4, 79, 166, 278, 284
James, C. L. R., travels of: in Britain,
  xviii, 1, 2, 4, 15, 24, 31, 33, 95, 97, 226,
  304; in Cuba, 219, 234n45; in France,
  5, 6–7, 20, 81, 189, 229; at Ghana Independence Day celebrations, 23–24,
  264; limits to, 31; plans to visit Haiti,
  25–26; tours and lectures in United
  States, 16, 17, 19, 31, 33, 47n103; in
  Trinidad, 28, 179–80, 186; in
  Uganda, 33
James, C. L. R., works of, 95; *American
  Civilization*, 303; autobiography of, 4,
  7, 308; "Black Sansculottes" (1964),
  191n7; *The Case for West Indian
  Self-Government* (1933, 1967), 5, 7,
  32, 110n7, 265–66, 267, 268, 276n67;
  edited collection of, xix, 256, 273n7;

Hill on, 265–66, 268; *A History of Negro Revolt*, 42n49, 144, 260; *A History of Pan-African Revolt*, 140, 154, 160n35, 166; introduction to and translation of Guérin's work, 23; "Lenin and the Problem," 248; *The Life of Captain Cipriani: An Account of British Government in the West Indies* (1932), 4–5, 110n7, 189, 276n67, 295n32; *Mariners, Renegades, and Castaways*, 268; *Minty Alley* (1936 novel), 39n3, 266, 267–68, 323; *Nkrumah and the Ghana Revolution* (1977), 24, 303, 353–66; *Notes on Dialectics* (1966), 80, 83n26, 211, 251, 256, 268; preface/introduction to Fouchard's *The Haitian Maroons* (1981), 34, 208–9, 228; responds to Harland in *The Beacon* (1931), 2–3, 187–88, 200, 226, 269–70; reviews by, 111n22; "The Revolution in Theory," 24; *State Capitalism and World Revolution*, 303; *Walter Rodney and the Question of Power*, 300; *World Revolution, 1917–1936: The Rise and Fall of the Communist International* (1937), 1, 10, 15, 128, 140, 142, 144, 148–49, 152, 154, 201, 261, 303, 305, 326. See also *Beyond a Boundary*; James, C. L. R., lectures by; James, C. L. R., plays by

James, C. L. R., as writer, 200; answers reviewers, 21–22; aphorism and, xiv, xv; alleged Communist bias of, 16; as cricket reporter, 5, 8, 323; of fiction, 39n3, 226, 266, 267–68, 316, 323; Hill as literary executor of, xix, 298; letters to editors by, 28; literary style of, xiv, 143; on revisions to *The Black Jacobins*, 28–29, 34, 65

James, Selma, 27, 31, 413; on *The Black Jacobins*, 73–82; on James's political legacy, 37–38

Japan, 378

Jaurès, Jean, 5, 89, 151, 336

Jean-François, 65, 145, 166, 347, 357

Jefferson, Thomas, 102, 147

Johnson, James Weldon, "Self-Determining Haiti" (1920), 128, 137n41

Johnson, Linton Kwesi, on *The Black Jacobins*, 32–33

Johnson, Wallace, 198

Journal of Negro History, *The Black Jacobins* reviewed in, 17–18

Julian, Herbert, 275n51

Kamenev, Lev, 99

Kaye, Anthony, 216

Kemp, Martin, 220, 223

Kenya, 8, 27, 33, 274n49, 358

Kenyatta, Jomo, xvi, 16, 198, 263, 274n49, 339; in London, 8, 305, 353

Keynes, John Maynard, 362

King, Coretta Scott, 25

King, Martin Luther, Jr., 23, 24, 25, 57, 276n56

Knight, Franklin, 37, 119, 120

Korda, Alberto, 222, 223

Korngold, Ralph, *Citizen Toussaint*, 313

Kouyate, G., 198

Kremlin, 353, 357

Kropotkin, Peter, 236, 253n3

labor movement, 10: in Britain, 3, 8, 355; in British West Indies, 7–8, 32; in Detroit, 55–57; James and, 8; in Trinidad, 5, 276n67

Labour Party, 17, 340, 355, 362

Lacroix, Pamphile de, 229, 317

Ladner, Joyce, 298

La Luzerne, César Henri, comte de, 347, 356

Lamartine, Alphonse de, 317

Lamming, George: on *The Black Jacobins*, 26–27; in Ghana, 46n97; James and, 25, 29; *The Pleasures of Exile*, 29, 109n4

language and literature, xv; African, 82n12; cultural studies and, xvii; James on, xv–xvi; Lenin and, 148; linguistic turn and, 134n14

Laos, 375

Latin America, 82, 87, 98, 322, 323, 327, 346

Lawrence, Jacob, 128, 213n25, 224, 229, 233n31

League of Nations, Haiti and, 5–6, 40n21, 189

League of Revolutionary Black Workers, 31, 55–56, 57n2

Leclerc, Charles, 91, 132, 229, 345; on Haitian slave leaders, 36; race war of, 170–71

Lefebvre, Georges, 35–36, 152, 153, 155; James and, 62–63, 151, 158n8, 251–52

Legum, Colin, 29

Lenin, Vladimir, 92, 103, 106, 200, 207, 243, 245, 249, 267, 360, 362; death of, 145; James on, 148–49, 154, 159n17, 248, 249–50; as leader of mass revolution, 141, 143, 144, 147; *Letters from Afar*, 103–4; returns to Russia, 99, 101, 103, 111n22; Trotsky and, 79; "Where to Begin," 56

Leninism, 156, 249, 315; colonial revolution in, 24; of James, 249, 251, 253n7, 355; Marxism-, 170, 279, 315; vanguard and, 153, 211, 279

Les Temps Modernes, *The Black Jacobins* reviewed in, 21, 22

Lewis, Arthur, 46n97, 274–75n49

Lewis, David Levering, 31

liberté, égalité, fraternité, 147, 373; in Haiti, 10, 283

Lincoln, Abraham, 75, 303

Lindenberger, Herbert, 286

Livingstone, Ken, 217, 218

Loederer, Richard, *Voodoo Fire in Haiti*, 117

Logan, Rayford W., reviews *The Black Jacobins*, 18

London: Africans in, 305, 353, 365; Gandhi in, 80; IASB in, 199; James in, 1, 2, 9, 24, 31, 33, 323, 324, 351, 355; Hall in, 32; King in, 25; labor movement in, 8, 9; leftist demonstrations in, 20; mayor of, 217; Padmore in, 128, 355; *Toussaint Louverture* play performed in, 41n29

Louis, Joe, 276n56

Louis XIV, 371

Louis XV, 369, 371

Louis XVI (Louis Capet), 155; flees to Varennes, 63; overthrow of, 144

Louis-Philippe, 371

Louverture, Toussaint, 2, 6, 10, 27, 67, 71–72, 154, 220, 305, 370, 379; in *The Beacon*, 187–88; betrays masses, 145; biographies of, 3, 135n19, 221; as black Spartacus, 89, 145; cultural afterlife of, 215–30; demythologization of, 279; as dictator, 91, 161n36, 172, 245, 249; documents of, 90–91, 342–43; exceptionalism of, 3; figuration of, 125, 130; as freeman and slave owner, 88, 149–50, 227, 318–20; gifts and talents of, xiii, xv, 139, 178–79, 240; as global icon, 218–21; as greatest black West Indian, xviii, xix, 180, 183; idealization and mythologization of, 184, 186, 218, 221, 223; imprisonment and death of, 91, 221, 281, 287, 345; as inspiration, 56; James on, 21, 22–23, 179, 248–49, 285, 314, 338–48; James's treatment of, 35, 65, 77, 79–80, 91, 102, 109n4, 122, 130–32, 138n48, 139, 141–49, 161n36, 165, 270, 284, 316–17, 320, 325; labor policy of, 171, 208, 237, 243–47, 286; leadership of, 75, 189, 237, 240, 242–43, 244–45, 285, 286; master of, 146, 149; Maurin lithograph of, 223–24, 233n31; memoirs of, 221; mistakes, flaws, and weaknesses of, 64, 80, 147, 163, 244, 248, 286, 308, 317–18, 320–21, 343–44; Moïse and, 131–32, 207, 248, 250, 262, 283, 285–86, 315; in popular culture, 222, 224–25, 313; psychology of, 12; Phillips on, 183, 185, 188, 317; as populist autocrat, 241–43; reads Raynal, 89–90, 92, 130, 145, 148, 165, 338; repeated self-reinvention of, 146, 150; restoration of slavery and, xviii, 79; revolutionary accomplishments of, xiv; Rousseau and, 244; as tragic hero, 91, 317, 318; as world-historical figure, 147, 200

Love, Joseph Robert, 184–85

Lovinsky, Pierre-Antoine, 81

Luddism, Luddites, 12, 243

Lukács, Georg, *History and Class Consciousness* (1923), 38

Luxemburg, Rosa, 103, 106

Lyndersay, Dexter, 30, 288, 290–91

Macaya, 206, 282

Mackandal, François, 76, 239, 241

Madagascar, 372

Maddox, Lester, 299

Madhubuti, Haki, 297, 299

Madiou, Thomas, 5, 317; *Histoire d'Haïti*, 188

Makonnen, Ras (George T. N. Griffith), 46n97, 198, 275n49, 305, 364

Malcolm X, 330

Manchester, 364; Fifth Pan-African Congress in (1945), 20, 363, 364

Manchester Guardian, James as cricket reporter for, 5, 8, 323

Mandela, Nelson, 263, 276n56

Maoism, 31, 56, 148; Mao Zedung and, 142

Marable, Manning, 31; on *The Black Jacobins*, 48n135

Maran, René, 34, 178, 330

maroons: in Brazil, 76; free, 239; in Haitian Revolution, 22, 34, 76–77, 166–67, 208–9; as intellectuals, 272–73n4; of Suriname, 117

Marques, João Pedro, 171

Marryshow, T. Albert, 198

Marseillaise, 10, 360

Martelly, Michel, 81, 82

Martinique, 27, 51n158, 135n19, 318, 372

Martin Luther King Memorial Center, 298, 300

Marx, Karl, 102, 107, 160n29, 207, 267; *Capital*, 140, 158n4, 211, 238; *Communist Manifesto*, 90, 237; *Eighteenth Brumaire of Louis Bonaparte*, 204, 205–6, 211; historical system of, 99; James quotes, 89; James's study of, 80

Marxism, Marxist theory, 201, 207, 245, 278–79, 294n19, 314, 340; *The Black Jacobins* and, 28, 36–37, 179, 257, 323; capital in, 140; classical, 105, 142, 164, 362; defining controversy of, 98–101; dialectics of, 164; French Revolution and, 151; Haitian history and, 22; Hegelian, 103, 303; historical time in, 99; James's study of and turn to, xvii, 1, 4, 5, 11, 80, 97, 102, 201; -Leninism, 170, 279, 315; in London, 32; of Marx, 107; permanent revolution in, 24; positivism and, 103; revolutionary, 4, 13; theater and, 280, 281; vanguard in, 23, 55–56, 75, 80, 153–54, 239–40, 247, 279, 282, 307; Wolf and, 19–20; world revolution in, 128–29. *See also* Leninism; Maoism; Marxists; Stalinism, Stalinists; Trotskyism, Trotskyists

Marxists, 151, 361; anarchists and, 100; Blacks as, 299; in Britain, 16, 19; classical, 165; in Europe, 324, 325; general strikes and, 360–61; in Jamaica, 50n148; orthodox, 251

masses: black, xvi, 12, 56–57, 63, 91, 139, 237, 246, 323, 326; movements of, 36–37, 279, 289; revolutions and, 141, 155, 361–62; in Russian Revolution, 98

materialism: of *The Black Jacobins*, 143–44, 146, 163–64, 203–5; dialectical, 163–64, 166; historical, 170, 203

Mathiez, Albert, 155, 160n36

Maurepas, 157

Maxwell, John, 48n123

Maxwell, Marina, 30, 48n123

Mbanefo, Louis, 305

Mbeki, Thabo, 82; on *The Black Jacobins*, 74

McAuley, Chris, 302

McClelland, Keith, 37

McGill University, 61

McLemee, Scott, 33, 168

Meeks, Brian, 271

Ménard, Louis: James responds to, 21–22; reviews *The Black Jacobins*, 21

Mercier, Louis Sebastien, *L'An 2440*, 89

metropole, metropolis, 354, 357, 370, 376; colony and, 37, 97; culture of, 3; in Europe, 10, 360, 379; French, 13, 165, 166, 167, 208, 209, 358, 375; intellectuals of, 104

Mexican Revolution, 15, 43n55

Michelet, Jules, 5, 111n22, 130, 203, 236, 257; *History of the French Revolution* (1847–53), 129–30; *The People* (1846), 239

middle class, 141, 152, 154, 251, 376; black West Indian, 180, 182, 185, 187, 188. *See also* bourgeoisie

Middle Passage, 67, 76–77, 130, 306, 331, 340

Mignet, François, 151, 159n20

Milliard, Peter, 198, 364

Mintz, Sidney, 19

Mirebalais, Haiti, 117

Mirzoeff, Nicholas, 230

Moïse, 23, 154, 157, 163, 227, 229; execution of, 131–32, 207, 248, 250, 262, 283, 286–87, 315; in James's play, 79, 284–87, 288; revolt of, 63, 236, 237, 247–48, 249–50

Montague, Ludwell Lee, reviews *The Black Jacobins*, 18

Montgomery bus boycott, 25

Moreau de Saint-Méry, Médéric Louis Élie, 347, 357

Morisseau-Leroy, Félix, 26

Morocco, 371, 372, 374, 375, 377, 378

Moscow, 128, 129, 218

Moyn, Samuel, 120

mulattoes, 131, 269; complexities of, 88, 264; as generals, xv, 157; Haiti and, 6, 22, 24, 67, 168, 315–16, 319; Haitian Revolution and, 79, 157, 168, 169, 243, 331; James on, 170–71, 272, 335, 341–42, 356

Mussolini, Benito, 315; Ethiopian war of, 7, 8

Myrdal, Gunnar, *An American Dilemma*, 302

Naipaul, V. S.: James corresponds with, 47–48n119; reviews *Beyond a Boundary*, 48n119

Napoleon III, 371

narrative, narration, 136n24; biographical, 201; in *The Black Jacobins*, 87, 94, 171–73, 174, 267–68; Hegel and, 107; Scott on, 120, 121; White and, 136n23

National Black Political Convention, 298

Naville, Pierre: on *The Black Jacobins*, 20–21; forewords by, 367–81; translates *The Black Jacobins* into French, 36, 73

Nazis, 20–21, 110n8, 378. *See also* Germany; Hitler, Adolf

Négritude, 5, 29, 94, 219, 225, 330, 348–49

Nehru, Jawaharlal, xvi

Nelson, Lancashire, 3; James in, 5, 200, 270

Nemours, Alfred Auguste, 5–6, 40n21, 189–90, 193n32

Nesbitt, Nick, 109n2, 120, 221, 413; *Caribbean Critique* (2013), 158n8; on equality in *The Black Jacobins*, 139–58; on universal emancipation, 119, 225

Nevis, 182

New International, review of *The Black Jacobins* in, 19

New Left, 30, 260

New Negro, 297

New Statesman: James's letter to editor in, 28–29; review of *The Black Jacobins* in, 16

New York Times, review of *The Black Jacobins* in, 19

Ngũgĩ wa Thiong'o, 33, 49n141

Niang, Philippe, 222

Nielsen, Aldon Lynn, 35, 297–309, 413

Nietzsche, Friedrich, 97

Nigeria, 288, 354; University of Ibadan in, 30, 278

Nkrumah, Kwame, xvi, 70, 243, 248, 263, 275nn49, 308, 350; *The Black Jacobins* and, 356; at Fifth Pan-African Conference, 363–64; Ghana revolution and, 365–66; James and, 20, 23, 24–25, 303, 332, 340, 364–65; at University of Pennsylvania, 332, 365

North Africa, 356, 377

Northern Rhodesia, 10, 348. *See also* Zambia

Northwestern University, James as visiting scholar at, 31, 300–301, 330, 351

Novack, George, 209

Nwankwo, Ifeoma Kiddoe, 180

Nyerere, Julius, xvi, 70, 78, 248

O'Neill, Eugene, *Emperor Jones* (1920), 127

Opportunity: Journal of Negro Life, review of *The Black Jacobins* in, 18

Ott, Thomas O., on *The Black Jacobins*, 36–37, 50n152

Padmore (Pizer), Dorothy, 303, reviews *The Black Jacobins*, 16

Padmore, George (Malcolm Ivan Meredith Nurse), 16, 20, 34, 65, 186, 258, 275n49, 304, 305, 330, 332, 333, 339; breaks with Comintern, 128, 353–54; at Ghana Independence Day celebrations, 23; *Haiti, An American Slave Colony*, 129; IASB and, 355, 363; James and, 8, 257, 263, 265, 302, 303, 324, 353; Pan-Africanism and, 198–99, 354; publications of, 355; reviews *The Black Jacobins*, 15–16; U.S. occupation of Haiti and, 128–29

Paine, Thomas, 90, 102

Palmer, R. R., *Age of Democratic Revolution* (1964), 30; *The World of the French Revolution* (1971), 60, 68n5

Pan African Federation, 198

Pan-Africanism, 94, 219; *The Black Jacobins* and, 20, 27; in Britain, 8; Du Bois and, 363; Fifth Pan-African Congress and, 20, 263, 363, 364; James and, 4, 16, 324; militant, 4; modern, 225; in South Africa, 23; after World War I, 128

Panier, Jean, 282, 284

Papillon, Jean-François, 241

Paris, 13, 173, 218, 219, 375; Archives Nationales in, 62, 66; Cordeliers in, 13, 62, 207, 248; Jacobins of, 13, 251; James in, 5, 6–7, 20, 81, 189, 229; masses of, 251; sans-culottes of, 63–64, 252

Patisson, John G., 28

Paton, Diana, 217

Paul, Emmanuel, 22

Pauléus Sannon, Horace, *Histoire de Toussaint Louverture* (1920–33), 188, 318

Pearce, Brian, 44n71

Penguin Books, xix; publishes *The Black Jacobins*, 36

People, The (Trinidadian newspaper), 16

People's National Movement (Trinidad), 26

Péralte, Charlemagne, 117

Pericles, 90, 102

Perspectives socialistes, James's writings in, 23

Pétion, Alexandre, 13, 82, 152, 346

Petrograd, 250; Soviet of, 236, 249; Vyborg workers in, 13, 207, 248, 249

Peynier, Louis-Antoine Thomassin, comte de, 347, 356

Philipson, Morris: corresponds with James, 28, 29, 47n111, 234n46; as James's editor, 28, 234n46

Phillips, Wendell, on Louverture (1861), 183, 185, 188, 317

plantations, 91, 93, 130, 144, 332; in Atlantic economy, 89, 141, 337; destruction of, 74, 81, 157, 239, 243; James on, 140, 144, 238, 336–37; Louverture and, 77–79, 172, 207, 208, 245, 246–47, 286; as modern capitalist institutions, 11, 12, 102, 139, 141–42, 157; in Northern Province, 248; slaves as workers on, 63–64; of South Province, 66–67

Pluchon, Pierre, 221

Pontecorvo, Gillo, *Quemada/Burn!* (1969), 230

positivism, 101, 106; Marxism and, 103, 107, 112n33

poststructuralism, 133

Pravda, 99

Price-Mars, Jean, 22; Herskovits and, 117

primitive, primitivism, 96–97, 101, 103, 111n15, 113n41, 117; African, 78, 94; Haiti and, 95, 101–2, 117, 127, 322; James and, 96–97; Russian, 99–100; Trotsky on, 101

prisons and prisoners, 33, 77, 285; Abu-Jamal as, 58, 411; *The Black Jacobins* and, 58, 70–72; James as, 300; Louverture as, 91, 262, 345; Shoatz as, 70–72, 82, 414

Pritchard, Hesketh, *Where Black Rules White* (1900), 126

Profintern (Red International of Labour Unions), 353

proletariat: bourgeoisie vs., 79, 315; European, 360, 362; Lenin on, 267; Marx on, 160n29; revolution by, 12, 169; sans-culottes and, 251; slaves as proto-, 12, 21, 67, 75, 102, 141–42, 238, 315; Trotsky on, 261

Puerto Rico, 31

Quest, Matthew, 413; on democracy and liberation in *The Black Jacobins*, 235–52

race, 172; debates on, in Trinidad, 186–87; historiography of, 37; Louverture's use of, 320; nexus of class and, 6, 11, 167–71, 260, 299, 369; pseudoscience of, 2–3; question of, xiv; war between, 168–69

racism, 57, 162; civilization and, 80, 93; Froude's, 11; James on, 167–68; of Red Summer 1919, 128; scientific, 125, 226;

Stoddard's, 50n152; struggle against, 82; in U.S. occupation of Haiti, 127; white supremacism and, 327

Ramchand, Kenneth, 273n9

Random House: as James's publisher, 28; publishes *The Black Jacobins* (1963), 30

Rawick, George, 37, 254n12, 332

Raynal, Abbé Guillaume Thomas François, 342; Louverture inspired by writings of, 89–90, 92, 130, 145, 148, 165, 338

Reddick, Lawrence Dunbar, 25, 47n103

Rediker, Marcus, 77, 229

Renton, Dave, 226

revolution, revolutions, 10, 37, 87, 156; anti-imperial, 142; in *The Black Jacobins*, 142–49; cultural, xvii, xviii, xix; cultural study of, xvii; as event, 205–9; logic of, 1; mass, 141–42, 155; permanent, 13, 267; in philosophy, 93, 94, 103; universality of, 120, 140, 154; world, 128–29; writing of, 202–5. *See also* counterrevolution; *and names of revolutions*

Rhodesia, 27, 73

Rigaud, Benoit Joseph André, xiv, 347, 357

Roberts, Alfie, 30, 256, 257

Robeson, Paul, 15, 219, 324; performs in production of James's play, 41n29, 128, 201, 263, 305

Robespierre, Maximilien, 63, 150–55, 158n8, 159n21, 161n144, 173, 236, 245, 251, 338; James on, 160–61n36

Robinson, Cedric, 267

Rochambeau, Donatien-Marie-Joseph de Vimeur, vicomte de, 347, 356

Rodney, Walter, 256, 260, 272n3, 298–99, 300, 302; on *The Black Jacobins*, 32; at IBW, 304, 308

Romanticism, 122, 124, 135n19, 146

Roosevelt, Elliott, 376–77

Roosevelt, Franklin D., 376–77, 378

Rose, Jacqueline, 93, 107

Rosengarten, Frank, 227

Rousseau, Jean Jacques, 244

Roux, Jacques, 236, 251

Rudder, David M., xxi-xxii, 37

Rudé, George, 214n43, 281, 294n19; *The Crowd in the French Revolution* (1969), 60; James and, 61–62; at Sir George Williams University, 61

ruling class, 80, 243, 245, 246, 249; crisis of, 66; as exploiters, 150; white, 167. *See also* elites

Russia, 353; backwardness of, 99–100; imperialism of, 372–73. *See also* Russian Revolution; Soviet Union

Russian Revolution, 1, 10, 24, 103, 112n33, 140, 150, 156, 207, 248; James on, 236; masses in, 98; Marxist theory and, 99–100; October Revolution, 147, 315; Trotsky and, 261

Said, Edward, 3, 38; on *The Black Jacobins*, 13, 134n14

Saint-Domingue, 88, 101, 139, 140, 189, 206, 315, 380; culture of, 155; French colonialism and, 373–74; independence of, 204; James and, 95; maroons of, 66; masses of, 63, 67, 91, 101–2, 142, 323; mulattoes in, 170; plantation production in, 141, 142; race and class in, 11, 168, 315; resistance in, 217; restoration of slavery in, xiv, xviii; revolution and revolutionary culture in, xvii, xviii, 21, 60, 64, 65–66, 67, 89, 91, 93, 94, 96, 97, 105, 112n34, 130, 147, 148, 149, 152, 154, 157, 166–67, 178, 203, 204, 304, 324, 367, 371; slaves of, 10, 13, 21, 101, 102, 119, 131, 155, 164, 166, 167, 173, 200, 266, 271, 306, 370. *See also* Haiti; San Domingo

Saint-Rémy, Joseph, 317

Sala-Molins, Louis, 89–90, 92n3

Salkey, Andrew, 256, 273n9

Salmon, C. S., 182–83, 184, 185

Salvemini, Gaetano, *The French Revolution, 1788–1792* (1954), 60

Sam, Guillaume, 127

San Domingo, xv, 79, 325–26, 331, 334; independence of, 285, 286; James on, xviii, 28, 35, 89, 112, 139, 141, 169, 228, 307, 335–38, 340–46, 348, 351, 356–58, 360; masses in, 131, 166; racism in, 168, 172, 272; slave revolution in, 1, 10, 21, 23, 32, 135n19, 270, 284, 329, 335–36, 358; slaves in, 10, 112, 156, 283; Spanish, 146. *See also* Haiti; Saint-Domingue

sans-culottes, 60, 63–64, 154, 229, 236, 251, 252, 281, 341; black, 167, 236, 250–52

Sans Souci, 154, 282, 284

Santiago-Valles, W. F., 256, 272n4

Saturday Review of Literature, The Black Jacobins reviewed in, 18

Savacou, 257, 273n9

Schoelcher, Victor, 317

Scholes, Theophilus, *Glimpses of the Ages* (1905), 183, 185

Schomburg Center for Research in Black Culture, 298

Schwarz, Bill, 5, 413; on Haiti and historical time, 93–108; interviews Hall, 3–4

Scott, David, 227, 277n88, 414; on *The Black Jacobins* and the poetics of universal history, 115–33, 258–59, 273–74n23; *Conscripts of Modernity*, 28, 120, 132, 259; on tragic dimension of Haitian Revolution, 91, 259

Seabrook, William: *The Magic Island* (1929), 17, 117, 202; reviews *The Black Jacobins*, 17–18

Secker and Warburg, 17, 28, 43; as publisher of *The Black Jacobins* (1938 ed.), 1, 14, 16; as publisher of Isaacs's *Tragedy of the Chinese Revolution*, 43n55; as publisher of *Minty Alley* (1936), 39n3. *See also* Warburg, Fredric

Selassie, Haile, 275n51

Selden, Dan, 4

Sembène, Ousmane, *Xala*, 287

Senegal, 371, 374

Shaka, 70–71

Shakespeare, William, 143, 308, 317

Shoatz, Russell Maroon, 70–72, 82, 414

Sierra Leone, 8, 16, 354

Silone, Ignazio, *Fontamara* (1934), 17

Singham, A. W.: Hill vs., 256–62, 267, 271, 273n9; on *The Black Jacobins*, 191n5

Sir George Williams University (Concordia University), 61

slavery and slave trade, 309; apologies for, 217; Greco-Roman, 168; historiography of, 37, 88, 163; James on, 331, 337; Marxist analysis of, 11; power of, 23; restoration of, xiv, xviii, 79, 207; in United States, 307. *See also* Atlantic history; slaves

slaves, 10, 112, 156, 283; agency of, 88, 101, 139; in *The Black Jacobins*, 74–75; foregrounding of, 36, 64; James on, 228; as leaders of Haitian Revolution, xvii–xviii, 34, 282; Lincoln and, 75; natural intelligence of, xviii; organization of, 62; political philosophy of, 88; as proto-proletariat, 12, 67, 75, 102, 141–42, 238, 315; resistance by, 238, 268; as revolutionary mass, 13, 102, 144, 280–81; sources by, 279. *See also* Saint-Domingue: slaves of

Small Axe, James's "Lectures on *The Black Jacobins*" in, 35, 36, 301, 302, 304

Smith, Ian, 73

Smith, Matthew J., 2, 414; on Haitian Revolution in British West Indian thought, 178–90

Smith, Samedi, 227, 282, 284, 287, 289, 294n26, 295n27

Soboul, Albert, 35–36, 151, 229, 281; *The Parisian Sans-Culottes and the French Revolution, 1793–4* (1964), 60

socialism, socialists, 3, 17, 21, 43n55, 83n18, 99–100, 111n22, 357, 375; in America, 213n41; in Britain, 353; end of, 133; in Europe, 261, 262, 265, 354, 376; as historians, 5, 64; international, 258–61, 263, 272, 374; James and, 128, 258, 262, 270; proto-, 247; revolution and, 13, 44n70, 107, 129, 201, 208–9, 354, 358; tribal, 78

Socialist Workers Party (U.S.), 304

Solzhenitsyn, Aleksandr, *Gulag Archipelago*, 308

Sonthonax, Léger-Félicité, 342

South Africa, 27, 220, 275n51; black Americans and, 276n56; *The Black Jacobins* in, 23–24, 33, 74, 263–64, 305; James and, 264; Mbeki and, 74, 82. *See also* apartheid

Souvarine, Boris, *Stalin* (1939), 245

Soviet Union, 16–17, 78, 226, 245, 261, 315, 376. *See also* Russia

Spain, Spanish, 184, 261, 369; in Caribbean, 329; Haiti and, 206, 329, 331, 341, 370; negotiations with, 131; Spanish Civil War and, 10, 15, 73, 267; Toussaint and, xiv, 73, 102, 145, 163, 285, 335

Spencer, Harry, 5, 304

Spengler, Oswald, *The Decline of the West*, 5, 97–98, 101, 102

Spivak, Gayatri Chakravorty, "Can the Subaltern Speak?," 280

Stalin, Joseph: anti-Stalinists and, 17, 149, 155, 236, 315; 78, 99, 128, 245, 250, 261, 262, 315, 353–54; Stalinism and, 1, 245, 257, 267, 354, 362, 379

Steward, Thomas, *The Haitian Revolution, 1791–1804* (1914), 202

Stoddard, T. Lothrop, 50n152, 110n8, 209; *The French Revolution in San Domingo* (1914), 42n45, 95, 202

Strickland, William, 298

Styron, William, *Confessions of Nat Turner*, 309

subalternity, subalterns, 96, 161n40, 163, 164, 280

Surkin, Marvin, 31

Sweezy, Paul, *The Theory of Capitalist Development* (1942), 20

Sylla, 282, 284

Syria, 372

Tambo, Oliver, 220

Tanzania, 70, 78, 83n18, 248, 298

Tarantino, Quentin, *Django Unchained*, 230

temporalities: *The Black Jacobins* and, 132; historical time and, 106–7

Terkel, Studs, 414; interviews James (1971), 227, 329–52, 352n

Thackeray, William Makepeace, *Vanity Fair*, James and, 268–69, 316

Thierry, Augustin, 151, 159n20

Third World, 31, 57, 260, 380

Third World Press, 297

Thomas, John Jacob, 226; *Froudacity* (1889), 2, 183

Thompson, E. P., xv, 94, 281, 294n19; *The Making of the English Working Class*, 30, 197, 325

Thornton, John, 36

Time magazine, *The Black Jacobins* reviewed in, 19

Tolson, Melvin B., 302

Trinidad, 186, 275n51, 289, 335; debates on race in, 186–87; Garvey in, 333; Imperial College of Tropical Agriculture in, 269; independence of, 27, 29; James leaves, 97, 179–80, 323; James's research and writing in, 5, 266; James's return to, 28; labor movement in, 5, 189, 276n67; nationalist movement in, 26; origins of *The Black Jacobins* in, 1–4, 259, 269–70; postcolonial, 229; prime minister of, 268; reviews of *The Black Jacobins* in, 16, 43n62

Trinidadian, Trinidadians, xxi, 2, 35, 49n138, 268, 302; *The Black Jacobins* and, 20, 30, 73–74; Carmichael as, 31; James as, 1, 56, 168, 318; Padmore as, 263.

Trinidad Workingmen's Association, 5

Tripp, Luke, 56

Trotsky, Leon, 79, 92, 106, 154, 200, 207, 250, 267, 360, 362; assassination of, 17, 315; introduction to Isaacs's *Tragedy of the Chinese Revolution* (1938) by, 43n55; Stalin and, 262; temporalities and, 107; world revolutionary movement and, 128; on writing revolution, 11; writings of, 15

Trotsky, Leon, *The History of the Russian Revolution*, 5, 113n41, 129–30, 257, 274n49; as inspiration, 15; James's reading of and comments on, 12, 17, 97, 98, 102, 107, 201, 203, 261–62; law of combined development in, 100–101; Russian proletariat in, 12; translation of, 98

Trotskyism, Trotskyists, 245, 261; *The Black Jacobins* and, 16, 19, 20–21; in Britain, 6; Fourth International, 323, 326; James and, 1, 6, 17, 73, 78, 80, 96, 107–8, 155, 201, 246, 267, 314, 323, 354; Johnson-Forest tendency within, 19, 279, 282, 294n19; law of uneven

capitalist development in, 12, 238–39; newspapers of, 44n71

Trouillot, Michel-Rolph, 36, 133n4, 180, 189, 228; on Haitian Revolution, 202, 221; on Haiti's exceptionalism, 115–16

Trujillo, Rafael, 28

Tubman, Harriet, 222

Tunapuna, Trinidad, xxi, 2

Tunisia, 371, 374, 377

Turner, Nat, 222

Tyson, George, 223

UAW (United Auto Workers), 55–56

UN (United Nations), xvi; Haiti and, 81, 82

United States: American Socialist Workers' Party in, 43n55; *The Black Jacobins* in colleges in, 31; *The Black Jacobins* published in, 17; black radicalism in, 55–56; civil rights movement in, 25, 27, 31, 73, 224, 306, 331; Civil War in, 75, 154, 166, 307, 346, 363; Communist Party in, 353; Declaration of Independence of, 90; Garvey and, 185; Haiti and, 57, 80–81, 82, 322; Haiti occupied by, 7, 17, 18, 117, 127, 128–29, 134n11, 137n40, 184, 189, 213n26, 225; hegemony of, 376–78; James lectures in, 31, 33, 351; James lives pseudonymously in, 19, 300; James teaches in, xix; James tours, 16, 17, 168, 323; James's troubles with, 300, 323; racism and racial segregation in, 184, 215, 359, 363; Red Summer 1919 in, 128; slaves in, 307; Southern fears of slave revolt in, 57, 346; Vietnam and, 160n33, 341, 345; War for Independence and, 13; in World War II, 376–77

Universal Negro Improvement Association, 128, 275n51

University of Toronto, 256
University of the West Indies, 32, 192n22, 256

vanguard, 23, 80; Haitian Revolution and, 153–54, 239–40, 247; James and, 307; leadership of, 75; party of, 55–56, 80, 154, 279; popular, 23; rejection of, 282
Varlet, Jean-François, 236, 251
Venezuela, 82 83n28, 323
Vietnam, 160n33, 341, 345, 374. *See also* Indochina
vindicationism, 122–28, 190n4, 199, 224, 270, 277n88; *The Black Jacobins* and, 125, 179, 237
Vinogradov, Anatolii, *The Black Consul* (1935), 16–17
Vintage Books, as publisher of *The Black Jacobins*, 55, 349, 351
Vodou (Vodun), 12, 17, 78, 102, 134n11, 155, 295n27, 295n32, 351–52; Boukman and, 165–66; Fick on, 112n26; James on, 340; sensationalism of, 127

Walcott, Derek, 98, 271
Walker, Margaret, 298
Wallace-Johnson, I. T. A., 8, 16, 354
Walsh, John, 218
Walvin, James, 36
Warburg, Fredric, 17, 261, 305; James writes to, 27, 31; supports republication of *The Black Jacobins*, 27. *See also* Secker and Warburg
Washington, DC, James in, xix, 31
Watson, John, 56
Waxman, Percy, *The Black Napoleon* (1931), 3, 127, 226–27
Wayne State University, 56
Webb, Constance, 211
Welles, Orson, 218
West, Fred, 187

West Africa, 8, 29, 354, 372, 375
West African Standard, 16
West African Youth League, 16
West Indian Federation, 288
West Indians: Africa question and, 364; Britain and, xvii, 32; Césaire as, 349; education of, 185; Garvey as, 334; in Ghana, 46n97; intelligence of, xviii; James as, xvii–xviii, 190, 239–30; James on, xix, 34, 266, 330; Louverture as greatest, xviii, xix, 179; thinking of, 305
West Indies, 27, 178, 288; Africa and, 258; Africans in, xv–xvi; cricket and, xvi–xvii; Haitian Revolution in thought of, 178–90; James and, xvii–xviii, xix, 31, 32; James on history and intellectualism of, 8, 181, 300; labor rebellions in, 7–8; middle class of, 182, 185; nationalist movements in, xix, 2, 26, 180–81, 185; Nkrumah and, 353; revolution and, 22; working-class movement in, 73. *See also* Caribbean; West Indians; *and names of individual islands*
Wilberforce, William, 217
Williams, Eric, 26, 88, 217, 308; as prime minister, 268; *Capitalism and Slavery* (1944), 11, 32, 89, 44n71, 162, 171, 268; "The Economic Aspect of the Abolition of the West Indian Slave Trade and Slavery" (1938), 7, 11; economic determinism and, 164; *From Columbus to Castro* (1970), 30; on James's work, 26, 47n107, 174n2
Williams, Raymond, 38, 96
Williams, Robert, 57
Wilson, William Julius, 299
Wilson, Woodrow, 127, 128
Winter, Sylvia, 298
Wittfogel, Karl, *Wirtschaft und Gesellschaft Chinas* (1931), 20

Wolf, Eric R., 19–20
Wordsworth, William, 317
Workers' and Farmers' Party (WFP) (Trinidad), 289
working class, workers, 13, 55–56, 73, 76, 207, 248, 368, 376; black, 56; definition of, 76; interests of, 245; international movement of, 73, 148, 265; organizing, 80. *See also* masses; proletariat
World War I, 128, 363

World War II, xvi, 20, 67, 73, 184, 263, 360, 379
Worrell, Frank, 274n49

Young Socialist League (Jamaica), 272n1

Zambia, 10. *See also* Northern Rhodesia
Žižek, Slavoj, 134–35n15
zombies, 58, 202
Zulus, 70